ETHICS AND LAW FOR SCHOOL PSYCHOLOGISTS

ETHICS AND LAW FOR SCHOOL PSYCHOLOGISTS

Sixth Edition

Susan Jacob
Dawn M. Decker
Timothy S. Hartshorne

WILEY

John Wiley & Sons, Inc.

Library of Congress Cataloging-in-Publication Data:

Jacob, Susan, 1949–

    Ethics and law for school psychologists / Susan Jacob, Dawn M. Decker, and Timothy S. Hartshorne. — 6th ed.
      p.   cm.
    Includes bibliographical references and index.
    ISBN 978-0-470-57906-0 (cloth); 978-0-470-91087-0 (ePDF); 978-0-470-91088-7 (eMobi); 978-0-470-91089-4 (ePub)
  1. School psychologists—Professional ethics—United States. 2. School psychologists—Legal status, laws, etc.—United States. I. Decker, Dawn M. II. Hartshorne, Timothy S. III. Title.
    LB3013.6.J33 2011
    174'.93717130683—dc22

                                                   2010019081

Printed in the United States of America

10 9 8 7 6 5 4 3 2

This book is dedicated to the memory of Tim and Nancy Hartshorne's children, Michael David Salem Hartshorne (1984–1992) and Katherine Swift Hartshorne (1991–1992)

And to the memory of Susan Jacob's son, Andrew Alan Neal (1982–2009)

The brevity of their lives reminds us just how precious are all children.

Contents

Preface ———————————————

There are a number of excellent texts, journal articles, and book chapters on ethics in psychology, legal issues in school psychology, and special education law. However, our experience as school psychology trainers suggested a need for a single sourcebook on ethics and law specifically written to meet the unique needs of the psychologist in the school setting. Consequently, *Ethics and Law for School Psychologists* was written to provide up-to-date information on ethical principles and standards and law pertinent to the delivery of school psychological services. Our goals for this sixth edition of the book remain unchanged. We hope that the book will continue to be useful as a basic textbook or supplementary text for school psychology students in training and as a resource for practitioners.

As stated in the preface to the first edition, one goal in writing the book was to bring together various ethical and legal guidelines pertinent to the delivery of school psychological services. We also introduce an ethical-legal decision-making model. We concur with the suggestion that the educated practitioner is the best safeguard against ethical-legal problems (Diener & Crandall, 1978; Koocher & Keith-Spiegel, 2008). School psychologists with a broad knowledge base of ethics and law are likely to anticipate and prevent problems. Use of a decision-making model allows the practitioner to make informed, well-reasoned choices in resolving problems when they do occur (Eberlein, 1987; McNamara, 2008; Tymchuk, 1986).

WHAT'S IN THE BOOK

Chapter 1 provides an introduction to ethical codes, an ethical-legal decision-making model, and the four broad ethical principles of respect for the dignity and rights of all persons, professional competence and responsibility, honesty and integrity in professional relationships, and responsibility to schools, families, communities, the profession, and society. We also describe ethics committees and sanctions for unethical conduct. Chapter 2 provides an introduction to the legal underpinnings of school-based practice and to public school law that protects the rights of students and their parents. We also address certification and licensure of school psychologists—mechanisms that help to ensure that psychologists meet specified qualifications before they are granted a legal sanction to practice. The chapter closes with a brief discussion of tort liability of schools and practitioners. In Chapter 3, we discuss privacy, informed consent, confidentiality, privileged communication, and record keeping— ethical-legal concerns that cut across all of the school psychologist's many roles.

The remaining chapters focus on ethical-legal issues associated with specific roles. Chapters 4 and 5 focus on the delivery of services to students with disabilities. Psychoeducational assessment within the context of a school psychologist–client relationship is discussed in Chapter 6. Chapter 7 addresses school-based interventions, including classroom interventions for students who require academic and behavioral support to succeed in the general education classroom, and therapeutic interventions such as counseling. Chapters 8 and 9 focus on indirect services. We discuss ethical-legal issues associated with consultative services to teachers and parents in Chapter 8 and systems-level consultation in Chapter 9. A number of special consultation topics are covered in Chapter 9, including the ethical-legal concerns associated with student proficiency assessment programs; school entry and grade retention decisions; efforts to foster safe schools (discipline, school violence prevention, and the problem of harassment and discrimination); and schooling for pupils with other special needs (limited English proficiency, gifted and talented students, and students with communicable diseases). In Chapter 10, ethical-legal issues associated with research are discussed, and Chapter 11 provides a brief overview of issues associated with school-based supervision of school psychologists in training. And, finally, in the Epilogue, we discuss advocacy.

WHAT'S NOT IN THE BOOK

We have chosen to focus on ethical-legal issues of interest to current and future school-based practitioners. Consistent with this focus, we did not include a discussion of issues associated with private practice. Interested readers are encouraged to consult Fisher (2003); Koocher and Keith-Spiegel (2008); Knapp and VandeCreek (2006); and Sales, Miller, and Hall (2005). We also did not address the legal rights of psychologists as employees in the public schools.

SIXTH EDITION REVISIONS

There have been a number of changes in codes of ethics and law pertinent to the practice of school psychology since we completed work on the fifth edition in 2006. Perhaps of most importance, the National Association of School Psychologists (NASP) adopted a revised version of its *Principles for Professional Ethics* in March 2010, and the language of the new code was incorporated into this edition of the book. In addition, many other changes were made in the content and organization of the book. Chapter 3 includes new material on the management of sensitive private student information and a revised section on privileged communication. Chapters 4 and 5 now address ethical and legal issues in the education of pupils with disabilities. The final federal regulations implementing Part B of the Individuals with Disabilities Education Improvement Act of 2004 are cited in Chapter 4, and Chapter 5 was updated to include changes in school law following the passage of the Americans with Disabilities Amendments Act of 2008. In this edition, Chapter 6 addresses school psychological assessment of individual students. Chapter 7 was expanded to provide broader coverage of ethical-legal issues in school-based intervention, including a new section on interventions in the general education classroom. A discussion of advocacy appears in the revised Epilogue.

Throughout the text we incorporated citations to recent publications. However, we also continued to cite older works that provided the foundation for more recent scholarship in the area of ethics and law for school psychologists. As Koocher and Keith-Spiegel (2008, p. 524) observed, ignoring important older publications on a topic is disrespectful of the efforts of early scholars. Furthermore, researchers and writers "who pass over earlier work may conclude that they discovered something fresh and innovative when in fact the same findings were published many years ago."

An updated instructor's manual and Microsoft PowerPoint slides are available for trainers who adopt the textbook. These supplements are available by contacting your John Wiley & Sons sales representative (visit http://www.wiley.com).

A number of the changes made in the sixth edition were suggested by readers. We welcome your suggestions for improving future editions of *Ethics and Law for School*

Psychologists. Please contact Susan Jacob, Professor of Psychology, 104 Sloan Hall, Central Michigan University, Mt. Pleasant, MI 48859. E-mail: jacob1s@cmich.edu.

TWO DISCLAIMERS

This text provides an overview and summary of constitutional, statutory, and case law pertinent to the practice of psychology in the schools. It does not provide a comprehensive or detailed legal analysis of litigation in education or psychology. The material included in the book, particularly the portions on law, is based on our review of the available literature. We are not attorneys. We often consulted the writings of attorneys and legal scholars for guidance in the interpretation of law rather than attempting to interpret it ourselves. However, original sources also were consulted when feasible, and citations have been provided so that interested readers can do the same.

Nothing in this text should be construed as legal advice. School psychology practitioners are encouraged to consult their school attorneys through the appropriate administrative channels when legal questions arise. Our interpretations of ethical codes and standards should not be viewed as reflecting the official opinion of any specific professional association.

CAST OF CHARACTERS

Throughout the text, we have included a number of case incidents to illustrate specific principles. Some of the incidents are from case law, some were suggested by practitioners in the field, and others are fictitious. To make it easier for the reader to follow who's who in the vignettes, we have used the same six school psychologists throughout the book:

SAM FOSTER worked as a school psychologist for several years and then returned to school to pursue his PsyD degree. He is currently a doctoral intern in a suburban school district.

CARRIE JOHNSON provides school psychological services in a rural area. She faces the special challenges of coping with professional isolation and works in a community where resources are limited.

HANNAH COOK serves as a member of a school psychological services team in a medium-sized city. She is particularly interested in school-based consultative services.

CHARLIE MAXWELL, a school psychologist in a large metropolitan district, is a strong advocate of school efforts to prevent mental health problems.

WANDA ROSE provides services at the preschool and elementary level in a small town. Children, babies, parents, and teachers love Wanda Rose. She has been a school psychology practitioner for many years. Wanda needs an occasional push from her colleagues to keep current with changing practices, however.

PEARL MEADOWS is a school psychologist in a small university town. She works with a diverse student population, including pupils from farm families who live on the district's outskirts, Native American students from the neighboring Indian reservation, and children from many different cultures whose parents are part of the university community. Pearl also provides on-site supervision to school psychology interns.

SUSAN JACOB

DAWN M. DECKER

TIMOTHY S. HARTSHORNE

Central Michigan University

Mt. Pleasant, Michigan

Acknowledgments

We would like to acknowledge the research assistance provided by Central Michigan University school psychology program graduate students Megan M. Kleinheksel, Abbie C. Barrett, and Robin Kuhn.

We also extend a special thanks to the editor of the sixth edition, Isabel Pratt, and we are grateful for the excellent copyediting work done by the staff at Cape Cod Compositors. A special thank you also is due to family members for their support during the completion of this and previous editions of the book.

Chapter 1

ETHICS IN SCHOOL PSYCHOLOGY: AN INTRODUCTION

Because the decisions made by school psychologists have an impact on human lives, and thereby on society, the practice of school psychology rests on the public's trust. To build and maintain society's trust in school psychology, it is essential that every school psychologist is sensitive to the ethical and legal components of his or her work, knowledgeable of broad ethical principles and rules of professional conduct, and committed to a proactive stance in ethical thinking and conduct.

The term *school psychologist* has been defined in many different ways (Fagan & Wise, 2007). For the purposes of this book, we adopted the definition developed by the National Association of School Psychologists (NASP): "*School psychologists* provide effective services to help children and youth succeed academically, socially, behaviorally, and emotionally. School psychologists provide direct educational and mental health services for children and youth, as well as work with parents, educators, and other professionals to create supportive learning and social environments for all children" (NASP, 2010a).

QUALITY CONTROL IN SCHOOL PSYCHOLOGY

A number of sources of quality control are available in the provision of school psychological services. Professional codes of ethics for the delivery of psychological services are discussed in this chapter. Chapter 2 provides an introduction to law that protects the rights of students and their parents in the school setting. Educational law provides a second source of quality control. Chapter 2 also addresses the credentialing of school psychologists, a third mechanism of quality assurance. Credentialing helps to ensure that psychologists meet specified qualifications before they are granted a legal sanction to practice (Fagan & Wise, 2007). Training-program accreditation is an additional mechanism of quality control. Program accreditation helps to ensure the adequate preparation of school psychologists during their graduate coursework and field experiences. (For a discussion of training-program accreditation, see Fagan & Wise, 2007.)

This chapter focuses on the what and why of professional ethics, ethics training and competencies, and the codes of ethics of the National Association of School Psychologists (NASP) and the American Psychological Association (APA). We introduce four broad ethical principles, along with an ethical-legal decision-making model. We also describe ethics committees and sanctions for unethical conduct.

WHAT AND WHY OF PROFESSIONAL ETHICS

The term *ethics* generally refers to a system of principles of conduct that guide the behavior of an individual. *Ethics* derives from the Greek word *ethos*, meaning character or custom, and the phrase *ta ethika*, which Plato and Aristotle used to describe their studies of Greek values and ideals (Solomon, 1984). Accordingly,

> ethics is first of all a concern for individual character, including what we call "being a good person," but it is also a concern for the overall character of an entire society, which is still appropriately called its "ethos." Ethics is participation in, and an understanding of, an ethos, the effort to understand the social rules which govern and limit our behavior. (p. 5)

A system of ethics develops in the context of a particular society or culture and is connected closely to social customs. Ethics is composed of a range of acceptable (or unacceptable) social and personal behaviors, from rules of etiquette to more basic rules of society.

The terms *ethics* and *morality* are often used interchangeably. However, according to philosophers, the term *morality* refers to a subset of ethical rules of special importance. Solomon (1984) suggested that moral principles are "the most basic and inviolable rules of a society." Moral rules are thought to differ from other aspects of ethics in that they are more important, fundamental, universal, rational, and objective (pp. 6–7). W. D. Ross (1930), a twentieth-century Scottish philosopher, identified a number of moral duties of the ethical person: *nonmaleficence, fidelity, beneficence, justice,* and *autonomy.* These moral principles have provided a foundation for the ethical codes of psychologists and other professionals (Bersoff & Koeppl, 1993; also Callan & Callan, 2005).

Our focus here is on *applied professional ethics*, the application of broad ethical principles and specific rules to the problems that arise in professional practice (Beauchamp & Childress, 2001). Applied ethics in school psychology is, thus, a combination of ethical principles and rules, ranging from more basic rules to rules of professional etiquette, that guide the conduct of the practitioner in his or her professional interactions with others. Furthermore, although school psychologists are employed in a variety of settings, in this text we emphasize the special challenges of school-based practice.

Professionalism and Ethics

Professionalization has been described as:

> the process by which an occupation, usually on the basis of a claim to special competence and a concern for the quality of its work and benefits to society, obtains the exclusive right to perform a particular kind of work, to control training criteria and access to the profession, and to determine and evaluate the way the work is to be performed. (Chalk, Frankel, & Chafer, 1980, p. 3)

Professional associations or societies function to promote the profession by publicizing the services offered, safeguarding the rights of professionals, attaining benefits for its members, facilitating the exchange of and development of knowledge, and promoting standards to enhance the quality of professional work by its members (Chalk et al., 1980).

Codes of ethics appear to develop out of the self-interests of the profession and a genuine commitment to protect the interests of persons served. Most professional associations have recognized the need to balance self-interests against concern for the welfare of the consumer. Ethical codes are one mechanism to help ensure that members of a profession will deal justly with the public (Bersoff & Koeppl, 1993; Koocher & Keith-Spiegel, 2008).

However, the development of a code of ethics also serves to foster the profession's self-interests. A code of ethics is an indicator of the profession's willingness to accept responsibility for defining appropriate conduct and a commitment to self-regulation of members by the profession (Chalk et al., 1980). The adoption of a code of ethics often has been viewed as the hallmark of a profession's maturity. Ethical codes thus may serve to enhance the prestige of a profession and reduce the perceived need for external regulation and control.

The field of psychology has shown a long-standing commitment to activities that support and encourage appropriate professional conduct. As will be seen in this chapter, both the NASP and the APA have developed and adopted codes of ethics. These codes are drafted by committees within professional organizations and reflect the beliefs of association members about what constitutes appropriate professional conduct. They serve to protect the public by sensitizing professionals to the ethical aspects of service delivery, educating practitioners about the parameters of appropriate conduct, and helping professionals to monitor their own behavior. Furthermore, the codes of ethics of psychologists can now be accessed using the Internet, and for this reason they also increasingly serve to educate the public and recipients of services about the parameters of expected professional conduct by school psychologists. Finally, professional codes of ethics also provide guidelines for adjudicating complaints (Bowser, 2009; Koocher & Keith-Spiegel, 2008).

By encouraging appropriate professional conduct, associations such as the NASP and the APA help to ensure that each person served will receive the highest quality of professional service. As a result, the public's trust in psychologists and psychology is enhanced and maintained.

Ethical Codes Versus Ethical Conduct

Codes of ethics serve to protect the public. However, ethical conduct is not synonymous with simple conformity to a set of rules outlined in professional codes and standards (J. N. Hughes, 1986). As Kitchener (2000) and others (Bersoff, 1994; J. N. Hughes, 1986; Koocher & Keith-Spiegel, 2008) have noted, codes of ethics are imperfect guides to behavior for several reasons. First, ethical codes in psychology are composed of broad, abstract principles along with a number of more specific statements about appropriate professional conduct. They are at times vague and ambiguous (Bersoff, 1994; J. N. Hughes, 1986).

Second, competing ethical principles often apply in a particular situation (Bersoff & Koeppl, 1993; Haas & Malouf, 2005), and specific ethical guidelines may conflict with federal or state law (Kitchener, 2000; Koocher & Keith-Spiegel, 2008). In some situations, a primary or overriding consideration can be identified in choosing a course of action. In other situations, however, no one principle involved clearly outweighs the other(s) (Haas & Malouf, 2005). For example, the decision to allow a minor child the freedom to choose or refuse to participate in psychological services often involves a consideration of law, ethical principles (respect for autonomy and self-determination versus the welfare of the child), and the likely practical consequences of affording choices (enhanced treatment outcomes versus refusal of treatment).

A third reason ethical codes are imperfect is because they tend to be reactive. They frequently fail to address new and emerging ethical issues (Bersoff & Koeppl, 1993; Eberlein, 1987). Committees within professional associations often are formed to study the ways existing codes relate to emerging issues, and codes may be revised in response to new ethical concerns. Concern about the ethics of behavior modification techniques was a focus of the 1970s; in the 1980s, psychologists scrutinized the ethics of computerized psychodiagnostic assessment. In the 1990s, changes in codes of ethics reflected concerns about sexual harassment and fair treatment of individuals, regardless of their sexual orientation. In recent years, codes have emphasized the need for practitioner competence in the delivery of services to individuals from diverse experiential, linguistic, and cultural backgrounds. Codes also have been scrutinized to ensure relevance to the use of electronic media.

Ethical codes thus provide guidance for the professional in his or her decision making. Ethical conduct, however, involves careful choices based on knowledge of broad ethical principles and code statements, ethical reasoning, and personal values. In many situations, more than one course of action is acceptable. In some situations, no course of action is completely satisfactory. In all situations, the responsibility for ethical conduct rests with the individual practitioner (Eberlein, 1987; Haas, Malouf, & Mayerson, 1986; Koocher & Keith-Spiegel, 2008).

ETHICS TRAINING AND COMPETENCIES

Prior to the late 1970s, many applied psychology graduate programs (e.g., clinical psychology, school psychology) required little formal coursework in professional ethics. Ethics was often taught in the context of supervised practica and internship experiences, a practice Handelsman (1986) labeled "ethics training by 'osmosis'" (p. 371). A shortcoming of this approach is that student learning is limited by supervisor awareness and knowledge of ethical-legal issues and the types of situations encountered in the course of supervision (Handelsman, 1986). Consensus now exists that ethics, legal aspects of practice, and a problem-solving model need to be explicitly taught during graduate training (Dailor & Jacob, 2010; Haas et al., 1986; Tymchuk, 1985). Both the NASP and the APA graduate program training standards require coursework in professional ethics. Furthermore, in *School Psychology: A Blueprint for Training and Practice* (Ysseldyke et al., 2006), prepared by a task force composed of leaders in the field, knowledge of the ethical and legal aspects of professional practice was identified as a foundational competency for school psychologists, one that permeates all aspects of the provision of services.

In the 1980s, psychology trainers began to ask, "What should be the goals of ethics education in psychology?" (Haas et al., 1986; Kitchener, 1986); "What are the desired cognitive, affective, and behavioral 'ethics competencies' for school psychologists?" More recently, trainers have raised these questions: "How do school psychology students and practitioners gain competence, and ultimately expertise, in ethical decision making?" (Dailor & Jacob, 2010); "How do they gain a sense of themselves as ethical professionals?" (Handelsman, Gottlieb & Knapp, 2005, p. 59); and "How should ethics be taught?" A number of goals for ethics training have been suggested in the literature. An emerging picture of desired competencies includes the following:

- Competent practitioners are sensitive to "the ethical components of their work" and are aware that their actions "have real ethical consequences that can potentially harm as well as help others" (Kitchener, 1986, p. 307; also Welfel & Kitchener, 1992).
- Competent psychologists have a sound working knowledge of the content of codes of ethics, professional standards, and law pertinent to the delivery of services (Fine & Ulrich, 1988; Welfel & Lipsitz, 1984).
- Competent practitioners are committed to a proactive rather than a reactive stance in ethical thinking and conduct (Tymchuk, 1986). They use their broad knowledge of codes of ethics and law along with ethical reasoning skills to anticipate and prevent problems from arising.
- Skilled practitioners are able to analyze the ethical dimensions of a situation and demonstrate a well-developed "ability to reason about ethical issues" (Kitchener,

1986, p. 307). They have mastered and make use of a problem-solving model (de las Fuentes & Willmuth, 2005; McNamara, 2008; Tymchuk, 1981, 1986).

- Competent practitioners recognize that a system of ethical rules and ideals develops in the context of a specific culture, and they are sensitive to the ways their own values and standards for behavior may be similar to or different from those of individuals from other cultural groups. They "strive to understand the manner in which culture influences their own view of others and other's view of them" (Ortiz, Flanagan, & Dynda, 2008, p. 1721).

- Competent psychologists are aware of their own feelings and beliefs. They recognize that personal feelings, beliefs, and values influence professional decision making (Handelsman et al., 2005; Kitchener, 2000).

- Competent practitioners do their best to engage in *positive ethics*; that is, they strive for excellence rather than meeting minimal obligations outlined in codes of ethics and law (Knapp & VandeCreek, 2006).

- Competent practitioners appreciate the complexity of ethical decisions and are tolerant of ambiguity and uncertainty. They acknowledge and accept that there may be more than one appropriate course of action (de las Fuentes & Willmuth, 2005; Kitchener, 2000).

- Competent practitioners have the personal strength to act on decisions made and accept responsibility for their actions (de las Fuentes & Willmuth, 2005; Kitchener, 1986).

Two paradigms describe how students and school psychology practitioners develop ethical competence: the acculturation model (Handelsman et al., 2005) and a stage model (Dreyfus, 1997). Handelsman et al. (2005) describe ethics training of psychology graduate students as a dynamic, multiphase acculturation process.[1] They suggested that psychology, as a discipline and profession, has its own culture that encompasses aspirational ethical principles, ethical rules, professional standards, and values. Students develop their own "professional ethical identity" based on a process that optimally results in an adaptive integration of personal moral values and the ethics culture of the profession. Trainees who do not yet have a well-developed personal sense of morality, and those who do not understand and accept critical aspects of the ethics culture of psychology, may have difficulty making good ethical choices as psychologists.

The stage model describes a process whereby practitioners progress through five levels (Dreyfus, 1997). *Novice* practitioners are rules-bound and slow to make decisions. With some experience in applying rules of practice, *advanced beginners* become more capable of identifying multiple aspects of a complex situation and taking context into account, but they are still focusing on technical mastery of their skills. *Competent* practitioners are better able to identify key elements of a situation, see relationships among elements, recognize subtle differences between similar situations, balance skills and empathy, and consider the long-term effects of their decisions. However, because they are more skilled in considering relevant elements, competent practitioners are at times overwhelmed by the complexity of real-world problems. Practitioners who are *proficient* recognize situational patterns and subtle differences more quickly and they are able to prioritize elements in decision making more effortlessly. Proficient practitioners may not be conscious of the knowledge and thinking processes that provide the foundation for choices.

---

[1]Portions of this section appeared previously in Dailor and Jacob (2010).

Finally, because of many experiences with diverse situations, *experts* are able to rely on past decisions to inform future decisions, base decisions on subtle qualitative distinctions, and often have an intuitive grasp of what needs to be done without extensive analyses. Based on their review of research on the acquisition of expertise, Ericsson and Williams (2007) suggested that expertise is acquired by early supervised practice coupled with deliberate practice over an extended period of time, usually 10 years.

How should ethics be taught? Growing professional support exists for a planned, multilevel approach to training in ethics and law (Conoley & Sullivan, 2002; Dailor & Jacob, 2010; Fine & Ulrich, 1988). Tryon (2000) and others (Jacob-Timm, 1999) recommend that formal coursework in ethics and law be required at the beginning of graduate training to prepare students to participate in discussions of ethical and legal issues throughout their program. Because many aspects of school-based practice are regulated by law as well as ethics, we recommend integrated rather than separate instruction in ethics and law; furthermore, key concepts such as privacy, informed consent, and confidentiality have roots in both ethics and law. A foundational course can introduce students to broad ethical principles, codes of ethics, the major provisions of school law pertinent to practice, and an ethical-legal decision-making model. In addition, Handelsman et al. (2005) recommended that early coursework include activities to heighten self-awareness of personal values and beliefs. For example, they suggest asking students to write an ethics autobiography in which they reflect on their own values, as well as those of their families and cultures of origin, and consider what it means to be an ethical professional (p. 63; also Bashe, Anderson, Handelsman, & Klevansky, 2007). (For a discussion of methods in teaching ethical and legal issues in school psychology, see Williams, Sinko, & Epifanio, 2010).

A foundational course in ethics and law can provide opportunities for students to apply what they are learning about the ethical-legal aspects of practice by role-playing difficult situations and analyzing case incidents (Dailor & Jacob, 2010). However, while such coursework provides a critically important foundation for subsequent training, it is not sufficient to achieve desired practitioner competencies in ethics and law. If students have only one course, they may not be prepared to apply this knowledge across various domains of practice. In order for students to progress beyond the stage of advanced beginner, discussion of ethical-legal issues associated with diverse situations and professional roles must be a component of coursework in assessment, academic remediation, behavioral interventions, counseling, and consultation. For this reason, Tryon (2000) recommended that all graduate program course instructors discuss ethical issues related to their specialty areas.

Supervised field experiences provide a vitally important opportunity for students to apply their knowledge to multiple real-world situations (Harvey & Struzziero, 2008). With appropriate supervisory support, internship is "a prime time to develop ethical frameworks that will be useful throughout a professional career" (Conoley & Sullivan, 2002, p. 135). Field- and university-based supervisors consequently have a special obligation to model sound ethical-legal decision making and to monitor, assist, and support supervisees and early-career practitioners as they first encounter real-world challenges (Conoley & Sullivan, 2002; Handelsman et al., 2005; Harvey & Struzziero, 2008).

Although growing professional support exists for a planned, multilevel approach to graduate preparation in ethics, Dailor (2007) surveyed a nationally representative sample of public school psychology practitioners and found that only 24% of the 208 respondents reported receiving multilevel university ethics training that included all of the following: coursework in ethics, discussion of ethical issues in multiple courses, and supervised discussion of ethical issues in practica and internships.

Only a few empirical investigations of the effectiveness of formal ethics training have appeared in the literature (Tryon, 2001; Welfel, 1992). Baldick (1980) found that clinical and counseling interns who received formal ethics training were better able to identify ethical issues than interns without prior coursework in ethics. Tryon (2001) surveyed school psychology doctoral students from APA-accredited programs and found that students who had taken an ethics course and those who had completed more years of graduate study felt better prepared to deal with the ethical issues presented in the survey than those who had not taken an ethics course and who had completed fewer years of graduate education. Student ratings of their preparedness to deal with ethical issues were positively associated with the number of hours of supervised practicum experience completed. More recently, Dailor (2007) found an association between the types of university training school psychology practitioners had received and their preparedness to handle ethical issues on the job, with those who had received multilevel university preparation in ethics reporting higher levels of preparedness to handle ethical issues. Preparedness was not associated with degree level (doctoral or nondoctoral) or years of experience on the job (five or fewer years versus more than five years).

Several studies, however, have reported a gap between knowledge of the appropriate course of action and willingness to carry out that action (Bernard & Jara, 1986; Smith, McGuire, Abbott, & Blau, 1991; Tryon, 2000). Even when practitioners can identify what ought to be done, many would choose to do less than they believe they should (Bernard & Jara, 1986). Thus, at this time, additional research is needed to identify the types of ethics training that are most effective in developing the skills and necessary confidence for psychologists to take appropriate actions in ethically difficult situations (Handelsman et al., 2005; Tymchuk, 1985; Welfel, 1992).

CODES OF ETHICS

D. T. Brown (1979) suggested that school psychology emerged as an identifiable profession in the 1950s. Two professional associations, the APA and the NASP, have shaped the development of the profession. Each professional association has formulated its own code of ethics. Within the APA, Division 16 is the Division of School Psychology.[2]

APA and NASP Codes of Ethics

In joining the APA or the NASP, members agree to abide by that association's ethical principles. Additionally, psychologists who are members of the National School Psychologist Certification System and those who are members of state associations affiliated with the NASP are obligated to abide by the NASP's code of ethics. We believe school psychology practitioners should be thoroughly familiar with the NASP's (2010a) "Principles for Professional Ethics" and the APA's (2002) "Ethical Principles of Psychologists and Code of Conduct," whether or not they are members of a professional association. A psychologist with a broad knowledge base of ethical principles may be better prepared to make sound choices when ethically challenging situations arise. Furthermore, regardless of association membership or level of training, trainees and practitioners may be expected to know and abide by both the APA and NASP ethics codes in their work setting (Flanagan, Miller, & Jacob, 2005).

---

[2]For information about the history of APA's Division 16 and NASP, see Fagan and Wise (2007).

Professional codes of ethics apply "only to psychologists' activities that are part of their scientific, educational, or professional roles as psychologists. . . . These activities shall be distinguished from the purely private conduct of psychologists, which is not within the purview of the Ethics Code" (APA, 2002, Introduction and Applicability). Similarly, the NASP's code states: "School psychologists, in their private lives, are free to pursue their personal interests, except to the degree that those interests compromise professional effectiveness" (III.4.1). The boundaries between professional and personal behaviors are sometimes "fuzzy" (Pipes, Holstein, & Aguirre, 2005, p. 332). For example, when a psychologist engages in socially undesirable behavior in a public setting (e.g., a school psychologist is verbally abusive of the referee at a high school football game), the behavior may negatively impact his or her credibility, diminish trust in school psychologists in general, and confuse students and others who hear about or witness the event. Pipes et al. consequently encourage psychologists to aspire to high standards of ethical conduct in their personal, as well as professional, lives. They also recommended that practitioners think critically about the boundaries between personal and professional relationships and take care to identify when they are speaking "as a matter of personal opinion as opposed to speaking as experts" (p. 329).

NASP's "Principles for Professional Ethics"

The NASP "Principles for Professional Ethics" (NASP-PPE) was first adopted in 1974 and revised in 1984, 1992, 1997, 2000, and 2010 (also see Williams, Armistead, & Jacob, 2008, for a brief history of the early development of the code). The 2010 code is reprinted in Appendix A. NASP's code of ethics focuses on the special challenges of school-based practice. *School-based practice* is defined as "the provision of school psychological services under the authority of a state, regional, or local educational agency" whether the school psychologist "is an employee of the schools or contracted by the schools on a per-case or consultative basis" (NASP-PPE Definition of Terms).

The team of NASP members responsible for drafting the 2010 revision of the "Principles for Professional Ethics" shared a commitment to ensuring that the code, like its precursors, would address the unique circumstances associated with providing school-based psychological services and would emphasize protecting the rights and interests of schoolchildren and youth (NASP-PPE Introduction). More specifically, they attempted to incorporate the following special considerations of school-based practice:

- School psychologists must "balance the authority of parents to make decisions about their children with the needs and rights of those children, and the purposes and authority of schools." Within this framework, school psychologists "consider the interests and rights of children and youth to be their highest priority in decision making, and act as advocates for all students" (NASP-PPE Introduction).
- The mission of schools is to maintain order, ensure pupil safety, and educate children (*Burnside v. Byars*, 1966). As school employees, "school psychologists have a legal as well as an ethical obligation to take steps to protect all students from reasonably foreseeable risk of harm" (NASP-PPE Introduction).
- As school employees, school psychology practitioners are *state actors*; that is, their actions are seen to be an extension of the state's authority to educate children. This creates a special obligation for school psychologists to know and respect the rights of schoolchildren under federal and state law (NASP-PPE Introduction).
- Like other mental health practitioners, school psychologists often provide assessment and intervention services within the framework of an established psychologist-client

relationship. However, at other times, as members of a school's instructional support team, school psychologists may provide consultative services to student assistance teams, classrooms, schools, or other recipients of service that do not fall within the scope of an established psychologist-client relationship (NASP-PPE Definition of Terms). This distinction is particularly important for school practitioners because, in law and ethics, the rules for informed consent are linked to whether services are provided within the context of a school psychologist–client relationship.

- Recent years have witnessed growing interest in better protection of sensitive student information. Partly as a result of changes that have occurred in health care settings, many parents now have a greater expectation of control of physical and mental health information about their children, even when information is to be shared internally in the school setting (Gelfman & Schwab, 2005b; Schwab & Gelfman, 2005a, 2005b; Schwab et al., 2005). In addition, since 1999, many states have broadened the scope of their laws governing privilege to include confidential communications that occur within a school psychologist–client relationship.
- "School-based practitioners work in a context that emphasizes multidisciplinary problem solving and intervention" (NASP-PPE Introduction).

The NASP's 2010 code of ethics is organized around four broad ethical themes: Respecting the Dignity and Rights of All Persons; Professional Competence and Responsibility; Honesty and Integrity in Professional Relationships; and Responsibility to Schools, Families, Communities, the Profession, and Society. These themes were derived from the literature on ethical principles (e.g., Bersoff & Koeppl, 1993; Prilleltensky, 1997; W. D. Ross, 1930) and other ethical codes, especially that of the Canadian Psychological Association (CPA). The four broad themes subsume 17 ethical principles, and each principle is then further articulated by specific standards. The "broad themes, corollary principles, and ethical standards are to be considered in ethical decision making" (NASP-PPE Introduction). However, the broad themes statements are aspirational; NASP will seek to enforce only the 17 ethical principles and associated standards of conduct. NASP's broad ethical themes, corollary principles, and associated standards of conduct will be discussed in more detail in this and subsequent chapters.

APA's "Ethical Principles of Psychologists and Code of Conduct"

The "Ethical Standards of Psychologists" was first adopted by the APA in 1953. Eight revisions of the APA's code of ethics were published between 1959 and 1992. The current version, "Ethical Principles of Psychologists and Code of Conduct" (APA-EP), was adopted in 2002 and amended in 2010. (See Appendix B.) The APA's "Ethical Principles" differs from the NASP's "Principles for Professional Ethics" in that it was developed for psychologists with training in diverse specialty areas (clinical, industrial-organizational, and school psychology) and who work in a number of different settings (private practice, industry, hospitals and clinics, public schools, university teaching, and research).

The "Ethical Principles of Psychologists and Code of Conduct" consists of the following sections: Introduction and Applicability, Preamble, General Principles, and Ethical Standards. The General Principles section includes five broadly worded aspirational goals to be considered by psychologists in ethical decision making, and the Ethical Standards section sets forth enforceable rules for conduct. General Principle A, Beneficence and Nonmaleficence, means that psychologists engage in professional actions that are likely to benefit others, or at least do no harm (Flanagan et al., 2005).

Principle B is Fidelity and Responsibility. Consistent with this principle, psychologists build and maintain trust by being aware of and honoring their professional responsibilities to clients and the community. Principle C, Integrity, obligates psychologists to be open and honest in their professional interactions and faithful to the truth and to guard against unclear or unwise commitments. In accordance with Principle D, Justice, school psychologists seek to ensure that all persons have access to and can benefit from what psychology has to offer, and strive for fairness and nondiscrimination in the provision of services. Principle E, Respect for People's Rights and Dignity, encourages psychologists to respect the worth of all people and their rights to privacy, confidentiality, autonomy, and self-determination (Flanagan et al., 2005).

The APA's Ethical Standards (enforceable rules for conduct) are organized into six general sections: Resolving Ethical Issues, Competence, Human Relations, Privacy and Confidentiality, Advertising and Other Public Statements, and Record Keeping and Fees. These are followed by four sections on Education and Training, Research and Publication, Assessment, and Therapy (APA, 2002). (For additional information on the APA's 2002 ethics code, see C. B. Fisher, 2003; Knapp & VandeCreek, 2006; and Koocher & Keith-Spiegel, 2008.)

Professional Models or Guidelines for Service Delivery

Professional models or guidelines for the delivery of school psychological services differ from ethical codes in both scope and intent. The NASP's *A Model of Comprehensive and Integrated Services by School Psychologists* (2010a) represents a consensus among practitioners and trainers about the roles and duties of school psychologists, desirable conditions for the effective delivery of services, the components of a comprehensive school psychological services delivery system, and standards for best practices. This document can be used to inform practitioners, students, trainers, administrators, policy makers, and consumers about the nature and scope of appropriate and desirable services. The NASP and the APA seek to ensure that members abide by their respective ethical codes and investigate and adjudicate code violations. In contrast, *A Model of Comprehensive and Integrated Services by School Psychologists* identifies standards for excellence in the delivery of comprehensive school psychological services, and it is recognized that not all school psychologists or all school psychological service units will be able to meet every identified standard.

FOUR BROAD ETHICAL PRINCIPLES

The four broad themes that appear in the NASP's 2010 "Principles for Professional Ethics" provide an organizational framework for the introduction to ethical issues in school psychology in this section of the chapter. As noted previously, these themes also can be found in the literature on ethical principles (e.g., Bersoff & Koeppl, 1993; Prilleltensky, 1997; W. D. Ross, 1930) and other ethical codes, especially that of the Canadian Psychological Association (CPA) (2000). In this book we emphasize principles-based ethics. We encourage readers to think about the spirit and intent of broad ethical themes outlined in this section and to enhance their understanding of ethics by becoming familiar with other philosophical systems (see Knapp & VandeCreek, 2006).

Respect for the Dignity of Persons

Psychologists "accept as fundamental the principle of respect for the dignity of persons" (CPA, 2000; also see APA-EP Principle E). "School psychologists are committed to the application of their professional expertise for the purpose of promoting improvement in the quality of life for students, families, and school communities. This objective is pursued in ways that protect the dignity and rights of those involved. School psychologists consider the interests and rights of children and youth to be their highest priority in decision making . . . " (NASP-PPE Introduction). The general principle of respect for the dignity of all persons encompasses respect for the rights of individuals to *self-determination and autonomy*, *privacy and confidentiality*, and *fairness and justice* (NASP-PPE I; also CPA, 2000).

Self-Determination and Autonomy

"In their words and actions, school psychologists demonstrate respect for the autonomy of persons and their right to self-determination" (NASP-PPE I). They "respect the right of persons to participate in decisions affecting their own welfare" (NASP-PPE I.1).School psychologists apply the ethical principle of respect for self-determination and autonomy to their professional practices by seeking informed consent to establish a school psychologist–client relationship, and by ensuring that the individuals with whom they work have "a voice and a choice" in decisions that affect them.

Except for urgent situations, school psychologists generally seek the informed consent of an adult (the parent or guardian of a child) to establish a school psychologist–client relationship (NASP-PPE I.1.2). They respect the right of the individual providing consent to choose or decline the services offered (NASP-PPE I.1.5). School psychologists also honor, to the maximum extent appropriate, the right of children to assent to or decline school psychological services. (See Chapters 3 and 7.)

However, when working with children, sometimes it is necessary to balance the rights of self-determination and autonomy against concerns for the welfare of the child. The NASP's code of ethics states: "Ordinarily, school psychologists seek the student's assent to services; however, it is ethically permissible to bypass student assent to services if the service is considered to be of direct benefit to the student and/or is required by law" (NASP-PPE I.1.4; also see CPA, 2000). If a child's assent is not solicited, school psychologists nevertheless ensure that the child is informed about the nature of the services being provided, and is afforded opportunities to participate in decisions that affect him or her (NASP-PPE I.1.4, II.3.11).

As noted previously, school psychologists often provide services within the framework of an established school psychologist–client relationship. However, as members of a school's instructional support team, practitioners also provide consultative services to student assistance teams, classrooms, or schools that do not fall within the scope of an established school psychologist–client relationship (NASP-PPE Definition of Terms). Thus, while school practitioners encourage parental participation in school decisions affecting their children (NASP-PPE I.1.1, II.3.10), not all of their consultative services require informed parent consent, particularly if the resulting interventions are under the authority of the teacher and within the scope of typical classroom interventions (NASP-PPE I.1.1; also Corrao & Melton, 1988). (See Chapter 7.)

During their careers, school psychologists will encounter dilemmas regarding how to balance the rights of parents to make informed decisions about their children with the rights and needs of those children. For example: Under what circumstances should minors have the right to seek school psychological services on their own, without parent permission? When should a minor be afforded the opportunity to make a choice whether to participate in or refuse the psychological services being offered?

Privacy and Confidentiality

Psychologists "respect the right of persons to choose for themselves whether to disclose their private thoughts, feelings, beliefs, and behaviors" (NASP-PPE I.2; also

APA-EP Principle E), and every effort is made to avoid undue invasion of privacy (APA-EP Principle E; NASP-PPE I.2.2). School psychologists "do not seek or store private information about clients that is not needed in the provision of services" (NASP-PPE I.2.2; APA-EP 4.04).

Practitioners also use appropriate safeguards to protect the confidentiality of client disclosures. Except for urgent situations, they inform clients of the boundaries of confidentiality at the outset of establishing a school psychologist–client relationship. They seek a shared understanding with clients regarding the types of information that will and will not be shared with third parties and recognize that it may be necessary to discuss how confidential information will be managed at multiple points in an ongoing professional relationship (NASP-PPE I.2.3).

Carrie Johnson (Case 1.1) will assure Joanne that her disclosure of drug use during pregnancy will be held in strict confidence and not shared with anyone else, and not included in Samantha's school psychology records (NASP-PPE I.2.2; APA-EP 4.04). Carrie recognizes that she has a special ethical obligation to safeguard the confidentiality of sensitive and private medical information (NASP-PPE I.2.7). Furthermore, the information that Joanne disclosed about her pregnancy is not needed for the purpose of determining eligibility for special education services or for planning appropriate educational interventions (NASP-PPE I.2.2, I.2.5), and could have negative repercussions for Joanne and Samantha if made available to others.

In situations in which confidentiality is promised or implied, school psychologists do not reveal information to third parties "without the agreement of a minor child's parent or legal guardian (or an adult student), except in those situations in which failure to release information would result in danger to the student or others, or where otherwise

---

Case 1.1

Samantha's first- and second-grade teachers observed that she experienced difficulties with concentration and memory. She frequently failed to remember letter sounds and math facts she had previously mastered. Now in third grade, Samantha continues to perform well below grade level even after multiple individualized interventions were attempted in the classroom. Samantha's mother, Joanne, agrees with the third-grade teacher that Samantha should be evaluated to determine whether she is eligible for special education services.

Carrie Johnson, the school psychologist, meets with Joanne to ensure she is informed about the nature and scope of the psychoeducational evaluation, and to gather information about Samantha's developmental history. Joanne is employed as a classroom teacher aide at the same small, rural school her daughter attends. In the meeting with Carrie, Joanne discloses that she was involved "with the wrong boyfriend" during her first semester away at college. She "partied a lot, used all kinds of drugs, and got pregnant." Because she was "too messed up" to realize she was pregnant, she continued to use drugs during the early months of her pregnancy, but then moved back home with her parents and "got straightened out." Joanne goes on to say, "Please don't tell anyone about this. I've never even told any of my doctors because my mom said it would be difficult for me to get health insurance if drug abuse showed up in my medical records. And if my drug use history gets out at this school—you know how this community is and how people talk—it could hurt Samantha and I might even lose my job."

required by law." Furthermore, when practitioners share information with third parties, they "discuss and/or release confidential information only for professional purposes and only with persons who have a legitimate need to know" (NASP-PPE I.2.5).

The ethical and legal issues of privacy, confidentiality, and privilege will create challenges for practitioners. For example, what information do teachers and other instructional staff need to know about a child's physical health, mental health, and family background to provide effective individualized instruction? Do parents have a right to know what their child tells a school psychologist? What if a young teenager discloses that he or she is planning to hurt someone or has committed a crime? These issues will be further explored in the chapters ahead.

Fairness and Justice

Respect for the dignity of all persons also encompasses the ethical obligation to ensure fairness, nondiscrimination, and justice. School psychologists "use their expertise to cultivate school climates that are safe and welcoming to all persons regardless of actual or perceived characteristics, including race, ethnicity, color, religion, ancestry, national origin, immigration status, socioeconomic status, primary language, gender, sexual orientation, gender identity, gender expression, disability, or any other distinguishing characteristics" (NASP-PPE I.3; also APA-EP Principle E). They do not engage in or condone actions or policies that discriminate against persons, including students and their families, other recipients of service, supervisees, and colleagues based on these or any other actual or perceived characteristics (I.3.1). Furthermore, school psychologists "work to correct school practices that are unjustly discriminatory . . ." (NASP-PPE I.3.3).

The school psychologist's obligation to students from diverse cultural, linguistic, and experiential backgrounds goes beyond striving to be impartial and unprejudiced in the delivery of services. Practitioners have an ethical responsibility to actively "pursue awareness and knowledge of how diversity factors may influence child development, behavior, and school learning" (NASP-PPE I.3.2), and to pursue the skills needed to promote the mental health and education of diverse students (NASP-PPE II.1.2). Ignoring or minimizing the importance of characteristics such as ethnicity, disabilities, sexual orientation, or socioeconomic background may result in approaches that are ineffective and a disservice to children, parents, teachers, and other recipients of services (see NASP-PPE I.3.2; also Erickson Cornish et al., 2008; Esquivel, Lopez, & Nahari, 2007; Jacob, Drevon, Abbuhl, & Taton, 2010; Rogers & Lopez, 2002).

Consistent with the broad ethical principle of justice, school psychologists also "strive to ensure that all children have equal opportunity to participate in and benefit from school programs and that all students and families have access to and can benefit from school psychological services" (NASP-PPE I.3.4, IV; also APA-EP Principle D; Shriberg et al., 2008).

Responsible Caring (Professional Competence and Responsibility)

A shared theme in ethical codes of the helping professions is that of beneficence. *Beneficence*, or responsible caring, means that psychologists engage in actions that are likely to benefit others, or at least do no harm (CPA, 2000; Welfel & Kitchener, 1992; also APA-EP Principle A; NASP-PPE II). "To do this, school psychologists must practice within the boundaries of their competence, use scientific knowledge from psychology and education to help clients and others make informed choices, and accept responsibility for their work" (NASP-PPE II).

Competence

NASP's code of ethics requires that school psychologists "engage only in practices for which they are qualified and competent" (II.1; also APA-EP 2.01). As noted previously, the term *competent* generally suggests that the practitioner is able to integrate professional knowledge and skills with an understanding of the client and situation and make appropriate decisions, based on a consideration of both the immediate and long-term effects (Dreyfus, 1997; also see Barnett, Doll, Younggren, & Rubin, 2007; Kaslow et al., 2007). Practitioners must consider their competence to provide various types of services and to use techniques that are new to them. They also must consider whether they are competent to provide services in light of client characteristics such as age; disability; ethnic, racial, and language background; and sexual orientation and gender identity. Hannah Cook (Case 1.2) needs to seek assistance in evaluating Melissa to ensure a fair and valid assessment. Psychologists who step beyond their competence in assessing children place the student at risk for misdiagnosis, misclassification, miseducation, and possible psychological harm (see Chapter 6).

The students who attend our nation's schools have become increasingly diverse in terms of race, ethnicity, language, national origin, and family composition (Ortiz, 2008). In addition, gay, lesbian, and transgender youth now "come out" at earlier ages than previous generations, often during their middle or high school years (Jacob et al., 2010). Consequently, all practitioners must assess and periodically reassess their competence to provide services to a diverse clientele, and seek the knowledge necessary to provide culturally sensitive services in the schools where they work. Where understanding of age, gender, race, ethnicity, national origin, religion, sexual orientation, gender identity or expression, disability, language, or socioeconomic status is essential for providing effective services, school psychologists have or obtain the training, experience, consultation, or supervision necessary to ensure the competence of their services, or they make appropriate referrals (APA-EP 2.01; also NASP-PPE I.3.2).

School psychologists are ethically obligated to "remain current regarding developments in research, training, and professional practices that benefit children, families, and schools. They also understand that professional skill development beyond that of the novice practitioner requires well-planned continuing professional development and professional supervision" (NASP-PPE II.1.4; also APA-EP 2.03). Our codes of ethics encourage practitioners to engage in the lifelong learning that is necessary to achieve and maintain expertise in the field of school psychology. (See Armistead, 2008.)

Responsibility

In all areas of service delivery, school psychologists strive to maximize benefit and avoid doing harm. Consistent with this principle of responsible caring, school psychologists use the science of psychology to assist students, teachers, parents, and others in making

---

Case 1.2

Hannah Cook, school psychologist, received a referral to evaluate Melissa Gardner, a four-year-old. Melissa receives special education and related services because she is hearing impaired; now her parents and teachers have begun to suspect she has learning and emotional problems as well. Hannah has no formal training or supervised experience working with hearing-impaired preschoolers, and she is uncertain how to proceed with the referral.

informed choices (APA-EP Preamble; NASP-PPE II). In addition, practitioners monitor the impact of their professional decisions and the consequences of those decisions, work to correct ineffective recommendations, and strive to offset any harmful consequences of decisions made (APA-EP Principle B; NASP-PPE II.2, II.2.2).

Under the broad principle of professional competence and responsibility, NASP's code of ethics has specific standards for responsible assessment and intervention practices (II.3), school-based record keeping (II.4), and use of professional materials (II.5).

Honesty and Integrity in Professional Relationships

A psychologist-client relationship is a *fiduciary* relationship, that is, one based on trust. To build and maintain trust, school psychologists must demonstrate integrity in professional relationships. The broad principle of integrity encompasses the moral obligations of fidelity, nonmaleficence, and beneficence. *Fidelity* refers to a continuing faithfulness to the truth and to one's professional duties (Bersoff & Koeppl, 1993). Practitioners are obligated to be open and honest in their interactions with others and to adhere to their professional promises (CPA, 2000; APA-EP Principle B; NASP-PPE III).

Consistent with the broad principle of honesty in professional relationships, school psychologists provide a forthright explanation of the nature and scope of their services, roles, and priorities (NASP-PPE III.2). They "explain all professional services to clients in a clear, understandable manner" (NASP-PPE III.2.1). Case 1.3 illustrates the importance of openly defining the parameters of the services to be offered in the school setting. Madeleine has become Hannah's consultee in this consultant-consultee relationship. Hannah is bound by the obligation and expectation that what is shared and learned in their professional interaction is confidential; she may not share information about her consultee with the principal without Madeleine's explicit consent to do so.

In defining their job roles to the school community, school psychologists also identify the services they provide and those that are outside the scope of their job roles (NASP-PPE III.2.2; APA-EP Principle E). It is the job role of the building principal, not the school psychologist, to gather information on teacher effectiveness (also NASP-PPE III.2.4). If Hannah violates the confidentiality of the consultative relationship and shares information about Madeleine's teaching with the school administration, her actions would most likely undermine teacher trust in school psychologists and diminish her ability to work with other teachers in need of consultative services. The ethical issues associated with the consultation role are also discussed in Chapters 8 and 9.

Case 1.3

Madeleine Fine, a new first-grade teacher, asks Hannah Cook, the school psychologist, for some ideas on handling Kevin, a child who has become a behavior problem in the classroom. After observing in the classroom, it is evident to Hannah that Madeleine needs some help working with Kevin and developing effective classroom management strategies. Hannah offers to meet with Madeleine once a week over a six-week period to work on classroom management skills, and Madeleine agrees. Shortly after their third consultation session, the building principal asks Hannah for her assessment of Madeleine's teaching competence. The principal indicates that she plans to terminate Madeleine during her probationary period if there are problems with her teaching effectiveness. Hannah is not sure how to respond to the principal's request.

Furthermore, consistent with the general principle of integrity in professional relationships, psychologists must be honest and straightforward about the boundaries of their competencies (NASP-PPE III.1.1, III.2.1). "Competency levels, education, training, experience, and certification and licensing credentials are accurately represented to clients, recipients of services, and others" (NASP-PPE III.1.1; also APA-EP Principle C). School psychology interns and practicum students identify themselves as such when seeking to establish a school psychologist–client relationship. Practitioners inform clients if they are offering a service that is new to them so that the client can make an informed choice about whether to accept the service. Hannah Cook (Case 1.2) is obligated to inform her supervisor and Melissa's parents that she has little expertise in the assessment of hearing-impaired preschoolers so that a course of action can be pursued that is in the best interests of the child.

School psychologists also respect and understand the areas of competence of other professionals in their work settings and communities, and they work in full cooperation with others "in relationships based on mutual respect" to meet the needs of students (NASP-PPE III.3; also APA-EP Principle B). As noted previously, school-based practitioners work in a context that emphasizes multidisciplinary problem solving and intervention. Consistent with their professional duties, they "encourage and support the use of all resources to serve the interests of students" (NASP-PPE III.3.1).

In addition, the principle of integrity in professional relationships also requires school psychologists to avoid multiple relationships and conflicts of interest that may interfere with professional effectiveness (NASP-PPE III.4; APA-EP 3.05a). "School psychologists attempt to resolve such situations in a manner that provides greatest benefit to the client" (NASP-PPE III.4.2). Multiple relationships occur when a psychologist is in a professional role with a client and at the same time is in another role with that person or in a relationship with an individual related to or closely associated with the client. The APA's ethics code states that a psychologist should refrain from entering into a multiple relationship "if it can reasonably be expected to impair the psychologist's objectivity, competence, or effectiveness" in providing services (APA-EP 3.05a; also NASP-PPE III.4.2). For example, it would not be appropriate to provide services to a friend's child. However, the APA's code recognizes that multiple relationships are not always unethical. School psychologists must think carefully about whether the existence of multiple roles (e.g., professional, social, business) in relation to a client or his or her family will impair professional objectivity or effectiveness (Flanagan et al., 2005).

Practitioners also avoid conflicts of interest. "When personal beliefs, conflicts of interests, or multiple relationships threaten to diminish professional effectiveness or would be viewed by the public as inappropriate, school psychologists ask their supervisor for reassignment of responsibilities, or they direct the client to alternative services" (NASP-PPE III.4.2).

Furthermore, school psychologists "do not exploit clients, supervisees, or graduate students through professional relationships or condone these actions by their colleagues. They do not participate in or condone sexual harassment . . . " (NASP-PPE III.4.3; also see APA-EP 3.02, 3.08). They "do not engage in sexual relationships with individuals over whom they have evaluation authority" and "do not engage in sexual relationships with their current or former pupil-clients; the parents, siblings, or other close family members of current pupil-clients; or current consultees" (NASP-PPE III.4.3; also APA-EP 3.02, 3.08).

Consistent with the general principle of honesty and integrity, psychologists also do not take credit for work that is not their own (APA-EP Principle C; NASP-PPE IV.5.8, IV.5.9). "When publishing or presenting research or other work, school psychologists do not plagiarize the works or ideas of others" (NASP-PPE IV.5.8). Furthermore, they take credit "only for work they have actually performed or to which they have contributed" (APA-EP 8.12; also NASP-PPE IV.5.9).

Responsibility to Schools, Families, Communities, the Profession, and Society

"Psychology functions as a discipline within the context of human society. Psychologists, both in their work and as private citizens, have responsibilities to the societies in which they live and work, such as the neighborhood or city, and to the welfare of all human beings in those societies" (CPA, 2000; also APA-EP Principle B; Prilleltensky, 1991). Consistent with these ideas, the NASP's fourth broad aspirational principle states:

> School psychologists promote healthy school, family, and community environments. They assume a proactive role in identifying social injustices that affect children and schools and strive to reform systems-level patterns of injustice. They maintain the public trust in school psychologists by respecting law and encouraging ethical conduct. School psychologists advance professional excellence by mentoring less experienced practitioners and contributing to the school psychology knowledge base. (NASP-PPE IV)

Under the fourth broad principle of responsibility to schools, families, communities, the profession, and society, NASP's code of ethics has specific standards for promoting healthy school, family, and community environments (IV.1); respecting law and the relationship of law and ethics (IV.2); maintaining public trust by self-monitoring and peer monitoring (IV.3); contributing to the profession by mentoring, teaching, and supervision (IV.4); and contributing to the school psychology knowledge base (IV.5).

Charlie's conduct (Case 1.4) is consistent with our ethical responsibility to speak up for the needs and rights of students even when it is difficult to so (NASP-PPE Introduction) and to use our professional expertise "to promote school, family, and community environments that are safe and healthy for children" (NASP-PPE IV.1). School psychologists are ethically obligated to help ensure that all youth can attend school, learn, and develop their personal identities in an environment free from discrimination, harassment, violence, and abuse (NASP-PPE IV.1.2). Through advocacy and education of staff and students, Charlie will work to foster a school climate that promotes not only understanding and acceptance of individual differences, but also a respect for and valuing of those differences.

In keeping with our responsibilities to the communities in which we live and work, school psychologists know and respect federal and state law and school policies (NASP-PPE IV.2; see "Relationship Between Ethics and Law," later in this chapter).

Case 1.4

After several incidents of harassment of gay teens and students who do not conform to gender-role expectations, Charlie Maxwell, school psychologist, became increasingly convinced that the schools in his district were not a safe or supportive place for lesbian, gay, biattractional, or transgender (LGBT) youth. He began to read about the developmental needs and challenges of LGBT youth and those questioning (Q) their sexual orientation or gender identity, and he spent time talking with LGBTQ teens about their experiences at school. He then formed alliances with school and community leaders who shared his concerns. Although he will face opposition, Charlie will advocate for districtwide changes to reduce harassment and improve the school climate for LGBTQ youth.

Also consistent with the broad principle of responsibility to schools, families, communities, the profession, and society, school psychologists monitor their own conduct to ensure that it conforms to high ethical standards, and they monitor the conduct of their professional colleagues. Self- and peer monitoring for ethical compliance safeguards the welfare of others and fosters trust in psychology. If concerns about unethical conduct by another psychologist cannot be resolved informally through a collegial problem-solving process, practitioners take further action appropriate to the situation, such as notifying the practitioner's worksite supervisor of their concerns or filing a complaint with a professional ethics committee (NASP-PPE IV.3.3; also APA-EP 1.04). (See "Unethical Conduct," later in this chapter.)

School psychologists also contribute to the profession by mentoring, teaching, and supervision: "As part of their obligation to students, schools, society, and their profession, school psychologists mentor less experienced practitioners and graduate students to assure high quality services, and they serve as role models for sound ethical and professional practices and decision making" (NASP-PPE IV.4).

Finally, psychologists accept the obligation to contribute to the knowledge base of psychology and education in order to further improve services to children, families, and others and, in a more general sense, promote human welfare (CPA, 2000; APA-EP Principle B; NASP-PPE IV.5). For this reason, they are encouraged to participate in, assist in, or conduct and disseminate research (NASP-PPE IV.5). When school psychologists engage in research activities, they "respect the rights, and protect the well-being, of research participants" (NASP-PPE IV.5.2). (See Chapter 10.)

SUMMARY

In this section, four broad ethical principles were introduced. The first was respect for the dignity of persons. Consistent with this principle, we value client autonomy and safeguard the client's right to self-determination, respect client privacy and the confidentiality of disclosures, aspire to fairness in interactions with the client and others, and promote justice in the environments where we work and live. The second broad principle was responsible caring. We engage in actions that are likely to benefit others. To do so, we work within the boundaries of our professional competence and accept responsibility for our actions. The third principle was integrity in professional relationships. We are candid and honest about the nature and scope of the services we offer and work in cooperation with other professionals to meet the needs of children in the schools. The fourth principle was responsibility to schools, families, communities, the profession, and society. We recognize that our profession exists within the context of society and work to ensure that the science of psychology is used to promote human welfare.

ETHICAL AND LEGAL DECISION MAKING

In this portion of the chapter, we address the following questions: What makes a situation ethically challenging? When the needs and rights of multiple parties conflict, is our primary responsibility to the student, parent, teacher, or school system? How do we evaluate whether a course of action is ethical? And how can we make good choices when ethical-legal dilemmas arise?

What Makes a Situation Ethically Challenging?

Jacob-Timm (1999) surveyed school psychology practitioners and asked them to describe ethically challenging situations that they had encountered in their work. She found that ethical-legal dilemmas can be created by situations involving competing ethical principles, conflicts between ethics and law, the conflicting interests of multiple parties, dilemmas inherent in the dual roles of employee and pupil advocate, poor educational practices resulting in potential harm to students, and because it is difficult to decide how broad ethics code statements apply to a particular situation (Jacob-Timm, 1999; also Dailor, 2007). In her more recent survey of school psychology practitioners, Dailor (2007) found that almost three-fourths of the 208 respondents indicated they had encountered at least one of eight types of ethical dilemmas within the previous year. Whereas some ethical dilemmas are quickly and easily resolved, others are troubling and time-consuming (Sinclair, 1998). These findings support the view that, in addition to knowledge of the content of ethical codes, skill in using a systematic decision-making procedure is needed.

Relationship Between Ethics and Law

As noted previously, *professional ethics* is a combination of broad ethical principles and rules that guide the conduct of a practitioner in his or her professional interactions with others. *Law* is a body of rules of conduct prescribed by the state that has binding legal force. Both the APA and NASP codes of ethics require practitioners to know and respect the law (APA-EP Introduction and Applicability; NASP-PPE Introduction, IV.2.2). Professional codes of ethics are generally viewed as requiring decisions that are "more correct or more stringent" than required by law (Ballantine, 1979, p. 636). The APA's ethics code states that if the code "establishes a higher standard of conduct than is required by law, psychologists must meet that higher ethical standard" (APA-EP Introduction and Applicability; also NASP-PPE Introduction).

In the delivery of school psychological services, practitioners may face decisions involving possible conflicts between codes of ethics and law. In such circumstances, practitioners are encouraged to ask themselves: "Do I understand my legal obligations correctly? What actions does the law specifically require or prohibit (*must* do, *can't* do)? What actions does the law permit (*can* do)? Even if an action is legal, is it ethical? Do I understand my ethical obligations correctly?" (Knapp, Gottlieb, Berman, & Handelsman, 2007; Stefkovich, 2006).

If the ethical responsibilities of psychologists conflict with law, regulations, or other governing legal authority, psychologists clarify the nature of the conflict, make known their commitment to their code of ethics, and take steps to resolve the conflict in a responsible manner. The APA code states, "Under no circumstances may this standard be used to justify or defend violating human rights" (APA-EP 1.02, also 1.03; also see NASP-PPE Introduction, IV.2.3). The NASP's code of ethics states: "When conflicts between ethics and law occur, school psychologists take steps to resolve the conflict through positive, respected, and legal channels. If not able to resolve the conflict in this manner, they may abide by the law, as long as the resulting actions do not violate basic human rights" (NASP-PPE IV.2.3).

Ethical Challenge of Multiple Clients

School psychologists frequently face the challenge of considering the needs and rights of multiple clients and other recipients of services, including children, parents, teachers, and systems (Jacob-Timm, 1999; NASP-PPE Introduction; also see M.A. Fisher, 2009). The Canadian Code of Ethics states, "Although psychologists have a responsibility to respect the dignity of all persons with whom they come in contact in their role as psychologists, the nature of their contract with society demands that their greatest responsibility be to those persons in the most vulnerable position" (CPA, 2000, Principle I). Consistent with the idea that ethical priority should be given to the most vulnerable persons, NASP's code of ethics states, "School psychologists consider the interest and rights of children and youth to be their highest priority in decision making, and act as advocates for all students" (NASP-PPE Introduction; also see APA-EP Principle E).

How Do We Evaluate Whether a Course of Action Is Ethical or Unethical?

Ethics involves "making decisions of a moral nature about people and their interactions in society" (Kitchener, 1986, p. 306). Individuals may make choices of a moral nature primarily on an intuitive level or a critical-evaluative level (Hare, 1981; Kitchener, 1986). Choices made on the intuitive level are based on "people's immediate feeling responses to situations," along with personal beliefs about what they should or should not do (Kitchener, 1986, p. 309).

Psychologists, however, have special obligations when making ethical choices in the context of a professional relationship (Haas & Malouf, 2005). In the provision of psychological services, decision making on a critical-evaluative level is consistent with sound professional practice. The critical-evaluative level of ethical decision making involves following a systematic procedure. This procedure may involve the exploration of feelings and beliefs, but also includes consideration of general ethical principles and codes of ethics and possibly consultation with colleagues. Psychologists need to be aware of their own feelings and values and how they may influence their decisions (N. D. Hansen & Goldberg, 1999; Newman, 1993). However, reliance on feelings and intuition alone in professional decision making may result in poor decisions or confusion (Kitchener, 1986).

How do we evaluate whether a course of action is ethical or unethical? Haas and Malouf (2005, p. 3) suggested that an act or a decision is likely to be viewed as ethical if it has the following three characteristics: (1) The decision is *principled*, based on generally accepted ethical principles; (2) the action is a *reasoned* outcome of a consideration of the principles; and (3) the decision is *universalizable*, that is, the psychologist would recommend the same course of action to others in a similar situation. The consequences of the course of action chosen must also be considered—namely, will the action chosen result in more good than harm? Evaluation of whether a course of action is ethical thus involves consideration of characteristics of the decision itself (based on accepted principles and universality), the process of decision making (reasoned), and the consequences of the decision.

Knapp and VandeCreek (2006) have called for a greater emphasis on *positive ethics* in choosing a course of action. A positive approach to ethics encourages psychologists to focus on moral excellence rather than meeting minimal obligations outlined in codes of ethics. Psychologists are encouraged to become familiar with philosophical systems of ethics, to internalize schemas for moral excellence, and to integrate schemas of moral excellence into their professional decision making.

Eight-Step Problem-Solving Model

Three broad types of ethical-legal challenges arise in professional practice: ethical dilemmas, ethical transgressions, and legal quandaries. Ethical dilemmas occur when "there are good but contradictory ethical reasons to take conflicting and incompatible courses of action" (Knauss, 2001, p. 231; also Beauchamp & Childress, 2001), and may foster moral distress among psychologists (Austin, Rankel, Kagan, Bergum, & Lemermeyer, 2005). Ethical transgressions or violations are those acts that go against professional expectations for ethical conduct and violate enforceable ethics codes. Ethical transgressions can result in harm to students or others and create a problematic situation for colleagues who must decide whether and how to confront the misconduct (Dailor & Jacob, 2010). Finally, disregard for federal or state law can result in infringement of the legal rights of pupils and families; parent-school disputes, especially with regard to special education law; and legal action against the school or school psychologist.

Sinclair (1998) observed that "some ethical decision making is virtually automatic and the individual may not be aware of having made an ethical decision. In other situations, ethical decision making is not automatic but leads rapidly to an easy resolution," particularly if a clear-cut standard exists. However, "some ethical issues . . . require a time-consuming process of deliberation" (p. 171). Eberlein (1987) and others (Kitchener, 1986; Knapp & VandeCreek, 2006; Tymchuk, 1986) suggested that mastery of an explicit decision-making model or procedure may help the practitioner make informed, well-reasoned choices when dilemmas arise in professional practice. Tymchuk has also noted that in difficult situations the course of action chosen may be challenged. Use of a systematic problem-solving strategy will allow the practitioner to describe *how* a decision was made. This may afford some protection when difficult decisions come under the scrutiny of others. Furthermore, practitioners may find a systematic decision-making model helpful in anticipating and preventing problems from occurring (Sinclair, 1998).

The following eight-step problem-solving model is adapted from Koocher and Keith-Spiegel (2008, pp. 21–25):

1. Describe the parameters of the situation.
2. Define the potential ethical-legal issues involved.
3. Consult ethical and legal guidelines and district policies that might apply to the resolution of each issue (N. D. Hansen & Goldberg, 1999). Consider the broad ethical principles as well as specific mandates involved (N. D. Hansen & Goldberg, 1999; Kitchener, 1986).
4. Evaluate the rights, responsibilities, and welfare of all affected parties (e.g., pupil, teachers, classmates, other school staff, parents, siblings). N. D. Hansen and Goldberg (1999) encouraged consideration of the cultural characteristics of affected parties that may be salient to the decision.
5. Generate a list of alternative decisions possible for each issue.
6. Enumerate the consequences of making each decision. Evaluate the short-term, ongoing, and long-term consequences of each possible decision, considering the possible psychological, social, and economic costs to affected parties (Tymchuk, 1986). Eberlein (1987, p. 353) advised consideration of how each possible course of action would "affect the dignity of and the responsible caring for all of the people involved." Consultation with colleagues may be helpful.
7. Consider any evidence that the various consequences or benefits resulting from each decision will actually occur (i.e., a risk-benefit analysis).
8. Make the decision. Consistent with codes of ethics (APA, NASP), the school psychologist accepts responsibility for the decision made and monitors the consequences of the course of action chosen.

In recent years, a number of ethical decision-making models have appeared in the literature (e.g., McNamara, 2008). Although many appear useful (Barnett, Behnke, Rosenthal, & Koocher, 2007), it is important to recognize that, to date, it has not been established that the use of a decision-making model necessarily improves the quality of practitioner choices (Cottone & Claus, 2000). Dailor (2007) asked school psychology survey participants to identify the types of problem-solving strategies they used when handling difficult situations in the previous year. Less than one-quarter of respondents reported using a systematic decision-making model. Respondents who had received multilevel university training (coursework in ethics, discussion of ethical issues in multiple courses, and supervised discussion of ethical issues in practica and internships) were more likely to report use of a systematic decision-making model than those who had not received multilevel ethics preparation. However, most survey participants indicated that they did consult with colleagues when faced with a challenging situation. Gottlieb (2006) identified best practices in providing consultation to colleagues who are facing a difficult ethical situation.

UNETHICAL CONDUCT

As noted previously, one of the functions of professional associations is to develop and promote standards to enhance the quality of work by its members (Chalk et al., 1980). By encouraging appropriate professional conduct, associations such as the APA and the NASP strive to ensure that each person served will receive the highest quality of service and, thus, build and maintain public trust in psychology and psychologists. Failure to do so is likely to result in increased external regulation of the profession.

Appropriate professional conduct is defined through the development and frequent revision of codes of ethics and professional standards.

> But the presence of a set of ethical principles or rules of conduct is only part, albeit an important one, of the machinery needed to effect self-regulation. The impact of a profession's ethical principles or rules on its members' behavior may be negligible . . . without appropriate support activities to encourage proper professional conduct, or the means to detect and investigate possible violations, and to impose sanctions on violators. (Chalk et al., 1980, p. 2)

The APA and NASP support a range of activities designed to educate and sensitize practitioners to the parameters of appropriate professional conduct. Both include ethics coursework as a required component in their standards for graduate training, and each organization disseminates information on professional conduct through publications and the support of symposia. In addition, continued professional training in the area of ethics is required for renewal of a Nationally Certified School Psychologist (NCSP) credential, and many states require continuing education credits in ethics for renewal of licensure.

The APA and NASP also each support a standing ethics committee. Ethics committees are made up of volunteer members of the professional association. Ethics committees respond to informal inquiries about ethical issues, investigate complaints about possible code of ethics violations by association members, and attempt to educate and/or impose sanctions on violators.

Ethics Committees and Sanctions

The APA (2001) developed an extensive set of "Rules and Procedures" for investigation and adjudication of ethical complaints against APA members. According to the "Rules and Procedures," the primary objectives of the ethics committee are to "maintain ethical conduct by psychologists at the highest professional level, to educate psychologists concerning ethical standards, [and] to endeavor to protect the public against harmful conduct by psychologists" (Part I, #1). The ethics committee investigates complaints alleging violation of the ethics code by APA members. Possible sanctions for ethics violations include issuance of an educative letter, reprimand or censure, expulsion, and stipulated resignation (APA, 2001).

The purpose of the NASP's Ethical and Professional Practices Committee is: "(1) to promote and maintain ethical conduct by school psychologists, (2) to educate school psychologists regarding NASP ethical standards, and (3) to protect the general well-being of consumers of school psychological services" (NASP, 2008, p. 1). The NASP's ethics committee responds to questions regarding appropriate professional practices and is committed to resolving concerns informally, if possible. The committee investigates alleged ethical misconduct of NASP members or any psychologist who holds a Nationally Certified School Psychologist (NCSP) credential (p. 2). If, after investigation, the committee determines that a violation of NASP's "Principles for Professional Ethics" has occurred, the committee may require the respondent to engage in remedial activities such as education or training and to provide restitution or apology. The committee also may recommend probation, suspension, or termination of NASP membership, and/or revocation of the NCSP.

The legality of ethical complaint adjudication was tested in court in the case of *Marshall v. American Psychological Association* (1987). The plaintiff in this case claimed that the APA had no legal right to expel him or to publicize his expulsion from the association following an investigation of ethical misconduct. The court upheld the authority of the APA to expel the plaintiff, noting that he agreed to be bound by the APA's ethical principles when he joined the association, that the principles were repeatedly published, and that he had detailed hearing rights to respond to any and all charges.

Complaints to Ethics Committees

The APA's ethics committee periodically publishes an analysis of its actions in the *American Psychologist*. In 2008, there were 288 inquiries regarding members, 85 complaints against members, and 25 new preliminary cases opened. Complaints were filed against one member per thousand. Based on categorization of the underlying behaviors (rather than the basis for processing the case), problem areas were sexual misconduct; sexual harassment; nonsexual dual relationships; insurance and fees; child custody; inappropriately controlling clients; inappropriate follow-up/termination; and false, fraudulent, or misleading public statements (APA, 2009).

The NASP's Ethical and Professional Practices Committee responded to approximately 50 inquires during the 2008–2009 academic year. Two complaints alleging ethical misconduct by NASP members and/or NCSPs were resolved using mediation facilitated by committee members. Two additional complaints were investigated by the committee and resolved, and an appeal by a respondent in a complaint from the previous year also was resolved (McNamara, 2009). In recent years, inquiries to the committee included questions regarding the maintenance and disposal of confidential records, the disclosure of psychiatric diagnoses of students to teachers and other instructional staff, the privileged communication status of disclosures by students in the context of a school psychologist–client relationship, dual relationships with family members of coworkers, consent and information release provisions pertaining to noncustodial parents, the adequacy of supervision and field experiences of school psychology trainees, providing consultation services in the classroom without parent permission, the use of outdated tests, misrepresentation of professional credentials, and conflicts with school administrators about appropriate school psychological professional practices.

Reasons for Unethical Conduct

In her survey of school psychology practitioners, Dailor (2007) found that more than 90% of the respondents in her sample had witnessed at least one of nine types of ethical transgression by a school psychologist within the past year. According to Koocher and Keith-Spiegel (2008), no one profile describes psychologists who become ethics violators. Ethics violations may occur because the psychologist is unaware of the parameters of appropriate conduct or not competent to provide the services being offered. This may occur because the psychologist is poorly trained, is inexperienced, or fails to maintain up-to-date knowledge. Violations also may occur when a psychologist who usually works within the parameters of appropriate practice fails to think through a situation carefully. Some psychologists suffer from emotional problems or situational stressors that impair professional judgment and performance (also see Barnett, Baker, Elman, & Schoener, 2007). Some practitioners lack sensitivity to the needs and rights of others; others may engage in unethical conduct because they are irresponsible or vengeful. Finally, a few psychologists (fortunately only a few) are self-serving and knowingly put their needs before those of their clients.

Peer Monitoring

Both the APA and the NASP require members to monitor the ethical conduct of their professional colleagues (APA-EP Principle B; NASP-PPE IV, IV.3). Both associations also support attempts to resolve concerns informally before filing a complaint. The NASP's code of ethics states: "When a school psychologist suspects that another school psychologist or another professional has engaged in unethical practices, he or she attempts to resolve the suspected problem through a collegial problem solving process, if feasible" (NASP-PPE IV.3.2; also see APA-EP 1.04). If, however, an apparent ethical violation cannot be resolved informally, school psychologists take further action appropriate to the situation, such as discussing the situation with a supervisor in the employment setting or other institutional authorities, referral to a professional ethics committee, or referral to a state certification or licensing board (APA-EP 1.05; NASP-PPE IV.3.3). If a decision is made to file an ethics complaint, the appropriate professional organization is contacted for assistance and its procedures for resolving concerns about ethical practices are followed (see APA, 2001; NASP, 2008).

Although most psychologists are aware of their obligation to report unethical practices if the situation cannot be resolved informally, many are reluctant to do so (Pope, Tabachnick, & Keith-Spiegel, 1987). In her study of students' beliefs about their preparation to deal with ethical issues, Tryon (2001) found that fewer than half of the advanced students in school psychology doctoral programs (fifth year and beyond) believed they were prepared to deal with ethical violations by colleagues. Similarly, Dailor (2007) found that about 25% of public school psychology practitioners had witnessed multiple instances of unethical conduct by a colleague within the past year but only 38% of the respondents perceived themselves to be "very well prepared" to address unethical conduct by colleagues. Survey participants who reported receiving multilevel training in ethics (coursework in ethics, discussion of ethical issues in multiple courses, and supervised discussion of ethical issues during field experiences) were more likely to report that they felt prepared to address unethical conduct by others than those who did not receive multilevel ethics training. Koocher and Keith-Spiegel (2008) provided helpful suggestions for engaging in informal peer monitoring.

CONCLUDING COMMENTS

Students and practitioners often complain that codes of ethics are bothersome to read, a confusing and boring list of "shoulds" and "should nots." Wonderly (1989) suggested, however, that codes of ethics in psychology are not so overwhelming if we remember their primary purpose: namely, to protect the public. Professionals do not have *rights* under a code of ethics, only *obligations*. We will be exploring those obligations in more detail in the chapters ahead.

STUDY AND DISCUSSION

Questions for Chapter 1

1. What are the sources of quality control in the provision of school psychological services?
2. What does the term *ethics* mean?
3. What does the term *applied professional ethics* mean?
4. Why do professional groups, such as school psychologists, develop a code of ethics?
5. Summarize the desired ethics competencies of school psychology practitioners.
6. Why are codes of ethics imperfect guides to behavior?
7. Summarize the broad ethical principles discussed in Chapter 1.
8. How do you evaluate whether a course of action is ethical?
9. What are some of the reasons for unethical conduct?
10. What are your responsibilities with regard to peer monitoring?

Discussion

You and a fellow student (a friend) are placed at the same school for your first practicum experience. You are aware that she is a problem drinker, but thus far, she has been able to conceal her problem from the program faculty. You discover that your fellow student drinks before coming to practicum, and you have observed some erratic behavior and poor judgment at the practicum site. What should you do? What will you do? Why? (Adapted from Bernard & Jara, 1986.)

Vignettes

Eberlein (1987) and others have suggested that mastery of an explicit decision-making model or procedure may help the practitioner make well-reasoned ethical choices when difficult situations arise in professional practice. In this chapter, we introduced an eight-step problem-solving model adapted from Koocher and Keith-Spiegel (2008). The incidents that follow are included to provide an opportunity to practice the problem-solving model. At first, use of a decision-making model may seem quite cumbersome. However, it is important for practitioners to remember that ethical decision making "applies to almost everything psychologists do," and, over time, if practiced regularly, it is likely to become almost automatic (Tryon, 2000, p. 278).

In the situations described, assume the role of the school psychologist and then follow a decision-making model to determine the course of action most appropriate. Compare your decisions with those of colleagues or fellow students.

1. A few months after Carrie Johnson was hired as the school psychologist in a rural school district, the district superintendent of schools asked to meet with her. During this meeting, he said, "You'll be working closely with the principal at Pine Lake. Rumor has it he drinks a lot on the job. He's been caught twice and fined for driving while intoxicated. I think he's nuts, and we've got to get rid of him. Keep notes on what he says and does. I want a report later." How should Carrie handle this situation? (Vignette source unknown.)

2. After a series of devastating floods destroyed homes and schools in a nearby community, many Native American families moved into Carrie Johnson's school district. Carrie began receiving referrals from a number of teachers because the Native American children were having difficulty coping with the loss of their homes and adjusting to their new school and community. Carrie has no experience working with Native American children and their families, or with anyone who had suffered such losses. How should Carrie handle the referrals for assessment and counseling of the Native American pupils now attending her school?

3. As part of her effort to build a strong working relationship with school staff and community members, Hannah Cook joined the Parent-Teacher Association (PTA) and regularly attends its meetings. During a public meeting of the PTA, a parent openly complained about the treatment her daughter was receiving in a world history class at a school where Hannah is the school psychologist. The parent contended that the history teacher lacked mental stability and consequently was causing her child much anguish. How should Hannah handle this situation? (Adapted from Bailey, 1980.)

4. Michelle Phillips was born with Sanfilippo syndrome, a genetic disorder that results in progressive neurological deterioration and limited life expectancy. No effective treatment for the disorder exists. Wanda Rose, a school psychologist, has worked with the Phillips family since Michelle was diagnosed six years ago, and she has formed a warm working relationship with them. Michelle is now in the third and final phase of the disorder. She is severely mentally impaired, unable to communicate, and unable to sit or walk without support. She has difficulty swallowing and chokes frequently.

Mr. and Mrs. Phillips have made an appointment with Wanda. They believe Michelle is experiencing much pain and suffering. Although they want all comfort care to continue for their daughter, they do not want medical interventions that would prolong her life. They have brought along do not resuscitate (DNR) orders (do not institute basic choking rescue) from Michelle's physician, and they would like Wanda's help in ensuring that the orders will be honored at school. How should Wanda respond to this situation? (See Schwab & Gelfman, 2005b.)

Activities

To learn more about the APA and the NASP, visit their web sites: http://www.apa.org and http://www.nasponline.org.

For additional cases to practice use of a problem-solving model, see Williams, Armistead, and Jacob (2008).

Chapter 2

LAW AND SCHOOL PSYCHOLOGY: AN INTRODUCTION

As noted in Chapter 1, codes of ethics are one source of quality control in the provision of school psychological services. This chapter explores two other mechanisms of quality assurance: public school law and the credentialing of school psychologists. We also further explore the legal implications of school-based practice. The term *school-based practice* means that the school psychologist is an employee of the schools, whether full-time, part-time, or on a per-case or consultative basis. In contrast, the term *private practice* refers to situations in which a school psychologist enters into an agreement with a client rather than an educational agency to provide services, and the fee for services is the responsibility of the client or his or her representative (NASP-PPE Definition of Terms).

In this chapter the reader will learn that in the United States, state governments, rather than the federal government, have assumed the duty to educate children and the power to do so. This authority to educate children and ensure pupil safety is further delegated by state governments to school boards. When principals, teachers, and school psychologists employed by a school board make decisions in their official roles, such acts are seen as an extension of the authority of state government; in legal parlance, school-based practitioners are considered to be *state actors* (Russo, 2006).

In our discussions with school psychologists, we have found that the subtle but important differences between school-based practice and private practice (or employment in other nonschool settings) often are misunderstood. Under the U.S. Constitution and federal and state statutory law, pupils and their parents have many legal rights in our public schools. School-based practitioners, as state actors, must know and respect those legal rights. Furthermore, as employees of a school board, school-based practitioners have a legal obligation to protect all students from reasonably foreseeable risk of harm. This duty extends to all students, not just clients (Russo, 2006).

THE U.S. CONSTITUTION

The three basic sources of public school law are the U.S. Constitution, statutes and regulations, and case law. The U.S. Constitution is the supreme law of the land. All statutes enacted by the U.S. Congress, state governments, and even regulations adopted by boards of education are subject to the provisions of the Constitution (Russo, 2006). The original Constitution outlined the duties and powers of the federal government. Concern that the Constitution provided the foundation for a federal government that was too powerful led to the passage in 1791 of 10 amendments to the Constitution, the Bill of Rights. The Bill of Rights was created to provide a more distinct balance of power between the federal government and the states and to safeguard the rights of individual citizens. The remaining amendments, 11th through 26th, were adopted between 1795 and 1971.

No fundamental right to an education is guaranteed to citizens in the Constitution (see *San Antonio Independent School District v. Rodriguez*, 1973). Nevertheless, the Constitution has been the foundation for many decisions affecting public school education, including the right to equal educational opportunity, student rights in the school setting, and church-state-school relationships. Portions of the Constitution most pertinent to education law are shown in Exhibit 2.1. The 10th, 14th, 1st, and 4th Amendments are discussed in the following paragraphs.

Exhibit 2.1 The U.S. Constitution: Selected Amendments

Amendment 1

Freedom of Religion, Speech, and the Press; Rights of Assembly and Petition

Congress shall make no law respecting an establishment of religion, or prohibiting the free exercise thereof; or abridging the freedom of speech, or of the press; or the right of the people peaceably to assemble, and to petition the government for a redress of grievances.

Amendment 4

Search and Arrest Warrants

The right of the people to be secure in their persons, houses, papers, and effects, against unreasonable searches and seizures, shall not be violated, and no warrants shall issue, but upon probable cause, supported by oath or affirmation, and particularly describing the place to be searched, and the persons or things to be seized.

Amendment 9

Powers Retained by the People

The enumeration in the Constitution, of certain rights, shall not be construed to deny or disparage others retained by the people.

Amendment 10

Powers Retained by the States and the People

The powers not delegated to the United States by the Constitution, nor prohibited by it to the states, are reserved to the states respectively, or to the people.

Amendment 14

Civil Rights

No state shall make or enforce any law which shall abridge the privileges or immunities of citizens of the United States; nor shall any state deprive any person of life, liberty, or property, without due process of law; nor deny to any person within its jurisdiction the equal protection of the laws.

The 10th Amendment

The Constitution does not specifically refer to education as a duty of the federal government. Under the 10th Amendment, "The powers not delegated to the United States by the Constitution, nor prohibited by it to the states, are reserved to the states respectively, or to the people." Thus, under the 10th Amendment, state governments have assumed the duty to educate, the power to tax citizens of the state to finance education, and the power to compel school attendance.

Both federal and state governments have an interest in an "educated citizenry," as educated citizens are more capable of self-government and of making a positive contribution to community life (Hubsch, 1989). Most states delegate much of the authority for the management of public schools to local school boards. Public schools consequently are considered to be an arm of the government (Russo, 2006). Thus, when school boards, principals, teachers, and school psychologists make decisions in their official roles, their actions are seen as actions by the state. A public education is considered to be an *entitlement* given by the state to its citizens under state constitutional or statutory law. On the basis of state law, all children within a state have a legitimate claim of entitlement to a public education. This right to a public education given by state law is considered to be a *property right*.

The 14th Amendment

As previously noted, the Bill of Rights was passed to ensure a clearer balance of power between the federal government and the states and to safeguard the rights of individual citizens. The 14th Amendment was created to prevent state governments from trespassing on the rights of individual citizens: "No state shall make or enforce any law which shall abridge the privileges or immunities of citizens of the United States . . . without due process of law."

Because education is a duty left to the states, the courts have long held the position that "judicial interposition in the operation of the public school system requires care and restraint" (*Epperson v. State of Arkansas*, 1968). As the Supreme Court stated in *Epperson*,[1] "By and large, public education in our Nation is committed to the control of state and local authorities. Courts do not and cannot intervene in the resolution of conflicts which arise in the daily operation of school systems and which do not directly and sharply implicate basic constitutional values" (p. 104).

The 1950s, 1960s, and 1970s were decades of increasing federal court involvement in school-related issues, however, because of school actions that violated the constitutional rights of students and their parents. Two aspects of the 14th Amendment have been extremely important in decisions regarding schools: the *equal protection clause* and the requirement for *procedural due process*.

Equal Protection Clause

The equal protection clause provides that no state shall "deny any person within its jurisdiction the equal protection of the laws." Beginning in the years of the Warren Court (1953–1969), this clause has been interpreted to mean that a state may not make a free

---

[1]This case concerned an Arkansas state law that prohibited the teaching of the Darwinian theory of evolution in the schools. The Supreme Court held the law to be an unconstitutional violation of 1st Amendment safeguards of freedom of speech and inquiry and belief.

public education available to some children but not to others in the state and that the state must provide equal educational opportunity to all citizens within its jurisdiction.

In the 1954 landmark Supreme Court ruling *Brown v. Board of Education*, the Court made it clear that each state must provide equal educational opportunity to all children in its jurisdiction regardless of race. The Court ruled that the assignment of African American children to separate and inferior public schools is a denial of equal protection under the 14th Amendment of the Constitution. In two important subsequent cases, *Pennsylvania Association for Retarded Children v. Commonwealth of Pennsylvania* (1971, 1972) and *Mills v. Board of Education of District of Columbia* (1972), the courts ruled that exclusion of children with handicaps from public school education is a denial of equal protection.

In the years since *Brown*, the courts have sent an unwavering message to the states that they have a duty to provide equal educational opportunities to all children regardless of race, color, national origin, native language, sex, and disability under the 14th Amendment. The 14th Amendment equal protection clause also protects the school access rights of pregnant and married students.

Due Process

The 14th Amendment also provides that no state shall "deprive any person of life, liberty, or property, without due process of law." Courts have identified two aspects of due process: substantive and procedural. *Substantive due process* applies to the content of a law. A state may not pass a law that deprives citizens of life, liberty, or property if the law is not related to a legitimate governmental purpose; arbitrary and capricious laws that impact on citizens' rights will be ruled unconstitutional. In the public schools, substantive due process has been interpreted to mean that school rules restricting student rights must be reasonably related to the purpose of schooling. (See the discussion of *Tinker v. Des Moines Independent Community School District* [1969] later in this chapter.)

Procedural due process means that a state may not take away life, a liberty interest, or a property right without some sort of procedural fairness to safeguard citizens from unfair or wrongful infringement of rights by the government (Reschly & Bersoff, 1999). The requirement for procedural due process applies only to the infringement or deprivation of a liberty or property interest protected by the 14th Amendment; citizens are guaranteed procedural due process only if a substantive liberty or property interest is affected. The specific liberty and property interests protected under the umbrella of the 14th Amendment have been identified in court interpretations of the scope of substantive rights. In *Goss v. Lopez* (1975), the Supreme Court held that education is a property right protected by the 14th Amendment.

Procedural due process "is a flexible concept whose precise contours change relative to the nature and gravity of the interest infringed" (Bersoff & Prasse, 1978, p. 402). Notice (being told what action the state proposes to take and the reason for that action) and the opportunity to be heard are basic components of due process when state action may deprive a citizen of a liberty or property interest.

Under the due process clause of the 14th Amendment, schools may not suspend or expel children from school (and therefore deprive them of their property interest) without some sort of fair, impartial due process procedures. The due process procedures required for school suspension or expulsion generally do not have to be complex or elaborate but must include notice and the opportunity to be heard (*Goss v. Lopez*, 1975). (The suspension or expulsion of students with disabilities for more than 10 days requires more formal procedures because of the protections afforded students with disabilities under statutory law. See Chapter 9.)

The due process clause of the 14th Amendment also protects individuals from arbitrary or unwarranted stigmatization by the state that may interfere with the ability to acquire property (*Wisconsin v. Constantineau*, 1971). More specifically, the courts have ruled that a school may not label a child as "mentally retarded" or "emotionally disturbed" without due process, that is, without some sort of fair decision-making procedure that includes parent notice of the proposed classification and the right to an impartial hearing to protest the classification (see Chapter 4).

As noted previously, the 14th Amendment also protects the basic personal freedoms of citizens outlined in the Bill of Rights from arbitrary infringement by the state. The 1st and 4th Amendments are important sources of fundamental rights.

The 1st and 4th Amendments

In 1969, the Supreme Court decided an important case concerning student rights in the public schools, *Tinker v. Des Moines Independent Community School District*. This case involved three students who were suspended from school for violating a school policy prohibiting pupils from wearing black armbands in protest of the war in Vietnam. In *Tinker*, the Court recognized the need to balance the school's interest in maintaining discipline in order to foster learning and the fundamental personal freedoms guaranteed citizens in the Bill of Rights. In the Court's view, the school's policy of banning armbands was seen as an unreasonable violation of the students' constitutional right to freedom of expression because there was no evidence that the silent wearing of armbands interfered with or disrupted the functioning of the school.

Thus, although children in the school setting are not afforded the full range of personal freedoms guaranteed citizens by the Bill of Rights, they do maintain certain fundamental rights in the school setting. In *Tinker*, the Court stated that "students in school as well as out of school are 'persons' under our Constitution . . . possessed of fundamental rights which the State must respect" (p. 511).

Freedom of Speech and Assembly

The 1st Amendment prohibits the government from interfering with the rights of free speech and assembly and freedom of religious choice. In *Tinker* and subsequent cases, the courts generally have acknowledged the right of students to free speech and assembly, as long as the exercise of those rights does not significantly interfere with or disrupt the functioning of the school. Freedom of speech and assembly can be restricted when their exercise "materially and substantially" interferes with schooling. The right to free speech does not protect the use of "obscene" language, gestures, or materials (see Russo, 2006; also *Bethel School Dis. No. 403 v. Fraser*, 1986).

Privacy Rights

No "right to privacy" is mentioned expressly in the Constitution. A number of different privacy rights have been carved out of the 1st Amendment concept of "liberty," 5th Amendment protections against self-incrimination, 9th Amendment reservation of rights to the people, and 4th Amendment prohibition against unreasonable search and seizure (Hummel, Talbutt, & Alexander, 1985).

In a case that received considerable attention from legal scholars, a federal district court ruled that parents of schoolchildren have a right to be free from the invasion of family privacy by the school (*Merriken v. Cressman*, 1973; see Chapter 10). This right to privacy was recognized only for the parents or family unit; the courts generally have not recognized an independent student right to privacy in the schools. However, federal education law (e.g., the Family Educational Rights and Privacy Act [FERPA], discussed later in this chapter) now provides some guidance regarding protection of the privacy rights of pupils and their parents.

Under the Constitution, the courts generally have held that students have a 4th Amendment right to be free from unreasonable search and seizure in the schools. The courts have ruled that students have a legitimate expectation of privacy rights with regard to their person and possessions, but they have allowed a more lenient standard of "reasonable suspicion" as opposed to "probable cause" for conducting searches in school. (Privacy is discussed further in Chapter 3.)

Freedom of Religion

The 1st Amendment also ensures the basic right to free exercise of religious choice, and, under the 14th Amendment, both Congress and the states are prohibited from passing laws "respecting an establishment of religion." As Russo (2006) notes, the 1st Amendment is the source of two types of church-school-state cases: those involving the use of public funds for parochial schools and those involving school policies or classroom procedures objected to on religious grounds. (For a discussion of cases involving school-sponsored prayer or other religious activities, see Russo, 2006.)

In general, court interpretations of the 1st Amendment suggest that the state is not allowed to provide funds directly to parochial schools. However, under the "child benefit theory," the state may provide educational services (e.g., remedial instruction and school psychological services) for pupils attending parochial schools as long as those services directly aid the pupil, they are not used for the purpose of religious instruction, and there is no impermissible entanglement of church and state (*Agostini v. Felton*, 1997; *Wolman v. Walter*, 1977).

In 2002, the Supreme Court decided *Zelman v. Simmons-Harris*, a case concerning whether the 1st Amendment prohibition against Congress establishing a religion prevents a state from providing tuition monies to parents and allowing them to use that aid to enroll their children in a private school of their own choosing, without regard to whether the school is religiously affiliated. In a narrow 5–4 ruling, the Court held that such school voucher plans are constitutionally permissible, so long as the money that flows to the parochial schools results from the true choice of schools by parents.

STATUTES AND REGULATIONS

A second source of law in the U.S. legal system is statutory law. The U.S. government is composed of three parallel systems of government at the federal and state levels, a form of government known as *federalism* (Turnbull & Turnbull, 2000). At the federal level, the Constitution is the basic law of the land. Congress is empowered to enact federal laws as long as they do not violate the U.S. Constitution. Similarly, each state has its own constitution and legislative body for enacting laws at the state level. State laws may not violate either the state or federal constitutions.

Many countries have a nationalized school system operated by the central government (Hubsch, 1989). Under the 10th Amendment of the Constitution, Congress is forbidden from creating a nationalized school system. However, the U.S. Congress has the power to shape educational policy and practices by offering monies to states contingent on compliance with federal mandates. Congress has passed two types of legislation that have had a dramatic impact on the public schools, *antidiscrimination legislation* and *federal education legislation*. Key federal statutes affecting the schools are highlighted in the paragraphs that follow.

Federal Education Legislation

Some federal education legislation is grant legislation; that is, funds are provided to states on the condition that schools comply with certain educational policies and practices. The Elementary and Secondary Education Act of 1965 and the Individuals with Disabilities Education Improvement Act of 2004 are important examples of this type of legislation. Other federal education legislation stipulates that no federal funds will be made available to schools unless they adhere to specific educational policies and practices outlined in the law; the Family Educational Rights and Privacy Act of 1974 (FERPA) is an example of this type of legislation.

Elementary and Secondary Education Act of 1965

As noted previously, education generally has been regarded as a responsibility of state governments. The Elementary and Secondary Education Act of 1965 (ESEA; Pub. L. No. 89-750) was one of the first major federal programs to aid education. With the passage of ESEA, Congress accepted the proposition that although "education is primarily a state function . . . the Federal Government has a secondary obligation to see that there is a basic floor under those essential services for all adults and children in the United States" (Taft, 1965, p. 1450). The ESEA was initially a permissive law that gave the schools much latitude in how funds would be spent. A major thrust of early amendments of the law was to target funds more specifically for economically disadvantaged schoolchildren.

The No Child Left Behind Act of 2001 (Pub. L. No. 107-110) includes the most recent set of amendments to ESEA. Like its precursors, the Act provides financial assistance for schools with high concentrations of children from disadvantaged homes. Its purpose is "to close the achievement gap with accountability, flexibility, and choice, so that no child is left behind." Resources are targeted for high-poverty school districts, and monies are provided to meet the educational needs of children with limited English proficiency; children of migrant workers; Native American children; children who are homeless, neglected, delinquent, or at risk of dropping out; and young children and their parents who are in need of family literacy services. Unlike previous amendments of ESEA, the No Child Left Behind Act of 2001 requires statewide reading and mathematics tests each year in grades 3 through 8. Each state must attain academic proficiency for all students within 12 years, and districts must document progress toward that goal each year. Districts must make public school choice available to pupils in schools that fail to demonstrate progress for two consecutive years and offer supplemental tutoring after a third year of failure to demonstrate progress. (Also see "Student Proficiency Assessment Programs," Chapter 9.) In March 2010, President Barack Obama issued his administration's blueprint for the reauthorization of ESEA (U.S. Department of Education, 2010).

Individuals with Disabilities Education Improvement Act

Prior to 1990, the Education for the Handicapped Act (EHA) referred to a series of federal statutes concerning the education of children with handicapping conditions (e.g., Pub. L. No. 94-142). In 1990, President George H.W. Bush signed into law the Education of the Handicapped Act Amendments of 1990 (Pub. L. No. 101-476), which changed the name of EHA to the Individuals with Disabilities Education Act (IDEA). In 1997, President Bill Clinton signed into law the Individuals with Disabilities Education Act Amendments of 1997 (Pub. L. No. 105-117). This Act reauthorized IDEA and introduced a number of changes to improve the law. Most recently, President George W. Bush signed into law the

Individuals with Disabilities Education Improvement Act of 2004 (Pub. L. No. 108-445), referred to as IDEA 2004 or simply IDEA in this book.

The IDEA–Part B allocates funds to states that provide a free and appropriate education to all children with disabilities as defined by the law. To receive funds, each state must have developed a plan that offers every child with disabilities an opportunity to receive special education and related services in conformance with an individualized education program (IEP). Children must be assessed on the basis of nondiscriminatory testing and evaluation procedures and provided with an individualized education program in the least restrictive environment appropriate for the child. The least restrictive environment is the educational setting selected from a continuum of alternative placements (ranging from a residential facility to the general education classroom) that is closest to the general education classroom but also meets the special education needs of the child with a disability. Individualized education planning decisions are made by a multidisciplinary team that includes the pupil's parents, and a number of safeguards are required in the law to ensure parent participation in decision making. The IDEA–Part C provides funds to states that offer early intervention programs for infants and toddlers with known or suspected disabilities in conformance with an individualized family service plan (see Chapter 4).

Family Educational Rights and Privacy Act of 1974

The Family Educational Rights and Privacy Act of 1974 (FERPA) was an amendment to the Elementary and Secondary Education Act of 1965 (Pub. L. No. 93-380). Under FERPA, no federal funds will be made available to schools unless they adhere to the pupil record-keeping procedures outlined in the law. FERPA record-keeping guidelines are designed to safeguard confidentiality of records and parent access to school records concerning their children. In accordance with FERPA, parents have access to all school education records of their children, the right to challenge the accuracy of those records, and the right to a hearing regarding their accuracy. Aside from parents, pupil records are to be available only to those in the school setting with a legitimate educational interest in the student, and parent consent must be obtained before records are released to agencies outside of the school (see Chapter 3).

Protection of Pupil Rights Act

The Protection of Pupil Rights Act was a 1978 amendment to the Elementary and Secondary Education Act of 1965. It was amended in 1994 and 2001 (Pub. L. No. 107-110 § 1061). The Act requires schools to obtain written parental consent before a pupil can be required to submit to a survey, analysis, or evaluation that reveals certain types of personal information (e.g., political affiliation, potentially embarrassing psychological problems, sexual or criminal behavior, religious practices, family income) if the survey, analysis, or evaluation is funded by the U.S. Department of Education. It also requires school districts that receive any federal funds to develop policies ensuring parents the opportunity to review the content of surveys prior to their distribution if the survey requests certain types of private information from students. Such policies must allow parents to have their child opt out of survey participation (see Chapter 3).

Federal Antidiscrimination Legislation

Congress also has passed antidiscrimination or civil rights legislation that has had an impact on public school policies and practices. These statutes prohibit state and school authorities from discriminating against individuals on the basis of race, color, or national origin;[2] sex;[3] or disability[4] in any program or activity receiving any federal funding. A state department of education may choose not to pursue monies available under federal grant statutes (e.g., funds for infants and toddlers with disabilities). School districts must comply with antidiscrimination legislation if they receive *any* federal funds for any purpose, however.

Federal antidiscrimination laws also protect students from harassment based on race, color, national origin, sex, or disability. The term *harassment* means oral, written, graphic, or physical conduct relating to an individual's race, color, national origin, sex, or disability that is sufficiently severe, pervasive, or persistent so as to interfere with or limit the ability of an individual to participate in or benefit from the district's programs or activities (see U.S. Department of Education & Bias Crimes Task Force of the National Association of Attorneys General, 1999). *Sexual harassment* means unwanted and unwelcome sexual advances that are sufficiently severe, pervasive, or persistent so as to interfere with or limit the ability of an individual to participate in or benefit from the district's programs or activities. The federal laws cited make schools responsible for taking reasonable steps to remedy harassment. Federal statutory law does not currently protect public school students from discrimination or harassment based on sexual orientation, gender identity, or gender expression. However, many courts have ruled that harassment on the basis of sexual orientation violates Title IX of the Education Amendments of 1972, state laws, or the U.S. Constitution (e.g., *Nabozny v. Podlesny*, 1996; see Chapter 9).

Rehabilitation Act of 1973

Section 504 of the Rehabilitation Act of 1973 (Pub. L. No. 93-112) specifically prohibits discrimination against any otherwise qualified individual solely on the basis of a handicapping condition in any program or activity receiving federal financial assistance. Section 504 is discussed in Chapter 5.

Americans with Disabilities Act of 1990

The Americans with Disabilities Act of 1990 (ADA) (Pub. L. No. 101-336; amended in 2008 by Pub. L. No. 110-325) is considered to be the most significant federal law ensuring the civil rights of all individuals with disabilities. The ADA guarantees equal opportunity to individuals with disabilities in employment, public accommodation, transportation, state and local government services, and telecommunications. Title II, Subtitle A, is the portion of the law most pertinent to public schools (see Chapter 5).

Civil Rights Act of 1871

School personnel also should be familiar with Section 1983 of the Civil Rights Act of 1871. This statute was passed following the Civil War as a reaction to the mistreatment of African Americans, and it originally was known as the Ku Klux Klan Act. Under Section 1983, any person whose constitutional rights (or rights under federal law) have been violated by a government (school) official may sue for damages in federal court, and the official may be held liable for damages (see the section "Civil Lawsuits Against Schools and School Psychologists," later in this chapter).

---

[2]Title VI of the Civil Rights Act of 1964.
[3]Title IX of the Education Amendments of 1972.
[4]Title II of the Americans with Disabilities Act of 1990.

Rules and Regulations

When federal legislation is enacted, an executive agency is charged with the responsibility for developing rules and regulations implementing the law. For example, rules and regulations implementing IDEA and FERPA are issued by the Department of Education. For all intents and purposes, *rules and regulations have the same impact as actual legislation.* School psychologists need to be familiar with both the statute itself and the regulations implementing the law.

Federal statutes are compiled and published in the *United States Code* (U.S.C.). Rules and regulations implementing a law first appear in a daily publication called the *Federal Register* (FR) and subsequently are published in the *Code of Federal Regulations* (C.F.R.). The *Code of Federal Regulations* has 50 titles, and each volume is updated once each calendar year. These government publications can be found at www.gpoaccess.gov and in state and university libraries. The U.S. Department of Education web site also has links to statutes and regulations pertinent to education (www.ed.gov). Citations for important federal statutes are provided in the "Table of Federal Legislation" in Appendix D.

State Education Laws

As Hubsch (1989) noted, the majority of public school *statutory* law is enacted at the state level. School psychologists must become familiar with the laws pertinent to the delivery of school psychological services in the state where they are employed, in addition to federal statutes and regulations. Copies of state laws affecting education typically can be purchased from a state's department of education, downloaded from its web site, or located in a college library law collection.

CASE LAW

A third source of law is case law. Case law, or common law, is law that emerges from court decisions (Russo, 2006). The common law system can be traced back to medieval England. At that time, it was widely accepted that there were "laws of nature" to guide solutions to problems if those laws could be discovered. Legal scholars studied past court decisions for the purpose of discovering these "natural laws." The rules and principles that judges customarily followed in making decisions were identified and, at times, articulated in case decisions, and judges tended to base new decisions on these earlier legal precedents. Common law is thus discovered law rather than enacted law (Russo, p. 1). Many aspects of public school law today are based on common law rather than enacted law, as Russo pointed out. For example, the courts generally have upheld a teacher's right to use corporal punishment to discipline students where no state laws or school board policies prohibit its use. The court's acceptance of the use of corporal punishment in the schools has a long history in case law (see Chapter 9).

In the United States, the federal court system has three tiers or layers; most state court systems also have three tiers or layers. As Turnbull and Turnbull (2000, p. 6) observed, "Why a case may be tried in one court, appealed or reviewed by another, and finally disposed of by yet another is a matter of great complexity." The following is a brief discussion of the state and federal court systems.

State court systems vary in organization and complexity. Cases filed in the lowest court may be appealed to an intermediate-level court, if a state has one. Decisions then may be appealed to the supreme court of the state, the "court of last resort" (Russo, 2006). The U.S. Supreme Court may review cases from a state court if a question of federal law is involved.

Within the federal system, at the lowest level are the trial courts, called district courts. Nearly 100 federal district courts exist. At the intermediate level are 11 numbered federal circuits or geographical areas and the District of Columbia. Each court at this level is called a Circuit Court of Appeals. These courts hear appeals from the district courts. They decide issues of law, not fact. The highest court in the federal system is the U.S. Supreme Court. A party who loses a case in a federal court of appeals or the highest state court may submit a written petition requesting the Supreme Court to review the case. The Court agrees to review a case by granting a *writ of certiorari* (an order calling up a case from a lower court for review). However, the Supreme Court selects only those cases it considers most important to review, and consequently, only a small percentage of the requests for review are granted.

The federal court system decides both civil and criminal cases. Criminal cases involve crimes prosecuted by the government, not private citizens (e.g., murder, theft, and assault). Civil cases are lawsuits brought by private parties. Federal courts rule only on cases that involve federal constitutional or statutory law or cases that involve parties from two different states. The U.S. Supreme Court has the final authority in interpreting the U.S. Constitution and federal statutes. State courts also decide both civil and criminal cases. State courts rule on cases involving state constitutional and statutory law, but also may rule on cases involving the federal Constitution and statutory laws.

The role of the courts is to resolve disputes involving citizens, organizations, and the government. Courts also decide the guilt or innocence of those accused of crimes. In education, most disputes are decided in civil court. Courts decide conflicts by applying law to a given set of facts and interpreting the meaning of the law in that context. It is the function of courts to say what the Constitution or statute means in a given case, set forth the findings of fact that the interpretation is based on, and enter an order commanding the parties in the case to take certain action (or, if the case is on appeal, the judge may enter an order for another court to take action). If there is no *codified* law (no constitutional or statutory provision) found controlling in a case, the court is likely to rely on common law (legal precedents) in rendering a decision (Hubsch, 1989; Turnbull & Turnbull, 2000).

In reading about court rulings, remember that decisions of the U.S. Supreme Court are binding throughout the country. The decisions of the lower federal courts are binding only within their jurisdictions, and the decisions of state courts are binding only within the state (Russo, 2006).

SUMMARY

We have explored the three basic sources of public school law within the American legal system, namely, the Constitution, statutes and regulations, and case law. It is evident from the material presented that the federal courts and legislature have had a powerful impact on public schools, particularly since *Brown* in 1954. But, as Hubsch (1989) pointed out, the role that the federal government can play in fostering quality public education in our nation's schools is limited. Court decisions spanning almost 60 years have sent a clear message that our schools must provide equal educational opportunities for all children. Equal educational opportunity for all children is not the same as a quality education for all, however, as Hubsch noted. By providing grants and resources, the federal government can encourage quality educational programs, but the bulk of the responsibility for ensuring a quality education for all children must be carried at the state and local levels. Individual teachers, principals, and school psychologists must accept and share in this responsibility.

CREDENTIALING OF SCHOOL PSYCHOLOGISTS

As part of the obligation to protect the health and welfare of their citizens, state governments enact laws to regulate the provision of psychological services. State credentialing of professionals, such as school psychologists, protects the consumer by requiring individuals to hold specified qualifications before they are granted a legal sanction to practice in the state.

Credentialing for School-Based Practice

Certification laws typically regulate public school professionals. In most states, the state department of education (SDE) certifies school psychologists for practice in the school setting. An SDE certificate generally permits school-based practice only; that is, the practitioner may work for the schools either as a regular school employee or on a contractual basis. A state department of education certificate typically does not authorize a school psychologist to engage in private practice. An SDE certificate is the credential most commonly held by school psychology practitioners (Fagan & Wise, 2007).

The credentialing of school psychologists for school-based practice is a state matter. Although commonalities in credentialing standards exist across states, equivalence of requirements between states is the exception rather than the rule. Furthermore, different states may use different titles or designations (e.g., school psychologist, school diagnostician), and some states have more than one level of certification, depending on the level of graduate preparation and years of experience.

Fagan and Wise (2007) identified two models of certification: *transcript review* and *program approval*. *Transcript review* requires submission of transcripts and other supporting materials to a state certifying agency. The agency then determines whether the applicant successfully has completed the prescribed set of courses and field experiences outlined in the state's certification standards. The *program approval* process means that applicants who have the recommendation from an approved state training program will be certified by the state agency. The procedure used for certification may be different for applicants from in-state training programs and those from out-of-state programs.

Because certification and licensure are controlled at the state level, students and practitioners need to contact the state in which they wish to practice for up-to-date information about credentialing. The National Association of School Psychologists maintains a National School Psychology Certification and Licensure Online Resource List that provides a summary of the requirements for licensure and certification in various states (see http://www.nasponline.org/certification/state_info_list.aspx).

Credentialing for Private Practice

Licensure acts typically regulate the private practice of psychology. Licenses usually are issued by a state psychology board. Only a few states license school psychologists for private practice at the subdoctoral level. Information on licensing boards is available at http://www.nasponline.org/certification/state_info_list.aspx and http://www.asppb.org.

Nonpractice Credentials

In addition to state credentials to practice, nonpractice credentials also recognize the quality of professional preparation (Fagan & Wise, 2007). The National School Psychology Certification System allows school psychologists who complete training consistent with

NASP standards, who achieve a passing score on the National School Psychology Examination, and who meet continuing education requirements to be identified as a Nationally Certified School Psychologist (NCSP). Currently more than 9,800 school psychologists hold the NCSP credential (NASP, 2009). It is important to recognize that the NCSP title alone does not authorize a school psychologist to render services (Fagan & Wise, 2007); practitioners must hold a valid certificate or license in the state where they wish to practice. However, 31 states use the NCSP as part of their standards for certification (NASP, 2009). For more information, visit NASP's web site at http://www.nasponline.org.

CIVIL LAWSUITS AGAINST SCHOOLS AND SCHOOL PSYCHOLOGISTS

In the last portion of this chapter, we discuss civil lawsuits against schools and school psychologists. Civil liability, simply stated, "means that one can be sued for acting wrongly toward another or for failing to act when there was a recognized duty to do so" (Hopkins & Anderson, 1985, p. 21). Civil liability rests within the basic framework of the law of tort. A tort is a civil (not criminal) wrong that does not involve a contract. It is a complex area of law. In general, the court considers four questions in tort cases: (1) Did injury occur? Injury means a wrong or damage done to the student's person, rights, reputation, or property. (2) Did the school owe a duty in law to the student? (3) Was there a breach of duty? That is, did the school fail to do what it should have done? A tort can arise when either an improper act or a failure to act causes injury to the student. (4) Is there a proximate cause relationship between the injury and the breach of duty? (Evans, 1997; Turnbull & Turnbull, 2000).

Lawsuits Against Schools Under State Laws

The most common tort committed by school personnel is negligence (Evans, 1997). Negligence suits often are precipitated by a physical injury to a student (e.g., injury resulting from student-on-student violence). When a student suffers harm and his or her parents seek vindication in court, the parents are most likely to file a negligence lawsuit in state court (Schill, 1993). Such lawsuits generally allege that the school had a duty (under state common or statutory law) to protect students from foreseeable harm, had knowledge of a specific danger, negligently failed to take reasonable precautions to protect the student, and thus caused the injury by allowing the incident to occur (Schill, 1993; Wood & Chestnutt, 1995).

As noted previously, public schools are an arm of state government. Historically, under common law, a school district could not be held liable for torts committed by the district, officials, or other employees (Russo, 2006). In some states, the immunity of school districts was based on the old English doctrine of *sovereign immunity*: "The king (state) can do no wrong; you can't sue the king." In other states, immunity of school districts was based on the fact that state law provides no funds for the payment of damages; funds for education could not be diverted to pay legal claims (Russo, 2006).

Currently, the doctrine of immunity of school districts has been modified by legislation or case law in most states. However, the exceptions to the doctrine of immunity vary from state to state, making it extremely difficult to make generalizations about the kinds of tort actions that will be successful against school districts in various states. Immunity usually exists to the extent that the school's or school board's liability insurance does not cover the particular injury suffered (Schill, 1993, p. 1). This means that, in many states, state legislation or case law permits lawsuits against school districts but allows recovery only up to the limits of the school's liability insurance (see Russo, 2006).

School-based practitioners must remember that they are state actors and district employees. As a result of a long history of negligence lawsuits against schools, school-based practitioners, like other school employees, have a legal duty to take steps to protect pupils from *reasonably foreseeable risk of harm*. This obligation extends to all students, not just student clients. Furthermore, school employment contracts often contain a provision whereby any act or failure to act that jeopardizes pupil health, safety, or welfare can result in the suspension or termination of employment. Schools are not likely to be held liable when spontaneous, unforeseeable acts by students result in injury (Wood & Chestnutt, 1995).

Whether a state will allow recovery of damages in lawsuits against school districts is a complicated matter. Whether individual school employees can be sued is also a complicated matter, determined by state legislation and case law. Michigan courts, for example, typically have held teachers and other individual school employees immune from liability during performance of duties within the scope of their employment. They may, however, be disciplined by their district for inappropriate actions.

While school-based practitioners have a duty to protect students from reasonably fore-seeable risk of harm, psychologists in nonschool settings also may have a professional obligation under the laws of the state where they practice to take steps to protect their clients from self-harm and to forewarn individuals whom their client has threatened to harm. However, where they exist, state laws governing mental health practitioners often use language that requires the psychologist to take preventive actions only in situations suggesting "clear and imminent" danger to the client or a targeted victim. Thus, a difference may exist between school-based practitioners and those in nonschool settings with regard to the threshold for breaking confidentiality of the psychologist-client relationship to protect a student or others from harm (i.e., reasonably foreseeable risk of harm versus imminent danger). (Also see Chapter 3.)

As previously noted, many of the negligence suits filed against school districts by parents are precipitated by a physical injury to a student (Evans, 1997). In the 1970s and 1980s, however, a number of so-called instructional malpractice suits were decided. These suits were filed by students or their parents when a student graduated from high school but was unable to read or write well enough to secure employment, or when the student did not achieve academically what his or her parents expected. The plaintiffs in these cases claimed that poor instruction (instructional malpractice) was the cause of the injury (student failure to learn). Such claims generally failed for several reasons. First, the courts prefer not to intervene in the administration of the public schools except in unusual circumstances involving clear violations of constitutional rights or federal law. Second, the courts have held that the award of monetary damages for instructional malpractice suits would be overly burdensome to the public education system in terms of both time and money (*Peter W. v. San Francisco Unified School District*, 1976). In addition, as noted in *Donohue v. Copiague Union Free School District* (1979), it would be difficult, if not impossible, to prove a causal link between a school's instructional practices and student academic failure.

Lawsuits Under Federal Law (Section 504, ADA, IDEA, and Section 1983)

Federal antidiscrimination laws such as Section 504, ADA, and Title IX of the Education Amendments of 1972 allow parents to sue a school district for violation of their child's rights under those laws. In successful suits, parents have been able to secure a court order commanding the school to take steps to comply with the law, and they have at times been awarded monetary damages (see Chapters 5 and 9).

The IDEA also allows parents of special education students to file a lawsuit when they believe their child's rights under the law have been violated. Except for unusual circumstances, parents are required to exhaust administrative remedies (e.g., due process hearings) available to them before they pursue a court action under IDEA. If parents prevail in a court action under IDEA, they may recover their attorney fees and/or be reimbursed for private school tuition or compensatory education for their child (see Chapter 4). Parents typically have not been able to recover monetary damages under IDEA.

In addition to claims filed under Section 504, ADA, and IDEA, an increasing number of lawsuits are filed against schools and school personnel under Section 1983 of the Civil Rights Act of 1871. In accordance with Section 1983, any person whose constitutional rights (or rights under federal law) have been violated by a government official may sue for damages in federal court, and the official may be held liable for the actual damages. Thus, a pupil whose civil rights were violated under Section 1983 may sue the school board, principal, teacher, and/or the school psychologist responsible in federal court, thereby bypassing any state law granting school personnel immunity from liability during performance of their job duties.

A number of student lawsuits concerning school disciplinary actions (e.g., illegal search and seizure, unreasonable corporal punishment) have been filed under Section 1983. School officials may have qualified immunity from Section 1983 lawsuits. The standard for qualified immunity applicable to government (school) officials is as follows: "Government officials performing discretionary functions are shielded from liability for civil damages unless their conduct violated clearly established statutory or constitutional rights of which a reasonable person would have known" (*Harlow v. Fitzgerald*, 1982, p. 2738). Hummel et al. (1985, p. 78) suggested that school personnel generally will not be held liable in Section 1983 lawsuits as long as they are "acting clearly within the scope of their authority for the betterment of those they serve" (e.g., *Landstrom v. Illinois Department of Children and Family Services*, 1990).

Paul D. Coverdell Teacher Protection Act of 2001

The 2001 amendments to ESEA, the No Child Left Behind Act, include the Paul D. Coverdell Teacher Protection Act (Pub. L. No. 107-110 §§ 2361–2368). The purpose of the Act is to provide a limitation on liability for teachers, principals, or other school professionals when they undertake reasonable actions to maintain order, discipline, and an appropriate educational environment. As a condition for accepting ESEA monies, the Act states that no punitive damages may be awarded against a school professional for harm caused by an act or omission if the school professional was acting on behalf of the school, within the scope of his or her authority, and in furtherance of efforts to maintain order in the school, and if the actions were carried out in conformity with federal, state, and local laws, unless clear and convincing evidence shows that the harm was proximately caused by willful or criminal misconduct on the part of the school professional or a conscious, flagrant indifference to the rights or safety of the individual harmed.

Professional Malpractice

Professional malpractice suits are filed against individual practitioners under state statutory and common law. Professional malpractice occurs when, in the context of a psychologist-client relationship, a client suffers harm and it is determined that the harm was caused by departure from acceptable professional standards of care. The APA Insurance Trust reports that the likelihood of a psychologist being sued for malpractice is small, less than one half of 1% (Bennett, Bryant, VandenBos, & Greenwood, 1990). As noted previously, whether an individual school-based practitioner is immune from liability under state law during performance of his or her job duties varies from state to state. Psychologists in private practice, however, can be held liable for malpractice in all states. Also, school psychologists who disclose privileged information to others without first obtaining consent may put themselves at risk for a malpractice suit under privileged communication laws whether they are employed by the schools or work in nonschool settings (see Chapter 3).

When a professional-client relationship exists and the psychologist is acting in a professional capacity, he or she is expected to provide "due care," or a level of care that is "standard" in the profession. To succeed in a malpractice claim, the plaintiff must prove four facts: (1) a professional relationship was formed between the psychologist and plaintiff so that the psychologist owed a legal duty of care to the plaintiff; (2) the duty of care was breached; that is, a standard of care exists and the practitioner breached that standard; (3) the client suffered harm or injury; and (4) the practitioner's breach of duty to practice within the standard of care was the proximate cause of the client's injury; that is, the injury was a reasonably foreseeable consequence of the breach (Bennett et al., 1990).

How does the court determine the standard of care? As Bennett et al. (1990) noted, in most cases, the courts look to the profession itself to identify the customary standard of care used by others in the same field. Expert testimony may be used to establish the customary standard of care. In addition, codes of ethics may be presented as evidence of the parameters of accepted practice. Sometimes the client's condition is a key factor in determining the expected standard of care (e.g., acceptable and reasonable actions in handling a suicidal adolescent). If the psychologist is not qualified to work with a particular type of problem situation, he or she is obligated to refer the client to someone with appropriate training (Bennett et al., 1990).

According to Woody (1988), the key words related to defining the appropriate standard of care are *ordinary*, *reasonable*, and *prudent*. *Ordinary* pertains to what is accepted or customary practice. *Reasonable* relates to the appropriate and adequate use of professional knowledge and judgment. *Prudent* means the exercise of caution, not in the sense of being traditional or conservative, but rather maintaining adequate safeguards. It is important to recognize that the courts do not expect psychologists to be all-knowing and perform without error (Knapp, 1980). They do not decide professional malpractice from the application of standard techniques. Sales, Miller, and Hall (2005) provide advice for psychologists on how to avoid malpractice suits.

Professional Liability Insurance

To protect themselves and perhaps ease their fear of litigation, some school psychologists purchase professional liability insurance. Prior to purchasing a policy, school psychologists should investigate what type of coverage, if any, is provided by their employers and whether any professional liability insurance is provided by their membership in a professional union, such as the National Education Association or American Federation of Teachers. Both the National Association of School Psychologists (www.nasponline.org) and the American Psychological Association (www.apa.org) have information about professional liability insurance on their web sites. Internship students are well advised to consider purchasing liability insurance (often available at a student rate) because they may not be covered by their school district's policies.

In choosing an insurance policy, several points should be kept in mind. First, be sure to study the policy carefully to know what is and is not covered. Some professional liability policies cover school psychologists only when their services are performed during school-based practice. In other words, they do not cover private practice. Such policies are generally much less expensive than those that cover private work. Second, policies may be either based on claims made or occurrence based. Under the former, the practitioner is covered only if insured when the alleged malpractice took place *and* when the claim was filed. Under the latter, an occurrence-based policy, the practitioner is covered as long as he or she was insured when the alleged malpractice took place, regardless of when the claim was filed. Third, many policies reserve the right to select legal counsel and to settle the case. This may be discouraging to practitioners who want their day in court. The psychologist may still hire his or her own attorney to work with the one supplied by the insurance carrier, but that is an additional expense.

CONCLUDING COMMENTS

This chapter has provided a brief overview of public school law pertinent to school psychology. School psychologists are ethically and professionally obligated to be familiar with law and to keep abreast of changes in law affecting practices. We concur with Reschly and Bersoff's (1999) view that understanding of law is important "as means to protect precious rights, as well as a method to resolve disagreements over rights and responsibilities. The better understanding of legal influences is one way to enhance opportunities for implementing the best professional practices" (p. 1077).

STUDY AND DISCUSSION

Questions for Chapter 2

1. What are the three sources of public school law in the U.S. legal system?
2. Why was the Bill of Rights passed? What is the significance of the 10th Amendment with regard to public education? Do citizens have a right to a public education under the U.S. Constitution?
3. Identify the two aspects of the 14th Amendment that have been extremely important in court decisions regarding public schools.
4. What was the significance of the Supreme Court decision in *Tinker v. Des Moines Independent Community School District* (1969)?
5. If public education is a duty of the states, how does the U.S. Congress have the power to shape educational policy and practices? Cite two examples of federal education legislation and two examples of federal antidiscrimination legislation.
6. What is case law, and why is it important?
7. What is civil liability?
8. What is professional malpractice? What aspects of the situation do courts evaluate to determine whether malpractice occurred? How is appropriate standard of care generally determined?

Activities

1. The majority of public school statutory law is enacted at the state level. School psychologists must become familiar with the laws pertinent to the delivery of school psychological services in the state where they are employed. Obtain a copy of the rules

governing special education and school psychological services in the state where you live. Copies of state laws affecting education typically can be purchased from a state's department of education, downloaded from its web site, or located in a college library law collection.

2. During the course of their careers, many school psychologists will be asked to provide testimony in legal proceedings, such as a special education due process hearing. Read about school psychologists' involvement in special education due process hearings (Havey, 1999) and the legal and ethical issues associated with being an expert witness in the courtroom (Sattler, 2008).

3. Visit the U.S. Department of Education web site at www.ed.gov. Can you locate information about the most recent amendments to the Elementary and Secondary Education Act of 1965 and to IDEA?

Chapter 3 ———————————————————————————————

PRIVACY, INFORMED CONSENT, CONFIDENTIALITY, AND RECORD KEEPING

This chapter explores four important ethical-legal concepts in the delivery of psychological services in the schools: *privacy, informed consent, confidentiality*, and *privileged communication*. School record keeping also is discussed. Privacy, informed consent, confidentiality, and record keeping are discussed together in this chapter because they are ethical-legal concerns that cut across all of the school psychologist's many roles. The chapter closes with a discussion of parent access to test protocols and the use of technology in communication and record keeping.

PRIVACY

The term *privacy* meshes together complicated concepts from case law, statutory law, and professional ethics. We first briefly explore privacy as a legal concept and then discuss respect for privacy as an ethical mandate.

Privacy and Law

The privacy rights of students and their parents have been addressed in case and statutory law. However, there are many areas in which the legal boundaries of pupil privacy are not clearly delineated. Furthermore, some tension between the school's perceived need for personal information about pupils and the right of students and parents to be free from unnecessary intrusions on their privacy is likely inevitable, even as additional privacy guidelines become available.

Case Law

As noted in Chapter 2, "right to privacy" is not mentioned explicitly in the Constitution. However, a number of privacy rights have been carved out of the 1st Amendment concept of liberty, the 5th Amendment protections against self-incrimination, the 9th Amendment reservations of rights to the people, and the 4th Amendment prohibition against unreasonable search and seizure (Hummel, Talbutt, & Alexander, 1985).

Court decisions regarding the rights of students have recognized the need to balance the interest of the state (school) in fulfilling its duty to educate children, maintain order, and ensure pupil safety against the personal freedoms and rights generally afforded citizens. Thus, in the school setting, students do not have the full range of privacy rights afforded adult citizens. Two court cases that addressed the issue of privacy rights are *Merriken v. Cressman* (1973) and *New Jersey v. T.L.O.* (1985); a third case, *Sterling v. Borough of Minersville* (2000), also may have implications for the privacy rights of students.

In *Merriken v. Cressman* (1973), a case decided in federal district court, a school district planned to administer a questionnaire to students as part of a program designed to identify drug abusers. The questionnaire inquired about the nature of the parent-child relationship and parenting practices and was to be administered without parent consent. The court ruled that parents of schoolchildren have a right to be free from invasion of family privacy by the school. However, this right to privacy was recognized for the parents only; the court did not address the issue of an independent student's right to privacy in the schools. (This case is discussed further in Chapter 10.)

In *New Jersey v. T.L.O.* (1985), the Supreme Court held that students have the 4th Amendment right to be free from unreasonable search and seizure in the schools. The case concerned whether school officials had the right to search a student's purse. The Court engaged in a two-part inquiry to determine the legality of the search, namely, "Was the search justified at its inception?" and "Was the search, as actually conducted, reasonably related in scope to the circumstances which justified the search in the first place?" While holding that students have a legitimate expectation of privacy rights with regard to their person and possessions in school, the Court in *T.L.O.* upheld the standard of *reasonable suspicion* as opposed to *probable cause* for conducting individual searches, thus giving more latitude in the case of students than provided adults by the 4th Amendment. School officials must, however, have reasonable grounds to suspect that a search will produce evidence that the student violated school rules or committed a crime; the search must be justified at its inception by more than a rumor or hunch.

The Court also noted that a search must not be "excessively intrusive in light of the age and gender of the pupil and the nature of the infraction" (*T.L.O.*, 1985, p. 342). The more personal the search (the closer the search comes to the body), the more serious the reasons the school must have for conducting the search. Thus, a search of a student's body for a weapon would more likely be viewed as legally permissible than an intrusive search for missing money. In our opinion, strip searches should be avoided if at all possible because they may result in emotional distress, anger, and alienation (Hyman & Perone, 1998). (Also see *Safford Unified School District No. 1 v. Redding*, 2009, and Pinard, 2003.)

A case decided in federal appeals court may have implications for the privacy rights of students with regard to sexual orientation. In *Sterling v. Borough of Minersville* (2000), the court determined that police may have violated a gay teen's constitutional right to privacy when they threatened to tell his family that he was gay. The boy committed suicide after the threat was made. In the majority opinion, the judge stated that disclosure of an individual's sexual orientation by government officials is a violation of the individual's constitutional right to privacy unless there is a "genuine, legitimate, and compelling" government interest in making the disclosure (*Sterling*, 2000, p. 196). This case has been interpreted to suggest that principals, teachers, school psychologists, and other school personnel should not divulge information about a student's sexual orientation without his or her permission (Bradley, 2001).

Statutory Law

The Individuals with Disabilities Education Improvement Act (IDEA 2004), the Protection of Pupil Rights Act (PPRA), and the Family Educational Rights and Privacy Act of 1974 (FERPA) provide some statutory protection for the privacy rights of students and their parents. The IDEA requires informed consent for an initial evaluation to determine whether a pupil is eligible for special education and protects the privacy of student education records (see Chapters 4 and 6). The requirements of FERPA are discussed in "Record Keeping in the Schools" later in this chapter.

The PPRA, enacted in 1978, provides protection from school actions that intrude on pupil or family privacy. It was amended in 1994 (Pub. L. No. 103-227) and 2001 (Pub. L. No. 107-110 § 1061). The Act has two major provisions regarding the collection of sensitive information from students. First, in accordance with PPRA, no student may be required to submit without prior consent to a survey, analysis, or evaluation funded by the Department of Education (DOE) that reveals one or more of eight types of information: (1) political affiliations or beliefs of the student or the student's parent; (2) mental and psychological problems potentially embarrassing to the student or his or her family; (3) sex behavior and attitudes; (4) illegal, antisocial, self-incriminating, and demeaning behavior; (5) critical appraisals of other individuals with whom respondents have close family relationships; (6) legally recognized privileged and analogous relationships; (7) religious practices, affiliations, or beliefs of the student or student's parent; or (8) income, other than required by law to determine eligibility for participation in a program or for receiving financial assistance under a program. *Prior consent* is defined as the prior consent of the student if the student is an adult or emancipated minor, or prior written consent of the parent or guardian if the student is an unemancipated minor (20 U.S.C. § 1232h). These privacy protections of PPRA apply only to schools that receive and use federal funds in connection with the use or administration of surveys, analyses, or evaluations concerning one or more areas listed in the statute (*Altman v. Bedford Central School District*, 1999).

A second provision of the PPRA requires local school districts that receive *any* federal funds to develop policies, in consultation with parents, to notify parents when the school intends to administer a survey that reveals one or more of the eight types of information listed in the preceding paragraph. The parent of a student must be given the opportunity to inspect the survey, upon request, prior to its distribution. Parents must be given the opportunity to have their student opt out of the information-gathering activity.

If an adult or emancipated student, or the parent of a minor child, feels that he or she has been affected by a violation of PPRA, he or she may file a complaint with the Family Policy Compliance Office, U.S. Department of Education.

Privacy as an Ethical Issue

Privacy is also an ethical issue. Siegel (1979, p. 251) defined privacy as "the freedom of individuals to choose for themselves the time and the circumstances under which and the extent to which their beliefs, behaviors, and opinions are to be shared or withheld from others."

Consistent with the general principle of respect for the dignity of all persons and the valuing of autonomy, psychologists respect the right of the client to self-determine whether to disclose private information (NASP-PPE I.2; also APA-EP Principle E). Furthermore, every effort is made to minimize intrusions on privacy (APA-EP Principle E, 4.04; NASP-PPE I.2.2). School psychologists do not seek or store private information about pupils, parents, teachers, or others that is not needed in the provision of services (NASP-PPE I.2.2; APA-EP 4.04).

INFORMED CONSENT TO ESTABLISH A SCHOOL PSYCHOLOGIST–CLIENT RELATIONSHIP

Ethical codes and law are consistent in respecting the individual's right to self-determine whether to share private thoughts, behaviors, and beliefs with others. In ethics and law, the requirement for informed consent grew out of deep-rooted notions of the importance of individual privacy. As Bersoff (1983, p. 150) noted, "It is now universally agreed, though not always honored in practice, *that human beings must give their informed consent prior to any significant intrusion of their person or privacy* [emphasis added]."

As mentioned in Chapters 1 and 2, school psychologists often, but not always, provide services within the framework of an established school psychologist–client relationship (NASP-PPE Definition of Terms). When a school psychologist—whether employed by the schools or in private practice—establishes a psychologist-client professional relationship, he or she assumes special ethical and legal obligations to the parties who enter the relationship (Haas & Malouf, 2005), such as the obligation to ensure informed consent for services (NASP-PPE I.1.2; APA-EP Principle E, 3.10–3.11). This ethical obligation to obtain consent to establish a school psychologist–client relationship for the purpose of individualized psychological assessment and intervention is consistent with IDEA. Codes of ethics and law thus show agreement that, with the exception of urgent and certain special situations, informed consent should be obtained to establish a school psychologist–client relationship.

However, as one of the members of a school's instructional support team, a practitioner also provides consultative services to student assistance teams, classrooms, or schools that do not fall within the scope of an established school psychologist–client relationship (NASP-PPE Definition of Terms). Not all school-based consultative services require informed parent consent, particularly if the resulting interventions are under the authority of the teacher, within the scope of typical classroom interventions, and not intrusive of pupil or family privacy beyond what might be expected in the course of ordinary school activities (NASP-PPE I.1.1; also Corrao & Melton, 1988). (See Chapter 7.)

The Meaning of Informed Consent

Case law and statutory regulations concur that the three key elements of informed consent are that it must be *knowing, competent,* and *voluntary* (Dekraai, Sales, & Hall, 1998). *Knowing* means that the individual giving consent must have a clear understanding of what he or she is consenting to. The person seeking consent must make a good-faith effort to disclose enough information to the person from whom consent is sought so that the individual can make an *informed choice* whether to enter a school psychologist–client relationship (Barnett, Wise, Johnson-Greene, & Bucky, 2007; Dekraai et al., 1998).

In seeking consent to establish a professional relationship with a client (or clients) for the provision of psychological services, the practitioner is obligated to provide information about the nature and scope of services offered, assessment-intervention goals and procedures, the expected duration of services, any foreseeable risks or discomforts (including any risks of psychological or physical harm), the cost of the services (if any), the benefits that reasonably can be expected, the possible consequences and risks of not receiving services, and information about alternative treatments or services that may be beneficial. The extent to which confidentiality of information will be maintained also should be discussed as part of the informed consent procedures. This information must be provided in language (or by other mode of communication) understandable to the person giving consent (Weithorn, 1983; also NASP-PPE I.1.3).

The individual giving consent must also be *legally competent* to give consent. As Bersoff and Hofer (1990) observed, the law presumes that every adult is competent to consent, unless judged incompetent following a full hearing conducted by an impartial fact finder. However, in the legal system, children generally are presumed to be incompetent and not capable of making legally binding decisions (Bersoff, 1983). Consequently, in the school setting, informed consent to establish a school psychologist–client relationship typically is sought from the parent or guardian of a minor child, or from the student if an adult. Parent consent may be bypassed in emergency situations (see NASP-PPE I.1.2).

NASP's code of ethics notes that the term *parent* may be defined in law (e.g., special education law) or district policy, "and can include the birth or adoptive parent, an individual acting in the place of a natural or adoptive parent (a grandparent or other relative, stepparent, or domestic partner), and/or an individual who is legally responsible for the child's welfare" (NASP-PPE Definition of Terms). Practitioners should consult their school administrator or attorney if there are questions regarding who can make educational decisions for a child.

The third element of informed consent is that it must be *voluntary*. Consent must be "obtained in the absence of coercion, duress, misrepresentation, or undue inducement. In short, the person giving consent must do so freely" (Bersoff & Hofer, 1990, p. 951).

When establishing a school psychologist–client relationship, practitioners are ethically obligated to appropriately document oral or written consent (NASP-PPE I.1.3). It is important for school psychologists to recognize that consent is an ongoing process, particularly if there is a significant change in the previously agreed-on assessment or intervention goals or procedures. Furthermore, consent is freely given; clients must be allowed to withdraw consent at any time without negative repercussions (NASP-PPE Definition of Terms; also Barnett, Wise, et al., 2007; IDEA). Specific ethical and legal requirements for informed consent vary across different situations within the school setting. Informed consent for release of student education records is discussed in this chapter. Consent for psychoeducational assessment is addressed in Chapter 6, consent for school-based interventions in Chapter 7, and participation in research in Chapter 10.

The Consent of Minors for Psychological Services

In this portion of the chapter, we explore children's competence to consent to psychological services from legal, ethical, and cognitive-developmental perspectives.

Consent of Minors as a Legal Issue

As noted earlier, legally, in the school setting, informed consent to establish a school psychologist–client relationship typically rests with the parent of a minor child. Legislators and the courts generally have presumed that minors are not developmentally competent to make sound judgments on their own regarding their need for psychological services. The courts have viewed parents as typically acting in their children's best interests and have reasoned that allowing minors a right to refuse services or treatment independent of parental wishes might be disruptive to the parent-child relationship and interfere with effective treatment programs (*Parham v. J.R.*, 1979).

Parham (1979) was an important case regarding the competence of minors to participate in decisions affecting their own welfare. In *Parham*, the Supreme Court upheld a Georgia statute allowing parents to commit a minor child to a mental institution for treatment (with the approval of a physician) in the absence of a formal or quasi-formal hearing to safeguard the child from arbitrary commitment. Although the Court recognized that children have an interest in being free from misdiagnosis and unnecessary confinement, the Court viewed minors as incompetent to make decisions concerning their own need for treatment. (Also see Redding, 1993.)

It should be noted, however, that minors are granted access to psychological or medical treatment without parental consent in emergency situations (Knapp & VandeCreek, 2006), and most states allow minors access to treatment independent of parent notice or consent for certain health-related conditions (e.g., venereal disease, alcohol abuse, drug abuse). Many states also permit minors to consent to mental health treatment at an age earlier than 18 years (see Boonstra & Nash, 2000; Cohn, Gelfman, & Schwab, 2005). The National Association of School Psychologists (NASP)'s code of ethics recommends "that school district parent handbooks and websites advise parents that a minor student may be seen by school health or mental health professionals (e.g., school nurse, counselor, social worker, school psychologist) without parent notice or consent to ensure that the student is safe or is not a danger to others" (NASP-PPE footnote at I.1.2).

Consent of Minors as an Ethical Issue

Although minors are not generally seen as legally competent to consent autonomously to or refuse psychological services in the schools, practitioners are ethically obligated to respect the dignity, autonomy, and self-determination of their clients. As discussed in the paragraphs that follow, we find the notion of developmentally appropriate rights to self-determination and autonomy suggested in the *Canadian Code of Ethics for Psychologists* (CPA, 2000) more satisfactory than an absolute stance that children should always (or never) be afforded the choice to accept or refuse psychological services. The term *assent*, rather than *consent*, typically is used to refer to a minor's affirmative agreement to participate in psychological services. (Also see NASP-PPE Definition of Terms.)

Minors and Capacity to Consent: A Research Perspective

What standards are used to determine whether a client is competent to provide consent to psychological treatment? In law and professional practice, the following four tests or standards of competency to consent have been applied in psychological treatment situations involving adult clients: (1) there is a simple expression of a preference relative to alternative treatment choices; (2) the choice is seen as one a reasonable person might make; (3) a logical or rational decision-making process was followed; and (4) the person giving consent demonstrates understanding (factual or abstract) of the situation, choice made, and probable consequences (adapted from Weithorn, 1983, pp. 244–245). Evidence of a preference is probably the most lenient standard, and evidence of understanding the most stringent (Weithorn, 1983).

Findings from cognitive-developmental research suggest that many children have a greater capacity to make competent choices about psychological treatment than is recognized in law. Research suggests that a child's capacity to effectively participate in treatment decisions depends on a number of factors, including cognitive and personal-social development and functioning, motivation to participate, prior experiences with decision making, and the complexity of the situation and choices under consideration (Melton, Koocher, & Saks, 1983).

Preschoolers have limited language and reasoning abilities. However, they may be able to express preferences when choices are presented in concrete, here-and-now terms (Ferguson, 1978). Although children in middle childhood (ages 6 to 11) have not attained adult reasoning capabilities, research suggests they typically are able to make sensible treatment choices (Weithorn, 1983), and parents and professionals have judged the participation of children this age in treatment decisions to be effective (Taylor, Adelman, & Kaser-Boyd, 1985).

The years between ages 11 and 14 are seen as transitional ones with much individual variation in cognitive development and the ability to make truly voluntary choices. Students in this age range, like younger children, may defer to authority in decisions, or they may make choices based on anti-authority feelings. Minors age 14 and older typically have reasoning capabilities similar to adults, and many are capable of participating in treatment decisions as effectively as adults (Grisso & Vierling, 1978; Steinberg, Cauffman, Woolard, Graham, & Banich, 2009; also Abramovitch, Freedman, Henry, & Van Brunschot, 1995). Cooper (1984) proposed the use of a written therapist-child agreement as a strategy for involving minors ages 9 and older in treatment decisions.

Research findings not only suggest that minors have greater capacity to make treatment decisions than generally recognized in law, but that a child's participation in intervention decisions may lead to enhanced motivation for treatment, an increased sense of personal responsibility for self-care, greater treatment compliance, and reduced rates of early treatment termination (Holmes & Urie, 1975; Kaser-Boyd, Adelman, & Taylor, 1985; Weithorn, 1983). For these reasons, Weithorn suggested that practitioners permit and encourage student involvement in decision making within the parameters of the law and the child's capacity to participate. However, psychologists must guard against overwhelming children with choices they do not wish to make for themselves. Furthermore, when children are given a choice of whether to accept school psychological services, it is important to recognize that they may have little knowledge of, or perhaps misconceptions about, the services offered. The practitioner should ensure that the pupil understands what participation means before soliciting assent so that the child can make an informed choice. For example, a psychologist might ask a pupil to attend a counseling group session before making a choice about participation (see NASP-PPE I.1.4; also APA-EP 3.10d).

In sum, the decision to allow a minor child the opportunity to choose or refuse psychological services and participate in treatment decisions involves a consideration of law, ethical issues (self-determination versus welfare of the client), the child's competence to make choices, and the likely consequences of affording choices (enhanced treatment outcomes versus choice to refuse treatment). As suggested in the *Canadian Code of Ethics* (CPA, 2000), it may be ethical to proceed without the child's explicit assent if the service is considered to be of direct benefit to the child. We concur with Corrao and Melton (1988) that it is disrespectful to solicit assent from the child if refusal will not be honored (NASP-PPE I.1.4).

It also is important to distinguish between the right to consent to (or refuse) services and *the right to be informed about the services offered* (Fleming & Fleming, 1987). Practitioners have an ethical obligation to inform student-clients of the scope and nature of psychological services whether or not they are given a choice about participating (NASP-PPE I.1.4).

Informed Consent Versus Notice

Informed consent differs from notice. *Notice* means that the school supplies information about impending actions. *Consent* requires "affirmative permission before actions can be taken" (Bersoff & Hofer, 1990, p. 950). Wanda's letter to parents (Case 3.1) does not meet the requirements for informed consent to establish a school psychologist–client relationship. If parents do not receive the letter, they have no opportunity to deny consent (J. H. Correll in Canter, 1989).

In seeking informed consent from the parents, Wanda is obligated to describe the nature, scope, and goals of the counseling sessions, their expected duration, any foreseeable risks or discomforts for the pupil (e.g., loss of pupil and family privacy), any cost to parent or student (e.g., loss of classroom instructional time), any benefits that can reasonably be expected (e.g., the possibility of enhanced adjustment to parent separation), alternative services available, and the likely consequences of not receiving services. After consideration of the ethical issues involved and the possible consequences of her decision,

---

Case 3.1

Wanda Rose is concerned about the children in her elementary school experiencing adjustment difficulties related to parent separation and divorce. She decides to form counseling groups for children experiencing parent separation and those from single-parent homes. She asks teachers to identify pupils who might benefit from the group counseling and then sends letters home with the children, notifying parents that their child will be seen for group counseling sessions. She asks parents to contact her if further information about the counseling is desired.

Wanda also must decide whether to offer each child the opportunity to make an informed choice about participating (or not participating) in the counseling groups.

CONFIDENTIALITY

Siegel (1979, p. 251) described confidentiality as "an explicit promise or contract to reveal nothing about an individual except under conditions agreed to by the source or subject." Although primarily a matter of professional ethics, in some states psychologists can be held civilly liable under state law for impermissible breach of client confidentiality (see "Privileged Communication," later in this chapter). The National Association of School Psychologists code of ethics states:

> School psychologists respect the confidentiality of information obtained during their professional work. Information is not revealed to third parties without the agreement of a minor child's parent or legal guardian (or an adult student), except in those situations in which failure to release information would result in danger to the student or others, or where otherwise required by law. Whenever feasible, student assent is obtained prior to disclosure of his or her confidences to third parties, including disclosures to the student's parents. (NASP-PPE I.2.4; also APA-EP 4.05)

The interpretation of the principle of confidentiality as it relates to the delivery of psychological services in the school setting is a complicated matter. However, three guidelines can be found in our codes of ethics and the literature on confidentiality in school-based practice. First, with the exception of urgent situations, school psychologists define the parameters of confidentiality at the onset of establishing a school psychologist–client professional relationship (J. M. Davis & Sandoval, 1982; also APA-EP Principle E, 4.02; NASP-PPE I.2.3). The parameters of the promise of confidentiality will vary depending on the nature of the services offered.

Second, if information learned within a school psychologist–client relationship is shared with third parties, such information is disclosed only on a *need-to-know* basis. "School psychologists discuss and/or release confidential information only for professional purposes and only with persons who have a legitimate need to know" (NASP-PPE I.2.5). Furthermore, only information "essential to the understanding and resolution" of a student's difficulties is disclosed (J. M. Davis & Sandoval, 1982, p. 548; also APA-EP Principle E, 4.04, 4.05; NASP-PPE I.2; Schwab & Gelfman, 2005a).

Third, in recent years there has been increased concern about protecting sensitive information about a student or his or her family from disclosure to others, including disclosure to others within the school setting (Jacob & Powers, 2009; Schwab & Gelfman,

2005a). School physical and mental health professionals, including school psychologists, must recognize that medical or other sensitive personal information "belongs to the student and family, not the school. Therefore, it is generally the student's (or parent's) right to control who has access to that information, especially when disclosure might cause harm" (Schwab & Gelfman, 2005a, p. 266–267; also see NASP-PPE I.2).

In the paragraphs that follow, we discuss confidentiality and its limits when school-based services are provided within the context of the following types of school psychologist–client relationships: direct services to the student, collaboration with the parent and/or teacher, and consultative services to a teacher-consultee.

Confidentiality and Direct Services to the Student

For our purposes here, the provision of direct services to the student means that the practitioner works with the student directly (e.g., individual counseling) as part of a process of ongoing, planned interactions between a school psychologist and student. When establishing a school psychologist–client relationship, the initial interview "should include a direct and candid discussion of the limits that may exist with respect to any confidences communicated in the relationship" (Koocher & Keith-Spiegel, 2008, p. 194; also M. A. Fisher, 2008; APA-EP 4.02; NASP-PPE I.2.3).[1] Because a student who is a minor generally has no legal right to confidentiality independent of the parents, it is critically important to discuss confidentiality and its limits with parents when seeking consent to provide direct services to a minor. The practitioner must explain to parents why a promise of confidentiality to the child can be essential to an effective helping relationship and seek parent understanding and agreement that the psychologist will not share with the parent specific confidences disclosed by the child without the child's assent to do so. Parents need to be reassured, however, that the practitioner will let them know what they can do to help their child and that the practitioner will inform them immediately if there is a serious situation, such as one suggesting that their child is in danger.

Much has been written about the importance of confidentiality for building and maintaining the trust essential to a helping relationship (M. A. Fisher, 2008; Siegel, 1979). However, a promise of confidentiality can help or hinder the psychologist's effectiveness when the client is a minor child (Taylor & Adelman, 1989). As Pitcher and Poland (1992) observed, for a troubled student, candor about the limits of confidentiality may be more important in fostering trust in adult helpers than a promise of absolute confidentiality that is later broken. Consequently, school psychologists must weigh a number of factors in deciding the boundaries of a promise of confidentiality (e.g., age and maturity of the student, self-referral or referral by others, reason for referral). Whatever the parameters, the circumstances under which the psychologist might share student confidences with others must be clear.

In the provision of direct services to the student, there are three situations in which the school psychologist may be obligated to share confidential student disclosures with others. First, it is usually appropriate to disclose student confidences to others when the student requests it. Second, as noted previously, confidential information may be disclosed when there is a situation involving danger to the student or others. Situations involving danger

---

[1]It is generally not necessary to discuss confidentiality with preschool-age student/clients. Preschool children lack cognitive awareness that their own thoughts and feelings differ from those of the people around them, and consequently, discussions of confidentiality have little meaning for this age group.

are discussed in the next subsection, "Duty to Protect." Third, it may be necessary for the psychologist to disclose confidential information when there is a legal obligation to testify in a court of law. This is discussed in the next main section, "Privileged Communication."

Taylor and Adelman (1989) provided suggestions regarding how to create an atmosphere of safety and trust in which the pupil knows and understands the exceptions to the promise of confidentiality, yet is motivated to disclose personal thoughts, feelings, and important information. Findings from a study by Muehleman, Pickens, and Robinson (1985) suggested that discussion of the limits of confidentiality with clients does not limit self-disclosure if self-disclosure is encouraged verbally.

As Poland (1989) noted, the ideal situation is for mental health professionals to discuss the limits of confidentiality at the onset of establishing a psychologist-client relationship. However, students at times are referred for assessment of whether they are a threat to self or others, or self-refer because they are in immediate need of assistance. In such situations, Poland suggested gathering the most complete information possible about the student's thoughts and plans first and then dealing with the issue of the limits of confidentiality (also APA-EP 4.02; NASP-PPE I.2.1). If students offer to disclose personal matters "on the condition that the counselor promises not to tell anyone," the practitioner should not enter into such an agreement, as the student is likely to feel betrayed if the promise cannot be kept.

If it becomes apparent in working with a student that confidentiality must be broken, only information essential to the resolution of the student's difficulties is disclosed to others and only to persons who need to know (J. M. Davis & Sandoval, 1982, p. 548; also APA-EP 4.05; NASP-PPE I.2.5). The decision to divulge information also should be discussed with the student. NASP's code of ethics states, "*Whenever feasible* [emphasis added], student assent is obtained prior to disclosure of his or her confidences to third parties, including the student's parents" (I.2.4). Taylor and Adelman (1989) suggested three steps: (1) explaining to the pupil the reason for disclosure, (2) exploring with the pupil the likely repercussions in and outside the student-psychologist relationship, and (3) discussing with the pupil how to proceed in a manner that will minimize negative consequences and maximize potential benefits. In their work with troubled youth, Pitcher and Poland (1992) found that if handled with sensitivity, most students come to understand that a decision to disclose confidential information to others is based on the need to help the student or protect others.

Duty to Protect

School psychologists have an ethical obligation to safeguard the confidentiality of information learned in a psychologist-client relationship. However, as discussed in Chapter 2, school-based practitioners also have a legal obligation to protect all students from reasonably foreseeable risk of harm (Russo, 2006). For this reason, NASP's code of ethics allows disclosure of confidences "in those situations in which failure to release information would result in danger to the student or others, or where otherwise required by law" (NASP-PPE I.2.4; also APA-EP 4.05). In contrast, depending on state statutory and common law, psychologists in nonschool settings may or may not have a legal duty to breach confidentiality to protect a client or others from danger (see Benjamin, Kent, & Sirikantraporn, 2009). Historically, most state *duty to protect* mandates governing the practice of psychology were a result of the *Tarasoff* case, summarized here as Case 3.2.

The *Tarasoff I* court decision triggered a lengthy debate between American Psychological Association (APA) psychologists who asserted that confidentiality is absolute and can be broken under no circumstances and those who insisted that limits to confidentiality be built into APA's ethical code. The 1981 revision of APA's code of ethics included

---

Case 3.2

Prosenjit Poddar, a foreign student from India attending the University of California–Berkeley, was in psychotherapy with a psychologist at the university's health center. The psychologist recognized that Poddar was quite dangerous, based in part on his pathological attachment to Tatiana Tarasoff, his ex-girlfriend, toward whom he made some threats. After consultation with his supervisor, the psychologist notified the campus police that Poddar was dangerous and should be committed. The police visited Poddar, who denied he had any intentions of harming Tarasoff. Poddar subsequently refused to return for therapy and two months later killed Tarasoff. Tarasoff's parents brought suit against the regents, the student health center staff members involved, and the campus police. Ultimately, the California Supreme Court ruled twice on the case.

The 1974 ruling (*Tarasoff I*) held that the therapists had a duty to warn Tarasoff. The court held that "public policy favoring protection of the confidential character of patient-psychotherapist relationships must yield in instances in which disclosure is essential to avert danger to others; the protective privilege ends where the public peril begins" (*Tarasoff v. Regents of California*, 1974, p. 566). The second ruling, in 1976 (*Tarasoff II*), held that a therapist has a "duty to exercise reasonable care to protect the foreseeable victim" from harm (*Tarasoff v. Regents of California*, 1976, p. 345).

---

the statement that psychologists reveal confidential information to others "only with the consent of the person or the person's legal representative, *except in those unusual circumstances where not to do so would result in clear danger to the person or others* [emphasis added]." The current code states, "Psychologists disclose confidential information without the consent of the individual only as mandated by law, or where permitted by law for a valid purpose, such as to . . . protect the client/patient, psychologist, or others from harm" (APA-EP 4.05; also NASP-PPE I.2.4). Psychologists refer to this obligation to breach confidentiality to ensure the safety of the client or others as the *duty to warn* (*Tarasoff I*) or, more generally, a *duty to protect* (*Tarasoff II*). Following the *Tarasoff* decisions, some, but not all, states enacted laws requiring psychologists to make reasonable efforts to warn potential victims of violent clients, and in some states, appropriate law enforcement agencies must be notified as well.

In summary, although direct service to the student is in many ways analogous to the psychologist-client relationship in nonschool settings, it is important to recognize that a school-based practitioner has special duty-to-protect obligations. Furthermore, most students are minors. Consequently, in school-based practice, student confidences must be shared with others when necessary to safeguard students from *reasonably foreseeable risk of harm* to self or others, a less stringent standard for disclosure of confidential information than *clear* or *imminent danger*, terms often used in state laws regulating mental health providers.

Collaboration and Confidentiality

As noted earlier, school psychologists may provide direct services to the student. However, they typically work in collaboration with teachers, parents, and others to assist the student, a situation that complicates the translation of the principle of confidentiality into appropriate action. In collaboration, the individuals involved carry joint responsibility for assisting the student (J. C. Hansen, Himes, & Meier, 1990). Thus, if the psychologist is working in collaboration with the teacher and/or parent in assisting the student, information will most likely be shared by those involved in the collaborative effort.

At the outset of establishing a professional relationship with a client, the school psychologist needs a clear prior agreement about confidentiality and its limits among those involved in the collaborative effort. The student is informed of those who will receive information regarding the services and the type of information they will receive (NASP-PPE I.2.3, II.4.1). In interactions with the parent, practitioners discuss confidentiality and its limits and parent and student rights regarding "creation, modification, storage, and disposal of psychological and educational records that result from the provision of services" (NASP-PPE II.4.1). Teachers and other staff involved in the collaborative effort also need a clear understanding of the parameters of confidentiality. "School psychologists recognize that it may be necessary to discuss confidentiality at multiple points in a professional relationship to ensure client understanding and agreement regarding how sensitive disclosures will be handled" (NASP-PPE I.2.3).

If information received in a confidential situation subsequently is disclosed to assist the teacher or parent in meeting the needs of a student, it is recommended that *only generalizations*, not specific confidences, are shared (J. M. Davis & Sandoval, 1982; also APA-EP 4.04; NASP-PPE I.2.5). Zingaro (1983) suggested that the psychologist share insights about pupils with others in terms of what they can do to help the child.

In sum, information obtained in a professional relationship and subsequently shared with others is discussed only for professional purposes and only with persons clearly concerned with the situation (APA-EP 4.04). Disclosure of information is "limited to the minimum that is necessary to achieve the purpose [of the disclosure]" (APA-EP 4.04; NASP-PPE I.2.5), called the *need-to-know* principle. Furthermore, in accordance with NASP's code of ethics, school psychologists "do not share information about the sexual orientation, gender identity, or transgender status of a student (including minors), parent, or school employee with anyone without that individual's permission" (I.2.6), and they "respect the right of privacy of students, their parents and other family members, and colleagues with regard to sensitive health information" (I.2.7).

In Case 3.3, Carrie may wish to discuss the parent conference with Amy's teacher in a private setting, but she must take care not to disclose specific information conveyed during her conferences with Mrs. Farwell. For example, Amy's teacher, in working with Mrs. Farwell, may need to know about her difficulty in accepting Amy's disabilities. She does not need to know about Mrs. Farwell's specific disclosures (e.g., the details of her search for a miracle cure).

As J. M. Davis and Sandoval (1982) observed, sometimes social pressures to gossip exist, particularly in the teacher's lounge or lunchroom, in order to be accepted as part of the school staff. Resisting the temptation to join in when teachers and other staff share their frustrations about pupils, parents, and school life may be particularly difficult for Carrie because of her professional isolation in a rural area. However, to safeguard confidential disclosures and maintain teacher trust in her as a professional, Carrie must avoid discussing her knowledge of pupils, parents, or school staff in casual conversations with others.

Confidentiality and Teacher Consultation

Maintaining confidentiality can be particularly problematic for practitioners when the teacher is the primary client. In consultation with the teacher, the parameters of confidentiality should be discussed at the onset of the establishment of the school psychologist-consultee relationship with the teacher, and, consistent with the notion of integrity in professional

---

Case 3.3

Carrie Johnson is exhausted. She just completed another parent conference with Mrs. Farwell. Mrs. Farwell's daughter, Amy, age 3, was diagnosed as having a rare genetic disorder characterized by mild to moderate mental retardation. After the diagnosis was made more than a year ago, Mr. Farwell soon focused his attention on how to best help his daughter, but Mrs. Farwell has not yet been able to accept her daughter's diagnosis. She has spent thousands of dollars during the past year shopping for a different diagnosis and seeking miracle cures. She continues to refuse Carrie's referrals for family counseling and involvement with a support group for parents of children with disabilities. Although she finally acquiesced to Amy's special education placement, she continues to insist that Amy will "grow out of it" and doesn't seem to hear Carrie's careful explanations of Amy's abilities, limitations, and needs. Today, Carrie learned that Mr. and Mrs. Farwell have separated and that Amy's older siblings are showing many adjustment problems at home and in school. She enters the teacher's lounge for a cup of coffee and is greeted by Amy's teacher, who asks, "How's it going with the Farwells?" What, if anything, should Carrie disclose?

---

relationships, the psychologist should have a clear prior agreement about those parameters with others in the school setting (e.g., principal).

In general, in consultation with the teacher, the guarantees of client confidentiality apply to the consultant-consultee relationship. All that is said between the psychologist and teacher must be kept confidential by the psychologist, particularly when the psychologist is confronted by requests for information about the teacher from administrators (J. M. Davis & Sandoval, 1982). As noted in Chapter 1, violation of confidentiality in consultation with teachers is likely to result in a loss of trust in the school psychologist and impair his or her ability to work with the consultee and other staff (also see Chapter 8).

PRIVILEGED COMMUNICATION

As discussed previously, psychologists have long recognized that a promise of confidentiality to the client, along with an explanation of its limits, is essential to establishing psychologist-client trust and an effective helping relationship. Confidentiality is a matter of professional ethics. In contrast, the term *privilege* refers to the *legal* right of the client to prevent disclosure to other parties of information revealed in an established psychologist-client relationship. In the course of a school psychological assessment or intervention, a child or his or her parents may divulge sensitive information, including information that, if disclosed to third parties, would create risks of harm to the child or family members (see Exhibit 3.1). Privilege can be established by common law (judicial decisions) or by statutory law. A distinction is made here between professional-client privilege and evidentiary (or testimonial) privilege.[2]

Professional-client privilege is not found in all states, but may be established in state codes that regulate the delivery of physical and mental health services, including occupation

---

[2]Portions of this section appeared previously in Jacob and Powers (2009).

Exhibit 3.1 Risks of Disclosing Confidential Communications

The following are examples of confidential communications to a school psychologist that create risk to the client's rights or reputation if disclosed to third parties.

Legal Risk

As a result of conversations with a child referred for academic assessment, the school psychologist becomes aware that the child's father is an illegal immigrant who fears deportation.

Risk to Right to Attend School and Academic Standing

A high school student referred for depression confides that he plagiarized several term papers because of parental pressure to get A's and acceptance at a prestigious college.

Social Risk (Risk to Reputation, Loss of Social Standing)

In a meeting with parents regarding their teen who may be suicidal, the parents confide that they are divorcing because one parent is leaving the marriage for a same-sex partner, resulting in turmoil at home.

---

codes, mental health codes, and health and safety codes. Where found, such laws create a legal right for clients to prevent disclosure of confidential information shared in a psychologist-client relationship except under certain circumstances. The parent or guardian of a minor child typically holds the legal right to prevent or allow disclosure of privileged information to third parties. These laws mean that a psychologist can be held civilly liable under state law for an impermissible breach of client confidentiality. Impermissible breach of confidentially also can result in loss of practice credentials (license or certification to practice) (Dekraai et al., 1998). *McDuff v. Tamborlane* (1999) provides an illustration of a civil suit filed against a school psychologist for violation of professional-client privilege as established by state law regulating the delivery of mental health services (see Case 3.4).

The duty for witnesses to testify in judicial proceedings in order to ensure justice at times conflicts with the need to safeguard the trust and privacy essential to special relationships (e.g., attorney-client, husband-wife, psychotherapist-patient). Evidentiary (or testimonial) privilege laws govern the admissibility of evidence in a trial or legal procedure. *Evidentiary privilege* is a legal term that refers to the right of a person in a special relationship to prevent the disclosure in court of information given in confidence in the special relationship. Where evidentiary privilege is extended to school psychologists, it generally means that a client can prevent the psychologist from disclosing information shared in a psychologist-client relationship in a legal proceeding. The client may voluntarily waive privilege (i.e., give consent for the psychologist to disclose privileged communications), and then the psychologist must provide relevant testimony. The waiver belongs to the *client*, and the psychologist has no independent right to invoke privilege against the client's wishes (Knapp & VandeCreek, 1985).

Rules of evidence are used to determine what evidence is admissible in a trial or other legal proceeding. Federal courts follow the Federal Rules of Evidence, while state courts may follow their own rules (Legal Information Institute [LII], 2007). At the federal level,

Case 3.4

McDuff v. Tamborlane (1999). A school psychologist employed by a public school district was providing psychological counseling to a high school student. In order to assist the school psychologist in providing appropriate treatment for her daughter, the girl's mother informed the school psychologist that her daughter had been involved in a larceny. The mother assumed that this disclosure was confidential. The school psychologist subsequently shared the information about the student's crime with the vice principal, who notified the police, and the student was arrested. The student's family filed a malpractice suit against the school psychologist alleging she had violated the confidential nature of the communication by the mother to the psychologist, as well as the state's privileged communication statutes. Although this case was subject to further review by the courts, in the opinion of a Superior Court of Connecticut, the communication of a client's past criminal activity is privileged whether the information is disclosed by the client or by a member of his or her family. The judge also noted that there was no imminent risk of injury to the student, others, or property that would justify the breach of confidentially.

except as required by the Constitution or the U.S. Congress, privilege, including whether communications between a psychologist and client are protected from disclosure, is determined by case law (Article V. Privileges, Rule 501. General Rule; LII, 2007). Prior to the late 1990s, federal case law recognized "psychotherapist-patient privilege," with the term *psychotherapist* meaning a psychiatrist or licensed doctoral-level psychologist. In 1996, however, in *Jaffee v. Redmond*, the Supreme Court ruled that communications between a psychotherapist who was a master's-level social worker and her client were privileged and protected from disclosure in federal court cases. Subsequent decisions in the lower federal courts extended privilege to the clients of a broad range of nondoctoral mental health providers.

State courts follow their own rules of evidence. At the state level, rules governing evidentiary privilege are established by common law or found in one section or several different sections of state codes. In 1892, a nongovernmental body, the National Conference on Commissioners on Uniform State Laws, was formed to promote uniformity in state laws (LII, n.d.). This group, comprised of attorneys from each state, drafted and continues to draft "uniform laws" on various subjects that are sometimes, but not always, adopted in whole or in part by states. As a result of the *Jaffee v. Redmond* decision and parallel developments in state law, the Uniform Rules of Evidence were revised in 1999 to broaden the scope of mental health provider privilege (Aronson, 2001). The components of the 1999 Uniform Rules of Evidence addressing mental health provider privilege are described in the paragraphs that follow. It is important to remember, however, that states rarely use the verbatim language of a uniform law (LII, n.d.).

The Uniform Rules now recognize privileged communication status for "mental health providers," identified as "a person authorized, in any State . . . , or reasonably believed by the patient to be authorized, to engage in the diagnosis or treatment of a mental or emotional condition, including addiction to alcohol or drugs" (1999; Rule 503[a][5]). The general rule of evidentiary privilege is that a client has a privilege to refuse to disclose, and to prevent a mental health provider from disclosing, confidential communications made for the purpose of diagnosis or treatment of the client's physical, mental, or emotional condition (Rule 503[b]). Privilege includes the confidential communications of family members who are participating in the diagnosis and treatment of the client (Rule 503[a][1]). Note that under the Uniform Rules, the mental health provider does not have to be licensed or certified; the only requirement is that the client "reasonably believes" that the person is an authorized mental health provider.

Thus, under the Uniform Rules, privilege communication status for school psychologists generally means that a psychologist cannot disclose confidential information about the client without client consent (or the consent of a minor's parents) to do so. There are, however, exceptions to privilege. First, to fall within the Uniform Rules scope of privileged communication, *the communication must occur in the context of a practitioner-client relationship, and privilege applies only if the client has a reasonable expectation that his or her communications are privileged* (Uniform Rules, 1999, Rule 503[a][5]). Case 3.5, *People v. Vincent Moreno* (2005), and Case 3.6, *J.N. v. Bellingham School District No. 501* (1994) exemplify this exception to privilege.

Case 3.5

People v. Vincent Moreno (2005). A student, Vincent, confessed to a school psychologist that he shot and killed a man during an attempt to rob the victim of his necklace. However, the school psychologist had forewarned Vincent of the limits of confidentiality. More specifically, she had cautioned him that if he were to tell her something "really serious" she would be obligated to take it to a higher level ("Psychologist-Patient Privilege," 2002). The defense attorneys for Vincent argued that his confession to the school psychologist was privileged communication. The court held that a psychologist-patient privilege did not exist in this case because, among other things, a client-psychologist relationship did not exist at the time of the confession, and the school psychologist had forewarned Vincent that her professional obligations prevented her from keeping such an admission confidential.

Case 3.6

J.N. v. Bellingham School District No. 501 (1994). A student, "A.B.," sexually assaulted another student, "J.N." The victim's parents subsequently filed suit against the school district, alleging that the school had prior knowledge that A.B. posed a threat to other pupils and, in light of this knowledge, was negligent in supervision of A.B. When the attorney for the victim's parents asked to see A.B.'s school psychological records to establish that A.B was a foreseeable risk to others, the school refused to release them on the basis that the records were privileged communication between the school psychologist and A.B.'s parents, although released with parent consent to members of the school's multidisciplinary special education assessment team. The court held that psychologist-patient privilege "does not apply where it is manifest that the communication was not intended to be confidential" (1994, p. 26). When information is recorded and shared for the purpose of making a recommendation to a teacher or school multidisciplinary team, the information is not privileged.

The Uniform Rules also identify other exceptions to privilege. Psychologist-client privilege is typically waived when the school psychologist is obligated to report information under state law (e.g., suspected child abuse or other state-mandated reporting), when the client has expressed an intent to engage in conduct likely to result in imminent death or serious bodily injury to the client or others, during legal proceedings to hospitalize a client for mental illness, for court-ordered psychological examination of a client, when a client claims mental illness as part of a legal defense, and during malpractice suits filed by a client against the psychologist (1999, Rule 503[d]). Judges also may waive privilege in child custody proceedings. While state laws include these exceptions to privilege, other exceptions may exist as well (Glosoff, Herlihy, & Spence, 2000). For example, in some states, psychologist-client privilege does not apply in serious felonies such as homicide (e.g., D.C. Code § 14-307 [2006]; Illinois, 735 ILCS 5/8-802 [2005]).

In sum, privileged communication laws are designed to protect the client and the therapeutic process. With regard to evidentiary privilege, the communications between a school psychologist and client are protected in federal courts, and may or may not be protected in state courts, depending on state law. If a client waives privilege or a judge rules that client communications to a school psychologist do not have privileged communication status, the psychologist is then required to testify in court, and refusal to testify may result in the psychologist being held in contempt of court. Furthermore, in some states, if school psychologists disclose privileged client information to others without first obtaining consent to do so (consent of the parents of a minor child), they may put themselves at risk for a malpractice suit (e.g., *McDuff v. Tamborlane*, 1999; Case 3.4) or sanction by their state credentialing board, including possible loss of certification or licensure.

Jacob and Powers (2009) analyzed trends in state privilege laws and found that most states (75%) have broadened the scope of their laws governing patient-psychotherapist privilege with language that would likely include nondoctoral as well as doctoral school psychologists. They also provided a framework to use in deciding whether a confidential client disclosure might be protected by privileged communication laws. In accordance with NASP's code of ethics (I.2.2), school psychologists "recognize that client-school psychologist communications are privileged in most jurisdictions, and do not disclose information that would put the student or family at legal, social, or other risk if shared with third parties, except as permitted by the mental health provider-client privilege laws in their state." Practitioners thus have an ethical and legal obligation to be informed of the scope, language, and exemptions of privilege law in the state where they work and to consult an attorney for advice when difficult situations arise.

Subpoenas and Court Orders

In the course of their professional careers, school psychologists may receive a subpoena or court order regarding a client's records. A *subpoena* is a command to produce certain documents or to appear at a certain time and place to give testimony, which is typically issued by the clerk of a court. Attorneys use subpoenas to gather information relevant to a case. It is important to understand that the client (parent of a minor child) has a right to challenge a subpoena.

The psychologist is the custodian of privilege for the client and, in the absence of written release from the client, must assume that privilege is to be maintained. Therefore, receipt of a subpoena in a situation in which the client has not explicitly waived privilege may still require the psychologist to assert privilege on behalf of the client. (APA Committee on Professional Practice and Standards, 2003, p. 598)

A subpoena differs from a *court order*, a legal document issued by a judge that compels the psychologist to appear in court or produce documents. Failure to comply with a court order can result in being held in contempt of court. However, practitioners may appeal a court order (APA Committee on Professional Practice and Standards, 2003). Strategies for coping with subpoenas or compelled testimony regarding client records are outlined by the APA Committee on Legal Issues (1996). School practitioners are encouraged to seek legal advice immediately if they receive a subpoena for student records or to testify in a legal proceeding regarding a client.

RECORD KEEPING IN THE SCHOOLS

In 1925, the National Education Association recommended that schools maintain health, guidance, and psychological records on each student so that information would be available about the "whole child" along with the academic record (Schimmel & Fischer, 1977). Although these records were made available to governmental agents, employers, and other nonschool personnel, they were to be closed to parents and students. In 1969, the Russell Sage Foundation (1970) convened a conference on the ethical and legal aspects of school record keeping, and many abuses of school records began to be identified:

- Public elementary and secondary school officials released student records to law enforcement agencies, creditors, prospective employers, and others without obtaining permission from parents or students.
- Parents and students typically had little knowledge of the contents of student records or how those records were used. Parent and student access to records usually was limited to attendance and achievement records.
- The secrecy with which the records were maintained made it difficult for parents or students to ascertain the accuracy of information contained in them. Because procedures for challenging the veracity of the information did not exist, an unverified allegation of misconduct could become part of a student's permanent record and be passed on—unknown to the student or parents—to potential employers, law enforcement agencies, and other educational institutions.
- Few provisions existed for protecting school records from examination by unauthorized persons.
- Formal procedures for regulating access to records by nonschool personnel did not exist in most schools.

Family Educational Rights and Privacy Act

In 1974, the Family Educational Rights and Privacy Act (FERPA) was passed as an amendment to the Elementary and Secondary Education Act of 1965 (20 U.S.C. § 1232g; 34 C.F.R. Part 99). This legislation specifically addresses the privacy of student records and access to those records. The Individuals with Disabilities Education Improvement Act (IDEA 2004) outlines similar requirements for parent access to records. The summary of FERPA in this chapter is based on the regulations published in the *Federal Register* on December 9, 2008, and focuses on FERPA as it applies to elementary and secondary schools.

Although FERPA was passed more than 35 years ago, it still generates considerable confusion among teachers, school officials, and school psychologists. In the text that follows, FERPA is discussed under the following five headings: (1) Education Records Defined, (2) Right to Inspect and Review Records, (3) Right to Confidentiality of Records, (4) Right to Request Amendment of Records, and (5) Complaints. Practitioners also need to be familiar with their state's laws regarding student records.

Education Records Defined

Under FERPA, *education records* are defined as any records maintained by the schools (or agencies or consultants to whom a school has outsourced services) that are directly related to the student (34 C.F.R. §§ 99.3, 99.35). At the elementary and secondary levels, the term *education records* typically includes student education records maintained by the school nurse, school psychologist, and special education student records[3] (U.S. Department of Health and Human Services [HHS] & U.S. Department of Education [DOE], 2008).

However, there are a number of different types of records maintained by schools that are explicitly excluded from the definition of education records under FERPA. For example, FERPA excludes records maintained by a school-based law enforcement unit for the purpose of law enforcement and records of employees who are not also students. In the case of an eligible student (one who is 18 or attending a postsecondary institution), the term *education record* does not apply to records made or maintained by a physician, psychiatrist, psychologist, or paraprofessional in connection with treatment of the student, unless that treatment is in the form of remedial education or is a part of the instructional program. The term *education record* also excludes grades on papers corrected by classmates before they are collected and recorded by a teacher.

The Act also excludes *directory information* from its definition of education record. Directory information is "information contained in an education record of a student that would not generally be considered harmful or an invasion of privacy if disclosed" (34 C.F.R. § 99.3). This category includes information such as name, address, telephone number, electronic mail address, activities and sports participation, and degrees and awards received. As long as the school informs parents or eligible students about what kind of directory information they maintain and gives them an opportunity to object to the release of this information, the school may freely release such information (34 C.F.R. § 99.3).

The definition of *education record* under FERPA also does not include *sole possession records*, which are described as follows: "Records that are kept in the sole possession of the maker, are used only as a personal memory aid, and are not accessible or revealed to any other person except a temporary substitute for the maker of the record" (34 C.F.R. § 99.3). In its comments regarding "sole possession records," "personal notes," or "private notes," made in 2000, the Department of Education stated:

> The main purpose of this exception to the definition of "educational records" is to allow school officials to keep personal notes private. For example, a teacher or a counselor who observes a student and takes a note to remind himself or herself of the student's behavior has created a sole possession record, so long as he or she does not share the note with anyone else. (65 FR 41856)

Under FERPA, it is permissible for school psychologists to keep personal notes about their contacts with pupils, parents, or other recipients of service (Martin, 1979).

---

[3]See U.S. Department of Health and Human Services and U.S. Department of Education (2008) for information regarding some of the differences in FERPA regulations for postsecondary institutions as compared with elementary and secondary schools.

Case 3.7

Dillon Rupert, a fourth grader, has always tested the patience of his teachers with his classroom antics. This year, however, his attention-seeking behavior appears to be spiraling out of control. Before planning a behavioral intervention with Dillon's teacher, Pearl Meadows meets with Mrs. Rupert, a divorced single mother who has sole custody of her three young boys. In her meeting with Pearl, Mrs. Rupert discloses that she is feeling overwhelmed by the pressures of her job and parenting, and confides that on occasion she has had four or five alcoholic drinks after the children are in bed at night. She is worried about Dillon's behavior at school and home and her own drinking habits. Mrs. Rupert asks Pearl to help her locate a counselor for herself and other sources of support.

Private notes are to jog the memory and include *information that is to be kept absolutely confidential*. If a practitioner believes that it is necessary to keep notes regarding privileged communications by a client, such information should be recorded in the school psychologist's private notes and not shared with anyone, be kept separately from student education records and in a secure file not accessible to anyone but the psychologist, and be destroyed as soon as the information is no longer needed. For example, Pearl (Case 3.7) may want to make private notes regarding her promise to help Mrs. Rupert locate an appropriate counselor and to remind herself to follow up with Mrs. Rupert in several weeks. Mrs. Rupert's confidential and privileged disclosure should not be shared with anyone (also see NASP-PPE I.2.2).

In contrast, because parents must have access to the data that forms the basis of educational decisions regarding their child, information that the psychologist discloses or makes available to others in the school setting should be placed in the student's education record (Martin, 1979; also see *Parents Against Abuse in Schools v. Williamsport Area School District*, 1991). As noted previously, information included in the student's school psychological file or other education record as defined by FERPA cannot be considered privileged because it is accessible to parties outside of an established school psychologist–client professional relationship (see Case 3.6, *J.N. v. Bellingham School District No. 501*, 1994). Also, as discussed under "Parental Access to Test Protocols" (later in this chapter), test data and a student's answers recorded on test protocols are not considered to fall within the category of private notes.

School psychologists who keep private notes need to be aware that a psychologist's personal notes can be subpoenaed. In a court of law, the problem reverts to one of privilege. Let's suppose that, several months after Pearl's meeting with Mrs. Rupert, her former husband attempts to have Pearl's private notes subpoenaed as part of a child custody suit. If Pearl has shared information from her private notes with anyone, she can no longer claim that the notes are privileged, and it would be difficult to prevent their disclosure in a legal proceeding.

Right to Inspect and Review Records

FERPA was developed to ensure appropriate access to school education records by parents or eligible students. *Parent* is defined as a parent of a student and includes "a natural parent, a guardian, or an individual acting as a parent in the absence of a parent or guardian" (34 C.F.R. § 99.3). Parental separation, divorce, and custody do not affect the right to inspect records, unless a court order or legally binding document specifically revokes parental right to access records (34 C.F.R. § 99.4). In the absence of an official legal notification to the contrary, school personnel may assume that a noncustodial parent has access to the records of his or her child (see *Fay v. South Colonie Central School District*, 1986).

An *eligible student* is a student who is 18 years of age or older, or enrolled in a post-secondary school. When a student reaches the age of 18, the rights of the parent transfer to the student (34 C.F.R. § 99.5). Parents maintain the right to inspect and review the files of a high school student age 18 or older, however, as long as the student is a dependent as defined by federal tax law (34 C.F.R. § 99.31[a][8]). Also, schools may disclose information to the parents of a student age 18 or older in a health or safety emergency, regardless of whether the student is a dependent as defined by tax law (34 C.F.R. § 99.31[a][10]). At age 18, a student may have psychological treatment records that are under his or her own control and not accessible to parents, but only if his or her treatment is not part of the school's instructional program for the student (34 C.F.R. § 99.3[b][4]).

Under FERPA, schools must provide annual notice to parents and eligible students of their right to inspect, review, and request amendments of the student's education records (34 C.F.R. § 99.7). When parents or eligible students make a request to inspect records, the school must comply with the request for access to records "within a reasonable period of time, but in no case more than 45 days after it has received the request" (34 C.F.R. § 99.10[b]). The school must respond to "reasonable requests for explanations and interpretations of the records" (34 C.F.R. § 99.10[c]). Also, if "circumstances effectively prevent the parent or eligible student from exercising the right to inspect and review the student's education records," the school must "provide the parent or eligible student a copy of the records requested" or make "other arrangements" for them to review and inspect the records (34 C.F.R. § 99.3[d]). The school may charge a fee for copies unless the fee effectively prevents parents or eligible students from exercising their right to inspect records (34 C.F.R. § 99.11). The school may not destroy any records if there is an outstanding request to review them (34 C.F.R. § 99.10[e]).

Right to Confidentiality of Records

FERPA was designed in part to protect the privacy of students and their parents. The school may not disclose personally identifiable information from student education records without the informed consent of the parent or eligible student, except for disclosures specifically authorized by FERPA. *Disclosure* means permitting access to, or the release, transfer, or other communication of personally identifiable information by any means, including oral, written, or electronic (34 C.F.R. § 99.3[c]). Information in an education record is considered to be *personally identifiable* if it includes or is linkable to direct personal identifiers, such as student name or Social Security number, or indirect identifiers, such as mother's maiden name, that alone or in combination would allow identification of the individual student (see 34 C.F.R. 99.3). FERPA allows schools to outsource record-keeping functions to an external agency.

When student education records are disclosed to specific persons or agencies at the request of the parent or an eligible student, the school must obtain the signed and written consent of the parent or eligible student. Electronic signatures are permitted. The written consent must specify the records to be disclosed, state the purpose of the disclosure, and identify the party to whom the disclosure may be made (34 C.F.R. § 99.30).

Certain disclosures of education records are authorized by FERPA and do not require the permission of the parent or eligible student. Schools may disclose information from education records without consent to school officials, including teachers, who have been determined to have "legitimate educational interests" in the information. It is important to recognize that although FERPA permits disclosure of information from student education records to teachers without the consent of the parent or eligible student, school psychologists are ethically obligated to release student information to others in the school setting only on a need-to-know basis (NASP-PPE I.2.5, II.4.5).

FERPA (34 C.F.R. § 99.31) also permits schools to disclose information from education records without consent to certain parties or under specific circumstances, such as:

- Appropriate officials in cases of health and safety emergencies
- State and local authorities within a juvenile justice system in accordance with state law
- Organizations conducting certain studies for or on behalf of the school, as long as personally identifiable information concerning students or their families is used only for the purpose of the study as stated in a written agreement with the school, the study is conducted in a manner that does not permit personal identification of students or parents by anyone other than the researchers or school officials with legitimate educational interests, and personally identifiable information is returned to the school or destroyed when no longer needed for research purposes
- Other schools to which a student is transferring
- Specified officials for audit and evaluation purposes

Also, if a school initiates a legal action against a parent or eligible student, or a parent or eligible student initiates a legal action against the school, information may be disclosed to the court without a court order or subpoena if the records are relevant to the legal action. In addition, schools may be required to release education records in compliance with a valid subpoena or judicial order. However, under FERPA, the school must notify parents and eligible students before records are released in response to a subpoena or judicial order, because they may be entitled to a hearing regarding the release (34 C.F.R. § 99.31[9]).

FERPA regulations also specify that schools must maintain a list of the names of educational and other authorities who may access education records without parent consent, and a record of each request for access to and each disclosure of personally identifiable information from the education records of each student (see 34 C.F.R. § 99.32; also §§ 99.34–99.39).

Right to Request Amendment of Records

A parent or eligible student has three bases for requesting an amendment to records: that the information (1) is inaccurate, (2) is misleading, or (3) violates the privacy or other rights of the student. The school then may agree and so amend the record, or disagree and so advise the parent or eligible student and inform the parent or student of their right to a hearing on the matter (34 C.F.R. §§ 99.20–99.21).

The hearing is to be conducted by an individual who has no direct interest in the outcome, but it may be an official of the school. The parent or eligible student may present any evidence he or she chooses and be represented by any individual he or she chooses. The school then makes a decision about whether to amend the record and must present written findings related to its decision. If the school agrees with the parent or student, the record is then amended. If it disagrees, the parent or student may then place in the file a statement commenting on the record (34 C.F.R. §§ 99.21–99.22).

Complaints

Persons may file complaints about violations of FERPA with the Family Policy Compliance Office, U.S. Department of Education (DOE). Complaints are investigated by the Family Policy Compliance Office, and the DOE may terminate federal funds to schools that do not comply with FERPA within a specified time period (34 C.F.R. § 99.63). Prior to 2002, some federal courts allowed parents to pursue Section 1983 lawsuits against school districts because of alleged FERPA violations. In 2002, however, the Supreme Court ruled that FERPA does not confer a personal right to enforcement under Section 1983 (*Gonzaga University v. John Doe*, 2002).

Summary

Schools must have a written policy consistent with FERPA regarding parent access to education records and confidentiality of records and provide annual notice to parents and eligible students of their right to inspect records.

Parental Access to Test Protocols

Two questions often arise with regard to school psychological records: (1) Do parents have the right to inspect and review their child's school psychological test protocols? and (2) Is it ever ethically and legally permissible to make copies of test protocols?

Right to Inspect and Review Protocols

The U.S. Department of Education (DOE) Office of Special Education Programs and Office for Civil Rights (OCR) have responded to numerous inquiries from school personnel, parents, and attorneys regarding parent access to school psychological test protocols. Their responses to letters of inquiry and reports subsequent to complaints are published in the *Individuals with Disabilities Education Law Report* (*IDELR*). Reschly and Bersoff (1999) reviewed 115 interpretations of the issue of parent access to test protocols that appeared in the *IDELR* and concluded that it is "unequivocal" that a student's psychological test protocol on which the child's answers were recorded is part of the student's education record under FERPA and IDEA. In the Analysis of Comments and Changes section of the 1999 IDEA regulations (*Federal Register*, March 12, 1999, p. 12641) and in more recent responses to letters of inquiry (Guard, 2007; Rooker, 2008), the DOE again reiterated its long-standing policy that the form on which an individual student's answers are recorded is an education record as defined by FERPA. Thus, parents have a legal right to inspect and review their child's responses recorded on a school psychological test protocol. Protocols cannot be considered private notes. (Also see *John K. and Mary K. v. Board of Education for School District #65, Cook County*, 1987; *Newport-Mesa Unified School District v. State of California Department of Education*, 2005).

Is it permissible for schools to simply destroy school psychological test protocols so as to avoid allowing parents to review their child's answers written on those protocols? Under FERPA, "if the school were to maintain a copy of a student's test answer sheet (an 'educational record') the parent would have a right under FERPA and IDEA to an explanation and interpretation of the record" (*Federal Register*, March 12, 1999, p. 12641). FERPA does not require parent notification prior to the destruction of an education record such as a test answer sheet. The language "if the school were to maintain a copy of a student's test answer sheet" thus allows schools to send schoolwide or gradewide test answer sheets to the company that produced the test for electronic scoring, with the school receiving only a report that shows the resulting student scores.

However, under IDEA–Part B, a school must inform parents when any personally identifiable information collected, maintained, or used in accordance with Part B is no longer needed *before* it destroys that information (34 C.F.R. § 99.10[e]). Furthermore, as noted earlier, FERPA and IDEA require schools to respond to requests by parents for explanation of their child's education records (34 C.R.F. § 99.10[c]). For these reasons, schools are cautioned against destroying protocols from individually administered psychological or educational tests if such actions could deny parents their legal right to access to information used in educational decision making about their child (Reschly & Bersoff, 1999; also see Rooker, 2005, 2008).

The legal right of parents to review their child's answers recorded on school psychological test protocols thus appears to be in conflict with the practitioner's ethical obligation to maintain test security and to respect purchase agreements with test publishers that prohibit test users from revealing the assessment principles or content of the instruments purchased. However, less conflict exists between the legal right of parents to inspect test protocols and ethical standards than practitioners might imagine. NASP's code of ethics requires school psychologists to maintain test security (II.5.1), but it also allows school-based practitioners to comply with education laws regarding the right of parents (and eligible students) to inspect answers on a school psychological test even if those answers are recorded on a test protocol (II.4.4). Similarly, purchase agreements with test publishing companies recognize that practitioners may be legally required to review test answers with the parent of a child who has taken a test (e.g., "Maintenance of Test Security and Test Use," at http://pearsonassess.com).[4]

When school-based psychologists must balance the obligation to protect test security against the parent's (or eligible student's) legal right to inspect answers on a test protocol, we believe the right to inspect education records is of paramount importance. Practitioners may be able to avoid parent requests to inspect test protocols, however, by establishing a good collaborative relationship early in the evaluation process, by explaining the conflict between their professional obligation to maintain test security and the parents' right to review their child's answers on test protocols, and by communicating assessment findings in a manner that satisfies the parents' need for information about their child. Providing handouts for parents that describe what a test measures with fictitious sample items may be helpful (e.g., Sattler, 2008, pp. 268–269).

If, nevertheless, parents do request to see their child's test protocols, parents should be encouraged to review protocols under the supervision of the school psychologist or other appropriately trained person (see *Newport-Mesa Unified School District v. State of California Department of Education*, 2005; Case 3.8). This review might include a discussion of sample questions and answers. Parents have a right to review the test questions "where the test booklet includes both the test questions and the student's written answers. . . . No exception under FERPA would permit the district to redact [to obscure or remove] the test questions from the test booklet" (Rooker, 2008, p. 1). However, school psychologists have no obligation under FERPA to disclose "nonidentifying information" to parents. Thus, it is appropriate to deny parent requests to inspect test materials (e.g., manuals and stimulus materials) that are not part of the child's individual performance record (Hehir, 1993).

Many states have adopted freedom of information laws to ensure that citizens have access to information regarding the activities of government and to safeguard against abuse of power by officials. Parents and others occasionally request access to test questions and answers under such laws. Tests used in academic settings typically are exempt from disclosure under freedom of information acts unless a court determines that public

---

[4]School psychologists in private practice or who work in other nonschool settings are advised to consult the APA's code statements on client access to test protocols (APA-EP 9.04, 9.11; also Behnke, 2003).

Case 3.8

In *Newport-Mesa Unified School District v. State of California Department of Education* (2005), a federal district court addressed the issue of parents' rights to copies of their child's test protocols under IDEA and California state law. In this case, Mr. Anthony, a parent of a child with special education needs, requested copies of his child's test protocols to review before a scheduled individualized education program meeting. Section 56504 of California's Education Code allows parents of special education students to have copies of their child's test protocols. The district declined to provide Mr. Anthony with copies of the test protocols, however, citing its potential liability for copyright violations. Mr. Anthony subsequently filed a complaint with the California Department of Education (CDOE), and CDOE subsequently ordered the school district to revise its policies regarding student records to comply with Section 56504. The school district brought the matter to a U.S. district court, contending that federal copyright law prevents it from providing copies of copyrighted test protocols to parents. The court invited Harcourt Assessment and Riverside Publishing, copyright holders of assessment instruments such as the Wechsler Intelligence Scale for Children IV (Wechsler, 2003), to intervene and assert a copyright interest. After a review of relevant case decisions and federal copyright law and weighing the competing interests involved, the court found that giving a copy of a copyrighted test protocol to the parents of special education students falls within the "fair use doctrine" of federal copyright law (17 U.S.C. § 107). Schools need to provide a copy of only those portions of the protocol that show the child's answers. Furthermore, "To minimize the risk of improper use, the District may choose to use appropriate safeguards, such as requiring a review by parents of the original test protocols before obtaining a copy, a written request for a copy, a nondisclosure of confidentiality agreement, or other reasonable measures" (p. 1179). It is important to note, however, that the court did not issue an opinion on whether the test publishing companies have a trade secret interest in the test protocols. Consequently, additional litigation can be anticipated.

---

interest in disclosure outweighs public interest in nondisclosure. Practitioners need to consult their state laws on this matter, however.

Making Copies of Test Protocols

As Canter (2001a, p. 30) observed, "One of the more controversial issues regarding release of school psychologists' records concerns the actual copying of test protocols for parents, other professionals or attorneys." Under FERPA, a school is not legally required to provide copies of a child's test protocols to parents except under the following unusual circumstances:

If circumstances effectively prevent the parent or eligible student from exercising the right to inspect and review the student's education records, the educational agency or institution, or SEA [state educational agency] or its component, shall—

1. Provide the parent of eligible student with a copy of the records requested; or
2. Make other arrangements for the parent or eligible student to inspect and review the requested records. (34 C.F.R. § 99.10)

Thus, a school must provide parents a copy of a student's education records, including a child's answers on school psychological test protocols, if the parent is unable to come into the school because of unusual circumstances such as extended travel or serious illness, or make other arrangements for the parent to review the requested records. Making a copy of a test protocol, rather than simply allowing parents to review it, raises additional ethical and legal concerns. Test publishers warn users that any reproduction of a test protocol without permission is a violation of copyright law (e.g., "Copyright Notice" at http://www.psychcorp.com).

However, in 1999, Reschly and Bersoff suggested that providing a single copy of a used protocol would probably fall under the fair use provisions of copyright law. The judge in a 2005 court ruling agreed (see Case 3.8). In *Newport-Mesa Unified School District v. State of California Department of Education*, a federal district court found that giving a copy of the child's test protocol to the parent of a special education student falls within the "fair use doctrine" of federal copyright law. However, schools may implement safeguards such as requiring a nondisclosure of test content agreement with parents.

In summary, some states allow parents to obtain copies of their child's test protocols. One court has ruled that providing a copy of a child's answers on his or her test protocol to parents is not a violation of federal copyright law. At this time, however, there is no definitive answer whether making copies of a used test protocol for parents might be viewed as a violation of the test publishers' trade secret (intellectual property) rights. Because there are many unanswered questions, it is important for school districts to have policies on parent access to test protocols that are consistent with evolving federal and state law and that are communicated to parents and school staff.

It also is important for school-based practitioners to recognize that it is *ethically permissible (and* good practice) to provide a copy of a student's test protocol to another professional who is qualified to interpret it (e.g., a psychologist in private practice), as long as consent to release the record has been obtained from the parents. Providing a protocol to another psychologist may allow parents to obtain a second opinion on their child's educational needs without additional testing. This parallels our right to have a second medical opinion without having to retake medical tests that were already done. Furthermore, because our primary concern is the welfare of the student, we must recognize that it is not appropriate to subject a child to retesting if parent concerns about the school's psychological evaluation might be resolved with an external review of existing data. Furthermore, a second assessment can result in less valid findings because the instruments used in the first evaluation should have been the best and most appropriate for the student, and retesting with the same instrument can result in a practice effect. Finally, the cost of retesting a student is likely to be significantly higher than simply having another psychologist review existing data. A second full and independent evaluation can be done if a review of existing records (including protocols) does not result in clear answers about the child's needs.

Privacy of Sensitive Health Information in Schools: New and Complex Challenges

The Health Insurance Portability and Accountability Act (HIPAA, Pub. L. No. 104-191) is a 1996 federal law created to protect the privacy and security of patient physical and mental health information and to ensure the efficient electronic exchange of patient information and health care claims. Psychologists who work in health care settings and private practice typically are required to comply with HIPAA. The law has three components: *privacy rules* requiring procedures to effectively control access to and disclosure of personally identifiable patient information, *security rules* addressing standards for creation and maintenance of electronic private health records, and *transmission rules* assuring secure and uniform electronic transmission of patient information.

The U.S. Department of Health and Human Services (HHS) together with the Department of Education (DOE) have determined that FERPA provides adequate privacy protection for elementary and secondary education records, and that HIPAA privacy rules generally do not apply to elementary and secondary education records protected by FERPA. More specifically, HIPAA privacy rules do not apply to an elementary or secondary school because it is not a HIPAA-covered entity or it is a HIPAA-covered entity, but maintains health information only in education records as defined by FERPA (see HSS & DOE, 2008, for a detailed discussion of this issue, including implications of HIPAA for Medicaid billing, school-operated health clinics, and contracted health services). Additional information about HIPAA can be found at http://www.hhs.gov/ocr/hipaa/.

Thus, school psychologists who are employed in schools that receive federal funds are generally required to comply with FERPA, but not HIPAA (HSS & DOE, 2008). At the elementary or secondary school level, FERPA does not make a distinction between pupil health records and other types of education records (HSS & DOE, 2008). Because education records created or maintained by K–12 schools may include sensitive health information about a student, some states have experienced pressure for state legislation and district policies to better protect the privacy of physical and mental health information maintained by elementary and secondary schools. Furthermore, most parents have received information regarding their privacy rights under HIPAA during visits to health care providers, and now many have *a greater expectation of ownership and control of physical and mental health information about their children in the school setting*. For example, a complaint by parents regarding health information privacy rights triggered an investigation by the DOE Office for Civil Rights (OCR), and OCR held that the disclosure of confidential health information concerning a student with a disability to others in the school setting without parent consent was discriminatory because students without disabilities were not subject to such disclosures (Pine-Richland [PA] School District, 2009). For these reasons, district policies may be more protective of the privacy of education records maintained by school physical and mental health professionals than other school education records (see Schwab & Gelfman, 2005a; Schwab et al., 2005).

It also is important for school psychologists to know that in many states penalties exist for unauthorized disclosure of certain types of public health status information by school personnel. Such laws are often located in the state's public health code. For example, in Michigan, with the exception of unusual circumstances, the passing of information about a person with a serious communicable disease by school personnel is a felony punishable by a prison term of up to three years and a $5,000 fine or both (Public Act 488, § 5131[10]).

Sensitive physical or mental health information might be received by a school psychologist in a report written by a physician or mental health provider that was released by the parents to the school; the information might be communicated orally by the parent or student (e.g., Case 1.1, in which the mother disclosed drug abuse during pregnancy); or a practitioner might uncover sensitive information as a result of the assessment process (e.g., Dr. Foster's mental health diagnosis of a somatoform disorder, Case 6.2). Although FERPA has specific requirements for the written consent of the parent (or eligible student) prior to disclosure of personally identifiable student information to external (nonschool) professionals and agencies, FERPA regulations provide little guidance regarding what, if any, sensitive student physical or mental health information to share with others who have "legitimate educational interests" in the student *within* the school setting (Schwab & Gelfman, 2005a).

Consistent with the need-to-know principle that appears in our codes of ethics (NASP-PPE I.2.5), Schwab and Gelfman advised school-based physical and mental health professionals to disclose sensitive student health information to others within the school setting only "when necessary in order to benefit the student" (Schwab & Gelfman, 2005a, p. 267). Information disclosure should focus on communicating the student's functional health, academic, and behavioral difficulties and how to respond. Furthermore, in keeping with recommended standards for the management of sensitive student health information in K–12 schools (see Exhibit 3.2), it is appropriate to have a certified or licensed school-based physical or mental health professional review, *in collaboration with the parent or eligible student,* any sensitive medical or mental health information received, to determine what information within those records should be disclosed, and to whom, in order to assist the student.

In summary, consistent with ethical obligations to respect family privacy and the need-to-know principle, school nurses, school psychologists, and other school health professionals should be allowed to serve as gatekeepers who, in partnership with parents or eligible students, control disclosure of sensitive information about students to others within the school setting. Exhibit 3.2 identifies guidelines for managing sensitive physical and mental health information.

Exhibit 3.2 Protecting Confidential Student Health Information

School psychologists have both ethical and legal obligations to safeguard the confidentiality of sensitive student physical and mental health information. Eight guidelines follow:

1. "School psychologists recognize that it may be necessary to discuss confidentiality at multiple points in a professional relationship to ensure client understanding and agreement regarding how sensitive disclosures will be handled" (NASP-PPE I.2.3).
2. School-based practitioners advocate for school record-keeping policies that distinguish student physical and mental health information from other types of school education records and that give school psychologists the authority to control access to school psychological records (National Task Force on Confidential Student Health Information [National Task Force], 2000; Schwab et al., 2005).
3. Consistent with ethical obligations, school psychologists release student information internally only for professional purposes and only with persons who have a legitimate need to know (NASP-PPE I.2.5). When preparing school psychological evaluation reports for a multidisciplinary evaluation team, student assistance team, teachers, or other school staff, school psychologists focus on providing information that will be useful in determining the student's school-related needs, such as the information required for determining eligibility for special education, planning individualized instruction, and identifying recommended school services and accommodations (also see Schwab et al., 2005).

4. School psychologists advocate for district policies that *generally* require "written, informed consent from the parent and, when appropriate, the student, to release medical and psychiatric diagnoses to other school personnel" (Schwab ct al., 2005; National Task Force, 2000, Guideline V).

5. School psychologists advocate for district policies and clear procedures for protecting confidentiality during the creation, storage, transfer, and destruction of electronic and paper student health and mental health records (see Schwab et al., 2005; National Task Force, 2000).

6. School psychologists advocate for the establishment of standard districtwide procedures "for requesting needed health information from outside sources and for releasing confidential health information, with parental consent, to outside agencies and individuals" (National Task Force, 2000, Guideline VII). They recommend the district use HIPAA-compliant authorization forms when requesting health information from outside persons and agencies. This form should identify the names of the certified or licensed school staff (e.g., school nurse, school psychologist) who are being given permission to receive and use the health information. The form also should identify the specific type of information requested, why the information has been requested, and how it will be used. As Schwab et al. (2005) noted, requesting a child's complete medical or mental health records is rarely appropriate.

7. School psychologists advocate for school districts to provide "regular, periodic training for all new staff, contracted service providers, substitute teachers, and school volunteers concerning the district's policies and procedures for protecting confidentiality" (Schwab et al., 2005; National Task Force, 2000, Guideline VIII).

8. School psychology practitioners begin meetings to discuss the needs of an individual student with a brief review of the boundaries of the confidentiality of information to be shared during the meeting and ensure that such meetings are private and cannot be overhead by others.

Adapted from *Guidelines for Protecting Confidential Student Health Information* (National Task Force on Confidential Student Health Information, 2000) and *Protecting and Disclosing Student Health Information: How to Develop School District Policies and Procedures* (Schwab et al., 2005).

Storage and Disposal of Psychological Records

Psychologists ethically are obligated to maintain records to document their professional work with sufficient detail to be useful in decision making by another professional (NASP-PPE II.4.2; also APA, 2007; APA-EP 6.01). Furthermore, because school psychological records may be used in special education due process hearings or other legal proceedings, practitioners have a responsibility to maintain records "with sufficient detail to withstand scrutiny if challenged in a due process or other legal procedure" (NASP-PPE II.4.2; also APA, 2007). However, practitioners respect privacy and do not seek or store sensitive information that is not needed in the provision of services (NASP-PPE I.2.2; also APA-EP Principle E, 4.04), and they include "only documented and relevant information from reliable sources" in their records (NASP-PPE II.4.3). School psychologists also are obligated to "discuss with parents and adult students their rights regarding creation, modification, storage, and disposal of psychological and educational records that result from the provision of services" (NASP-PPE II.4.1).

School psychologists have an ethical obligation to "safeguard the privacy of school psychological records and to ensure parent access to the records of their own children" (NASP-PPE II.4). Under federal special education law (IDEA), schools must establish policies regarding the storage, retrieval, and disposal of education records, and parents of pupils with disabilities must be provided a summary of the school's record-keeping policies (34 C.F.R. § 300.612[a][3]). The federal government provides little guidance, however, regarding how school education records should be stored to ensure compliance with FERPA and IDEA. Thus, policies for the retention and destruction of student education records are largely a state matter. Some states have detailed policies for school record keeping; others only specify minimal requirements regarding the retention of records of attendance, grades, and graduation (Gelfman & Schwab, 2005b).

School-based practitioners occasionally receive reports from professionals or agencies outside the school setting that include sensitive information about a student or a student's family (e.g., information regarding marital problems or parent incarceration, sensitive private health information) that is not needed in the school setting. This may pose a dilemma for the practitioner who believes the report should not become part of the student's education record, yet it also includes information about the student that is helpful in addressing educational needs. A strategy for handling this dilemma is to return the report to the sender with a request that the sender delete any information that is not needed in the school setting (see Schwab et al., 2005, Standard 3).

How long should psychological records be maintained? We are not aware of any federal guidance with regard to how long school psychological records should be maintained, except that the school may not destroy any records if an outstanding request to review them exists. Also, under IDEA, schools must notify parents when personally identifiable information is no longer needed for providing special educational services, and, upon parent request, obsolete records must be destroyed (34 C.F.R. § 300.624).

In the absence of laws controlling how long psychological records must be retained, the APA (2007) suggests psychologists retain full records on adult clients until seven years after the last date of service, and retain the records of minor clients for three years after the minor has reached the age of majority (the age at which an individual legally ceases to be a minor) in the state where the psychologist practices. The APA points out that decisions must be made on a case-by-case basis, however, after consideration of the risks associated with storage of outdated information and the possible benefits of having a record of the early manifestation of a disorder. Bernstein and Hartsell (1998) advise retaining records beyond the state statute of limitations for filing a lawsuit against the psychologist. The statute of limitations for filing a due process complaint under IDEA 2004 is two years unless different explicit time limitations are identified in state law (34 C.F.R. § 300.507[a][2]).

NASP's code of ethics encourages school psychologists to work in collaboration with school administrators and other staff "to establish district policies regarding the storage and disposal of school psychological records that are consistent with law and sound professional practice" (NASP-PPE II.4.9; also Exhibit 3.2). As Canter suggested (2001b), it may be desirable to specify different time lines for storage of different types of psychological records in the district's policies. She recommended that reports and summaries of psychological services be maintained "at least five years beyond the student's graduation or last day of enrollment, or until the date required by state law" (p. 19). If permitted under state law, test protocols and other raw data might be maintained for a shorter period. However, in our opinion, it is advisable to retain a student's test protocols until there is a pattern of relatively stable findings across multiple reevaluations, at which time protocols and other raw data from early evaluations might be destroyed. (See NASP-PPE II.4.9 for a list of recommended practices and policies regarding storage and disposal of school psychological records.)

Technology in Communication and Record Keeping

Electronic management of student education records is a reality in many districts. In some school districts, school psychological assessment results, along with the assessment results of other evaluation team members, are entered into a multidisciplinary report preparation program on the district's server, and an integrated evaluation report is then prepared and disseminated electronically to student assistance or individualized education program (IEP) team members. Similarly, some districts have implemented networked data collection systems to monitor the problem behaviors (e.g., truancy, tobacco use, fighting) of individual students and to evaluate school management at the building or district level (McWilliams, 2003).

Computerized record keeping makes it easier for schools to store and transmit pupil information. FERPA explicitly allows districts to outsource record-keeping functions. Electronic transmission and storage of education records pose the same general risks as paper record keeping, namely unauthorized access to personally identifiable student information or accidental destruction and loss of student education records. In accordance with codes of ethics, parents and adult students should be notified by the school or the school psychologist of the electronic storage and transmission of personally identifiable school psychological records and any known risks to privacy (NASP-PPE II.4.1; APA-EP 4.02c).

Furthermore, "To the extent that school psychological records are under their control, school psychologists protect electronic files from unauthorized release or modification (e.g., by using passwords and encryption), and they take reasonable steps to ensure that school psychological records are not lost due to equipment failure" (NASP-PPE II.4.7; also see APA-EP 6.01; Schwab et al., 2005, Standard 7). Although FERPA, not HIPAA, generally applies to the records of school-based psychologists, the U.S. Department of Health and Human Services (HHS), U.S. Department of Commerce, and security experts have published guidelines for the electronic exchange of health information that may be of assistance in identifying reasonable approaches to risk assessment and management of the electronic creation, storage, and sharing of confidential student information within a networked school system, or on devices that allow "data in motion" outside that network (e.g., Scarfone, Souppaya, & Sexton, 2007).

School psychologists often serve multiple schools within a district or regional cooperative, making it necessary and efficient for them to use portable devices for record keeping, report writing, and communication. For this reason, they must take special care to ensure that their files are always encrypted and password-protected, especially when using laptops and storage devices such as USB flash drives, memory cards, floppy disks, CDs, and DVDs. Word-processing software typically has information rights management procedures that allow users to encrypt and password-protect files and prevent others from modifying or copying restricted files. In addition, they should avoid creating and sending sensitive information when using unsecured wireless access and personal digital assistant (PDA) devices (handheld mobile communication and computing devices) (HHS, 2006).

Practitioners also must take reasonable steps to ensure that no one can recover confidential information from old or failed computers (or other hardware) after their disposal (NASP-PPE II.4.9).

CONCLUDING COMMENTS

In light of the ethical-legal issues of privacy, confidentiality, and school record keeping, Eades's (1986) recommendation is helpful: School psychologists need to ensure that the statements they make orally or in writing are necessary, permitted, and required as a part of their employment and their professional responsibility to their clients.

STUDY AND DISCUSSION

Questions for Chapter 3

1. What is *privacy?*
2. Do schoolchildren have a legal right to privacy in the public schools?
3. The chapter states, "Codes of ethics and law thus show agreement that . . . informed consent should be obtained to establish a school psychologist–client relationship." What does *informed consent* mean?
4. Under what circumstances is it ethically permissible to provide psychological services to a child without his or her explicit assent for services?
5. Research suggests that involving children in treatment decisions may result in better treatment outcomes. What factors affect a child's capacity to participate effectively in treatment decisions?
6. What does *confidentiality* mean? Identify three situations in which the school psychologist is obligated to share student disclosures with others.
7. What is the *need-to-know* principle?
8. What is *privileged communication*? Who has the right to waive privilege in a legal proceeding?
9. Briefly discuss school responsibilities under FERPA with regard to: (a) ensuring parent access to pupil's records, (b) safeguarding the privacy of pupil's records, and (c) affording parents opportunities to ensure the accuracy of records.

Discussion

In this chapter, we recommended that school psychology practitioners encourage a child's participation in treatment decisions to the maximum extent appropriate to the child and the situation. This statement reflects our belief that children are individuals who should be given choices when feasible. This valuing of autonomy, choice, and independence has its foundation in Anglo-European culture and American psychology. In contrast, in many other cultures, children are seen as an extension of the parent; they are expected to obey authority, and they are not offered choices to make on their own (Lynch & Hanson, 1998). Discuss how contrasting beliefs about allowing a child to participate in decisions might affect psychologist-parent communication and collaboration when working with families from culturally diverse backgrounds (see Lynch & Hanson, 1998).

Vignettes

1. Todd, a student with a history of behavior problems, made an appointment with Sam Foster. Now that he has turned 18, he would like to see all of the school psychological reports that have been written about him over the years. He also would like to restrict

his parents' right of access to his school records. How should Sam respond? What are the ethical-legal issues involved? (Adapted from J. L. Davis & Mickelson, 1994.)

2. Pearl Meadows opens her door to a man who states that he is the father of Jeff Blume, a child Pearl recently evaluated. The man asks politely to see the test results, including protocols, that Pearl obtained. He also wants to know what comments, if any, Jeff may have made about his parents, as they are divorced and Mr. Blume plans to go to court seeking custody of Jeff. What, if anything, should Pearl share with this man?

3. During a school vacation day, Sam Foster returns to campus to meet with his faculty advisor about completion of his PsyD degree. Because he is concerned about upcoming deadlines for school psychological reports of students he has been evaluating in the district where he is an intern, Sam takes several pupil folders with him to campus, completes the reports using a computer in the campus computer lab, and then e-mails the reports back to his secretary at work. What are the potential ethical-legal problems associated with this situation?

4. As a result of Hannah Cook's assessment and other information gathered by the school's multidisciplinary team, the school has recommended that John Malamo be classified as cognitively impaired in the team meeting with his parents. John's father, furious with Hannah and the school, has made an appointment with Hannah to review the results of the school psychological evaluation in more detail. When he appears for his appointment, Mr. Malamo demands copies of all information in John's psychological file, including the WISC-IV (Wechsler, 2003) test protocol, so that he can seek an independent opinion about John's needs from a psychologist in private practice. How should Hannah handle this situation?

Chapter 4

ETHICAL-LEGAL ISSUES IN THE EDUCATION OF STUDENTS WITH DISABILITIES UNDER IDEA

Education law is one thing; educational action is quite another. Between the two events, the passing of a law and the behavior of the school, must occur a chain of intermediate events: the interpretation of the law in terms of practice; the study of the feasibility of the interpretation; the successive adjustments, reorganizations, retrainings, and redesign of administrative procedures; the self-monitoring and reporting—the reality testing. (Page, 1980, p. 423)

This chapter provides a summary of law pertinent to providing services to children with disabilities. It focuses on the Individuals with Disabilities Education Improvement Act (IDEA 2004). Special education services for children with disabilities ages 3 through 21 are discussed first in some detail (IDEA–Part B). This is followed by a summary of the federal legislation that provides funds for early intervention services for infants and toddlers with disabilities (IDEA–Part C).

EDUCATION OF CHILDREN WITH DISABILITIES: A HISTORICAL PERSPECTIVE

It is important for school psychology practitioners to have some knowledge of the history of IDEA to appreciate fully the meaning of current law. In the text that follows, we have summarized case law and early legislation that foreshadowed the most important special education law, the Education for All Handicapped Children Act of 1975 (Pub. L. No. 94-142), which was renamed the Individuals with Disabilities Education Act in 1990.

Right-to-Education Case Law

As discussed in Chapter 2, no fundamental right to an education is mentioned in the U.S. Constitution. Public education is an entitlement granted to citizens of a state under state law. However, on the basis of state laws, all children within a state have a legitimate claim to an education at public expense. In legal terms, education is a property right protected by the 14th Amendment of the Constitution, which provides that no state shall "deny to any person within its jurisdiction the equal protection of the laws."

For many years, children with disabilities, particularly those with severe or multiple impairments, were routinely excluded from a public education. School districts typically had policies that required a child to meet certain admissions standards (e.g., toilet trained, ambulatory, mental age of at least five years) before they were allowed to enter school. One of the responsibilities of many school psychologists prior to 1975 was to evaluate children to certify that they were not eligible to attend public school and, therefore, excused from school attendance. Children who were behavior problems in the classroom or simply too difficult to teach were often expelled from school.

Few options existed for the parents of children who did not qualify to attend public school. Institutionalization was the recommended treatment for children with disabilities prior to the 1960s. Affluent families often placed their children in private schools. Others kept their children at home.

In the 1960s, following successful court challenges to racial discrimination in the public schools (e.g., *Brown v. Board of Education*, 1954), parents of children with disabilities began to file lawsuits against public school districts, alleging that the equal protection clause of the 14th Amendment prohibits states from denying school access to children because of their disabilities. Two landmark court cases, *Pennsylvania Association for Retarded Children (P.A.R.C.) v. Commonwealth of Pennsylvania* (1971, 1972) and *Mills v. Board of Education of District of Columbia* (1972), marked a turning point in the education of children with disabilities and gave impetus to the development of federal legislation ensuring a free and appropriate education for all children with disabilities.

Pennsylvania Association for Retarded Children (P.A.R.C.) v. Commonwealth of Pennsylvania

In *P.A.R.C.* (1972), parents of children with mental retardation brought suit against the state of Pennsylvania in federal court because their children were denied access to public education. In a consent decree (where parties involved in a lawsuit consent to a court-approved agreement), parents won access to public school programs for children with mental retardation, and the court ordered comprehensive changes in policy and practices regarding the education of children with mental retardation within the state. The consent decree in *P.A.R.C.* marked the beginning of a redefinition of education in this country, broadened beyond the "three Rs" to include training of children with disabilities toward self-sufficiency (Martin, 1979). The consent decree in *P.A.R.C.* stated:

> Expert testimony in this action indicates that all mentally retarded persons are capable of benefiting from a program of education and training; that the greatest number of retarded persons, given such education and training, are capable of achieving self-sufficiency, and the remaining few, with such education and training, are capable of achieving some degree of self-care; that the earlier such education and training begins, the more thoroughly and the more efficiently a mentally retarded person can benefit at any point in his life and development from a program of education and training. (P.A.R.C., 1971, p. 1259)

The *P.A.R.C.* case is a particularly important because it foreshadowed and shaped subsequent federal laws regarding schools' responsibilities in educating children with disabilities. The state of Pennsylvania was required to locate and identify all school-age persons excluded from the public schools, to place all children in a "free program of education and training appropriate to the child's capacity" (1971, p. 1258), to provide home-bound instruction if appropriate, and to allow tuition grants for children who needed alternative school placements. The *P.A.R.C.* consent decree also required parent notice before children were assigned to special education classes and an opportunity for an impartial hearing if parents were unsatisfied with the placement recommendation for their child.

Mills

Mills (1972) was a lawsuit filed on behalf of seven children with behavioral, emotional, and learning impairments in the District of Columbia.[1] The court order in *Mills* reiterated

---

[1]The suit was initially resolved by a consent decree in 1972. However, the District of Columbia Board of Education failed to comply with the consent decree, and the suit ultimately resulted in a contempt of court judgment against the school board.

many of the requirements of *P.A.R.C.*, and a number of additional school responsibilities in educating children with disabilities were identified. The decision required the schools to "provide each handicapped child of school age a free and suitable publicly supported education regardless of the degree of the child's mental, physical or emotional disability or impairment" (p. 878). The decision also required the schools to prepare a proposal outlining a suitable educational program for each child with a disability, and set limits on the use of disciplinary suspensions and expulsions of children with disabilities.

Following the successful resolution of *P.A.R.C.* and *Mills*, 36 right-to-education cases were soon filed in 27 jurisdictions (Martin, 1979). These cases signaled to Congress that a need existed for federal laws to ensure educational opportunities for all children with disabilities.

Early Legislation

Congress's attempts to address the needs of pupils with disabilities took two routes: the passage of antidiscrimination legislation and the amendment of federal education laws (Martin, 1979). One of the first bills that attempted to ensure equal educational opportunity for children with handicaps in the public schools was an amendment to Title VI of the Civil Rights Act of 1964. The bill later became Section 504 of the Rehabilitation Act of 1973, civil rights legislation that prohibits discrimination against pupils with handicaps in school systems receiving federal financial assistance. School responsibilities under Section 504 to pupils with physical or mental impairments are discussed in Chapter 5.

In addition to antidiscrimination legislation, Congress attempted to meet the needs of pupils with disabilities by amending federal education laws. In 1966, Congress amended the Elementary and Secondary Education Act of 1965 (Pub. L. No. 89-750) to provide grants to states to assist them in developing and improving programs to educate children with disabilities.

In 1970, Congress repealed the 1966 law but established a similar grant program to encourage states to develop special education resources and personnel (Pub. L. No. 91-230; Turnbull & Turnbull, 2000). Four years later, Congress passed the Education Amendments of 1974 (Pub. L. No. 93-380), which increased aid to states for special education and served to put the schools on notice that federal financial assistance for special education would be contingent on the development of state plans with "a goal of . . . full educational opportunities to all handicapped children." Congress intended that this interim legislation would encourage states to begin a period of comprehensive planning and program development to meet the needs of pupils with disabilities. The Education Amendments of 1974 are primarily of historical interest now, except for Section 513, the Family Educational Rights and Privacy Act, discussed in Chapter 3 (Martin, 1979).

INDIVIDUALS WITH DISABILITIES EDUCATION ACT

The most important federal statute concerning the education of children with disabilities is the Education for All Handicapped Children Act of 1975 (Pub. L. No. 94-142). This legislation was introduced as a Senate bill in 1972. A Senate subcommittee on the handicapped held extensive hearings on the proposed legislation. The witnesses (numbering more than 100) included teachers, parents, education associations, parent organizations, and legislators (Martin, 1979). Their testimony made it increasingly evident that more clear-cut federal incentives were needed to assure educational opportunities for children with disabilities. As of 1975, it was estimated that there were more than eight million children with handicaps in the United States. More than half were not receiving an appropriate education, and one million were excluded from public education entirely (Pub. L. No. 94-142, § 601[b]).

In 1975, Congress passed the Education for All Handicapped Children Act, and President Gerald Ford signed it into law. The purpose of the law was to assure that all handicapped children have available to them:

> a free appropriate education which emphasizes special education and related services designed to meet their unique needs; to assure that the rights of handicapped children and their parents or guardians are protected; to assist States and localities to provide for the education of all handicapped children; and to assess and assure the effectiveness of efforts to educate handicapped children. (Pub. L. No. 94-142, § 601[c])

In 1990, President George H. W. Bush signed into law the Education for the Handicapped Act Amendments of 1990 (Pub. L. No. 101-476), which changed the name of the Education for All Handicapped Children Act to the Individuals with Disabilities Education Act (IDEA). Throughout the law, the term *handicap* was replaced by *disability*. In 1997, President Bill Clinton signed into law the Individuals with Disabilities Education Act Amendments of 1997 (Pub. L. No. 105-17). The 1997 amendments focused on improving educational outcomes for students with disabilities.

In 2004, President George W. Bush signed into law the Individuals with Disabilities Education Improvement Act of 2004 (Pub. L. No. 108-446). This set of amendments to IDEA was based on congressional findings that education of children with disabilities can be made more effective by having high achievement expectations; ensuring access to the general education curriculum; making special education a service rather than a place; and providing funds for whole-school approaches, evidence-based early reading programs, positive behavioral interventions, and early intervening services. The authors of the 2004 amendments also recognized that the increasing diversity of the nation's population requires greater responsiveness to the needs of ethnic minority or limited English-proficient schoolchildren (Pub. L. No. 108-446, § 682[c]).

The IDEA provides funds to state and local educational agencies that provide a free and appropriate education to children with disabilities in conformance with the requirements of the law. The law has four parts: Part A, General Provisions; Part B, Assistance for Education of All Children with Disabilities; Part C, Infants and Toddlers with Disabilities; and Part D, National Activities to Improve Education of Children with Disabilities. The IDEA–Part B refers to special education legislation that provides funds for services to children with disabilities ages 3 through 21. The IDEA–Part C provides funds for early intervention services for infants and toddlers. The IDEA–Part C is discussed later in this chapter.

It is important to recognize that IDEA is not a fully funded federal statute; it funds only a modest portion of the extra expenses schools incur in providing special education to students with disabilities. Prior to the 2004 amendments, the level of funding provided to states by the law never exceeded 14% of the additional costs for special education services borne by state governments and school districts (Reschly & Bersoff, 1999). The 2004 amendments allowed each state to receive 40% of the average per-pupil expenditure in public elementary schools and secondary schools multiplied by the number of children ages 3 to 21 with disabilities in the state who receive special education and related services (Pub. L. No. 108-446, § 611[a]). However, there is no guarantee that Congress will make these funds available. For example, the approved final funding for 2005 fell far short of the 40% per-pupil funding allowed under IDEA and was at about 19% (Klotz & Nealis, 2005). The current level of per-pupil funding is unknown because additional federal dollars for IDEA were made available under the American Recovery and Reinvestment Act of 2009.

Under IDEA 2004, states may set aside up to 10% of their monies for a "high-cost" fund. This account can be used to reimburse districts when the cost of providing special education and related services to a high-need child with a disability is greater than three times the average pupil expenditure (34 C.F.R. § 300.704[c]). School districts also are allowed to allocate up to 15% of their federal funds to develop and implement coordinated early intervening services (34 C.F.R. § 300.226[a]).

Parts of IDEA are funded permanently and can be changed only if Congress repeals or amends that portion of the law. Other parts are funded for a specified time period. Part A, the general provisions of the law, does not contain funding and does not require periodic reauthorization. Part B, the portion that provides funds to states for children with disabilities ages 3 through 21, is funded permanently. Part C, infant and toddler programs, and Part D, National Activities to Improve Education of Children with Disabilities, are funded for a limited time period (usually four or five years) and must be reauthorized when the specified period ends.

Reauthorizations of IDEA funds are often accompanied by amendments to the statute. In the years since 1975, some of these amendments have been minor; others have resulted in significant changes in the law (Yell, Drasgow, & Ford, 2000). Rules and regulations implementing IDEA are developed by the U.S. Department of Education (DOE) and are revised following changes in the law. The Part B and Part C regulations are codified at Title 34 of the Code of Federal Regulations (34 C.F.R. Parts 300 and 303, respectively).

Part B final regulations implementing IDEA 2004 were published in 2006. The Office of Special Education and Rehabilitative Services (OSERS) in the U. S. Department of Education created a "one-stop shop" web site for resources concerning IDEA and its implementation (http://idea.ed.gov). The Part B regulations can be accessed through this web site as well as changes that have occurred since the final regulations were published. Additionally, the web site includes topic briefs on selected regulations, training materials, model forms, video clips, webcasts, presentations, dialogue guides, and Q&A documents. It is intended to be a living web site that changes and grows with the implementation of IDEA. Readers also are encouraged to become familiar with special education law in the state where they practice.

The major provisions of IDEA–Part B are discussed under the following headings: "State Plans and Single-Agency Responsibility," "The Zero Reject Principle," "Children Eligible for Services," "Early Intervening Services," "Evaluation Procedures," "Individualized Education Program," "Least Restrictive Environment," "The Meaning of Appropriate Education," "The Scope of Required Related Services," "Procedural Safeguards," and "Right to Private Action."

Proposed regulations for IDEA–Part C were published in 2007 but then withdrawn. As of February 2010, revised proposed new rules for Part C had not been published.

State Plans and Single-Agency Responsibility

Each state must develop a plan to provide special education and related services to pupils with disabilities and identify the state agency responsible for carrying out the plan.

State Plans

To receive funds, IDEA requires each state educational agency (SEA) to have on file with the U.S. Department of Education (DOE) a plan that describes state policies and procedures to assure a free appropriate public education for all children with disabilities residing within the state between the ages of 3 and 21, inclusive, including children with disabilities who have been suspended or expelled from school. The SEA is not required to provide special education and related services to children in the 3- to 5- and 18- to 21-year age groups if the provision of services to those age groups is in conflict with the state law or practice. In addition, states are not required to provide special education and related services to youth ages 18 through 21 who are incarcerated in adult correctional facilities if they were not identified as disabled or did not have an individualized education program (IEP) prior to their incarceration (34 C.F.R. § 300.102[a][2]).

Under IDEA–Part B, federal funds are provided to all states that had an acceptable state plan on file with the DOE prior to the 2004 amendments (34 C.F.R. § 300.176[a]). The DOE may require revisions to state plans, but only as necessary to achieve compliance with the 2004 amendments or new interpretations of the law by a federal court or a state's highest court, or following a finding of noncompliance problems (34 C.F.R. § 300.176[c]). To ensure responsiveness to the needs of children with disabilities and their parents, the SEA must provide opportunities for public comment prior to a revision of its plan (34 C.F.R. § 300.165[a]). Each state also must maintain an advisory panel for the purpose of providing policy guidance with respect to special education and related services for children within the state (34 C.F.R. § 300.167).

The Office of Special Education Programs (OSEP) within the DOE monitors compliance with IDEA at the level of the state and only indirectly (e.g., through the review of the state plan). States are responsible for monitoring local school districts to ensure compliance with IDEA regulations and the state's plan (see Reschly & Bersoff, 1999). The OSEP responds to written inquiries regarding interpretation of IDEA, but it does not attempt to enforce compliance at the level of the individual school district (Zirkel & Kincaid, 1993).

Single-Agency Responsibility

In legislating Pub. L. No. 94-142, Congress sought to ensure that a single state agency was responsible for carrying out the requirements of the law (Turnbull & Turnbull, 2000). The single-agency responsibility aspect of the law has several implications. First, under IDEA–Part B, the SEA is the agency responsible for monitoring all educational programs for children with disabilities ages 3 through 21 within the state and ensuring that they meet IDEA standards (34 C.F.R. §§ 300.101, 300.149). The IDEA–Part B allows the SEA to delegate the responsibility to provide special education and related services to intermediate school districts (or other regional units) and local educational agencies (LEAs). An LEA is usually the board of education of a public school district; the educational administrative unit of a public institution (e.g., school for the deaf or blind); or a charter school that is established as an LEA under state law (34 C.F.R. § 300.28). The SEA must ensure that policies and programs administered by intermediate and local education agencies are in conformance with IDEA–Part B requirements. If an LEA is unable or unwilling to provide appropriate services under IDEA–Part B, the SEA must ensure that special education and related services are available to students with disabilities residing in those areas (Turnbull & Turnbull, 2000). If a charter school is a part of an LEA, the LEA is required to serve children with disabilities who attend the charter school and provide funds to charter schools in the same manner as funds are provided to other schools (34 C.F.R. § 300.209[b]).

Second, consistent with the idea of single-agency responsibility, the SEA also must ensure IDEA–Part B rights and protections to children with disabilities who are enrolled in programs administered by other state agencies. As illustrated by the Joseph McNulty case (see Case 6.1), prior to 1975, many state residential facilities provided custodial care but little training or education for children with disabilities. With the exception of children unilaterally placed in schools or facilities by their parents, the SEA is now responsible for making available an appropriate education for all children with disabilities in the state, including those who are homeless, are residing in mental health facilities or hospitals, and are in homes for individuals with developmental disabilities. The IDEA, however, allows an SEA to delegate its responsibility for providing special education to youth in adult prisons to another agency (e.g., the prison system; 34 C.F.R. § 300.149[d]).

Third, the SEA must ensure that special education and related services are available to children with disabilities enrolled in private schools or facilities. Congress identified two types of private school placements: A child with a disability may be placed in a private school or facility by the SEA or LEA as a means of providing special education and related services, or children may attend private schools or facilities by parental choice.

Private School Placement by the State Educational Agency or Local Educational Agency

Some children with disabilities are placed in a private school or facility as a means of providing the child with appropriate special education and related services. Children placed in a private school or facility by the SEA or LEA must be provided special education and related services in conformance with an IEP developed by an IEP team as described in the law. Publicly placed private school students are entitled to the same benefits and services as those attending public schools. The child must retain all IDEA rights in the private school setting, and the SEA or LEA must monitor the services provided to ensure compliance with IDEA requirements (34 C.F.R. § 300.146). When the placement is made by the SEA or LEA, the placement must be at no cost to the parents, including the program, nonmedical care, and room and board if placement is in a residential facility (34 C.F.R. § 300.146[a][2], 300.104).

Unilateral Placement by Parents

If an LEA makes available a free appropriate public education for a child with a disability but the parents choose to place their child in a private school, the child does not have an individual right to receive some or all of the special education and related services the child would receive if enrolled in a public school (34 C.F.R. §§ 300.137[a]). A school system must provide parentally placed private school students Part B programs and services in accordance with a service plan (34 C.F.R. §§ 300.132[b]). Amounts expended for the provision of services by the LEA must be equal to a proportionate amount of available federal funds, excluding funds expended for child find activities (34 C.F.R. §§ 300.133 [a–b], 300.131[d]).

Decisions about the services that will be provided to parentally placed private school children with disabilities are made in consultation with representatives of the private school (34 C.F.R. §§ 300.134). However, the LEA makes the final decision with respect to the services to be provided to eligible children (34 C.F.R. §§ 300.137[b][2]). Based on this consultation and the funding available, the LEA decides which children will receive services; what services will be provided; and how, where, and by whom the services will be provided (34 C.F.R. § 300.134[d]). If a child enrolled in a private school will receive special education or related services from an LEA, the LEA initiates and conducts meetings to develop, review, and revise a service plan for the child and ensures that a representative of the private school attends or otherwise participates (e.g., by telephone) in each meeting (34 C.F.R. § 300.137[c]).

Thus, parentally placed private school students with disabilities may receive a different amount and range of services than children with disabilities in public school (34 C.F.R. § 300.138 [a][2]). School systems are given broad discretion with regard to which private school students with disabilities will receive services and what services will be provided. Parentally placed private school children may receive services on-site at the child's school, including a religious school, to the extent consistent with law (34 C.F.R. § 300.139[a]). LEAs may not use federal funds to benefit private schools and LEAs must maintain control over any property, equipment, and supplies that are used to benefit private school students with disabilities (34 C.F.R. §§ 300.141, 300.144). LEAs may count the cost of transporting children to participate in services as part of their required expenditure on private school students (34 C.F.R. § 300.139 [b]).

Parents have, at times, recovered private school tuition costs from the SEA or LEA through administrative hearings or lawsuits in which they demonstrated that the SEA or LEA failed to offer their child an appropriate education program in the public schools, leaving them no option but to place him or her at their own expense (see *Forest Grove School District v. T.A.*, 2009). The IDEA specifically addresses this issue. If the parents of a child with a disability who previously received special education under the authority of a public agency enroll the child in a private school without the consent or referral of the agency, a court or hearing officer may require the agency to reimburse the parents for the cost of enrollment if it is found that the agency failed to make a free appropriate public education available to the child in a timely manner prior to that enrollment (34 C.F.R. § 300.148[c]).

However, IDEA also states that the cost of reimbursement may be reduced or denied if:

- At the most recent IEP meeting the parents attended prior to removal of the child from the public school, the parents did not inform the IEP team that they were rejecting the placement proposed by the public agency, including stating their concerns and their intent to enroll their child in a private school at public expense.
- The parents did not give the public agency written notice of their concerns and their intent to enroll their child in a private school at public expense at least 10 business days prior to the removal of the child from the public school.
- The public agency notified the parents of its intent to evaluate the child (and the reasons for the evaluation) prior to the parents' removal of the child from the public school, but the parents did not make the child available for such evaluation.
- Or a judicial finding is made that the actions taken by the parents were unreasonable (34 C.F.R. § 300.148[d]).

The cost of reimbursement may not be reduced or denied if the school prevented the parents from providing notice, the parents had not received notice, compliance would likely result in physical or serious emotional harm to the child, or the parents are not literate or cannot write in English (34 C.F.R. § 300.148[e]).

The Zero Reject Principle

The zero reject principle requires states to locate and evaluate pupils with disabilities and provide them with full educational opportunity, regardless of the severity of the disability.

Child Find

Consistent with the court decisions in *P.A.R.C.* and *Mills*, Congress recognized that to assure special education was available to all children with disabilities (i.e., the zero reject principle), it was necessary for the SEA to actively seek to locate all children with disabilities within the state. This aspect of the law is called the *child find* requirement. The IDEA requires the SEA to implement policies and procedures to assure that all children with disabilities (including those who are homeless, wards of the state, or attending private schools) are identified, located, and evaluated (34 C.F.R. § 300.111[a]). The SEA also must identify pupils who are suspected of being disabled and in need of special education services, even though they are advancing from grade to grade, and highly mobile children, including migrant children (34 C.F.R. § 300.111[c]). Finally, the SEA must ensure that accurate child counts of children receiving services under IDEA are made to Washington each year (34 C.F.R. § 300.640).

Severity of the Disability

The zero reject principle also encompasses the notion that the SEA must provide full educational opportunity to all children with disabilities, regardless of the severity of their disability. A 1989 court case raised the question of whether some children are so severely impaired that they do not qualify for services under IDEA. *Timothy W. v. Rochester, New Hampshire School District* (1989) concerned a child who was profoundly retarded, deaf, blind, spastic, and subject to convulsions. The school alleged that Timothy was so impaired he was "not 'capable of benefiting' from an education, and therefore was not entitled to one" (p. 956). In a surprise ruling, the district court agreed with the school. On appeal, however, this decision was reversed. In a lengthy opinion the court stated, "The language of the Act [IDEA] in its entirety makes clear that a 'zero-reject' policy is at the core of the Act" (p. 960). As the court noted in *Timothy W.*, there is no requirement under IDEA that a child be able to demonstrate that he or she will benefit from special education in order to be eligible for services.

Exception to the Zero Reject Principle

When Pub. L. No. 94-142 was passed in 1975, its purpose was to assure a free and appropriate education for *all* pupils with disabilities within a state. If parents failed to consent to the initial special education placement, schools were expected to use due process procedures (e.g., hearings) to override parent refusal of services. Based on a review of case law and special education regulations in the late 1970s, Martin (1979) concluded that "the parent cannot be allowed to block needed services any more than the school can be allowed to offer inadequate services" (p. 103).

In contrast, IDEA 2004 *prohibits* schools from using procedural safeguards to overrule a parent's failure to consent to the initial provision of services (34 C.F.R. § 300.300[b][3]). Parents now have "the ultimate choice" as to whether their child will receive special education services. The IDEA 2004 states that a school is not required to convene an IEP meeting or develop an IEP for a pupil whose parents do not consent to the initial evaluation or provision of special education services (34 C.F.R. § 300.300[b][4][ii]). Also, the school will not be considered in violation of the requirement to make available a free appropriate public education to the child if the parent withholds consent to the initial evaluation or placement (34 C.F.R. § 300.300[b][4][i]).

In summary, Pub. L. No. 94-142 assured a free and appropriate education to all students with disabilities. Federal special education law is now more accurately described as assuring that all states *offer* or *make available* a free and appropriate education to all children with disabilities. The IDEA 2004 presumes that parents can and will make educational decisions that are in the best interest of their child.

Children Eligible for Services

The funds available under IDEA–Part B are earmarked to provide special education and related services only for children with disabilities as defined by the law. Under IDEA–Part B, a *child with a disability* means a child evaluated in accordance with the procedures in the law as having:

> mental retardation, a hearing impairment (including deafness), a speech or language impairment, a visual impairment (including blindness), a serious emotional disturbance (referred to in this part as "emotional disturbance"), an orthopedic impairment, autism, traumatic brain injury, an other health impairment, a specific learning disability, deaf-blindness, or multiple disabilities, and who . . . needs special education and related services. (34 C.F.R. § 300.8[a])

It is important to note that eligible children under IDEA–Part B must have a disability as outlined in one of the 13 disability categories (see Exhibit 4.1), and they must need special education and related services because of that disability. Identification of a pupil as needing special education is thus "a two-pronged determination: (a) A disability in obtaining an education must be documented, and (b) a need for special education must be established" (Reschly, 2000, p. 87). Also, a child is not eligible for special education and related services if "the determinant factor for that determination is lack of appropriate instruction in reading, including the essential components of reading instruction (as defined in ESEA); lack of appropriate instruction in math; or limited English proficiency" (34 C.F.R. § 300.306[b]).

Exhibit 4.1 Disability Categories Under IDEA 2004 Part B

Definitions of disability terms. The terms used in this definition are defined as follows:

(1)(i) *Autism* means "a developmental disability significantly affecting verbal and nonverbal communication and social interaction, generally evident before age three, that adversely affects a child's educational performance. Other characteristics often associated with autism are engagement in repetitive activities and stereotyped movements, resistance to environmental change or change in daily routines, and unusual responses to sensory experiences.

(ii) Autism does not apply if a child's educational performance is adversely affected primarily because the child has an emotional disturbance, as defined in paragraph (c)(4) of this section.

(iii) A child who manifests the characteristics of autism after age three could be identified as having autism if the criteria in paragraph (c)(1)(i) of this section are satisfied."

(2) *Deaf-blindness* means "concomitant hearing and visual impairments, the combination of which causes such severe communication and other developmental and educational needs that they cannot be accommodated in special education programs solely for children with deafness or children with blindness."

(3) *Deafness* means "a hearing impairment that is so severe that the child is impaired in processing linguistic information through hearing, with or without amplification, that adversely affects a child's educational performance."

(4) *Emotional disturbance.* See text later in this chapter.

(5) *Hearing impairment* means "an impairment in hearing, whether permanent or fluctuating, that adversely affects a child's educational performance but that is not included under the definition of deafness in this section."

(6) *Mental retardation.* See text later in this chapter.

(7) *Multiple disabilities* means "concomitant impairments (such as mental retardation–blindness, mental retardation–orthopedic impairment), the combination of which causes such severe educational needs that they cannot be accommodated in special education programs solely for one of the impairments. Multiple disabilities does not include deaf-blindness."

(8) *Orthopedic impairment* means "a severe orthopedic impairment that adversely affects a child's educational performance. The term includes impairments caused by a congenital anomaly, impairments caused by disease (e.g., poliomyelitis, bone tuberculosis), and impairments from other causes (e.g., cerebral palsy, amputations, and fractures or burns that cause contractures)."

(9) *Other health impairment.* See text later in this chapter.

(10) *Specific learning disability.* See text later in this chapter.

(11) *Speech or language impairment* means "a communication disorder, such as stuttering, impaired articulation, a language impairment, or a voice impairment, that adversely affects a child's educational performance."

(12) *Traumatic brain injury* means "an acquired injury to the brain caused by an external physical force, resulting in total or partial functional disability or psychosocial impairment, or both, that adversely affects a child's educational performance. Traumatic brain injury applies to open or closed head injuries resulting in impairments in one or more areas, such as cognition; language; memory; attention; reasoning; abstract thinking; judgment; problem-solving; sensory, perceptual, and motor abilities; psychosocial behavior; physical functions; information processing; and speech. Traumatic brain injury does not apply to brain injuries that are congenital or degenerative, or to brain injuries induced by birth trauma."

(13) *Visual impairment including blindness* means "an impairment in vision that, even with correction, adversely affects a child's educational performance. The term includes both partial sight and blindness." (Adapted from 34 C.F.R. § 300.8)

The IDEA–Part B allows states to use a broader definition of disability for children ages 3 through 9 years, or for a subset of that age range (e.g., ages 3 through 5) (34 C.F.R. § 300.111[b]). States may use the term *developmental delay* for a three- to nine-year-old who is experiencing delays (as defined by the state) in one or more areas of development—physical, cognitive, communication, social or emotional, or adaptive—and who, for that reason, needs special education and related services (34 C.F.R. § 300.8).

The IDEA–Part B definitions that concern sensory, motor, and speech or language impairments typically pose few problems. The definitions of *mental retardation*, *specific learning disability (SLD)*, *emotional disturbance (ED)*, and *other health impairment* frequently have been a source of confusion and disagreement, and they are discussed in the text that follows.

The present discussion focuses on the federal definitions of disability categories under IDEA–Part B. School psychologists also must be knowledgeable of the broader definition of disability under Section 504 of the Rehabilitation Act of 1973 (see Chapter 5) and their state code eligibility requirements. Different states use different names for special education categories (e.g., mental retardation, cognitive impairment, or developmental cognitive delay), and state classification criteria vary as well (Reschly & Bersoff, 1999). It is important to note that IDEA does not require states to label pupils, and some states have adopted a noncategorical system for the delivery of special education services (34 C.F.R. § 300.111[d]). However, states must nevertheless provide data to the DOE each year regarding the number of children with disabilities by disability category (34 C.F.R. § 300.641[a]).

Finally, it also is important to note that a medical diagnosis is not required by *federal* law, nor is it sufficient for determining whether a child is eligible for special education and related services under IDEA–Part B (Zirkel, 2009b, p. 336). Federal special education law allows schools to use means other than a medical evaluation by a licensed physician to determine whether a child has a disability. States may, however, require a medical evaluation to determine whether a child has a medically related disability. If a medical evaluation is required, it must be done at no cost to the parent. Similarly, a *Diagnostic and Statistical Manual of Mental Disorders* diagnosis (American Psychiatric Association, 2000) may assist in determining eligibility under IDEA, but it is neither legally required nor sufficient to determine whether a student is eligible for special education under IDEA–Part B (Zirkel, 2009b).

Mental Retardation

> Mental retardation means significantly subaverage general intellectual functioning, existing concurrently with deficits in adaptive behavior and manifested during the developmental period, that adversely affects a child's educational performance. (34 C.F.R. § 300.8[c][6])

Prior to the passage of Pub. L. No. 94-142, many children were labeled mentally retarded on the basis of a single IQ score (see Case 6.1). The use of an IQ score as the sole criterion for classifying mental retardation in the schools resulted in the overidentification of children as mentally retarded, particularly pupils from ethnic minority backgrounds and those with limited English proficiency. In the 1950s and 1960s, the American Association of Mental Deficiency argued persuasively for a change in the definition of *mentally retarded*. The group recommended that a diagnosis of mental retardation be based on the finding of deficits in both intellectual functioning and adaptive behavior. This view gained wide acceptance and was incorporated into the IDEA–Part B regulations.

Under IDEA–Part B, eligibility for special education is determined by a team of qualified professionals and the parents of the child. The team must consider three types of assessment information in determining whether a child has mental retardation: general intellectual functioning, adaptive behavior, and school performance. To be eligible for special education under the mental retardation category, the child must show subaverage performance on a measure of general intellectual functioning. Subaverage is usually further defined in state guidelines as performance at least two standard deviations below the population mean for the child's age group. Most states recommend the use of IQ tests for this measure. However, this evaluation can be accomplished by testing "or by means other than testing" as long as the procedures are valid and nondiscriminatory (Heumann, 1993, p. 539).

The child also must demonstrate concurrent deficits in adaptive behavior and school performance. Assessment of adaptive behavior focuses on the child's ability to meet age-appropriate standards of personal independence and social responsibility. Such measures typically are based on observations of behavior and competencies provided by an informant, usually a parent or teacher (Sattler & Hoge, 2006). Deficits in school performance are most often documented by individually administered achievement tests.

Specific Learning Disability

Specific learning disability means a disorder in one or more of the basic psychological processes involved in understanding or in using language, spoken or written, that may manifest itself in an imperfect ability to listen, think, speak, read, write, spell, or to do mathematical calculations, including conditions such as perceptual disabilities, brain injury, minimal brain dysfunction, dyslexia, and developmental aphasia. . . . Specific learning disability does not include learning problems that are primarily the result of visual, hearing, or motor disabilities, of mental retardation, of emotional disturbance, or of environmental, cultural, or economic disadvantage. (34 C.F.R. § 300.8[c][10])

Prior to the 2004 amendments, IDEA regulations stated that a team could determine that a child has a specific learning disability (SLD) only if the child had a severe discrepancy between an area of academic achievement and intellectual ability. Over the years since the regulations were first introduced in 1977, many experts expressed dissatisfaction with the IQ-achievement discrepancy model for identifying children with specific learning disabilities (U.S. Department of Education, Office of Special Education Programs, 2002). Criticisms included inadequate reliability and validity of the model; overidentification of children as having an SLD, particularly ethnic and racial minorities; delayed treatment for young children who do not yet evidence a score discrepancy between ability and achievement; and wide variability in SLD identification practices across schools and states. Under IDEA 2004, schools are no longer required to take into consideration whether a child has a severe discrepancy between achievement and intellectual ability; states "must permit the use of a process based on the child's response to scientific, research-based intervention" (34 C.F.R. § 300.307[a][2]). A response to intervention (RTI) model identifies children who are likely to qualify as learning disabled through (a) a documented slow rate of learning and (b) large differences from age or grade expectations even after high quality, scientifically based interventions are put in place for the child (Gresham et al., 2005).

In determining whether a student has a specific learning disability, the IDEA regulations specify the group (or team) members who should be involved in eligibility determination. The determination must be made by the child's parents and a team of qualified professionals, which includes the child's general education teacher (or if the child does not have a general education teacher, a general education teacher qualified to teach a child of his or her age), as well as at least one person qualified to conduct individual diagnostic examinations of children such as a school psychologist, speech-language pathologist, or remedial reading teacher (34 C.F.R. § 300.308).

The regulations go on to state that a team may determine a child has a specific learning disability if:

(1) The child does not achieve adequately for the child's age or to meet State-approved grade-level standards in one or more of the following areas, when provided with learning experiences and instruction appropriate for the child's age or State-approved grade-level standards:
(i) Oral expression.
(ii) Listening comprehension.

(iii)   Written expression.
(iv)   Basic reading skill.
(v)   Reading fluency skills.
(vi)   Reading comprehension.
(vii) Mathematics calculation.
(viii) Mathematics problem solving.
(2)(i) The child does not make sufficient progress to meet age or State-approved grade-level standards in one or more of the areas identified in paragraph (a)(1) of this section when using a process based on the child's response to scientific, research-based intervention; or

(ii) The child exhibits a pattern of strengths and weaknesses in performance, achievement, or both, relative to age, State-approved grade-level standards, or intellectual development, that is determined by the group to be relevant to the identification of a specific learning disability, using appropriate assessments . . . ; and

(3) The group determines that its findings under paragraphs (a)(1) and (2) of this section are not primarily the result of—
(i)   A visual, hearing, or motor disability;
(ii) Mental retardation;
(iii) Emotional disturbance;
(iv) Cultural factors;
(v)   Environmental or economic disadvantage; or
(vi) Limited English proficiency. (34 C.F.R. § 300.309)

To ensure that the underachievement in a child suspected of having a specific learning disability is not due to lack of appropriate instruction in reading or math, the group must consider whether data demonstrate that prior to (or as a part of) the referral process, the child was provided appropriate instruction in general education settings. The team also must consider, as part of the evaluation, data-based documentation of repeated assessments (at reasonable intervals) of the student's progress during instruction, information that also was provided to the child's parents (34 C.F.R. § 300.309).

Furthermore, the regulations require an observation of the child's academic performance and behavior in the child's learning environment, including the general education classroom, or an age-appropriate setting if not in school (34 C.F.R. § 300.310[a], [c]). The group (team) report and documentation for a child suspected of having a specific learning disability must include a statement covering seven items: (1) whether the child has a specific learning disability; (2) the basis for making the determination; (3) the relevant behavior, if any, noted during the observation of the child and the relationship of that behavior to the child's academic functioning; (4) the educationally relevant medical findings, if any; (5) whether the child does not achieve adequately and does not make sufficient progress to meet age or state-approved grade-level standards, or whether the child exhibits a pattern of strengths and weaknesses in performance, achievement, or both, relative to age, state-approved grade-level standards, or intellectual development; (6) the determination of the group concerning the effects of a visual, hearing, or motor disability; mental retardation; emotional disturbance (ED); cultural factors; environmental or economic disadvantage; or limited English proficiency on the child's achievement level; and (7) the instructional strategies used and the student-centered data collected if a response to a scientific, research-based intervention process was implemented, and documentation showing that the parents were notified regarding this process (34 C.F.R. § 300.311[a]). Each team member is required to certify in writing whether the report reflects his or her conclusion (34 C.F.R. § 300.311[b]). If it does not reflect his or her conclusion, the team member must submit a separate statement presenting his or her conclusions (34 C.F.R. § 300.311[b]).

Emotional Disturbance

Emotional disturbance is defined as follows:

(i) The term means a condition exhibiting one or more of the following characteristics over a long period of time and to a marked degree that adversely affects a child's educational performance:
  (A) An inability to learn that cannot be explained by intellectual, sensory, or health factors.
  (B) An inability to build or maintain satisfactory interpersonal relationships with peers and teachers.
  (C) Inappropriate types of behavior or feelings under normal circumstances.
  (D) A general pervasive mood of unhappiness or depression.
  (E) A tendency to develop physical symptoms or fears associated with personal or school problems.
(ii) Emotional disturbance includes schizophrenia. The term does not apply to children who are socially maladjusted, unless it is determined that they have an emotional disturbance. (34 C.F.R. § 300.8)

The IDEA–Part B definition of emotional disturbance (ED) has been controversial since it was adopted in 1975. It is a modification of a definition of the emotionally disturbed schoolchild first outlined by Bower (1982). Bower's definition grew out of a California study in the late 1950s of children identified by school personnel as emotionally disturbed. This study found that children with emotional disturbances differed from their classmates on a number of characteristics: They were poor learners; they had few, if any, satisfactory interpersonal relationships; they behaved oddly or inappropriately; they were depressed or unhappy; and they developed illnesses or phobias. These characteristics also were found among nondisturbed children; however, the disturbed children displayed the characteristics "to *a marked degree over a long period of time*" (Bower, 1982, p. 57).

Bower (1982) did not differentiate between emotionally disturbed and socially maladjusted children in his definition. He believed that emotionally disturbed and socially maladjusted children were not separate entities. Federal policy makers, however, feared that a definition of emotionally disturbed based on Bower's original description would result in a category of special education eligibility that was too broad and costly for schools. They consequently added a clause excluding children who are socially maladjusted unless they also are emotionally disturbed.

The ED definition, particularly the exclusionary clause, has generated classification disagreements and confusion (Hughes & Bray, 2004). Slenkovich (1988a) advocated for a narrow, legally correct interpretation of *emotionally disturbed*. She advised the team to consider the IDEA requirements point by point when making eligibility decisions for the ED classification. Under IDEA–Part B, the term *emotional disturbance* means that the child suffers from an emotional "condition exhibiting one or more . . . characteristics over a long period of time and to a marked degree." Slenkovich (1988a) suggested that, consistent with the psychiatric diagnosis of schizophrenia, six months might be seen as the minimum period of time. Also, according to Bower's (1982) original definition, the disturbance must be present to a marked degree; it must be overt and observable. The definition of *emotionally disturbed* "avoids presumptions about the child's intrapsychic condition, psychiatric nosology, or clinical designation. It does not presume to go beyond what is observable in the school setting. . . . It accepts as given that emotional disturbance is disturbing to others" (p. 57). Simply put, school personnel can perceive that the child is experiencing a problem (Slenkovich, 1988a).

Also consistent with Bower's (1982) original definition, the emotional disturbance must adversely affect educational performance. If a student is performing within his or her expected range for age and ability, then he or she does not qualify as ED under IDEA–Part B (Slenkovich, 1988a). The child with emotional disturbance under IDEA–Part B must exhibit one or more of five characteristics:

1. *An inability to learn* because of the ED. Emotional difficulties interfere with the school performance of many children. However, to qualify as ED using this part of the definition, the child must be so disturbed that he or she cannot learn.
2. *An inability to build or maintain satisfactory interpersonal relationships with peers and teachers.* Children who are simply unpopular or associate with an undesirable peer group do not manifest this characteristic. The child must be so disturbed that he or she cannot enter into or maintain relationships with peers and teachers.
3. *Inappropriate types of behavior or feelings under normal circumstances.* This appears to mean odd, bizarre, unusual behavior, not simply behavior that is disturbing to the class and teacher.
4. *A general or pervasive mood of unhappiness or depression.* The mood of unhappiness or depression must be observable.
5. *A tendency to develop physical symptoms or fears associated with personal or school problems.* Again, the fears or symptoms must be marked and occur over a long period of time. (Adapted from Slenkovich, 1988a, pp. 153–164.)

The ED definition also expressly includes children diagnosed as schizophrenic. Children with autism are eligible under a separate disability category.

The last element of the ED definition excludes children who are socially maladjusted unless they also are emotionally disturbed. This portion of the definition has generated much discussion because the federal regulations do not define *socially maladjusted*, and, despite recent advances in differentiation of emotionally disturbed and socially maladjusted children (e.g., Gacono & Hughes, 2004; J. A. Miller, Williams, & McCoy, 2004), distinguishing between the two continues to be problematic. Furthermore, the two categories are not mutually exclusive; some children are emotionally disturbed *and* socially maladjusted (Clarizio, 1987; Merrell & Walker, 2004).

Bower (1982), as noted, believed that attempts to differentiate between emotionally disturbed and socially maladjusted children are artificial and that such distinctions miss the more important point that both groups of children are in need of special help (also Hughes & Bray, 2004; Olympia et al., 2004). Over the past 30 years, a number of experts and concerned professional associations have called for replacing "emotional disturbance" in IDEA with "emotional or behavior disorders" and adopting new criteria for classification; others have challenged general education to develop better programs for socially maladjusted students who are not emotionally disturbed (Clarizio, 1987; Merrell & Walker, 2004). Response to intervention (RTI) has also been proposed as an alternative method to identify students who are at risk for emotional disturbance (Gresham, 2007). At the present time, the definition of emotional disturbance varies across states, with some states eliminating the social maladjustment exclusion from their definition (Olympia et al., 2004).

Thus, aspects of the ED definition are vague, subjective, and controversial. Confusion also arises from the fact that nonschool mental health professionals typically are trained to use a system for classifying childhood disorders that differs from IDEA. The system of classification that is most frequently used outside the schools is the *Diagnostic and Statistical Manual of Mental Disorders* (*DSM-IV*) (American Psychiatric Association, 2000). As Slenkovich (1988a) observed, psychologists and psychiatrists in nonschool settings often assume (and state in reports to schools) that a child diagnosed as suffering from an emotional problem under *DSM-IV* automatically qualifies for special education and related services as emotionally disturbed. However, to qualify for special education as ED under IDEA–Part B, a child must be found eligible under the IDEA–Part B definition (also see Zirkel & Rose, 2009).

Other Health Impairment

Other health impairment means having limited strength, vitality or alertness, including a heightened alertness to environmental stimuli, that results in limited alertness with respect to the educational environment, that—

(i) Is due to chronic or acute health problems such as asthma, attention deficit disorder or attention deficit hyperactivity disorder, diabetes, epilepsy, a heart condition, hemophilia, lead poisoning, leukemia, nephritis, rheumatic fever, sickle cell anemia, Tourette syndrome; and

(ii) Adversely affects a child's educational performance. (34 C.F.R. § 300.8)

Beginning in the 1980s, the courts and the Office of Special Education Programs (OSEP) began to address questions regarding whether students with acquired immune deficiency syndrome (AIDS), alcohol and chemical dependency, and attention deficit disorder or attention deficit/hyperactivity disorder (ADD/ADHD) qualify as having a health impairment under Part B. Court rulings have determined that students with conditions such as AIDS qualify under the "other health impairment" classification only if their physical condition is such that it adversely affects educational performance (*Doe v. Belleville Public School District No. 118*, 1987). However, as will be seen in Chapter 5, students with AIDS are protected by Section 504 of the Rehabilitation Act of 1973.

The OSEP also has addressed the question of whether chemically dependent pupils (alcohol or drug addicted) qualify as having a health impairment under IDEA. According to OSEP, chemical dependency does not, in and of itself, qualify a child for special education and related services within the "other health impairment" classification (cited in Slenkovich, 1987a). However, students who are receiving treatment for drug or alcohol dependency may be protected by Section 504 (see Chapter 5).

A third question was whether students with ADD/ADHD qualify for special education and related services under the "other health impairment" classification of IDEA–Part B. Unlike its precursors, IDEA 1997 specifically included ADD/ADHD among the disabling conditions listed under "other health impairment." To be eligible within this category, the child must have limited strength, vitality, or alertness due to the ADD/ADHD, and the condition must adversely impact the child's education performance and result in the need for special education and related services. Thus, some pupils with ADD/ADHD qualify within the IDEA definition of *other health impairment*. Other students do not qualify under the "other health impairment" classification but may be eligible for accommodations in general education under Section 504 if the ADD/ADHD *substantially limits* (rather than *adversely affects*) their educational performance (see Chapter 5; "ADD/ADHD Students," 1999).

Early Intervening Services

In the mid-1980s, some schools began to introduce building-based "child study" teams to assist teachers in planning interventions for pupils with learning or behavior problems. Such programs provided early assistance to students who were struggling to succeed in the general education classroom, reduced referrals to special education, and were seen as a safeguard against unnecessary referral, testing, and possible misclassification (see Chalfant & Pysh, 1989).

In 2004, IDEA was amended to allow school districts to use up to 15% of their federal special education funds each year to develop and implement coordinated *early intervening services*. These services are for all students, with a focus on kindergarten through third grades. The services are targeted to those pupils who "need additional academic and behavior support to succeed in the general education environment" but who have not been identified as needing special education and related services (34 C.F.R. § 300.226[a]). Funds may be used for professional development to enable staff to deliver "scientifically based academic and behavioral interventions, including scientifically based literacy instruction," and to provide "educational and behavioral evaluations, services, and supports, including scientifically based literacy instruction" services (34 C.F.R. § 300.226[b][1][2]). It is hoped that IDEA's early intervening services will result in effective assistance to pupils before their problems become severe, a reduction of inappropriate referrals for special education, and less misclassification of children as having disabilities for the purpose of providing individualized help. (Also see Chapter 7.)

Evaluation Procedures

This portion of the chapter describes a series of lawsuits concerning the misclassification of racial and ethnic minority pupils as "mentally retarded," including students whose native language was not English, and the safeguards that Congress subsequently included in IDEA to protect against misclassification.

Problem of Misclassification

As noted previously, right-to-education court cases signaled to Congress that federal legislation was needed to ensure educational opportunities for all children with disabilities. A second type of court case was important in shaping the nondiscriminatory testing, classification, and placement procedures required by IDEA–Part B. These cases concerned the misclassification of ethnic minority group children as "mentally retarded" and their placement in special classes for the educable mentally retarded (EMR). They raised questions regarding school violations of the due process and equal protection guarantees of the 14th Amendment (Bersoff, 1979).

Due Process.   The due process clause of the 14th Amendment protects individuals from arbitrary or unwarranted stigmatization by the state that may interfere with the ability to acquire property (*Wisconsin v. Constantineau*, 1971). Under the protections of the 14th Amendment, the state (school) may not assign a negative label such as "mentally retarded" without due process, that is, without some sort of fair and impartial decision-making procedures (Bersoff & Ysseldyke, 1977). In the *P.A.R.C.* ruling, a number of procedural safeguards against misclassification were required. For example, parents were given the right to an impartial hearing if they were dissatisfied with their child's special education classification or placement.

Equal Protection.   With the landmark *Brown v. Board of Education* decision in 1954, the Supreme Court ruled that school segregation by race was a denial of the right to equal protection (equal educational opportunity) under the 14th Amendment. Following this decision, the courts began to scrutinize school practices that suggested within-school seg-regation, that is, where ethnic minority group children were segregated and treated differ-ently within the schools. A number of suits against the public schools were filed in which minority group children were overrepresented in lower education tracks and special educa-tion classes. These lower tracks and special education classes were seen as educationally inferior and a denial of equal education opportunities. The claimants in these cases main-tained that many children were misclassified and inappropriately placed based on racially and culturally discriminatory classification and placement procedures (see Exhibit 4.2).

Exhibit 4.2 Cases Concerning Misclassification of Ethnic Minority Children

Hobson v. Hansen (1967, 1969)

The first significant legal challenge to the use of aptitude tests for assigning minority group children to low-ability classes was *Hobson v. Hansen*. In this case, African American and poor children were disproportionately assigned to the lower tracks in the Washington, D.C., public schools on the basis of scores on group-administered aptitude tests. Federal Judge Wright noted that the tracking system was rigid, that it segregated students by race, and that the lower tracks were edu-cationally inferior. He further stated that because the aptitude tests were "stand-ardized primarily on and are relevant to a white middle-class group of students, they produce inaccurate and misleading test scores when given to lower class and Negro students" (*Hobson*, 1967, p. 514). He ruled that the tracking system was a violation of equal protection laws and ordered the system abolished.

Diana v. State Board of Education (1970)

Diana was a class action suit filed in California on behalf of nine Mexican American children placed in classes for the educable mentally retarded (EMR) on the basis of Stanford-Binet or Wechsler Intelligence Scale for Children IQ scores. Diana, one of the plaintiffs, came from a Spanish-speaking family and was placed in an EMR classroom based on an IQ score of 30. When she was later retested in Spanish and English by a bilingual psychologist, she scored 49 points higher on the same test and no longer qualified for special class placement (Bersoff & Ysseldyke, 1977). The consent decree in *Diana* required that children be assessed in their primary language or with sections of tests that do not depend on knowl-edge of English (Reschly, 1979).

Guadalupe Organization, Inc. v. Tempe Elementary School District NO. 3 (1972)

Guadalupe was a class action suit filed on behalf of Yaqui Indian and Mexican American pupils. The consent decree in *Guadalupe* also required assessment in the

(Continued)

Exhibit 4.2 (*Continued*)

child's primary language or the use of nonverbal measures if the child's primary language was not English. *Guadalupe*, however, went further than *Diana* in requiring a multifaceted evaluation that included assessment of adaptive behavior and an interview with the parents in the child's home (Reschly, 1979). *Guadalupe* also required due process procedures, including informed consent for evaluation and placement.

Larry P. v. Riles (1984)

Larry P. was a class action suit filed on behalf of African American pupils placed in classes for the educable mentally retarded (EMR) in the San Francisco School District. The plaintiffs claimed that many African American children were misclassified as mentally retarded and that IQ tests were the primary basis for classification as EMR. The court asked the schools to demonstrate that their methods of classification (i.e., use of IQ test scores) were "rational" or valid for the purpose of classifying African American children as mentally retarded and in need of special education. The school district was unable to convince the court that IQ tests were valid for the purpose of placing African American children in EMR classes, and in 1972 the court temporarily enjoined the schools from any further placement of African American children in EMR classes on the basis of IQ test results.

In the second phase of *Larry P.*, the trial on the substantive issues, the plaintiffs requested that the court consider their claims under both the 14th Amendment and the new federal statute, Pub. L. No. 94-142. More than 10,000 pages of testimony were presented during this phase. In his lengthy opinion, Judge Peckham characterized the EMR classes as "inferior" and "dead-end." Based on his analysis of the expert testimony, he found IQ tests to be racially and culturally discriminatory. He ruled that the school failed to show that IQ tests were valid for the purpose of selecting African American children for EMR classes, and, in his view, IQ scores weighed so heavily in decision making that they "contaminated" and biased the assessment process. He permanently enjoined the state from using any standardized intelligence tests to identify African American children for EMR classes without prior permission of the court (Bersoff, 1982; Reschly, 1979). In 1986, Judge Peckham banned the use of IQ tests to assign African American children to any special education program except for the state-supported gifted and talented program. In 1988, a group of parents filed a suit claiming that the state's ban on IQ tests discriminated against African American children by denying them an opportunity to take the tests helpful in determining special education needs. In 1992, Judge Peckham issued an order allowing African American children to be given IQ tests with parent consent (*Crawford v. Honig*, 1994). The California State Department of Education continued to prohibit the use of IQ tests with African American children, however. The California Association of School Psychologists made an unsuccessful attempt to challenge the state's ban on IQ testing in 1994 (*California Association of School Psychologists v. Superintendent of Public Instruction*, 1994).

Parents in Action in Special Education (P.A.S.E.) v. Hannon (1980)

This case was filed on behalf of African American children in the Chicago public schools. As Bersoff (1982, p. 81) notes, "the facts, issues, claims and witnesses" were similar to those in *Larry P.*, but the outcome was different. Judge Grady carefully listened to the same expert witnesses who testified in San Francisco. He decided that the issue of racial and cultural bias could best be answered by examining the test questions himself. He proceeded to read aloud every question on the WISC, WISC-R, and Stanford-Binet and every acceptable response. As a result of his analysis, he found only eight items on the WISC or WISC-R to be biased and one item on the Stanford-Binet. He concluded that the use of IQ tests in the context of a multifaceted assessment process as outlined in IDEA was not likely to result in racially or culturally discriminatory classification decisions and found in favor of the school system (Bersoff, 1982).

The first three court cases summarized in Exhibit 4.2, along with *P.A.R.C.* and *Mills*, were extremely influential in shaping the IDEA–Part B requirements for nondiscriminatory testing and classification and the procedural or due process safeguards against misclassification. *Larry P. v. Riles* (1984) and *Parents in Action in Special Education (P.A.S.E.) v. Hannon* (1980) addressed the question of whether IQ tests are valid for the purpose of classifying and placing minority group children in special classes. The court in *P.A.S.E.* ruled that the use of IQ tests in the context of the assessment process outlined in IDEA–Part B was not likely to result in racially or culturally discriminatory placement decisions.

As an additional safeguard against misclassification of ethnic minority children, IDEA requires each state to gather and examine data to determine whether significant disproportionality based on race and ethnicity is occurring in the state in relation to the identification and/or placement of children with disabilities (34 C.F.R. § 300.646[a]). If it is determined that a significant disproportionality exists, the state must provide for the review and, if appropriate, revision of policies, procedures, and practices (34 C.F.R. § 300.646[b]). (See Losen & Orfield, 2002; Skiba et al., 2008.)

Conduct of Evaluation

The early court cases concerning the misclassification of pupils as mentally impaired prompted Congress to include a number of standards with regard to both the content and the process of assessment, classification, and special education placement in IDEA. The IDEA–Part B requires each SEA or LEA to establish procedures to assure a full and individual evaluation of each child who may qualify as having a disability (34 C.F.R. § 300.301[a–c]). These procedures must yield the information necessary to determine if the child has a disability and his or her educational needs. The evaluation must be completed prior to the initial provision of special education and related services and within the time frame identified in state law, or within 60 days of receiving parental consent for the evaluation if no deadline is specified by the state (34 C.F.R. § 300.301[c]). Informed parental consent for an initial assessment and the nondiscriminatory testing and assessment procedures required by IDEA–Part B are discussed in Chapter 6.

Student Evaluations and Eligibility Determination

In conducting an evaluation, IDEA–Part B requires the LEA to:

use a variety of assessment tools and strategies to gather relevant functional, developmental, and academic information about the child, including information provided by the parent that may assist in determining whether the child has a disability . . . and the content of the child's

IEP, including information related to enabling the child to be involved in and progress in the general curriculum (or, for preschool children, to participate in appropriate activities); not use any single procedure as the sole criterion for determining whether a child has a disability or determining an appropriate educational program for the child; and use technically sound instruments that may assess the relative contribution of cognitive and behavioral factors, in addition to physical or developmental factors. (34 C.F.R. § 300.304[b])

In addition, assessment tools must be validated for the purpose used and be fair, and the child must be assessed in all areas related to the suspected disability (34 C.F.R. § 300.304[c]; see Chapter 6). The assessment strategies must provide information that directly assists in determining the education needs of the child (34 C.F.R. § 300.304[c]).

After completion of the administration of tests and other evaluation procedures, the determination of whether the child has a disability is made by a team that includes qualified professionals and the parent (34 C.F.R. § 300.306). The composition of this team will vary depending on the nature of the child's suspected disability. Some or all of the persons who serve on this eligibility determination team may also serve on the IEP team. The parent is given a copy of the evaluation report and documentation of determination of eligibility (34 C.F.R. § 300.306[a][2]).

Under IDEA–Part B, parents have the right to obtain an independent educational evaluation (IEE) of their child, and those findings must be considered by the school "in any decision made with respect to the provision of [a free appropriate public education] to the child" (34 C.F.R. § 300.502[a], [c][1]). An IEE is an evaluation conducted by a qualified examiner who is not employed by the district responsible for the education of the child in question (34 C.F.R. § 300.502 [a][3][i]). The school, on request, must provide parents with information about where an independent educational evaluation may be obtained and the district's criteria for an IEE (34 C.F.R. § 300.502[a][2]).

Depending on the circumstances, an IEE may be conducted at parent or school expense. If the parent disagrees with the evaluation done by the school, the district is required, with no unnecessary delay, to either ensure that an IEE is conducted at public expense or initiate a due process hearing if it believes its evaluation was appropriate (34 C.F.R. § 300.502[b][2]). If the hearing officer determines that the evaluation was appropriate, parents may proceed with an IEE, but at their own expense (34 C.F.R. § 300.502[b][3]). It should be noted that a parent is entitled to only one independent educational evaluation at school expense each time the LEA conducts an evaluation with which the parent disagrees (34 C.F.R. § 300.502[b][5]).

When a child is seen for reevaluation, the IEP team and other qualified professionals, as appropriate, review existing evaluation data on the child and, on the basis of that review (along with input from the parents), identify what additional data are needed to determine: (a) whether the child continues to have a disability and the educational needs of the child; (b) the present levels of academic achievement and related developmental needs of the child; (c) whether the child continues to need special education and related services; and (d) whether any additions or modifications to special education and related services are needed to enable the child to meet the measurable annual goals set out in his or her IEP and to participate, as appropriate, in the general education curriculum (34 C.F.R. § 300.305[a]). For reevaluations, the group may conduct its review without a meeting (34 C.F.R. § 300.305[b]).

If, as part of a reevaluation, it is determined that no additional data are needed to determine whether a child continues to have a disability, the school ensures that the parents are notified of that determination and the reasons for it, along with their right to request an assessment of the child (34 C.F.R. § 300.305[d]). In this situation, the school is not required to conduct an assessment unless requested by the child's parents (34 C.F.R. § 300.305[d][2]). A school is required, however, to evaluate a child before determining that the child no longer qualifies as disabled under Part B (34 C.F.R. § 300.305[e][1]). If a pupil graduates from high school with a regular diploma or exceeds age eligibility for special education under state law, an evaluation is not needed (34 C.F.R. § 300.305[e][2]). Schools must provide the graduating student with a summary of his or her academic achievement and functional performance, along with recommendations on how to assist the student in meeting postsecondary goals (34 C.F.R. § 300.305[e][3]).

Placements

In determining the educational placement of a child with a disability, including preschool children, the LEA is required to ensure that the placement decision is made by a group of persons (including the parents and other persons knowledgeable regarding the child) who consider the evaluation data and the placement options (34 C.F.R. § 300.116[a][1]). Placement must be determined at least annually based on the child's IEP, must be in the least restrictive environment, and must be as close as possible to the child's home (34 C.F.R. § 300.116[c–e]). The child must be educated in the school that he or she would attend if not disabled unless the parent agrees otherwise, or the child requires some other arrangement because of his or her special education needs (34 C.F.R. § 300.116[b–c]). In selecting the least restrictive environment, consideration is given to any potential harmful effect on the child or the quality of services that he or she needs, and a child is not removed from education in an age-appropriate general classroom solely because of needed modifications in the general curriculum (34 C.F.R. § 300.116 [d–e]; also see "Least Restrictive Environment," later in this chapter).

Individualized Education Program

As previously noted, in the *P.A.R.C.* consent decree, the court required that instructional programs for each child with disabilities be "appropriate for his learning capabilities," and the *Mills* ruling required that a disabled child's education be "suited to his needs." This policy of providing an appropriate education for children with disabilities is achieved in IDEA–Part B by the IEP. Congress viewed the IEP as a means of preventing functional exclusion of children with disabilities from opportunities to learn, and the yearly review of the IEP was seen as a safeguard against misclassification and as a way to encourage continued parent involvement (Turnbull & Turnbull, 2000). As noted previously, students placed in private schools by the SEA or LEA must receive special education and related services in conformance with an IEP; in contrast, school districts are given broad latitude in developing a service plan that determines which parentally placed private school students with disabilities will receive special education and related services and the types of services to be provided. (See Weber, 2007.)

The Meeting

The SEA or LEA is responsible for initiating and conducting a meeting for the purpose of developing the child's initial IEP. The initial IEP meeting must be held within 30 calendar days after the determination that the child needs special education and related services (34 C.F.R. § 300.323[c][1]). Schools are not required to hold the IEP meeting within 30 days of the *referral* for evaluation; the 30-day countdown to the IEP starts the day that the group making the eligibility determination finds that the child qualifies for and needs special education. Schools must have an IEP for each child with a disability in effect at the beginning of each school year (34 C.F.R. § 300.323[a]).

The Team

The IEP team is composed of: (a) the parents of the child; (b) at least one general education teacher of the child (if the child is, or may be, participating in a general education environment); (c) at least one special education teacher of the child, or, if appropriate, at least one special education provider of the child; (d) a representative of the LEA who is qualified to provide, or supervise the provision of, specially designed instruction to meet the unique needs of children with disabilities, and who is knowledgeable about the general curriculum and the availability of resources of the LEA; (e) an individual who can interpret the instructional implications of evaluation results (who may already be a member of the team in another capacity); (f) at the discretion of the parent or the LEA, other individuals who have knowledge or special expertise regarding the child, including related services personnel as appropriate; and (g) whenever appropriate, the child (34 C.F.R. § 300.321[a]).

If private school placement is under consideration by the IEP team, the LEA must ensure that a representative of the private school attends the meeting or in some way participates in the meeting to develop the initial IEP (e.g., telephone conference call) (34 C.F.R. § 300.325[a][2]). After a child with a disability enters a private school or facility, any meetings to review and revise the child's IEP may be initiated and conducted by the private school or facility at the discretion of the LEA, as long as the LEA and parents are involved in any decisions about the IEP (34 C.F.R. § 300.325[b]).

If the purpose of the IEP meeting is to consider transition services for the student (services to promote movement from school to postschool activities), the school must invite the student to attend (34 C.F.R. § 300.321[b]). If the student is not able to attend, the school must take steps to ensure that the student's preferences and interests are considered (34 C.F.R. § 300.321[b][2]). With the consent of the parents or the adult student, schools also must invite representatives of agencies responsible for providing or paying for transition services to attend the meeting or in some way participate in the planning of any transition services (34 C.F.R. § 300.321[b][3]).

Prior to 1975, parents often were not included in special education placement decisions, and school policies of closed records made it difficult for parents to gain access to information about how such decisions were made. Initially clarified in IDEA 1997, the law states that each SEA or LEA must ensure that the parents of a child with a disability are members of any group that makes decisions on the identification, evaluation, and educational placement of their child (34 C.F.R. § 300.501[b]). To ensure parent participation and shared decision making in the development of the IEP, IDEA–Part B requires the school to provide adequate prior notice of team meetings, and the meeting must be scheduled at a mutually agreed-upon time and place (34 C.F.R. § 300.322[a]). Notice must include the purpose, time, place, and location of the meeting and who will be in attendance (34 C.F.R. § 300.322[b]). A meeting does not include informal or unscheduled conversations among school personnel or conversations on issues such as teaching methodology, lesson plans, or coordination of services (34 C.F.R. § 300.501[a][3]). A meeting also does not include preparatory activities that school personnel engage in to develop a proposal (or a response to a parent proposal) that will be discussed at a later meeting (34 C.F.R. § 300.501[a][3]).

Schools must make reasonable efforts to ensure that parents understand, and are able to participate in, any group discussions relating to the educational placement of their child, including providing interpreters for parents who are deaf or whose native language is other than English (34 C.F.R. § 300.322[e]). If neither parent can attend, the school must attempt to ensure parent participation using other means such as telephone conference calls or videoconferencing (34 C.F.R. § 300.501[b][3]). The IEP meeting may be conducted without parent participation only if the school is unable to convince the parents to attend (34 C.F.R. § 300.322[d]). The school must document its efforts to arrange a mutually agreed-upon meeting. This documentation might include records of telephone calls and the results of those calls, copies of correspondence to parents and responses, or records of home visits or visits to the parents' place of employment (34 C.F.R. § 300.322[d]).

The IDEA 2004 introduced greater flexibility with regard to IEP meetings. First, a member of the IEP team is not required to attend the IEP meeting if the parent and the school agree, in writing, that the attendance of that member is not necessary (34 C.F.R. § 300.321[e][1]). If the meeting involves discussion related to the excused member's area of expertise, he or she must submit written input to the parent and IEP team prior to the meeting (34 C.F.R. § 300.321[e][2]). Second, consolidation of the reevaluation and IEP team meetings is encouraged (34 C.F.R. § 300.324[a][5]). Third, after the annual IEP meeting for the school year and if the parent and school agree, a child's IEP may be modified in writing without convening additional meetings (34 C.F.R. § 300.324[a][4]).

Development of the Individualized Educational Program

The IDEA–Part B outlines a number of factors the IEP team is obligated to consider in developing each child's IEP. The team must consider the strengths of the child, the concerns of the parents, the results of the initial evaluation or most recent evaluation of the child, and the academic, developmental, and functional needs of the child (34 C.F.R. § 300.324[a][1]). In addition, the team should consider the following five special factors: (1) In the case of a child whose behavior impedes his or her learning or that of others, the team should consider strategies, including positive behavioral interventions and supports, to address that behavior; (2) in the case of a child with limited English proficiency, the team should consider the language needs of the child as those needs relate to his or her IEP; (3) in the case of a child who is blind or visually impaired, the team should consider providing instruction in Braille and the use of Braille, unless the IEP team determines after evaluation of reading and writing skills, needs (including future needs), and media that use of Braille is not appropriate for the child; (4) in the case of the child who is deaf or hard of hearing, the team should consider the child's full range of needs, including language and communication needs, opportunities for direct communications with peers and professional personnel in the child's language and communication mode, opportunities for direct instruction in the child's language and communication mode, and academic level; and (5) whether the child requires assistive technology devices and services (34 C.F.R. § 300.324[a][2]).

Content of the Individualized Educational Program

Parents must be given a copy of the IEP at no cost (34 C.F.R. § 300.322). The written IEP must include the following:

- A statement of the child's present levels of academic achievement and functional performance, including how the child's disability affects the child's involvement and progress in the general education curriculum, or for preschool children, as appropriate, how the disability affects the child's participation in appropriate activities.
- For a child who will take regular state and districtwide assessments, a statement of measurable annual goals, including academic and functional goals designed to

meet the child's needs that result from his or her disability, to enable the child to be involved in and make progress in the general education curriculum, and to meet each of the child's other educational needs that result from the child's disability. For a child who will take alternate assessments aligned to alternative achievement standards, the IEP includes a description of benchmarks or short-term objectives.

- A description of how the child's progress toward meeting the annual goals will be measured, and when periodic reports on the progress the child is making toward meeting the annual goals (such as through the use of quarterly or other periodic reports, concurrent with the issuance of report cards) will be provided.

- A statement of the special education and related services and supplementary aids and services, based on peer-reviewed research to the extent practicable, to be provided to the child or on behalf of the child, and a statement of the program modifications or supports for school personnel that will be provided to enable the child to advance appropriately toward attaining the annual goals, to be involved in and make progress in the general curriculum, to participate in extracurricular and other nonacademic activities, and to be educated and participate with other children with disabilities and nondisabled children.

- An explanation of the extent, if any, to which the child will not participate with nondisabled children in general education and in nonacademic activities.

- A statement of any individual accommodations that are necessary to measure the academic achievement and functional performance of the child on state and districtwide assessments. If the IEP team determines that the child must take an alternate assessment instead of a particular regular state or districtwide assessment of achievement, a statement of why the child cannot participate in the regular assessment and why the particular alternate assessment selected is appropriate for the child.

- The projected date for the beginning of the services and modifications and the anticipated frequency, location, and duration of those services and modifications.

- Beginning not later than the first IEP to be in effect when the child turns 16, or younger if determined appropriate by the IEP team, and updated annually thereafter, the IEP must include appropriate measurable postsecondary goals based on age-appropriate transition assessments related to training, education, employment, and, where appropriate, independent living skills, and the transition services (including courses of study) needed to assist the child in reaching those goals.

- In a state that transfers rights at the age of majority, beginning not later than one year before the child reaches the age of majority under state law, the IEP must include a statement that the child has been informed of his or her rights that will transfer to the child on reaching the age of majority. (Adapted from 34 C.F.R. § 300.320[a].)

Special Education.   The IEP must include a statement of the specific special education and related services to be provided to the child. The term *special education* is defined as "specially designed instruction, at no cost to the parents, to meet the unique needs of a child with a disability, including instruction conducted in the classroom, in the home, in hospitals and institutions, and in other settings" (34 C.F.R. § 300.39[a][1][i]). Special education includes instruction in physical education, vocational education, and travel training (i.e., instruction in the skills necessary to move effectively and safely from place to place), if designed to meet the unique needs of a child with a disability (34 C.F.R. § 300.39[a][1][ii], [a][2][ii–iii]). Speech pathology instruction is included as special education; however, speech pathology also can be a related service (34 C.F.R. § 300.39[a][2][i]).

The IDEA–Part B requires schools to provide a statement of needed transition services for pupils with disabilities beginning at age 16 (or younger if appropriate) as part of the IEP. *Transition services* means a coordinated set of activities for a child with a disability that:

(1) is designed to be within a results-oriented process, that is focused on improving the academic and functional achievement of the child to facilitate the child's movement from school to post-school activities, including postsecondary education, vocational education, integrated employment (including supported employment), continuing and adult education, adult services, independent living or community participation;

(2) is based on the individual child's needs, taking into account the child's strengths, preferences, and interests; and includes instruction; related services; community experiences; the development of employment and other post-school adult living objectives; and, if appropriate, acquisition of daily living skills and provision of a functional vocational evaluation. (34 C.F.R. § 300.43[a][1–2])

Related Services. *Related services* means:

transportation and such developmental, corrective, and other supportive services as are required to assist a child with a disability to benefit from special education, and includes speech-language pathology and audiology services, interpreting services, psychological services, physical and occupational therapy, recreation, including therapeutic recreation, early identification and assessment of disabilities in children, counseling services, including rehabilitation counseling, orientation and mobility services, and medical services for diagnostic or evaluation purposes. Related services also include school health services and school nurse services, social work services in the schools, and parent counseling and training. (34 C.F.R. § 300.34[a])

Under IDEA–Part B, a related service cannot "stand alone—it must be attached to a special education program, and it must be a necessary service for the child to benefit from special instruction" (Slenkovich, 1988b, p. 168). If the child is not eligible for special education under IDEA–Part B, there can be no related services, and the child (lacking a disability) is not covered under the IDEA.

Supplementary Aids and Services. *Supplementary aids and services* means "aids, services, and other supports that are provided in general education classes or other education-related settings, and in extracurricular and nonacademic settings, to enable children with disabilities to be educated with nondisabled to the maximum extent appropriate" (34 C.F.R. § 300.42).

Implementation of the Individualized Educational Program

The IEP must be made accessible to each of the child's teachers and service providers, and each must be informed of his or her responsibilities under the IEP and of the specific accommodations, modifications, and supports that must be provided under the IEP (34 C.F.R. § 300.323[d]). The school is accountable for providing the special education instruction and related services outlined in the IEP. The description of services to be provided is an "enforceable promise." However, neither the school nor the teacher may be held liable if a student fails to achieve his or her IEP goals (Slenkovich, 1988b, p. 168). Recommendations for nonspecial education services the school is not required to provide (e.g., for family therapy) should be made separately from the IEP (Slenkovich, 1987b).

Special education and related services are made available as soon as possible following the development of the IEP (34 C.F.R. § 300.323[c][2]). If the parents and school do not agree on the content of the IEP, either party may request mediation or a due process hearing. Unless parents and the school agree otherwise, the student remains in his or her present placement during any due process proceeding. This is the *stay put* rule (34 C.F.R. § 300.518[a]).

Each child's IEP must be reviewed and revised at least annually, and each child must be seen for reevaluation at least once every three years, or more often if warranted (34 C.F.R. § 300.324[b][1], 300.303[b][2]). However, as noted previously, if the IEP team determines that no additional assessment data are needed as part of a reevaluation, the LEA is not required to conduct additional assessments unless requested by the child's parents or teacher. During the annual review of the IEP, the team must determine whether the annual goals for the child are being achieved and revise the IEP as appropriate to address: (a) any lack of expected progress toward annual goals and progress in the general curriculum, (b) the results of any reevaluations conducted, (c) information about the child provided by the parents, or (d) the child's anticipated needs (34 C.F.R. § 300.324[b][1]). The general education teacher is required to participate in the IEP review as appropriate (34 C.F.R. § 300.324[b][3]). The LEA also must convene an IEP meeting if an agency fails to provide the transition services described in a child's IEP (34 C.F.R. § 300.324[c]).

Least Restrictive Environment

As noted earlier in the chapter, prior to 1975, children with moderate or severe impairments were often routinely excluded from school. Children with mild disabilities frequently were segregated in special classes with few opportunities to interact with their nondisabled peers. In some cases, these classes were located in a separate corridor of the school. At times, the less capable teachers were assigned to teach children with disabilities, and typically the classroom facilities and equipment were less adequate than for nondisabled children (Turnbull & Turnbull, 2000). Few special class children ever returned to the mainstream.

The "least restrictive alternative" doctrine evolved from court decisions starting in the 1960s (e.g., *Wyatt v. Stickney*, 1971). Turnbull and Turnbull (2000, p. 243) summarized this constitutionally based doctrine as follows: "Even if the legislative purpose of a government action is appropriate . . . the purpose may not be pursued by means that broadly stifle personal liberties if it can be achieved by less oppressive restrictive means." The doctrine of least restrictive alternative was at the foundation of the deinstitutionalization movement in the field of mental health in the late 1960s and early 1970s. The doctrine recognizes that it may be necessary to restrict personal freedoms when treating a mentally ill individual, but the state should deprive the patient of his or her liberties only to the extent necessary to provide treatment (Turnbull & Turnbull, 2000).

This principle also was applied to the education of children with disabilities in IDEA– Part B with the requirement that special education and related services be provided in a setting that is the least restrictive environment (LRE) appropriate for the child. Congress recognized that integration of children with disabilities into the educational mainstream was not likely to occur without a legal mandate. Many educators and nondisabled pupils and their parents held negative stereotypes and attitudes toward special education students (Martin, 1979). Consequently, IDEA–Part B requires the SEA or LEA to ensure the following:

To the maximum extent appropriate, children with disabilities, including children in public or private institutions or other care facilities, are educated with children who are nondisabled; and special classes, separate schooling, or other removal of children with disabilities from the regular educational environment occurs only when the nature or severity of the disability is such that education in regular classes with the use of supplementary aids and services cannot be achieved satisfactorily. (34 C.F.R. § 300.114[a][2])

Congress intended that the SEA or LEA make available a continuum of alternative placements to meet the needs of children with disabilities, including instruction in general education classes with supplementary services, special classes, special schools, home instruction, and instruction in hospitals and institutions (34 C.F.R. § 300.115). Congress also intended that decisions about the extent to which pupils with disabilities can be educated with nondisabled children be made on the basis of the child's individual needs and capabilities.

A number of court decisions have addressed the school's responsibility to ensure that children with disabilities are educated in the least restrictive appropriate environment (e.g., *Daniel R.R. v. Texas Board of Education, El Paso Independent School District*, 1989; *Greer v. Rome City School District*, 1991; *Sacramento City Unified School District, Board of Education v. Rachel H.*, 1994). In *Greer*, the judge noted that "Congress created a statutory preference for educating handicapped children with nonhandicapped children" (1991, p. 695). In *Sacramento City Unified School District, Board of Education v. Holland* (1992), the court stated that the IDEA's preference for inclusion of children with disabilities in the general educational environment "rises to the level of a rebuttable presumption" (pp. 877–878). This means that placement decision making must begin with the assumption that the child can be educated in the general education classroom:

> Before the school district may conclude that a handicapped child should be educated outside the regular classroom, it must consider whether supplemental aids and services would permit satisfactory education in the regular classroom. The school district must consider the whole range of supplemental aids and services, including resource rooms and itinerant instruction, for which it is obligated under the Act. . . . Only when the handicapped child's education may not be achieved satisfactorily, even with one or more of these supplemental aids and services, may the school board consider placing the child outside of the regular classroom. (*Greer*, 1991, p. 696)

[handwritten margin note: Removing child from reg. class]

In *Holland* (1992) and, on appeal, *Sacramento City Unified School District, Board of Education v. Rachel H.* (1994), the courts established a four-part test for determining compliance with the IDEA's mainstreaming requirement. These rulings concerned Rachel, an elementary school child with moderate mental impairment (IQ 44), whose parents requested full-time placement in a general education classroom with supplemental services. The school district, however, believed that Rachel was too severely disabled to benefit from full-time placement in the general education classroom and recommended special education placement for all academic instruction. The Hollands appealed the school's placement decision to a state hearing officer, who ordered the district to place Rachel in a general education classroom with supportive services. The school district appealed this determination to the district court (1992), to the circuit court (1994), and to the Supreme Court (*certiorari denied*, 1994). The courts affirmed the hearing officer's decision that Rachel should be educated in the general education classroom.

In *Holland* (1994, p. 1404), the courts considered the following four factors in determining the least restrictive appropriate environment: (1) the educational benefits available in a general education classroom, supplemented with appropriate aids and services, as compared with the educational benefits of a special education classroom; (2) the nonacademic benefits of interaction with children who are not disabled; (3) the effect of the child's presence on the teacher and other children in the classroom; and (4) the cost of educating the child in a general education classroom.

In evaluating the educational benefit of inclusion in the general education classroom, the *Holland* rulings considered the learning opportunities available in alternative settings and the child's likely progress toward IEP goals if placed in the general education classroom. In evaluating nonacademic benefits, the court considered whether the child was likely to interact with and learn from other children in the inclusive placement. As noted in an earlier case, the presumption of inclusion in the general education classroom is not rebutted unless the school shows that the child's disabilities are so severe that he or she will receive little or no educational benefit from inclusion (e.g., *Devries v. Fairfax County School Board*, 1989).

With regard to the effect of the child's presence on the teacher and other children, the court in *Holland* (1994, p. 1401) considered two aspects of disruptive behavior: (1) whether there was detriment because the child was disruptive, distracting, or unruly, and (2) whether the child would take up so much of the teacher's time that the other students would suffer from lack of attention. *Holland* thus suggested that an IEP team may consider the impact of the child's behavior on the setting where services are provided in determining an appropriate placement. However, the education of the other children must be impaired significantly by the inclusion of the child with a disability to justify exclusion on this basis. The child may be excluded from the general education environment only if "after taking all reasonable steps to reduce the burden to the teacher, the other children in the class will still be deprived of their share of the teacher's attention" (*Holland*, 1992, p. 879; see also *Daniel R.R. v. Texas Board of Education, El Paso Independent School District*, 1989). According to Turnbull and Turnbull (2000), IDEA 1997 codified the *Holland* decision. It required implementation of a positive behavior intervention plan to remedy problem behaviors, but also allowed a more restrictive placement when, despite such efforts, the student's behavior had a detrimental impact on other students and the teacher.

Schools also may consider the cost of providing an inclusive education. However, the cost must be *significantly* more expensive than alternative placements to justify an exclusion from the general education classroom on the basis of cost (*Holland*, 1994).

The IDEA regulations state that "in selecting the [least restrictive environment], consideration is given to any potential harmful effect on the child or on the quality of services that he or she needs; and . . . [the] child with a disability is not removed from education in age-appropriate regular classrooms solely because of needed modifications in the general education curriculum" (34 C.F.R. § 300.116[d–e]). However, several court cases suggest that the law does not require general education teachers to "modify the curriculum beyond recognition" (*Daniel R.R. v. Texas Board of Education*, 1989, p. 1048). *Daniel R.R.* and *Brillon v. Klein Independent School District* (2004) suggested that a fifth factor can be considered in making placement decisions, namely, whether the child can benefit from the general education curriculum *without substantial and burdensome curricular modifications*. In *Daniel R.R.*, the court noted: "Mainstreaming would be pointless if we forced instructors to modify the regular education curriculum to the extent that the handicapped child is not required to learn any of the skills normally taught in regular education" (1989, p. 1049). In the more recent *Brillon* case, the court noted that placement of a second grader with disabilities in general education for social studies and science "required the school district to make unduly burdensome modifications to the regular curriculum" (2004, p. 314). For this reason, the court held that providing social studies and science instruction to the child in the special education setting did not violate the least restrictive environment requirement.

As Turnbull and Turnbull (2000) noted, the courts have recognized that appropriate sometimes means more, rather than less, separation from the general education classroom. The LRE favors integration but allows separation when separation is needed to achieve a satisfactory educational program for the child. In *A.W. v. Northwest R-1 School District* (1987, p. 163), the judge noted that the mainstreaming requirement is "inapplicable" where it cannot be achieved satisfactorily.

A school placement that allows a child to remain with his or her family is considered to be less restrictive than a residential placement. The IDEA also indicates a preference for a neighborhood school. Part B regulations state that unless "the IEP of a child with a disability requires some other arrangement, the child is educated in the school that he or she would attend if not nondisabled" (34 C.F.R. § 300.116[c]). However, although the law indicates a preference for neighborhood schooling, proximity of the school is only one factor the IEP team must consider in making placement decisions. The court in *Flour Bluff Independent School District v. Katherine M.* (1996, p. 675) noted, "Distance remains a consideration in determining the least restrictive environment. . . . The child may have to travel farther, however, to obtain better services."

The SEA or LEA also must ensure that a child with a disability has opportunities to participate with nondisabled children in nonacademic and extracurricular activities (e.g., meals, recess, clubs, and interest groups) to the maximum extent appropriate to the needs of the child (34 C.F.R. § 300.117). However, in several cases (e.g., *Rettig v. Kent City School District*, 1986), the courts ruled that IDEA–Part B does not require schools to provide nonacademic and extracurricular activities to children with disabilities without regard for their ability to benefit from the experience.

The Meaning of Appropriate Education

The IDEA–Part B also requires that children with disabilities be offered a free appropriate public education (FAPE) in the least restrictive environment. Since the passage of Pub. L. No. 94-142, a number of court cases have provided further interpretation of *appropriate education*. In their decision making about what is appropriate, the courts have considered several different factors, including whether IDEA–Part B procedures were followed in developing the IEP and whether the IEP is consistent with the intent of the law (Turnbull & Turnbull, 2000).

Board of Education of the Hendrick Hudson Central School District v. Rowley (1982) was the first case to reach the Supreme Court in which the Court attempted to define appropriate education (see Exhibit 4.3). The Supreme Court's interpretation of appropriate education in *Rowley* has shaped all subsequent court decisions concerning the meaning of *appropriate education* under Part B. *Rowley* suggested that IDEA ensures only an education program reasonably designed to benefit the student, not the best possible or most perfect education. The *Rowley* decision set forth a two-pronged test of appropriate education, namely, "Were IDEA procedures followed in developing the IEP?" and "Is the program reasonably designed to benefit the child?"

Since *Rowley*, in a number of court cases parents have challenged whether their child's special education program was reasonably calculated to enable their child to receive educational benefits. Consistent with the majority opinion in *Rowley*, these decisions suggest that the determination of whether a program is reasonably designed to confer benefit must be made on the basis of the individual child's potential. Furthermore, the program must be likely to provide meaningful benefit, that is, more than de minimis or trivial benefit, in relation to the child's potential (e.g., *Cordrey v. Euckert*, 1990). Also, as foreshadowed in the *Rowley* opinion, schools, not parents, have the authority to select

---

Exhibit 4.3 Board of Education of the Hendrick Hudson Central School District v. Rowley (1982)

The case involved Amy, a deaf child with minimal residual hearing, who understood about 50% of spoken language by lip-reading. During her kindergarten year, the school provided an FM hearing aid to amplify speech. Her IEP for first grade included continued use of the hearing aid, instruction from a tutor for the deaf one hour each day, and speech therapy three hours each week.

Amy's parents also requested that the school provide an interpreter for the deaf in the classroom in order for her to make optimal school progress. The school and a hearing officer agreed that an interpreter was too costly and not needed because "Amy was achieving educationally, academically, and socially without such assistance" (*Rowley*, p. 3040). A district court, however, found in favor of the parents and noted that without the interpreter Amy was not afforded the opportunity to achieve her full potential.

Based on a review of the history of IDEA, the Supreme Court concluded that Congress intended only to provide an education program "reasonably calculated to enable the child to receive educational benefits" (p. 3051) or a "basic floor of opportunity" (p. 3047). It was noted that there is no requirement under IDEA that the school provide services that maximize the potential of a child with disabilities; the "furnishing of every special service necessary to maximize each handicapped child's potential is, we think, further than Congress intended to go" (p. 3047). The Court found in favor of the school.

---

specific instructional methodologies as long as the methods chosen are considered to be acceptable evidence-based practice.

The courts also have ruled that when two or more appropriate placements are available, IEP team members may consider costs to the school in determining a child's education placement (e.g., *Clevenger v. Oak Ridge School Board*, 1984).

Extended School Year

The IDEA requires extended school year (ESY) services for a child with a disability if they are necessary to ensure an appropriate public education for the child (34 C.F.R. § 300.106[a]). ESY services are provided beyond the normal school year, in accordance with the child's IEP and at no cost to the child's parents. Such services must be provided only if a child's IEP team determines, on an individual basis, that the services are necessary for the child to receive a free and appropriate public education (34 C.F.R. § 300.106[a][2]). The following standard for determining whether a child with disabilities is entitled to ESY services has gained acceptance:

> If a child will experience severe or substantial regression during the summer months in the absence of a summer program, the handicapped child may be entitled to year-round services. The issue is whether the benefits accrued to the child during the regular school year will be significantly jeopardized if he is not provided an educational program during the summer months. (*Alamo Heights Independent School District v. State Board of Education*, 1986, p. 261)

According to *Cordrey* (1990) and *Reusch v. Fountain* (1994), "This standard is satisfied when it is shown that the student will suffer a significant regression of skills or knowledge without a summer program, followed by an insufficient recoupment of the same during the next school year" (*Reusch*, 1994, p. 1434). The courts have ruled that parents do not need empirical data demonstrating regression during summer and slow recoupment to establish that their child is entitled to ESY services (*Cordrey*, 1990; *Johnson v. Independent School District No. 4 of Bixby, Tulsa County, Oklahoma*, 1990). The court in *Cordrey* noted that it is unfair to require that a child demonstrate regression in the absence of summer programming in order to be entitled to such programming in subsequent summers and suggested that decisions about whether a child is entitled to ESY services can be based on predictive factors (i.e., the child is likely to show significant regression and slow recoupment of skills). Furthermore, decisions about whether a child is likely to show regression and slow recoupment may rely on "expert opinion, based on professional individual assessment" when empirical data are not available (*Cordrey*, 1990, p. 1472). Thus, rulings suggest schools may not require definitive empirical evidence of prior regression and slow recoupment in determining whether a child is entitled to ESY services.

Assistive Technology

The IDEA requires schools to ensure that assistive technology devices and services are made available to a child with a disability if the child requires the devices and services to receive an appropriate public education. *Assistive technology device* is "any item, piece of equipment, or product system, whether acquired commercially off the shelf, modified, or customized, that is used to increase, maintain, or improve the functional capabilities of a child with a disability. The term does not include a medical device that is surgically implanted" (34 C.F.R. § 300.5). Schools are not obligated to provide eyeglasses, hearing aids, or braces. However, they must ensure that hearing aids are functioning properly (34 C.F.R. § 300.113[a]). *Assistive technology service* is "any service that directly assists a child with a disability in the selection, acquisition, or use of an assistive technology device" (34 C.F.R. § 300.6). Assistive technology services include evaluation of the needs of a child with a disability; purchasing, leasing, or otherwise providing for the acquisition of an assistive technology device; selecting, designing, fitting, or customizing such devices; coordinating and using devices with other therapies or interventions; and training the child and the professionals involved in the use of the device (34 C.F.R. § 300.6). (For additional information, see McGivern & McKevitt, 2002.)

Freedom from Harassment

In *Shore Regional High School v. P.S.* (2004) (Exhibit 4.4), a federal court of appeals held that a school district failed to offer a free and appropriate education within the meaning of IDEA for a student who was subjected to severe and prolonged harassment by other students. P.S. was harassed primarily because of his effeminate appearance rather than on the basis of a disability. As will be seen in Chapter 5, Section 504 cases concerning harassment based on disability are on the rise. Under IDEA and Section 504, schools must take reasonable steps to prevent bullying and harassment of students with disabilities.

Summary

Schools are required to offer a child with a disability an appropriate education reasonably designed to confer benefit. However, consistent with *Rowley*, IDEA does not require that the school provide a program designed to maximize the potential of a child with disabilities.

Exhibit 4.4 Shore Regional High School v. P.S. (2004)

P.S. was teased and bullied by other pupils in the early elementary grades, and the physical and verbal harassment intensified in the middle school. He was called names such as "Loser," "Bit Tits," and "Fat Ass"; bullies threw rocks at him; and a student hit him with a padlock in gym class. Bullies warned other students not to interact with him, and when he sat down at a cafeteria table, other pupils moved away. Despite repeated complaints by P.S.'s parents, the school administration failed to address the bullying.

Because of the severe and relentless harassment by other students, P.S. became depressed in middle school, his grades declined, and he attempted suicide. P.S. was placed in special education, with his school day modified so he could avoid situations where he would likely be harassed. P.S. was scheduled to attend the high school in his district, Shore Regional High School, beginning in ninth grade. Unhappy with the constant and continuing harassment of their son and the school district's failure to address the problem, P.S.'s parents requested a transfer to a public school in a neighboring district. When Shore High refused the transfer, P.S.'s parents unilaterally placed him in an out-of-district school and then took steps to recover out-of-district tuition, related costs, and attorney fees from Shore High. In requesting reimbursement, P.S.'s parents argued that Shore High had not offered P.S. a free appropriate public education (FAPE) in the least restrictive environment. The courts ultimately upheld this request for reimbursement, noting that Shore High failed to offer "an education sufficiently free from the threat of harassment to constitute a FAPE" (p. 199).

Scope of Required Related Services

As noted earlier in the chapter, a child must be found eligible for special education before he or she qualifies to receive related services, and the related services must be necessary to assist the child with disabilities to benefit from special education. The related services provision includes school health, school nurse, and counseling services, but medical services are provided only for diagnostic and evaluation purposes to determine a child's medically related disability (34 C.F.R. § 300.34[a]). This is the *medical exclusion*.

Whether certain services fall within the parameters of school health or counseling services (and are thus provided under IDEA–Part B) has been the focus of a number of court cases. *Irving Independent School District v. Tatro* (1984) (Exhibit 4.5) was a key case in determining the scope of school health services required under IDEA–Part B. In this case, the Supreme Court ruled that the school must provide clean intermittent catheterization (CIC) for a disabled child as a related service needed for her to benefit from special education. In the Court's opinion, CIC is not a medical service because it can be performed by a trained layperson and requires only several minutes every three or four hours.

Thus, in accordance with *Tatro*, schools are not responsible for providing school health services that must be performed by a physician rather than a nurse or trained layperson. But what if a child requires *full-time* nursing care? Until 1999, courts ruled that full-time nursing care was beyond the scope of the services that must be provided by the schools (e.g., *Detsel v. Board of Education of the Auburn Enlarged City School District*, 1987). However, in 1999, the Supreme Court decided *Cedar Rapids Community School*

Exhibit 4.5 Irving Independent School District v. Tatro (1984)

Amber Tatro was born with spina bifida and suffered from orthopedic and speech impairments and a neurogenic bladder. Because she was unable to empty her bladder voluntarily, she required clean intermittent catheterization (CIC) every three or four hours. This procedure involves insertion of a catheter into the urethra to drain the bladder and can be performed in a few minutes by a trained layperson.

Amber first received special education services at age 3, and her IEP provided early child development classes, occupational therapy, and physical therapy. There was no provision for CIC as requested by Amber's parents, however. The school held that CIC is a medical service and, under IDEA, the school is required to provide medical services only for the purpose of diagnosis to determine the child's medically related disability.

Tatro ultimately reached the Supreme Court, and the Court decided in favor of the parents. The Court reasoned that Amber could not attend class (and, therefore, could not benefit from special education) without CIC as a related supportive service, and held that CIC is not a medical service because it can be performed by a trained layperson or school nurse (i.e., a physician is not required).

District v. Garret F. by Charlene F., a case concerning a ventilator-dependent student who required continuous, one-on-one nursing services to remain in school. Contrary to previous lower court rulings, the Supreme Court held that the school must provide full-time nursing services if such services are necessary for a child with a disability to benefit from special education. The Court reiterated *Tatro* in stating that schools are not responsible for services that must be performed by a physician but made clear that the nursing services a child needs to benefit from special education must be provided without regard to the cost to the school.

Another question that arises under the related services provision of IDEA–Part B is: When is the school responsible for the cost of psychotherapy as a related service? Counseling services identified as related services in the regulations include "services provided by qualified social workers, psychologists, guidance counselors, and other qualified personnel" (34 C.F.R. § 300.34[c][2]). Psychological services include "planning and managing a program of psychological services, including psychological counseling for children and parents" (34 C.F.R. § 300.34[c][10][v]). Schools are required to provide these services at no cost to the parents when they are included in the child's IEP.

However, more difficult questions have arisen with regard to psychotherapy provided by a physician (i.e., psychiatric treatment) and that provided in a residential facility. Court rulings on these issues have been inconsistent (Turnbull & Turnbull, 2000). In *Darlene L. v. Illinois State Board of Education* (1983, p. 1345), the court ruled that "states may properly consider psychiatric services as medical services and therefore not related services which the state must provide as part of a free appropriate education." The court in this case saw the cost of psychiatric treatment as overly burdensome to the schools.

In another case, however, the court ruled that psychotherapy provided by a psychiatrist does not automatically mean that the service is a medical service. In *Max M. v. Thompson* (1984, p. 1444), the court held, "The simple fact that a service *could be* or *actually is* rendered by a physician rather than a non-physician does not dictate its removal from the list of required services under EAHCA [IDEA]." The court went on to say that the limit to psychiatric services is cost: "A school board can be held liable for no more than the cost of the service as provided by the minimum level health care personnel recognized as competent to perform the related service" (p. 1444). Thus, this ruling suggests that in states where a psychologist or social worker is recognized as competent to provide psychotherapy, the school is responsible only for the amount it would cost for a psychologist or social worker to perform the service.

Whether the school is responsible for the cost of psychotherapy when a pupil is placed in a residential facility also has been addressed by the courts. The key issue in these cases appears to be whether the psychotherapy provided in the facility is seen as necessary for educational reasons, that is, to assist the child in benefiting from special education (Weirda, 1987). In *In re the "A" Family* (1979), the court ruled that the school must pay for psychotherapy provided at a residential facility for a seriously emotionally disturbed child who was placed there as a way of meeting his education needs. In contrast, in *McKenzie v. Jefferson* (1983), a child was hospitalized in a treatment facility for serious mental illness. The court in this case held that the placement was not made in support of a special education program. The primary purpose of the placement was for "much needed *medical* treatment" (p. 411). Psychiatric treatment costs were not seen as a related service in this case.

Coordination of IDEA, Medicaid, and Private Health Insurance

When a child with disabilities has multiple health-related needs, the cost of school health and nursing services can be extraordinarily high. The IDEA, however, typically funds only a small portion of the extra expenses involved in educating a child with disabilities. States may set aside up to 10% of their monies for a so-called high-cost fund to be used to reimburse districts when the cost of providing special education and related services to a high-need child with a disability is greater than three times the average pupil expenditure (34 C.F.R. § 300.704[c][i]).

In 1990, the U.S. Department of Health and Human Services (HHS) signaled greater willingness to allow Medicaid coverage for health-related services for children receiving special education (see the 1991–1992 "HHS Policy Clarification" prepared by HHS in cooperation with OSEP and DOE). In this policy clarification, HHS stated that school districts can bill the Medicaid program for medically necessary health-related services provided at school, at home, or in a residential facility if the child is eligible under the state's Medicaid plan. Medicaid now covers a broad range of medical services (e.g., physician's services, prescription drugs, therapeutic interventions such as occupational therapy, psychological services), and states have considerable flexibility in defining Medicaid eligibility groups. Under IDEA, the state's governor must ensure interagency agreements regarding Medicaid and other public insurance agencies. Medicaid precedes the financial responsibility of the LEA and SEA, but the SEA remains the payer of last resort (34 C.F.R. § 300.154[d]).

Schools must obtain parent consent to bill Medicaid or public insurance and may not require parents to sign up for or enroll in public insurance programs in order for their child to receive a free and appropriate education under Part B (34 C.F.R. § 300.154[d][2][i]). The school must pay any deductibles or copays (34 C.F.R. § 300.154[d][2][ii]). Schools also may not use a child's benefits under a public insurance program if that use would decrease the lifetime coverage available, result in the family's paying for care outside of school that would otherwise be covered, or result in increased premiums or discontinuation of insurance (see 34 C.F.R. § 300.154[d][iii]).

In addition, under IDEA, it is permissible for schools to ask parents to use their own private health insurance to cover the costs of health services provided at school. However, because related services must be provided at no cost to the parent, the school must pay copays or other deductibles (34 C.F.R. § 300.154[e]).

Procedural Safeguards

A number of Part B procedural safeguards to ensure the rights of children with disabilities and their parents were foreshadowed in the *P.A.R.C.* and *Mills* decisions. Under IDEA–Part B, the SEA must ensure that each LEA establishes and implements procedures to safeguard the parents' right to confidentiality of records and right to examine records; right to participate in meetings with respect to the identification, evaluation, and placement of their child; right to consent to the initial pupil evaluation and the initial placement; right to written prior notice before changes are made in identification, evaluation, placement, and special services; right to present findings from an independent evaluation; right to resolution of complaints by mediation; right to resolution of complaints by an impartial hearing officer; and right to bring civil action in court. Notice and consent, transfer of parental rights at age of majority, surrogate parents, and mediation and due process hearings are discussed next.

Consent and Notice

Depending on the proposed school action or refusal to act, IDEA may require consent or written notice and procedural safeguards notice.

Consent.   Under IDEA–Part B, parental written consent (permission) must be obtained before conducting a preplacement evaluation and before the initial placement of a child in special education (34 C.F.R. § 300.300[a][1]). If the parent refuses consent to the initial preplacement evaluation, the LEA may request mediation or a hearing to override a parent's refusal to consent (34 C.F.R. § 300.300[a][3]). However, if the parent of a child who is homeschooled or parentally placed in a private school does not provide consent for the initial evaluation or reevaluation, or if the parent fails to respond to a request to provide consent, the LEA may not use the consent override procedures (34 C.F.R. § 300.300[d][4]).

Parent consent also is required for subsequent reevaluations of a child, unless the school can demonstrate that it has taken reasonable measures to obtain consent and the child's parent failed to respond (34 C.F.R. § 300.300[c][2]). It should also be noted that if the parent refuses to consent to the initial placement of a child in special education, the school may not use mediation or due process procedures to override parent consent (34 C.F.R. § 300.300[b][2–3]). Thus, consent for initial evaluation should not be misconstrued as consent for placement (34 C.F.R. § 300.300[a][1][ii]).

Notice.   The IDEA divides information sent to parents into two different types of notice: prior written notice and procedural safeguards notice. Prior written notice is required a reasonable time before the proposed school action whenever the SEA or LEA proposes to initiate or change the identification, evaluation, education placement, or program of the child or refuses to change the identification, evaluation, placement, or program (34 C.F.R. § 300.503[a][1–2]). Notice must be provided in a mode of communication understandable to the parent (unless it is clearly not feasible to do so) and must include a description of the proposed action (or refusal to act); an explanation of why the school proposes or refuses to take action; a description of each evaluation procedure, test, record, or report used as the basis for the school's action; a statement that the parents have protection under procedural safeguards and, if the notice is not an initial referral for evaluation, the means by which a copy of a description of the procedural safeguards can be obtained; sources for parents to contact to obtain assistance in understanding these provisions (e.g., nonprofit group that could assist the parents); a description of any other options considered and why those were rejected; and a description of other factors that the IEP team considered and the reasons those options were rejected (34 C.F.R. § 300.503[b]).

A procedural safeguards notice includes information on protections available to the parents of a child with a disability. This information must be provided only one time a school year, except that a copy also must be given to the parents at the time of initial referral or parent request for an evaluation, following registration of a complaint, when a decision is made to make a removal that constitutes a change of placement because of violation of a code of student conduct, and upon parent request (34 C.F.R. § 300.504[a]; also see 34 C.F.R. § 300.530[h]). A copy of the procedural safeguards notice may be placed on the school's web site (34 C.F.R. § 300.504[b]).

The procedural safeguards notice must include a full explanation of the procedural safeguards written in an understandable manner (34 C.F.R. § 300.504[d]). The content of the notice must include information pertaining to all the procedural safeguards relating to independent educational evaluations, prior written notice, parental consent, access to education records, opportunity to present and resolve complaints, the availability of mediation, the child's placement during the pendency of any due process complaint, procedures for students who are subject to placement in an interim alternative educational setting, requirements for unilateral placements by parents of children in private schools at public expense, hearings on due process complaints, state-level appeals, civil actions, and attorneys' fees (34 C.F.R. § 300.504[c]). Parents of a child with a disability may choose to receive notices by electronic mail, if the school makes that option available (34 C.F.R. § 300.505).

Transfer of Parent Rights at Age of Majority

Under IDEA, a state may require that when an individual with a disability reaches the age of majority or a child with a disability is incarcerated in an adult or juvenile correctional facility, all rights accorded to parents transfer to the individual with a disability (34 C.F.R. § 300.520[a]). The school or other agency must notify the individual and parents of the transfer of rights (34 C.F.R. § 300.520[a][3]). For youth who have reached the age of majority and who have not been determined to be incompetent, but who are determined not to have the ability to provide informed consent with respect to their education program, the state will establish procedures for the appointment of the parent of the youth (or other appropriate person if the parent is not available) to represent the educational interest of the youth as long as he or she is eligible for special education under IDEA (34 C.F.R. § 300.520[b]).

Surrogate Parents

Under IDEA–Part B, the school must ensure that the rights of a child with disabilities are protected when no parent can be identified; when, after reasonable efforts, the school cannot locate the parents; when the child is a ward of the state under state laws; or when the child is an unaccompanied homeless youth (34 C.F.R. § 300.519[a]). The school (or a judge overseeing the case of child who is a ward of the state) must assign a surrogate parent for the child (34 C.F.R. § 300.519[b]). The surrogate may not be an employee of the school or have interests that conflict with the interests of the child (34 C.F.R. § 300.519[d]).

Complaints, Resolution Meetings, Mediation, and Due Process Hearings

The school and parents may attempt to resolve disputes regarding the identification, evaluation, educational placement, or program of a child through resolution meetings, the mediation process, due process hearings, or civil action. The school and parents may agree to mediation of a disagreement prior to filing a due process complaint or after filing a due process complaint.

Complaints.   A due process complaint must allege that a violation occurred not more than two years before the date the parent or school knew or should have known about the action that forms the basis of the complaint, unless different explicit time limitations are identified in state law (34 C.F.R. § 300.507[a][2]). The IDEA requires the school to have procedures that require either party (school or parent) to provide the other party a written due process complaint, which must remain confidential (34 C.F.R. § 300.508[a]). The complaint must include: (a) the name and address of the child and the name of the school he or she is attending; (b) a description of the nature of the problem of the child relating to the proposed or refused initiation or change, including facts relating to the problem; and (c) a proposed resolution of the problem to the extent known and available to the parents at that time (34 C.F.R. § 300.508[b]). Within five days of receipt of notification, a hearing officer reviews the complaint to determine if it is sufficient or needs amendment (34 C.F.R. § 300.508[d][2]). The party receiving the complaint has 10 days to send the other party a response that specifically addresses the issues raised in the due process complaint (34 C.F.R. § 300.508[f]).

Resolution Meetings.   Within 15 days of receiving notice of the parents' due process complaint, and prior to the initiation of a hearing, the school must convene a resolution meeting with the parents and members of the IEP team who have knowledge of the facts identified in the complaint (34 C.F.R. § 300.510[a]). The purpose of the resolution meeting is to give the school an additional opportunity to attempt to resolve the dispute without a due process hearing (34 C.F.R. § 300.510[a][2]). The meeting does not have to be held if the parent and school agree in writing to waive the meeting, or if the parent and the school agree to use the mediation process (34 C.F.R. § 300.510[a][3]). If a resolution of the dispute is reached at the meeting, the parties sign a legally binding agreement that is enforceable in any state or federal court (34 C.F.R. § 300.510[d]). If the complaint is not resolved during the resolution meeting, a due process hearing is held within 30 days of the receipt of the due process complaint (34 C.F.R. § 300.510[b][1]).

Mediation.   Any SEA or LEA that receives IDEA funds must ensure that procedures are established and implemented to allow parties to resolve disputes regarding the identification, evaluation, educational placement, or program of a child through a mediation process. This process must be available to resolve disputes arising prior to the filing of a due process complaint (34 C.F.R. § 300.506[a]). The procedures must ensure that the mediation process is: (a) voluntary on the part of the parties; (b) not used to deny or delay a parent's right to a due process hearing, or to deny any other parental rights; and (c) conducted by a qualified and impartial mediator who is trained in effective mediation techniques (34 C.F.R. § 300.506[b]).

The SEA or LEA may establish procedures to offer parents and schools that choose not to use the mediation process an opportunity to meet, at a time and location convenient to the parents, with a disinterested party who is under contract with an appropriate alternative dispute resolution agency to explain and discuss the benefits of the mediation process (34 C.F.R. § 300.506[b][2]). The SEA is responsible for maintaining a list of qualified mediators and bears the costs of the mediation process (34 C.F.R. § 300.506[b][4–5]). The mediator must be selected on a random, rotational, or other impartial basis (34 C.F.R. § 300.506[b][3][ii]). The mediator must not be an employee of the school, and no individual with a personal or professional conflict of interest may serve as mediator (34 C.F.R. § 300.506[c]). An agreement reached by the parties as a result of mediation is a legally binding document (34 C.F.R. § 300.506[b][7]). Discussions that occur during mediation are confidential and may not be used as evidence in any subsequent due process hearing or civil proceeding that arises from the dispute (34 C.F.R. § 300.506[b][8]).

Due Process Hearings.   IDEA–Part B also grants parents and the school a right to an impartial due process hearing on any matter regarding the identification, evaluation, educational placement, or program of a child. In a 2005 Supreme Court decision, the Court held that the burden of persuasion in an administrative hearing challenging a child's IEP falls on the party seeking relief, whether it is the parent of child with a disability or the school (*Schaffer v. Weast*, 2005). Under IDEA–Part B, the due process hearing must be conducted by the SEA or other school agency responsible for the child (34 C.F.R. § 300.511[b]). Each SEA or LEA must maintain a list of hearing officers and their qualifications (34 C.F.R. § 300.511[c][3]). The hearing officer may not be an employee of the school, and no person with a personal or professional interest in the outcome may serve as the hearing officer (34 C.F.R. § 300.511[c][1]). The school must inform the parents of any free or low-cost legal and other relevant services available (34 C.F.R. § 300.507[b]) and that they may be able to recover attorney fees if they prevail in a hearing or judicial proceeding (34 C.F.R. § 300.517).

The IDEA–Part B further specifies a number of hearing rights. The hearing must be held at a time and place reasonably convenient to the parents. Each party has a right to be accompanied and advised by legal counsel and other experts and to present evidence and confront, cross-examine, and compel the attendance of witnesses (34 C.F.R. § 300.512[a][1–2]). The party requesting the due process hearing may not raise issues at the hearing that were not raised in the due process complaint, unless both parties agree otherwise (34 C.F.R. § 300.511[d]). No evidence may be introduced by any party unless it was disclosed at least five business days before the hearing; each party must disclose to all other parties all evaluations completed by that date and the recommendations based on those evaluations if the findings from such evaluations will be used at the hearing (34 C.F.R. § 300.512[b][1]). The parents are afforded the right to have their child present and to have the hearing open to the public (34 C.F.R. § 300.512[c][1–2]).

The hearing generally must be held and a final decision reached within 45 days after the expiration of the resolution period (30 days after the receipt of the due process complaint) (34 C.F.R. § 300.515[a]). Each party has a right to a written record of the hearing (or an electronic verbatim recording if the parent so chooses) and to a copy of the written findings of fact and the decision (34 C.F.R. § 300.512[a][3–4]). The decision of the hearing officer is final unless a party initiates an appeal or begins a court action (34 C.F.R. § 300.514[a]). An appeal may be filed by the parent or the school to the SEA for an impartial review of the findings and the decision appealed (34 C.F.R. § 300.514[b]).

Right to Private Action

The IDEA grants the parents and the school the right to civil action if they are not satisfied with the SEA decision. This means that parents may initiate a court action against the school on behalf of a child with a disability if they believe the school has violated the provisions of IDEA with respect to their child (34 C.F.R. § 300.516). Except for very unusual circumstances, parents are required to exhaust administrative remedies (e.g., due process hearings) available to them before they pursue a court action. In *Schaffer v. Weast* (2005), the Supreme Court ruled that the burden of proof (the burden of persuasion) in cases challenging the appropriateness of an IEP rests with the challenging party. In *Winkelman v. Parma City School District* (2007), the Supreme Court ruled that parents may pursue a court action under IDEA without being represented by an attorney.

Recovery of Attorney Fees

In 1986, Congress enacted the Handicapped Children's Protection Act (Pub. L. No. 99-372), an amendment to IDEA that provides: "In any action or proceeding brought under this subsection, the court in its discretion, may award reasonable attorneys' fees as part of the costs to the parents or guardian of a handicapped child or youth who is the prevailing party" (20 U.S.C. 1415[a][4][B]). In *Hensley v. Eckerhart* (1983, p. 433), the Supreme Court found that "plaintiffs may be considered 'prevailing parties' for the purposes of recovery of attorney fees if they succeed on any significant issue in litigation which achieves some of the benefit the parties sought in bringing the suit." The IDEA prohibits recovery of attorney fees for an IEP meeting unless the meeting is convened as a result of an administrative proceeding or a judicial action; for mediation that is conducted prior to filing a complaint; or if the parent declines a written settlement offer and the court later awards the parent a lesser amount (34 C.F.R. § 300.517[c][2–3]). In addition, attorney fees may be reduced if the parent unreasonably protracted the resolution of the dispute, the fees unreasonably exceeded the prevailing rate in the community, the time spent on legal services was excessive in light of the nature of the proceedings, or the attorney representing the parent did not provide the required information to the school district (34 C.F.R. § 300.517[c][4]).

Abrogation of State Sovereign Immunity

Under IDEA, states and their departments of education can be sued by private citizens if they violate the law. This provision in IDEA waives the traditional immunity from private lawsuits that states enjoy under the 11th Amendment to the Constitution.

INFANTS AND TODDLERS WITH DISABILITIES

Pub. L. No. 99-457, the Education for the Handicapped Act Amendments of 1986 (now IDEA–Part C), provides grants to states to develop and implement a statewide, comprehensive system of early intervention services for infants and toddlers with disabilities and their families. The purpose of IDEA-Part C is fivefold: (1) to enhance the development of infants and toddlers with disabilities and to minimize their potential for developmental delay; (2) to reduce the education costs to our society, including our nation's schools, by minimizing the need for special education and related services after infants and toddlers with disabilities reach school age; (3) to maximize the potential for individuals with disabilities to live independently in society; (4) to enhance the capacity of families to meet the special needs of their infants and toddlers with disabilities; and (5) to enhance the capacity of state and local agencies and service providers to identify, evaluate, and meet the needs of all children, particularly minority, low-income, inner-city, and rural children, and infants and toddlers in foster care (Pub. L. No. 105-17; § 631; 111 Stat. 106 [1997]).[2]

---

[2]As noted previously, new IDEA–Part C regulations had not been issued at the time this section was written in February 2010.

A number of similarities and differences exist between legislation providing a free and appropriate education for children with disabilities in the 3- to 21-year age group (IDEA–Part B) and the legislation providing grants for early intervention services for infants and toddlers (IDEA–Part C). Part C is described under the following sections: "Statewide System," "Child Find," "Eligible Children," "Evaluation and Assessment," "Individualized Family Service Plan," "Early Intervention Services," and "Procedural Safeguards."

Statewide System

Prior to 1986, services for infants and toddlers with disabilities typically were provided by a number of different agencies in each state (social services, public health, education), often resulting in service gaps or unnecessary duplication (Gallagher, 1989). The IDEA–Part C was designed to encourage states to develop and implement a statewide, comprehensive, coordinated, multidisciplinary, interagency program of early intervention services for infants and toddlers with disabilities and their families (34 C.F.R. § 303.1).

The law requires each state to identify a lead agency responsible for administration, supervision, coordination, and monitoring of programs and activities in the state. Different states have chosen different lead agencies, including state departments of health, education, and social welfare (Gallagher, 1989). To receive funds, each state must have submitted an application to the U.S. Department of Education (DOE) that outlines state policies and procedures for the delivery of services consistent with the requirements of Part C. Part C also requires the development of an interagency coordinating council to advise and assist the lead agency, identify and coordinate financial resources, and promote interagency agreements (34 C.F.R. §§ 303.141–142).

Child Find

The IDEA–Part C requires each state to establish a public awareness program and a comprehensive child find system to ensure that eligible children are identified and referred for evaluation in a timely manner. Each state also must develop a central directory of public and private early intervention services, resources, research and demonstration projects, and experts in the state that is accessible to parents of infants and toddlers with disabilities and to the general public (34 C.F.R. § 303.301; §§ 303.320–321).

Eligible Children

The IDEA–Part C defines *infant or toddler with a disability* to mean a child from birth through two years of age who needs early intervention services because he or she (a) is experiencing developmental delays, as measured by appropriate diagnostic instruments and procedures, in one or more of the areas of cognitive, physical, communication, social or emotional, or adaptive development, or (b) has a diagnosed physical or mental condition that has a high probability of resulting in developmental delay. The term also may include, at a state's discretion, at-risk infants and toddlers. The term *at-risk infant or toddler* means a child from birth through two years of age who would be at risk of experiencing a substantial delay if early intervention services were not provided. The factors that put the child at risk may be biological or environmental (34 C.F.R. § 303.16).

Evaluation and Assessment

IDEA–Part C requires a multidisciplinary assessment of the unique strengths and needs of each child and the identification of services appropriate to meet such needs. The evaluation must be based on nondiscriminatory procedures, be conducted by personnel trained to utilize appropriate methods and procedures, be based on informed clinical opinion, and include a review of pertinent records related to the child's current health status and medical history. The evaluation must include an assessment of the unique needs of the child in each of the following five developmental areas: cognitive, physical (including hearing and vision), communication, social or emotional, and adaptive. The evaluation includes the identification of services appropriate to meet the needs of the child in each of these areas (34 C.F.R. §§ 303.322–323).

The IDEA–Part C also requires a family-directed assessment of the resources, priorities, and concerns of the family and the identification of the supports and services necessary to enhance the family's capacity to meet the developmental needs of the infant or toddler. Any assessment that is conducted must be voluntary on the part of the family. If an assessment of the family is carried out, the assessment must be conducted by personnel trained to utilize appropriate methods and procedures, be based on information provided by the family through a personal interview, and incorporate the family's description of its resources, priorities, and concerns related to enhancing the child's development (34 C.F.R. § 303.322).

With the exception of unusual circumstances, the evaluation and initial assessment of each child (including the family assessment) must be completed within 45 days after the lead agency receives the referral (34 C.F.R. § 303.321).

Individualized Family Service Plan

The IDEA–Part C requires a written individualized family service plan (IFSP) rather than an IEP for each infant or toddler. The IFSP is developed at a meeting that includes the parents of the child; other family members, as requested by the parents, if feasible to do so; an advocate or person outside of the family, if the parents request that the person participate; the service coordinator; a person directly involved in conducting the evaluations and assessment; and, as appropriate, persons who will be providing services to the child or family. If one of these persons is unable to attend, arrangements are made for his or her involvement via telephone conference calls or other means. Agencies must provide adequate prior written notice regarding meetings, and IFSP meetings must be conducted in settings and at times that are convenient to families and in the native language of the family or other mode of communication used by the family, unless it is clearly not feasible to do so. For the child who has been referred for evaluation for the first time and found eligible, the meeting to develop the IFSP must be conducted within 45 days of the referral (34 C.F.R. § 303.342). With the consent of the parent, services maybe provided prior to the completion of the assessment (34 C.F.R. § 303.345).

The IFSP includes the following: (a) a statement of the infant's or toddler's present levels of physical, cognitive, communication, social or emotional, and adaptive development, based on professionally acceptable objective criteria; (b) with the concurrence of the family, a statement of the family's resources, priorities, and concerns relating to enhancing the development of the infant or toddler; (c) a statement of the major outcomes expected to be achieved for the infant or toddler and the family and the criteria, procedures, and time lines used to determine the degree to which progress toward achieving the outcomes is being made and whether modifications of the outcomes or services are necessary; (d) a statement of the specific early intervention services necessary to meet the unique needs of the infant or toddler and the family, including the frequency, intensity, and method of delivering services; a statement of the natural environments in which early intervention services will appropriately be provided, including a justification of the extent, if any, to which services will not be provided in a natural environment; the location of services; and payment arrangements, if any; (e) as appropriate, medical and other services that the child needs but that are not provided under IDEA–Part C, and how those services might be obtained through public or private sources; (f) the projected dates for the initiation of services and the anticipated duration of those services; (g) the identification of the service coordinator from the profession most immediately relevant to the child's or family's needs (or who is otherwise qualified to carry out all applicable responsibilities) who will be responsible for the implementation of the plan and coordination with other agencies and persons; and (h) the steps to be taken to support the transition of the toddler with a disability to preschool or other appropriate services (34 C.F.R. § 303.344).

The content of the IFSP must be explained fully to the parents, and informed written consent from the parents must be obtained prior to the provision of the early intervention services described in the plan. If the parents do not provide consent for a particular service, then the early intervention services to which consent is obtained are provided (34 C.F.R. § 303.342). An annual meeting is conducted to evaluate the IFSP, and the family is provided with a review of the plan every six months, or more often if needed.

Early Intervention Services

Under Part C, early intervention services include both special instruction and related services; an infant or toddler can receive a related service under Part C without receiving special instruction. (This differs from the requirement under Part B that children with disabilities ages 3 to 21 only receive related services in order to benefit from special education.) The term *early intervention services* means services that are: (a) designed to meet the developmental needs of the child and the needs of the family related to enhancing the child's development, (b) selected in collaboration with the parents, (c) provided under public supervision by qualified personnel in conformity with an individualized family service plan, and (d) provided at no cost, unless federal or state law provides for a system of payments by families. Types of services include family training, counseling, and home visits; special instructions; speech-language pathology and audiology services; occupational therapy; physical therapy; psychological services; service coordination services; medical services only for diagnostic or evaluative purposes; early identification, screening, and assessment services; health services necessary to enable the infant or toddler to benefit from the other early intervention services; nursing services, nutrition services, and social work services; vision services; assistive technology devices and services; and transportation and related costs that are necessary to enable the infant or toddler and his or her family to receive other early intervention services (34 C.F.R. §§ 303.12–13).

Procedural Safeguards

The procedural safeguards under Part C are similar to those under Part B. Parents are afforded the right to confidentiality of personally identifiable information; the right to examine records; the right to consent to or decline any early intervention service without jeopardizing the right to other services; the right to written prior notice before changes are made in identification, evaluation, placement, or provision of services; the right to use mediation; the right to timely administrative resolution of complaints; and the right to bring civil action in state or federal court (34 C.F.R. §§ 303.400–406).

CONCLUDING COMMENTS

Pub. L. No. 94-142 was enacted more than 35 years ago. Amendments, court interpretations, changing rules and regulations, and policy statements have further shaped special education law. Education law will continue to change. School psychologists must keep abreast of these changes to ensure that the educational rights of pupils are safeguarded.

STUDY AND DISCUSSION

Questions for Chapter 4

1. Why did Congress require single-agency responsibility for children with disabilities?
2. What is the zero reject principle?
3. What is the purpose of the IEP meeting? Who attends? Briefly describe the content of the IEP.
4. Briefly describe what is meant by *least restrictive appropriate environment* in special education law. Does this aspect of the law mean that all children with disabilities must be integrated into the general education classroom? What are the guiding principles for determining a child's educational placement?
5. How is *appropriate education* defined in *Rowley*?
6. What is the medical exclusion?
7. Under federal law, what is the role of a *DSM-IV* diagnosis in determining whether a student is eligible for special education under IDEA–Part B?
8. What are some of the ways that Part C and Part B differ?

Activities

1. Compare the 13 disability categories under IDEA–Part B with the categories and eligibility criteria that appear in the special education guidelines of your state.
2. Does your local school district distribute a special education handbook or pamphlet to parents outlining their rights and the school's responsibilities under special education law? Obtain and review copies of informational materials given to parents and review forms used by school districts for referral for special education evaluation, parent consent for evaluation under special education law, and team meeting decisions.

Chapter 5

SECTION 504 AND THE AMERICANS WITH DISABILITIES ACT

This chapter begins with a summary of those portions of Section 504 of the Rehabilitation Act of 1973 most pertinent to school psychological practice. Special attention is given to similarities and differences between Section 504 and the Individuals with Disabilities Education Improvement Act (IDEA 2004) regarding school responsibilities to students with disabilities. We also provide a brief overview of the Americans with Disabilities Act of 1990 (ADA) and the Americans with Disabilities Amendments Act of 2008 (ADAA).

SECTION 504

Section 504 of the Rehabilitation Act of 1973 is civil rights legislation that prohibits discrimination against pupils with disabilities in school systems receiving federal financial assistance. Contemporary interpretations suggest that schools must attend to three types of potential discrimination prohibited by law. First, Section 504 prohibits public schools from excluding students from participating in school programs and activities solely on the basis of a disability. Second, it requires schools to take reasonable steps to prevent harassment on the basis of disability. Third, it requires schools to make accommodations to ensure that pupils with disabilities have equal opportunity to benefit from its programs and activities.

Passed in 1973, Section 504 was initially misunderstood or ignored by the schools. Beginning in the late 1980s, however, Office for Civil Rights (OCR) enforcement activities, court decisions, and parent advocacy efforts heightened awareness of Section 504, and the law subsequently began to impact school practices. Because of changes in IDEA 1997 and 2004 (e.g., funds for early intervening services), we anticipate that Section 504 may become less important as a means of ensuring educational assistance for students in general education classrooms who have learning and behavioral problems. However, claims based on disability harassment in the schools appear to be on the rise, and the expanded definition of *disability* under Section 504/ADAA may increase the number of requests for 504 plans from parents of students with health-related impairments (see Zirkel, 2009a). School psychologists must be knowledgeable about Section 504 and its role in safeguarding the right to equal educational opportunity for students with a broad range of physical and mental impairments.

Historical Framework

One way Congress attempted to ensure a free and appropriate education for all children with disabilities was through federal grant legislation such as Pub. L. No. 94-142 (now IDEA). A second way the federal government attempted to address the problem of discrimination against pupils with disabilities was through antidiscrimination laws. One of the first bills that attempted to ensure equal educational opportunity for children with disabilities in the public schools was an amendment to Title VI of the Civil Rights Act of 1964. The bill was introduced in the House of Representatives by Congressman Vanek and in the Senate by Senator Humphrey and later became part of the Rehabilitation Act of 1973 (Pub. L. No. 93-112; Martin 1979). Section 504 of the Rehabilitation Act states, "No otherwise quali-fied handicapped individual in the United States...shall, solely by reason of his handicap, be excluded from the participation in, or be denied the benefits of, or be subjected to discrimina-tion under any program or activity receiving Federal financial assistance" (29 U.S.C. § 794).

Both Vanek and Humphrey saw Section 504 as requiring all states to provide educational services to all children. However, the Rehabilitation Act of 1973 is concerned primarily with discrimination in employment settings, and many interpreted Section 504 as a prohibition against employment discrimination in the schools. The 1974 amendments to the Rehabilitation Act (Pub. L. No. 93-516) clarified the intent of the law by specifically prohibiting discrimi-nation against pupils with physical or mental impairments in schools receiving federal funds (Martin, 1979).

There was still no immediate impact on school policies regarding children with disabilities, however. Advocates for the rights of pupils with disabilities staged wheelchair sit-ins to encourage the quick development of regulations implementing the law, while school officials quietly protested this legislation as too costly for the public schools (Martin, 1979). The Department of Health, Education, and Welfare (HEW), caught in the middle, was slow to develop and approve regulations implementing Section 504. As Martin noted, HEW did not require compliance with Section 504 until the 1978–1979 school year, a full five years after the law was passed.

During the same years that HEW was struggling to develop regulations for Section 504, Congress debated and passed several laws providing funds to states to assure educa-tional opportunities for children with disabilities. Following the passage of the Education for All Handicapped Children Act of 1975 (Pub. L. No. 94-142, now IDEA), public school districts typically concentrated on fulfilling their obligation to provide special educa-tion and related services to pupils with disabilities in conformance with its requirements. Many school administrators were unaware that the broad definition of *handicapped* under Section 504 included a number of students who did not qualify as disabled under Pub. L. No. 94-142. They falsely believed that compliance with special education law meant the school was in full compliance with Section 504 (Martin, 1992).

In the late 1980s, a number of lawsuits and complaints to the OCR were filed on behalf of pupils in general education programs because schools failed to make accommodations for their handicapping conditions under Section 504 (e.g., *Elizabeth S. v. Thomas K. Gilhool*, 1987; Lake Washington [WA] School District No. 414, 1985; Rialto [CA] Unified School District, 1989).[1] Advocacy efforts on behalf of children with attention deficit disorder (ADD) and attention deficit/hyperactivity disorder (ADHD) also were an important trigger for increased attention to Section 504 requirements.

When Congress considered the 1990 amendments of Pub. L. No. 94-142, parents of children with ADD/ADHD testified to Congress that many schools were unwilling to make even simple modifications of educational programming because their children did not qual-ify under special education law (Martin, 1992). The U.S. Department of Education (DOE, 1991) subsequently issued a memorandum to clarify DOE policy regarding appropriate education for children with ADD/ADHD under Section 504 and special education law. The memorandum stated that some pupils with ADD/ADHD qualify within the IDEA definitions of other health impairment, specific learning disability, or emotional disturbance. Others

---

[1]References to court cases are italicized; references to OCR opinions and administrative hearings are not.

might require a variety of special accommodations in the classroom under Section 504. The memorandum went on to identify more than 20 strategies to meet the needs of 504-only children with learning and behavior problems in the general education classroom. The kinds of accommodations identified by DOE were classroom modifications that a teacher, student assistance team, and/or school psychologist might recommend (e.g., repeating and simplifying instructions, using applied behavior analysis techniques).

Passage of the Americans with Disabilities Act of 1990 (ADA; Pub. L. No. 101-336) further heightened attention to the requirements of Section 504. As will be seen later in this chapter, ADA generally requires full compliance with Section 504, but at times it requires more than Section 504 does with regard to the school's obligations to students with physical or mental impairments. In 2008, the Americans with Disabilities Amendments Act (ADAA, Pub. L. No. 110-325) was passed, further defining and clarifying the criteria for determining whether a student has a disability under ADAA and is eligible for Section 504 protections and accommodations.[2]

Section 504 of the Rehabilitation Act of 1973 prohibits discrimination against physically or mentally *handicapped* pupils in federally supported school systems. The ADA and IDEA use the term *disability*. In the next portion of this chapter, we will use the umbrella term *disability* to mean students who qualify under Section 504 (as amended by the ADAA) *and* under IDEA. The term *504/ADAA impairment* will be used to refer to those students who qualify as having a disability under Section 504/ADAA, but who are not eligible for special education and related services under IDEA. The term *IDEA disability* will be used to refer to those students who qualify for special education and related services.

Overview of Section 504

Section 504 is antidiscrimination legislation; it is not a federal grant program. Unlike IDEA, Section 504 does not provide funds to schools. A state department of education may choose not to pursue monies available under federal grant statutes (e.g., IDEA–Part C funds for infants and toddlers). However, school districts must comply with antidiscrimination legislation if they receive any federal funds for any purpose.

With respect to public school educational services, Section 504 protections against discrimination apply to all pupils with a 504/ADAA disability who are the same age as nondisabled pupils receiving a public education, or who are eligible for educational services for pupils with a 504/ADAA disability under state law or eligible for special education in the state under IDEA. Students who have an IDEA disability are thus "double covered" under Section 504 and IDEA (Zirkel, 2009a).

The Office for Civil Rights (OCR), an agency within the U.S. Department of Education (DOE), is charged with investigating Section 504 and ADA complaints pertaining to DOE programs or activities. Although an OCR investigation may be triggered by a complaint regarding possible discriminatory treatment of an individual student with a disability, OCR may choose to expand its investigation to encompass school policies and practices regarding all students within the district who have a particular type of disability (e.g., mental retardation, ADD/ADHD). The OCR has the authority to remove federal funds from a district if it is not in compliance with Section 504.

Section 504 does not require states to develop a written plan to meet the requirements of the law. However, under 504, each school district must designate at least one

---

[2]The ADAA language quoted in this chapter is based on the text of United State Code (Title 42, Chapter 126) as amended by ADAA and was retrieved from http://www.ada.gov/pubs/adastatute08mark.htm on April 17, 2009.

person to coordinate its efforts to comply with the law and adopt grievance procedures that incorporate appropriate due process standards and provide for the prompt and equitable resolution of complaints alleging violations of Section 504 (34 C.F.R. § 104.7). Each school district also must take appropriate and continuing steps to notify students and their parents that it does not discriminate in its programs and activities on the basis of disability (34 C.F.R. § 104.8).

Preventing Discrimination in Access to Programs and Services

As previously noted, Section 504 of the Rehabilitation Act of 1973 was designed to eliminate discrimination on the basis of disability in any program or activity receiving federal financial assistance. Subpart D applies to preschool, elementary, and secondary education programs and activities and requires schools to make special accommodations for students with disabilities to ensure that they are afforded educational opportunity equal to their nondisabled peers.

Section 504 specifically prohibits schools from discriminating on the basis of disability (see Exhibit 5.1 for the 504/ADAA definition of disability) in providing any aid, benefit, or service, either directly or through contractual arrangements. Schools may not deny pupils with disabilities an opportunity to participate in or benefit from any of the services or benefits it affords others. This means that schools must provide aids, benefits, or services that are equal to and as effective as those provided to nondisabled pupils. Schools are not required to produce the identical result or level of achievement for pupils with and without disabilities, but they *must afford students with disabilities equal opportunity* to obtain the same result, to gain the same benefit, or to reach the same level of achievement, in the most integrated setting appropriate to the student's needs. Schools may not provide different or separate aid, benefits, or services to pupils with disabilities unless such action is necessary to provide them with services that are as effective as those provided to others. When separate programs or activities exist to meet the needs of students with disabilities, a school may not deny a qualified student with a disability the opportunity to participate in programs or activities that are not separate or different (34 C.F.R. § 104.4; also see *Baird v. Rose*, 1999). For example, in recent years, some school districts refused to allow qualified students with disabilities to enroll in advanced placement or other accelerated programs. Such practices are a violation of Section 504 (Monroe, 2007).

Case 5.1 is based on a real-life incident. The school's policy of barring special education classes from the school's computer lab was clearly in violation of Section 504. The policy was changed quickly after it was challenged by the special education teacher and the school psychologist.

Case 5.1

Mrs. Drew, a middle school special education teacher, teaches an English class for students with cognitive impairments who cannot keep pace in the general education English curriculum. After observing that several of Mrs. Drew's students had problems with handwriting, Hannah Cook offered to take Mrs. Drew and her students to the school's computer lab to show them how to use a simple word processing program for English writing assignments. When Hannah contacted the teacher responsible for scheduling the school's computer lab, she was told that, in accordance with school policy, special education classes were not allowed to use the computer lab because the students were too likely to damage the expensive equipment.

Protection from Disability Harassment

Section 504 and the ADA protect students from harassment based on disability. As noted in Chapter 2, the term *harassment* means oral, written, graphic, or physical conduct *relating to an individual's disability* that is sufficiently severe, pervasive, or persistent so as to interfere with or limit the ability of an individual to participate in or benefit from the district's programs or activities. Section 504 and the ADA require schools to take reasonable steps to remedy harassment (see U.S. Department of Education & Bias Crimes Task Force of the National Association of Attorneys General, 1999). Weber (2002) suggested that disability harassment in the public schools is common, and he detailed a number of cases in which teachers or other school staff inflicted verbal harassment and physical abuse on pupils with disabilities or encouraged or tolerated disability harassment by peers.

To date, there have been complaints to OCR following disability harassment of a student ("Is District to Blame," 2003) and several court cases in which parents have sought monetary damages following disability harassment of their child. Some courts have recognized the right of parents to seek monetary damages or another remedy for disability harassment under Section 504 and the ADA (e.g., *Biggs v. Board of Education of Cecil County*, 2002; *K.M. ex rel. D.G. v. Hyde Park Central School District*, 2005; *Werth v. Board of Directors of the Public Schools of the City of Milwaukee*, 2007). In 1999, the U.S. Supreme Court opinion in *Davis v. Monroe County Board of Education* (a case involving student-on-student sexual harassment) identified five specific elements or tests for determining whether student-on-student harassment resulted in a denial of equal educational opportunity (see Chapter 9). Thus far, some claims of student-on-student harassment on the basis of disability were not successful because of failure to exhaust other remedies or failure to prove that the harassment resulted in a denial of equal educational opportunity consistent with the standards outlined in *Davis v. Monroe County Board of Education* (1999).

It also is important to remember that under IDEA persistent harassment of a student eligible for special education and related services may be interpreted by the courts to mean that the student's placement does not provide a free, appropriate education in the least restrictive environment (*Shore Regional High School v. P.S.*, 2004; see Chapter 4).

Eligibility for 504 Accommodations

To be eligible for special education and related services under IDEA–Part B, students must be evaluated in accordance with procedures outlined in Part B and found eligible under one of the 13 categories of disability, and they must need special education because of that disability (see Chapter 4). The definition of *disability* under Section 504/ADAA is broader and more open-ended than under IDEA (Zirkel, 2009b). Under 504/ADAA the term *disability* means a physical or mental impairment that substantially limits one or more of the major life activities of the individual (see Exhibit 5.1). *Major life activities* include, but are not limited to, functions such as caring for oneself, performing manual tasks, seeing, hearing, eating, sleeping, walking, standing, lifting, bending, speaking, breathing, learning, reading, concentrating, thinking, communicating, and working.

The ADAA (2008) clarified that the definition of *disability* should be "construed in favor of broad coverage of individuals" (Sec. 12102[4][A]). Furthermore, the determination whether a physical or mental impairment substantially limits a major life activity is made without regard to the "ameliorative effects of mitigating measures" such as medication; medical devices (except for ordinary glasses and corrective lens); assistive technology; accommodations, aids, or services; or learned behavioral or adaptive neurological modifications (Sec. 12102[4][E]). Thus, a student with attention deficit/hyperactivity disorder

---

Exhibit 5.1 Definition of *Disability* as Amended by the ADAA

Sec. 12102. Definition of disability

As used in this chapter:

(1) Disability
   The term "disability" means, with respect to an individual
   (A) a physical or mental impairment that substantially limits one or more major life activities of such individual;
   (B) a record of such an impairment; or
   (C) being regarded as having such an impairment (as described in paragraph (3)).

(2) Major Life Activities
   (A) In general
      For purposes of paragraph (1), major life activities include, but are not limited to, caring for oneself, performing manual tasks, seeing, hearing, eating, sleeping, walking, standing, lifting, bending, speaking, breathing, learning, reading, concentrating, thinking, communicating, and working.
   (B) Major bodily functions
      For purposes of paragraph (1), a major life activity also includes the operation of a major bodily function, including but not limited to, functions of the immune system, normal cell growth, digestive, bowel, bladder, neurological, brain, respiratory, circulatory, endocrine, and reproductive functions.

(3) Regarded as having such an impairment
   For purposes of paragraph (1)(C):
   (A) An individual meets the requirement of "being regarded as having such an impairment" if the individual establishes that he or she has been subjected to an action prohibited under this chapter because of an actual or perceived physical or mental impairment whether or not the impairment limits or is perceived to limit a major life activity.
   (B) Paragraph (1)(C) shall not apply to impairments that are transitory and minor. A transitory impairment is an impairment with an actual or expected duration of 6 months or less.

Note: Retrieved from http://www.ada.gov/publications/adastatute08mark.htm on April 17, 2009.

---

might qualify as having a disability under 504/ADAA even though his or her ADHD is generally well controlled by medication.

Under 504/ADAA, the term *disability* also includes persons who can document that they experienced illegal discriminatory actions against them because of the perception of a disability, whether or not they have an actual impairment. For example, if a high school senior was denied admission to college solely on the basis of school education records showing a history of special education placement, Section 504/ADAA safeguards would be triggered. This prong of the definition of Section 504/ADAA disability is most pertinent to discrimination in employment and settings other than elementary and secondary schools.

The ADAA also clarifies that the term *substantially limits a major life activity* does not apply to impairments that are transitory, defined as an actual or expected duration of six months or less, and minor (Sec. 12102[3][B]). However, an impairment that is "episodic or in remission is a disability if it would substantially limit a major life activity when active" (Sec. 12102[4][D]).

Furthermore, in the portion of the law that addresses discrimination in employment settings, the ADAA states that its protections do not extend to individuals who are disabled by drug addiction if they are "currently engaged in the illegal use of drugs" (Sec. 12114[a]). However, the ADAA does protect individuals from discrimination if they have undergone drug rehabilitation successfully and no longer engage in illegal drug use (Sec. 12114[b][1][2][3]). Other exclusions from the 504/ADAA definition of disability include homosexuality, bisexuality, gender identity disorders, and transgender status. (See Zirkel, 2009b.)

In sum, Section 504 prohibits schools from discriminating on the basis of disability in providing aids, benefits, or services and requires schools to take reasonable steps to prevent harassment of students with disabilities. Any student who has a disability as defined by 504/ADAA and who needs special assistance at school because of his or her impairment may be eligible for individual accommodations under Section 504. All students who are disabled under IDEA are considered to be disabled under 504/ADAA, and are, therefore, afforded the protections of Section 504. Students who are not disabled under IDEA may nevertheless have a disability under 504/ADAA. The students who are likely to qualify for accommodations under 504/ADAA but not be eligible for special education under IDEA are those with *physical and mental health impairments* and *communicable diseases*.

Physical and Mental Health Impairments

A number of schoolchildren have health conditions that substantially impair major life activities such as caring for oneself, performing manual tasks, walking, seeing, hearing, speaking, breathing, or learning. Pupils with a wide range of physical health conditions (e.g., diabetes, asthma, severe allergies, impairments from an accident, arthritis, epilepsy) *may* qualify for accommodations under 504/ADAA. A student with a temporary 504/ADAA impairment also may qualify for accommodations if the impairment has an actual or expected duration of more than six months. (See Zirkel, 2009b.)

Similarly, the 504/ADAA definition of *mental impairment* is broad and includes any mental impairment that substantially limits a major life activity, including learning, reading, concentrating, thinking, or communicating. For example, a general education student may have a disability within the meaning of 504/ADAA because of a condition that impairs reading, thinking, or concentration such as ADHD or dyslexia. Or a general education student may fail to attend school or be otherwise unable to participate in his or her education because of a mental illness such as depression, a sleeping disorder, an anxiety disorder, or oppositional defiant disorder, and therefore require 504 accommodations (see Zirkel, 2009b).

It is critically important for school psychologists to be knowledgeable about the eligibility determination criteria under 504/ADAA, and to seek competent consultation when they are unsure. In a recent due process hearing, the hearing officer awarded compensatory education at district expense to a student, noting that "the District's school psychologist... did not fully understand the eligibility requirements under Section 504" (Bristol Township School District Pennsylvania State Education Agency, 2009, p. 12).

Communicable Diseases

Section 504/ADA prohibits schools from discriminating against any "otherwise qualified" student with a communicable disease. This means that schools may not remove an infected child from the general education classroom unless a significant risk of transmission of the disease would still exist in spite of reasonable efforts by the school to accommodate the infected child (see also Chapter 99).

Evaluation of Students to Determine Eligibility for Accommodations

The evaluation regulations that implement Section 504 are difficult to interpret because they are limited in scope and detail. Although they specifically address evaluation with regard to *placement* in special or general education, procedures for determining 504 eligibility or needed special accommodations are not clearly addressed. Beginning in the early 1990s, education law experts (Council of Administrators of Special Education, 1999; Zirkel, 2009a, 2009b) and a series of OCR rulings provided guidance regarding how to determine whether a student has a 504/ADA disability. However, the passage of ADAA raises some new and unanswered questions regarding best practices in identifying students eligible under Section 504/ADAA.

An evaluation of a student is required if it is believed that the student may qualify as having a disability under 504/ADAA and may need special school services or accommodations. If a student is evaluated and found not eligible for special education under IDEA, the school should consider whether the student might be eligible for accommodations under 504/ADAA (e.g., Yukon [OK] Public Schools, 2007). However, a student should not be "504'd" (found eligible) unless he or she meets the eligibility criteria outlined in 504/ADAA. School personnel with good intentions may mislabel a pupil as having a 504/ADAA disability so that the student can receive individualized help at school. Unfortunately, such actions result in unnecessary stigmatization of the child and create an unwarranted legal entitlement to special treatment.

Schools are required to advise students with suspected disabilities and their parents of their rights and the school's duties under Section 504/ADAA (34 C.F.R. § 104.32). Schools must notify parents of their rights regarding the identification, evaluation, and placement of children with suspected disabilities prior to initiating a Section 504 evaluation. The OCR has recommended that parents be notified of their procedural safeguard rights under Section 504 at the time the district requests parental permission for an evaluation (e.g., Cobb County [GA] School District, 1992) or when a parent requests an evaluation. When a pupil is suspected of having a disability under IDEA, parent rights and school duties under both IDEA and 504 should be clearly identified.

A school must evaluate a student only when the school has reason to believe a child may have a 504/ADAA disability (Lim, 1993). Like IDEA, schools are not required to evaluate children based only on parental suspicion of an impairment. However, when a school does not agree with a parental request for evaluation, it must still inform parents of their right to contest that decision and the procedures for a fair and timely resolution of the evaluation dispute.

When it is suspected that a student may have a 504/ADAA disability, Martin (1992) interpreted the evaluation regulations to require three determinations: (1) Is there a physical or mental impairment? (2) Does that impairment substantially limit a major life activity? (3) What kind of accommodations would be needed so that the student will be able to enjoy the benefits of the school program? Section 504 does not require a specific categorical label or diagnosis, only the determination that a condition exists that substantially impairs one or more major life activities at school. (Also see Zirkel, 2009b.)

School psychologists, along with other members of the group of persons involved a making a Section 504/ADAA eligibility determination, should be aware that federal law does not require a medical diagnosis for the purpose of determining whether a child has a disability; the OCR "expressly allows for alternative assessment methods in lieu of medical diagnosis" for determining whether a child has an impairment that substantially limits a major life activity (Zirkel, 2009b, p. 336). The school should, however, consider the findings from a medical evaluation if shared with the school by the parents as part of the eligibility determination process. Furthermore, like IDEA, if the school believes that a medical diagnosis is necessary to determine eligibility, the school must assure that the diagnosis is made at no cost to the parent. Also, as noted previously, while a *DSM-IV* (American Psychiatric Association, 2000) diagnosis may assist in determining eligibility under 504/ADAA or IDEA, it is neither legally required nor sufficient to make an eligibility determination under federal law (Zirkel, 2009b).

Section 504 requires schools to establish standards and procedures for the evaluation of pupils who, because of a suspected impairment, are believed to need special school accommodations. The 504 regulations regarding evaluation procedures (34 C.F.R. § 104.35) are almost identical to those implementing the IDEA–Part B. Test and evaluation materials must be valid for the purpose used, administered by trained personnel, and fair. The evaluation must be comprehensive enough to assess the nature and extent of the impairment and the needed accommodations and services. In interpreting data and in making placement decisions, schools must "draw upon information from a variety of sources," "establish procedures to ensure that information obtained from all such sources is documented and carefully considered," and ensure that decisions are made by a "group of persons, including persons knowledgeable about the child, the evaluation data, and the placement options" (34 C.F.R. § 104.35). As Zirkel (2009b, p. 340) noted, "use of a systematic eligibility form facilitates a defensible determination" of whether a child is eligible for accommodations under 504/ADAA.

Time lines for the completion of an evaluation and determination of a child's needs are not specified in 504 regulations. The OCR has held that although "504 does not specify the time periods permitted at each stage of the process of identification, evaluation, and placement, it is implicit that the various steps in the process will be completed within a reasonable time period" (Cobb County [GA] School District, 1992, p. 29). It also has held that it is reasonable to expect schools to complete evaluations under Section 504 within the same time frame outlined in state guidelines for completion of IDEA evaluations (East Lansing [MI] Public Schools, 1992).

Section 504 does not require reevaluation of the student every three years, only periodic reevaluation and reevaluation prior to any significant change in placement (34 C.F.R. § 104.35). Courts have ruled that expulsion or long-term suspension (more than 10 days) of a student with a 504/ADAA disability is a change of placement.

Free Appropriate Public Education

The IDEA and Section 504 both require schools to offer a free appropriate public education (FAPE) to every student with a disability. *Appropriate education* is defined in Section 504 as "the provision of regular or special education and related aids and services (i) that are designed to meet individual educational needs of handicapped persons as adequately as the needs of nonhandicapped persons are met and (ii) [that] are based on adherence to procedural safeguards" outlined in the law (34 C.F.R. § 104.33). Thus, under Section 504, appropriate education is more broadly defined than under IDEA–Part B, and it can consist of education in general education classes, placement in the general education classes with the use of supplementary services, or special education and related services (see also Lake Washington [WA] School District No. 414, 1985).

Section 504, like IDEA, also requires schools to "educate, or provide for the education of, each qualified handicapped person in its jurisdiction with persons who are not handicapped to the maximum extent appropriate to the needs of the handicapped person"

(34 C.F.R. § 104.34). Students with disabilities must be placed in the general educational environment unless it is determined that the education of the student in the general education classroom with the use of supplementary aids and services cannot be achieved satisfactorily. In providing or arranging for the provision of nonacademic services (e.g., lunch, recess) and extracurricular activities, schools must ensure that students with disabilities participate with nondisabled students to maximum extent appropriate to their needs (34 C.F.R. §§ 104.34, 104.37). Furthermore, students with disabilities must be afforded opportunities to participate in after-school activities and informed that those opportunities are available (e.g., Kenowa Hills [MI] Public Schools, 1992–1993). They also must be given equal opportunity to participate in school field trips compared to their nondisabled peers (e.g., Clovis [CA] Unified School District, 2009).

Section 504 requires the provision of general or special education and related aids and services designed to meet the individual needs of pupils with impairments. A question raised by parents of children with 504/ADAA impairments and school administrators is whether school districts may use IDEA programs and services in making accommodations for 504-only students. The court ruling in *Lyons by Alexander v. Smith* (1993), OCR complaint investigation findings (e.g., Lake Washington [WA] School District No. 414, 1985), and OCR policy statements indicate that children with 504/ADAA impairments may have access to all IDEA programs and services, even if they do not qualify under IDEA. As the court noted in *Lyons* (1993), a school system may have to provide special education to a 504-only student if such services are necessary to prevent discrimination, that is, to meet the individual educational needs of the student with 504 impairments as adequately as those of nondisabled students.

Under Section 504, when a school district places a student with a disability in a program not operated by the school district, the district retains responsibility for assuring that Section 504 rights and protections are afforded to the student placed elsewhere (34 C.F.R. § 104.33). When selecting a child's placement, proximity to the child's home must be considered (34 C.F.R. § 104.34). When school districts refer or place pupils with disabilities in programs not operated by the school itself, the placement must be at no cost to the parent. Schools also must ensure adequate transportation to the placement site at no greater cost to the parent than would be incurred if the student were placed in a program operated by the school (34 C.F.R. § 104.33).

Accommodation Plan

Under Section 504, schools must provide a free, appropriate education for children with 504/ADAA impairments, designed to meet the individual education needs of children with 504 impairments as adequately as those of nondisabled students. The law itself does not specifically require a written accommodation plan; however, education experts recommend that a written plan be developed for students with 504/ADAA disabilities (Zirkel, 2009c).

As noted previously, the 504/ADAA student accommodation plan must be developed by a group of persons, including persons knowledgeable of the child and the evaluation data. The Council of Administrators of Special Education (1999) suggested that this plan include: (a) a description of the nature of the concern, (b) a description of the basis for the determination of the impairment, (c) a description of how the impairment substantially affects a major life activity, (d) a description of the reasonable accommodations that are necessary, (e) the date when the plan will be reviewed or reassessed, and (f) the names and titles of the participants at the accommodation plan meeting. The accommodation plan should be reviewed on the predetermined date.

Nature of the Required Accommodations

Specific accommodations for a child must always be determined by a group of persons and based on individual student need. However, the court settlement in *Elizabeth S. v. Thomas K. Gilhool* (1987) provided early guidance regarding school responsibilities *to students with physical and health impairments* who do not qualify under the IDEA. The court stated that the required school accommodations and services for students with physical or health impairments might include, but are not limited to, development of a plan to address any medical emergencies, school health services including assistance in monitoring of blood sugar levels and arrangements for a child to take injections or medications, assistance with toileting, adjustment of class schedules, home instruction, use of an elevator or other accommodations to make school facilities accessible, adaptive transportation, and adaptive physical education and/or occupational therapy.

Some schools have been reluctant to allow staff to administer medications and to allow students to self-medicate (e.g., use their nebulizer or inhaler in an asthma attack) because of concerns about district legal liability. While medical diagnosis is not necessary or controlling in determining eligibility under 504/ADAA, schools may require a physician's diagnosis for medical treatment at school, such as providing medication. However, based on a review of OCR opinions, Gelfman and Schwab (2005a) concluded that under Section 504 schools "no longer have a choice of whether to agree to administer medication when the student has a condition that interferes with a major life function and administration of medication during school hours is necessary" (p. 361). The OCR also has held that schools may not require parents to attend a school program to provide health services to their child (e.g., diabetes monitoring) because this imposes an obligation on the parents of a child with a health impairment that is not imposed on other parents (e.g., Clovis [CA] Unified School District, 2009). (For additional discussion of services for students with 504 health impairments, see Gelfman & Schwab, 2005a.)

Several administrative hearings and OCR investigations have addressed *accommodations for students with mental health impairments*. These cases concerned students who did not qualify under IDEA–Part B as having an emotional disturbance but who were deemed to have a mental impairment that substantially affected a major life activity. Accommodations and services for a student with a mental health impairment under Section 504 also must be based on individual need. However, schools must, at a minimum, provide assistance to ensure equal educational opportunity. For example, as a result of a hearing involving Howard County, Maryland, Public Schools ("Failure to Provide," 2005), parents of a high school student diagnosed with depression were awarded funds to cover all expenses they incurred from unilaterally placing their son in a private facility (tuition, room and board, psychological services) after it was determined that the school failed to offer any services to address the student's depression and inability to participate in his education. (See Zirkel, 2009b, for additional examples.)

Procedural Safeguards Under Section 504

Procedural safeguards in Section 504 regulations are stated in more general terms than those in IDEA–Part B. Under 504, schools are required "to make available a system of procedural safeguards that permit parents to challenge actions regarding the identification, evaluation, or educational placement of their handicapped child whom they believe needs special education or related services" (DOE, 1991; also 34 C.F.R. § 104.36). The system of procedural safeguards must include "notice, an opportunity for the parents or guardian to examine relevant records, an impartial hearing with opportunity for participation by the person's parents or guardian and representation by counsel, and a review procedure" (34 C.F.R. § 104.36). School districts may not require parents to exhaust their internal complaint resolution procedures such as mediation before requesting a due process hearing under Section 504 (e.g., Talbot County [MD] Public Schools, 2008).

As noted previously, the Office for Civil Rights (OCR) is charged with investigating Section 504 complaints pertaining to DOE programs or activities. The OCR investigates individual complaints, and a parent may trigger an investigation of school district compliance with 504 by filing a complaint with the OCR (Zirkel & Kincaid, 1993).

In addition, parents have the right to initiate a court action against the school on behalf of a child with 504/ADAA impairments if they believe the school has violated the provisions of Section 504 with respect to their child. In accordance with the Handicapped Children's Protection Act of 1986 (Pub. L. No. 99-372), if a Section 504 claim can be remedied under IDEA, parents must first attempt to remedy the problem under IDEA before filing a civil action on a Section 504 claim. The courts may award reasonable attorney fees as part of the costs to parents when they are the prevailing party in a Section 504 suit. Zirkel & Rose (2009) reported an increase in 504/ADA claims in recent years, including in increase in cases in which parents sought money damages from schools under 504/ADA along with an increase in claims of illegal retaliation by the school in the aftermath of parent efforts to advocate for their child's rights.

AMERICANS WITH DISABILITIES ACT

Congress passed more than 20 laws prohibiting discrimination against individuals with disabilities between 1973 and 1990 (Burgdorf, 1991). The Americans with Disabilities Act of 1990 (ADA) (Pub. L. No. 101-336) is considered to be the most significant federal law ensuring the civil rights of all individuals with disabilities.

The ADA was first introduced as a bill in Congress in 1988. In its statement of findings, Congress reported widespread discrimination against individuals with disabilities in all spheres of life, including employment, housing, public accommodations, education, transportation, communication, recreation, health services, and access to public services (Pub. L. No. 101-336 § 2[a][1]). Additionally, testimony to Congress documented a strong link between disability and poverty, joblessness, lack of education, and failure to participate in social and recreational opportunities (Burgdorf, 1991). President George H. W. Bush signed the ADA into law in 1990.

The ADA guarantees equal opportunity to individuals with disabilities in employment, public services, transportation, state and local government services, and telecommunications. It prohibits discrimination on the basis of disability in public and private schools that are not controlled by a religious entity, regardless of whether the private school receives federal funds (Zirkel, 2009a). The ADA thus differed from earlier laws because it extended to programs and activities outside the federal sphere and includes a detailed set of standards prohibiting discrimination (Burgdorf, 1991).

The protections of ADA extend only to those persons who have a disability as defined by the law. Following several Supreme Court decisions that narrowed the interpretation of disability under the ADA, particularly in employment settings (e.g., *Sutton v. United Air Lines, Inc.*, 1999; *Toyota Motor Manufacturing, Kentucky, Inc. v. Williams*, 2002), Congress passed the Americans with Disabilities Amendments Act (ADAA) of 2008. The purpose of the 2008 ADA amendments was to restore the original, broad scope of the definition of *disability* as intended by Congress in 1990 and to explicitly reject the narrower interpretations enunciated in Supreme Court decisions. The ADAA definition of *disability* also applies to Section 504 of the Rehabilitation Act of 1973.

The ADA regulations state that, unless otherwise noted, the ADA "shall not be construed to apply a lesser standard" than Section 504 (28 C.F.R. § 35.103). Thus, ADA generally requires full compliance with 504, but at times it requires more than 504 in school obligations to students with disabilities. The ADA stresses the removal of architectural barriers as a top priority (Martin, 1992).

The Office for Civil Rights within the U.S. Department of Education was designated as the agency responsible for enforcing the ADA with regard to public and nonreligious private schools. Complaints regarding ADA violations may be filed with the OCR. The remedies of Section 504 are the remedies of Title II of ADA.

Whistle-Blowers Protection

School psychologists also should be familiar with the ADA's protection against retaliation or coercion for whistle-blowers:

(a) No private or public entity shall discriminate against any individual because that individual has opposed any act or practice made unlawful by this part or because that individual made a charge, testified, assisted, or participated in any manner in an investigation, proceeding or hearing under the Act or this part.

(b) No private or public entity shall coerce, intimidate, threaten, or interfere with any individual in the exercise or enjoyment of, or on account of his having exercised or enjoyed, or on account of his or her having aided or encouraged any other individual in the exercise of enjoyment of, any right granted or protected by the Act or this part. (28 C.F.R. § 35.134)

This portion of the law was designed in part to protect individuals who advocate for the rights of persons with disabilities from retaliation by the agency involved. Thus, if a school district failed to meet its obligations to pupils with disabilities under the ADA and a school employee assisted those students in obtaining their rights under the Act, the school district would be prohibited from retaliating against the employee. If the school did retaliate by firing or in some way demoting the employee, the employee would have the right to file a lawsuit against the school district under the ADA's protection against retaliation. For example, in 2001, a federal jury awarded almost $1 million to a former special education teacher who was fired after persistently complaining that students with disabilities received less adequate time, equipment, and facilities for physical education than their nondisabled peers (Chestnut, 2001; *Settlegoode v. Portland Public Schools*, 2004).

CONCLUDING COMMENTS

Contemporary interpretations of Section 504 suggest that schools must attend to three types of potential discrimination prohibited by the law. First, Section 504 prohibits public schools from excluding students from participating in school programs and activities solely on the basis of a disability. Second, it requires schools to take reasonable steps to prevent harassment on the basis of disability. Third, it requires schools to make accommodations to ensure that pupils with disabilities have equal opportunity to benefit from its programs and activities.

STUDY AND DISCUSSION

Questions for Chapter 5

1. What type of legislation is Section 504 of the Rehabilitation Act of 1973? How does it differ from the IDEA in purpose, scope, and funding?
2. How is pupil eligibility determined under 504/ADAA?
3. Must a child have a permanent mental or physical impairment to be eligible for accommodations under 504/ADAA?
4. What is the meaning of *free appropriate public education* within 504/ADAA?
5. Describe the content of an accommodation plan under 504/ADAA and how one is developed.
6. Briefly describe the scope and purpose of the ADA as it relates to public school students.

Activities

Does your local school district distribute a handbook or pamphlet to parents outlining their rights and school responsibilities under Section 504 of the Rehabilitation Act of 1973? Obtain and review copies of informational materials given to parents.

Chapter 6

ETHICAL AND LEGAL ISSUES IN PSYCHOEDUCATIONAL ASSESSMENT

Psychological testing and assessment techniques, in common with most tools, can be used for a diversity of purposes, some destructive and some constructive, and their use cannot be separated from the training, competence, and ethical values of the clinical-user. (Matarazzo, 1986, p. 18)

This chapter focuses on ethical and legal issues associated with the assessment of individual students within the context of an established school psychologist–client relationship.

TESTING VERSUS ASSESSMENT

In their work with teachers, parents, and children (and in their own thinking), it is important for school psychologists to distinguish between *testing* and *assessment*. Testing and assessment are not synonymous, interchangeable terms (Matarazzo, 1986). A test is a tool that may be used to gather information as part of the assessment process. Assessment is a broader term. Mowder (1983, p. 145) defined the assessment process as "the planning, collection, and evaluation of information pertinent to a psychoeducational concern." A psychoeducational assessment of a student referred for individual evaluation is conducted by a psychologist trained to gather a variety of different types of information (e.g., review of school history and health records, observations, interviews, and test results) from a number of different sources (e.g., pupil, teacher, and parents) and to interpret or give meaning to that information in light of the unique characteristics of the pupil and his or her situation.

Practitioners also need to be familiar with the distinction between the medical and ecological models of school psychological assessment. In past years, practitioners often were trained to accept a medical model that views learning and behavior problems as a result of within-child disorders or disabilities (Ysseldyke & Christenson, 1988). In contrast, the ecological model encourages an assessment approach that takes into account the multiple factors that affect learning and behavior, including classroom variables, teacher and instructional variables, characteristics of the referred student, and support available from the home for school achievement. The ecological perspective has gained acceptance because it is viewed as potentially more beneficial to the child. To reverse a student's pattern of poor progress, systematic assessment of factors in the child's learning environment is needed (Ysseldyke & Christenson, 1988). Messick (1984) suggested that, ethically, a child should not be exposed to the risk of misdiagnosis unless deficiencies in instruction first have been ruled out (also NASP-PPE II.3.1).

The psychologist has certain preassessment responsibilities to the parent and pupil. After discussing these, we address ethical-legal concerns associated with assessment planning, selection of technically adequate tests and evaluation procedures, data collection and interpretation, report writing, and sharing findings. Nonbiased assessment and projective personality assessment then are discussed. The final portions of the chapter focus on the professional issues of competence and autonomy in conducting psychoeducational evaluations and the use of computers in assessment.

Codes of ethics, professional testing standards, and law provide guidelines for psychological assessment in schools. The National Association of School Psychologists (NASP) "Principles for Professional Ethics" (2010a) and the American Psychological Association (APA)'s "Ethical Principles of Psychologists and Code of Conduct" (2002) each include ethical principles for psychological assessment. The *Standards for Educational and Psychological Testing*, or *Standards* (American Educational Research Association, American Psychological Association, & National Council on Measurement in Education, 1999), provide criteria for psychologists and educators to use in the evaluation of assessment practices. The *Standards* have no official legal status. However, the *Standards* have been referred to in federal regulations concerning acceptable testing practices, and they have been cited in Supreme Court cases as an authoritative source on issues concerning the technical adequacy of testing practices (Adler, 1993). As this book goes to press, the *Standards* are being revised and updated. Citations here are to the 1999 edition.

The Individuals with Disabilities Education Improvement Act of 2004 (IDEA) and Section 504 of the Rehabilitation Act of 1973 each outline legal requirements for evaluation procedures used in the identification of children with disabilities. The regulations for IDEA–Part B pertaining to tests and evaluation procedures are shown in Exhibit 6.1.

Exhibit 6.1 Excerpts from IDEA Regulations on Evaluation Procedures

§ 300.304 Evaluation procedures

(a) *Notice.* The public agency must provide notice to the parents of a child with a disability, in accordance with § 300.503, that describes any evaluation procedures the agency proposes to conduct.

(b) *Conduct of evaluation.* In conducting the evaluation, the public agency must—
  (1) Use a variety of assessment tools and strategies to gather relevant functional, developmental, and academic information about the child, including information provided by the parent, that may assist in determining—
    (i) Whether the child is a child with a disability under § 300.8; and (ii) The content of the child's IEP [individual education program], including information related to enabling the child to be involved in and progress in the general education curriculum (or for a preschool child, to participate in appropriate activities);
  (2) Not use any single procedure as the sole criterion for determining whether a child is a child with a disability and for determining an appropriate educational program for the child; and
  (3) Use technically sound instruments that may assess the relative contribution of cognitive and behavioral factors, in addition to physical or developmental factors.

(c) *Other evaluation procedures.* Each public agency must ensure that—
  (1) Assessments and other evaluation materials used to assess a child under this part—

(i) Are selected and administered so as not to be discriminatory on a racial or cultural basis;

(ii) Are provided and administered in the child's native language or other mode of communication and in the form most likely to yield accurate information on what the child knows and can do academically, developmentally, and functionally, unless it is clearly not feasible to so provide or administer;

(iii) Are used for the purposes for which the assessments or measures are valid and reliable;

(iv) Are administered by trained and knowledgeable personnel; and

(v) Are administered in accordance with any instructions provided by the producer of the assessments.

(2) Assessments and other evaluation materials include those tailored to assess specific areas of educational need and not merely those that are designed to provide a single general intelligence quotient.

(3) Assessments are selected and administered so as best to ensure that if an assessment is administered to a child with impaired sensory, manual, or speaking skills, the assessment results accurately reflect the child's aptitude or achievement level or whatever other factors the test purports to measure, rather than reflecting the child's impaired sensory, manual, or speaking skills (unless those skills are the factors that the test purports to measure).

(4) The child is assessed in all areas related to the suspected disability, including, if appropriate, health, vision, hearing, social and emotional status, general intelligence, academic performance, communicative status, and motor abilities;

(5) Assessments of children with disabilities who transfer from one public agency to another public agency in the same academic year are coordinated with those children's prior and subsequent schools, as necessary and as expeditiously as possible, consistent with § 300.301(d)(2) and (e), to ensure prompt completion of full evaluations.

(6) In evaluating each child with a disability under §§ 300.304 through 300.306, the evaluation is sufficiently comprehensive to identify all of the child's special education and related services needs, whether or not commonly linked to the disability category in which the child has been classified.

(7) Assessment tools and strategies that provide relevant information that directly assists persons in determining the educational needs of the child are provided. (Authority: 20 U.S.C. 1414[b][1–3], 1412[a][6][B])

PREASSESSMENT RESPONSIBILITIES

Consistent with the ethical obligation "to respect the right of persons to participate in decisions affecting their own welfare" (NASP-PPE I.1), school psychologists "encourage and promote parent participation in school decisions affecting their children" (NASP-PPE I.1.1). However, as will be discussed here and in Chapter 7, not all of their assessment services require informed parent consent.

Parental Involvement and Consent

Practitioners are ethically obligated to seek informed consent to establish a psychologist-client relationship for the purpose of conducting a school psychological evaluation of a student (NASP-PPE I.1.2), and consent, oral or written, should be appropriately documented (APA-EP 3.10d, 9.03; NASP-PPE I.1.3; *Standards*, p. 85). Consent is given by the parent of a minor child or another adult acting in the place of a parent. A student who has reached the age of majority or who is an emancipated minor typically may consent on his or her own behalf (see Chapter 3).[1] Under IDEA, written consent (34 C.F.R. § 300.9) of the parent is needed to conduct an initial evaluation of a child to determine if the child has a disability as defined in the law. However, it is important to understand that parent consent for an initial evaluation "must not be construed as consent for the initial provision of special education and related services" (34 C.F.R. § 300.300[a][1][ii]); that is, parents have a legal right to consent to an evaluation but may later refuse special education and related services even if their child is found to be a child with a disability under IDEA.

Parent consent also is required for subsequent reevaluations, unless the school can demonstrate that it has taken reasonable measures to obtain consent and the child's parent failed to respond (34 C.F.R. § 300.300[c]). Parent consent is not required for a review of existing student data as part of an evaluation or reevaluation (34 C.F.R. § 300.300[d][1][i]). In addition, the screening of a student by a teacher or specialist to determine appropriate instructional strategies for curriculum implementation is not considered to be an evaluation requiring parental consent under IDEA (34 C.F.R. § 300.302). (Also see Chapter 7.)

Professional standards and IDEA are highly similar with regard to the necessary components of the informed consent agreement for psychoeducational assessment. According to the *Standards* (Standard 8.4) and consistent with IDEA (34 C.F.R. § 300.9), the parent granting permission for the psychoeducational evaluation should be made aware of the reasons for the assessment, the type of tests and evaluation procedures to be used, what the assessment results will be used for, the types of records that will be created, and who will have access to those records. This information must be presented to the parent in his or her native language or other mode of communication (also see NASP-PPE I.1.3). Parents must be informed that their consent is voluntary and they may revoke it at any time (34 C.F.R. § 300.9; also NASP-PPE I.1). School psychologists also are ethically obligated to "respect the wishes of parents who object to school psychological services and attempt to guide parents to alternative resources" (NASP-PPE I.1.5).

Many states and school districts have developed materials for parents describing their evaluation procedures and the assessment instruments used by multidisciplinary team members. Many districts also have developed forms for parents to sign to consent to a school psychological evaluation of their child. However, school-based practitioners are cautioned to ensure that they have a shared understanding with the individual providing consent regarding the nature and scope of the proposed psychological evaluation. For example, are parents providing informed consent for an evaluation of whether their child has a disability as defined by IDEA, or a disability as defined by Section 504 of the Rehabilitation Act of 1973? Or are they providing consent for psychological diagnosis (e.g., *Diagnostic and Statistical Manual of Mental Disorders* (*DSM-IV*) (American Psychiatric Association, 2000)? Although *DSM-IV criteria* may be used in identifying children with disabilities under IDEA or Section 504 (e.g., autism or attention deficits),

---

[1]The term *parent* will be used here to refer to an individual who has the legal authority to provide consent and make decisions.

parents and eligible students should be given an explicit choice regarding whether they consent to a *DSM-IV diagnosis* as part of a school district's psychoeducational evaluation.

Most parents cooperate with school attempts to secure approval for psychoeducational assessment. However, under IDEA, if the parent fails to provide consent for an initial evaluation of a child with a suspected disability, the school *may* use mediation and other due process procedures (e.g., a hearing by an impartial hearing officer) in an effort to overrule parent failure to consent (34 C.F.R. § 300.300[a][3][i]). However, schools are *not required* to pursue an initial evaluation of a child with a suspected disability if the parent fails to provide consent to do so (34 C.F.R. § 300.300[a][3][i]). Furthermore, if the parent of a child who is homeschooled or parentally placed in a private school does not provide consent for an initial evaluation or reevaluation under IDEA, or fails to respond to a request for consent, the school may not use IDEA consent override procedures and it is not required to consider the child as eligible for services (34 C.F.R. § 300.300[d][4]).

Consistent with our ethical standards for consent, school psychologists should be aware that under IDEA the parents or an adult student may withdraw consent for assessment or special education placement or services at any time, and this withdrawal of consent must be honored (34 C.F.R. 300.9[c][1]). If a parent revokes consent for assessment, it is "not retroactive," that is, "it does not negate an action that has occurred after the consent was given and before the consent was revoked" (34 C.F.R. 300.9[c][2]). School psychologists should not destroy records of a partially completed evaluation without first notifying the parent.

School psychologists also should be aware that the requirement for parent consent prior to initiating an individual psychoeducational assessment does not extend to educational testing that is done as part of regular school activities (Standard 8.4; also IDEA 34 C.F.R. § 300.300[d][1][ii]). Ethically, parents should "be notified prior to the administration of school-or classroom-wide screenings for mental health problems and given the opportunity to remove their child or adolescent from participation" because such screenings may be more intrusive of personal and family privacy than expected in the course of typical school activities (NASP-PPE I.1.1; also see Chapter 9). Parental permission for testing done as part of school-based research is discussed in Chapter 10.

Responsibilities to the Student

In addition to prior parental consent to initiate a psychoeducational evaluation of an individual student, school psychologists also have a number of obligations to the student. As noted in Chapter 3, children are not seen as *legally* competent to make autonomous decisions about whether to participate in a psychological assessment; minors have no *legal* right "to consent, assent, or object to proposed psychoeducational evaluations" (Bersoff, 1983, p. 153). In our opinion, it is ethically permissible to assess a minor child without his or her explicit assent if the assessment promises to benefit his or her welfare (e.g., the planning of an individualized instructional program to enhance student learning). We concur with Corrao and Melton (1988) that it is disrespectful to solicit the assent of the child if refusal will not be honored (NASP-PPE I.1.4). Consistent with good testing practices, practitioners need to make full use of their professional skills to gain the active cooperation of the student.

Every student has the right to be fully informed about the scope and nature of the assessment process, whether or not the student is given a choice to assent to or refuse services. Practitioners are obligated ethically to explain the assessment process to the pupil in a manner that is understood by the student (NASP-PPE I.1.4). This explanation includes how the assessment results will be used, who will receive information, and possible implications of results. Even preschoolers and children who are developmentally disabled should receive an explanation in a language they can understand as to why they are being seen by the school psychologist (Standard 8.4).

ASSESSMENT PLANNING

Each phase of the assessment process—assessment planning, information gathering, and interpretation of findings—requires data-based decision making and professional judgment (Ysseldyke et al., 2006). School psychologists are obligated to make decisions that promote the welfare of the student in each phase of the assessment process and to accept responsibility for decisions made (NASP-PPE I, II.2, II.3). Case 6.1 illustrates how psychological test results can have a powerful impact on the lives of children.

Five Ethical-Legal Concerns

Psychologists have long recognized that the use of an IQ score in isolation is not sound practice in the identification of cognitive impairment. However, prior to the passage of Pub. L. No. 94-142 in 1975 (now IDEA), IQ test scores were frequently the sole basis for labeling children as mentally retarded (Matarazzo, 1986). The 1960s and 1970s were years of increasing court and federal government involvement in the regulation of school psychological testing as a result of this type of misuse of tests.

Five broad ethical-legal concerns emerge from an analysis of our codes of ethics, professional standards, and federal laws that address psychological assessment: Psychologists must strive to ensure that psychoeducational evaluations are *multifaceted, comprehensive, fair, valid,* and *useful.* We address each of these concerns briefly in the following pages, and then discuss the selection of technically adequate assessment instruments.

Multifaceted

Psychoeducational assessment of a child with learning or behavior problems must be based on information "gathered from multiple measures and multiple informants"

Case 6.1

Joseph McNulty was the unwanted child of a woman who was raped. He was placed in Willowbrook State Hospital in 1966 at the age of 4, after being diagnosed as "an imbecile" on the basis of an IQ score of 32. Subsequent reevaluations suggested that Joseph had some hearing problems, but those findings were "initially ignored or simply not seen." Joseph grew up among children and adults diagnosed with severe mental retardation, and during his stay at Willowbrook, he was given high doses of drugs, including Valium, Thorazine, and Haldol. In 1976, when Joseph was 14, an audiologist observed that Joseph showed a greater interest in learning than other youth with severe cognitive impairments and confirmed that Joseph was hearing impaired. After years of intensive therapy, Joseph's IQ tested in the normal range in 1980. In his late 20s, Joseph was not yet able to live independently, and he continued to need therapy and training. In 1988, he won a $1.5 million damage suit against the state of New York for medical malpractice. (Adapted from Bauder, 1989, p. B-1.)

(Miller & Nickerson, 2007, p. 48). Under IDEA and consistent with codes of ethics, evaluation procedures must include findings from a variety of assessment tools and strategies "to gather relevant functional, developmental, and academic information, including information provided by the parent" (34 C.F.R. § 304[b][1], also [c][2]; NASP-PPE II.3.3). School psychologists base their opinions on "information and techniques sufficient to substantiate their findings" (APA-EP 9.01). No important decisions (e.g., special education eligibility) should be made on the basis of findings from a single test score or assessment procedure (34 C.F.R. § 300.304[b][2]; NASP-PPE II.3.3; Standard 13.7).

Comprehensive

Children with suspected disabilities must be assessed "in all areas related to the suspected disability, including, if appropriate, health, vision, hearing, social and emotional status, general intelligence, academic performance, communicative status, and motor abilities" (34 C.F.R. § 300.304[c][4]; also NASP-PPE II.3.4). As was apparent in Case 6.1, failure to have a child evaluated for possible sensory impairments can result in misdiagnosis with tragic consequences for the child.

Fair

School psychologists strive to conduct fair and valid assessments. "They actively pursue knowledge of the student's disabilities, and developmental, cultural, linguistic, and experiential background and then select, administer, and interpret assessment instruments and procedures in light of those characteristics" (NASP-PPE II.3.5; also APA-EP 9.02). The IDEA outlines requirements for the assessment of children with limited English proficiency, pupils with disabilities, and those from culturally different backgrounds.

Limited English Proficiency. Under IDEA, tests and other assessment tools used in the evaluation of children with suspected disabilities are "provided and administered in the child's native language or other mode of communication and in the form most likely to yield accurate information on what the child knows and can do academically, developmentally, and functionally, unless it is not feasible to so provide or administer" (34 C.F.R. § 300.304[c][1][ii]; also APA-EP 9.02; *Standards*, pp. 91–100; NASP-PPE II.3.5). Furthermore, materials and procedures used to assess a child with limited English proficiency are selected and administered to ensure that they measure the extent to which the child has a disability and needs special education, rather than measuring the child's English language skills (34 C.F.R. § 300.304[c][3]). For the purpose of an evaluation of a child, *native language* is defined as "the language normally used by the child in the home or learning environment" (34 C.F.R. § 300.29[a][2]).

According to Dana (2000), Ortiz (2008), and Paredes Scribner (2002), among others, competent assessment of children from culturally and linguistically diverse backgrounds requires the practitioner to gather information about the family's degree of acculturation and to assess the child's language proficiency *prior* to selecting assessment tools. For children who come from homes where English is not the primary language, it is important to assess both the child's native and English language proficiency. This assessment should include evaluation of spoken and written language skills in each language, using both formal and informal measures, to obtain a full picture of functional language usage (Lopez, 1997). Language proficiency information is needed to guide selection and interpretation of measures of aptitude, achievement, and adaptive behavior and in planning instruction and interventions (see Paredes Scribner, 2002). Even if a child from a culturally different background demonstrates some proficiency in spoken or written English, it is important to remember that commonly used tests (e.g., Wechsler Intelligence Test for Children IV, Wechsler, 2003) tap the language, symbols, and knowledge children encounter in the dominant U.S. culture and schools. Consequently, practitioners must also consider the degree of acculturation of the child and his or her family in selecting and interpreting assessment tools (see "Nonbiased Assessment" later in this chapter).

The NASP maintains a directory of bilingual school psychologists who may be available to assist in the assessment of a child with limited English proficiency. When a bilingual psychologist is not available and the services of an interpreter are used during psychological assessment, the psychologist is obligated ethically to obtain consent for the use of the interpreter, ensure that the interpreter is adequately trained to assist in the assessment (including training in maintaining confidentiality), and describe any limitations regarding the validity of the results obtained (APA-EP 9.03; NASP-PPE II.3.6; also *Standards*, pp. 95–96). In addition, the practitioner is obligated to ensure that he or she has the necessary skills to work effectively with an interpreter (Lopez, 2008).

When assessing the cognitive abilities, adaptive behavior, or achievement of a child whose native language is not English, the examiner should select tests or portions of tests that do not require knowledge of English. Practitioners are advised not to translate (or have an interpreter translate) items from a test developed for English-speaking examinees into the child's native language, because translation of an item is likely to change item difficulty (Figueroa, 1990; Rogers et al., 1999; *Standards*, pp. 92, 95). An on-the-spot translation of a test or subtest thus results in scores of unknown validity. In accordance with the *Standards*, when a test is translated, it must be restandardized in the new language. The test publisher is obligated to describe the methods used in establishing the adequacy of the translation and the evidence for reliability and validity of the translated test's scores. Since many dialects and differences in word usage exist among groups with the same official language (e.g., Spanish), the test producer should identify the intended target linguistic groups for the test (e.g., Cubans, Puerto Ricans, or Mexicans) and provide evidence of score validity for each linguistic group (Standard 9.7). (See Rhodes, Ochoa, & Ortiz, 2005, for additional information on assessing linguistically diverse children.)

Children with Disabilities.   IDEA–Part B also mandates careful selection of assessment procedures for children with sensory, motor, or speech impairments. Children with deafness or blindness or no written language must be evaluated using the mode of communication that he or she uses, such as sign language, Braille, or oral communication (34 C.F.R. § 300.29). Furthermore, assessments are "selected and administered so as best to ensure that if an assessment is administered to a child with impaired sensory, manual, or speaking skills, the assessment results accurately reflect that child's aptitude or achievement level or whatever other factors the test purports to measure, rather than reflecting the child's impaired sensory, manual, or speaking skills (unless those are the factors which the test purports to measure)" (34 C.F.R. § 300.304[c][3]; also see *Standards*, 1999).

Ethnic Minority Children.   Codes of ethics, professional standards, and special education law also mandate *nonbiased* assessment of children from diverse cultural, ethnic, and racial backgrounds. As the issue of bias is complex, it is discussed separately later in the chapter.

Valid

"School psychologists use assessment techniques and practices that the profession considers to be responsible, research-based practice" (NASP-PPE II.3.2). They "select assessment instruments and strategies that are reliable and valid for the child and the purpose of the assessment" (NASP-PPE II.3.2; also 34 C.F.R. § 300.304[c][1][iii]; APA-EP 9.02; *Standards*, pp. 9–24). To ensure reliable and valid findings, IDEA also requires that assessment and evaluation materials be administered by trained and knowledgeable personnel, in accordance with any instructions provided by the producer of such assessments (34 C.F.R. § 300.304[c][1][iv, v]; also NASP-PPE II.3.2, II.5.2).

Useful

School psychologists use their expertise in assessment for the purpose of improving the quality of life for the child (NASP-PPE Introduction). Evaluation procedures are selected to provide a profile of the child's strengths and difficulties that will assist parents, educators, and other helping professionals to make informed decisions about the child's needs and aid in instructional planning. The IDEA requires that assessment tools and strategies "provide relevant information that directly assists persons in determining the educational needs of the child" (34 C.F.R. § 300.304[c][7]).

Selecting Technically Adequate Instruments

School psychology practitioners select assessment techniques that are consistent with the highest standard for responsible professional practices (APA-EP 9.02; NASP-PPE II.3). The *Standards* were developed to guide selection of instruments for a variety of different measurement applications (e.g., psychodiagnosis, applicant selection for jobs and colleges, program evaluation, research) in diverse settings. Consequently, absolute psychometric standards of technical adequacy based on specific statistical procedures are not prescribed. Evaluating the adequacy of assessment practices ultimately rests with the test user and involves professional judgment based on knowledge of behavior science, psychometrics, and assessment standards for the field; the degree to which the test developer has met the intent of the *Standards*; and knowledge of alternatives (*Standards*, p. 4).

When assessment results play an important role in decision making for the individual pupil, the school psychologist is obligated to choose the best available assessment procedures. Considerable agreement exists in the school psychology literature that a variety of different types of information are appropriate within the framework of a *successive-levels model* of psychoeducational assessment. Consistent with this model, primary emphasis is given to scores and information from the most reliable and valid sources (composite scores on technically adequate measures) in interpretation and decision making. However, findings from less reliable and valid sources (scores on various subtest groups, individual subtest scores, performance on individual items, observations, and impressions) may also play a role in generating hypotheses about the student's profile of abilities, skills, and needs. These hypotheses then may be confirmed or abandoned by collecting additional information that verifies (cross-validates) or disconfirms the hypothesis (Kaufman, 1994).

According to the *Standards*, evaluating the technical adequacy of assessment instruments and procedures involves careful consideration of the evidence of test *reliability*, *validity*, and the *adequacy of the standardization norms*.

Test Reliability

Test reliability refers to the consistency of test scores when a testing procedure is repeated on a group of individuals. Two types of reliability information should be reported in the manuals for tests to be used in psychoeducational decision making: test stability and internal consistency reliability. *Test stability* or *test-retest reliability* studies provide information about the consistency of scores from one testing session to another. This information typically is obtained by administering the same test to the same group of examinees on two occasions and correlating the resultant test scores (Sattler, 2008).

Internal consistency reliability is based on scores obtained during one administration of the test. The reliability coefficient obtained in this manner provides information about the extent to which items on the test are intercorrelated. According to the *Standards* (p. 28), coefficients of internal consistency should not be substituted for estimates of stability unless evidence supports that interpretation in a particular context.

How reliable must a test be? There is no simple answer to this question. Shorter, less time-consuming, and less reliable measures may be adequate when tests are selected to provide information about groups rather than individuals (as in program evaluation and research) or when the results are used for decisions that are tentative and reversible (as when teacher-made tests are used to group children for reading instruction). A review of the literature suggests that some consensus exists in the field of school psychology about desirable levels of reliability for tests used in the schools. Reliability coefficients of .60 to .65 are seen as adequate for measures of group performance, coefficients of .80 to .85 are acceptable for screening instruments, and correlations of .90 or above are desirable for instruments that play a key role in making educational decisions about individual pupils (Hammill, Brown, & Bryant, 1989; Sattler, 2008).

Test producers have primary responsibility to obtain and report reliability information (*Standards*, p. 30). Unlike some types of validity information (e.g., predictive validity) that require a longitudinal design, reliability data can be gathered during test development and standardization and should be included in the supporting manuals when the test is marketed. The *Standards* recommend that reliability estimates be provided for each total score, subscore, or combination of scores that the test reports (Standard 2.1). Both internal consistency and test stability estimates should be reported for each age or grade level and population for which the test is intended, along with a description of the research procedures and sample used in the reliability studies (Standards 2.4, 2.12). The test user is responsible for evaluating this information to ensure that the test selected is reliable for its intended use (NASP-PPE II.3.2).

Test Validity

Validity is the single most important consideration in evaluating tests and assessment procedures (*Standards*, p. 9). Validity refers to the degree to which a test or assessment procedure measures what it purports to measure. However, "no test is valid for all purposes or valid in the abstract"; tests are valid (or not valid) for a specific purpose (Sattler, 2008, p. 117). The IDEA requires that assessment materials used in the identification of children with suspected disabilities "are used for purposes for which the assessments or measures are valid and reliable" (34 C.F.R. § 300.304[c][iii]).

As noted in the *Standards* (p. 11), "Validity is a unitary concept. It is the degree to which all the accumulated evidence supports the intended interpretation of test scores for the proposed purpose." However, test producers gather and report validity information in a number of different ways. A distinction is often made among content-related, criterion-related, and construct-related validity. *Content-related validity* refers to the degree to which the sample of items, tasks, or questions on a test is representative of the domain that the test is supposed to measure (Sattler, 2008). Test authors are obligated to specify adequately the universe of content that a test is intended to represent and provide evidence that the test content agrees with specifications of what the test should measure (Standard 1.6).

Criterion-related validity refers to evidence that test scores are related systematically to one or more other measures (Sattler, 2008). Criterion-related validity typically is reported as a correlation between scores on the test and scores on some type of outcome of interest called the "criterion" measure. As suggested in the *Standards*, the key issue is: "How accurately do test scores predict criterion performance?" (p. 14). Two types of criterion-related evidence may be provided. Concurrent validity studies involve obtaining information from the predictor and criterion measures at the same point in time. Predictive validity studies involve administering the criterion measure after a specified time interval to evaluate how well a test correlates with future performance.

What levels of criterion-related validity are acceptable for tests used in psychoeducational assessment? Again, no simple answer exists. Estimates of criterion-related validity are affected by a number of factors, including the extent to which the predictor and criterion tests measure the same traits and abilities, the reliability of the predictor and criterion measures, the heterogeneity or spread of scores on either measure, and the time interval between the administration of the two measures (see Gregory, 2007).

According to the *Standards*, criterion-related validity studies should be described by the test producer in enough detail to evaluate the adequacy of the research design and findings. This description should include the types of test takers; research procedures, including the time interval between tests; and statistical analysis, including any correction for attenuation of range of scores (Standards 1.15, 1.18). The psychometric characteristics of the criterion measure also should be described in detail (Standard 1.16).

Construct-related validity is "a term used to indicate that the test scores are to be interpreted as indicating the test taker's standing on the psychological construct measured by the test" (*Standards*, p. 174). This type of validity focuses on the test score as a measure of a construct (psychological characteristic or trait) such as intelligence, scholastic ability, reading comprehension, anxiety, or sociability. No single study can establish the construct validity of a test or other measure (Messick, 1995). Evidence for construct validity may be based on studies of test content (item analysis, factor analysis) and an accumulation of evidence based on a multitrait, multimethod construct validation paradigm. This model of construct validation suggests that evidence should be provided showing that the test correlates well with other measures of the same construct (convergent evidence) but does not correlate highly with measures of theoretically unrelated constructs (discriminate evidence) (Campbell & Fiske, 1959).

How do you decide whether a test instrument is valid? Both the quality and quantity of the supporting evidence are important in evaluating the validity of a test for the child being evaluated (*Standards*, p. 17). Although the test manual and supportive materials are starting points for test review, practitioners are obligated ethically to keep abreast of the research related to the validity of tests used in psychoeducational assessment (NASP-PPE II.3.2).

Adequacy of Test Norms

Norm-referenced tests allow us to interpret a child's test performance in comparison with a reference group of children of the same age, in the same grade, or perhaps with the same type of disability. In selecting norm-referenced instruments, the school psychologist has a responsibility to evaluate the adequacy and appropriateness of the test norms for the intended use of the test. Test norms must be: (a) based on a sample representative of the intended target population for the test, (b) recent, and (c) appropriate for the child being evaluated.

Test producers have a responsibility to identify the intended target population for a test and to describe fully the extent to which the norm group is characteristic of that specific population. Norming studies should be described in the test manual or supportive materials in sufficient detail for the user to evaluate their adequacy and appropriateness for intended test use (Standard 4.6). Test users have a responsibility to evaluate the extent to which the children they test are represented in the published norms (NASP-PPE II.3.2).

INFORMATION GATHERING

Ethical-legal concerns that arise during information gathering include ensuring that assessment procedures are administered by qualified examiners under appropriate conditions and that family and pupil privacy are respected.

Invasion of Privacy

The school psychologist seeks to gather the information needed to develop a picture of the pupil that is comprehensive enough to be useful in decision making and in planning appropriate interventions. However, in responsible psychological assessment, the practitioner also remains sensitive to pupil and family privacy (Matarazzo, 1986). School psychologists are obligated ethically to respect the privacy of others (APA-EP Principle E; NASP-PPE I.2). They do not seek or store personal information about the student, parents, or others that is not needed in the provision of services (APA-EP 4.04; NASP-PPE I.2.2).

Assessment Conditions

School psychologists must ensure that the assessment conditions are in the best interests of the pupil being evaluated. The testing environment should be of "reasonable comfort and with minimal distractions" (Standard 5.4); otherwise, findings may not be accurate and valid. Testing done by computers should be monitored to ensure that results are not adversely affected by a lack of computer test-taking skills or by problems with the equipment (*Standards*, p. 62; also NASP-PPE II.3.2).

In accordance with professional standards and law, tests and other assessment procedures must be "administered by trained and knowledgeable personnel . . . in accordance with any instructions provided by the producer of the assessments" (34 C.F.R. § 300.304[c][1][iv, v]). Practitioners are obligated to "follow carefully the standardized procedures for administration and scoring specified by the test developer, unless the situation or test taker's disability dictates that an exception should be made" (Standard 5.1). Modifications are based on carefully considered professional judgment. Furthermore, if an assessment is not conducted under standard conditions, a description of the extent to which it varied from standard conditions should be included in the evaluation report (APA-EP 9.06; NASP-PPE II.3.2; Standard 5.2).

Psychological and educational tests should be administered only by individuals qualified to do so (APA-EP 9.07). "School psychologists do not promote or condone the use of restricted psychological and educational tests or other assessment tools or procedures by individuals who are not qualified to use them" (NASP-PPE II.5.2).

Test Security

The development of valid assessment instruments requires extensive research and considerable expense. Disclosure of the underlying principles or specific content of a test is likely to decrease its validity for future examinees. Disclosure of test content also may infringe on the intellectual property and/or copyright interests of the test producer (APA, 1996). The APA's code states that psychologists are obligated to "make reasonable efforts to maintain the integrity and security of test materials and other assessment techniques consistent with law, contractual obligations, and in a manner that permits adherence to this Ethics Code" (APA-EP 9.11; also NASP-PPE II.5, II.5.1–3; Standards 11.7, 11.8). (Also see Chapter 3, "Parent Access to Test Protocols.")

ASSESSMENT INTERPRETATION

"School psychologists adequately interpret findings and present results in clear, understandable terms so that the recipient can make informed choices" (NASP-PPE II.3.8). Psychologists also are obligated to ensure that assessment results are useful in planning interventions (34 C.F.R. § 300.304[c][7]). Response to intervention (RTI), curriculum-based assessment, and criterion-referenced testing are assessment strategies that have gained popularity because they facilitate the linking of data gathered to appropriate instructional strategies.

As noted previously, in reporting assessment results, psychologists indicate any reservations that exist concerning validity or reliability due to assessment circumstances or norm appropriateness (APA-EP 9.06; NASP-PPE II.3.2). School psychologists may be asked to make recommendations for a student based on findings from a psychoeducational evaluation conducted by another psychologist. This might happen, for example, when a child moves from one locale to another. According to NASP's code of ethics, "It is permissible for school psychologists to make recommendations based solely on a review of existing records. However, they should utilize a representative sample of records, and explain the basis for, and the limitations of, their recommendations" (NASP-PPE II.3.7; also APA-EP 9.01b, 9.01c).

Classification

Depending on his or her work setting and prior training, a school psychologist might use one or more of several different diagnostic or classification systems. In school-based practice, practitioners are most typically involved in determination of whether a student is eligible for special education under the IDEA and/or whether the student has an impairment and is eligible for accommodations in accordance with Section 504 of the Rehabilitation Act of 1973. Some school psychologists also have been trained to use the *Diagnostic and Statistical Manual of Mental Disorders* (*DSM-IV*, American Psychiatric Association, 2000) to diagnose mental disorders. As noted previously, *decisions regarding eligibility under the IDEA or Section 504 must be based on the disability criteria outlined in those laws.*

When included in a report written by or for a physician or mental health care provider, a *DSM-IV* diagnosis may be helpful in assisting a student to acquire appropriate services. However, school-based practitioners should not render a *DSM-IV* diagnosis without the prior consent of the parent (or adult student). Dr. Foster (Case 6.2), like other school psychologists, needs to think carefully about the privacy rights of students and their families and the meaning of the "need to know" principle when making decisions about what information to disclose to others within the school setting. For this reason, school-based practitioners, in collaboration with parents, should decide whether it is in the child's best interests to include a *DSM-IV* diagnosis in a multidisciplinary report for use by the group of persons determining eligibility under the IDEA or Section 504, and whether others in the school setting "need to know" the *DSM-IV* diagnosis.

Legally and ethically, practitioners also are obligated to ensure that when classification labels are assigned they are based on valid assessment procedures and sound professional

---

Case 6.2

After completing his PhD, Sam Foster became a licensed psychologist as well as a certified school psychologist and has continued to work as a school-based practitioner. He has received a referral to evaluate Ana, a 12-year-old student in sixth grade, to determine whether she might be eligible for special education services as a student with a learning disability in mathematics calculation and reasoning under the IDEA. Ana's school records indicated that she is a shy and anxious student who has struggled in math since first grade. Her mathematics achievement test scores are below the 4th percentile, even after multiple individualized interventions were attempted in the fourth and fifth grades. Ana's father has consented to a school psychological evaluation in hopes that his daughter will receive additional individualized help in mathematics.

As a result of his interview with Ana, her father, and her teachers, Dr. Foster learns that Ana's mother died after a long battle with cancer when Ana was in third grade. Ana's school records show many absences due to illness and that she frequently goes home early from school because of complaints of a headache or upset stomach. Ana's father reports that their family doctor has found no medical cause for these recurring symptoms.

Based on his observations, assessment results, and interview findings, Dr. Foster determines that, in addition to possible eligibility under the IDEA as learning disabled in mathematics, Ana meets the diagnostic criteria for somatoform disorder, a diagnosis based on the *Diagnostic and Statistical Manual of Mental Disorders* (American Psychiatric Association, 2000). Dr. Foster recognizes that he has a number of ethical-legal decisions to make regarding what information to include and what to exclude from his section of the multidisciplinary report that is being prepared for the individualized education program (IEP) team.

---

judgment. Furthermore, when labels are used, "The least stigmatizing labels, consistent with accurate representation, should always be assigned" (Standard 8.8).

Report Writing and Sharing Findings

School psychologists typically share their assessment findings in written reports and orally in meetings with the individuals involved.

Report Writing

The written psychological report documents the assessment process and outcomes and outlines recommendations to assist the child. A school psychological evaluation report may be used in making special education decisions and identifying instructional needs. It may serve as a history of performance for subsequent evaluations of pupil progress or deterioration. It also may be used as a communication tool in referrals to professionals outside the school setting (e.g., neurologist, clinical psychologist) and as documentation in legal proceeding such as hearings and court procedures (Sattler, 2008).

In preparing school psychological evaluation reports, practitioners must consider their obligation to ensure that their findings are understandable and useful to the intended recipient (NASP-PPE II.3.8), as well as their obligation to safeguard the confidentiality of sensitive private information about the student and family (NASP-PPE I.2). While parents (and eligible students) have access to all school psychological assessment findings, school-based practitioners, in collaboration with parents, need to make careful choices about what information to include in psychological reports prepared for different purposes. It may be ethically appropriate (and legally advisable) to exclude sensitive family and student information from a report written for the purpose of making special education decisions or identifying instructional needs. However, *with parent permission*, this information could be shared with others in the school setting or included in a school psychological report prepared for a professional outside the school. (Also see Chapter 3.)

School psychologists also accept responsibility for their professional work (NASP-PPE II.2). They "review all of their written documents for accuracy, signing them only when correct. They may add an addendum, dated and signed, to a previously submitted report if information is found to be inaccurate or incomplete" (NASP-PPE II.2.1). School psychologists who supervise students and interns are responsible for the professional practices of their supervisees (NASP-PPE II.2.4; IV.4.2). Reports prepared by school psychology graduate students should be cosigned by the supervising school psychologist. The IDEA requires that parents be given a copy of their child's evaluation report (34 C.F.R. § 300.306[a][2]).

Sharing Findings with the Parent and Pupil

School psychologists secure continuing parental involvement by honest and forthright reporting of their findings within the promised time frame (APA-EP 9.10; NASP-PPE III; Standard 5.10), and they "encourage and promote parental participation in designing interventions for their children" (NASP-PPE II.3.10). Practitioners "discuss with parents the recommendations and plans for assisting their children. This discussion takes into account the ethnic/cultural values of the family and includes alternatives that may be available" (NASP-PPE II.3.10). (Also see Chapter 8.)

School psychologists also discuss the outcomes of the psychoeducational evaluation with the child. Recommendations for program changes or additional services are discussed with the student, along with any alternatives that may be available (NASP-PPE II.3.11). Consistent with ethical principles, students should be afforded opportunities to participate in decisions that affect them.

NONBIASED ASSESSMENT

In Chapter 1, we suggested that psychologists have an ethical obligation to help ensure that the science of psychology is used to promote human welfare in the schools, neighborhoods, and communities in which they work and in the larger society (also NASP-PPE IV). Unfortunately, American history is replete with examples of the ways the supposed science of psychology has been used to oppress ethnic, racial, and linguistic minorities in the United States and to justify discriminatory practices in society and in our schools. For example, following the introduction of the Stanford-Binet Intelligence Scales in 1916 and the development of group ability tests, IQ tests were used to characterize Negroes as a genetically inferior race and justify discriminatory treatment in society, to characterize non-Anglo immigrants as intellectually inferior and therefore undesirable, and in support of laws allowing sterilization of women of below-normal IQ without their consent (Gould, 1996). In schools, IQ and other mental ability tests have been used to segregate ethnic, racial, and linguistic minority pupils in inferior, dead-end classes; to deny them access to the college preparatory curriculum; to misclassify them as retarded; and to justify their placement in poorly equipped special education classes taught by inadequately trained staff (see Exhibit 4.2). School psychology practitioners need to be knowledgeable about the history of the misuse of tests in the United States so that they can understand the roots of contemporary controversies regarding the use of IQ tests with children from diverse backgrounds, as well as the concerns of parents of ethnic, racial, and linguistic minority children referred for psychological testing (also see Ortiz, 2008).

Today, nonbiased assessment is both an ethical and a legal mandate. The IDEA requires that assessment and other evaluation materials must be "selected and administered so as not to be discriminatory on a racial or cultural basis" (34 C.F.R. § 300.304[c][1][i]). Our codes of ethics and professional standards include multiple statements regarding valid and fair assessment of clients from culturally diverse backgrounds. The APA's code of ethics addresses these issues in General Principles D (Justice) and E (Respect for People's Rights and Dignity), and in Standards 2.01 (Competence), 2.05 (Delegation of Work to Others), 3.01 (Unfair Discrimination), 9.02 (Use of Assessments), and 9.06 (Interpreting Assessment Results). The NASP's code also includes multiple statements with regard to valid and fair assessment of diverse students (NASP-PPE I.3, II.3.2, II.3.5, II.3.6). In addition, the *Standards* include extensive discussion of fairness in testing.

Although the ethical, professional, and legal mandate for nonbiased assessment is clear, it is not easy to translate the nondiscrimination principle into practice. As Reschly and Bersoff (1999, p. 1085) noted, "widely varying" interpretations of the meaning of nondiscriminatory assessment have appeared in the professional literature and court interpretations. Ortiz (2008) describes nondiscriminatory assessment as:

> a wide range of approaches that collectively seek to uncover as fairly as possible relevant information and data upon which decisions regarding functioning and performance can equitably be based. In other words, nondiscriminatory assessment is not a search for an unbiased test but rather a process that ensures every individual, not just those who are different in some way, is evaluated in the least discriminatory manner possible. (p. 662)

Culture and Acculturation

There appears to be growing agreement in the professional literature that competent assessment of children from culturally different backgrounds requires the practitioner to seek knowledge of the child's culture and how that background may influence development, behavior, and school learning and to gather information about the student's degree of acculturation (Dana, 2000; Ortiz, 2008; Rogers et al., 1999; *Standards*, p. 91).

With regard to the pupil's degree of acculturation, Dana (2000, p. 60) views *cultural orientation* on a continuum ranging from traditional (retention of original culture) to nontraditional (assimilation into the majority Anglo-American culture). Information about cultural orientation can be gathered through interviews with the pupil and his or her family. A number of acculturation measures also are available (see Aponte & Johnson, 2000). Information about acculturation should inform test selection, examiner interactional style, assessment interpretation, and intervention planning. The closer a pupil's cultural orientation falls toward the traditional end of the continuum, the greater the need for caution in use and interpretation of IQ measures that draw on knowledge of language, symbols, and information specific to the dominant U.S. culture. For some groups, such as African American children, information about *cultural identity* may assist in providing effective services (see Dana, 2000).

Test Bias

For the purposes of the following discussion, bias in assessment is discussed in terms of *test bias*, *bias in clinical application*, and *fairness of consequences*.

Test bias here refers to the psychometric adequacy of the instrument, that is, evidence that a test or procedure is not equally valid when used with children from differing ethnic or racial backgrounds (Messick, 1965, 1980; Reynolds, Lowe, & Saenz, 1999). In selecting tests for minority group children, the practitioner needs to ask, "Is this test a valid measure of what it purports to measure for examinees from this ethnic group?"

Test bias may be defined and evaluated in terms of content validity, criterion-related validity, and construct validity. "An item or subscale of a test is considered to be biased in content when it is demonstrated to be relatively more difficult for members of one group than another when the general ability level of the groups being compared is held constant and no reasonable theoretical rationale exists to explain group differences on the item (or subscale) in question" (Reynolds et al., 1999, p. 564).

The question of content bias is resolved by research that shows equal (or unequal) item difficulties for various groups (Flaugher, 1978). Biased items usually can be identified and eliminated during the test development phase. Reynolds et al. (1999) reviewed available studies and found little evidence of any consistent content bias in well-prepared, standardized tests when such tests are used with English-speaking examinees. When content bias was found, it accounted for a relatively small proportion of the variance (2% to 5%) in the group score differences associated with minority group membership.

Test bias may also be defined in terms of differential concurrent or predictive (criterion-related) validity. "A test is considered biased with respect to predictive validity if the inference drawn from the test score is not made with the smallest feasible random error or if there is constant error in an inference or prediction as a function of membership in a particular group" (Reynolds et al., 1999, p. 577). A test may be shown to be nonbiased in criterion-related validity if it predicts the criterion measure performance equally well for children from different ethnic backgrounds. Based on a review of the school psychology literature, R. T. Brown, Reynolds, and Whitaker (1999, p. 231) concluded that "empirical evidence overwhelmingly supports the conclusion that well-developed, currently-used mental tests are of equivalent predictive validity for American-born, English-speaking individuals regardless of their subgroup membership." Less is known about bias in adaptive behavior and personality assessment instruments.

Test bias may also be defined in terms of construct validity. "Bias exists in regard to construct validity when a test is shown to measure different hypothetical traits (psychological constructs) for different groups; that is, differing interpretations of a common performance are shown to be appropriate as a function of ethnicity, gender, or another variable of interest" (Reynolds et al., 1999, p. 573). Studies that show a test has the same factor structure for children from different ethnic backgrounds provide evidence that the test is measuring the same construct for different groups: that it is nonbiased with respect to construct validity. Reynolds et al. reported that "no consistent evidence of bias in construct validity" was found with any of the well-constructed and well-standardized tests they investigated (p. 577).

The *Standards* recommend that test developers research and report results of differential concurrent and predictive validity studies for various groups, particularly if test results may be used in making classification decisions (*Standards*, p. 79, Standard 7.1). The practitioner is obligated to evaluate the research on test bias when selecting instruments for ethnic minority children and to choose the fairest and most appropriate instruments available.

Bias in Clinical Application

Bias in clinical application refers to fairness in administration, interpretation, and decision making. The use of biased tests may lead to unfair decisions. However, poor decisions can be made on the basis of fair tests because of atmosphere bias and bias in interpretation or decision making. *Atmosphere bias* refers to factors in the testing situation that may inhibit performance of children from ethnic minority backgrounds (Flaugher, 1978). As noted previously, practitioners are obligated to seek knowledge of the child's background so that they can build and maintain rapport during testing in a culturally sensitive manner. Atmosphere bias may occur because of limited test-taking skills (e.g., lack of responsiveness to speed pressures); wariness of the examiner (e.g., race of the examiner effects, reluctance to verbalize); and differences in cognitive style and test achievement motivation that hinder optimal performance. Sattler (2008) suggested that atmosphere bias can be minimized by a competent, well-trained examiner who is sensitive to the child's personal, linguistic, and cultural background. (See Frisby, 1999a, 1999b, for a comprehensive review of the empirical literature on culture/ethnicity of the examinee, test session behaviors, and test performance.)

As Ortiz (2008, pp. 663–664) observed, "Although psychometric data are often viewed as objective, they have no inherent meaning and derive significance only from interpretation." To minimize bias in data collection and interpretation, he suggested that the process of assessment should "begin with the hypothesis that the examinee's difficulties are not intrinsic in nature, but rather that they are more likely attributable to external or environmental problems" (p. 664). Examiners must use their knowledge of a student's unique experiences and background to evaluate and interpret all information gathered. The hypothesis of normality is not rejected unless the data strongly suggest the contrary.

Fairness of Consequences

A third area of concern is *fairness of consequences* of test use. This involves an appraisal of the outcomes or consequences of test use for a particular group (Messick, 1980). If testing and assessment practices result in children from a particular ethnic group being placed in inferior educational programs, then the outcomes or consequences of testing are biased and unfair, no matter how adequate the tests and decision-making procedures are (Reschly, 1997; also *Standards*, p. 80).

Closing Comments on Nonbiased Assessment

In these closing comments on nonbiased assessment, we refer the reader back to Messick's (1984) statement that, consistent with responsible, ethical practice, no child should be seen for psychological evaluation unless deficiencies in instruction have first been ruled out. A service delivery model that emphasizes early intervening services may help safeguard ethnic, racial, and linguistic minority children from unnecessary testing and the risk of misdiagnosis or misclassification. By working with teachers and parents to pinpoint learning and behavior problems before they become severe and by intervening early, many problems can be remedied without formal psychological assessment.

If, however, such efforts to remediate problems are unsuccessful and a psychological assessment is needed, practitioners can minimize assessment bias by adhering to seven "best practice" recommendations: (1) be knowledgeable of the child's culture and able to establish and maintain rapport in a culturally sensitive manner; (2) consider the influence of culture and the degree of acculturation in selecting assessment methods; (3) gather developmental, health, family, and school history information; (4) observe the child in the classroom and other settings as appropriate to the problem; (5) consider teacher characteristics, instructional variables, classroom factors, and support available from the home in understanding the child's difficulties and possible interventions; (6) use a variety of formal and less formal assessment strategies, including interviews, behavioral assessments, evaluation of classroom work samples, curriculum-based assessment, testing the limits, and response to intervention; and (7) interpret findings in light of the child's background to ensure a valid and useful picture of the child's abilities and educational needs. Ortiz (2008) outlined a systematic, step-by-step procedure to guide school psychologists in conducting nondiscriminatory assessments. Practitioners also assume responsibility for monitoring the outcomes of assessment for culturally diverse pupils in their schools to ensure that the consequences of testing are fair and in the best interests of the children.

PERSONALITY ASSESSMENT

Three ethical-legal concerns associated with the use of personality tests in the schools, in particular projective techniques, have been identified in the literature. First, there has been a long-standing concern among psychologists that the use of personality tests may result in unwarranted invasion of privacy. Personality tests have been a special focus of concern because, unlike achievement or ability tests, questions on personality tests are often indirect, and the test taker may unknowingly reveal aspects of the self, including emotional problems, that he or she is not prepared to unveil (Messick, 1965). Two strategies to safeguard privacy in the use of personality tests have been suggested. First, consistent with ethical codes and legal requirements (e.g., IDEA), explicit informed consent should be obtained before administering such tests. Second, the school psychologist must consider carefully whether the use of such tests is justified in assisting the pupil; that is, weigh the risk of intrusion on pupil and family privacy against the likelihood that such techniques will result in information helpful in promoting student welfare.

A second ethical-legal issue specific to the use of projective personality tests in the schools focuses on whether such tests meet professional and legal standards for demonstrated test validity. A number of writers have argued that evidence for the technical adequacy of many projective techniques is lacking or does not support their use with children and that projective test results appear to lack educational relevance (Batche & Peterson, 1983). Miller and Nickerson (2007, pp. 50–51) questioned the use of projective techniques in school-based practice because of their lack of *incremental validity*, namely "the extent to which an assessment method contributes to the understanding of an individual beyond that which is already known, as well as the degree to which it can provide information that cannot be gained in some other, easier way." More specifically, are there other assessment procedures, such as direct observations and rating scales, that have better evidence of diagnostic validity and clearer implications for school-based interventions?

An additional concern about the use of personality tests, including projectives, is that school psychologists may not be adequately trained in their use. Consistent with the broad ethical principle of responsible caring, school psychologists must evaluate their own competence to use particular assessment strategies. Practitioners who use personality tests need to have skills in the administration and interpretation of the particular assessment tool and competent judgment about when to use the test or strategy. Projective tests should be used only by psychologists with verifiable training in their use.

PROFESSIONAL COMPETENCE AND AUTONOMY

To ensure valid results, psychologists must offer assessment services only within the boundaries of their competence, and they must insist on professional autonomy in the selection of assessment methods.

Competence

As noted previously, it has become increasingly important for practitioners to assess their competence to provide services to a diverse clientele and to acquire the knowledge and skills needed to conduct a valid psychoeducational assessment of the students whom they typically serve in their work setting (see APA-EP 2.01; also NASP-PPE II, II.1, II.1.1, II.1.2; Standard 11.3). Psychologists who step beyond their competence in assessing children place students at risk for misdiagnosis, misclassification, miseducation, and possible psychological harm. Practitioners are well advised to develop a directory of colleagues with expertise in evaluating children from special backgrounds or with low-incidence disabilities. Seeking assistance through supervision, consultation, and referral are appropriate strategies for psychologists faced with a difficult or unusual case (NASP-PPE II.1.1). However, practitioners who plan to shift or expand their services to a new age group or special pupil population are obligated to seek formal training or professional supervision before offering such services. Hannah Cook (Case 6.3) was obligated to clarify the scope of her expertise before accepting the position in Michigan and to make arrangements for training (coursework and/or supervised experience) before accepting referrals for infant assessments.

Professional Autonomy

The IDEA–Part B requires the consideration of certain types of pupil information in the evaluation of children with suspected disabilities. For example, intellectual ability, achievement, adaptive behavior, and developmental history all must be considered in the evaluation of children who may qualify for services as mentally impaired. State education laws and local district policy may specify additional *types* of information to be considered in evaluation of children with suspected disabilities. School psychologists need to be knowledgeable of these requirements. In some school districts, administrators have attempted to dictate the specific tests that psychologists must use to determine special education eligibility. To serve the best interests of students, however, school psychologists must insist on professional autonomy in the selection of specific assessment instruments.

Case 6.3

Hannah Cook accepted a position as a school psychologist with an intermediate school district in Michigan after working for several years as a school psychologist in another state. Her graduate coursework and prior work experiences focused only on preschool and school-age children; she had no training or experience in infant assessment. In her new job in Michigan, she began receiving referrals for the evaluation of infants with suspected developmental delays. She read the Bayley Scales manual and began conducting assessments of the referred babies. (Adapted from Koocher & Keith-Spiegel, 2008.)

District-mandated test batteries are inconsistent with our professional standards, may result in unsound assessment choices for the student being evaluated, and violate the intent of special education law that requires tests be selected in light of the unique characteristics of the individual child (APA-EP 9.02; NASP-PPE II.3.2, II.3.5; *Standards*, p. 20).

COMPUTERS IN PSYCHOEDUCATIONAL ASSESSMENT

A number of psychological and educational tests can now be administered, scored, and interpreted via the Internet or computer software programs. As additional instruments for schoolchildren become available online, Internet testing is likely to become more common (Naglieri et al., 2004). A special challenge of this technology has been to interpret our ethical codes, professional standards, and special education laws as they relate to computer-assisted assessment (Harvey & Carlson, 2003; Naglieri et al., 2004). The APA's *Guidelines for Computer-Based Tests and Interpretations* (*GCBTI*) (1986) were formulated to interpret the APA's *Ethical Principles* and the *Standards* as they relate to computer-based testing and test interpretation.

As Harvey and Carlson (2003) suggested, school practitioners have an ethical responsibility to consider the ways computers can improve assessment practices. Computer-administered tests and interviews can result in quick and accurate scores and facilitate fair assessment of students with disabilities as well as those from diverse linguistic backgrounds. For example, features such as variable text and image size and digitalized voice may improve testing of students with visual impairments; response devices such as joy sticks, the mouse, and touch-sensitive screens and pads can facilitate assessment of students with physical and communicative disabilities. A digitalized voice or video clips providing instructions or asking questions in the child's native language and dialect may assist in assessment of children from linguistically and culturally diverse backgrounds and permit parents who do not speak English to provide child history information in their native language (Black & Ponirakis, 2000). In addition, computer-administered tests allow easy and efficient use of adaptive testing formats (where the computer is programmed to select and administer test questions based on the examinee's pattern of correct answers) to assess academic skills or cognitive abilities. Furthermore, research suggests that some examinees are more candid when answering sensitive questions administered via computer (e.g., drug use, suicidal thoughts) when compared to in-person interviews, resulting in more valid results (see Black & Ponirakis, 2000).

Computer-assisted score analysis can provide interpretive guidance to the practitioner. Computer-generated interpretations, based on research findings and the knowledge of the expert clinicians who developed the underlying algorithms, can encourage the practitioner to consider appropriate alternative diagnostic hypotheses (Harvey & Carlson, 2003). Furthermore, Internet testing should allow test developers to offer less expensive products and revisions and translations more quickly (Naglieri et al., 2004).

In addition to the possible benefits of computer-assisted testing, practitioners must consider the potential ethical-legal pitfalls (Harvey & Carlson, 2003). First, and perhaps most important, it is the psychologist's responsibility to ensure that all assessment procedures, including those that are computer-assisted, yield valid results prior to using the results in decision making (*GCBTI*, p. 8; NASP-PPE II.3.2). Selection of Internet-based tests and psychodiagnostic software should be limited to those programs that have been reviewed by experts in the field and found to meet high standards for professional practice (Harvey & Carlson, 2003; NASP-PPE II.3.2; Schulenberg & Yutrzenka, 2004). Furthermore, computer-generated test interpretations should be considered a tool to be used in conjunction with the clinical judgment of a well-trained professional (NASP-PPE II.3.2; Schulenberg & Yutrzenka, 2004).

CONCLUDING COMMENTS

In recent years, many school psychologists have modified their job role so that more time is devoted to consultation and intervention activities and less time is devoted to student assessment to determine eligibility for special education services. Although current job roles may now place more emphasis on consultation and intervention, the school psychologist will continue to be one of the members of a school's staff who is most knowledgeable about assessment. Consequently, school psychologists must continue to accept responsibility for ensuring that tests and assessment procedures are used only in ways that protect the rights and promote the well-being of students.

STUDY AND DISCUSSION

Questions for Chapter 6

1. What is the difference between *testing* and *assessment*?
2. Identify the school psychologist's ethical-legal obligations to the parent prior to beginning an assessment and during interpretation of findings.
3. Describe five ethical-legal concerns a psychologist should consider in planning and conducting psychoeducational assessments.
4. What are test bias, bias in clinical application, and fairness of consequences?
5. Identify the ethical concerns associated with the use of projective personality tests with schoolchildren.
6. Identify the ethical-legal issues associated with the selection and use of computer-assisted test interpretation programs.

Discussion

Reread Case 6.2. What are the potential benefits and the potential problems associated with including a psychological diagnosis such as somatoform disorder in a multidisciplinary report being prepared for an IEP team? Is the diagnosis necessary for eligibility determination under the IDEA or Section 504?

Vignettes

1. Wanda Rose's school district has a backlog of referrals for children suspected of qualifying for special education services. To increase the number of evaluations she can complete, Wanda carefully trained a teacher's aide in the administration of the Wechsler Intelligence Scale for Children IV (Wechsler, 2003) and several achievement tests. She has used the results of the tests administered by the teacher's aide to determine whether the referred pupils qualify for special education services. What are the ethical-legal issues involved in this vignette?

2. Each May, the elementary schools in Carrie Johnson's district invite children who will enter kindergarten in the fall and their parents to a kindergarten roundup. During the roundup, hearing, vision, and speech screenings are conducted, and Carrie administers

the Vocabulary and Picture Completion subtests from the Wechsler Preschool and Primary Scale of Intelligence III (Wechsler, 2002) to identify children who might need further evaluation of their learning needs. A new resort-hotel complex is being built in the area, and the hotel management has recruited several families from Dominica for job openings. Carrie is delighted when a Dominican child comes to her screening table. Relying on the French she learned in college, Carrie speaks to the child in French and attempts an on-the-spot translation of the WPPSI-III subtests from English to French. What are the ethical issues in this situation?

3. Hannah Cook, school psychologist, and Bob Smoke, the reading consultant at the junior high school, were interested in decreasing the amount of time needed to complete individual assessment of reading achievement so that more time could be devoted to consultation activities. They contacted the high school computer sciences teacher, and the three of them worked together to create a computer-administered version of a popular, well-standardized, paper-and-pencil test of reading comprehension. Students referred for assessment of reading achievement are then routinely given the computer-administered version of the test in a testing carrel in the school library. The computer program computes raw scores, and the raw scores then are transformed to standard scores by the reading consultant using tables from the test manual. The test scores are used by the psychologist and reading consultant for both placement and program planning purposes. What are the ethical-legal issues involved in this vignette? (Adapted from Jacob & Brantley, 1989.)

4. During his internship in a suburban school district, Sam Foster receives a disproportionately high number of referrals for special education evaluation of children who live in federally funded low-income scatter-site housing in his district. Most of these children are African American or Hispanic, but attending predominately white elementary schools. Sam is concerned about potential overidentification of minority children for special education in his district. What are some strategies he might use to prevent this problem?

Activities

A seven-year old child has been referred for psychoeducational assessment because of her slow academic progress. Her teacher suspects that she may qualify for special education services as mentally impaired. Role-play your initial meeting with the child's parents during which you seek informed consent for assessment. Role-play your meeting with the child during which you describe the scope and nature of the assessment process.

Chapter 7

ETHICAL AND LEGAL ISSUES IN SCHOOL-BASED INTERVENTIONS

As noted in Chapter 1, school-based practitioners often provide consultative services to school districts, to student assistance teams, or within classrooms that are not within the scope of an established psychologist-client relationship. In Chapter 7, we first explore the ethical-legal aspects of providing classroom interventions for students who require additional academic and behavioral support to be successful in the general education program, but who have not been referred for evaluation of a suspected disability. The second portion of the chapter explores the ethical-legal issues associated with providing counseling and other therapeutic interventions within the context of a school psychologist–client relationship.

INTERVENTIONS FOR STUDENTS WHO REQUIRE ACADEMIC AND BEHAVIORAL SUPPORT TO SUCCEED IN GENERAL EDUCATION

In 2006, a task force composed of experts in the field of school psychology completed the document titled *School Psychology: A Blueprint for Training and Practice III* (Ysseldyke et al.), in which the authors suggested that the goals of improving educational and mental health outcomes for all students, and the capacity of systems to meet the needs of all students, can best be achieved by a three-tier model of service delivery (p. 13). *Tier I* or *universal services* are systems-level programs and services designed to meet the academic and social-emotional needs of the majority of students. Examples include "use of evidence-based approaches to reading and math instruction or the implementation of a positive school-wide discipline program to reduce problems with behavior management" (Ysseldyke et al., 2006, p. 13; also Marston, 2003; Tilly, 2008). At Tier I, school psychology practitioners might assist in developing a universal (districtwide) screening process to identify students at risk of not making adequate progress in the general education curriculum. *Tier II* or *targeted interventions* are for students who do not succeed in response to Tier I services and address "specific academic or social-emotional skill or performance deficits" (Ysseldyke et al., 2006, p. 13). At Tier II, school psychologists might provide consultation to student assistance teams or in classrooms with the goal of implementing evidence-based interventions and monitoring their effectiveness. *Tier III or intensive interventions* are tailored to the needs of the individual student (Marston, 2003; Tilly, 2008). Tier III interventions might include special education and related services, therapeutic interventions in the context of a school psychologist–client relationship, and/ or assistance provided through interagency collaborations.

Classroom Interventions

Beginning in the mid-1980s, some school districts introduced building-based prereferral child study teams to assist teachers in planning academic and behavioral interventions for students in general education classes. Researchers found that such efforts were a safeguard against inappropriate referral for special education eligibility evaluation, unnecessary testing, and misclassification (e.g., Chalfant & Pysh, 1989; Graden, Casey, & Bonstrom, 1985). A statewide system of prereferral intervention also was found to be one means of reducing the overrepresentation of African American students in special education (e.g., *Lee v. Lee County Bd. of Education*, 2007). Federal policy makers encouraged schools to implement prereferral child study teams as a component of a district's child find procedures under the Individuals with Disabilities Education Act (IDEA) and Section 504 in the 1990s (Shrag, 1991). The 2004 amendments to IDEA allow school districts to use up to 15% of their federal special education funds each year to develop and implement coordinated *early intervening services*. These services are for students in all grades who require additional academic and behavior support to be successful in general education, but who have not been identified as needing special education and related services (34 C.F.R. § 300.226).

Many school districts are implementing a three-tier service delivery model that includes *response to intervention* (RTI) as part of its early intervening services. The RTI process generally involves providing effective instruction for students within general education, monitoring student progress, providing more individualized assistance for students who do not demonstrate adequate progress, and again monitoring progress. Students who still do not respond satisfactorily might be referred for a special education or Section 504 eligibility evaluation (Burns, Jacob, & Wagner, 2008; Fuchs, Mock, Morgan, & Young, 2003).

The following portion of the chapter focuses on ethical-legal issues associated with academic and behavioral interventions in the classroom including: (1) selecting interventions; (2) monitoring and documenting interventions; (3) parent involvement, consent, and child find obligations under IDEA and Section 504 of the Rehabilitation Act of 1973; and (4) special considerations associated with the use of behavioral interventions. Ethical and legal issues associated with using RTI as part of the procedure to determine whether a student is eligible as learning disabled under the IDEA are discussed in Burns et al. (2008).

Selecting Classroom Interventions

Both the No Child Left Behind Act of 2001 (NCLB, Pub. L. No. 89-10) and IDEA 2004 called on school psychologists and other educational specialists to use scientifically based academic and behavioral interventions. A reliance on applied learning sciences in making intervention choices also is consistent with our codes of ethics. Standard II.3.9 of the NASP's code requires school psychologists to "use a problem-solving process to develop interventions appropriate to the presenting problems and that are consistent with data collected" and to give preference "to interventions described in the peer-reviewed professional research literature and found to be efficacious" (also APA-EP 2.04). However, while practitioners give preference to interventions reported to be effective, they also must adapt those interventions to the setting and the individual needs of the child. In other words, practitioners must strive for fidelity to the treatment program as it is described in the research literature while at the same time adapting the intervention to the unique characteristics of the setting and student.

Although there is no government-approved list of research-based classroom interventions, the U.S. Department of Education (DOE) has funded the development of several helpful practice guides that are available at the Institute of Education Sciences web site (http://ies.ed.gov/ncee/wwc/publications/practiceguides). Examples include *Reducing Behavior Problems in the Elementary School Classroom* (Epstein, Atkins, Cullinan, Kutash, & Weaver, 2008) and *Assisting Students Struggling with Reading: Response to Intervention (RTI) and Multi-Tier Intervention in the Primary Grades* (Gersten et al., 2009).

Monitoring and Documenting Interventions

School psychologists are ethically obligated to use a data-based problem-solving process to plan and monitor the effectiveness of interventions. The NASP's code of ethics specifically requires practitioners to:

actively monitor the impact of their recommendations and intervention plans. They revise a recommendation, or modify or terminate an intervention plan, when data indicate the desired outcomes are not being attained. School psychologists seek the assistance of others in supervisory, consultative, or referral roles when progress monitoring indicates that their recommendations and interventions are not effective in assisting a client. (NASP-PPE II.2.2)

Furthermore, *documenting* student response to an intervention and *modifying* that intervention when it does not achieve the desired results are essential components of legally defensible RTI practices. For example, in a due process hearing under IDEA, a parent sought compensatory education for her child because the school failed to provide her with notice of parent rights under IDEA and failed to evaluate her child for special education services during the academic year, even though her child exhibited extensive and continuing behavioral problems from the first day of school. In its defense, the school argued in part that the child had not been referred for evaluation of IDEA eligibility because RTI methods were being implemented prior to initiating an evaluation. However, the school had no written documentation of an RTI plan and no evidence of progress monitoring or that the RTI interventions were modified based on student progress. The hearing officer found in favor of the parent, awarding considerable compensatory education for the child at school district expense (Delaware College Preparatory Academy and the Red Clay Consolidated School District Delaware State Educational Agency, 2009).[1]

Parent Involvement, Consent, and Child Find Obligations under IDEA and Section 504

As discussed in Chapters 1 and 3, school psychologists are ethically obligated to promote parental participation in school decisions affecting children (NASP-PPE, I.1.2, II.3.10). However, consistent with IDEA, where school psychologists are members of the school's instructional support staff, not all of their services require informed parent consent. It is ethically and legally permissible "to provide school-based consultation services regarding a child or adolescent to a student assistance team or teacher without informed parent consent as long as the resulting interventions are *under the authority of the teacher* [emphasis added] and within the scope of typical classroom interventions" (NASP-PPE I.1.1).

Furthermore, consistent with IDEA:

Parent consent is not ethically required for a school-based school psychologist to review a student's education records, conduct classroom observations, assist in within-classroom interventions and progress monitoring, or to participate in educational screenings conducted as part of a regular program of instruction. Parent consent is required if the consultation about a particular child or adolescent is likely to be extensive and ongoing and/or if school actions may result in a significant intrusion on student or family privacy beyond what might be expected in the course of ordinary school activities. (NASP-PPE I.1.1)

---

[1]Court cases are italicized; Office for Civil Rights and state due process hearing officer decisions are not italicized.

The NASP's code of ethics goes on to recommend that a school district's parent handbook informs families that school psychologists routinely assist teachers in planning classroom instruction and monitoring its effectiveness, and that district policy does not require parent notice or consent for such involvement in student support (NASP-PPE, footnote to I.1.2).

Although based on a limited number of decisions, the courts have supported the use of "less drastic alternatives" such as RTI prior to evaluation of a student for eligibility under IDEA or Section 504 as long as the student's progress is monitored and a referral for evaluation is made as soon as a disability is suspected (e.g., *A.P. v. Woodstock Board of Education*, 2008; *Johnson v. Upland* [an unpublished decision], 2002).[2] If, at any point during the process of providing early intervening services, a student is suspected of having a disability, then the school is required to conduct an individual evaluation in accordance with IDEA or Section 504 procedures and time lines. Under IDEA, parents have a right to be notified if RTI is being implemented as part of the process to determine whether their child has a disability (34 C.F.R. § 300.311[a]). Furthermore, if parents request a special education or 504 eligibility evaluation during the RTI process and the school decides not to evaluate the student, the school must provide parents with written notice of its refusal to evaluate along with information describing parent rights to challenge that decision (see Burns et al., 2008).

School districts may not require that RTI be implemented for a predetermined number of weeks before responding to a parent request for an evaluation under IDEA or Section 504. For example, an Office for Civil Rights (OCR) investigation was triggered by a parent's complaint that the school did not respond to her request for evaluation of her child under Section 504 or provide notice of parent rights under the law. The investigation found that the school required an eight-week RTI intervention period before a student could be considered for a Section 504 evaluation, at which time parents would be provided notice of their rights. The complaint resolution stated that "the use of RTI does not offend Section 504," but RTI may not, without violating Section 504, be implemented in such a manner that denies parents notice of their rights under 504 at the time they request an evaluation of their child, including their right to "persist in their request for an evaluation or to seek procedural safeguards" (Acalanes [CA] Union High School District Office for Civil Rights, Western Division, San Francisco [California], 2009, p. 8).

In sum, the implementation of prereferral recommendations by student assistance teams or the use of RTI is not likely to be seen as an unreasonable delay of the child find requirements of IDEA and Section 504/Americans with Disabilities Amendments Act (ADAA) as long as academic progress is documented and a referral for evaluation is made as soon as a disability is suspected. If parents request a special education or 504 eligibility evaluation during the RTI process and the school decides not to evaluate the child, the school must provide parents with written notice of the refusal to evaluate along with information describing parent rights to challenge that decision.

Special Considerations Associated with the Use of Behavioral Interventions

For many years, school psychologists have provided consultation to teachers and other behavior change agents on the use of behavioral techniques (e.g., applied behavior analysis) to reduce problematic student behaviors. For the purpose of this discussion,

---

[2]Although the *Johnson* opinion is reported in case digests, it was designated as "unpublished," meaning that it may not be cited as legal precedent except in accordance with the rules of the Ninth Circuit (2002, p. 690).

behavioral intervention means the planned and systematic use of learning principles, particularly operant techniques and modeling theory, to change the behavior of students. This portion of the chapter provides a brief overview of the ethical-legal issues associated with the use of behavioral interventions in school-based practice. Readers are encouraged to also consult the "Guidelines for Responsible Conduct for Behavior Analysts" adopted by the Behavior Analysis Certification Board (BACB, 2004).

Selection of Goals   An ethical concern that arises in the use of behavioral interventions is whether the goals of the intervention are in the best interests of the student. Classroom behavior modification programs introduced in the late 1960s often focused on teaching children to "be still, be quiet, and be docile" (Winett & Winkler, 1972), what Conoley and Conoley (1982) later referred to as "dead man behaviors." Such goals may assist the teacher in maintaining a quiet, orderly classroom, but they are not likely to improve learning or foster the healthy personal-social development of children (Winett & Winkler, 1972). The school psychologist is obligated ethically to ensure replacement behaviors are selected that "enhance the long-term well-being of the child" (A. Harris & Kapche, 1978, p. 27) and are consistent with the long-range goal of self-management. Goals must be selected to ensure that the student will develop appropriate adaptive behaviors and not just suppress inappropriate ones (Van Houten et al., 1988).

Selection of Interventions   Considerable research support exists for the practice of selecting behavioral interventions based on a systematic evaluation of the function a problem behavior serves for the child (Tilly, Knoster, & Ikeda, 2000). Two assessment methodologies have been developed to assist in identifying the functions served by a behavior. *Functional assessment* is based on naturalistic observations and involves direct observation and the use of informants (e.g., teacher interviews and rating scales) to gather information. *Functional analysis* involves controlled observation; that is, the factors that are believed to maintain the behavior are experimentally manipulated (Martens, Witt, Daly, & Vollmer, 1999). Both assessment strategies allow evaluation of the child and the environmental factors associated with the problem behavior, including examination of the setting events, antecedents, and consequences of behavior (also see Steege & Watson, 2008).

As noted previously, school psychologists are obligated ethically to select (or assist in the selection of) change procedures that have demonstrated effectiveness (NASP-PPE II.3.9). Consistent with the least restrictive alternative doctrine that evolved from court decisions (e.g., *Wyatt v. Stickney*, 1971) and the broad ethical principle of nonmaleficence, practitioners are obligated to select the least drastic procedures and those that minimize the risk of adverse side effects and also are likely to be effective. The literature reflects some consensus about the acceptability of various behavior-change procedures. First-choice strategies are *positive behavioral interventions* typically based on differential reinforcement (reinforcing appropriate behaviors incompatible with problem behaviors). Second-choice strategies are based on extinction (withdrawing of reinforcement for undesired behavior). Third-choice strategies include removal of desirable stimuli (e.g., time-out procedures). The least acceptable strategies are those that involve presentation of aversive stimuli (BACB, 2004; Repp & Singh, 1990).

Under IDEA, if a child's behavior impedes his or her learning or that of others, the individualized education plan (IEP) team is required to consider "the use of positive behavioral interventions and support, and other strategies to address that behavior" in developing the IEP (34 C.F.R. § 300.324[a][2][i]). It is important for school psychologists to ensure that a functional behavioral assessment is conducted and to assist in the development of a behavior intervention plan when such strategies are essential to the provision of quality early intervening services or to the development of a student's IEP or 504 plan (e.g., *Denita Harris v. District of Columbia*, 2008). In addition, functional behavioral assessment and intervention services are required following a disciplinary infraction that was determined to be a manifestation of the student's disability (34 C.F.R. § 300.530[d][ii]).

In the 1970s, a number of behavioral control or change procedures came under the scrutiny of the courts. These early cases concerned youth in juvenile correction facilities (e.g., *Morales v. Turman*, 1974; *Pena v. New York State Division for Youth*, 1976) or residential mental health facilities (e.g., *New York State Association for Retarded Children v. Carey*, 1975) and provided some insight into the minimal standards that must be adhered to in the use of behavioral methods so as not to violate the constitutional rights of the children involved. More specifically, these rulings suggested that behavioral control methods must not deprive students of their basic rights to food, water, shelter (including adequate heat and ventilation), sleep, and exercise periods (also see APA-EP 1.03).

In the 1980s, the court addressed the use of behavioral methods in the public schools. As noted previously, the systematic use of differential reinforcement is considered to be a first-choice strategy. Access to privileges (e.g., use of a computer to play games), special luxuries (e.g., colorful stickers), and social reinforcers (e.g., smiles and praise) are types of reinforcers that typically present no special concerns. However, court rulings have been interpreted to suggest that not all types of reinforcers are acceptable. Some teachers use token economies to manage behavior. In token economies, tokens or points may be earned for appropriate behavior, and the tokens subsequently are exchanged for rewards. The use of token economies should not result in denial of basic rights (e.g., access to food at lunchtime), and students should not be denied educational opportunities that are part of the child's expected program, such as gym or art (Hindman, 1986).

Time-out is a behavioral intervention based on removal of desirable stimuli. K. R. Harris (1985) identified three different types of time-out: (1) nonexclusion, which involves removing the child from the reinforcing situation but still allowing the child to observe the ongoing activity; (2) exclusion, which involves removing the child from the reinforcing situation but not from the room; and (3) isolation, which involves the removal of the child from the reinforcing situation and placing him or her in a different area or room (see Turner & Watson, 1999). Discussion here focuses primarily on the use of exclusion and isolation time-out procedures.

Legal challenges to the use of time-out in the public schools found it to be an acceptable procedure to safeguard other students from disruptive behavior (*Dickens by Dickens v. Johnson County Board of Education*, 1987; *Hayes v. Unified School District No. 377*, 1987; see also *Honig v. Doe*, 1988).[3] In *Dickens*, the court noted that "judicious use of behavioral modification techniques such as 'time-out' should be favored over expulsion in disciplining disruptive students, particularly the handicapped" (p. 158). However, the use of time-out must meet reasonable standards safeguarding the rights and welfare of pupils. In finding the use of time-out permissible, the judge in *Dickens* also noted, "This is not to say that educators may arbitrarily cage students in a corner of the classroom for an indeterminate length of time" (p. 158). The court considerations in *Dickens*, *Hayes*, and

---

[3]In *Dickens*, time-out procedures involved having the child sit at a desk placed inside a three-sided refrigerator carton in the corner of the classroom, where the child could not see classmates but could hear the teacher and sometimes see the teacher and chalkboard. *Hayes* involved removing the child to a different room.

earlier cases suggest some general parameters for the use of time-out: School personnel must monitor a secluded student to ensure his or her well-being; the room must have adequate ventilation (*Morales*, 1974); the time-out room itself must not present a fire or safety hazard (*Hayes*, 1987); students must be permitted to leave time-out for appropriate reasons (*Dickens*, 1987); and the door to the time-out room must remain unlocked (*New York State Association for Retarded Children*, 1975).

Students should be given prior notice about the types of behaviors that will result in being placed in time-out (*Hayes*, 1987), and school personnel must ensure that time-out, when used as punishment, is "not unduly harsh or grossly disproportionate" to the offense (*Dickens*, 1987, p. 158). Placement in time-out should not result in "a total exclusion from the educational process for more than a trivial period" (*Goss v. Lopez*, 1975, p. 575). Use of time-out combined with instruction in the time-out room, or requiring the child to do schoolwork while segregated or secluded, is recommended (*Dickens*, 1987). (See Turner & Watson, 1999, for a review of research-based best practices in the use of time-out.)

The past several years have witnessed renewed concern about the misuse of isolation time-out, in particular, seclusion rooms. In 2009, the U.S. Government Accountability Office provided a report to Congress on documented cases of death and trauma that resulted from the misuse of seclusion and restraints with students, often involving students with disabilities (Kutz, 2009). The report also examined state laws on the use of seclusion rooms and restraints, and found wide variability across states, with many states having no laws regulating the use of these techniques in schools.

A highly controversial area in behavioral intervention is the use of *aversive conditioning*, in which a discomforting stimulus is presented contingent on the student's undesirable behavior. Some psychologists and educators believe that aversive conditioning must never be used; others believe its use may be justified in the treatment of extremely self-injurious or dangerously aggressive behaviors. It is beyond the scope of this book to explore the controversy fully; interested readers are referred to Jacob-Timm (1996), National Institutes of Health (1991), and Repp and Singh (1990).

Evaluation of Intervention Integrity and Effectiveness   Consistent with our codes of ethics, school psychologists ensure that intervention integrity is monitored, and modify or terminate the intervention plan when data indicate it is not achieving the desired goals (NASP-PPE II.2.2, II.2.3; see Roach & Elliot, 2008). The monitoring of intervention integrity and effectiveness is particularly important when students evidence difficult behaviors. Change agents, including teachers and parents, may resort to more punitive behavior control practices if they are frustrated by a lack of success using positive behavioral interventions or the intervention plan is too difficult to implement.

THERAPEUTIC INTERVENTIONS WITHIN THE CONTEXT OF A SCHOOL PSYCHOLOGIST–CLIENT RELATIONSHIP

We first address ethical and legal issues associated with providing counseling in the schools and then explore challenging special situations, such as suspected child abuse and working with students who are potentially dangerous to others or a threat to themselves. The chapter concludes with a brief discussion of psychopharmacologic interventions, using Ritalin as an example.

Counseling: Ethical and Legal Issues

Tharinger and Stafford (1995) described counseling in the schools as a process of ongoing, planned interactions between a student and a mental health professional. The school psychologist works to alleviate the student's distress by improving the child's psychological functioning and/or facilitating change in his or her environment, in particular the school and family systems. More specifically, the goals of counseling may include:

> alleviating the child's emotional and cognitive distress, changing the child's behavior, assisting with self-understanding, helping the child meet current developmental tasks successfully, supporting needed environmental changes, and promoting a more positive fit between the child and the systems in which she or he resides (e.g., school and family). (p. 896)

School psychologists have a number of ethical and legal obligations to students and their parents prior to providing ongoing counseling services. The NASP's code of ethics states:

> Except for urgent situations or self-referrals by a minor student, school psychologists seek parent consent (or the consent of an adult student) prior to establishing a school-psychologist client relationship . . . to provide ongoing individual or group counseling or other non-classroom therapeutic intervention. (NASP-PPE I.1.2)

In the school setting, informed consent to establish a school psychologist–client relationship usually rests with the parents of a minor. However, the practitioner is ethically obligated to respect the dignity, autonomy, and self-determination of the student. The decision to allow a student the opportunity to choose or refuse psychological intervention may involve consideration of a number of factors, including law, ethical issues (self-determination versus welfare of the student), the child's competence to make choices, and the likely consequences of affording choices (e.g., enhanced functioning versus choice to refuse treatment). We concur with Weithorn's (1983) suggestion that practitioners permit and encourage student involvement in decision making to the maximum extent appropriate to the child and the situation. Practitioners have an ethical obligation to inform students of the scope and nature of the proposed intervention, whether or not they are given a choice about participating (see NASP-PPE I.1.4).

Self-Referrals for Counseling

Young children are unlikely to seek help or initiate a counseling relationship on their own. However, at the high school level, many referrals for counseling are self-referrals. Students may wish to see a school psychologist on the condition that their parents are not notified. This raises the question of whether students who are minors can ever be seen by the school psychologist for counseling without parental permission. We are not aware of any case law decisions that specifically address this question. The NASP's code of ethics states:

> When a student who is a minor self-refers for assistance, it is ethically permissible to provide psychological assistance without parent notice or consent for one or several meetings to establish the nature and degree of the need for services and assure the child is safe and not in danger. It is ethically permissible to provide services to mature minors without parent consent where allowed by state law and school district policy. However, if the student is *not* old enough to receive school psychological assistance independent of parent consent, the school

psychologist obtains parent consent to provide continuing assistance to the student beyond the preliminary meetings or refers the student to alternative sources of assistance that do not require parent notice or consent. (NASP-PPE I.1.2)

The preliminary meetings can serve to ensure that the child is not in danger (C. Osip, quoted in Canter, 1989). During these meetings, the school psychologist also can discuss the need for parental consent for further counseling sessions, offer to contact the parent on behalf of the student, or offer to meet jointly with the student and parents to discuss consent and ensure ongoing parent support. Unless there is a conflict with state law, we believe school districts should adopt written policies stating that students may be seen by the school psychologist or other mental health professional for one or several meetings without parent notice or consent to ensure that the student is not in danger (e.g., child abuse, suicidal) or if it is suspected the student may be a danger to others (see footnote, NASP-PPE I.1.2).

Practitioners should be aware that under federal and state law community-based providers may be permitted to treat minors for certain health and mental health conditions (e.g., mental illness, drug and alcohol abuse, pregnancy management, treatment of sexually transmitted diseases) independent of parent notice or consent, with the minor's treatment records considered to be under his or her own control (Boonstra & Nash, 2000). Because of the Family Educational Rights and Privacy Act of 1974, it may be problematic for school-based practitioners to keep records about individual students that are not accessible by the parent (see Chapter 3). For this reason, school-based practitioners at times may need to refer students who desire assistance without parent involvement to community-based providers (NASP-PPE I.1.2).

Planning Counseling and Other Therapeutic Interventions

School psychologists are obligated to use counseling or other therapeutic intervention techniques that the profession considers to be "responsible, research-based practice" (NASP-PPE II.3.9; also APA-EP 2.04). Practitioners "encourage and promote parental participation in designing interventions for their children" (NASP-PPE II.3.10) and, to "the maximum extent appropriate, students are invited to participate in selecting and planning interventions" (II.3.11). The proposed options should consider all resources (school and community) available to assist the student and family and take into account the academic performance and conduct expectations of the school, the support and assistance that can be made available to the teacher, and the values and skills of the parents (NASP-PPE II.3.10). School practitioners "respect the wishes of parents who object to school psychological services and attempt to guide parents to alternative resources" (NASP-PPE I.1.5).

Interventions with Culturally Diverse Clientele

School psychologists have special obligations when working with students and families whose background characteristics are different from their own (NASP-PPE I.3.2). First, psychologists need to be aware of how their own cultural heritage, gender, class, ethnic-racial identity, sexual orientation, and age cohort shape personal values and beliefs, including assumptions and biases related to those who are different (N. D. Hansen, Pepitone-Arreola-Rockwell, & Greene, 2000; Rogers et al., 1999). Second, practitioners need to learn about the student's background, values, beliefs, and worldview and how those cultural and experiential factors may influence development and behavior. Third, to provide sensitive and effective services, practitioners must be able to demonstrate an understanding and respect for cultural and experiential differences in interacting with the student.

Fourth, practitioners are obligated to seek knowledge of best practices in selecting, designing, and implementing intervention plans for diverse clientele with learning or behavior problems (N. D. Hansen et al., 2000; Lynch & Hanson, 1998; Rogers et al., 1999). And fifth, when working with diverse students, practitioners should assist the students and their parents to better understand the culture of the school and community so that they can make informed choices relevant to schooling and mental health services (Hays, 2001; Rogers et al., 1999).

Practitioners also are obligated to self-assess their multicultural competence (N. D. Hansen et al., 2000). More specifically, they need to consider when circumstances (e.g., personal biases, lack of requisite knowledge, skills, or language fluency) may negatively influence professional practice and adapt accordingly, that is, by obtaining needed information, consultation, or supervision, or referring the student to a better qualified professional (NASP-PPE II.1.2; N. D. Hansen et al., 2000).

DUTY TO PROTECT

As noted in Chapter 2, school-based practitioners have a legal as well as an ethical obligation to take reasonable steps to protect all students from reasonably foreseeable harm.

Child Abuse

The Child Abuse Prevention, Adoption, and Family Services Act of 1988 defined child maltreatment as "the physical or mental injury, sexual abuse or exploitation, negligent treatment, or maltreatment of a child by a person who is responsible for the child's welfare, under circumstances which indicate that the child's health or welfare is harmed or threatened" (Pub. L. No. 100-294, § 14). States are required to use a similar definition of abuse in their reporting laws to be eligible for federal child protection funds. There is some variation among states, however, with regard to the way abuse is defined (Kalichman, 1999). All 50 states have enacted legislation requiring school professionals to report suspected cases of child abuse to child welfare or protection agencies.

In 2002 there were about 2,600,000 reports to child protective service agencies of possible maltreatment, with an estimated 896,000 substantiated cases of child maltreatment that year (U.S. Department of Health and Human Services, 2004). Most child abuse goes unreported, however. Researchers estimate that reported cases of child abuse constitute only about 40% of all cases (Kalichman, 1999). School psychologists are legally required to report all cases of suspected child abuse. As mandated reporters, their role is to ensure a report is made to child protective services each time an incident of child abuse is suspected. For example, in *Phillis P.* (1986; Case 7.1), the California Supreme Court held that the school psychologist had a mandatory duty to report a student who was sexually molesting another student to the state child protection agency. In *Pesce v. J. Sterling Morton High School* (1987), the court held that the duty to protect schoolchildren by reporting suspected child abuse outweighs any right to confidentiality of the school psychologist–client relationship.

In her survey of NASP school psychology practitioners, Dailor (2007) found that, of eight types of ethical dilemmas experienced in the previous year, the dilemma reported by the largest percentage of respondents was whether there was a reasonable suspicion of child abuse that would warrant contacting child protective services. Kalichman (1999) reviewed studies of reporting decisions, and found that physical signs of abuse were most influential in the decision to report, followed by child verbal reports of physical

---

Case 7.1

An eight-year-old girl, Celia, complained to her teacher that another pupil (a 13-year-old boy) was "playing games" with her. As it was apparent that the games involved inappropriate sexual contact, the teacher informed the school psychologist. The school psychologist counseled Celia without notifying her mother of the problem. The school principal was informed of the incidents and told the boy involved not to "bother" Celia any more. The principal also failed to notify Celia's mother about the incidents. Meanwhile, the assaults on Celia continued over a three-month period, both on school premises and en route to school. Celia became increasingly despondent and withdrawn. The sexual assaults ultimately led to rape. The victim's mother, after learning what had happened, filed a lawsuit against the school psychologist, teacher, and principal.

The California Supreme Court ruled that the school had had a mandatory duty to warn Celia's mother that her daughter was being sexually molested, a duty to report the assaults to a child protective agency, a duty to obtain written parent consent prior to psychological treatment dealing with matters of a sensitive sexual nature, and a duty to properly supervise the molesting student and ensure Celia's safety. (Adapted from *Phillis P. v. Claremont Unified School District*, 1986).

---

or sexual abuse. Parent or other adult reports that a child was abused also were likely to trigger a report.

In many situations, however, the determination of whether a reasonable suspicion of child abuse exists is complicated. In general, teachers and other school staff who work closely with children should be encouraged to respond to ambiguous child disclosures with open-ended questions and in a warm, calm, nonjudgmental manner. For example, a child's statement that "Mommy hurt me" might be followed by "Oh, I'm sorry to hear that. What happened?" (See Horton & Cruise, 2001, pp. 39–52.) Schools are well advised to ensure that each building has a physical or mental health professional with expertise in child abuse and a positive working relationship with child protective services. This individual can seek guidance from child protective services when difficult questions arise and also assist in making reports when abuse is suspected.

It is critically important for school staff to recognize that it is the responsibility of the child protection agency, not school personnel, to confirm or disconfirm the existence of suspected abuse or neglect. The courts have held that it is not necessary for school personnel to be certain that the abuse took place, only that there is reason to suspect abuse (e.g., *State v. Grover*, 1989). In a news story described as a wake-up call for educators, a school principal asked the school psychologist and several teachers to interview a nine-year-old to confirm a parent's report of suspected abuse prior to contacting child protective services. Six educators, including the school psychologist, were subsequently investigated by the school district for failing to promptly report suspected child abuse. Although the school psychologist and teachers were cleared of any wrongdoing, the principal was dismissed (Saunders, 2007).

School attorneys advise school psychologists to promptly report suspected abuse and to document that the call was made rather than to attempt to confirm abuse suspicions on their own (Saunders, 2007). Experts in law and developmental psychology have crafted research-based protocols for use when interviewing children if abuse is suspected. These interview protocols are based on a *forensic* (rather than a clinical) perspective. To meet forensic standards, interviews with suspected victims of abuse should be conducted by individuals specifically trained to gather, evaluate, and interpret evidence of child abuse using accepted interview techniques (e.g., Poole & Dickinson, 2005; State of Michigan's Governor's Task Force on Children's Justice, Department of Human Services, 1998/2004).

All states provide immunity from civil or criminal action for filing a child abuse report to the appropriate authorities. This means that a school psychologist who files a report of suspected abuse cannot be sued for damages that might arise from making such a report (e.g., defamation), as long as the report is made in good faith and the procedures for filing a report under state law are followed (Small, Lyons, & Guy, 2002). Penalties for not reporting may include civil or criminal liability and loss of certification or license. Fines for failure to report range from $25 to $5,000; possible jail sentences range from 10 days to one year (Small et al., 2002).

One concern about making a report about suspected child abuse by a family member is the potential loss of rapport with the student and his or her family as a result of making a report. However, based on a review of the available studies, Kalichman (1999, p. 61) concluded, "Little evidence exists to support the popular perceptions that reporting abuse has detrimental effects on the quality and efficacy of professional services. In fact, studies specifically addressing these issues in clinical settings find that reporting sometimes benefits the treatment process." Similarly, Meddin and Rosen (1986, p. 30) noted, "After their initial and appropriate anger at the intervention of the agency, most parents feel a sense of relief that the problems has [sic] been identified, and they are usually very willing to work toward a solution."

Threat to Self or Others and Risky Behaviors

In Chapter 3 we noted that at about age 14 adolescents show the cognitive capacity to make informed decisions about as well as adults, especially if adults are available to assist them in making informed choices. Why, then, do so many adolescents engage in risky behaviors? Steinberg, Cauffmann, Woolard, Graham, and Banich (2009) measured both cognitive performance and psychosocial maturity in a sample of 935 individuals aged 10 to 30 years, and found that adolescents aged 14 and older performed about as well as adults on measures of cognitive abilities, including logical reasoning, but did not perform as well as adults on measures of social and emotional maturity. More specifically, 14-year-olds were less mature than young adults in their mid-20s or older on a composite measure of sense of responsibility, impulse control, resistance to pressure from others (including peer pressure), immediate—as compared to future—orientation, and thrill seeking. Although additional research is needed, such findings highlight the importance of adult support, mentoring, and supervision for adolescents at school, at home, and in the community, particularly when students evidence risky behaviors.

Threat to Self

Suicide is one of the three leading causes of death among adolescents. It is estimated that in 2006 there were approximately 8.2 completed suicides per 100,000 adolescents in the 15- to 19-year age group and 1.3 suicides per 100,000 children in the 10- to 14-year age group (National Institute of Mental Health, 2009). The *Kelson v. The City of Springfield* (1985) and *Eisel v. Board of Education of Montgomery County* court decisions (Cases 7.2. and 7.3), among others (e.g., *Wyke v. Polk County School Board*, 1997), have been interpreted to suggest that schools should develop clear suicide prevention policies and procedures that include notifying parents and should ensure adequate staff orientation to district policy and procedures.

Case 7.2

Brian, a 14-year-old, confronted his teacher during class with a .38-caliber revolver. The teacher persuaded Brian to talk with the vice principal alone in an empty classroom. Brian showed the vice principal a suicide note he had written and asked to speak with his favorite teacher; he was not allowed to do so. When they left the classroom, Brian was met by a police officer who told him he was "in trouble with the law." Brian (still armed with the gun) entered the boy's restroom, where he shot himself. He died later that morning. (Adapted from *Kelson v. The City of Springfield*, 1985.)

Case 7.3

"Nina," a 13-year-old middle school student, became involved in Satanism and developed an obsessive interest in death. She told several friends that she intended to kill herself. Nina's friends reported her suicidal intentions to their school counselor (at a different school), who conveyed the information to Nina's school counselor. Both counselors met with Nina and questioned her about her statements concerning suicide, but she denied making them. Neither counselor informed Nina's parents about her suicidal statements. One week after telling her friends about her suicidal intentions, Nina and another 13-year-old girl consummated a murder-suicide pact in a public park some distance from the middle school she attended. (Adapted from *Eisel v. Board of Education of Montgomery County*, 1991.)

In *Kelson* (1985; Case 7.2), Brian's parents filed a negligence suit against the school and city in state court and a Section 1983 lawsuit against the school and city in federal court, alleging that the state interfered with their constitutionally protected liberty interest in the companionship of their son. When the Section 1983 lawsuit reached the U.S. Court of Appeals, the judge advised Brian's parents to file an amended claim against the school district after ruling on several legal questions raised by the case. In so doing, he raised the question of a possible relationship between school policy (namely, inadequate suicide training for its staff) and Brian's death.

In *Eisel* (1991; Case 7.3), Nina's father filed a negligence suit against the two school counselors based on their failure to communicate information to him concerning Nina's contemplated suicide. Nina's father believed he could have prevented his daughter's death had he been told about her statements. The court held that a school has a special duty to protect a pupil from harm and that "school counselors have a duty to use reasonable means to attempt to prevent a suicide when they are on notice of a child or adolescent's suicidal intent" (p. 456). The school counselors were viewed as having little discretion regarding whether to contact parents once information suggested a potential suicide.[4]

When it is suspected that a student is suicidal, the situation should be reported to a designated professional who has training in assessment of suicide lethality and suicide prevention.

---

[4] This decision did not determine the school's liability; the decision only allowed action in another court to rule on the school's liability. The school counselors ultimately were not held liable for the $1 million in damages the father sought.

The school psychologist might serve as one of the designated staff members. The student should be assessed for the lethality of suicidal ideation because the degree of lethality determines the appropriate course of action (Poland, 1989). Most methods of assessing lethality involve seeking answers to a series of critical questions, such as: Is there a preoccupation with death? Does the student have a suicide plan? Has the student made previous suicide attempts? Is the student involved with drugs? Has there been a precipitating event? Why does the student want to die? (See Poland, 1989; also see Lieberman, Poland, & Cassel, 2008.)

Research has shown that assessments to predict youth suicide yield high false-positive rates (Miller & Eckert, 2009). Consequently, although practitioners cannot be expected to predict suicide attempts with a high degree of accuracy (Knapp, 1980, p. 609), they are expected to apply "skill and care in assessing suicidal potential and . . . a reasonable degree of care and skill in preventing the suicide." Some psychologists recommend asking suicidal clients to sign a "no-suicide contract." Although "do no harm" contracts may be clinically useful, it is important to recognize that such contracts do not substitute for a careful risk assessment and appropriate intervention based on the assessed risk (Simon, 1999).

Parents must be contacted in all cases, whether the risk is determined to be low or high. As Poland (1989) noted, the question is not whether to tell the parents, but how to elicit a supportive reaction from them. Parents of medium- or high-risk students should be contacted as soon as possible. The high-risk student should not be left alone, and his or her parents should be required to come to school for a conference and to pick up their child (Poland, 1989). Poland recommended that two staff members conduct the parent notification conference and noted that some districts have parents sign a form acknowledging that they have been notified that their child is suicidal. The psychologist needs to ensure that parents understand the seriousness of the situation, and parents should be advised to increase supervision at home and remove access to weapons and other means of self-harm, such as medications. The practitioner should be prepared to refer the family to a community mental health professional who has expertise in working with suicidal youth. Poland also provided a number of recommendations for eliciting a supportive response from the parents.

School psychologists are well advised to develop consultative relationships with clinicians who have expertise in suicide assessment and management whom they can contact for assistance in evaluating and managing a potential suicide situation (Jobes & Berman, 1993). Practitioners also are advised to document their actions regarding risk assessment and management of students who may be suicidal. School-based practitioners should become familiar with community resources for referral, including the procedures for hospitalization of suicidal minors and adult students. Furthermore, school psychologists also need to consider the long-range needs of the suicidal student with regard to follow-up educational and mental health services. Unfortunately, as Miller and Eckert (2009) noted, many youths do not receive any form of treatment following a suicide attempt. Additionally, many questions remain regarding the most effective treatment for suicidal youth.

The courts generally have not held schools liable for failure to prevent a student suicide. One notable exception is when school actions are so reckless as to "shock the conscience" by placing the student at substantial increased risk of immediate self-harm. In *Armijo v. Wagon Mound Public Schools* (1998), a 13-year-old boy shot and killed himself after he was driven home by the school counselor and left alone even though both the school principal and the counselor knew that the boy was upset about a disciplinary infraction, had a history of suicide attempts, and had access to firearms at his house.

In a national survey of school psychology practitioners, Debski, Spadafore, Jacob, Poole, and Hixson (2007) found that most respondents had participated in a suicide-risk assessment in the previous two years. It has become increasingly important for school practitioners to obtain professional competence in assessment and management of suicidal students. Additionally, psychologists who acquire special expertise in suicide prevention can play an important role in the development of their school district's planned response to suicidal students. Recent publications have addressed best practices in school-based suicide prevention programs (see Lieberman et al., 2008; Miller & Eckert, 2009).

Threat to Others

Schools are one of the safest places for children (Mulvey & Cauffman, 2001; National Center for Education Statistics [NCES], 2008). However, violence in our schools is a concern of educators and parents. In 2006, students ages 12 to 18 years were victims of approximately 767,000 violent crimes at school, including simple assault and serious violent crimes. In 2007, 8% of students in grades 9 through 12 reported that they were threatened or injured with a weapon at school during the previous 12 months (NCES, 2008). Our focus here is on assessment of whether an individual student poses a danger to others; schoolwide programs to identify students who may be at risk for violent acts are discussed in Chapter 9.

The assessment of whether a student poses a danger to others is not an easy task. School personnel may become concerned about a student because of his or her aggressive, antisocial behavior (e.g., fighting, explosive temper). For such students, the task is to determine the risk for future violent acts and how to reduce the likelihood of future violence. Borum (2000) provided guidelines regarding how to conduct a systematic assessment of violence potential in such situations. His approach takes into account the student's past violent acts, the precipitants to those acts, and the protective factors—that is, factors that would help the student avoid situations likely to trigger violent actions. A student also may come to the attention of the school psychologist because the student made direct or indirect threats to injure others. The term *targeted violence* is used to refer to situations in which both the potential perpetrator and the target(s) are identifiable prior to a violent attack (Vossekuil, Reddy, Fein, Borum, & Modzeleski, 2000). As Borum (2000) noted, a different assessment approach is recommended in situations involving targeted violence.

When students make threats to injure others, such threats should be taken seriously (*Mirand v. Board of Education of the City of New York*, 1994; Reddy et al., 2001). A report sponsored by the Federal Bureau of Investigation recommended a multidisciplinary team approach to threat assessment (FBI Academy, 2000). This team might include mental health professionals, school administrators, and law enforcement professionals. In *Milligan et al. v. City of Slidell* (2000), a federal court ruled that it is permissible for school officials and police to detain and question a student thought to be planning an act of violence at school because the school's interest in deterring school violence outweighs a student's limited 4th Amendment privacy rights in such situations.

The risk factors for targeted violence do not appear to be the same as the risk factors associated with general aggression and violence recidivism among youth (Reddy et al., 2001). Reddy et al. outlined a model for evaluating whether a student is on a path to targeted violence. Their model is based on three principles: (1) Targeted violence is a result of an interaction among the student, situation, target, and setting; there is no single type of student prone to such acts; (2) evaluators must make a distinction between a student who makes threats versus one who actually poses a threat; and (3) targeted violence is often the product of an understandable pattern of thinking and behavior. The model involves evaluating the student's behavior and pattern of conduct using information from multiple sources. Information gathering might involve interviewing the student and his or her family, teachers, and friends and reviewing student records. Key questions that guide the threat assessment evaluation include the following: Does the student have ideas about or plans for targeted violence? Has the student shown an interest in violence, acts of violence by others, or weapons? Has the student engaged in any attack-related behavior, including menacing, harassing, or stalking? Is the student cognitively and physically capable of carrying out a plan of violence? Has the student experienced a recent loss or loss of status, and has this led to feelings of desperation and despair? What factors in the student's life and/or environment might increase or decrease the likelihood of the student becoming violent? (Also see Borum, Fein, Vossekuil, & Berglund, 1999.)

In making a decision whether a student is potentially dangerous, the psychologist is well advised to consult with other professionals. In court decisions, therapists have not been held liable for failure to warn "when the propensity toward violence is unknown or would be unknown by other psychotherapists using ordinary skill" (Knapp & VandeCreek, 1982, p. 515).

Consistent with the guidelines for other situations involving danger, schools need to develop written procedures regarding when and how to notify school officials and legal authorities (e.g., police, the student's probation officer) if school staff become aware of a potentially assaultive student. These procedures should ensure that the intended victim is warned. If a student poses a threat to a minor child, the parents of the threatened child should be notified (see Case 7.1). Parents of a potentially assaultive student also must be informed of the situation. The potentially violent student should be supervised in the school setting and at home, with steps taken to ensure that there is no access to weapons. School psychology practitioners should know and follow school policies regarding dangerous students and document their actions in the management of a student who may become violent. In addition, they should be prepared to refer the family to a community mental health agency and be knowledgeable of procedures for the involuntary commitment of minors and adult students (Pitcher & Poland, 1992).

Practitioners also must consider the long-range needs of students at risk for violence with regard to follow-up educational and mental health services. They need to ensure that the student receives well-coordinated assistance from the family, school, and community mental health professionals. Furthermore, as is true of many mental health concerns in the school setting, efforts aimed at preventing student violence on a systemwide basis are preferable to the dilemmas of managing the assault-prone student (see Jimerson & Furlong, 2006; also see Chapter 9).

Substance Abuse

Alcohol is the substance most commonly used illegally by minors. In 2008, 32% of eighth graders, 53% of tenth graders, and 66% of students in grade 12 reported having consumed alcohol within the year. In the same year, 14% of eighth graders, 27% of tenth graders, and 37% of students in grade 12 reported using illicit drugs (National Institute on Drug Abuse, 2008). School psychologists (particularly those who work with middle and senior high students) need to be knowledgeable about drugs commonly used by adolescents and the symptoms of alcohol and drug abuse.

Forman, Bry, and Urga (2006, p. 1011) defined *substance abuse* as "the use of alcohol or other drugs in ways that negatively affect life functions" and go on to note that most youth "who use alcohol and drugs do not use them in ways that are considered abuse." At times, however, the frequency, duration, or type of substance used (e.g., amphetamines) may pose a threat to the student's physical or mental health.

Unfortunately, the laws regarding disclosure of a student's substance abuse to his or her parents are complicated. If a minor student discloses risky substance abuse to a school-based psychologist within the context of a professional relationship, the school psychologist may disclose this information to the child's parent and work with the parent in locating treatment. However, with the exception of a medical emergency, federal law provides confidentiality protection to students, *including minors*, who specifically seek drug and alcohol evaluation and treatment (part of the Public Health Service Act codified at 42 U.S.C. § 290dd; 42 C.F.R. Part 2). For this reason, if a student requests drug or alcohol treatment or a referral for treatment and he or she does not want his or her parents to be notified, the request is absolutely confidential, and the school psychologist should identify treatment options for the student that do not require parental notice or consent (Cohn, Gelfman, & Schwab, 2005; also see Boonstra & Nash, 2000).

If a school psychologist gains knowledge of substance abuse that involves other students in the school setting, the practitioner may need to discuss the situation with appropriate school authorities (without disclosing the identity of the student client) to ensure the safety of others. Practitioners must be cautious to avoid involvement in searches of students for illegal drugs, particularly if such activities are not part of their formal job responsibilities (see Chapter 2). School-based practitioners can, however, assume a leadership role in the development and implementation of educational programs for school staff and parents regarding substance abuse, prevention, and intervention programs for students, and developing liaisons with community resources (Forman et al., 2006).

Students Who Disclose Criminal Acts

If, within the context of a psychologist-client relationship, a student or other client discloses that he or she committed a crime and was never arrested, does the psychologist have a legal obligation to report the crime to the police or the building principal? If there is no legal duty to report a past crime to the police, is it permissible for the school psychologist to do so without risking a malpractice lawsuit? (See Appelbaum & Meisel, 1986.)

In 1790, the U.S. Congress passed *misprision of felony* laws, making it a criminal offense "to conceal and . . . not as soon as possible make known" a felony committed by another person (U.S.C., Title 18, § 4). Subsequent court decisions have held that misprision of felony occurs only if an individual takes affirmative steps to conceal a felony committed by another person (e.g., suppressing evidence, providing false statements to authorities, hiding stolen property); simple failure to report a felony is not a crime (*U.S. v. Farrar*, 1930). Although state laws vary with regard to misprision of felony statutes, Applebaum and Meisel (1986, p. 227) concluded, "American law at the federal and state levels rejects the imposition of criminal liability for mere failure to report a crime and requires overt assistance rendered to a felon for there to be a criminal offense." Thus, school psychologists generally do not have a legal duty to report a crime committed by student clients or their parents, unless it involves suspected child abuse or other state-mandated reporting. In *McDuff v. Tamborlane* (1999; Case 3.4), the school psychologist had no legal duty to report the student's past crime of larceny.

If there is no legal duty to report a past crime, is it permissible for the school psychologist to do so without becoming liable for malpractice (Appelbaum & Meisel, 1986)? As noted in Chapter 3 under "Privileged Communication," if a psychologist discloses privileged client information to others without first obtaining client consent to do so (consent of an adult student or the parents of a minor child), they put themselves at risk for a malpractice suit. In *McDuff v. Tamborlane* (1999; Case 3.4), the parents of a student client filed a malpractice suit against a school psychologist after she disclosed information about the student's past crime without parent consent to do so, and the student was arrested.

Exceptions to the requirement of consent for disclosure of privileged information include child abuse reporting and when a client is deemed to be a danger to self or others.

What can practitioners do to avoid ethical-legal dilemmas that arise when student clients disclose past criminal acts? As noted in Chapter 3, practitioners must carefully define confidentiality and its limits to student clients and their parents. Our federal courts have recognized that individuals who receive mental health services generally expect their disclosures to a psychologist to be held in strict confidence unless they are told otherwise (see Uniform Rules of Evidence, 1999). In *McDuff* (Case 3.4), the mother assumed that the information she provided to the school psychologist was confidential, and the judge supported her contention, noting that a parent would naturally assume that communications to the school psychologist were confidential. In contrast, in *People v. Vincent Moreno* (2005; Case 3.5), the school psychologist had forewarned a student (who was no longer one of her clients) that if he disclosed anything "really serious," she was bound to "take it to a higher level" ("Psychologist-Patient Privilege," 2002, p. 17). As happened in *Moreno*, student clients may confess to criminal acts even after they are warned about the limits of confidentiality.

If a school-based psychologist believes the past crimes of a minor student should be reported to legal authorities, the issue should be discussed with the student and parents. For example, most practitioners would be uncomfortable keeping quiet if an innocent individual had been wrongly convicted of the crime that the student client committed. The student's parents *should be encouraged to report the crime but to obtain legal representation for their child before they contact legal authorities* (Applebaum & Meisel, 1986). If the parents cannot be persuaded to report the crime themselves and the psychologist believes the situation is so serious that it must be reported, the practitioner should consult the school's attorney regarding how to proceed.

As noted in Chapter 3, state law extending privileged status to nondoctoral mental health workers is evolving. Consistent with evolving law, "School psychologists recognize that client–school psychologist communications are privileged in most jurisdictions and do not disclose information that would put the student or family at legal . . . or other risk if shared with third parties" without prior consent to do so, "except as permitted by the mental health provider-client privilege laws of their state" (NASP-PPE I.2.2).

Pregnancy, Birth Control, and Sexually Transmitted Disease

In the following paragraphs we provide a brief overview of the legal issues associated with student pregnancy, birth control counseling, and sexually transmitted disease (STD).

Pregnancy

In 2002, there were an estimated 252,170 pregnancies in the 15- to 17-year-old age group, and 17,340 pregnancies for girls under age 15 (Alan Guttmacher Institute, 2006). School psychologists who work with adolescents must be knowledgeable about area physicians and family planning clinics that provide teens with sensitive and supportive care. If a student discloses to a school psychologist that she suspects she is pregnant, the practitioner should refer the student to a physician or clinic to confirm or disconfirm the pregnancy. Parent notification or consent is not needed for a minor to visit a family planning clinic. It is important, however, to refer students to a neutral agency, not one perceived as an abortion clinic (Hummel, Talbutt, & Alexander, 1985).

In *Arnold v. Board of Education of Escambia* (1990; Case 7.4), the court noted that federal law does not require school personnel to notify the parents of a student who is pregnant. However, practitioners must be familiar with state law and district policy

---

Case 7.4

In *Arnold v. Board of Education of Escambia* (1990), a 15-year-old female student ("Jane Doe") was referred to a school counselor because a physical education coach suspected Jane might be pregnant. After the pregnancy was confirmed, the counselor encouraged Jane to inform her mother, or her aunt, with whom she lived. The student refused to do so because she had already been thrown out of her mother's home, where there also was a history of physical abuse, and she feared her aunt would ask her to leave if she was pregnant. The counselor and a social worker explored options with the student, including adoption. The student made her own decision to choose an abortion. A grandparent of the unborn child later filed suit against the school, claiming that the school counselor and social workers coerced Jane to have an abortion and refrain from notifying parents about the pregnancy and that their actions interfered with parental guidance. The court decided for the school, noting that Jane was of age to consent to an abortion under state law and that there was no requirement for a school to notify the parents of the pregnancy of a minor student under federal or state law.

---

regarding parental notification when an unemancipated minor is pregnant. Except for situations in which disclosure to the parent might mean more harm to the student than nondisclosure, a student should be encouraged to disclose her pregnancy to a parent. In some circumstances, it may be necessary for school personnel to inform parents about their daughter's pregnancy to safeguard the student's health and well-being.

If a school psychologist continues to work with the student after her pregnancy is confirmed, all alternatives to pregnancy management should be discussed and explored (*Arnold*, 1990; Case 7.4). The Alan Guttmacher Institute provides state-by-state information regarding a minors' right to consent to confidential prenatal care, the right of minors to place their children for adoption, and state laws regarding access to abortion for minors (see http://www.guttmacher.org).

There have been numerous court cases involving minors and access to abortion. In *Planned Parenthood of Central Missouri v. Danforth* (1976), the Supreme Court held that a Missouri statute requiring parental consent prior to an abortion in the case of an unmarried minor was unconstitutional. As of 2009, parent consent or notice for a minor to obtain an abortion is required in 34 states. However, all of the 34 states that require parent consent or notice provide for a *judicial bypass* procedure as an alternative to parent notice or consent for minors seeking an abortion (Alan Guttmacher Institute, 2009c). A judicial bypass to parental involvement in a minor's decision to have an abortion was described in the 1979 *Bellotti v. Baird* Supreme Court decision as:

> an alternative procedure whereby authorization for the abortion can be obtained. A pregnant minor is entitled to such a proceeding to show either (1) that she is mature enough and well enough informed to make her abortion decision, in consultation with her physician, independently of her parents' wishes; or (2) that even if she is not able to make this decision independently, the desired abortion would be in her best interests. (p. 4973)

In addition to judicial bypass procedures, six states allow a minor to have an abortion without parent notice or consent if a grandparent or other adult relative is involved in the decision, 31 states allow a minor to obtain an abortion without parental involvement in a medical emergency, and 14 states permit access to an abortion without parent involvement in cases of assault or incest. Information on state policies regarding parental involvement in minors' abortions can be found at http://www.guttmacher.org.

Birth Control Information

Most states allow minors to consent to contraceptive services without parent notice or consent (Alan Guttmacher Institute, 2009a). The issue of *school* involvement in the provision of family planning information is highly controversial and involves deep-rooted family and community values. School policies run the gamut, from those that forbid discussion of birth control with individual students to programs that allow easy student access to family planning information and contraceptives (e.g., health clinics on or adjacent to school grounds).

Practitioners who work with adolescents must be knowledgeable about state law and local school policy regarding the provision of birth control information by school staff and be sensitive to community and family values. Providing competent advice on contraception to a minor in the school setting is probably permissible unless it conflicts with state or local policies (Fischer & Sorenson, 1996).

Sexually Transmitted Disease

In the United States, an estimated 19 million new cases of sexually transmitted disease (STD) occur each year, and almost half of them are among teenagers and young adults 15 to 24 years of age (Centers for Disease Control and Prevention, 2009a). The spread of human immunodeficiency virus (HIV) among adolescents is a cause of national concern. If a psychologist believes that a student client may have or is at risk of contracting an STD, the student should be referred to a public health clinic or area physician known to provide teens with sensitive care. It is important to remember that young adolescents often think they are invincible and may deny any risk. All states allow minors to consent to confidential testing and treatment of STDs. Eighteen states allow a physician to inform a minor's parents that their child is seeking or receiving STD services if the physician believes it is in the best interests of the minor, and one state requires parent notification of a positive HIV test (Alan Guttmacher Institute, 2009b).

What if a student client has tested positive for HIV and engages in unprotected sex with partners who are uninformed of his or her HIV status? First-step strategies for the school psychologist include encouraging the student to discontinue sexual activity unless sexual partners are informed about his or her HIV status and to practice safe sex. The student should be reminded that, under most state laws, knowingly transmitting an STD could result in legal action against him or her.

Little consistency exists in the laws of various states regarding a psychologist's duty to protect a client's sexual partner from exposure to HIV, and ethical opinions on the matter are contradictory (see Huprich, Fuller, & Schneider, 2003). If the student client fails to take responsibility to protect others from exposure to possible infection, the psychologist may have a duty to protect the student client's sexual partners from risk of HIV. As noted in Chapter 3, a minor has no *legal* right to confidentiality independent of the parent. If the student client with HIV is a minor, talking with his or her parents about the situation may be appropriate. If the parents are uncooperative or not likely to be of assistance or the student is an adult, practitioners are advised to seek guidance regarding how to handle the situation from their state public health agency. Penalties may exist under state law if school personnel disclose to third parties that a student client is infected with an STD. However, these same state laws typically allow school personnel to contact public health for assistance without penalty (also NASP-PPE I.2.7).

School psychologists can play an important role in encouraging the development of programs to prevent teen pregnancies and reduce the incidence of STDs among teenagers. Interested readers are referred to Stoiber and McIntyre (2006).

Summary

Within the protection of a confidential relationship, students may report any number of behaviors that, although not immediately dangerous, have that potential. Such actions as failure to take prescribed medications, eating disorders, criminal activity, engaging in unprotected sex, and sexual promiscuity might fall into this category.

Anticipating all possible circumstances in counseling that may prove to be a problem is not possible. The keys to dealing with most cases successfully are, first, a candid discussion of confidentiality and its limits at the outset of offering services; second, a good working relationship with the student; third, knowledge of state laws and regulations as well as school policies; fourth, familiarity with resources in the community and how to access them; and fifth, dealing openly and honestly with the student about your concerns and possible courses of action.

COMPETENCE AND RESPONSIBILITY

Consistent with the principle of responsible caring, school psychologists are obligated to "recognize the strengths and limitations of their training and experience, engaging only in practices for which they are qualified" (NASP-PPE II.1.1; also APA-EP 2.01).

Competence

A problem for psychologists is to determine what constitutes an acceptable and recognized level of competency to provide specific services. Seeking assistance through supervision, consultation, and referral is an appropriate strategy for handling a difficult case (NASP-PPE II.1.1). However, practitioners who plan to introduce new counseling techniques or expand the scope of their services must complete appropriate and verifiable training before offering such services (APA-EP 2.01).

Is Carrie (Case 7.5) competent to provide group counseling to teens with eating disorders? The question of her competence relates to both the adequacy of the workshop she attended and her background. If she has had extensive training in group counseling, including prior supervised experience, she is able to claim more competence to attempt this new technique than if this workshop was her first exposure to the group counseling process. Group counseling techniques require a high degree of skill and prior supervised experience (Fischer & Sorenson, 1996).

========================= Case 7.5 =========================

Carrie Johnson, school psychologist, has developed expertise in eating disorders and has successfully counseled a number of students on a one-to-one basis. She became interested in providing a counseling group for students with eating disorders and attended a one-day workshop on using group counseling methods with anorexic and bulimic teens. She is now using this group counseling technique with students in her schools.

Case 7.6

Tamika, a new student in Mr. March's fifth-grade class, recently transferred from an inner-city school located in a poverty-ridden neighborhood. She came to live with her grandparents after her mother's death. She is one of only a few African American students in her new school, which, along with her Black English, sets her apart from her classmates. Tamika's records from her previous school indicate that she was an average student, and there is no mention of disciplinary problems. According to Mr. March, Tamika appears to be scared and angry. She refuses to talk in class, has made no friends, and does not complete assignments. Her classmates complain that she is "mean," that she shoves or punches when no teachers are in sight. When Hannah Cook, the school psychologist, phoned Tamika's grandparents to discuss her school adjustment and invite them in for a conference, Tamika's grandmother responded, "The Lord brought Tamika to us, and He will show us the way." She declined to come in for a conference but agreed to allow Hannah to work with Tamika to identify possible interventions. Hannah has received training in helping children cope with grief and loss, but she has little experience working with African American students or their families, particularly students from low-income, inner-city homes who may be mistrusting of white school professionals.

Practitioners also must evaluate their competence to provide services to students whose background characteristics are outside the scope of their supervised experience. Is Hannah competent to provide psychological counseling to Tamika (Case 7.6)? Ignoring or minimizing the importance of client characteristics such as race, ethnicity, sexual orientation, or socioeconomic background may result in approaches that are ineffective (NASP-PPE II.1.2; N. D. Hansen et al., 2000; Rogers et al., 1999).

An issue related to the question of competence is whether the school psychologist is the most competent professional available to provide the counseling service. School psychologists recognize the competence of other professionals and encourage the use of all resources to best meet the needs of students (NASP-PPE III.3.1). Hannah Cook (Case 7.6) may have some expertise in helping children cope with loss. However, she should consider whether Tamika might benefit more from counseling provided by a professional who has experience working with African American children and their families.

School psychologists also are ethically obligated to refrain from any activity in which their personal problems or conflicts may interfere with professional effectiveness. "When personal beliefs, conflicts of interest, or multiple relationships threaten to diminish professional effectiveness . . . school psychologists ask their supervisor for a reassignment of responsibilities, or they direct the client to alternative services" (NASP-PPE III.4.2).

Responsibility

The APA code of ethics states, "Psychologists terminate therapy when it becomes reasonably clear that the client/patient . . . is not likely to benefit, or is being harmed by continued service" (APA-EP 10.10). If the practitioner determines that he or she is not able to be of professional assistance to the client, the psychologist should "suggest alternative service providers as appropriate" (APA-EP 10.10; also NASP-PPE II.2.2).

PSYCHOPHARMACOLOGIC INTERVENTIONS IN THE SCHOOLS

Beginning in the 1990s, there was an increase in the use of psychotropic agents to treat a variety of mental disorders in children. As Kral, LaRosa, Brown, and Kubiszyn (2006) noted, this rise in the use of psychotropic agents occurred despite the fact that many of these medications have not been adequately tested for safety and effectiveness in children. This portion of the chapter alerts the practitioner to ethical and legal issues associated with the use of medications to treat children with school learning or behavior problems. Discussion here is limited to the use of Ritalin (methylphenidate hydrochloride), a drug that has been approved by the Food and Drug Administration for the treatment of attention deficit/hyperactivity disorder (ADHD) in children aged six years and older (*Physicians' Desk Reference*, 2010). Ritalin is widely prescribed for schoolchildren in the United States (Marshall, 2000), and it provides an excellent example of both the promise and potential pitfalls of drug therapy.

Substantial research has shown that stimulant medication can be effective in the treatment of ADHD (e.g., Angold, Erkanli, Egger, & Costello, 2000). Many school psychology practitioners and teachers have witnessed the dramatic improvements that occur for some children after they are placed on Ritalin. However, the use of Ritalin or other drugs to treat difficulties such as ADHD places the child at risk for physical or psychological harm because of the problems of potential misdiagnosis and drug side effects. A number of different types of hyperactivity exist, and stimulant medication is not appropriate for all types. Some children may be placed on Ritalin because of misdiagnosis, and use of the drug may consequently mask the child's true problems (Angold et al., 2000; Marshall, 2000).

Although Ritalin is generally considered safe, harm can result from its side effects. Potential side effects include nervousness, insomnia, anorexia, nausea, dizziness, headache, cardiac arrythmia, blood pressure changes, skin rash, abdominal pain, and growth suppression. Although rare, toxic psychosis, the development of Tourette's syndrome, abnormal liver function, and cerebral arteritis (inflammation) also have been reported (*Physicians' Desk Reference*, 2010).

A number of lawsuits have been filed against public schools and physicians by parents of children prescribed Ritalin. In many of these suits, children suffered physical (e.g., Tourette's syndrome) or psychological harm (e.g., suicidal behavior) as a result of drug treatment recommended to them by school personnel (see Case 7.7). In some instances, parents report that they were pressured by school officials to seek drug treatment for their son or daughter with threats of exclusion from school if they failed to comply (*Valerie J. v. Derry Coop. School District*, 1991).

Pediatricians report that schools overrefer students to them for treatment of ADHD, and many believe ADHD is overdiagnosed (HaileMariam, Bradley-Johnson, & Johnson, 2002). Barkley and Edwards (1998) recommended that identification of students with ADHD be based on *DSM-IV* criteria (American Psychiatric Association, 2000) following a comprehensive psychological assessment and pediatric medical examination. The psychological evaluation to identify children with ADHD should be based on multiple assessment methods across settings, including teacher, parent, and child interviews; behavior rating scales; cognitive and educational assessment; direct observation in the classroom; and functional behavioral assessment (Barkley & Edwards, 1998; Hoff, Doepke, & Landau, 2002). DuPaul, Barkley, and Connor (1998) provided a list of child, family, and situational factors that should be examined when drug therapy is under consideration, and it is likely that the school psychologist can play a valuable role in collecting this information (also see HaileMariam et al., 2002).

Case 7.7

In 1980, a California court approved the settlement of a lawsuit filed by 18 students and their parents against the school district. In the suit, the parents made claims against the school district and staff (including the school psychologist) stemming from the district's intrusion into the decision whether a child should take Ritalin to control what the schools alleged was hyperactive behavior. The parents contended that they had been subjected to extremely strong pressure to agree to the administration of the drug. One parent reported being called in before an array of school district staff and told that she would be a "foolish parent" if she refused to give the drug to her son. Others were told that their children could not possibly succeed in school without the drug, or that they would not be able to remain in general education classes unless they took it. Nothing was mentioned about the potentially dangerous side effects of the drug, and when parents asked about this, they were told that the drug was as harmless as aspirin. Only the most superficial of medical examinations of the children were done prior to prescribing or recommending the drug, and no follow-up monitoring at all was done. No efforts were made to alter any environmental factors (such as poor teaching) that might have contributed to the children's difficult behavior.

The suit was filed after two of the children experienced their first grand mal epileptic seizures while taking the drug. Other children complained of aches and pains, insomnia, loss of appetite, apathy, moodiness, nosebleeds, and other problems associated with the drug Ritalin. Expert witnesses for the parents testified that many of the children were perfectly normal and should never have been candidates for drug therapy and that the school's procedures for diagnosis and prescription were woefully inadequate.

The settlement agreement ordered by the court included a lump sum of $210,000, which the court allocated among the plaintiffs according to the severity of harm each child suffered. In addition, the settlement agreement set forth a number of policy clarifications that precluded the school district from diagnosing hyperactivity or recommending in any way that a child take behavior-modification drugs. (Adapted from *Benskin v. Taft City School District*, 1980.)

To receive IDEA 2004 funds, states must prohibit school personnel from requiring parents to obtain a prescription for a controlled substance as a condition of attending school. The law does not, however, prohibit school personnel from consulting or sharing classroom-based observations with parents or guardians regarding a student's behavior in the school (34 C.F.R. § 300.174). Thus, decisions to prescribe drugs must be made by a physician (a point that should be clearly communicated to parents), and parents must be free to choose or refuse the use of such medication without pressure from the school.

The court settlement in *Benskin* (1980) provides some guidance to schools regarding psychopharmacological interventions with students. Drug treatment requires careful physician-school-parent collaboration. The school psychologist should ensure that parents have been provided information regarding the potential benefits of drug treatment (e.g., enhanced academic productivity, reduced disruptive behavior) and any known risks (drug side effects and adverse reactions). Through cooperative efforts with the physician, school psychologists can assist in the monitoring of the effectiveness of drug treatments and thereby provide important feedback to the physician and parents (see Carlson, 2008; Kral et al., 2006).

Research findings indicate that drugs such as Ritalin are generally effective in improving the academic productivity of children with ADHD (DuPaul et al., 1998). However, individualized instruction may be needed to translate improved productivity into enhanced academic achievement. Based on their review of the research, Henker and Whalen (1989) concluded that most children with ADHD need individualized interventions to promote improved academic achievement and foster social competence, whether or not they are given medication. (See Power, 2009.)

CONCLUDING COMMENTS

> Teenaged parents. Academic failure. Substance abuse. Youth suicide. Divorce. AIDS. Childhood depression. Juvenile delinquency. Sexual abuse. The list of problems facing students in our schools today continues to grow and seemingly is endless. Yet, our time and resources remain limited. (Zins & Forman, 1988, p. 539)

Today we must add fear of terrorism and school shootings, and the problem of student-on-student harassment and victimization, including cyberbullying. Partly in response to court decisions and high-profile crisis events, many schools are beginning to recognize the importance of a planned response to crisis situations and many are beginning to place a greater emphasis on the prevention of student academic and mental health problems.

STUDY AND DISCUSSION

Questions for Chapter 7

1. When a school psychologist becomes aware of a potentially assaultive student, what actions are appropriate?
2. When a school psychologist becomes aware of a potentially suicidal student, what actions are appropriate?
3. When a school psychologist suspects child abuse or child neglect, what actions are appropriate?
4. Develop a list of guidelines for teachers on how to safeguard the ethical and legal rights of pupils when behavioral interventions are planned and implemented.
5. May a school require a child to take medication as a precondition for school attendance? Identify the ethical-legal issues associated with the use of medications to treat schoolchildren with learning and behavior problems.

Vignettes

1. Mrs. McClure, a kindergarten teacher, stops by Wanda Rose's office. "Wanda," she says, "I need your advice. Mr. and Mrs. Clifford came in to see me about their son, Kyle, who is in my kindergarten class. Kyle is a sweet, effeminate boy who prefers to play with the girls in the doll corner rather than play with the boys. Dad isn't comfortable with Kyle's girlishness, so the Cliffords now have a psychologist from downstate working with them to change Kyle's feminine behaviors. They want me to carry out a

behavior-change program in class similar to the one they are using at home—I'm to give Kyle blue poker chips when he shows masculine behavior and red ones for feminine behavior. The Cliffords will then reward Kyle for the blue chips—minus the red ones—he brings home from school. Wanda, I'm just not comfortable with this. What do you think I should do? What should I tell the Cliffords?" How should Wanda respond to this situation? What are the ethical issues involved? (See LeVay, 1996, pp. 97–102.)

2. Sam Foster, the school psychologist, developed good rapport with Frank Green, a tenth grader, when he counseled Frank about some problems in adjusting to a new step-father. Later in the year, Frank makes an appointment to see Sam and reports that things seem to be going better at home. He confides that he stopped by to talk to Sam because he is worried about a girl in his woodshop class named Heidi. Heidi is a friendly 16-year-old who is cognitively impaired. Recently, three boys in the woodshop class began to show a special interest in her. Frank saw the boys take Heidi into a storeroom near the woodshop on two occasions after class, and he thinks the boys are doing something bad to Heidi. How should Sam handle this situation?

3. Cindy, a troubled 14-year-old whom Hannah Cook has seen previously for counseling, comes to her without an appointment. She is upset because two of her best friends, Tara and Trisha, have made plans to "ambush and beat up" another girl after school because of an argument about a boy. She knows that Tara and Trisha have been in trouble at school before for fighting, and she is worried they will be kicked out of school if they follow through on their plans, and that they may really hurt their intended victim. How should Hannah respond to this situation? What are the ethical-legal issues involved?

4. Nora Hudson, a 16-year-old, makes an appointment to see Charlie Maxwell, the school psychologist. Nora confides that she is worried that her friend Jason may be planning to kill himself. She reports that Jason has been upset since his parents announced their plans for divorce several weeks ago and that he has been talking about "ending it all" because life isn't worth living. Recently Jason gave her several books from his prized collection of science fiction because he "won't need them anymore." How should Charlie handle this situation?

Activities

According to the NASP's code of ethics, it is permissible to delay the discussion of the boundaries of confidentiality if a student is in immediate need of assistance (NASP-PPE I.2.3). Except for such situations, school psychologists "inform students and other clients of the boundaries of confidentiality at the outset of establishing a professional relationship" (NASP-PPE I.2.3). You, the school psychologist, are responsible for defining the boundaries of confidentiality and explaining them in a language that is understood by the client(s). Role-play the following situations:

1. A teenager (age 14) has made an appointment for a counseling session with you, the school psychologist. Role-play the initial meeting during which the psychologist defines the parameters of confidentiality and discusses parent consent issues.

2. A parent, Mrs. Fox, has made an appointment with you to discuss her concerns about Bill, her 15-year-old son. She reports that Bill has become moody and difficult and that his grades have recently declined markedly. She would like you to meet with Bill to see whether you can discover what the problems are and report your findings back to her. Role-play the initial meeting with Mrs. Fox, including a discussion of consent, assent, and confidentiality issues.

3. During a precounseling screening session, Joan Bellows, a 16-year-old, confides in you that she might be pregnant. Role-play how you might handle this situation.

4. A 13-year-old boy has been referred to you for counseling. The student has a history of truancy, running away from home, and being involved in physical fights at school, and he is suspected of stealing from other students. Role-play the initial meeting with the student's parents during which you seek consent to provide counseling and discuss confidentiality issues. Role-play your meeting with the student during which you seek assent and discuss confidentiality and its limits.

Chapter 8

INDIRECT SERVICES I
Ethical-Legal Issues in Working with Teachers and Parents

Chapter 8 first addresses ethical issues associated with professional-to-professional consultation, focusing on teachers as consultees, and then discusses issues in working with parents.

CONSULTATION WITH TEACHERS

The term *consultation* is used here to refer to a voluntary, nonsupervisory relationship between the consultant (school psychologist) and the consultee (teacher or other school professional) established to remediate learning or behavior problems of a student and/or to improve the professional skills of the consultee (Conoley & Conoley, 1982; Gutkin & Curtis, 1999). By "voluntary" we mean that the consultant makes an informed choice to enter the consultative relationship. Unlike supervision, consultation is nonhierarchical; the consultant and consultee share coordinate status. The consultee remains an autonomous professional and retains the right to accept or reject suggestions made by the consultant. Although the consultee retains responsibility for decisions, the consultant encourages alternative solutions until the goals of the consultative relationship are achieved. Like supervision, the goals of consultation in the schools should be work-related (Conoley & Conoley, 1982; Gutkin & Curtis, 1999).

Integrity in Consultative Relationships with Teachers

In providing school-based consultative services, the school psychologist is working within a network of relationships. Consistent with the broad ethical principle of integrity in professional relationships, the psychologist/consultant strives to be honest and straightforward in interactions with the consultee. Consultants "explain their professional competencies, roles, assignments, and working relationships to recipients of services and others in their work setting in a forthright and understandable manner" (NASP-PPE III.2.1, also III.2.4).

Gutkin and Curtis (1999) suggested that the consultation role be clearly defined to the school community prior to offering consultative services (APA-EP 3.11; NASP-PPE III.2). Discussions of consultative services should include role definition, the process of goal setting during consultation, the responsibilities of the consultant and consultee, and the parameters of confidentiality. Although initially this may occur at the level of the school, the same entry stage issues subsequently are discussed with individual teachers at the beginning of establishing a consultative relationship.

A means of ensuring a mutual understanding of the parameters of a consultative relationship is through contracting. "A contract is a verbal or written agreement between the consultant and the consultee that specifies the parameters of the relationship"

(Conoley & Conoley, 1982, p. 115). The contract might include the following five elements: (1) general goals of consultation and how specific goals will be selected; (2) tentative time frame; (3) consultant responsibilities (services to be provided, methods to be used, time commitment, and how the success of the consultation will be evaluated); (4) the nature of consultee responsibilities; and (5) confidentiality rules. (Adapted from Gallessich, 1982, pp. 272–273.)

Respect for the Dignity of Persons (Welfare of the Consultee and Student)

When providing consultation to teachers, the broad principle of respect for the dignity of persons encompasses the obligation to safeguard the autonomy and self-determination of the consultee and student(s); to make known and respect boundaries of confidentiality; and to promote understanding among consultants, consultees, and students from culturally and linguistically diverse backgrounds.

Student Welfare, Autonomy, and Self-Determination

Although in consultation the teacher is the recipient of services, student welfare "must be of primary importance to a school-based consultant" (J. M. Davis & Sandoval, 1982, p. 549; also NASP-PPE III.2.3).

Students   School psychologists consider the rights and welfare of students to be their primary responsibility. The school psychologist is obligated to work with the teacher to ensure that consultation goals and intervention strategies are selected that are likely to be ultimately beneficial to the student (NASP-PPE II.3, III.2.3). A number of strategies can be used for safeguarding student welfare, autonomy, and self-determination when providing consultative services. These include involving the student as much as is feasible in the selection of goals and intervention strategies and selecting goals to promote student self-management (Newman, 1993).

Teacher/Consultee   In providing consultation services to the teacher, the teacher/consultee remains an autonomous professional and retains the right to accept or reject suggestions made by the consultant. The psychologist discourages teacher dependence on the consultant (Fanibanda, 1976), and also is careful to avoid stepping into the role of counselor/therapist to the consultee (Gutkin & Curtis, 1999).

Consultants must be keenly sensitive to the ethical issues of manipulation and control of the consultee in providing consultative services to teachers (J. N. Hughes, 1986). The psychologist and teacher have differing fields of specialization, and they may have differing values. It is important that, as consultants, we "sufficiently understand the values of the community, institution, consultee, and clients with whom we work so that we will not merely impose our values on them" (J. M. Davis & Sandoval, 1982, p. 545; also NASP-PPE I.3.2, IV.1.1). As Fanibanda (1976) pointed out, our obligation to the welfare of the student may require us to advocate for certain decisions even if they conflict with the apparent value orientation of the consultee. Candid discussion of values and goals throughout consultation is a safeguard for teacher autonomy (D. Brown, Pryzwansky, & Schulte, 1987).

Consistent with our ethical codes, school psychologists work in full cooperation with teachers in a relationship based on *mutual respect* (NASP-PPE III, III.2.3). It is important to remember that teachers are our most important resource in helping children in the school setting.

Informed Consent

In consultative services to the teacher, the use of a verbal or written contract helps to ensure his or her informed consent for services. As discussed in Chapter 7, informed consent of the parent is needed if an intervention is planned for a student that diverges from ordinary, expected schooling.

Confidentiality

Confidentiality in providing consultative services to the teacher can be problematic. The parameters of confidentiality must be discussed at the outset of the delivery of services, and at a minimum, teachers should clearly understand what and how information will be used, by whom, and for what purposes (APA-EP 4.02; NASP-PPE I.2.3; Newman, 1993). In general, in consultation to the teacher or other school staff, the guarantees of client confidentiality apply to the consultant-consultee relationship (Fanibanda, 1976). All that is said between the school psychologist and the consultee is kept confidential by the psychologist, unless the consultee requests information be disclosed to others (J. M. Davis & Sandoval, 1982). Violation of confidentiality in consultation with teachers or other staff is likely to result in a loss of trust in the school psychologist and may impair his or her ability to work with the consultee and others.

Is there ever a duty to breach the confidentiality of the consultant-consultee relationship to safeguard the welfare of students? In providing consultative services to teachers, school psychology practitioners must identify limits to the promise of confidentiality (Conoley & Conoley, 1982; J. N. Hughes, 1986; Newman, 1993). More specifically, as a consultant, the school psychologist should inform the consultee that third parties (e.g., the building principal) may be notified if the consultee "chronically and stubbornly" persists in activities that put students at risk for foreseeable harm (Conoley & Conoley, 1982, p. 216).

However, "before breaching confidentiality, the consultant must have expended all resources at influencing the consultee to take collaborative action" (J. N. Hughes, 1986, p. 491). Such a breach of confidentiality would be appropriate only in unusual circumstances, namely when the consultee's actions are harmful or potentially harmful to students: "The consultee's approach toward the client [student] actually must be detrimental to the child rather than a less than optimal approach" (p. 491). The consultant is obligated to discuss the anticipated breach of confidentiality with the consultee prior to disclosure of information to third parties.

Fairness and Nondiscrimination

The broad ethical principle of respect for the dignity of persons also encompasses the values of fairness and nondiscrimination. School psychologists deal justly and impartially with each consultee regardless of his or her personal, political, cultural, racial, linguistic, or religious characteristics. As noted in Chapter 1, practitioners have an ethical obligation to become knowledgeable of the values, beliefs, and worldview of the consultee so as to be able to provide consultative services in a culturally sensitive manner (NASP-PPE I.3, II.1.2).

Providing consultation across culturally diverse consultant-consultee-student groups can pose special challenges. To provide consultation services that foster school success for all students, Charlie Maxwell (Case 8.1) needs to ensure that Mrs. Dolan and other teachers understand the backgrounds, cultures, prior school experiences, and interests of the African American and Hispanic students who now attend Littlefield Elementary and how to select materials and modify instruction as needed to meet their needs. He also can help families new to Littlefield better understand the culture and expectations of the

---

Case 8.1

In the 1980s, there was a change in the ethnic-racial composition of Littlefield Elementary, one of Charlie Maxwell's schools, from 60% white students to almost 90% African American and Hispanic students. Littlefield Elementary now has a dynamic African American principal and a staff composed of many new teachers of diverse racial and ethnic backgrounds, as well as older white teachers. Charlie is concerned because a white second-grade teacher, Mrs. Dolan, recommends five or six of her students for grade retention each year, all African American boys. (Adapted from Rogers et al., 1999.)

---

school and work to assist them in supporting their children's achievements. Conceptual frameworks for cross-cultural consultation and best practices in providing services across culturally diverse consultant-consultee-client groups have been addressed in the literature (see Ingraham & Meyers, 2000).

Responsible Caring

Psychologists are obligated ethically to provide consultation only within the boundaries of their competence, to evaluate the impact of consultative services on consultees and students, and to modify consultative plans as needed to ensure effectiveness.

Professional Responsibility in Teacher Consultation

Practitioners accept responsibility for their decisions and the consequences of their actions (APA-EP Principles A, B; NASP-PPE II.2), and they work to offset any harmful consequences of decisions made. School psychologists "revise a recommendation, or modify or terminate an intervention plan, when data indicate the desired outcomes are not being attained" (NASP-PPE II.2.2).

Models of consultation typically include four stages: an entry phase, problem identification/clarification, intervention/problem solution, and evaluation. The fourth stage of the consultation process, evaluation, encourages professional responsibility on the part of both the school psychologist and the consultee. During this final stage, the consultant and consultee assess whether the intervention was successful in meeting the agreed-on goals, and if not, the consultant and consultee recycle back to the stages of problem identification/clarification or intervention/solution.

However, in the course of the consultative process, it may become apparent to the psychologist that he or she is unable to assist the consultee. If so, the psychologist is obligated ethically to refer the consultee to another professional (NASP-PPE II.2.2). This could occur when the consultee has emotional difficulties that interfere with effective functioning. As noted earlier, the practitioner generally must avoid the dual roles of consultant and counselor/therapist to the teacher. It may also become apparent during the consultative process that another professional is better able to assist the consultee (e.g., another psychologist with different skills or perhaps a well-respected teacher with special expertise in the problem area).

Special problems with regard to professional responsibility sometimes occur when the practitioner steps into the role of *consultant/trainer* and provides an in-service education workshop to teachers in the school or district. Although at first it might seem that the use of informational methods such as in-service training raises no special ethical concerns, problems may arise when there is no planned follow-up on the way the information provided is understood and used by teachers or other staff. For example, a number of writers noted that brief workshop methods of teaching applied behavior analysis techniques to teachers are inadequate and may result in unintended harmful consequences for pupils. As Conoley and Conoley (1982, p. 134) suggested, consultant/trainers are well advised to view in-service training as "a *means*, not an *end*." A number of options exist for follow-up consultation to ensure that new ideas and techniques introduced during in-service training are used appropriately in the classroom (see J. C. Hansen, Himes, & Meier, 1990, for suggestions).

Competence

D. Brown et al. (1987) suggested that the following competencies are necessary to provide effective consultative services: knowledge of models of consultation, organizational theory, and change strategies; skills in communication, relationship building, contracting, mediating, and group leadership; and judgmental competencies with regard to problem identification and solution. In addition, to provide services effectively, practitioners must be knowledgeable about the organization, philosophy, goals, and methodology of their school (NASP-PPE, IV.1.1), and they must be familiar with the areas of competence of other professionals in their setting (also Curtis, Castillo, & Cohen, 2008). The personal characteristics of the consultant also are important in successful school-based consultation (see Conoley & Conoley, 1982). Rogers et al. (1999) provided a list of recommended competencies for consulting across multiculturally diverse consultant-consultee-client groups.

SPECIAL ISSUES IN WORKING WITH PARENTS

Family-school partnerships have been linked to improved student achievement and higher academic aspirations, higher rates of academic engagement and attendance, and a reduction of suspensions and early school withdrawals (Esler, Godber, & Christenson, 2008). In this chapter we generally use the terms *family* or *parent* to mean "the caregivers with whom educators build a relationship to enhance children's learning" (Esler et al., 2008, p. 917). The term *parent*, however, more specifically refers to the adults who take primary responsibility for a child's welfare:

> The term *parent* may be defined in law or district policy, and can include the birth or adoptive parent, an individual acting in the place of a natural or adoptive parent (a grandparent or other relative, stepparent, or domestic partner), and/or an individual who is legally responsible for the child's welfare. (NASP-PPE Definition of Terms)

Respect for the Dignity of Persons

We again utilize the framework provided by the code of ethics of the National Association of School Psychologists (NASP, 2010a) to discuss the issues involved in working with families.

Autonomy and Self-Determination

Historically, prior to the 1970s, parents were expected to simply be passive recipients of decisions made by school professionals. Parents were often considered to be the source of their children's problems and treated poorly. Today, however, parents are viewed as collaborative partners in school-family relationships (Fish, 2002; Turnbull & Turnbull,

2001). Sheridan, Cowan, and Eagle (2000, p. 314) defined school-parent collaboration as "a student-centered, dynamic framework that endorses collegial, interdependent, and co-equal styles of interaction between families and educators who work jointly together to achieve common goals."

However, if parents are to assume the role of "equal and full partners with educators and school systems" (Turnbull & Turnbull, 2001, p. 13), schools must actively encourage and enable parents to do so. School psychologists, along with other school personnel, may need to help parents acquire the knowledge and competencies "necessary to solve problems, meet needs, realize personal projects, or otherwise attain goals" (Dunst & Trivette, 1987, p. 451). Practitioners also must know the rights of parents under federal and state law and ensure that parents are informed of those rights. As a result of advocacy efforts by parents and court rulings, the presumption that parents should be viewed as collaborators in educational decision making for their children has been incorporated into our codes of ethics and education law (Fish, 2002).

The Individuals with Disabilities Education Act (IDEA) of 1997 placed greater emphasis on parent involvement in special education decision making than previous versions of the law (Sheridan et al., 2000). Establishing an effective working relationship with parents became even more essential with the 2004 changes in special education law. Under IDEA 2004, parents may withdraw consent for assessment or special education placement or services at any time, and this withdrawal of consent must be honored (34 C.F.R. 300.9[c][1]). Because addressing the needs of the student is the top priority of school psychologists, practitioners must ensure genuine and ongoing communication with parents, listening carefully to family concerns and questions, and emphasizing the shared goal of making decisions that are in the best interests of the child (see Blue-Banning, Summers, Frankland, Nelson, & Beegle, 2004).

In addition, according to NASP's code of ethics, when a pupil experiences school difficulties, school psychologists encourage parent involvement in all phases of the problem identification and remediation process (NASP-PPE I.1.1, II.3.10). They clearly explain their services so that they are understood by parents (NASP-PPE I.1.3, III.2.1) and "respect the wishes of parents who object to school psychological services," guiding them to alternative resources (NASP-PPE I.1.5). Findings and recommendations are communicated to parents in language they can understand, and when interpreters are used, school psychologists adhere to ethical guidelines and best practices regarding their use (APA-EP 2.05; NASP-PPE II.3.6). Furthermore, practitioners propose alternative recommendations to parents, ensuring that options take into account the values and cultural background of the family and the types of support for school achievement the family is able to provide the child (NASP-PPE II.3.10).

It is important to recognize, however, that not all educators are willing to grant parents a partnership role. Furthermore, because of individual and cultural differences, not all parents may wish to assume a coequal role, and some are not capable of doing so (Webb, 2001). In such situations, because the school psychologist's "greatest responsibility is to those persons in the most vulnerable position," practitioners have a special obligation to speak up for the rights and wishes of the parent and student (Canadian Psychological Association, 2000, Principle I).

Managing the Conflicting Interests of Parent, Child, and School

How do school psychologists provide guidance, advice, and intervention while respecting parent autonomy and encouraging parent empowerment? What if the wishes of the parent do not coincide with the school psychologist's view of what is best for the child? How do school-based practitioners balance the needs of the particular family with the larger needs of the school (Friedman, Helm, & Marrone, 1999)? The problem of conflicting interests of multiple parties (parent, student, school) can arise in a variety of contexts (Dailor, 2007; Jacob-Timm, 1999). We provide two examples here that focus on special education decision making.

In Case 8.2, consistent with the principle of respect for autonomy, Charlie should encourage the parents to exercise their right to make their wishes known and understood. One way to foster parents' autonomy and safeguard their legal rights in special education decision making is to ensure that parents understand the assessment findings, alternative recommendations, the process of decision making (including factors the team is legally required to consider), and their role in that process. For example, at the beginning of the individualized education program (IEP) team meeting to determine Jane's placement, Charlie might remind all team members that, as educators and parents, they share the goal of developing the best possible program the district can offer Jane—a program that, at a minimum, meets the legal standard of "reasonably designed to confer meaningful educational benefit." In addition, Charlie might summarize issues that must be considered by the team under IDEA in making the placement decision: The presumption is placement in general education with supplementary supports and services; placement in a more restrictive setting must be justified on the basis of greater academic or social benefit, or the presence of behavior that interferes with the learning of others in the general education classroom (see Chapter 4). The goal of providing such information is to put parents on an equal footing with other team members in the decision-making process.

Charlie must ensure that Jane's parents understand the benefits and shortcomings of the alternative decisions. However, he must take care not to usurp their right to an independent opinion and voice about desired services for their child. Hartshorne (2002) recommended that professionals encourage parents to choose the right answers for themselves, with the understanding there may be no absolute right answer or any way to find one. Professionals can, however, encourage parents to investigate all available information. Friedman et al. (1999, p. 355), in contrast, stated that "it is proper and ethical and, in fact, supportive of the concept of consumer or patient autonomy for the professional to actively seek to influence the decisions and actions of the person(s) being helped." They argue that professionals have a greater base of knowledge and skills than do parents and that equal and mutual relationships naturally involve attempts to influence the other. Lasser and Klose (2007, p. 497) identified social psychological phenomena that can influence decision making by parents and other members of an IEP team (e.g., deference to authority or experts, pressure for conformity). They encouraged school psychologists to gain greater awareness of such factors and to learn strategies "to promote meaningful involvement of all team members."

Case 8.2

Charlie Maxwell is asked to conduct a reevaluation of a girl, Jane, who is developmentally disabled and who will be entering junior high next fall. Consistent with parental wishes, Jane has been in an inclusive setting since kindergarten. Following his assessment, Charlie feels very strongly that Jane will receive much greater academic benefit from an outstanding self-contained program in the junior high. However, the parents have made it clear that they wish to continue with an inclusive program for their daughter.

Case 8.3

The parents of a five-year-old boy with developmental disabilities have requested that their child be fully included in the kindergarten at his neighborhood school. Because of the child's unique needs, Sam Foster, the school psychologist, and the boy's parents believe he should be in a full-day program. Consequently, the parents have requested that their son be in both sections of kindergarten, morning and afternoon. Prior to the boy's IEP meeting, the school district's assistant superintendent contacts Sam. She has heard about the possible request for a full-day kindergarten placement and is concerned because by teacher contract a child with special needs counts as two children in a classroom. This boy would take the space of four children in kindergarten. Because this is a desirable school in the district, this means that three children will be turned away by the school and assigned to other elementary schools in the district.

How do school psychologists balance the needs of the particular family with the larger needs of the school? The NASP's code of ethics recognizes that school-based practitioners provide services to multiple parties, including children, parents, and systems, and states that school psychologists should support conclusions that are in the best interests of the child (NASP-PPE Introduction, III.2.3). Sam Foster in Case 8.3, like Charlie Maxwell in Case 8.2, may want to remind IEP team members of the legal parameters of the placement decision at the IEP team meeting. A full-day program must be provided if that is what is necessary to confer meaningful benefit. Then, Sam should advocate for the full-day kindergarten program he believes meets the intent of IDEA and is in the best interests of the child, even if it puts him in conflict with district wishes. (Also see Minke & Anderson, 2008.)

Privacy and Confidentiality

School psychologists respect family privacy and do not seek information that is not needed in the provision of services (NASP-PPE I.2.2). Practitioners must be sensitive to cultural differences regarding the concept of privacy and recognize that, in some cultures, discussing personal problems with individuals outside of the family is "taboo" (Webb, 2001, p. 343). In such situations, it is critically important that practitioners follow culturally appropriate protocols to build a relationship with family members before initiating discussion of the student's difficulties. Practitioners also should discuss confidentiality and its limits with family members before seeking information from them, carefully identifying the types of information that might be shared with other school personnel or outside agencies, for what purpose, and under what circumstances (NASP-PPE I.2.3). The concept of confidentiality may not be familiar to parents from some cultures, whereas parents from other backgrounds may be very concerned that information will not be held in confidence (Webb, 2001).

Professional Competence and Responsibility

Consistent with the principle of beneficence (responsible caring), school psychologists must consider whether they are competent to provide services in light of family characteristics (e.g., language, cultural background) and the nature of the concern, or whether the family might benefit more from services provided by another professional (see Case 7.6; NASP-PPE II.1.2). Webb (2001) reviewed the available research on cultural matching

---

Case 8.4

Pearl Meadows received a referral for evaluation of a first grader, Brent, because of his slow academic progress in reading and math. Brent lives in a trailer with his grandparents and two-year-old brother in a small rural community known for its high unemployment and poverty. His mother is in prison, convicted of burglary and arson. Brent is initially slow to warm up to Pearl but becomes quite talkative during their second meeting. He shares that he recently got into "big trouble" with his grandpa because he snuck out his bedroom window after being put to bed and went to play with older boys who live down the road. He goes on to explain how his grandpa went *"whack, whack, whack, whack, whack"* on his rear with a wooden paddle when he got home.

---

of psychologist and client, and reported that, for some groups, racial matching between practitioner and client results in more positive outcomes (also see Behring, Cabello, Kushida, & Murguia, 2000). Webb goes on to note, however, that for most clients who participated in these studies, *"the practitioner's personal qualities of sensitivity and competence were more important than was similarity of ethnicity and race"* (p. 344).

In responsible practice, practitioners discern the potential harm as well as benefits of their work with families. They must be concerned about the effects of their actions on parents, other caregivers, and siblings, as well as student clients. Pearl (Case 8.4) is obligated ethically to be sensitive to cultural and generational differences in the use of physical punishment in discipline but is obligated legally to report suspected child abuse. She must consider what actions, if any, might be appropriate in responding to Brent's disclosure and the possible consequences of each alternative course of action for Brent, his brother, and his grandparents.

Integrity in Relationships with Parents

Practitioner-family partnerships are ideally based on honesty, trust, shared responsibility, and mutual support (Sheridan et al., 2000). Practitioners must avoid conflicts of interest; that is, they refrain from taking on a professional role when their own interests (personal, professional, financial) could reasonably be expected to impair their objectivity, competence, or effectiveness or expose clients to harm or exploitation (APA-EP Principle B, 3.06; NASP-PPE III.4, III.4.2–4.4). In situations where there is a potential conflict of interest, practitioners ask their supervisor to assign a different school psychologist. If that is not feasible or acceptable, the practitioner should attempt to guide the parents to alternative resources (NASP-PPE III.4.2).

School psychologists also must consider potential problems associated with multiple relationships. In working with parents, multiple relationships occur when the school psychologist is in a professional role in relation to a student's parents and at the same time has another relationship with the parents or a person closely associated with the parents. For example, a school psychologist might be asked to provide services to a student whose parents are his or her close personal friends, or the parent with whom the school psychologist is consulting might be the teacher of the psychologist's own child.

Psychologists refrain from entering into multiple relationships if the relationship could reasonably be expected to impair the psychologist's performance (APA-EP 3.05; NASP-PPE III.4.2). Again, in such situations, the parents should be offered the services

---

Case 8.5

Hannah Cook is trying to establish a working partnership with a Puerto Rican couple whose 15-year-old daughter is pregnant. The family has appreciated Hannah's openness with them and recently invited her to the girl's baby shower. Should Hannah attend? (Situation suggested by Congress, 2001.)

---

of another school psychologist in the district, and if that is not feasible, the practitioners should attempt to guide them to alternative resources. However, multiple relationships "that would not reasonably be expected to cause impairment or risk exploitation or harm are not unethical" (APA-EP 3.05). If, due to unforeseen circumstances, a potentially harmful multiple relationship arises, the school psychologist attempts to revolve it with due regard for the best interests of the client and others involved (APA-EP 3.05; NASP-PPE III.4.2).

For many years, psychotherapists were cautioned to avoid social or other nonprofessional contacts with their patients because a blurring of professional boundaries could impair the therapist's objectivity or effectiveness. More recently, however, codes of ethics have been modified to recognize that not all social contacts between psychologists and their clients pose a risk of harm. Social contacts with families may, in fact, improve family-school relationships. For example, Hispanic families may expect relationships with the school psychologist to involve *personalismo*, namely a warm, friendly relationship in which the psychologist demonstrates an interest and concern about the individual student and his or her family. Making a personal connection with the family may be the only way to establish a partnership (Congress, 2001). Hannah Cook (Case 8.5) should consider both the potential benefits and disadvantages of social interaction with her student client and family in deciding whether to attend the baby shower.

Diversity Issues

School psychologists are obligated ethically to provide services to students and their families that are respectful of diverse backgrounds and circumstances (APA-EP 2.01; NASP-PPE I.3, I.3.2). Living in a multicultural society makes this challenging. Webb (2001) identified four themes related to strains and obstacles in culturally diverse practice. One is "the practitioner's lack of understanding about the multidimensional reality and stresses of the client's situation in the context of the client's specific cultural and family environment" (p. 339). School psychologists must strive to understand family circumstances; they cannot assume that the parents' reality is the same as theirs (Ortiz, Flanagan, & Dynda, 2008).

When Charlie Maxwell is able to contact Adam's mother (Case 8.6), he learns that she is a widow who works the second shift as a press operator in a stamping plant. Adam and his sisters go to a neighbor's house after school where she picks them up after midnight. She noticed that Adam has had some congestion but did not want to take him out of school to see the doctor and cannot afford to miss work. Now that she knows he is having problems at school, she promises to take him to the doctor and contact the teacher.

A second theme concerns difficulties in "engaging, communicating, and agreeing about the problem" (Webb, 2001, p. 339). Practitioners must be able to establish rapport with parents, communicate the school's concerns in culturally sensitive ways, and seek to understand how the parents view their child's development, learning, and behavior,

---

Case 8.6

Charlie Maxwell received a referral for an African American boy, Adam, who is experiencing difficulty learning to read. Charlie arranges to meet with Adam's teacher, Mrs. Barbos, who reports that Adam does not seem to be able to distinguish different phonemes. Adam has a "nonstop" runny nose and congestion, and Mrs. Barbos wonders if he is experiencing ear infections and possible hearing difficulties. Mrs. Barbos goes on to explain that Adam's parents did not show up for school open house or fall conferences. She has tried to contact them by phone many times after school and at night, but no one answers. Exasperated, she comments, "How can we be expected to help these kids when their parents don't care?"

---

along with the school's concerns. In some school districts, considerably more children are classified as emotionally disturbed than in other districts. This is likely due in part to different understandings of particular behavior. When the community becomes diverse culturally, these understandings can create considerable confusion.

A third theme describes "different ideas about seeking help and dealing with the problem situation" (Webb, 2001, p. 339). School psychologists should examine their systems for making services available to families to ensure that they are usable by persons from different cultural groups (NASP-PPE I.3.4). In addition, it is likely that cultural modifications in the psychologist's approach will be needed to work effectively with families from different backgrounds. For some families, attempts to establish a collaborative partnership may not be culturally appropriate (Behring et al., 2000; Lynch & Hanson, 1998). For example, some families with Asian roots place great importance on expert opinion and prefer a directive rather than a collaborative approach (Behring et al., 2000).

It is also important to recognize that many families prefer to seek and receive help from other family members, friends, or religious leaders rather than schools or social service agencies. Some mistrust school personnel (Webb, 2001). Practitioners are obligated ethically to identify alternative sources of assistance available in the community (NASP-PPE, I.1.5) and should work to support, rather than supplant, existing community-based helping relationships.

The final theme concerns the "different values and worldviews of the practitioner and the client" (Webb, 2001, p. 339). School psychologists should recognize that the way they prioritize needs and services may differ considerably from the way this is done by parents (NASP-PPE I.3.2).

Lopez and Rogers (2001) developed a comprehensive list of cross-cultural competencies for school psychologists. Four apply to working with parents and would seem important practices for school psychologists who wish to be respectful of and sensitive to cultural differences of the families they work with. These are being aware "of roles parents play in child's country of origin," "understanding of differences in child rearing practices due to cultural differences," respecting "values that clash with dominant culture," and being aware "of the value placed in education by the parents of the client" (p. 302).

A greater number of gay and lesbian parents are identifying themselves to school personnel than in past years. Unfortunately, as Ryan and Martin (2000, p. 207) observed, "At present there are few school systems that have the information, experience, comfort level, or even willingness to address the needs of lesbian, gay, bisexual and transgender-parented families." To form effective home-school partnerships with families headed by

---

Case 8.7

The principal has asked Pearl Meadows to attend a conference with the parents of a first-grade girl, Sally. When Pearl enters the conference room, she is greeted by two women who introduce themselves as Sally's mother Fran and Sally's mother Lynnly, who then go on to identify themselves as lesbians. Fran explains that they requested a meeting because, although Sally has been accepted by her classmates, she is harassed repeatedly on the school bus and playground by older boys who call her "dyke tyke" and other names. They hope the principal and staff will take action to stop the harassment.

---

lesbian and gay parents, practitioners must discard "any traditional notions about what a family constellation should optimally be" (p. 208). Practitioners are encouraged to seek specialized knowledge of the social obstacles faced by families with gay and lesbian parents and their needs in the school system.

In an interview study with gay- and lesbian-headed families, respondents identified both benefits and risks of disclosure of their family constellations to school personnel. Some choose not to disclose that they are parents with same-sex partners because they fear discrimination in housing or employment, social rejection or harassment of their children, loss of child custody because of sexual orientation, or that they would not be welcome at school (Ryan & Martin, 2000). Others, such as Sally's mothers in Case 8.7, choose to disclose their family constellation in hopes of opening channels of communication with the school and directly addressing any problems that may arise.

In Case 8.7, the school principal, teachers, Pearl, and other school staff must work cooperatively to address the immediate issue of teasing and harassment. Pearl will also seek ways to promote positive partnerships with these and other gay-parented families and to foster a school climate that encourages acceptance of diversity of family constellations. (See Shriberg et al., 2008.)

Responsibility to Families, Community, and Society

As noted in Chapter 1, school psychologists have an ethical obligation to use psychological knowledge to benefit students and the larger school community. Family-school partnerships have been found to enhance the success of students. Practitioners can assist in developing a school environment that is welcoming to all families, identifying parent-involvement activities appropriate to their own school community, and implementing and evaluating school-family partnership efforts. An increasing number of resources are available to assist practitioners in pursuing these goals (e.g., Esler et al., 2008; D. D. Miller & Kraft, 2008).

CONCLUDING COMMENTS

Effective problem solving and intervention for students who are experiencing difficulties in social or emotional development, school learning, or behavior depend on using the combined skills and resources of teachers, other professionals, and the family. School psychologists can play an important role in drawing together these resources to bring about positive change for individual students, classrooms, and schools.

Practitioners will undoubtedly encounter difficult teachers and parents in the course of their careers. Regardless of their personal feelings and frustrations, school psychologists are ethically obligated to engage in conduct that is respectful of all persons (NASP-PPE I). Research with physicians has demonstrated the importance of sensitive and tactful communication with clients and consultees (Knapp & VandeCreek, 2006). For example, Levinson, Roter, Mullooly, Dull, and Frankel (1997) audiotaped two groups of physicians interacting with patients during routine office visits. One group of physicians had a history of one or more malpractice claims against them; the second group had no history of malpractice claims. Results indicated significant differences in the communication behaviors of no-claims physicians in comparison with the claims physicians. No-claims physicians spent more time educating their patients regarding what to expect, laughed and used humor more, showed better listening skills (e.g., asked patients their opinions, checked understanding, encouraged patients to talk). This and subsequent research suggests that physical and mental health care providers who are courteous, tactful, and good listeners are more likely to achieve excellence in their profession and are less likely to be the targets of complaints.

STUDY AND DISCUSSION

Questions for Chapter 8

1. What information should be provided in describing the consultant's role to the school, community, and individual consultees?

2. Under what circumstances, if any, might it be appropriate for the psychologist/consultant to breach the confidentiality of a consultative relationship with a teacher?

3. Although the idea that parents should be viewed as collaborators in educational decision making has been incorporated into education law and our codes of ethics, it is not always realized in practice. Identify two barriers to parents assuming the role of "equal and full partners with educators and school systems." (Also see Lasser & Klose, 2007.)

4. Throughout the text, the authors have stressed the idea that the school psychologist's responsibility goes beyond being impartial and unprejudiced in the delivery of services. Identify some of the practitioner's special obligations in working with families from backgrounds different from his or her own.

Vignettes

1. Mrs. French, a middle school English teacher, stops by to see the school psychologist, Charlie Maxwell. Mrs. French is upset about a love note she intercepted between two students in one of her classes. The note was written by a 14-year-old boy named Derek to another boy in the class. Derek knows that Mrs. French has read and kept the note, but she has not spoken with him about the matter. Mrs. French wants Charlie to confront Derek with the note and talk with Derek's parents so that he will "get help to cure him of this sick stuff before it's too late." How should Charlie respond to this situation? (Adapted from Eversole, 1993; also see *Sterling v. Borough of Minersville*, 2000, in Chapter 2.)

2. Victor and Margaret Lee attend school in Pearl Meadow's district. Their father, who speaks almost no English, is the cook at their family-owned Chinese restaurant, while their mother, who is fluent in English, manages the restaurant and is very actively involved in her children's education. One Monday morning, Pearl is saddened to hear of Mrs. Lee's

unexpected death over the weekend. While Margaret, in eighth grade, slowly adjusts to her loss, Victor, a fifth grader, continues to struggle with his grief many months after his mother's death, and he has begun to show signs of serious depression. Pearl would like to meet with Mr. Lee to discuss Victor's depression. The principal suggests that Margaret serve as the interpreter during the conference. What are the ethical issues regarding choice and use of interpreters? (See APA-EP 2.05; NASP-PPE II.3.6; Lopez, 2008.) Evaluate the appropriateness of the principal's suggestion in light of the hierarchical family structure of many Asian families (see Webb, 2001, p. 342) and the psychologist's ethical obligations to Victor.

Activities

Mrs. Finch, a first-grade teacher, is known to have a punitive classroom management style. One parent recently complained to the principal after Mrs. Finch spanked her son. Mrs. Finch has asked you (probably as a result of the principal's urging) to help her develop a more positive classroom discipline style. Role-play your initial meeting with Mrs. Finch during which you offer your consultative services and define the parameters of the consultant-consultee relationship.

Chapter 9

INDIRECT SERVICES II
Special Topics in Systems-Level Consultation

As used in this chapter, the term *systems-level consultation* refers to cooperative problem solving between the school psychologist (consultant) and consultee(s) (e.g., principal, district-level administrators) with a goal of improving school policies, practices, and programs so as to better serve the mental health and educational needs of all students. We concur with Prilleltensky's (1991, p. 200) suggestion that "school psychologists have a moral responsibility to promote not only the well-being of their clients but also of the environments where their clients function and develop." Similarly, the National Association of School Psychologists (NASP)'s code of ethics states:

> School psychologists use their professional expertise to promote changes in schools and community service systems that will benefit children and other clients. They advocate for school policies and practices that are in the best interests of children and that respect and protect the legal rights of students and parents. (NASP-PPE IV.1.2)

To be competent to provide systems-level consultation, school psychologists need expertise in understanding human behavior from a social systems perspective, well-developed skills in collaborative planning and problem-solving procedures, and knowledge of principles for organizational change (Curtis, Castillo, & Cohen, 2008; also NASP-PPE IV.1.1).

The first portion of the chapter summarizes the ethical and legal issues associated with the following special topics in school consultation: student proficiency assessment programs, grade retention, grouping students for instructional purposes, school discipline, school violence prevention and response, and pupil harassment and discrimination. The chapter closes with a brief discussion of issues associated with public schooling for three additional groups of children with special needs: children with limited English proficiency, gifted and talented pupils, and students with serious communicable diseases. The National Association of School Psychologists has adopted position statements on a number of these topics (NASP statements can be found at http://www.nasponline.org). These position statements are resolutions by the NASP to advocate for certain practices seen as promoting the mental health and educational needs of children and youth. Interested readers are encouraged to consult them.

STUDENT PROFICIENCY ASSESSMENT PROGRAMS

A heightened emphasis on school accountability gave impetus to the development of statewide student performance assessment programs. The No Child Left Behind Act of 2001 (NCLB) requires each state to develop challenging academic content standards for mathematics, reading or language arts, and science and measurable achievement standards for those content areas (Pub. L. No. 107-110 § 1111[a][1]). Each state also must implement a set of high-quality, yearly student academic assessments that include, at a minimum, assessment in mathematics, reading or language arts, and science, which will be used as the primary means of determining yearly performance of the state, school district, and school. Districts must make public school choice available to pupils in schools that fail to demonstrate progress for two consecutive years and offer supplemental tutoring after a third year of failure to demonstrate progress (see Braden & Tayrose, 2008). Since 1997, the Individuals with Disabilities Education Act (IDEA) has required children with disabilities to participate in statewide student proficiency assessment programs. Students with disabilities may take their statewide assessment with or without individualized testing accommodations, and/or with modified proficiency standards, or they may take an alternative assessment specifically designed to document progress in relation to the student's individualized education program (IEP) objectives (see Braden & Joyce, 2008; Braden & Tayrose, 2008).

Unfortunately, statewide testing programs can encourage school practices that are not in the best interests of children. Braden and Tayrose (2008) used the term *high-stakes testing* to refer to situations in which test outcomes have a direct impact on the lives of stakeholders. Results of statewide proficiency assessments have been used to evaluate the performances of individual teachers and schools. Low-scoring schools may suffer negative publicity and increased external scrutiny and control, while high-scoring schools receive public praise, increased autonomy, and, in some states, financial rewards. Unintended consequences of high-stakes testing can include limiting the district's curriculum to match test content (e.g., eliminating music and art); teacher and student demoralization due to repeated low performance; and dishonest school practices in test administration, scoring, and reporting of results (Braden & Tayrose, 2008; also see Decker & Bolt, 2008).

School psychologists can play a positive role in improving school test performance by assisting districts in evaluating the consistency among their goals, the curriculum, and the test demands; promoting quality evidence-based instructional practices; and providing consultation to improve student test-taking skills (see Braden & Tayrose, 2008). School psychologists also can assist districts by identifying reasonable test accommodations for students with disabilities (Braden & Joyce, 2008).

In addition to statewide student proficiency assessment programs, many districts have their own testing programs. Such testing programs can serve a number of purposes, including screening, student evaluation for instructional planning, and program evaluation and research. In many districts, the school psychologist is the professional with the greatest expertise in measurement. Consequently, practitioners may be asked to help administrators and teachers make decisions regarding whether a testing program is needed, clarify the purposes of a testing program, help select tests and assessment tools that are technically adequate and valid for the intended purpose, develop guidelines for appropriate test interpretation and use of results, and assist in reporting data to parents and the community. The *Standards for Educational and Psychological Testing*, or *Standards* (American Educational Research Association, American Psychological Association, & National Council on Measurement in Education, 1999, pp. 51–54), provides guidelines for school testing programs. Minimum competency testing and the use of school readiness screening tests pose special ethical-legal concerns.

Minimum Competency Testing

Minimum competency testing is the practice of requiring a student to achieve a certain score on a standardized test in order to be promoted or to receive a high school diploma

(Medway & Rose, 1986). There have been a number of legal challenges to the policy of requiring students to pass an examination before they are awarded a high school diploma. *Debra P. v. Turlington* (1984) is probably the most important decision in this area.

In Florida, high school seniors are required to pass a state-mandated competency test to receive a high school diploma. Students unable to pass the test are typically awarded a certificate of attendance. *Debra P.* was a class action suit filed on behalf of African American students in the state of Florida. The plaintiffs claimed to have a property interest in receiving a diploma and that use of the competency exam was a denial of the equal protection clause of the 14th Amendment because the test was discriminatory against African Americans.

The court ultimately upheld the right of the state to require students to pass a competency test to receive a diploma. The court identified several issues that must be addressed in evaluating whether such tests are legally permissible. The first is whether *adequate notice* exists, that is, an adequate phase-in period before the test is used to determine the award of a diploma. Other issues are whether the test has adequate curricular validity and whether the school can document acceptable instructional validity. *Curricular validity* addresses the question of whether the curriculum of the school matches what is measured by the test. *Instructional validity* is whether the students are, in fact, taught what is outlined in the curriculum, that is, whether the curriculum is implemented (Fischer & Sorenson, 1996; also *Debra P.*, 1984, p. 1408).

Legally, pupils with disabilities also may be required to pass a competency test to receive a high school diploma. The school must ensure that tests used with students who have disabilities are a valid measure of school achievement and that no student is penalized due to his or her disability (Fischer & Sorenson, 1996). Medway and Rose (1986) suggested that special education students who might be able to pass a high school competency test have appropriate instructional goals outlined in their IEPs and that teachers be able to document that adequate instruction was provided.

Developmental/Readiness Screening Tests

Many public school districts implemented prekindergarten developmental/readiness screening programs in the 1970s. Developmental screening tests are designed to determine quickly and tentatively whether a child's progress is age-appropriate (Casey, 2006). Children identified as having potential school problems on the basis of screening test results then are referred for a more comprehensive evaluation to reject or confirm the suspected problem and plan for appropriate intervention, if indicated.

Gredler (1997) identified criteria to use in the selection of screening instruments. As is apparent from his discussion, screening test scores alone do not have adequate technical adequacy for educational decision making about individual pupils and should be used only for identifying children in need of further evaluation or for decisions that are tentative and easily reversed. Unfortunately, our experience suggests that many schools have used screening test scores as the sole criterion for assigning a child to a developmental classroom (e.g., developmental kindergarten). Parent complaints about such unsound practices prompted several states (e.g., New York, Pennsylvania, Michigan) to enact policies stating that no child may be placed in a developmental kindergarten without parent approval (Gredler, 1992, 1997). Because of the limited predictive value of screening tests, decisions to assign a child to a developmental classroom are best made in cooperation with the parent, based on a consideration of multiple factors (e.g., physical, cognitive, personal-social development) and reliable and valid assessment information.

SCHOOL ENTRY AND GRADE RETENTION DECISIONS

Teachers and principals occasionally recommend delayed school entry for pupils who appear to be not ready to begin school, and grade retention often is recommended for pupils who demonstrate poor academic achievement. We now explore the legal and ethical issues associated with these practices.

School Entry

We are aware that some public school districts persist in the practice of advising or encouraging parents to postpone school entry an extra year. Such practices often stem from a misunderstanding of compulsory school attendance laws. Compulsory school attendance laws identify the ages (e.g., 7 to 16 years) during which the state (school) can compel school attendance; the school may hold the parent responsible for ensuring that his or her child receives schooling during those years in accordance with state requirements (Russo, 2006).

However, after a child reaches the age of school eligibility, the child has a property interest (created by the state or local school board) in receiving a public school education. The legal reasoning of *Pennsylvania Association for Retarded Children (P.A.R.C.) v. Commonwealth of Pennsylvania* (1972) consent decree can be seen to apply in all school districts (Kirp, 1973); that is, public school districts must offer an education program to all children who are age-eligible for school entry in their district under the equal protection clause of the 14th Amendment. The education program must be offered at district expense and no child can be turned away (see *P.A.R.C.*, 1972, p. 1262). (See Casey, 2006, for additional discussion of school readiness.)

Grade Retention

Grade retention, or nonpromotion, is the practice of requiring a student to repeat a grade due to poor academic achievement. A number of studies have found no lasting beneficial effect of grade retention (see Jimerson et al., 2006, for a review). Some research suggests that grade retention actually may be detrimental, especially in the areas of student self-concept and personal and social adjustment.

In general, the courts have preferred not to interfere with school promotion or retention decisions. However, the court considerations in *Sandlin v. Johnson* (1981) suggested that a decision to retain a child cannot be arbitrary; that is, the method for assignment to a particular grade must be reasonably related to the purpose of providing appropriate instruction and furthering education. Furthermore, any method of determining pupil retention that has a disproportionate impact on minorities may be scrutinized more closely as a possible denial of equal educational opportunities. School psychologists can assist in providing effective early intervention for students who are experiencing school difficulties and help ensure that retention is not used inappropriately. Alternatives to retention are discussed in Jimerson et al. (2006) and Picklo and Christenson (2005).

INSTRUCTIONAL GROUPING

With the landmark *Brown v. Board of Education* decision in 1954, the courts ruled that school segregation by race was a denial of the right to equal protection (equal educational opportunity) under the 14th Amendment. Following this decision, the courts began to scrutinize school practices that suggested within-school segregation—that is, where ethnic minority children were segregated and treated differently within the schools. A number of court cases were filed against the public schools in which minority group children were overrepresented in the lower educational tracks (ability groups) and special education classes (see Chapter 4).

Grouping, Minority Students, and Disproportionality

Hobson v. Hansen (1967, 1969) was the first significant challenge to the disproportionate assignment of minority group (African American) children to lower-ability tracks. The judge in this case noted that the tracking system was rigid, the lower tracks offered inferior educational opportunities, and children were grouped on the basis of racially biased group ability tests. He ruled that the tracking system was a violation of the equal protection clause of the 14th Amendment and ordered the system abolished. He did not find that ability grouping was per se unconstitutional.

Subsequent court rulings also found that ability grouping is not per se unconstitutional (*Georgia State Conference of Branches of NAACP v. State of Georgia*, 1985; *Simmons v. Hooks*, 1994). In these cases, the courts held that ability grouping that results in within-school segregation may be permissible if the school district can demonstrate that its grouping practices will remedy the results of past segregation by providing better educational opportunities for children. *Georgia* was a class action suit filed on behalf of African American students because of their disproportionate assignment to the lower-achievement groups, resulting in intraschool racial segregation. In this case, information about grouping practices showed that students typically were assigned to achievement rather than ability groups on the basis of a combination of factors, including assessment of skill level in a basal series, achievement test results, and teacher recommendations. In defending their grouping practices, the schools noted that the achievement groupings were flexible (students could move easily from one group to another) and likely to benefit students as instruction was matched to skill level. They also presented achievement data to show that pupils in the lower tracks did, in fact, benefit from the instructional grouping. The schools consequently were able to show that their grouping practices resulted in enhanced educational opportunities for African American students. The court found in favor of the schools.

Simmons (1994) involved a school district in which students were placed in whole-class ability tracks in kindergarten through third grade, with a disproportionate number of African American students placed in the low-ability classes. In grades 4 through 6, students were placed in heterogeneous classes, with within-class instructional grouping for reading, math, and language arts. The district was not able to show that whole-class ability grouping resulted in better educational opportunities for pupils in grades kindergarten through grade 3, and the court found this practice unconstitutionally segregative. The court did not find heterogeneous class assignment with within-class grouping for reading, math, and language arts unconstitutionally segregative.

Further, serious concerns have been expressed regarding the overrepresentation of minority students in special education. Overrepresentation can occur when the percentage of students in special education from a particular group is higher than one would expect based on that group's prevalence in a broader population, or it can occur when the rate of identification of a particular group of students is higher than the rate of identification for other groups of students (Skiba et al., 2008). The disproportionate representation of minority students in special education has been documented as a persistent problem since the late 1960s (e.g., Chinn & Hughes, 1987; Dunn, 1968; Finn, 1982; Hosp & Reschly, 2003; Mercer, 1973).

The disproportionate representation of minority students in special education is a complex problem with multiple factors contributing to its persistence (see Losen & Orfield, 2002, and Skiba et al., 2008, for reviews). Given the persistence of the disproportionate representation of minority students in special education, the Individuals with Disabilities Education Improvement Act of 2004 provides guidance to prevent and reduce its occurrence. In particular, states must have policies and procedures in place to prevent the inappropriate overidentification or disproportionate representation by race or ethnicity of students with disabilities (34 C.F.R. § 300.173). Each state that receives IDEA–Part B funds must collect and examine special education data to determine if significant disproportionality is occurring at the state or local levels with respect to disability, placement in particular settings, or disciplinary actions (e.g., suspensions, expulsions) (34 C.F.R. § 300.346[a]). If significant disproportionality is found, states must review and, if appropriate, revise the policies, practices, and procedures used in the identification and placement of students with disabilities. Local agencies that are found to have significant disproportionality must devote the maximum amount of funds (15% of IDEA–Part B) to providing comprehensive coordinated early intervening services directed particularly (but not exclusively) toward children from groups found to be disproportionately represented (34 C.F.R. § 300.646[b]).

Instructional Grouping and Children's Needs

As noted in *Simmons* (1994), a number of different types of instructional grouping practices exist. The grouping practice that has raised the most concern is ability-grouped class assignment, in which pupils are assigned to self-contained classes based on homogeneity of ability. Research suggests that assignment to self-contained classes based on ability level does not improve school achievement and may result in lowered self-esteem and educational aspirations for students placed in the lower tracks. School psychologists should be knowledgeable of the various types of instructional grouping and encourage the use of grouping methods that are in the best interests of all children (see R. P. Ross & Harrison, 2006).

In concluding this section, it is important to note that these cases concerning within-school grouping should not draw attention away from the sad fact that, today, many children of color attend underfunded, inferior, segregated schools in poverty pockets of the country. As Kozol (1991, p. 4) observed, our "nation, for all practice and intent, has turned its back on the moral implications, if not yet the legal ramifications, of the *Brown* decision." In many cities, the racial segregation of schools is largely ignored and uncontested; the presence of dilapidated, ill-equipped, inadequately staffed ghetto schools has been accepted as a "permanent American reality" (p. 4).

SCHOOL DISCIPLINE

Under the general mandate to operate the public school, school officials have been given "a wide latitude of discretion" to fulfill their duty to maintain order, ensure pupil safety, and educate children (*Burnside v. Byars*, 1966, p. 748). Historically, school administrators and teachers were allowed to function quite autonomously in maintaining school and classroom discipline. In recent years, however, the courts have been called on to consider the constitutionality of school rules and disciplinary methods.

In considering the constitutionality of school rules, the courts generally have held that school rules and regulations must be a reasonable exercise of the power and discretion of the school's authority, related to the purpose of maintaining order and discipline

(*Burnside*, 1966), and enforced in a nondiscriminatory manner. The courts also have generally held that school rules should be clearly stated, and the consequences for conduct code violations should be reasonably explicit. Students should be informed of expectations for appropriate conduct through written statements or instruction (Russo, 2006). The methods of school discipline that frequently have been the focus of judicial scrutiny include corporal punishment, suspension, and expulsion.

School discipline is the job responsibility of the building principal, not the school psychologist. However, because of their role as consultant to principals and teachers regarding mental health principles and pupils with behavior problems, practitioners need a sound working knowledge of the ethical-legal aspects of disciplinary practices.

Corporal Punishment

Why is it that school children remain the last Americans that can be legally beaten? (Messina, 1988, p. 108)

Corporal punishment by the teacher or other school official generally is defined as the infliction of pain on the body as a penalty for conduct disapproved of by the punisher. Forms of corporal punishment include spanking, beating, whipping, gagging, punching, shoving, knuckle rapping, arm twisting, shaking, and ear and hair pulling (Roy, 2001).

Social science evidence suggests that corporal punishment in the schools can be psychologically harmful to children and that alternative approaches to maintaining school discipline are preferable and more effective. Furthermore, children throughout the country have suffered severe and sometimes permanent physical injuries as a result of corporal punishment administered in the schools, including injuries to the head, neck, spine, kidneys, and genitals; perforated eardrums and hearing loss; facial and body scars; and chipped teeth (Hyman, 1990). Unfortunately, the use of corporal punishment in the schools is based on "social norms which are seeded deep within American culture" (Purcell, 1984, p. 188) and disciplinary practices that are deep-seated within the American schools (Messina, 1988).

The following subsections summarize case law and statutory law regarding corporal punishment, and then discuss the role of the school psychologist in promoting alternatives to corporal punishment.

Case Law

Historically, English common law viewed teachers as having the authority to use corporal punishment under the doctrine of in loco parentis. According to this doctrine, a child's father delegated part of his parental authority to the tutor or schoolmaster. The tutor or schoolmaster then "stood in the place of the parent" and was permitted to use "restraint and correction" as needed to teach the child (Zirkel & Reichner, 1986). In the United States, the notion that educators have the authority to use corporal punishment under the common law doctrine of in loco parentis dates back to Colonial times, but it has been replaced gradually with the view that the state (school) has the right to administer corporal punishment because of the school's legitimate interest in maintaining order for the purpose of education.

Baker v. Owen (1975) raised the question of whether the parent can "undelegate," or take away, the school's authority to use corporal punishment. In this case, Mrs. Baker told the school principal she did not want her son, Russell, corporally punished because he was a fragile child. Following a minor school infraction, his teacher took a drawer divider and spanked him twice, causing some bruises. Mrs. Baker filed a complaint in federal court alleging that her fundamental right to the care, control, and custody of her child had been violated when the school used corporal punishment despite her prohibition.

The court in *Baker* held that the school's interest in maintaining order by the use of reasonable corporal punishment outweighs parents' rights to determine the care and control of their child, including how a student shall be disciplined. Under this ruling, schools were free to use reasonable corporal punishment for disciplinary purposes, despite parental objections to the practice.

In *Ingraham v. Wright*, a 1977 Supreme Court ruling, the parents of two schoolchildren contended that corporal punishment was a violation of a child's basic constitutional rights. The Court in *Ingraham* agreed to consider whether corporal punishment in the schools is "cruel and unusual punishment" under the 8th Amendment, the extent to which paddling is constitutionally permissible, and whether paddling requires due process protection under the 14th Amendment.

The Court found that corporal punishment to maintain discipline in the schools does not fall under the "cruel and unusual punishment" prohibition of the 8th Amendment because the Amendment was designed to protect those accused of crimes. The Court noted that "the schoolchild has little need for the protection of the Eighth Amendment" because the openness of the schools and supervision by the community afford significant safeguards from the abuse of corporal punishment by teachers (*Ingraham*, 1977, p. 1412).

Justice Powell, who wrote the majority opinion, acknowledged that the 14th Amendment protects the right to be free from unjustified intrusions on personal security and that liberty interests are "implicated" if punishment is unreasonable. However, he went on to state that "there can be no deprivation of substantive rights as long as disciplinary corporal punishment is within the limits of common law privilege" (*Ingraham*, 1977, p. 1415) and held that due process safeguards do not apply. Thus, the Supreme Court in *Ingraham* found that corporal punishment of schoolchildren is not unconstitutional per se. However, the opinion left unanswered the question of whether corporal punishment *is ever* unconstitutional.

Subsequent court decisions at the level of the U.S. Circuit Court of Appeals suggest that excessive corporal punishment is likely to be viewed as unconstitutional. In *Hall v. Tawney* (1980) and *Garcia by Garcia v. Miera* (1987), for example, the parents of schoolchildren filed Section 1983 civil rights lawsuits against school officials after their children were severely beaten as a part of disciplinary actions. The actions of the school personnel in these cases were seen as a violation of the substantive rights of the child to be free of state intrusions into realms of personal privacy and bodily security through means the court viewed as "brutal and demeaning." (Also see Kutz, 2009, on misuse of restraints.)

Statutory Law

As of 2006, 29 states had adopted legislation or issued regulations banning the use of corporal punishment in public schools (Stefkovich, 2006). Most state laws that prohibit corporal punishment allow teachers and others in the school setting to use reasonable physical restraint as necessary to protect people from immediate physical danger or to protect property. Michigan's law, for example, allows an individual to use reasonable physical force for self-defense and in defense of others, to prevent self-injury, to obtain a weapon, and to restrain or remove a disruptive student who refuses to refrain from further disruptive behaviors when told to do so (Public Act 521 as amended by Act No. 6 of the Public Acts of 1992). The Paul D. Coverdell Teacher Protection Act of 2001, part of the No Child Left Behind Act (Pub. L. No. 107-110 §§ 2361–2368), provides a limitation on liability for teachers, principals, or other school professionals when they undertake reasonable actions to maintain order, discipline, and an appropriate educational environment (see Chapter 2).

Promoting Alternatives

School psychology practitioners can work to abolish corporal punishment by promoting alternatives to its use through in-service training and consultation (see Hyman, Barrish, & Kaplan, 1997). They also may serve an important role by sensitizing school staff to the potential legal sanctions for the use of corporal punishment. The use of corporal punishment can be costly to the principal or teacher in terms of time and legal defense fees, even if he or she is ultimately found innocent of any wrongdoing. In districts that have banned the use of corporal punishment, its use is likely to result in disciplinary action by the local school board, possibly including suspension or loss of employment. Even in states that allow the use of corporal punishment in the schools, parents who are upset by its use with their child may pursue several courses of legal action. The majority of corporal punishment cases are filed in state courts under charges of battery, assault and battery, or negligent battery. Parents also may file a complaint under state child abuse laws. In addition, a number of parents have filed actions in federal court under Section 1983 (Henderson, 1986).

Suspension and Expulsion

Schools have been given the authority to suspend or expel students to maintain order and carry out the purpose of education. Short-term suspension typically is defined as an exclusion of 10 days or less from school or from participation in classes and activities (in-school suspension). In most districts, school principals are given the authority to suspend students. Expulsion means exclusion of the student for a period longer than 10 consecutive school days or the equivalent, with "equivalent" determined by factors such as the number and proximity of excluded days (Hindman, 1986). Student expulsion usually requires action by the school board.

The specific grounds for disciplinary suspensions and expulsions vary from state to state. School codes are likely to allow suspension or expulsion of students guilty of persistent noncompliance with school rules and directives, weapon- and drug-related offenses, repeated use of obscene language, stealing or vandalizing property on school grounds, and using violence or encouraging the use of violence (Hindman, 1986; Russo, 2006). The No Child Left Behind Act of 2001 includes the Gun-Free Schools Act (Pub. L. No. 107-110 § 4141). This portion of the legislation requires each state receiving federal funds under the Act to have in effect a state law requiring schools to expel for a period of not less than one year a student who brings a firearm to school. However, the law must allow the chief school administrator to modify the expulsion requirement on a case-by-case basis, and states may allow students expelled from their regular schools to receive educational services in an alternative setting.

In 1975, *Goss v. Lopez* was decided by the Supreme Court. This case was filed on behalf of several high school students suspended without any sort of informal due process hearing. The Court ruled that because education is a state-created property right, a school may not suspend or expel pupils without some sort of due process procedures to protect students from arbitrary or wrongful infringement of their interests in schooling. In writing the majority opinion, Justice White outlined the minimal due process procedures required for suspensions of 10 days or less:

> Students facing temporary suspension have interest qualifying for protection of the Due Process Clause, and due process requires, in connection with a suspension of 10 days or less,

that the student be given oral or written notice of the charges against him and, if he denies them, an explanation of the evidence the authorities have and an opportunity to present his side of the story. The Clause requires at least these rudimentary precautions against unfair or mistaken findings of misconduct and arbitrary exclusion from school. (p. 740)

Justice White further noted that "longer suspensions or expulsions for the remainder of the school term, or permanently, may require more formal procedures" (p. 741). He also noted that, generally, the notice and hearing should precede the removal of the pupil from the school. However, students "whose presence poses a continuing danger to persons or property or an ongoing threat of disrupting the academic process may be immediately removed from school. In such cases, the necessary notice and rudimentary hearing should follow as soon as practicable" (p. 740).

When immediate removal of a student is under consideration, it is important to remember that suspension may serve as a trigger for suicide attempts or violence against others. Consequently, parents should be notified if it is necessary to remove their child from school, and students who are suspended during the school day should not be sent home to an empty house (see *Armijo v. Wagon Mound Public Schools*, 1998). Skiba and Rausch (2006) identified alternatives to suspension and expulsion.

Students with Disabilities

When Congress passed Pub. L. No. 94-142 in 1975, it was recognized that schools might rely on suspension and expulsion policies to exclude children with disabilities from public schools, particularly students with emotional and behavioral difficulties. Consequently, the IDEA includes special protections with regard to disciplinary removals of children with disabilities.

Disciplinary Removals

The IDEA Part-B regulations regarding disciplinary removals of students with disabilities are complex. A brief overview of the federal regulations is provided here.

Disciplinary Removals for 10 Days or Less.   The IDEA allows school officials to remove a child with a disability who violates a student conduct code from his or her current placement to an appropriate interim alternative educational setting, another setting, or suspension for not more than 10 consecutive school days to the extent that those alternatives are applied to children without disabilities (34 C.F.R. § 300.530[b][1]). A school is not required to provide services to a child with a disability who has been removed from his or her current placement for 10 school days or less in that school year, if services are not provided to children without disabilities who have been similarly removed (34 C.F.R. § 300.530[d][3]).

Additional Removals.   It is helpful for practitioners to be familiar with the term *change of placement because of disciplinary removals* before reading the text that follows. A change of placement occurs if:

(a)(1) The removal is for more than 10 consecutive school days; or
  (2) The child has been subjected to a series of removals that constitute a pattern—

(i) Because the series of removals total more than 10 school days in a school year;
(ii) Because the child's behavior is substantially similar to the child's behavior in previous incidents that resulted in the series of removals; and

(iii) Because of such additional factors as the length of each removal, the total amount of time the child has been removed, and the proximity of the removals to one another. (34 C.F.R. § 300.536[a][b])

The IDEA provides schools with the flexibility to consider any unique circumstances on a case-by-case basis when determining whether a change in placement is appropriate for a child with a disability following a disciplinary infraction (34 C.F.R. § 300.530[a]). More specifically, the law permits additional removals of not more than 10 consecutive school days in the same school year for separate incidents of misconduct as long as the child has not been subject to a series of removals that constitute a pattern indicative of a change of placement (34 C.F.R. § 300.530[b][1]). However, after a child with a disability has been removed from his or her current placement for more than 10 school days in the same school year, during any subsequent days of removal the school must provide education services so as to enable the child to continue to participate in the general curriculum, although in another setting, and to progress toward meeting his or her IEP goals and receive, as appropriate, a functional behavioral assessment and behavioral intervention services to address the behavior violation so that it does not recur (34 C.F.R. § 300.530[b][2], [d]).

If the current removal is not a change of placement, school personnel, in consultation with at least one of the child's teachers, determine the extent to which services are needed to enable the child to continue to participate in the general education curriculum, although in another setting, and to progress toward meeting the goals set out in the child's IEP (34 C.F.R. § 300.530[d][4]). If the removal is determined to be a change of placement, the child's IEP team decides what services are appropriate.

Manifest Determination Review

If a disciplinary action is contemplated as a result of weapons, drugs, or potential injury to self or others, or if a disciplinary action involving a change of placement is contemplated for a child with a disability who engaged in behavior that violated any school rule or code, a manifest determination review must be conducted. This review is conducted by the IEP team, including the parents, within 10 days of the decision to change the placement of a child with a disability because of a violation of a code of student conduct. For the purpose of a manifest determination, the IEP team reviews all relevant information in the student's file, including the child's IEP, teacher observations, and information provided by the parents, to determine if the conduct in question was caused by, or had a direct and substantial relationship to, the child's disability, or if the conduct in question was the direct result of the district's failure to implement the IEP (34 C.F.R. § 300.530[e]). School psychologists should not share information at the manifest determination review that was disclosed within the context of a school psychologist–client relationship with the expectation it would be held in confidence by the psychologist unless the parent grants permission to do so (see Chapter 3).

When Misconduct Is a Manifestation of a Disability.   If the IEP team determines that the disciplinary infraction was caused by the child's disability or failure to implement the IEP, the conduct is considered to be a manifestation of the child's disability. Furthermore, if the disciplinary infraction is determined to be a manifestation of the child's disability, the IEP team is required to conduct a functional behavioral assessment and implement a behavior intervention plan for the child (34 C.F.R. § 300.530[f][1][i]).

If the child had a behavior plan prior to the disciplinary action, the IEP team is required to review the plan and modify it as necessary to address the problem behavior.

The child is returned to the placement from which he or she was removed, unless the parent and school agree to a change of placement as part of the modification of the behavioral intervention plan, or special circumstances exist (described later) (34 C.F.R. § 300.530[f][1–2]).

When Misconduct Is Not a Manifestation of a Disability.   If, as a result of the manifestation review, it is determined that behavior of the child with a disability was not a manifestation of the child's disability, the relevant disciplinary procedures applicable to children without disabilities may be applied to the child in the same manner that they would be applied to other children (e.g., long-term suspension), except that children with disabilities under IDEA must continue to receive a free appropriate public education (34 C.F.R. § 300.530[c–d]). Educational services must be provided to enable the child to continue to participate in the general education curriculum, although in another setting, and to continue to progress toward meeting the goals set out in the child's IEP and receive, as appropriate, a functional behavioral assessment and interventions designed to address the behavior violation so that it does not recur. Services are determined by the IEP team. Schools may discontinue educational services to students who qualify as having a disability under Section 504, but who are not also eligible for special education under IDEA, as long as nondisabled students receive identical treatment ("Discipline Under Section 504,"1996).

Special Circumstances.   School officials may order placement of a child with a disability into an appropriate interim alternative educational setting (IAES) for not more than 45 days if the child carried a weapon to school or to a school function; inflicted serious bodily injury on another person while at school, on school premises, or at a school function; or knowingly possessed or used illegal drugs or sold or solicited the sale of a controlled substance while at school or a school function. Placement in an IAES for these reasons can be made without regard to whether the behavior is determined to be a manifestation of the child's disability (34 C.F.R. § 300.530[g]). Parents must be notified on the date which the decision is made to make a removal that constitutes a change of placement of a child with a disability because of a violation of a code of student conduct, and be provided with the procedural safeguards notice (34 C.F.R. § 300.530[h]). The interim alternative setting is determined by the IEP team (34 C.F.R. § 300.531).

Appeals

The parent of a child with a disability who disagrees with any decision regarding placement or the manifest determination, or a school that believes that maintaining a child's current placement is likely to result in injury to the child or others, may request a hearing (34 C.F.R. § 300.532[a]). A hearing officer makes a determination regarding the appeal. The officer may return a child with a disability to the placement from which the child was removed, or order a change in placement to an appropriate interim alternative setting for not more than 45 school days if he or she determines that maintaining the current placement is substantially likely to result in injury to the child or others (34 C.F.R. § 300.532[a][2]).

The school is responsible for arranging an expedited due process hearing, which must occur within 20 school days of the date the complaint requesting the hearing is filed. The hearing officer must make a determination within 10 school days after the hearing (34 C.F.R. § 300.532[c][2]). During an appeal, the child remains in the interim alternative setting pending the decision of the hearing officer or until the expiration of the 45-day time limit, whichever comes first, unless the parent and school agree otherwise (34 C.F.R. § 300.533).

Protections for Children Not Yet Eligible for Special Education

A child who has not been determined to be eligible for special education and who engaged in behavior that violated any school rule or code may seek IDEA protections by asserting that the school knew the child had a disability before the behavior leading to disciplinary action occurred. The school is "deemed to have knowledge" that a child has a disability if: (a) the parents had expressed concern in writing that their child is in need of special education, (b) the parents requested an evaluation of the child, or (c) the teacher or other school personnel expressed concern about the child to the special education director or by making a referral (34 C.F.R. § 300.534[b]). If a request is made for evaluation of a child during the time the child is subjected to disciplinary measures, the evaluation will be conducted in an expedited manner, and if found eligible, the child will receive special education and related services (34 C.F.R. § 300.534[d][2]).

Monitoring of Suspension and Expulsion Rates

Under IDEA, states are required to collect and examine data to determine if significant discrepancies are occurring in the rate of long-term suspensions and expulsions of children with disabilities among school districts or compared to the rates for children without disabilities. If discrepancies are occurring, the state educational agency (SEA) must review and if appropriate, revise policies, procedures, and practices related to the development and implementation of IEPs, the use of behavioral interventions, and procedural safeguards (34 C.F.R. § 300.170).

SCHOOL VIOLENCE PREVENTION

The NASP's code of ethics encourages school psychologists to "use their expertise in psychology and education to promote school, family, and community environments that are safe and healthy for children" (NASP-PPE IV.1). Schools "can provide a sense of safety, challenge, and mission; foster positive relationships between and among adults and students; and provide students with access to mental health supports and youth development opportunities" (Osher et al., 2008, p. 1263). This portion of the chapter touches briefly on ethical-legal issues associated with universal (Tier I) interventions to enhance the capacity of schools to promote positive mental health and reduce school violence, and ethical-legal concerns associated with selective (Tier II) interventions to identify and intervene with students at risk for violence.

Researchers have identified a number of modifiable school factors that may be protective against student self-harm or violence toward others. Schoolwide programs that emphasize positive behavioral supports likely contribute to enhanced school safety and student mental health. Such approaches "provide students with the knowledge, skills, and behavioral supports to meet the school's behavioral expectations and provide staff with the knowledge, skills, and structure to reinforce student behaviors positively" (Osher et al., 2008, p. 1268). Schoolwide interventions also can foster a sense of connectedness to school among students. For example, ensuring that caring teachers and other adults are available to all students, creating a climate accepting of diversity, and implementing policies and practices to prevent bullying may enhance feelings of belonging and connectedness among students and reduce the likelihood of harm to self or others (see Felix & Furlong, 2008; Larson, 2008; Miller & Eckert, 2009).

Exhibit 9.1 outlines recommendations for schools regarding violence prevention and response. These suggestions were based on a review of statutory and case law, recommendations from school attorneys, U.S. Department of Education policy recommendations, and expert opinion. (For additional information about the history and legal underpinnings of these recommendations, see Feinberg & Jacob, 2002.)

Exhibit 9.1 Preventing and Responding to School Violence

1. All school districts should have a comprehensive safe school plan that addresses violence prevention, intervention, and response. The plan should describe the procedures and personnel available to respond in the event that a crisis occurs, be developed by a school-community team, take into account the resources available to the district, and be consistent with federal, state, and local laws (see Stephens, 1994).

2. As part of its safe school plan, districts should ensure that their discipline practices foster a positive school climate and minimize the likelihood of student alienation and mistrust. School rules and regulations must be a reasonable exercise of the power of school authorities, be related to the purpose of maintaining order and discipline, and be enforced in a fair and nondiscriminatory manner. Policies should be clearly stated and publicized, must not violate the legal rights of pupils or their parents, and should be implemented in ways that are respectful of the rights and dignity of individual students (Jacob & Feinberg, 2002; Mulvey & Cauffman, 2001; Stefkovich, 2006).

3. Every district should establish an incident reporting and tracking system to determine the nature and scope of crime and violence in its schools and monitor progress toward establishing a safe school environment (Osher et al., 2008). Schools should implement policies that encourage staff and students to report incidents and concerns. The nature and scope of school crimes should be documented prior to the implementation of any safety measures that may compromise student freedoms. For example, if metal detectors are introduced but challenged in court, the school must demonstrate that use of metal detectors is justified by state (school) interests compelling enough to override students' privacy interests (e.g., a history of weapons incidents at school).

4. Districts should ensure adequate staff orientation to district violence prevention and response procedures and provide ongoing training for staff to improve violence prevention efforts through curricular and other interventions. Pulliam (1999) and Pitcher and Poland (1992) recommended that the violence prevention component of a safe school plan includes training for administrators and staff on how to recognize and defuse potential violence.

5. The violence prevention component should include written policies that protect students from harassment, including bullying, based on "actual or perceived characteristics including race; ethnicity; color; religion; ancestry; national origin; immigration status; socioeconomic status; primary language; gender; sexual orientation, gender identity, or gender expression;

mental, physical, or sensory disability; or any other distinguishing characteristics" (NASP-PPE I.3.1). The policy should specify how students, staff, and parents can report concerns about harassment and identify the school personnel responsible for ensuring that reasonable steps are taken to stop harassment and prevent future occurrences (see U.S. Department of Education & Bias Crimes Task Force of the National Association of Attorneys General, 1999).

6. The intervention component of the safe school plan should include written procedures for school personnel to follow if they suspect that a student is potentially dangerous to others or to self, or is a victim of abuse. Threats of violence and suicide should be taken seriously. When it is suspected that a student is suicidal, the student should be seen by a mental health professional with training in assessment of suicide lethality. When a student makes threats to harm others, procedures should ensure that the student is seen for evaluation by professionals knowledgeable of threat assessment. District policies should state that students may be seen by the school psychologist or other mental health professional without parent consent to determine whether the pupil is dangerous or in danger. If a student is determined to be a threat to self or others, school procedures should ensure that appropriate parties are informed of the situation (e.g., parents of a suicidal youth) and that there is a coordinated response, drawing on the resources of the school, family, and community as needed.

7. The job descriptions of school personnel should be written to include their likely roles in school violence prevention and crisis response (Pitcher & Poland, 1992). School employees are more likely to be shielded from liability in lawsuits if they are acting within the scope of their authority.

8. School personnel who are expected to assume special roles in violence prevention or response (e.g., psychologists who assess suicide lethality) should receive verifiable training to assume those roles and be encouraged to consult with experts in situations where the appropriate course of action is not clear.

9. The crisis response component of the safe school plan should identify a school-based core team responsible for crisis management, trained to respond to unforeseeable events (*Kelson v. The City of Springfield*, 1985). The plan should identify the individuals (or their alternates) who will be expected to take responsibility in a crisis situation, and how to contact medical, fire, and police emergency assistance, as well as community mental health providers (Pulliam, 1999).

10. The crisis response plan should be coordinated carefully with law enforcement. When a crime occurs on school grounds, the police are in charge. School officials should be prepared to assist police in their efforts to define and secure the crime zone (e.g., preserve evidence) (Pulliam, 1999).

11. The crisis response plan should identify a trained spokesperson responsible for answering questions from the media to ensure that there is no

(Continued)

Exhibit 9.1 (*Continued*)

disclosure of confidential information and that student, staff, and family privacy are respected (Pitcher & Poland, 1992).

12. The plan should emphasize the need for careful documentation of all steps taken to prevent a crisis situation, as well as the steps taken by the crisis team in the aftermath of a crisis. Such documentation can assist in improving crisis response procedures and serves as a record if there is a legal action against the school following a crisis event.

_____

Source: Adapted from "Administrative Considerations in Preventing and Responding to Crisis: A Risk Management Approach," by T. Feinberg and S. Jacob, in *Best Practices in School Crisis Prevention and Intervention*, S. E. Brock, P. J. Lazarus, and S. R. Jimerson (Eds.) (pp. 95–108), 2002, Bethesda, MD: National Association of School Psychologists.

One Tier II intervention strategy, the use of large-scale screening programs to identify students at risk for harm to self or others, raises legal and ethical concerns. As systems-level consultants, school psychologists should ensure that the school's protocol for large-scale screenings meets ethical-legal requirements for consent and assent.[1] The Protection of Pupil Rights Amendment (2001) requires schools that receive any federal funds to notify parents prior to administering a questionnaire or other measure to students that seeks information about mental or psychological problems potentially embarrassing to the student or his or her family (see Chapter 2). Parents must be given an opportunity to inspect the measure prior to its distribution and to remove their child from participation if they so desire. Also, school psychologists are ethically required to ensure that students are informed about the purpose of the screening and who, in addition to their parents, will have access to the results. Furthermore, because participation in a screening may not result in any direct benefit to an individual student, adolescents should be given a choice whether they wish to complete a mental health screening instrument.

Second, consistent with our codes of ethics, school psychologists must consider whether screening results are valid, fair, and useful for identification of students at risk for harm to self or others, and whether the potential benefits of such screenings outweigh possible harm. Although the emotional impact of student-on-student violence or student suicide is enormous, screening results are not highly predictive of suicide or targeted violence (e.g., Hanson, 2009; Miller & Eckert, 2009). Also, it is important for school psychologists to remember that students have a constitutional right to be free from unjustified stigmatization by the school. The risk-benefit analysis of large-scale screenings consequently must take into account the possibility that such screenings will result in harm to those students who are false positives (i.e., inaccurately identified as being at risk for violence), including the stigma and embarrassment of being subjected to an unnecessary follow-up mental health evaluation.

Finally, school psychologists must consider whether the school has access to the resources necessary to provide individualized evaluations of the students who are identified as at risk by large-scale screenings (Gutierrez & Osman, 2009). It is unethical to screen for risk of harm to self or others but then fail to provide individualized follow-up evaluation and intervention.

_____

[1]Portions of this material were adapted from Jacob (2009).

Many researchers have suggested that suicidal behavior and violence toward others are best understood within a dynamic ecological framework that encompasses multiple influences that combine over time to elevate or reduce risk (Ayyash-Abdo, 2002), what Fergusson, Beautrais, and Horwood (2003) called an "accumulative risk" model (p. 61). In contrast to large-scale screenings, we believe efforts to identify at-risk students should take into account a confluence of characteristics and behaviors, with special attention to the presence of proximal warning signs of violence to self or others. For example, in the Miami-Dade County Public Schools, a student intervention profile is developed for each student. This profile is based on a review of each student by school professionals in seven areas of concern, such as academic performance, effort, conduct, attendance, and involvement with school police (Zenere & Lazarus, 2009). Students identified as demonstrating difficulty in three or more areas are seen by a school counselor, who assesses student needs and works in collaboration with a student support team to plan individualized interventions such as counseling or more intensive mental health services.

We concur with Mulvey and Cauffman's (2001) conclusion that efforts to reduce the likelihood of school crime and violence should focus on fostering a positive, supportive school climate and healthy student-school relationships: "Students who are committed to school, feel that they belong, and trust the administration are less likely to commit violent acts than those who are uninvolved, alienated, or mistrustful" (p. 800). Furthermore, when students feel connected to school and an atmosphere of mutual trust and respect exists among students, teachers, and administrators, the "critical link between those who often know when trouble is brewing and those who can act to prevent it" has a chance to develop (p. 801).

HARASSMENT AND DISCRIMINATION

School psychologists "assume a proactive role in identifying social injustices that affect children and schools and strive to reform systems-level patterns of injustice" (NASP-PPE IV). Federal antidiscrimination law protects students from harassment based on race, color, national origin, sex, and disability. As noted in Chapter 2, the term *harassment* means oral, written, graphic, or physical conduct relating to an individual's race, color, national origin, sex, or disability that is sufficiently severe, pervasive, or persistent so as to interfere with or limit the ability of an individual to participate in or benefit from the district's programs or activities (U.S. Department of Education & Bias Crimes Task Force of the National Association of Attorneys General, 1999). Title VI of the Civil Rights Act of 1964 prohibits discrimination based on race, color, or national origin in programs or activities receiving federal financial assistance and makes schools responsible for taking reasonable steps to remedy racial harassment of students. Similarly, Title IX of the Education Amendments of 1972 prohibits discrimination on the basis of sex and makes schools responsible for taking reasonable steps to remedy sexual harassment of students. Section 504 of the Rehabilitation Act of 1973 and Title II of the Americans with Disabilities Act of 1990 prohibit discrimination based on disability. Federal statutory law does not currently protect public school students from discrimination or harassment based on sexual orientation, gender identity, or gender expression. However, as is evident from the ruling in *Nabozny v. Podlesny* (1996) (Case 9.3), harassment on the basis of sexual orientation may violate state laws or the U.S. Constitution.

Cases 9.1 through 9.3 summarize three court cases involving the failure of schools to protect students from harassment in school. The Supreme Court ruling in *Davis* (Case 9.1) along with the court ruling in *Davison* (Case 9.2) suggest that, to avoid

---

Case 9.1

In 1999, the U.S. Supreme Court heard *Davis v. Monroe County Board of Education*, a lawsuit filed against a school district under Title IX. The case was brought by the mother of a girl who, as a fifth grader, was subjected to a prolonged pattern of sexual harassment by one of her classmates. The unwanted sexual advances included attempts to touch the girl's breasts and genital areas and statements such as "I want to get in bed with you" and "I want to feel your boobs" (p. 1666). The girl reported each incident to her mother and classroom teacher. The teacher and school administrators did not respond to complaints from the mother; the school did not take steps to stop the harassment by disciplining the boy or separating the two (e.g., changing the girl's seat in class so she did not have to sit next to him); and the teacher did not allow other girls to report their complaints about the boy to the principal. The boy eventually was charged and convicted in juvenile court of sexual battery against the girl.

The Supreme Court ruled that Title IX applies to student-on-student sexual harassment. In her opinion, Justice Sandra Day O'Connor stated that "damages are not available for simple acts of teasing and name-calling among school children" but rather for behavior "so severe, pervasive, and objectively offensive" (p. 1675) that it denies its victims the equal access to education as guaranteed under Title IX. She went on to state that the school officials must have known of the harassment and, acting with "deliberate indifference," failed to take reasonable steps to stop it. The case was returned to a lower court for determination of the school district's liability.

Case 9.2

In 1998, the U.S. District Court of the Central District of California issued a ruling in *Davison v. Santa Barbara High School*, a case in which the school district was sued because of alleged racial discrimination in violation of Title VI and Section 1983. This lawsuit concerned an 11th-grade African American student, Cheron, who was the target of racial harassment at school. For example, classmates placed a drawing of an African American person hanging from a tree by a rope around the neck on Cheron's desk, with "Sharoon" (a combination of "Cheron" and "coon") written next to the hanging body. When Cheron and her parents complained to the vice principal, they were promised an investigation, but nothing was done. The school had a history suggesting a racially hostile environment. Prior incidents included racially offensive graffiti on students' lockers, racially derogatory remarks to other students, and the circulation of racist literature by white supremacist groups on campus. Furthermore, evidence suggested that school administrators knew about the racially hostile environment, but the district failed to take any action to remedy the problems. The court determined not to dismiss Cheron's Title VI claim and that the district was not immune from liability for claims under Title VI.

---

liability under federal antidiscrimination legislation, schools must take reasonable steps to prevent student-on-student harassment based on race, color, national origin, sex, and disability. The court in *Nabozny* (Case 9.3) indicated that, under the 14th Amendment of the Constitution, school personnel also must take reasonable steps

---

Case 9.3

In 1996, the U.S. Court of Appeals for the Seventh Circuit issued its ruling in *Nabozny v. Podlesny*. The case concerned Jamie, a boy who was harassed continually and physically abused by his fellow students throughout his middle school and high school years because he was homosexual. Classmates referred to him as "faggot" and "queer." In seventh grade, two students performed a mock rape on him in science class in front of 20 other students who looked on and laughed. When Jamie reported the incident, the principal told him that "boys will be boys" and that he should expect such treatment from his fellow students if he was going to be openly gay. No action was taken against the students involved. In eighth and ninth grades, Jamie suffered assaults in the school bathroom, including an incident in which he was pushed into a urinal and urinated on by his attackers. In tenth grade, he was pelted with steel nuts and bolts. That same year, he was beaten in school by eight boys while other students looked on and laughed. When Jamie reported the incident, the school official in charge of discipline laughed and told him that he deserved such treatment because he was gay. Jamie later collapsed from internal bleeding that resulted from the beating. Although a school counselor encouraged administrators to take steps to protect Jamie and discipline the perpetrators, nothing was done. For more than four years, Jamie and his parents repeatedly asked school officials to protect him and to punish his assailants. Despite the fact that the school had a policy of investigating and punishing student-on-student sexual harassment, the administrators turned a deaf ear to Jamie's requests. Jamie eventually filed suit against several school officials and the district under Section 1983, alleging, among other claims, that his 14th Amendment rights to equal protection had been violated by school officials because they denied him the protection extended to other students. The court concluded that it would allow a lawsuit for damages against school officials because, if the facts presented were true, school officials had violated Jamie's 14th Amendment right to equal protection by failing to protect him from harassment to the same extent as other students because he was gay. The court also concluded that the law establishing the defendant's liability was sufficiently clear for the defendants to know that their conduct was unconstitutional.

---

to prevent student-on-student harassment based on sexual orientation. Such preventive actions are necessary to ensure an environment in which all children have equal opportunities to learn and because student-on-student harassment may be a precursor to even more serious acts of sexual assault or physical violence (see U.S. Department of Education & Bias Crimes Task Force of the National Association of Attorneys General, 1999).

Consistent with these court rulings, federal antidiscrimination legislation, and ethical principles, safe school plans should include policies to ensure that all students and staff are free from verbal abuse and intimidation. However, in developing and applying policies to prevent harassment, schools must take care to avoid violating student 1st Amendment rights to free speech and expression. (See U.S. Department of Education & Bias Crimes Task Force of the National Association of Attorneys General, 1999, for guidance in developing appropriate policies.)

As noted in Chapter 1, school psychologists have an ethical responsibility to help ensure that *all* youths have equal opportunities to attend school, learn, and develop their personal identities in an environment free from discrimination, harassment, violence, and abuse (NASP-PPE I.3.4, IV.1; Shriberg et al., 2008). As systems-level consultants, school psychologists can help to develop and implement school policies, procedures, and programs to protect students from harassment and discrimination. Recent years have witnessed substantial growth in the literature on bullying prevention (e.g., Felix & Furlong, 2008; Power, 2007; Swearer & Espelage, 2008), including cyberbullying (Willard, 2007). Through advocacy and education of staff and students, we can work to foster a school climate that promotes not only understanding and acceptance of, but also respect for and valuing of, individual differences.

OTHER PUPILS WITH SPECIAL NEEDS

In the last portion of this chapter, we discuss the ethical-legal issues associated with public schooling for three other groups of students with special needs: children with limited English proficiency, gifted and talented pupils, and students with communicable diseases.

Children with Limited English Proficiency

In 1974, the Supreme Court decided a landmark case, *Lau v. Nichols*, concerning the education of children with limited English proficiency (LEP). This case was based on a class action suit filed by non-English-speaking Chinese students in the San Francisco Unified School District. At that time, more than half of the LEP Chinese pupils were taught solely in English and no instruction to help them learn the English language was provided. Furthermore, proficiency in English was a requirement for high school graduation. The plaintiffs in this case claimed that the school's practice was a denial of equal opportunity under the 14th Amendment.

The case was decided on statutory grounds (Civil Rights Act of 1964) rather than the equal protection clause of the 14th Amendment. The 1964 Civil Rights Act prohibits discrimination in programs receiving federal assistance. In his decision in favor of the plaintiffs, Justice William O. Douglas wrote, "There is no equality of treatment merely by providing students with the same facilities, textbooks, teachers, and curriculum; for students who do not understand English are effectively foreclosed from meaningful education" (*Lau*, 1974, p. 566). Lau has been interpreted to mean that schools must provide assistance or "take affirmative steps" to ensure that students with limited English proficiency have access to a meaningful education. It is not interpreted as requiring bilingual instruction for each LEP child.

Thus, no federal mandate requires bilingual education for a child with LEP. However, in 1968, the Bilingual Education Act was added as an amendment to the Elementary and Secondary Education Act of 1965 (ESEA) (Pub. L. No. 100-297), providing funds for bilingual education. Title III of the No Child Left Behind Act of 2001 provides funds for language instruction for LEP and immigrant students. Part A of Title III is the English Acquisition, Language Enhancement, and Academic Achievement Act (Pub. L. No. 107-110 §§ 3101–3102). The purpose of this portion of the statute is to provide funds to help children develop proficiency in English while meeting state academic content and achievement standards. Each state is given the flexibility to implement the research-based language instructional programs it believes to be most effective for teaching English, with the goal of preparing students to enter all-English instruction settings. It requires schools to demonstrate increased English proficiency of LEP children each year. School psychologists who serve children with limited English proficiency need to maintain up-to-date knowledge of best practices in assessment and instruction of the LEP child (see Paredes Scribner, 2002).

Gifted and Talented Pupils

No federal legislation requires schools to provide specialized education to gifted and talented students. In 1988, the Jacob K. Javits Gifted and Talented Students Education Act was passed (part of ESEA). This legislation provided funds for programs designed to meet the special instructional needs of gifted and talented students. The Jacob K. Javits Gifted and Talented Students Education Act of 2001 (Pub. L. No. 107-110 §§ 5461–5466) reaffirmed the purposes of the 1988 Act. The identification and provision of services to gifted and talented students who may not be identified and served through traditional assessment methods was a funding priority (e.g., pupils with limited English proficiency and those from economically disadvantaged backgrounds).

Many disagreements exist about how to identify gifted and talented children and how to provide them with effective educational programs (see Callahan, 2006). School psychologists involved in the identification of gifted and talented students and the development of instructional programs are obligated to keep abreast of literature in this area.

Students with Communicable Diseases

State and local school boards have the power and authority to adopt regulations to safeguard the health and safety of students. Schools may require vaccinations or immunizations prior to school attendance, and they may deny school access to children who pose a health threat to others (Russo, 2006). The difficulty with serious long-term communicable diseases is in determining whether the health threat posed by the infected child is significant enough to outweigh the student's right to schooling in the least restrictive setting. The discussion here focuses on students with human immunodeficiency virus (HIV), but the issues raised are pertinent to other communicable diseases (e.g., hepatitis B). We discuss HIV as a disability under Section 504 of the Rehabilitation Act of 1973 and IDEA, and the obligation of school personnel to safeguard the privacy of pupils with communicable diseases.

HIV and the Rehabilitation Act of 1973

Initially, some disagreement existed about whether Section 504 provides protection against discriminatory treatment for an individual with a communicable disease. However, in *School Board of Nassau County, Florida v. Arline* (1987), the Supreme Court made it clear that a person with a communicable disease is eligible for protection under Section 504. *Arline* was a case concerning a teacher dismissed from her job after she suffered a relapse of tuberculosis. In *Arline*, the Supreme Court judged it necessary to conduct a two-step individualized inquiry to determine whether a person with a communicable disease is otherwise qualified under Section 504 (p. 1131).

The two-step inquiry outlined in *Arline* suggests that in determining whether a pupil is otherwise qualified, it is first necessary to evaluate whether the student poses *a significant risk of transmission* of the disease to others in the school setting. This part of the inquiry must be based on medical judgment and include consideration of the nature, duration, and severity of the risk and the probabilities the disease will be transmitted and cause varying degrees of harm. The second step in evaluating whether a student with a contagious disease is "otherwise qualified" is to evaluate, in light of the medical findings, whether the school can reasonably accommodate the pupil. A pupil who poses a significant risk of communicating an infectious disease to others in school is not otherwise qualified to be placed in the regular school setting if *reasonable accommodation will not eliminate that risk*.

Court rulings have specifically found that students with HIV have a physical impairment within the meaning of Section 504 (e.g., *Doe v. Belleville Public School District No. 118*, 1987; *Martinez v. The School Board of Hillsborough County, Florida*, 1987; *Thomas v. Atascadero Unified School District*, 1987). Thus, schools that receive federal assistance may not discriminate against any otherwise qualified schoolchild with HIV. However, if a significant risk of transmission would still exist in spite of reasonable efforts by the school to accommodate the infected child, then the pupil is *not* "otherwise qualified," and removal from the normal classroom setting is permissible (*Thomas v. Atascadero Unified School District*, 1987).

Arline and other court rulings (e.g., *District 27 Community School Board v. Board of Education of the City of New York*, 1986) suggested that the decision of whether a child with HIV or a similar communicable disease should be excluded from the normal school setting must be made on a case-by-case basis. The Centers for Disease Control and Prevention (CDC) recommends a team approach to decision making, with the team being composed of the child's physician and parent or guardian, along with school health personnel.

The CDC's recommended guidelines for prevention of HIV transmission in day care, school, and athletics can be retrieved from its web site (http://www.cdc.gov; also Simmonds & Chanock, 1993). Simmonds and Chanock, authors of the recommended guidelines, suggested consideration of the following factors in placement decisions: the child's propensity for aggressive biting, the likelihood of uncontrollable bleeding episodes, the presence of oozing skin lesions that cannot be covered, and the child's immune function. No cases of HIV transmission in day care settings or schools have been reported and, worldwide, only one case of HIV transmission attributed to sports has been reported. Simmonds and Chanock concluded that, for most school-age children with HIV infection, the normal classroom setting is appropriate. Decisions regarding participation in contact sports should be made on a case-by-case basis (see CDC guidelines for considerations).

HIV and IDEA

Children with HIV do not qualify for special education and related services under the "other health impairment" classification of IDEA–Part B unless the disease adversely affects educational performance. As noted in *Doe v. Belleville Public School District No. 118* (1987, p. 345), "Based on the Department of Education's opinions and the tenor of the statutory language, the Court concludes that EAHCA [IDEA] would apply to AIDS [HIV] victims *only* if their physical condition is such that it adversely affects their educational performance (i.e., their ability to learn and to do the required classroom work)." (Also see *District 27*, 1986.)

Pupil Privacy

Schools must protect the privacy of students with HIV or other communicable diseases. Knowledge that a student is infected should be confined to those persons with a direct need to know. School personnel also must keep abreast of state policies regarding the disclosure of information about students with communicable diseases. In Michigan, for example, the passing of information about a person with a serious communicable disease by school personnel is a felony punishable by a prison term of up to three years and a $5,000 fine, or both (Public Act 488, § 5131[10]).

The School Psychologist and Students with HIV

Medical advances in the 1990s have almost eliminated perinatal infection of babies by their HIV-positive mothers (Lindegren et al., 1999). Today, only about 200 HIV-infected babies are born each year nationwide. This means that very few children will enter the school system who were born with HIV. On the other hand, babies born HIV-positive in the mid-1990s are living into adolescence and young adulthood. Their potential life spans are unknown. Their "unexpected adolescence" has resulted in unique psychological challenges as they struggle with a mature understanding of their own illness, whether to disclose their HIV status to peers, and how to disclose their status to potential sexual partners (Dee, 2005). Unfortunately, every year many new cases of HIV infection due to unprotected sex or injected drug use are diagnosed among youth. In 2007, there were more than 6,800 newly diagnosed cases of HIV among persons in the 13- to 24-year age range based on data from 34 states and five U.S. dependent areas (Centers for Disease Control and Prevention, 2009b).

School psychologists can potentially serve a number of important consultation roles with regard to students with HIV or other serious communicable diseases. Practitioners can work closely with school and community health professionals in promoting health education in the schools. They also may develop expertise on the psychological aspects of serious childhood disease such as HIV and provide consultation to teachers as well as counseling to enhance the psychological well-being of children with health impairments and their families. (Also see Landau, Meyers, & Pryor, 2006.)

CONCLUDING COMMENTS

As Dawson (1987, p. 349) observed some time ago, "School psychologists are often in a position to influence educational policy and administrative practices." Maintaining up-to-date knowledge of school policies and practices that have an impact on the welfare of children and sharing that expertise in consultation with school principals and other decision makers "may enable school psychologists to effect organizational change that can have a positive impact on large numbers of children" (p. 348).

STUDY AND DISCUSSION

Questions for Chapter 9

1. Under IDEA, must special education students participate in statewide assessment programs? May schools require special education students to pass a minimum competency test prior to the award of a high school diploma?
2. Is the use of paddling (spanking) for disciplinary purposes in the schools constitutionally permissible?
3. What strategies does a school have under IDEA for handling a special education student who violates school rules? What is a manifest determination review?

4. Are public schools required to provide bilingual instruction under federal law?

5. Do gifted children have a right to an individualized and appropriate education under federal law?

6. Do children with HIV qualify for special education? Under what circumstances does Section 504 allow schools to remove students with HIV from the general education classroom?

Chapter 10

RESEARCH IN THE SCHOOLS
Ethical and Legal Issues

In this chapter, we explore the ethical and legal aspects of research in the schools. There are a number of sources of guidance in the conduct of research with human participants. The codes of ethics of both the American Psychological Association (APA) and the National Association of School Psychologists (NASP) include standards for research. In recognition of some of the special problems posed by research with children, the Society for Research in Child Development (SRCD) also developed ethical standards specifically for research with children (SRCD, 2007).[1] *Ethical Principles in the Conduct of Research with Human Participants* (*RHP*) (APA, 1982) is an older text, but it continues to be a useful resource for identifying and understanding fundamental principles.

The National Research Act of 1974 (Pub. L. No. 93-348) outlines federal policies for research with human participants. It is interesting to note that the basic elements of the APA's *Ethical Principles in the Conduct of Research with Human Participants* and federal policies for research with human participants can be traced back to the Nuremberg Code, a judicial summary made at the war trials of Nazi physicians who conducted medical experiments on war prisoners and were indicted for crimes against humanity (Keith-Spiegel, 1983).

The National Research Act mandated the formation of the National Commission for the Protection of Human Subjects of Biomedical and Behavioral Research. One of the charges to the commission was to identify the basic ethical principles that should underlie the conduct of research involving human subjects; a second charge was to develop guidelines to ensure that research involving human participants is conducted in accordance with those principles. In 1979, the commission published *The Belmont Report: Ethical Principles and Guidelines for the Protection of Human Subjects of Biomedical and Behavioral Research* (http://www.hhs.gov/ohrp/belmontArchive.html). In *The Belmont Report*, three broad ethical principles relevant to research with human subjects were identified:

1. *Respect for persons*—the obligation to respect the autonomy of individuals and protect individuals with diminished autonomy.
2. *Beneficence*—the obligation to do no harm, to maximize possible benefits and minimize possible harm.
3. *Justice*—the obligation to ensure that all persons share equally in the burdens and benefits of research.

---

[1]The SRCD's (2007) "Ethical Standards for Research with Children" has 16 Principles that will be referred to by number in this chapter.

Federal regulations for the protection of human research participants are issued by the Department of Health and Human Services (HHS) and are published at 45 C.F.R. Subtitle A, Part 46. Several proposed and final rule changes appeared in the *Federal Register* in recent years, and consequently interested readers are encouraged to consult the HHS Office for Human Research Protections (OHRP) web site for up-to-date guidance (http://www.hhs. gov/ohrp/). Only institutions receiving federal research support are legally required to comply with the rules and regulations drafted under the National Research Act.

Beginning in 1981, institutions that receive federal research support were required to establish institutional review boards for research involving human subjects (IRBs). IRBs were originally created to protect human research participants from harm in risky biomedical research such as trials with experimental drugs (National Research Council, 2003). Unfortunately, between 1981 and 2005, IRB mission creep at many universities resulted in burdensome overregulation of research that posed little or no risk to participants, at times creating barriers to studies designed to improve our nation's schools. Many university IRBs focused "on procedures and documentation" and lost sight of their primary mission, namely to consider the ethical acceptability of proposed research with human participants (Gunsalus et al., n.d., pp. 2-4; also American Association of University Professors, 2006; Koocher & Keith-Spiegel, 2008; National Research Council, 2003). In 2004, the HHS Office for Human Research Protections and its Secretary's Advisory Committee on Human Research Protection (SACHRP) began to address some of these problems by providing clearer guidance on the regulation of low-risk studies, posting decision charts to assist in interpretation of federal requirements for review of human subjects research and proposing changes in the rules implementing the National Research Act (e.g., see SACHRP letters and the decision charts at the OHRP web site).

COMPETENCE, RESPONSIBILITY, AND WELFARE OF PARTICIPANTS

The broad ethical principles of respect for the dignity and welfare of persons and professional competence and responsibility provide the foundation for ethical decision making in the conduct of research in the schools.

Professional Competence and Responsibility

In all types of data-gathering activities, whether it is decision-oriented action research or more basic research, school psychologists are ethically obligated to conduct research "as well as they know how" (*RHP*, p. 15). As Koocher and Keith-Spiegel (2008) noted, poorly designed research is likely to result in invalid and perhaps misleading findings. Misleading findings may result in the introduction or continuation of ineffective practices and a potential disservice to students, teachers, parents, and others. Poorly designed studies also are unfair to research participants who volunteer in hopes of contributing to the knowledge base of psychology and education. For these reasons, school psychologists with limited expertise in research design should consult with experienced researchers to ensure that a planned study is methodologically sound.

Welfare of the Participant

In planning research and data collection, priority must always be given to the welfare of the participant (*RHP*, p. 18; also *The Belmont Report*, 1979). The researcher is obligated ethically to identify any potential risks for the research participants and collect data in ways that will avoid or minimize such risks (*RHP*, p. 17; SRCD Principle 1; 45 C.F.R. § 46.111). The six major types of risk are physical, psychological, social, economic, legal, and dignitary (National Research Council, 2003, pp. 27–28). Potential risks of research participation may include pain or physical injury, exposure to stressful procedures and possible emotional discomfort or harm, invasion of privacy, loss of community standing, exposure to criminal prosecution, loss of employment or potential monetary gain, denial of potentially beneficial treatment, and violations of confidentiality.

Ethical and legal standards for research are consistent in recommending that the researcher ask the advice of others regarding the acceptability of proposed research procedures (NASP-PPE IV.5.2). The greater the potential risks, the greater the obligation to seek advice and observe stringent safeguards. Consistent with the regulations implementing the National Research Act, colleges and universities typically have IRBs that evaluate the ethical acceptability of research proposed by their faculties and students. The NASP's code of ethics requires school psychologists and graduate students affiliated with a university or an agency subject to HHS regulation of human subjects research to first obtain IRB approval prior to initiating a study (NASP-PPE IV.5.2). In addition, research in the schools that is *funded* by the U.S. Department of Education also is required to comply with HHS protections of human subjects.

The NASP's code of ethics recommends peer review of any and all research involving children (NASP-PPE IV.5.2), even if a school-based practitioner is not required to obtain IRB approval. Policies and procedures for review and approval of research activities in the public schools vary; some school districts have their own research review boards. School practitioners should consult with principals, teachers, parents, and others about the acceptability of planned research studies and obtain formal school district approval for proposed research through appropriate administrative channels (NASP-PPE IV.5.2).

This chapter explores informed consent for research; the risks of invasion of privacy, exposure to stress or harm, and denial of beneficial treatment; post-data-collection responsibilities; concealment and deception; confidentiality of data; research with ethnic and linguistic minority populations; and scientific misconduct.

INFORMED CONSENT AND PRIVACY

Case 10.1 summarizes the circumstances that prompted Sylvia Merriken, the mother of an eighth grader named Michael, to file a complaint against the school system that was subsequently decided in a federal district court in Pennsylvania in 1973. Although this incident occurred almost 40 years ago, it is not hard to imagine the occurrence of similar events today as school districts continue to struggle with the problem of substance abuse.

Sylvia Merriken's complaint alleged that the school's drug abuse prevention program, particularly the research phase, violated her constitutional rights and those of her son, including the right to privacy. A central issue in this case was the school's failure to seek informed consent for the collection of personal, private information about Michael and his family. As mentioned in Chapter 3, case law, government regulations, and our codes of ethics concur that waiver of an individual's right to privacy must be based on informed consent. The key elements of informed consent are that it must be knowing, competent, and voluntary. The court held that the school's program violated Sylvia Merriken's right to privacy, and an injunction was issued.

Case 10.1

School administrators, teachers, and members of the school board were alarmed by reports of high levels of drug abuse by students in the school district. They decided to hire a private consultant in hopes of developing an effective drug abuse prevention program for junior high students. The initial phase of the program involved research to identify eighth graders at risk for drug abuse. As part of the research phase, questionnaires were administered to eighth graders and their teachers. Students were asked to rate themselves on a number of personality variables, such as level of self-confidence, and they were asked about their relationship to their parents (e.g., Did one or both of your parents hug and kiss you goodnight when you were small? Do they make you feel unloved?). Teachers were asked to identify students with antisocial behavior patterns, and students were asked to identify classmates with problem behavior patterns. The private consultant planned to collect and analyze the data and prepare a list of "potential drug abusers" for the school superintendent that could be used to identify pupils in need of drug abuse prevention therapy. The therapy program would use peer-pressure techniques to combat potential drug abuse, and teachers would serve as the therapists. A letter was sent to parents informing them of the diagnostic testing and prevention program and assuring confidentiality of the results. Parents' silence in response to the letter was construed as consent for their child to participate. (Adapted from *Merriken v. Cressman*, 1973; Bersoff, 1983.)

Consent Must be Knowingly Given

Informed consent in research is an agreement between the researcher and the research participant that identifies the obligations and responsibilities of each party. The investigator informs the participant of all aspects of the research that may be expected to influence willingness to participate and answers all questions about the nature of the research procedures (APA-EP 8.02; NASP-PPE IV.5.2; SRCD Principles 2, 3; 45 C.F.R. § 46.116).

Who Gives Consent?

The individual giving consent to volunteer for research must be legally competent to do so (Bersoff, 1983). In the HHS protections for children involved as research subjects, a distinction is made between *consent*, what a person may do autonomously, and *permission*, what a person may do on behalf of another, as when a parent or guardian grants permission for a child to participate in research (46 C.F.R. § 46.402). When research involves children (minors) as study participants, legal standards and codes of ethics (SRCD Principles 2, 3) suggest that the researcher should seek informed consent or permission of the parent or legal guardian for the child to participate, and the child's assent to participate. *Assent* is defined as "a child's affirmative agreement to participate in research" (46 C.F.R. § 46.402[b]). This means that the child "shows some form of agreement to participate without necessarily comprehending the full significance of the research necessary to give informed consent" (SRCD Principle 2). HHS regulations note that a child's ability to make informed decisions about participation in research depends on his or her age and maturity (46 C.F.R. § 46.408[a]).

Ferguson (1978) observed that individual level of cognitive development and the complexity of the research situation must be taken into account in determining a child's capacity to make choices regarding research participation. She suggested that informed parental permission is both necessary and sufficient for research with infants and toddlers. The preschool age child, however, is able to understand explanations stated in here-and-now concrete terms, with a straightforward description of what participation means for the child. The researcher is consequently obligated to seek both parental permission and affirmative assent for the child of preschool age or older. Ferguson provided some helpful guidelines for explaining research to children of various ages (pp. 118–120). (See V. A. Miller, Drotar, & Kodish, 2004, for a review of the empirical literature on children's competence to assent to research participation; also see Masty & Fisher, 2008.)

The SRCD suggested that the informed consent of any person whose interaction with the child is the subject of the study also be obtained (SRCD Principle 4). For example, a study of the association between children's positive or negative feelings about their classroom teacher and academic achievement would require parental permission, the child's assent to participate, and the teacher's informed consent.

Freedom from Coercion

The third characteristic of informed consent is that it must be voluntary. HHS regulations specify that research participants (the parent or legal representative in the case of a minor child) should be given "sufficient opportunity" to decide whether to choose to participate in the research, and should be informed that they may refuse to participate without incurring any penalty (46 C.F.R. § 46.116[a][8]). The investigator also must respect the individual's freedom to discontinue participation at any time (APA-EP 8.02; SRCD Principles 2, 3, 4; 45 C.F.R. § 46.116[a][8]). Consistent with the values of respect for self-determination and autonomy, researchers must attract consent and assent without coercion, duress, pressure, or undue enticement or influence (Koocher & Keith-Spiegel, 2008; also APA-EP 8.06; SRCD Principle 5).

In the school setting, it is important to allow potential volunteers (e.g., pupils, teachers) the opportunity to decline to participate without embarrassment (SRCD Principles 2, 3, 4). In the *Merriken* decision (1973, p. 915), Judge Davis noted that the school did not afford the students an opportunity to decline to participate without being marked for "scapegoating" and unpleasant treatment by peers.

It also is important to remember that researchers may not promise benefits from research participation unless they are able to ensure the promised outcomes. For example, a researcher may not guarantee that participation in an experimental counseling group for overweight teens will result in weight loss for each participant, although weight loss might be identified as a *possible* benefit from participation.

Minimal Risk Research

Informed consent is not always required for research in the schools. Legal standards suggest that minimal risk research in public school settings probably does not require informed consent as long as information is recorded and reported in a way that individuals cannot be identified. *Minimal risk research* generally means that the study poses little likelihood of invasion of privacy, exposure to stress, or psychological or physical harm as a result of participation in the study.

HHS regulations at A—Basic HHS Policy for Protection of Human Research Subjects exempt the following types of research from its informed consent requirements: "research conducted in established or commonly accepted educational settings, involving normal educational practices" and research involving "the use of educational tests (cognitive, diagnostic, aptitude, achievement)" if information taken from these sources is recorded in such a manner that subjects cannot be identified (45 C.F.R. § 46.101[b][1]). Similarly, *RHP* (p. 45) states, "Research participation that is incidental to systematic study of the effects of normal variations in a regular institutional program appears not to raise serious ethical concerns even when the principle of informed consent is compromised." Research involving the study of existing school records also would be viewed as minimal risk research under HHS regulations as long as information is recorded in such a manner that subjects cannot be identified directly or through identifiers linked to the subjects (45 C.F.R. § 46.101[b][4]).

The Family Educational Rights and Privacy Act of 1974 (FERPA) and the Protection of Pupil Rights Act (PPRA) were passed to protect privacy of student and family information in schools that receive any type of federal funds; they are not research acts. However, both have implications for research in schools. FERPA was amended in 2008 (*Federal Register*, Vol. 73, No. 237, pp. 74851–74855) to clarify, among other issues, the conditions under which consent is *not* required to disclose information to be used for research studies by the school or outside parties. The change allows more flexibly to permit non-school researchers to initiate studies using information from student education records as long as the school and the researcher enter into a written agreement about the use of the personally identifiable information disclosed for research purposes. More specifically, a school may disclose information protected by FERPA without consent if:

(A) The study is conducted in a manner that does not permit personal identification of parents and students by individuals other than representatives of the organization that have legitimate interests in the information;

(B) The information is destroyed when no longer needed for the purposes for which the study was conducted; and

(C) The educational agency or institution enters into a written agreement with the organization that—

(*1*) Specifies the purpose, scope, and duration of the study or studies and the information to be disclosed;

(*2*) Requires the organization to use personally identifiable information from education records only to meet the purpose or purposes of the study as stated in the written agreement;

(*3*) Requires the organization to conduct the study in a manner that does not permit personal identification of parents and students . . . by anyone other than representatives of the organization with legitimate interests; and

(*4*) Requires the organization to destroy or return to the educational agency or institution all personally identifiable information when the information is no longer needed for the purposes for which the study was conducted and specifies the time period in which the information must be returned or destroyed. . . .

(*iii*) An educational agency or institution is not required to initiate a study or agree with or endorse the conclusions or results of the study. (*Federal Register*, Vol. 73, No. 237, p. 74852)

As noted in Chapter 3, PPRA requires local school districts that receive any federal funds to develop policies, in consultation with parents, to notify parents when the school intends to request one or more of the following eight types of information from students, or if nonemergency invasive physical examinations of students will be conducted: (1) political affiliations or beliefs of the student or the student's parent; (2) mental and psychological problems potentially embarrassing to the student or his or her family; (3) sex behavior and attitudes; (4) illegal, antisocial, self-incriminating, and demeaning behavior; (5) critical appraisals of other individuals with whom respondents have close family relationships; (6) legally recognized privileged and analogous relationships; (7) religious practices, affiliations, or beliefs of the student or student's parent; or (8) income, other than required by law to determine eligibility for participation in a program or for receiving financial assistance under a program. The parent of a student must be given the opportunity to inspect the survey, on request, prior to its distribution. Parents also must be given the opportunity to have their student opt out of the information-gathering activity or physical examination.

Components of the Informed Consent Agreement

The HHS has outlined a number of requirements for informed consent for research (46 C.F.R. § 46.116). The consent agreement is a written agreement but it may be presented orally to the individual giving consent. Oral presentation should be witnessed by a third party. The informed consent information must be presented in a language understandable to the participant or guardian granting permission for the child to participate, and the researcher may not include language that implies a release from ethical and legal responsibility to the subjects of the study.

There are eight basic components of the informed consent agreement: (1) a description of the nature and purpose of the research and the procedures and expected duration of participation; (2) a description of "any reasonably foreseeable risks or discomforts" for the participant or to others; (3) a description of any potential benefits to the participant that can reasonably be expected; (4) a description of available alternative treatments that might be advantageous; (5) a description of the extent to which confidentiality of information will be maintained; (6) instructions concerning who may be contacted to answer questions about the research; (7) a statement that participation is voluntary and that the participant may discontinue the study at any time without penalty; and (8) for studies that involve more than minimal risk, a description of any compensation and medical treatment available if injury occurs as a result of participation (46 C.F.R. § 46.116[a]). The SRCD also suggested that the professional and institutional affiliation of the researcher be identified (SRCD Principle 3). The consent form should be signed by the parent or guardian of a minor child or by the research participant if he or she is an adult. HHS has procedures for requesting a waiver of the parent consent requirement if requesting parent consent might jeopardize subject welfare (e.g., research with abused children) (45 C.F.R. § 46.408). Grunder (1978) recommended using reading-level determination formulas to evaluate the readability of the consent form to ensure that it is understandable.

EXPOSURE TO STRESS OR HARM AND DENIAL OF BENEFICIAL TREATMENT

Consistent with the principle of responsible caring, researchers take steps to protect study participants from physical and emotional discomfort, harm, and danger (*RHP*, p. 51; SRCD Principle 1). We can think of no ethically permissible studies by school psychologists that involve exposing a study participant to harm and danger. Research on the use of medications in treatment of behavior or learning problems (e.g., the use of Ritalin in the treatment of hyperactivity) exposes the child to potentially dangerous medical side effects (see Chapter 7). Although data regarding the effects of medications might be gathered in the school setting, any research involving the administration of drugs must be conducted under the supervision of a physician knowledgeable in the necessary medical and legal safeguards (see *RHP*, pp. 57–58).

Prior to beginning a study, the researcher is obligated to determine whether proposed research procedures are stressful and to explore ways to avoid or minimize stress by modifying the research methodology (SRCD Principle 1). Psychological discomfort is likely to result from failure experiences; from temptations to lie, cheat, or steal; or if the investigator asks the research participant to reveal personal information that is embarrassing, or to perform disturbing tasks such as rating parents (*RHP*, pp. 58–59). The survey questions for students in the *Merriken* case, for example, were likely to be quite stressful for some eighth graders.

In evaluating the acceptability of a study that places the participants at risk for discomfort, the researcher is obligated to seek the advice of others and carefully consider whether the potential benefits of the study outweigh the risks, often called a risk-benefit analysis (SRCD Principle 1). The researcher must obtain fully informed consent for any study that exposes the subjects to potential discomfort or harm (*RHP*, p. 53). HHS regulations recommend that informed consent be sought for any research that exposes volunteers to risks greater than "those ordinarily encountered in daily life" (46 C.F.R. § 46.102[h][i]). The HHS Secretary's Advisory Committee on Human Research Protection further suggested that the evaluation of minimal risk for children "be indexed to risks in daily life and routine medical or psychological examinations experienced by children the same age and developmental status as the subject population" (Prentice, 2005).

Assessing the potential risks of research participation for children can be a difficult and complex task. The researcher is obligated to consider developmental factors, prior experiences, and individual characteristics of the study participants in evaluating children's vulnerability to research risk. The likelihood of distress, embarrassment, and diminished self-esteem should be evaluated within a developmental context. For example, after age 7 or 8, children have greater self-awareness and capacity to make inferences about the meaning of others' behavior, and consequently they become increasingly more sensitive to both explicit and implied judgments of their performance in research situations. There also are developmental changes with regard to embarrassment from intrusions on privacy. The privacy concerns of young children center on their bodies and possessions. As children mature, privacy concerns extend to include informational privacy, namely, a desire to keep private information about their peer group, activities, and interests. Adolescents are highly sensitive to privacy intrusions and may view requests for personal information as intrusive and threatening (Thompson, 1990; also Masty & Fisher, 2008).

The researcher also must be alert to the fact that the data-collection procedures may result in unanticipated discomfort or harm. It is important to monitor the research procedures, particularly when research involves children. Children are likely to be highly sensitive to failure, and "seemingly innocuous" questions may be stressful for some (*RHP*, p. 59). If a research participant appears to show a stressful reaction to the procedures, the researcher is obligated "to correct these consequences" and should consider altering the data-collection procedures (SRCD Principle 10).

In planning research investigations of the effectiveness of new treatments or interventions, school psychologists are obligated to select an alternative treatment known to be beneficial (a contrast group), rather than using a no-treatment control group, if at all feasible. If the new or experimental intervention is found to be effective, contrast or control group participants should be given access to the new treatment (*RHP*, p. 68; also see APA-EP 8.02).

POST-DATA-COLLECTION RESPONSIBILITIES

The investigator is obligated to end the data-collection session with "a positive and appropriate debriefing" (*RHP*, p. 67). After the data are collected, the investigator provides the participant with information about the nature of the study and attempts to remove any misconceptions participants may have (APA-EP 8.08). The investigator also is obligated to remove or correct any undesirable consequences that result from research participation (*RHP*, p. 66; SRCD Principles 10, 12). As Holmes (1976) observed, stress is likely to occur when participants acquire an awareness of their own inadequacies and weaknesses as a result of participation in research. Researchers are obligated to introduce procedures to desensitize participants when this occurs; that is, the investigator must eliminate any distress that results from self-knowledge acquired as a result of research (Holmes, 1976).

As the APA noted, there are special postexperimental responsibilities in research with children. The investigator must "ensure that the child leaves the research situation with no undesirable after-effects of participation" (*RHP*, p. 66). This may mean "that certain misconceptions should not be removed or even that some new misconceptions should be induced. If children erroneously believe that they have done well on a research task, there may be more harm than good in trying to correct this misconception than in permitting it to remain" (p. 66). When children feel that they have done poorly, corrective efforts are needed. Such efforts might include introducing a special experimental procedure "to guarantee the child a final success experience" (p. 66).

Investigators also are obligated to consider any long-range aftereffects from participation in research. Research that introduces the possibility of irreversible aftereffects should not be conducted (*RHP*, p. 59). In *Merriken* (1973), Judge Davis admonished the school for its failure to acknowledge the risks of harm introduced by its drug prevention program. He noted that on the basis of responses to an unvalidated survey a student could be erroneously labeled as a "potential drug abuser," possibly resulting in stigma, peer rejection, or a self-fulfilling prophesy and be subjected to group therapy sessions conducted by untrained and inexperienced therapists (the teachers) (p. 920).

CONCEALMENT AND DECEPTION

Case 10.2 provides an illustration of deception and concealment in research.

Case 10.2

Carrie Johnson, school psychologist, decides to conduct a study of differences in teacher behaviors toward general education and mainstreamed special education students to fulfill the research requirements for her PsyD degree. She plans to observe time samples of reading instruction in five second-grade classrooms in a district near her university and code the number of positive and negative comments the teachers make to general and special education pupils. She is concerned that knowledge of the purpose of the study might alter teacher behavior, so she misinforms the teachers that the purpose of the research is to study the peer interaction patterns of special education students. The findings from her study show that all teachers observed give special education students more negative and fewer positive comments during reading instruction compared with their general education classmates. Carrie places a form letter in the faculty mailbox of each teacher/participant and the building principal, thanking them for their help and briefly summarizing her findings. Two of the teacher/participants are angry about the deception and demand that their observation data be destroyed. A third teacher is dismayed and embarrassed by her biased treatment of students with disabilities and considers abandoning her career in teaching.

Concealment

The nature and purpose of a study may require a compromise of the principle of fully informed consent (*RHP*, p. 36; SRCD Principle 6). The term *concealment* is used to refer to studies in which the investigator gathers information about individuals without their knowledge or consent; that is, the study subject may not know he or she has participated in a research study (*RHP*, p. 36). These studies often involve covert (hidden) or unobtrusive observation. The National Research Act regulations and the APA's code of ethics (APA-EP 8.5; *RHP*, p. 39) suggest that covert observation or unobtrusive observational studies can be considered minimal risk research and exempt from informed consent requirements as long as data are recorded so that subjects cannot be identified directly or indirectly; the behaviors observed are public; the research does not deal with sensitive or illegal behaviors (e.g., sexual behaviors, drug abuse); the experience of the person is not affected by the research (i.e., the research procedures are nonreactive); and the person is not put at risk in the event of a breach of confidentiality (e.g., criminal or civil liability, financial damage, or loss of employment) (45 C.F.R. § 46.101[b][2]; *RHP*, pp. 36–39). The research described in Case 10.2 appears to present minimal risk for the pupils observed in the study.

Deception

The term *deception* is typically used to refer to studies in which the participants are misinformed about the purpose of the study or the meaning of the participant's behavior (*RHP*, p. 40). Carrie Johnson's study (Case 10.2) illustrates the use of deception with the teacher/participants; she deliberately misinformed them of the purpose of the study so as to avoid altering their typical teaching behaviors.

Studies that involve deception are controversial. The investigator has a responsibility to seek peer review and carefully evaluate whether the use of deception is justified by the value of the study and to consider alternative procedures (APA-EP 8.07; *RHP*, p. 41; SRCD Principle 6). C. B. Fisher and Fryberg (1994) suggested that researchers ask nonparticipants from the same subject pool about the acceptability of the deception before proceeding with the study. Another alternative is forewarning subjects—that is, gaining the informed consent of participants to use deception as part of the research procedure. Some researchers maintain that the intentional use of deception with children is never justified as "children may be left with the distinct impression that lying is an *appropriate* way for adults to achieve their goals" (Keith-Spiegel, 1983, p. 201).

If, after consultation with others, it is determined that the use of deception is necessary and justified by the value of the study, the researcher incurs additional obligation to the study participants. After the completion of the data collection, the researcher must fully inform each participant of the nature of the deception, detect and correct any stressful aftereffects, and provide an opportunity for the participant to withdraw from the study after the deception is revealed (*RHP*, p. 41). In studies involving deception, the postexperimental debriefing involves explaining to participants that they were deceived as part of the research procedures (APA-EP 8.08; SRCD Principle 6) and dealing with any resultant feelings.

In Case 10.2, Carrie did not fulfill her postexperimental obligations to the teacher/participants. An individual or small group meeting was needed to explain the nature of the deception, introduce appropriate desensitization procedures, and assure the confidentiality of the data gathered. It would have been beneficial for the teacher/participants to know that their differential treatment of low-achieving students is normal teacher behavior and most likely an unconscious response to student behavior; that is, student behavior may condition teacher behavior (Brophy & Good, 1974). Offering to work with the teachers to help modify these behaviors would have been appropriate and in the best interests of everyone involved.

CONFIDENTIALITY OF DATA

Codes of ethics, case law, and legal regulations are consistent in requiring a clear prior agreement between the investigator and the research participant about who will have access to information gathered during research and what types of information, if any, will be shared with others.

> Information obtained about the research participant during the course of an investigation is confidential unless otherwise agreed on in advance. When the possibility exists that others may obtain access to such information, this possibility, together with the plans for protecting confidentiality, is explained to the participants as part of the procedure for obtaining informed consent. (*RHP*, p. 70; also SRCD Principle 11)

In his *Merriken* (1973) decision, Judge Davis noted that the school made a blanket promise to parents that survey results would be confidential. However, documents describing the program indicated that, to the contrary, it was anticipated that a "massive data bank" would be developed and information would be shared with guidance counselors, athletic coaches, Parent-Teacher Association (PTA) officers, and school board members, among others (p. 916). The judge also noted that the list of "potential drug abusers" could be subpoenaed by law enforcement authorities. Investigators are obligated to forewarn research participants of any such risks of violation of confidentiality.[2]

RHP (p. 82) recommends removing identifying information from research protocols immediately. If a coding key that links the individual to his or her data is necessary because of the nature of the research, it should be kept in a secure location. The use of any permanent recordings during data collection (e.g., videotapes) increases the risk of loss of anonymity. The researcher should seek informed consent to create and maintain such records (*RHP*, p. 37; also APA-EP 8.03).

Codes of ethics and standards do not prohibit the sharing of research information if informed consent to do so is obtained. Information obtained in the course of research (e.g., test scores) may be helpful in educational planning for an individual child. However, it is of critical importance that researchers in the schools have a clear prior understanding with all parties involved, including students, parents, teachers, and administrators, regarding what research information will be shared and with whom, and what information will not be disclosed (*RHP*, pp. 70–71). School administrators may believe they have a legitimate right to information gathered about individual teachers, and parents are likely to believe they have a right to information about their child's performance in a research situation unless they are advised ahead of time that the research information gathered will be confidential.

Student researchers are advised against offering to share information from psychological tests with parents or teachers. The interpretation of psychological tests by students outside the supervised internship setting raises legal questions regarding the practice of psychology without certification or licensure (see also SRCD Principle 13).

In unusual circumstances, a researcher may choose to disclose confidential information deliberately for the protection of the research participant or the protection of others.

---

[2]Investigators planning research on sensitive topics such as drug abuse may apply to HHS's OHRP for a confidentiality certificate to protect subject identity from disclosure in legal proceedings.

"The protection afforded research participants by the maintenance of confidentiality may be compromised when the investigator discovers information that serious harm threatens the research participant or others" (*RHP*, p. 69). The researcher may uncover information about the participant that has important implications for his or her well-being, such as emotional or physical problems. Such situations are most likely rare in school settings. If deliberate disclosure is warranted, however, the research volunteer (parent or guardian of a minor child) should be counseled about the problem identified by someone qualified to interpret and discuss the information gathered and handle any resultant distress. If disclosure of information to a third party is anticipated, this also should be discussed with the research participant (or parent or guardian) (*RHP*, p. 72; also SRCD Principle 9).

School psychologists must be sensitive to potential loss of confidentiality as a result of presentation or publication of research findings. As the APA notes, there are rarely problems with loss of confidentiality when data on groups are published (*RHP*, p. 73). However, school psychology practitioners may be interested in presenting or publishing case studies. Often the data from case studies were obtained as part of an intervention plan and follow-up, and informed consent to use the data for research was not obtained. If a psychologist plans to present or publish case information, this should be discussed with the individuals involved (pupils, parents, teachers), and informed consent should be obtained. The researcher also should make a sincere effort to disguise the identity of the research participants (APA-EP 4.07; NASP-PPE IV.5.3; SRCD Principle 11).

It is usually appropriate to offer research participants a brief summary of the findings from the study based on the data from all study participants. This summary should preserve the anonymity of the participants and the confidentiality of the data gathered from individual participants (SRCD Principle 12).

RESEARCH WITH CULTURALLY AND LINGUISTICALLY DIVERSE POPULATIONS

In conducting research that involves culturally and linguistically diverse groups, researchers must give special consideration to the selection and recruitment of research participants, research methodology, evaluation of potential risks and benefits, and reporting of results. In the 1960s, a number of research investigations came to the attention of the U.S. Congress in which poor, minority, and other vulnerable groups carried the burden of research but were often denied its benefits. Perhaps the best known of these was the Tuskegee Study, conducted by the U.S. Public Health Service, in which 400 African American men with syphilis were observed until autopsy to determine the natural course of the disease. The study lasted from 1932 to 1972. The men were left untreated even when penicillin became available.

According to White (2000), the facts of the Tuskegee Study were more complex than presented in the public forum (e.g., penicillin treatment at that time typically was limited to early syphilis and many study participants had late-latent syphilis). However, growing concern about this and other research studies gave impetus to the formation of the National Commission for the Protection of Human Subjects of Biomedical and Behavioral Research (discussed earlier) and heightened awareness of the importance of the ethical principle of justice, namely, the obligation to ensure that all persons share equally in the burdens and benefits of research. In accordance with this principle, researchers must select and recruit participants in an equitable manner, or for reasons directly related to the research question, instead of selecting subjects because of their easy availability or tractability (Frankel & Siang, 1999).

Researchers also have special obligations when planning research studies of ethnic and linguistic minorities. Nonminority researchers must be sensitive to the ways their own background and biases may impact how they conceptualize and design research studies (Rogers et al., 1999). In addition, it is critically important for researchers to have or to acquire knowledge of the culture of the minority group under study, including an understanding of how to convey respect for that culture in the conduct of research. Researchers are advised to seek input from members of the group being studied in planning the research project. This can help to ensure that the research targets the needs of the study population, that research questions and methods are culturally appropriate, and that risks and benefits are evaluated in light of the special circumstances of the group participating in the study (Gil & Bob, 1999).

In addition, researchers must be cautious in interpretation of findings. According to Atkinson (1993, p. 220), "We each have our own way of interpreting data based on the cultural lenses through which we view the world." Again, seeking to understand the experiences and worldview of the study group and seeking input from members of that group regarding the possible meaning of data may help the researcher avoid inaccurate and biased interpretation (Gil & Bob, 1999). Also, in the dissemination of research, researchers should consider how their findings might be misrepresented and how to minimize the likelihood that their findings will result in unintended harm (Sieber, 2000).

SCIENTIFIC MISCONDUCT

Scientific misconduct here refers to reporting research findings in a biased or misleading way, fabricating or falsifying data, plagiarism, or taking credit for work that is not your own. Consistent with APA and NASP codes of ethics, school psychologists strive to collect and report research information so as to make an honest contribution to knowledge and minimize the likelihood of misinterpretation and misunderstanding. In publishing reports of their research, they acknowledge the limitations of their study and the existence of disconfirming data and identify alternate explanations of their findings (APA-EP Principle C; NASP-PPE IV.5.1, IV.5.6).

The publication of scientific misinformation based on false or fabricated data is a serious form of misconduct that can potentially result in harm to others. In 1988, Dr. Stephen Breuning, a psychopharmacologist, pleaded guilty to charges of fabricating research data. The charges followed an investigation of his research that reported improved functioning for children with mental retardation who were treated with Ritalin or Dexedrine, research that "helped shape drug treatment policy for mentally retarded" individuals in several states (Hostetler, 1988). This was the nation's first federal conviction for falsifying scientific data. Breuning was ordered to pay over $11,000 in restitution and was sentenced to 60 days in jail and five years' probation (Coughlin, 1988). Breuning's case triggered much discussion of the need to protect the public from misinformation. Psychologists and others involved in investigating the case hoped that it would serve as a warning to others about the seriousness of falsifying data in scientific research (Hostetler, 1988, p. 5). (See Koocher & Keith-Spiegel, 2008, for additional cases.)

Another type of scientific misconduct is plagiarism. Plagiarism "occurs when the words, ideas, or contributions of others are appropriated in writing or speech without proper citation or acknowledgment" (McGue, 2000, p. 83). Psychologists are ethically and legally obligated to acknowledge the source of their ideas when publishing or making a professional presentation (NASP-PPE IV.5.8; also APA-EP 8.11; McGue, 2000). Both published and unpublished material that influenced the development of the manuscript or presentation materials must be acknowledged.

Finally, psychologists take credit "only for work they have actually performed or to which they have contributed" (APA-EP 8.12). "Principal authorship and other publication credits accurately reflect the relative scientific or professional contributions of the individuals involved. . . . Minor contributions to the research or to the writing for publications are acknowledged appropriately, such as in footnotes or in an introductory statement" (APA-EP 8.12; also NASP-PPE IV.5.9). (See McGue, 2000.)

CONCLUDING COMMENTS

As in other areas of service delivery, school psychologists can most likely avoid ethical-legal dilemmas in research by maintaining up-to-date knowledge of relevant guidelines, by careful planning of proposed research activities, and by seeking consultation and advice from others when questions arise. School psychologists conducting research need to be knowledgeable of the organization and methodology of the school and to work within the organizational framework, taking care to build and maintain good public relations within and outside of the school community during all phases of a research project.

STUDY AND DISCUSSION

Questions for Chapter 10

1. Identify the key codes of ethics and legal documents that provide guidelines for research.
2. What is the single most important ethical consideration in conducting research?
3. Identify six types of potential risks for research participants.
4. What are the key elements of informed consent for research?
5. What is the difference between consent and assent for research participation?
6. We do not always seek children's assent for the provision of psychological services. Why should we seek their assent to participate in psychological research?
7. Do we always need informed parent consent for research in the schools? What is minimal risk research?

Discussion

In 2001, third and fifth graders in a California school participated in a study conducted by a school therapist as part of her graduate degree requirements. The consent form sent home to parents said nothing about the survey's content. Angry parents contacted the school after learning that the survey asked children questions such as whether they were "thinking about having sex," "touching my private parts too much," and "thinking about touching other people's private parts" (Bowman, 2002).

What are the ethical and legal issues associated with this research situation? What risks for children are associated with participation in this study? What mechanisms to protect schoolchildren in human subjects research apparently failed in this situation? What are some ways researchers can evaluate whether their research designs and data-gathering instruments are developmentally appropriate and appropriate in light of special characteristics (e.g., pupils with learning difficulties) that may heighten vulnerability to research risks? (See Thompson, 1990.)

Vignettes

1. Christa Jones, a second-year student in a school psychology program, administered IQ tests to children in area nursery schools as part of her thesis research. Two months after she completed the data collection, the director of one of the nursery schools requests IQ test information for a pupil she feels is delayed developmentally as a first step toward requesting a full evaluation of the child's developmental status. How should Christa respond? What are the ethical-legal issues involved?

2. After seeing a newspaper article on how Internet chat rooms reduced feelings of isolation for some lesbian, gay, and bisexual (LGB) youth, Brad Gilman, a school psychology student, decides to conduct his master's thesis research on the life stories of gay teens. To gather his data, he pretends to be a gay teen, enters several chat rooms popular among LGB youth, asks questions to prompt chat room participants to share information about their lives, and then records their conversations verbatim. In his thesis write-up, he identifies the chat rooms he visited and includes many direct quotes, attributing the quotes to the speakers' undisguised online pseudonyms. What are the ethical issues involved in this research project? (See Frankel & Siang, 1999.)

3. Marrisa Garcia, a school psychologist, is concerned about the failure of her district to successfully involve Hispanic families in home-school collaboration efforts. After receiving approval from her district and a small research grant from a private corporation, she began an interview study with Hispanic families to identify the barriers to their participation in school meetings, parent conferences, and school outreach activities. Perhaps because she is of Hispanic descent and fluent in Spanish, Marrisa was able to establish rapport with families, gain their trust, and solicit their informed consent for research participation. During the interviews, Marrisa has been surprised to learn that several of the families have avoided involvement with the schools because one or more family members entered the country illegally and they fear detection. What are the ethical and legal issues associated with this research situation? (See Henning-Stout, 1996.)

4. To complete the requirements for her specialist degree, Shantelle Brown has decided to conduct a study of the effectiveness of a drug education program in reducing substance abuse at the middle school level. She plans to individually interview middle school students to ask about their patterns of drug use before and after their participation in the new drug education program. What are the ethical and legal issues associated with a study of this type?

Activities

If you are required to complete a research project as part of your program of graduate studies and the project will involve human subjects, complete the research ethics training program (usually online) required by your university's institutional review board (IRB).

Chapter 11

ETHICAL AND LEGAL ISSUES IN SUPERVISION

Supervision can occur in a variety of settings (e.g., school, hospital, mental health clinic) and for a variety of different purposes (McIntosh & Phelps, 2000). School psychologists may serve as supervisors of interns or of practitioners seeking full certification or licensure; and, in larger school districts with more than one psychologist, they may assume a supervisory role as lead psychologist or director of school psychological services (Harvey & Struzziero, 2008). The goal of this chapter is to provide an introduction to some of the ethical and legal issues associated with field-based supervision of interns and beginning practitioners in a school setting. For comprehensive treatment of the topic of supervision in school psychology, readers are referred to Harvey and Struzziero's *Professional Development and Supervision of School Psychologists* (2008). For the purposes of the chapter, we adopt McIntosh and Phelps's (2000) definition of supervision:

> Supervision is an interpersonal interaction between two or more individuals for the purpose of sharing knowledge, assessing professional competencies, and providing objective feedback with the terminal goals of developing new competencies, facilitating effective delivery of psychological services, and maintaining professional competencies. (pp. 33–34)

Unlike consultation, in supervision the supervisor has ultimate responsibility for client welfare (Knapp & VandeCreek, 1997). "When supervising graduate students' field experiences or internships, school psychologists are responsible for the work of their supervisees" (NASP-PPE II.2.4). The supervisor is ethically obligated to take reasonable steps to ensure that supervisees "perform services responsibly, competently, and ethically" (Knapp & VandeCreek, 1997, p. 591; also APA-EP 2.05; NASP-PPE II.2.4, IV.4.2). Some differences exist, however, in the supervisor's role and duties depending on the type of supervision. The supervisor assumes greater control and is obligated to provide more intensive supervision to interns and other psychologists in training (e.g., practitioners with a preliminary credential to practice who are pursuing full certification or licensure) than to fully credentialed practitioners (Knapp & VandeCreek, 1997).

A supervisor's role may include clinical supervision (working with supervisees to promote skill development) and/or administrative functions (providing effective leadership and management of school psychological services, hiring, delegating work assignments, evaluation of job performance for contract renewal) (Harvey & Struzziero, 2008). Some psychologists routinely assume both roles, particularly those who serve as lead psychologist or director of psychological services. Numerous legal issues are associated with hiring employees, employee performance evaluation, and contract renewal or nonrenewal that are beyond the scope of this book. Interested readers are referred to Harvey and Struzziero (2008) and Russo (2006).

PROFESSIONAL STANDARDS FOR SUPERVISION

Both the American Psychological Association (APA) and the National Association of School Psychologists (NASP) include guidelines pertinent to supervision in their codes of ethics (APA-EP 7.06; NASP-PPE IV.4). NASP's code of ethics states, "As part of their obligation to students, schools, society, and their profession, school psychologists mentor less experienced practitioners and graduate students to assure high quality services, and they serve as role models for sound ethical and professional practices and decision making" (IV.4).

In addition, NASP (2010a) identified recommended professional standards for supervision in school psychology in its *Model of Comprehensive and Integrated Services by School Psychologists*. Organizational Principle 5 addresses supervision and mentoring, and outlines the following criteria for being a supervisor of school psychological services: Supervisors must be state certified and have three years of experience as a practicing school psychologist. The NASP *Model* Organizational Principle 6 goes on to state that professional development and supervision should be ongoing, and not simply restricted to students in training.

The NASP (2010b) *Standards for Graduate Preparation of School Psychologists* specify standards for field experiences and internships that must be met by school psychology training programs to receive NASP training program approval. Similarly, the APA's Commission on Accreditation (2009) publishes standards for internships that must be met to be eligible for doctoral training program and internship accreditation. In addition, NASP's (2010b) *Standards for the Credentialing of School Psychologists* outlines recommended predegree and postdegree supervision requirements for states to consider when developing their standards for the credentialing of school psychologists and describes the required supervised field experiences to become a Nationally Certified School Psychologist (NCSP).

PROFESSIONAL DISCLOSURE STATEMENT AND INDIVIDUALIZED LEARNING PLAN

Consistent with the ethical principles of integrity in professional relationships and respect for the supervisee's right to make informed choices, Cobia and Boes (2000) recommended that the parameters of the supervisory relationship be outlined in a *professional disclosure statement*. This written agreement is similar to an informed consent agreement between school psychologist and client (Chapter 3) or a consultative contract between psychologist and teacher/consultee (Chapter 8).

The professional disclosure statement is a means of ensuring a mutual understanding between the supervisor and supervisee regarding the rights and responsibilities of all parties and helps to ensure that the supervisee is able to make an informed choice about entering the supervisor-supervisee relationship. The professional disclosure statement might include the following nine components: (1) description of the supervision site, clientele, and types of services typically provided; (2) credentials of the supervisor; (3) general goals of supervision and how specific objectives will be selected; (4) time frame, frequency and length of supervision contacts, and type of supervision provided (i.e., individual versus group supervision); (5) rights and responsibilities of supervisor and supervisee; (6) potential risks and benefits of supervision; (7) parameters of confidentiality; (8) record keeping; and (9) methods of evaluation (Cobia & Boes, 2000; also NASP-PPE III, IV.4.4).

In addition to a professional disclosure statement, it is recommended that the supervisee, in cooperation with his or her supervisor, develop a written *individualized learning plan* outlining the supervisee's learning objectives; activities for the achievement of those objectives (e.g., supervised experiences, reading, attending workshops); and how progress toward mastery of objectives will be evaluated. This individualized learning plan provides further clarification of the expectations and responsibilities of both the supervisor and supervisee and sets the stage for the establishment of a collaborative supervisory relationship (Cobia & Boes, 2000). The plan should be reviewed and modified periodically and serve as the basis for ongoing feedback to the supervisee. As discussed in Chapter 1, school psychology practitioners are ethically obligated to engage in continuing professional development (NASP-PPE II.1.4). The individualized learning plan can provide a mechanism whereby the supervisor can teach self-supervision to the supervisee (Harvey & Struzziero, 2008). By periodic review of the learning plan, supervisees gain practice in self-assessing their skills, pinpointing areas in need further development, and identifying strategies to remediate skill deficit areas.

While the professional disclosure statement and individualized learning plan clarify rights and responsibilities of supervisors and supervisees, a written university–internship site affiliation agreement is advisable in those settings where school psychologists provide field supervision for graduate student interns. This agreement outlines the duties of the university as well as the internship site with regard to an intern's field experience (also see NASP's *Standards for Graduate Preparation of School Psychologists*, 2010b).

ETHICAL PRINCIPLES AND SUPERVISION

Ethical principles and standards pertinent to supervision in school psychology are discussed in the pages that follow.

Respect for the Dignity of Persons (Welfare of the Client and Supervisee)

In providing supervision, the supervisor must consider the rights and welfare of multiple parties (e.g., the pupil who is the recipient of services, parents, teachers, other students, and the supervisee). However, protecting the welfare of the schoolchildren is of primary importance. In Case 11.1, Wanda and Morgan have mutually agreed on a plan that ensures infants and their parents will receive school psychological services that meet high professional standards while Morgan is gaining competence in infant assessment and working with parents.

Case 11.1

Wanda Rose has agreed to supervise a school psychologist intern, Morgan LaLone, who is interested in infant assessment and intervention. Morgan administered the Bayley Scales a number of times as part of her university practicum experience but feels she is not yet ready to conduct an infant assessment on her own. Consequently, in preparing Morgan's individualized learning plan, Wanda and Morgan agree they will conduct a number of infant assessments together before Morgan undertakes such evaluations independently. This will afford Morgan the opportunity to observe Wanda interact with babies and their parents, as well as practice administration of infant scales, before she begins conducting infant assessments on her own.

A number of issues should receive attention early in supervision to help safeguard the well-being of schoolchildren. Supervisees should receive explicit instructions regarding how and under what circumstances to contact their supervisor immediately (Knapp & VandeCreek, 1997). School-based supervisees also should receive verifiable training in the school district's crisis prevention and response procedures, including written instructions regarding what to do in situations in which it is suspected a student might be a danger to self, a danger to others, or in danger (e.g., child abuse). Additionally, it is important to remind school psychology trainees not to leave schoolchildren unsupervised after they remove them from their classrooms for assessment or intervention services.

Although the welfare of schoolchildren is of primary importance, the supervisor is also obligated to consider the welfare of the supervisee. Supervisors are in a position of greater power than supervisees and are expected to advocate for the welfare of the supervisee (Barnett, Erickson Cornish, Goodyear, & Lichtenberg, 2007; Knapp & VandeCreek, 1997). In Case 11.2, Carrie needs to work with Ben to choose a course of action that will relieve Ben of the inappropriately assigned duties but still make it possible for him to have a positive working relationship with the assistant principal involved. Practitioners new to a school district may feel overwhelmed by requests for assistance from teachers and others, particularly when faced with a backlog of referrals. Consequently, it is advisable for supervisors to introduce beginning practitioners and interns at a school staff meeting and to clarify their role and how work assignments will be delegated and prioritized (NASP-PPE IV.4.2; also III.2).

Autonomy and Self-Determination

The use of a professional disclosure statement is a means of ensuring that the supervisee makes an informed choice when entering a supervisor-supervisee relationship. As described previously, this statement should include a description of the general goals of supervision. There is currently some consensus in the literature that a supervisor's training responsibilities encompass four broad areas: (1) competency; (2) ethical sensitivity, knowledge, decision making, and behavior; (3) understanding of and respect for individual and cultural differences; and (4) emotional awareness and personal functioning (Conoley & Sullivan, 2002; Lamb, Cochran, & Jackson, 1991; Vasquez, 1992). In addition, consistent with the principle of respect for autonomy and self-determination, the supervisor and supervisee should work together to identify specific objectives and experiences to include in the supervisee's individualized learning plan, taking into account the supervisee's current and desired competencies.

Case 11.2

When Carrie Johnson's cooperative special services unit hired a new school psychologist, Ben Pennington, Carrie agreed to serve as supervisor for his first year. A year of supervision by a certified school psychologist is required for Ben to be eligible for full rather than preliminary certification under state law. Carrie also recognizes the importance of providing professional support for her new colleague. During one of their weekly meetings, she learns that the assistant principal and special education coordinator in one of Ben's three schools has assigned Ben the responsibility of scheduling all individualized education program (IEP) team meetings in the building. Carrie is indignant, because IEP scheduling is part of the job description of the building special education coordinator, not the school psychologist. It appears the assistant principal is attempting to take advantage of a new employee.

Psychologists also have an obligation to ensure that parents and adult students have an opportunity to make an informed choice about whether to accept services provided by a graduate student or an uncertified intern under supervision. "Any service provision by interns, practicum students, or other trainees is explained and agreed to in advance, and the identity and responsibilities of the supervising school psychologist are explained prior to the provision of services" (NASP-PPE I.1.3). Parents should be given information about how to contact the supervisor in the event they are not satisfied with the services provided (Knapp & VandeCreek, 1997). In addition, written consent of the parents (or adult student) and child assent should be obtained prior to audio- or videotaping pupils as part of the supervision process, and, unless parents agree otherwise, such tapes should be destroyed as soon as they are no longer needed for supervision purposes (APA-EP 4.03; Harvey & Struzziero, 2008).

Privacy and Confidentiality

In general, the guarantees of client confidentiality apply to the supervisor-supervisee relationship. However, supervision often involves evaluations of supervisee performance that must be shared with others (e.g., the university intern supervisor). Consequently, the professional disclosure statement should identify the circumstances under which information regarding the performance of the supervisee will be disclosed to others and the nature and types of information that may be disclosed. Furthermore, supervisees should be informed that supervisors have a duty to breach confidentiality if such action is necessary to safeguard the welfare of clients.

Supervisors are well advised to review ethical and legal principles with supervisees regarding respect for privacy and maintaining client confidentiality and to discuss district policies regarding privacy of pupil education records. In a study of ethical transgressions by school psychology graduate students, Tryon (2000) found that failure to maintain the privacy and confidentiality of others was an area of difficulty for graduate students.

Fairness, Nondiscrimination, and Diversity Issues

Psychologists are ethically obligated to be respectful of cultural, racial, linguistic, and other differences in providing supervision to interns and employees (APA-EP Principle E; also NASP-PPE I.3). Like consultation across culturally diverse groups, supervision across culturally diverse supervisor-supervisee-client groups can be challenging, particularly with regard to building understanding and trust (Allen, 2007).

While Donita (Case 11.3) has been able to open channels of communication with African American parents, she has inadvertently alienated some teachers and administrators.

Case 11.3

Charlie Maxwell was pleased when asked to provide field-based supervision for an African American intern. His district has had difficulty recruiting African American school psychologists and he is hopeful that his new intern, Donita, might be interested in future employment with his district. Donita came to the internship with strong assessment and intervention skills for an entry-level prac-titioner. She had grown up in the inner city and was able to establish a warm, positive rapport with a number of African American parents who were previously uninvolved with the school. However, Sam received several negative evaluations of Donita from principals and teachers because they were unable to understand the Black English she used when conversing with parents during meetings.

Charlie needs to share with Donita the feedback he received from principals and teachers regarding their inability to understand her speech patterns, and explore strategies (such as speaking more slowly) to make sure all persons involved in parent meetings understand what is being said. His feedback and guidance are necessary to ensure that Donita will be able to build a good working relationship with school staff and provide effective services to teachers, pupils, and their families.

Responsible Caring in Supervision

To foster the supervisee's professional development and safeguard the well-being of clients, supervisors should offer and provide supervision only within the areas of their own competence (Cobia & Boes, 2000). The supervisor is obligated to be forthcoming and accurate in describing to potential supervisees the areas in which he or she is qualified to provide supervision and may wish to include this information in the professional disclosure statement. As illustrated by Case 11.4, supervision by another professional with appropriate credentials, training, and skills should be arranged if the supervisee would like to gain experience in areas outside of the competence of the supervisor; otherwise, such experiences should not be offered.

Also, with regard to supervisor competence, it is important to note that few school psychology supervisors receive formal training in how to supervise (Ward, 2001; also Falender & Shafranske, 2007). Harvey and Struzziero (2008, pp. 21–24) outlined the basic skills needed for supervision. School psychologists who wish to provide supervision should assess their competence to do so and possibly seek training in effective supervisory methods. In addition, supervisors are advised to seek feedback from former supervisees regarding the effectiveness of their supervision methods (also see Conoley & Sullivan, 2002).

The supervisor also is obligated to ensure that client welfare is not compromised because of the supervisee's lack of competence. In her study of school psychology graduate students, Tryon (2000) found that, in addition to respecting privacy and confidentiality, working within the boundaries of competence was also an area of difficulty. Supervisors must "delegate responsibilities carefully and deliberately to their supervisees" (Knapp & VandeCreek, 1997, p. 591). The supervisor has a duty to carefully assess the skill level of the supervisee by review of past training and experiences, face-to-face discussion, evaluation of work samples, use of audio- and videotape and direct observation, and inviting feedback from recipients of the supervisee's services (Conoley & Sullivan, 2002; Falender & Shafranske, 2007). As in Wanda's supervision of her intern Morgan (Case 11.1), it may be appropriate and necessary for the supervisor to work very

---

Case 11.4

Sam Foster's district accepted a school psychology intern, Roberto Otero, for the upcoming academic year. Roberto is Hispanic and bilingual. He would like to gain supervised experience working with pupils and families whose native language is Spanish and consulting with teachers in the district's English as a second language (ESL) classrooms. Because Sam is not competent to provide psychological services to bilingual students, he has arranged for Roberto to receive supervision from the district's Spanish-bilingual psychologist for the second half of his internship year.

closely with the supervisee in certain practice areas before allowing the supervisee to function more autonomously in providing services.

Furthermore, consistent with ethical obligations and the legal requirements of most states, supervisors review and cosign psychological reports prepared by interns and supervisees who do not yet hold a credential to practice in the state (NASP-PPE IV.4.2).

Bosk (1979) observed that there are dilemmas inherent in the supervisor's role of selecting and assigning responsibilities to the beginning practitioner. To master new skills and situations, beginners must be given the opportunity to try new experiences and learn from their successes and mistakes. At the same time, the supervisor must protect the client from the supervisee's errors and make sure the supervisee is not overly discouraged by his or her mistakes. *Technical* errors occur when trainees are performing their role conscientiously but their skills fall short of what the task requires. Similarly, *judgmental* errors occur when trainees are performing conscientiously but select an incorrect strategy or intervention. Supervisors should assure trainees that technical errors and errors in professional judgment are "inevitable and forgivable" during training and should seek to create an atmosphere in which supervisees can openly admit and discuss such mistakes without fear. Open discussion of errors encourages trainees to learn from their mistakes and take responsibility for them (Bosk, 1979; also Barnett, Erickson Cornish, et al., 2007).

In contrast, *normative errors* constitute a more serious failure, possibly resulting in the need for reprimand, probation, or dismissal (Bosk, 1979). Normative errors occur when a supervisee fails to discharge his or her role responsibilities conscientiously or violates fundamental expectations for proper conduct in the profession, such as covering up mistakes. Normative errors are a breach of psychologist-client and supervisor-supervisee trust.

Consistent with the principle of responsible caring, supervision must be provided "on a scheduled basis with additional supervision available as needed," and supervisees should be provided timely and straightforward evaluations of their progress (Knapp & VandeCreek, 1997, p. 593). Supervisors are ethically obligated to use accurate and fair methods for evaluating their supervisees (NASP-PPE IV.4.3, 4.4; also APA-EP 7.06; Barnett, Erickson Cornish, et al., 2007; Falender & Shafranske, 2007; Harvey & Struzziero, 2008) and, as recommended by Cobia and Boes (2000), the professional disclosure statement should outline the methods and timetable for evaluation. Evaluations should occur early and often enough in supervision to make and implement modifications in the individualized learning plan if the supervisee is not making the desired progress toward goals and objectives. As Knapp and VandeCreek (1997) suggested, the final evaluation of supervisee performance should "never come as a surprise to a supervisee" (p. 594).

Records of supervisee performance should be maintained on an ongoing basis and with sufficient detail to provide support for summative appraisals and any final recommendations (e.g., for or against approval for state certification). Supervisors should maintain a record of supervisory contacts to document that supervision was provided as promised in the professional disclosure statement and consistent with professional standards. In unusual circumstances, it may be necessary to terminate a supervisory relationship before the end of the agreed-on supervision period. In such situations, supervisors "should summarize the progress made by the supervisee, discuss the supervisee's additional need for supervision and training, draw generalizations from the supervision, resolve interpersonal issues, review the written evaluation with the supervisee in a personal interview, and bring supervision to a closure" (Harvey & Struzziero, 2008, pp. 59–60).

Integrity in Supervisor-Supervisee Professional Relationships

Supervisory relationships are ideally based on honesty, objectivity, and mutual respect. Supervisors "must be continually careful not to abuse the inherent power in the supervisor-supervisee relationship" (Vasquez, 1992, p. 200). Practitioners refrain from taking on a supervisory role when their own interests (e.g., personal, professional, financial) could reasonably be expected to impair their objectivity, competence, or effectiveness in providing supervision, or place the supervisee at risk of exploitation or harm (APA-EP Principles A, B; NASP-PPE III.4.2–4.4; Gottlieb, Robinson, & Younggren, 2007). Supervisors are cautioned not to step into the dual role of therapist and supervisor to the supervisee. When a supervisee displays signs of serious personal problems, the "appropriate role of the supervisor is to listen carefully, provide support, and refer the supervisee for additional counseling as appropriate" (Harvey & Struzziero, 2008, p. 46).

Psychologists also must consider potential problems associated with multiple relationships. In working with supervisees, multiple relationships occur when the psychologist is in a supervisory role and at the same time has another role with the same person, or a relationship with a person closely associated with or related to the supervisee (APA-EP 3.05; NASP-PPE III.4.2, III.4.4; Gottlieb et al., 2007). For example, a practitioner might be asked to accept the daughter or son of a close personal friend as a supervisee. The school psychologist is obligated to refrain from entering into a multiple relationship if the relationship could reasonably be expected to impair his or her performance as a supervising psychologist or might otherwise risk exploitation or harm to the supervisee (APA-EP 3.05).

Supervisors of school psychology trainees must take steps to ensure a training environment that is free of sexual harassment (NASP-PPE III.4.3). Sexual harassment in the workplace is a violation of Title VII of the Civil Rights Act of 1964. Under this Title, sexual harassment is defined as "unwelcome sexual advances, requests for sexual favors, and other verbal or physical conduct of a sexual nature…when this conduct explicitly or implicitly affects an individual's employment, unreasonably interferes with an individual's work performance, or creates an intimidating, hostile or offensive work environment" (U.S. Equal Opportunity Commission, 2005).

Title IX of the Education Amendments of 1972 prohibits sexual harassment of students by university trainers or other college staff. Under Title IX, sexual harassment in education can take two forms: quid pro quo and hostile environment.

> Quid pro quo harassment occurs when a school employee causes a student to believe that he or she must submit to unwelcome sexual conduct in order to participate in a school program or activity. It can also occur when an employee causes a student to believe that the employee will make an educational decision based on whether or not the student submits to unwelcome sexual conduct. For example, when a teacher threatens to fail a student unless the student agrees to date the teacher, it is quid pro quo harassment. Hostile environment harassment occurs when unwelcome conduct of a sexual nature is so severe, persistent, or pervasive that it affects a student's ability to participate in or benefit from an education program or activity, or creates an intimidating, threatening, or abusive educational environment. (Office for Civil Rights, n.d., p. 1)

It is not illegal for a supervisor to engage in a consensual sexual relationship with an adult supervisee or for a university faculty member to engage in a consensual sexual relationship with a graduate student. However, our ethical codes recognize the inherent imbalance of power between supervisors and supervisees and between professors and their students (C. B. Fisher, 2003). *Ethically*, school psychologists are prohibited from "engaging in sexual relationships with individuals over whom they have evaluation authority, including college students in their classes or program, or any other trainees, or supervisees" (NASP-PPE III.4.3; also APA-EP 3.02, 3.08, 7.07).

As Cobia and Boes (2000) and others (e.g., Harvey & Struzziero, 2008; Johnson et al., 2008) observed, the role of supervisor in psychology often involves the dual roles of evaluator and growth facilitator of the supervisee, and balancing these two roles may cause "ethical tugs" for the supervisor. As part of the supervision process, supervisors encourage supervisees to be open and self-disclosing, particularly regarding strengths and difficulties in professional functioning. However, as in Case 11.5, it is possible that the supervisee, as a result of the supervisor's encouragement, may disclose material that leads to the conclusion that the supervisee has serious skill deficits or personal problems and is perhaps not suited for the professional role of school psychologist (Cobia & Boes, 2000). Pearl (Case 11.5) may feel she has betrayed Jack's trust because, after encouraging his self-disclosure, she must now terminate his internship on the basis of the information disclosed.

However, in supervision, ethical priority must always be given to the welfare of current and future clients (Cobia & Boes, 2000). Knapp and VandeCreek (1997) distinguished between supervisee *distress* and *impairment*. A supervisee may be experiencing stress and discomfort but still be "able to perform his or her job responsibly" (p. 591). In such situations, the supervisee is able to provide services adequately and, with the support and guidance of the supervisor, make progress toward internship goals. *Impairment* refers to the inability of supervisees "to fulfill minimal responsibilities of their profession because of mental or physical disability" (p. 591), thus placing the client at risk for misdiagnosis, inappropriate and inadequate treatment, and possible harm. When a supervisee is suffering from impairment or engages in serious normative errors, it is ethically appropriate and necessary for the supervisor to recommend a failing internship grade, suspend or terminate the internship, deny endorsement for state credentialing, and/or recommend nonrenewal of an employment contract or immediate termination of employment. These risks, along with the potential benefits of supervision, should be outlined in the professional disclosure statement (Johnson et al., 2008; Sherry, 1991).

Case 11.5

Jack Western was a capable and conscientious intern during his first semester as Pearl Meadows's supervisee. After Christmas vacation, however, Jack was often late to school, was sporadically absent due to illness, and appeared disorganized and unprepared for meetings. When Pearl expressed concern about this change in his performance, Jack apologized, attributed his tardiness and disorganization to the stress of completing his master's thesis, and promised to do better. The following week, however, when reviewing a pupil assessment he had completed, Pearl noticed that Jack had failed to record any of the child's verbatim responses on the Vocabulary and Comprehension WISC-IV subtests and that his report was poorly written, with little attention to integration and interpretation of findings. Then, after lunch that day, Pearl thought she smelled alcohol on his breath. When Pearl queries Jack about the incomplete WISC-IV protocol and hastily written report during their supervision meeting, Jack discloses that his wife left him over the Christmas holidays and that he is devastated by their separation. He never administered all the WISC-IV subtests and simply fabricated the scores. When asked whether alcohol is a problem, he confides that he has been drinking heavily.

LIABILITY ISSUES

It is well established in common law that psychologists in private practice or health care settings may be held liable for their own actions or the actions of supervisees that result in harm to clients (Knapp & VandeCreek, 1997). The legal principle of *respondent superior* ("let the master answer" for the wrongful acts of his servant) provides the foundation for liability suits against a supervisor when the actions of a supervisee result in harm to a client (H. C. Black, 1983). As discussed in Chapter 2, however, whether a school employee can be sued is a complicated matter, determined by state legislation and case law. Many states hold individual school employees immune from liability under state law during the performance of duties within the scope of their employment. The provision of supervision to school psychology trainees or employees should be included in the job description of practitioners who provide such services.

Some, but not all, states permit tort actions against school districts and allow recovery up to the limits of the school's liability insurance. Consequently, inappropriate actions by a supervisee that result in harm to a schoolchild could trigger a negligence suit against the school under state law and possibly result in reprimand or suspension of employment of the supervisor if it is determined that the supervisor failed to provide proper supervision to the supervisee. Supervisees should be reminded that they have a legal duty to take steps to protect pupils from reasonably foreseeable risk of harm, and, as noted previously, supervisees should receive verifiable training regarding how to respond to situations that suggest a potential danger to students or others. In addition, if a supervisee violates a pupil's constitutional rights or other rights under federal law, parents could file suit against the supervisor and supervisee under Section 1983 of the Civil Rights Act of 1871.

Also, parents who are not satisfied with the identification, evaluation, or placement of their child with a disability under special education law may request mediation, initiate a due process hearing, and pursue court action when administrative remedies are exhausted (see Chapters 4 and 5). Supervisors are advised to select their cases for interns and beginning practitioners carefully, avoiding those that might be expected to trigger difficult school-parent disagreements.

Although the likelihood of an intern being involved in a lawsuit in the school setting is probably small, we encourage supervisors and interns to consider purchasing professional liability insurance. Interns may not be covered by the school district's liability insurance if they are not also employees of the district (see Chapter 2).

CONCLUDING COMMENTS

Quality supervision helps to ensure that practitioners are trained and prepared to provide school psychological services that meet high professional standards. Unfortunately, several studies have found that school psychology practitioners often do not receive as much supervision as other mental health practitioners. Furthermore, there is less research literature on effective supervision in school psychology than in the fields of counseling or clinical psychology (Fischetti & Crespi, 1999; McIntosh & Phelps, 2000). Consequently, school psychologists should consider ways they can contribute to the field by providing quality supervision to interns and beginning practitioners and ways they might contribute to our knowledge of effective supervision practices by conducting or participating in research on supervision.

STUDY AND DISCUSSION

Reread Case 11.5 about Pearl and her supervisee, Jack. What information do you think Pearl should share with Jack's university supervisor, and why? What information should Pearl disclose to the school district regarding the termination of Jack's internship, and why? Do you believe Pearl should recommend to the university that Jack be permanently dismissed from his graduate training program? Or do you believe Jack should be allowed to complete an internship after he has received treatment for alcohol abuse and personal problems? What are the ethical reasons for or against each course of action? See Lamb et al. (1991) for a discussion of suggested procedures for identifying and responding to a supervisee's problematic behaviors or impairment.

ETHICS, LAW, AND ADVOCACY

The code of ethics of the National Association of School Psychologists (NASP) states: "School psychologists consider the interest and rights of children and youth to be their highest priority in decision making and act as advocates for all students" (NASP-PPE Introduction). In addition, consistent with the general ethical principle of responsible caring and our commitment to building the capacity of systems, practitioners promote scientifically sound school policies to enhance the welfare of all students. They also are encouraged to work as advocates for change at the state and national level to better address the needs of children (NASP-PPE IV.1, IV.1.2; also Duncan & Fodness, 2008; Nastasi, 2008).

Many different definitions of *advocacy* exist. NASP's "Principles for Professional Ethics" describe advocacy as follows:

> School psychologists have a special obligation to speak up for the rights and welfare of students and families, and to provide a voice to clients who cannot or do not wish to speak for themselves. Advocacy also occurs when school psychologists use their expertise in psychology and education to promote changes in schools, systems, and laws that will benefit school children, other students, and families. Nothing in this code of ethics, however, should be construed as requiring school psychologists to engage in insubordination (willful disregard of an employer's lawful instructions) or to file a complaint about school district practices with a federal or state regulatory agency as part of their advocacy efforts. (NASP-PPE Definition of Terms).

In 1974, a special issue of NASP's *School Psychology Digest* (now *School Psychology Review*) addressed emerging ethical and legal issues in school psychology (Kaplan, Crisci, & Farling, 1974). One concern expressed by multiple authors was the challenge of managing conflicts inherent in the dual roles of child advocate and school employee. Not surprisingly, in several subsequent research studies, school-based psychologists reported pressure from their supervisors to put the administrative needs of the district (e.g., to contain costs, to maintain discipline) ahead of the rights and needs of students (Dailor, 2007; Helton, Ray, & Biderman, 2000; Jacob-Timm, 1999). Although school administrators also are committed to promoting the welfare of all students, they face pressures to base decisions on "the good of the whole" rather than the needs of individual students and to carefully manage limited resources (Denig & Quinn, 2001). As is evident from the F. L. Miller's (2009) experiences, the struggle to advocate for the best interests of the student and uphold ethical standards, while at the same time facing pressure from administrators to simply defer to their judgments, continues to be a challenge for school-based psychological practitioners (Exhibit E.1).

Throughout this book, we have focused on the ways in which our codes of ethics protect the rights and interests of children and their parents in the school setting. In this Epilogue, we discuss the uncertain legal landscape for school-based practitioners who wish to advocate for students when they encounter unjust or ineffective school practices and offer suggestions for

---

Exhibit E.1 Excerpt from "Advocacy: The Risks and Rewards" by Frank L. Miller

School psychologists are very different from other public school employees—teachers, counselors, and paraprofessionals. We are *required* by our ethical guidelines to speak up. While most employees defer to the administrator, we cannot, and as such we often stand out as the fly in the ointment. We must always be ready to offer reasonable alternatives to administrators frustrated in their attempts to maintain a safe and orderly building. We must, in a quiet and yet determined fashion, also help administrators to understand that in protecting the disabled student, we are also protecting the school district, and we are protecting them. The fine line between advocacy and insubordination is just that, a fine line, but as long as we understand our role, and communicate it loudly and clearly to our superiors, they can choose to respect what we have to say, or they can simply remove us from the case. They do this, however, at their own peril. And never give up; there's a reason school psychologists are part of this process: We know the law, we understand the psychological dynamics of behavior, and we understand our role as a powerful and sometimes lonesome advocate for students. (F. L. Miller, 2009, pp. 17–18).

---

speaking up effectively without facing disciplinary action or dismissal by their employers. We then identify several general guidelines for developing an ethical practice.

ADVOCACY AND AN UNCERTAIN LEGAL LANDSCAPE

The most important U.S. Supreme Court decision specifically addressing the right of a school employee to publicly criticize school practices is *Pickering v. Board of Education of Township High School District 205, Will County* (1968).[1] *Pickering* concerned a public school teacher who wrote a letter to the editor of a local newspaper criticizing the way in which the board of education handled proposals to increase revenue for the schools. He was subsequently dismissed on the grounds that the letter was detrimental to the operation of the school. When the case reached the Supreme Court, the Court held that "in the absence of proof of false statements knowingly or recklessly made by the teacher, his right to speak on issues of public importance could not furnish the basis for his dismissal, and that under the circumstances . . . his dismissal violated his constitutional right to free speech" (*Pickering*, p. 563).

However, a 2006 U.S. Supreme Court decision limits the free speech rights of state actors. In *Garcetti v. Ceballos* (2006, p. 1), the Court held that "When public employees make statements pursuant to their official duties, they are not speaking as citizens for First Amendment purposes, and the Constitution does not insulate their communications from employer discipline." The opinion goes on to state: "Without a significant

---

[1] Portions of this material previously appeared in Jacob (2008). Copyright 2008 by the National Association of School Psychologists, Bethesda, MD. Reprinted with permission of the publisher. www.nasponline.org.

degree of control over its employees' words and actions, a government employer would have little chance to provide public services efficiently. . . . Thus, a government entity has broader discretion to restrict speech when it acts in its employer role, but the restrictions it imposes must be directed at speech that has some potential to affect its operations." This ruling suggests that school psychologists, as state actors, could be disciplined for criticizing the policies and practices of the school district where they are employed if speaking in their official job role rather than as private citizens. It is important to note that the opinion did acknowledge the significance of federal and state whistle-blower protections of employees who expose unlawful actions by their employers (see *Settlegoode v. Portland Public Schools*, 2004, Chapter 5). In addition, speech related to teaching and scholarship was explicitly excluded from the decision. (Also see Zirkel, 2008.)

The implications of the *Garcetti* decision for school-based practice are not yet clear. As Justice Souter noted in his dissenting opinion, employers generally prefer that "employees voice their concerns about workplace practices openly and directly to a supervisor rather than disclosing their concerns to the public" (p. 8). We believe school psychologists and administrators should identify and agree on communication channels and forums that are appropriate within-district venues for school psychologists to voice concerns about ineffective school policies and practices without fear of disciplinary sanctions for speaking out.

Because of the uncertain legal landscape, school psychologists are wise to emphasize the potential positive effects of implementing new policies and practices in their systems-level advocacy efforts rather than simply criticizing existing practices. In addition, school psychologists must take care to identify when they are speaking as an employee versus speaking as a private citizen, recognizing that there are more constitutional protections for free speech as a private citizen than in their job role.

As noted previously, school-based practitioners are not ethically required to engage in insubordination (willful disregard of an employer's lawful instructions) as part of their efforts to advocate for children (NASP-PPE Definition of Terms). Although widely varying definitions of the term *insubordination* exist across states, dismissal of school employees for insubordination has been upheld in many court cases (McCarthy, Cambron-McCabe, & Thomas, 2004). If a school psychologist believes it is necessary to engage in insubordination to safeguard fundamental human rights, the practitioner should seek legal advice (APA Committee on Professional Practice and Standards, 2003).

DEVELOPING AN ETHICAL PRACTICE

The following guidelines for developing an ethical school psychology practice were first suggested in Jacob (2008, pp. 1930–1931) and are reprinted here with some modifications. By developing an ethical practice, we enhance our credibility and ability to effectively advocate for children on the individual and systems levels.

- Keep up-to-date regarding developments in ethics and law by reading professional publications and newsletters and attending conferences and workshops. Lifelong learning is necessary to achieve and maintain expertise in applied professional ethics (Armistead, 2008; Dailor & Jacob, 2010; Ysseldyke et al., 2006).
- Be sensitive to the ethical and legal components of service delivery and adopt a proactive stance; that is, work to anticipate and avoid ethical and legal problems. When difficult situations arise, use a decision-making model to choose the best course of action.

- Develop a positive approach to ethics; that is, strive for excellence rather than meeting minimal obligations outlined in codes of ethics and law (Knapp & VandeCreek, 2006). Be candid about commitments and priorities and foster a reputation for being a psychologist who is dedicated to high standards of service delivery and whose primary concern is to promote the best interests of children.

- Take care to discuss confidentiality and its limits with each student, his or her parents, and other clients at the outset of establishing a school psychologist–client relationship, and maintain confidentiality as promised.

- If at all feasible, negotiate a job description that encompasses advocacy for evidence-based practices and the freedom to adhere to NASP and APA codes of ethics. When advocating for changes in school policies or practices (or for services to better address the needs of a student client), emphasize the potential positive effects of new practices or new or modified services rather than simply criticizing existing practices.

- Consistent with the broad ethical principles of beneficence, responsible caring, and responsibility to community and society, work to build the capacity of systems to better address the academic, wellness, and mental health needs of children (Ysseldyke et al., 2006).

- As noted in Chapter 8, school psychologists encounter difficult teachers, administrators, colleagues, staff, parents, and students in the course of their careers. Regardless of personal feelings and frustrations, engage in conduct that is respectful of all persons at all times (NASP-PPE I). Practitioners who are courteous, tactful, sensitive, and good listeners are more likely to foster positive working relationships with their clientele, build and maintain trust, avoid client complaints, and achieve excellence in their profession.

CONCLUDING COMMENTS

In attempting to write as current a book as we could, we have been impressed by the speed with which law and ethics change. You, the school psychologist, must take it from here. This means maintaining your currency regarding new developments in ethics and law and also working proactively for school policies and law to better serve the interests and rights of children.

Appendix A

*NATIONAL ASSOCIATION OF SCHOOL PSYCHOLOGISTS PRINCIPLES FOR PROFESSIONAL ETHICS 2010**

CONTENTS

Introduction

Definition of Terms

Principles

I.   Respecting the Dignity and Rights of All Persons

School psychologists engage only in professional practices that maintain the dignity of all individuals. In their words and actions, school psychologists demonstrate respect for the autonomy of persons and their right to self-determination, respect for privacy, and a commitment to just and fair treatment of all persons.

Principle I.1. Autonomy and Self-Determination (Consent and Assent)

Principle I.2. Privacy and Confidentiality

Principle I.3. Fairness and Justice

II.   Professional Competence and Responsibility

Beneficence, or responsible caring, means that the school psychologist acts to benefit others. To do this, school psychologists must practice within the boundaries of their competence, use scientific knowledge from psychology and education to help clients and others make informed choices, and accept responsibility for their work.

Principle II.1. Competence

Principle II.2. Accepting Responsibility for Actions

Principle II.3. Responsible Assessment and Intervention Practices

Principle II.4. Responsible School-Based Record Keeping

Principle II.5. Responsible Use of Materials

III.   Honesty and Integrity in Professional Relationships

To foster and maintain trust, school psychologists must be faithful to the truth and adhere to their professional promises. They are forthright about their qualifications, competencies, and roles; work in full cooperation with other professional disciplines to meet the needs of students and families; and avoid multiple relationships that diminish their professional effectiveness.

Principle III.1. Accurate Presentation of Professional Qualifications

Principle III.2. Forthright Explanation of Professional Services, Roles, and Priorities

Principle III.3. Respecting Other Professionals

Principle III.4. Multiple Relationships and Conflicts of Interest

IV. Responsibility to Schools, Families, Communities, the Profession, and Society

School psychologists promote healthy school, family, and community environments. They maintain the public trust in school psychologists by respecting law and encouraging ethical conduct. School psychologists advance professional excellence by mentoring less experienced practitioners and contributing to the school psychology knowledge base.

Principle IV.1. Promoting Healthy School, Family, and Community Environments

Principle IV.2. Respect for Law and the Relationship of Law and Ethics

Principle IV.3. Maintaining Public Trust by Self-Monitoring and Peer Monitoring

Principle IV.4. Contributing to the Profession by Mentoring, Teaching, and Supervision

Principle IV.5. Contributing to the School Psychology Knowledge Base

Appendix A

INTRODUCTION

The mission of the National Association of School Psychologists (NASP) is to represent school psychology and support school psychologists to enhance the learning and mental health of all children and youth. NASP's mission is accomplished through identification of appropriate evidence-based education and mental health services for all children; implementation of professional practices that are empirically supported, data driven, and culturally competent; promotion of professional competence of school psychologists; recognition of the essential components of high-quality graduate education and professional development in school psychology; preparation of school psychologists to deliver a continuum of services for children, youth, families, and schools; and advocacy for the value of school psychological services, among other important initiatives.

School psychologists provide effective services to help children and youth succeed academically, socially, behaviorally, and emotionally. School psychologists provide direct educational and mental health services for children and youth, as well as work with parents, educators, and other professionals to create supportive learning and social environments for all children. School psychologists apply their knowledge of both psychology and education during consultation and collaboration with others. They conduct effective decision making using a foundation of assessment and data collection. School psychologists engage in specific services for students, such as direct and indirect interventions that focus on academic skills, learning, socialization, and mental health. School psychologists provide services to schools and families that enhance the competence and well-being of children, including promotion of effective and safe learning environments, prevention of academic and behavior problems, response to crises, and improvement of family-school collaboration. The key foundations for all services by school psychologists are understanding of diversity in development and learning; research and program evaluation; and legal, ethical, and professional practice. All of these components and their relationships are depicted in Appendix A [Figure A.1], a graphic representation of a national model for comprehensive and integrated services by school psychologists. School psychologists are credentialed by state education agencies or other similar state entities that have the statutory authority to regulate and establish credentialing requirements for professional practice within a state. School psychologists typically work in public or private schools or other educational contexts.

The NASP *Principles for Professional Ethics* is designed to be used in conjunction with the NASP *Standards for Graduate Preparation of School Psychologists*, *Standards for the Credentialing of School Psychologists*, and *Model for Comprehensive and Integrated School Psychological Services* to provide a unified set of national principles that guide graduate education, credentialing, professional practices, and ethical behavior of effective school psychologists. These NASP policy documents are intended to define contemporary school psychology; promote school psychologists' services for children, families, and schools; and provide a foundation for the future of school psychology. These

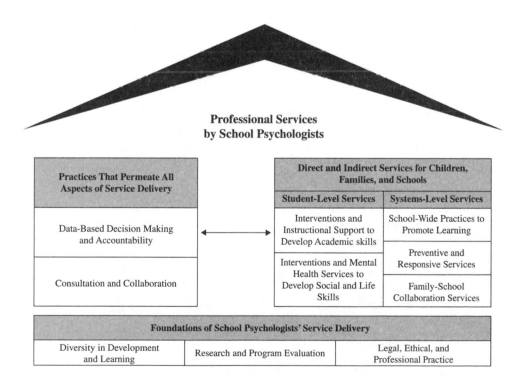

Figure A.1   Professional Services by School Psychologists

NASP policy documents are used to communicate NASP's positions and advocate for qualifications and practices of school psychologists with stakeholders, policy makers, and other professional groups at the national, state, and local levels.

The formal principles that elucidate the proper conduct of a professional school psychologist are known as *ethics*. In 1974, the National Association of School Psychologists (NASP) adopted its first code of ethics, the *Principles for Professional Ethics* (*Principles*), and revisions were made in 1984, 1992, 1997, and 2000. The purpose of the *Principles* is to protect the public and those who receive school psychological services by sensitizing school psychologists to the ethical aspects of their work, educating them about appropriate conduct, helping them monitor their own behavior, and providing standards to be used in the resolution of complaints of unethical conduct.[1] NASP members and school psychologists who are certified by the National School Psychologist Certification System (NCSP) are bound to abide by NASP's code of ethics.[2]

The NASP *Principles for Professional Ethics* were developed to address the unique circumstances associated with providing school psychological services. The duty to educate children and the legal authority to do so rests with state governments. When school psychologists employed by a school board make decisions in their official roles, such acts are seen as actions by state government. As state actors, school-based practitioners have special obligations to all students. They must know and respect the rights of students under the U.S. Constitution and federal and state statutory law. They must balance the authority of parents to make decisions about their children with the needs and rights of those children, and the purposes and authority of schools. Furthermore, as school employees, school psychologists have a legal as well as an ethical obligation to take steps to protect all students from reasonably foreseeable risk of harm. Finally, school-based practitioners work in a context that emphasizes multidisciplinary problem solving and intervention.[3] For these reasons, psychologists employed by the schools may have less control over aspects of service delivery than practitioners in private practice. However, within this framework, it is expected that school psychologists will make careful, reasoned, and principled ethical choices[4] based on knowledge of this code, recognizing that responsibility for ethical conduct rests with the individual practitioner.

School psychologists are committed to the application of their professional expertise for the purpose of promoting improvement in the quality of life for students, families, and school communities. This objective is pursued in ways that protect the dignity and rights of those involved. School psychologists consider the interests and rights of children and youth to be their highest priority in decision making, and act as advocates for all students. These assumptions necessitate that school psychologists "speak up" for the needs and rights of students even when it may be difficult to do so.

The *Principles for Professional Ethics*, like all codes of ethics, provide only limited guidance in making ethical choices. Individual judgment is necessary to apply the code to situations that arise in professional practice. Ethical dilemmas may be created by situations involving competing ethical principles, conflicts between ethics and law, the conflicting interests of multiple parties, the dual roles of employee and pupil advocate,

---

[1]Jacob, S., Decker, D. M., & Hartshorne, T. S. (in press). Ethics and law for school psychologists (6th ed.). Hoboken, NJ: John Wiley & Sons.

[2]National Association of School Psychologists. (2008). Ethical and Professional Practices Committee Procedures. Available: http://www.nasponline.org.

[3]Russo, C. J. (2006). Reutter's the law of public education (6th ed.). New York: Foundation Press.

[4]Haas, L. J., & Malouf, J. L. (2005). Keeping up the good work: A practitioner's guide to mental health ethics (4th ed.). Sarasota, FL: Professional Resource Press.

or because it is difficult to decide how statements in the ethics code apply to a particular situation.[5] Such situations are often complicated and may require a nuanced application of these *Principles* to effect a resolution that results in the greatest benefit for the student and concerned others. When difficult situations arise, school psychologists are advised to use a systematic problem-solving process to identify the best course of action. This process should include identifying the ethical issues involved, consulting these *Principles*, consulting colleagues with greater expertise, evaluating the rights and welfare of all affected parties, considering alternative solutions and their consequences; and accepting responsibility for the decisions made.[6,7]

The NASP *Principles for Professional Ethics* may require a more stringent standard of conduct than law, and in those situations in which both apply, school psychologists are expected to adhere to the *Principles*. When conflicts between ethics and law occur, school psychologists are expected to take steps to resolve conflicts by problem solving with others and through positive, respected, and legal channels. If not able to resolve the conflict in this manner, they may abide by the law, as long as the resulting actions do not violate basic human rights.[8]

In addition to providing services to public and private schools, school psychologists may be employed in a variety of other settings, including juvenile justice institutions, colleges and universities, mental health clinics, hospitals, and private practice. The principles in this code should be considered by school psychologists in their ethical decision making regardless of employment setting. However, this revision of the code, like its precursors, focuses on the special challenges associated with providing school psychological services in schools and to students. School psychologists who provide services directly to children, parents, and other clients as private practitioners, and those who work in health and mental health settings, are encouraged to be knowledgeable of federal and state law regulating mental health providers, and to consult the American Psychological Association's (2002) *Ethical Principles of Psychologists and Code of Conduct* for guidance on issues not directly addressed in this code.

Four broad ethical themes[9] provide the organizational framework for the 2010 *Principles for Professional Ethics*. The four broad ethical themes subsume 17 ethical principles. Each principle is then further articulated by multiple specific standards of conduct. The broad themes, corollary principles, and ethical standards are to be considered in decision making. NASP will seek to enforce the 17 ethical principles and corollary standards that appear in the *Principles for Professional Ethics* with its members and school psychologists who hold the NCSP credential in accordance with NASP's *Ethical and Professional Practices Committee Procedures* (2008). Regardless of role, clientele, or setting, school psychologists should reflect on the theme and intent of each ethical principle and standard to determine its application to his or her individual situation.

---

[5]Jacob-Timm, S. (1999). Ethical dilemmas encountered by members of the National Association of School Psychologists. Psychology in the Schools, 36, 205–217.

[6]McNamara, K. (2008). Best practices in the application of professional ethics. In A. Thomas & J. Grimes (Eds.), Best practices in school psychology V (pp. 1933–1941). Bethesda, MD: National Association of School Psychologists.

[7]Williams, B., Armistead, L., & Jacob, S. (2008). Professional ethics for school psychologists: A problem-solving model casebook. Bethesda, MD: National Association of School Psychologists.

[8]American Psychological Association. (2002). Ethical principles of psychologists and code of conduct. American Psychologist, 57, 1060–1073.

[9]Adapted from the Canadian Psychological Association. (2000). Canadian code of ethics for psychologists (3rd ed.). Available: http://www.cpa.ca.

The decisions made by school psychologists affect the welfare of children and families and can enhance their schools and communities. For this reason, school psychologists are encouraged to strive for excellence rather than simply meeting the minimum obligations outlined in the NASP *Principles for Professional Ethics*,[10] and to engage in the lifelong learning that is necessary to achieve and maintain expertise in applied professional ethics.

DEFINITION OF TERMS AS USED IN THE *PRINCIPLES FOR PROFESSIONAL ETHICS*

Client: The *client* is the person or persons with whom the school psychologist establishes a professional relationship for the purpose of providing school psychological services. A school psychologist–client professional relationship is established by an informed agreement with client(s) about the school psychologist's ethical and other duties to each party.[11] While not *clients* per se, classrooms, schools, and school systems also may be recipients of school psychological services and often are parties with an interest in the actions of school psychologists.

Child: A *child*, as defined in law, generally refers to a minor, a person younger than the age of majority. Although this term may be regarded as demeaning when applied to teenagers, it is used in this document when necessary to denote minor status. The term *student* is used when a less precise term is adequate.

Informed Consent: Informed consent means that the person giving consent has the legal authority to make a consent decision, a clear understanding of what it is he or she is consenting to, and that his or her consent is freely given and may be withdrawn without prejudice.[12]

Assent: The term *assent* refers to a minor's affirmative agreement to participate in psychological services or research.

Parent: The term *parent* may be defined in law or district policy, and can include the birth or adoptive parent, an individual acting in the place of a natural or adoptive parent (a grandparent or other relative, stepparent, or domestic partner), and/or an individual who is legally responsible for the child's welfare.

Advocacy: School psychologists have a special obligation to speak up for the rights and welfare of students and families, and to provide a voice to clients who cannot or do not wish to speak for themselves. *Advocacy* also occurs when school psychologists use their expertise in psychology and education to promote changes in schools, systems, and laws that will benefit school children, other students, and families.[13] Nothing in this code of ethics, however, should be construed as requiring school psychologists to engage in insubordination (willful disregard of an employer's lawful instructions) or to file a complaint about school district practices with a federal or state regulatory agency as part of their advocacy efforts.

---

[10]Knapp. S., & VandeCreek, L. (2006). Practical ethics for psychologists: A positive approach. Washington, DC: American Psychological Association.

[11]Fisher, M. A. (2009). Replacing "Who is the client?" with a different ethical question. Professional Psychology: Research and Practice, 40, 1–7.

[12]Dekraai, M., Sales, B., & Hall, S. (1998). Informed consent, confidentiality, and duty to report laws in the conduct of child therapy. In T. R. Kratochwill & R. J. Morris (Eds.), The practice of child therapy (3rd ed., pp. 540–559). Boston: Allyn & Bacon.

School-based versus Private Practice: School-based practice refers to the provision of school psychological services under the authority of a state, regional, or local educational agency. School-based practice occurs if the school psychologist is an employee of the schools or contracted by the schools on a per case or consultative basis. *Private practice* occurs when a school psychologist enters into an agreement with a client(s) rather than an educational agency to provide school psychological services and the school psychologist's fee for services is the responsibility of the client or his or her representative.

PRINCIPLES

I. Respecting the Dignity and Rights of All Persons

School psychologists engage only in professional practices that maintain the dignity of all with whom they work. In their words and actions, school psychologists demonstrate respect for the autonomy of persons and their right to self-determination, respect for privacy, and a commitment to just and fair treatment of all persons.

Principle I.1 Autonomy and Self-Determination (Consent and Assent)

School psychologists respect the right of persons to participate in decisions affecting their own welfare.

Standard I.1.1   School psychologists encourage and promote parental participation in school decisions affecting their children (see Standard II.3.10). However, where school psychologists are members of the school's educational support staff, not all of their services require informed parent consent. It is ethically permissible to provide school-based consultation services regarding a child or adolescent to a student assistance team or teacher without informed parent consent as long as the resulting interventions are under the authority of the teacher and within the scope of typical classroom interventions.[14] Parent consent is not ethically required for a school-based school psychologist to review a student's educational records, conduct classroom observations, assist in within-classroom interventions and progress monitoring, or to participate in educational screenings conducted as part of a regular program of instruction. Parent consent is required if the consultation about a particular child or adolescent is likely to be extensive and on-going and/or if school actions may result in a significant intrusion on student or family privacy beyond what might be expected in the course of ordinary school activities.[15] Parents must be notified prior to the administration of school- or classroom-wide screenings for mental health problems and given the opportunity to remove their child or adolescent from participation in such screenings.

---

[13]Masner, C. M. (2007). The ethic of advocacy. Doctoral dissertation, University of Denver. Available: http://www.dissertation.com.

[14]Burns, M. K., Jacob, S., & Wagner, A. (2008). Ethical and legal issues associated with using response-to-intervention to assess learning disabilities. Journal of School Psychology, 46, 263–279.

[15]Corrao, J., & Melton, G. B. (1988). Legal issues in school-based therapy. In J. C. Witt, S. N. Elliot, & F. M. Gresham (Eds.), Handbook of behavior therapy in education (pp. 377–399). New York: Plenum Press.

Standard I.1.2   Except for urgent situations or self-referrals by a minor student, school psychologists seek parent consent (or the consent of an adult student) prior to establishing a school psychologist-client relationship for the purpose of psychological diagnosis, assessment of eligibility for special education or disability accommodations, or to provide ongoing individual or group counseling or other non-classroom therapeutic intervention.*

- It is ethically permissible to provide psychological assistance without parent notice or consent in emergency situations or if there is reason to believe a student may pose a danger to others; is at risk for self-harm; or is in danger of injury, exploitation, or maltreatment.
- When a student who is a minor self-refers for assistance, it is ethically permissible to provide psychological assistance without parent notice or consent for one or several meetings to establish the nature and degree of the need for services and assure the child is safe and not in danger. It is ethically permissible to provide services to mature minors without parent consent where allowed by state law and school district policy. However, if the student is *not* old enough to receive school psychological assistance independent of parent consent, the school psychologist obtains parent consent to provide continuing assistance to the student beyond the preliminary meetings or refers the student to alternative sources of assistance that do not require parent notice or consent.

Standard I.1.3   School psychologists ensure that an individual providing consent for school psychological services is fully informed about the nature and scope of services offered, assessment/intervention goals and procedures, any foreseeable risks, the cost of services to the parent or student (if any), and the benefits that reasonably can be expected. The explanation includes discussion of the limits of confidentiality, who will receive information about assessment or intervention outcomes, and the possible consequences of the assessment/intervention services being offered. Available alternative services are identified, if appropriate. This explanation takes into account language and cultural differences, cognitive capabilities, developmental level, age, and other relevant factors so that it may be understood by the individual providing consent. School psychologists appropriately document written or oral consent. Any service provision by interns, practicum students, or other trainees is explained and agreed to in advance, and the identity and responsibilities of the supervising school psychologist are explained prior to the provision of services.[16]

Standard I.1.4   School psychologists encourage a minor student's voluntary participation in decision making about school psychological services as much as feasible. Ordinarily, school psychologists seek the student's assent to services; however, it is ethically

---

*It is recommended that school district parent handbooks and web sites advise parents that a minor student may be seen by school health or mental health professionals (e.g., school nurse, counselor, social worker, school psychologist) without parent notice or consent to ensure that the student is safe or is not a danger to others. Parents should also be advised that district school psychologists routinely assist teachers in planning classroom instruction and monitoring its effectiveness and do not need to notify parents of, or seek consent for, such involvement in student support.

[16]Weithorn, L. A. (1983). Involving children in decisions affecting their own welfare: Guidelines for professionals. In G. B. Melton, G. P. Koocher, & M. J. Saks (Eds.), *Children's competence to consent* (pp. 235–260). New York: Plenum Press.

permissible to by-pass student assent to services if the service is considered to be of direct benefit to the student and/or is required by law.[17]

- If a student's assent for services is not solicited, school psychologists nevertheless honor the student's right to be informed about the services provided.
- When a student is given a choice regarding whether to accept or refuse services, the school psychologist ensures the student understands what is being offered, honors the student's stated choice, and guards against overwhelming the student with choices he or she does not wish or is not able to make.[18]

Standard I.1.5   School psychologists respect the wishes of parents who object to school psychological services and attempt to guide parents to alternative resources.

Principle I.2 Privacy and Confidentiality

School psychologists respect the right of persons to choose for themselves whether to disclose their private thoughts, feelings, beliefs, and behaviors.

Standard I.2.1   School psychologists respect the right of persons to self-determine whether to disclose private information.

Standard I.2.2   School psychologists minimize intrusions on privacy. They do not seek or store private information about clients that is not needed in the provision of services. School psychologists recognize that client-school psychologist communications are privileged in most jurisdictions and do not disclose information that would put the student or family at legal, social, or other risk if shared with third parties, except as permitted by the mental health provider-client privilege laws in their state.[19]

Standard I.2.3   School psychologists inform students and other clients of the boundaries of confidentiality at the outset of establishing a professional relationship. They seek a shared understanding with clients regarding the types of information that will and will not be shared with third parties. However, if a child or adolescent is in immediate need of assistance, it is permissible to delay the discussion of confidentiality until the immediate crisis is resolved. School psychologists recognize that it may be necessary to discuss confidentiality at multiple points in a professional relationship to ensure client understanding and agreement regarding how sensitive disclosures will be handled.

Standard I.2.4   School psychologists respect the confidentiality of information obtained during their professional work. Information is not revealed to third parties without the agreement of a minor child's parent or legal guardian (or an adult student), except in those

---

[17]Weithorn, L. A. (1983). Involving children in decisions affecting their own welfare: Guidelines for professionals. In G. B. Melton, G. P. Koocher, & M. J. Saks (Eds.), Children's competence to consent (pp. 235–260). New York: Plenum Press.

[18]Weithorn, L. A. (1983). Involving children in decisions affecting their own welfare: Guidelines for professionals. In G. B. Melton, G. P. Koocher, & M. J. Saks (Eds.), Children's competence to consent (pp. 235–260). New York: Plenum Press.

[19]Jacob, S., & Powers, K. E. (2009). Privileged communication in the school psychologist–client relationship. Psychology in the Schools, 46, 307–318.

situations in which failure to release information would result in danger to the student or others, or where otherwise required by law. Whenever feasible, student assent is obtained prior to disclosure of his or her confidences to third parties, including disclosures to the student's parents.

Standard I.2.5   School psychologists discuss and/or release confidential information only for professional purposes and only with persons who have a legitimate need to know. They do so within the strict boundaries of relevant privacy statutes.

Standard I.2.6   School psychologists respect the right of privacy of students, parents, and colleagues with regard to sexual orientation, gender identity, or transgender status. They do not share information about the sexual orientation, gender identity, or transgender status of a student (including minors), parent, or school employee with anyone without that individual's permission.[20]

Standard I.2.7   School psychologists respect the right of privacy of students, their parents and other family members, and colleagues with regard to sensitive health information (e.g., presence of a communicable disease). They do not share sensitive health information about a student, parent, or school employee with others without that individual's permission (or the permission of a parent or guardian in the case of a minor). School psychologists consult their state laws and department of public health for guidance if they believe a client poses a health risk to others.[21]

Principle I.3 Fairness and Justice

In their words and actions, school psychologists promote fairness and justice. They use their expertise to cultivate school climates that are safe and welcoming to all persons regardless of actual or perceived characteristics, including race, ethnicity, color, religion, ancestry, national origin, immigration status, socioeconomic status, primary language, gender, sexual orientation, gender identity, gender expression, disability, or any other distinguishing characteristics.

Standard I.3.1   School psychologists do not engage in or condone actions or policies that discriminate against persons, including students and their families, other recipients of service, supervisees, and colleagues based on actual or perceived characteristics including race; ethnicity; color; religion; ancestry; national origin; immigration status; socioeconomic status; primary language; gender; sexual orientation, gender identity, or gender expression; mental, physical, or sensory disability; or any other distinguishing characteristics.

Standard I.3.2   School psychologists pursue awareness and knowledge of how diversity factors may influence child development, behavior, and school learning. In conducting psychological, educational, or behavioral evaluations or in providing interventions, therapy, counseling, or consultation services, the school psychologist takes into account

---

[20]Sterling v. Borough of Minersville, 232 F.3d 190, 2000 U.S. App. LEXIS 27855 (3rd Cir. 2000).
[21]Jacob, S., Decker, D. M., & Hartshorne, T. S. (in press). Ethics and law for school psychologists (6th ed.). Hoboken, NJ: John Wiley & Sons.

individual characteristics as enumerated in Standard I.3.1 so as to provide effective services.[22]

Standard I.3.3   School psychologists work to correct school practices that are unjustly discriminatory or that deny students, parents, or others their legal rights. They take steps to foster a school climate that is safe, accepting, and respectful of all persons.

Standard I.3.4   School psychologists strive to ensure that all children have equal opportunity to participate in and benefit from school programs and that all students and families have access to and can benefit from school psychological services.[23]

II. Professional Competence and Responsibility

Beneficence, or responsible caring, means that the school psychologist acts to benefit others. To do this, school psychologists must practice within the boundaries of their competence, use scientific knowledge from psychology and education to help clients and others make informed choices, and accept responsibility for their work.[24]

Principle II.1 Competence

To benefit clients, school psychologists engage only in practices for which they are qualified and competent.

Standard II.1.1   School psychologists recognize the strengths and limitations of their training and experience, engaging only in practices for which they are qualified. They enlist the assistance of other specialists in supervisory, consultative, or referral roles as appropriate in providing effective services.

Standard II.1.2   Practitioners are obligated to pursue knowledge and understanding of the diverse cultural, linguistic, and experiential backgrounds of students, families, and other clients. When knowledge and understanding of diversity characteristics are essential to ensure competent assessment, intervention, or consultation, school psychologists have or obtain the training or supervision necessary to provide effective services, or they make appropriate referrals.

Standard II.1.3   School psychologists refrain from any activity in which their personal problems may interfere with professional effectiveness. They seek assistance when personal problems threaten to compromise their professional effectiveness (also see III.4.2).

Standard II.1.4   School psychologists engage in continuing professional development. They remain current regarding developments in research, training, and professional practices that benefit children, families, and schools. They also understand that professional

---

[22]Flanagan, R., Miller, J. A., & Jacob, S. (2005). The 2002 revision of APA's ethics code: Implications for school psychologists. Psychology in the Schools, 42, 433–444.
[23]Flanagan, R., Miller, J. A., & Jacob, S. (2005). The 2002 revision of APA's ethics code: Implications for school psychologists. Psychology in the Schools, 42, 433–445.
[24]Jacob, S., Decker, D. M., & Hartshorne, T. S. (in press). Ethics and law for school psychologists (6th ed.). Hoboken, NJ: John Wiley & Sons.

skill development beyond that of the novice practitioner requires well-planned continuing professional development and professional supervision.

Principle II.2 Accepting Responsibility for Actions

School psychologists accept responsibility for their professional work, monitor the effectiveness of their services, and work to correct ineffective recommendations.

Standard II.2.1   School psychologists review all of their written documents for accuracy, signing them only when correct. They may add an addendum, dated and signed, to a previously submitted report if information is found to be inaccurate or incomplete.

Standard II.2.2   School psychologists actively monitor the impact of their recommendations and intervention plans. They revise a recommendation, or modify or terminate an intervention plan, when data indicate the desired outcomes are not being attained. School psychologists seek the assistance of others in supervisory, consultative, or referral roles when progress monitoring indicates that their recommendations and interventions are not effective in assisting a client.

Standard II.2.3   School psychologists accept responsibility for the appropriateness of their professional practices, decisions, and recommendations. They correct misunderstandings resulting from their recommendations, advice, or information and take affirmative steps to offset any harmful consequences of ineffective or inappropriate recommendations.

Standard II.2.4   When supervising graduate students' field experiences or internships, school psychologists are responsible for the work of their supervisees.

Principle II.3 Responsible Assessment and Intervention Practices

School psychologists maintain the highest standard for responsible professional practices in educational and psychological assessment and direct and indirect interventions.

Standard II.3.1   Prior to the consideration of a disability label or category, the effects of current behavior management and/or instructional practices on the student's school performance are considered.

Standard II.3.2   School psychologists use assessment techniques and practices that the profession considers to be responsible, research-based practice.

- School psychologists select assessment instruments and strategies that are reliable and valid for the child and the purpose of the assessment. When using standardized measures, school psychologists adhere to the procedures for administration of the instrument that are provided by the author or publisher or the instrument. If modifications are made in the administration procedures for standardized tests or other instruments, such modifications are identified and discussed in the interpretation of the results.
- If using norm-referenced measures, school psychologists choose instruments with up-to-date normative data.
- When using computer-administered assessments, computer-assisted scoring, and/or interpretation programs, school psychologists choose programs that meet professional standards for accuracy and validity. School psychologists use professional judgment in evaluating the accuracy of computer-assisted assessment findings for the examinee.

Standard II.3.3   A psychological or psychoeducational assessment is based on a variety of different types of information from different sources.

Standard II.3.4   Consistent with education law and sound professional practice, children with suspected disabilities are assessed in all areas related to the suspected disability.

Standard II.3.5   School psychologists conduct valid and fair assessments. They actively pursue knowledge of the student's disabilities and developmental, cultural, linguistic, and experiential background and then select, administer, and interpret assessment instruments and procedures in light of those characteristics (see Standards I.3.1 and I.3.2).

Standard II.3.6   When interpreters are used to facilitate the provision of assessment and intervention services, school psychologists take steps to ensure that the interpreters are appropriately trained and are acceptable to clients.[25]

Standard II.3.7   It is permissible for school psychologists to make recommendations based solely on a review of existing records. However, they should utilize a representative sample of records and explain the basis for, and the limitations of, their recommendations.[26]

Standard II.3.8   School psychologists adequately interpret findings and present results in clear, understandable terms so that the recipient can make informed choices.

Standard II.3.9   School psychologists use intervention, counseling and therapy procedures, consultation techniques, and other direct and indirect service methods that the profession considers to be responsible, research-based practice:

- School psychologists use a problem-solving process to develop interventions appropriate to the presenting problems and that are consistent with data collected.
- Preference is given to interventions described in the peer-reviewed professional research literature and found to be efficacious.

Standard II.3.10   School psychologists encourage and promote parental participation in designing interventions for their children. When appropriate, this includes linking interventions between the school and the home, tailoring parental involvement to the skills of the family, and helping parents gain the skills needed to help their children.

- School psychologists discuss with parents the recommendations and plans for assisting their children. This discussion takes into account the ethnic/cultural values of the family and includes alternatives that may be available. Subsequent recommendations for program changes or additional services are discussed with parents, including any alternatives that may be available.
- Parents are informed of sources of support available at school and in the community.

---

[25]American Psychological Association. (2002). Ethical principles of psychologists and code of conduct. American Psychologist, 57, 1060–1073.
[26]American Psychological Association. (2002). Ethical principles of psychologists and code of conduct. American Psychologist, 57, 1060–1073.

Standard II.3.11   School psychologists discuss with students the recommendations and plans for assisting them. To the maximum extent appropriate, students are invited to participate in selecting and planning interventions.[27]

Principle II.4 Responsible School-Based Record Keeping

School psychologists safeguard the privacy of school psychological records and ensure parent access to the records of their own children.

Standard II.4.1   School psychologists discuss with parents and adult students their rights regarding creation, modification, storage, and disposal of psychological and educational records that result from the provision of services. Parents and adult students are notified of the electronic storage and transmission of personally identifiable school psychological records and the associated risks to privacy.[28]

Standard II.4.2   School psychologists maintain school-based psychological and educational records with sufficient detail to be useful in decision making by another professional and with sufficient detail to withstand scrutiny if challenged in a due process or other legal procedure.[29]

Standard II.4.3   School psychologists include only documented and relevant information from reliable sources in school psychological records.

Standard II.4.4   School psychologists ensure that parents have appropriate access to the psychological and educational records of their child.

- Parents have a right to access any and all information that is used to make educational decisions about their child.
- School psychologists respect the right of parents to inspect, but not necessarily to copy, their child's answers to school psychological test questions even if those answers are recorded on a test protocol (also see II.5.1).[30]

Standard II.4.5   School psychologists take steps to ensure that information in school psychological records is not released to persons or agencies outside of the school without the consent of the parent except as required and permitted by law.

Standard II.4.6   To the extent that school psychological records are under their control, school psychologists ensure that only those school personnel who have a legitimate

---

[27]Weithorn, L. A. (1983). Involving children in decisions affecting their own welfare: Guidelines for professionals. In G. B. Melton, G. P. Koocher, & M. J. Saks (Eds.), Children's competence to consent (pp. 235–260). New York: Plenum Press.

[28]American Psychological Association. (2002). Ethical principles of psychologists and code of conduct. American Psychologist, 57, 1060–1073.

[29]Nagy, T. F. (2000). Ethics in plain English. Washington, DC: American Psychological Association.

[30]Reschly, D. J., & Bersoff, D. N. (1999). Law and school psychology. In C. R. Reynolds & T. B. Gutkin (Eds.), Handbook of school psychology (3rd ed., pp. 1077–1112). New York: John Wiley & Sons. Note: this chapter summarizes Department of Education policy letters on the matter of parent inspection of test protocols.

educational interest in a student are given access to the student's school psychological records without prior parent permission or the permission of an adult student.

Standard II.4.7   To the extent that school psychological records are under their control, school psychologists protect electronic files from unauthorized release or modification (e.g., by using passwords and encryption), and they take reasonable steps to ensure that school psychological records are not lost due to equipment failure.

Standard II.4.8   It is ethically permissible for school psychologists to keep private notes to use as a memory aid that are not made accessible to others. However, as noted in Standard II.4.4, any and all information that is used to make educational decisions about a student must be accessible to parents and adult students.

Standard II.4.9   School psychologists, in collaboration with administrators and other school staff, work to establish district policies regarding the storage and disposal of school psychological records that are consistent with law and sound professional practice. They advocate for school district policies and practices that:

- safeguard the security of school psychological records while facilitating appropriate parent access to those records;
- identify time lines for the periodic review and disposal of outdated school psychological records that are consistent with law and sound professional practice;
- seek parent or other appropriate permission prior to the destruction of obsolete school psychological records of current students;
- ensure that obsolete school psychology records are destroyed in a way that the information cannot be recovered.

Principle II.5 Responsible Use of Materials

School psychologists respect the intellectual property rights of those who produce tests, intervention materials, scholarly works, and other materials.

Standard II.5.1   School psychologists maintain test security, preventing the release of underlying principles and specific content that would undermine or invalidate the use of the instrument. Unless otherwise required by law or district policy, school psychologists provide parents with the opportunity to inspect and review their child's test answers rather than providing them with copies of the their child's test protocols. However, on parent request, it is permissible to provide copies of a child's test protocols to a professional who is qualified to interpret them.

Standard II.5.2   School psychologists do not promote or condone the use of restricted psychological and educational tests or other assessment tools or procedures by individuals who are not qualified to use them.

Standard II.5.3   School psychologists recognize the effort and expense involved in the development and publication of psychological and educational tests, intervention materials, and scholarly works. They respect the intellectual property rights and copyright interests of the producers of such materials, whether the materials are published in print or digital formats. They do not duplicate copyright-protected test manuals, testing materials, or unused test protocols without the permission of the producer. However, school psychologists understand that, at times, parents' rights to examine their child's test answers may supersede the interests of test publishers.[31,32]

III. Honesty and Integrity in Professional Relationships

To foster and maintain trust, school psychologists must be faithful to the truth and adhere to their professional promises. They are forthright about their qualifications, competencies, and roles; work in full cooperation with other professional disciplines to meet the needs of students and families; and avoid multiple relationships that diminish their professional effectiveness.

Principle III.1 Accurate Presentation of Professional Qualifications
School psychologists accurately identify their professional qualifications to others.

Standard III.1.1   Competency levels, education, training, experience, and certification and licensing credentials are accurately represented to clients, recipients of services, and others. School psychologists correct any misperceptions of their qualifications. School psychologists do not represent themselves as specialists in a particular domain without verifiable training and supervised experience in the specialty.

Standard III.1.2   School psychologists do not use affiliations with persons, associations, or institutions to imply a level of professional competence that exceeds that which has actually been achieved.

Principle III.2 Forthright Explanation of Professional Services, Roles, and Priorities
School psychologists are candid about the nature and scope of their services.

Standard III.2.1   School psychologists explain their professional competencies, roles, assignments, and working relationships to recipients of services and others in their work setting in a forthright and understandable manner. School psychologists explain all professional services to clients in a clear, understandable manner (see I.1.2).

Standard III.2.2   School psychologists make reasonable efforts to become integral members of the client service systems to which they are assigned. They establish clear roles for themselves within those systems while respecting the various roles of colleagues in other professions.

Standard III.2.3   The school psychologist's commitment to protecting the rights and welfare of children is communicated to the school administration, staff, and others as the highest priority in determining services.

---

[31]Reschly, D. J., & Bersoff, D. N. (1999). Law and school psychology. In C. R. Reynolds & T. B. Gutkin (Eds.), Handbook of school psychology (3rd ed., pp. 1077–1112). New York: John Wiley & Sons. Note: this chapter summarizes Department of Education policy letters on the matter of parent inspection of test protocols.
[32]Newport-Mesa Unified School District v. State of California Department of Education, 371 F. Supp. 2d 1170; 2005 U.S. Dist. LEXIS 10290 (C.D. Cal. 2005).

Standard III.2.4   School psychologists who provide services to several different groups (e.g., families, teachers, classrooms) may encounter situations in which loyalties are conflicted. As much as possible, school psychologists make known their priorities and commitments in advance to all parties to prevent misunderstandings.

Standard III.2.5   School psychologists ensure that announcements and advertisements of the availability of their publications, products, and services for sale are factual and professional. They do not misrepresent their degree of responsibility for the development and distribution of publications, products, and services.

Principle III.3 Respecting Other Professionals

To best meet the needs of children, school psychologists cooperate with other professionals in relationships based on mutual respect.

Standard III.3.1   To meet the needs of children and other clients most effectively, school psychologists cooperate with other psychologists and professionals from other disciplines in relationships based on mutual respect. They encourage and support the use of all resources to serve the interests of students. If a child or other client is receiving similar services from another professional, school psychologists promote coordination of services.

Standard III.3.2   If a child or other client is referred to another professional for services, school psychologists ensure that all relevant and appropriate individuals, including the client, are notified of the change and reasons for the change. When referring clients to other professionals, school psychologists provide clients with lists of suitable practitioners from whom the client may seek services.

Standard III.3.3   Except when supervising graduate students, school psychologists do not alter a report completed by another professional without his or her permission to do so.

Principle III.4 Multiple Relationships and Conflicts of Interest

School psychologists avoid multiple relationships and conflicts of interest that diminish their professional effectiveness.

Standard III.4.1   The *Principles for Professional Ethics* provide standards for professional conduct. School psychologists, in their private lives, are free to pursue their personal interests, except to the degree that those interests compromise professional effectiveness.

Standard III.4.2   School psychologists refrain from any activity in which conflicts of interest or multiple relationships with a client or a client's family may interfere with professional effectiveness. School psychologists attempt to resolve such situations in a manner that provides greatest benefit to the client. School psychologists whose personal or religious beliefs or commitments may influence the nature of their professional services or their willingness to provide certain services inform clients and responsible parties of this fact. When personal beliefs, conflicts of interests, or multiple relationships threaten to diminish professional effectiveness or would be viewed by the public as inappropriate, school psychologists ask their supervisor for reassignment of responsibilities, or they direct the client to alternative services.[33]

Standard III.4.3   School psychologists do not exploit clients, supervisees, or graduate students through professional relationships or condone these actions by their colleagues. They do not participate in or condone sexual harassment of children, parents, other clients, colleagues, employees, trainees, supervisees, or research participants. School psychologists do not engage in sexual relationships with individuals over whom they have evaluation authority, including college students in their classes or program, or any other trainees, or supervisees. School psychologists do not engage in sexual relationships with their current or former pupil-clients; the parents, siblings, or other close family members of current pupil-clients; or current consultees.

Standard III.4.4   School psychologists are cautious about business and other relationships with clients that could interfere with professional judgment and effectiveness or potentially result in exploitation of a client.

Standard III.4.5   NASP requires that any action taken by its officers, members of the Executive Council or Delegate Assembly, or other committee members be free from the appearance of impropriety and free from any conflict of interest. NASP leaders recuse themselves from decisions regarding proposed NASP initiatives if they may gain an economic benefit from the proposed venture.

Standard III.4.6   A school psychologist's financial interests in a product (e.g., tests, computer software, professional materials) or service can influence his or her objectivity or the perception of his or her objectivity regarding that product or service. For this reason, school psychologists are obligated to disclose any significant financial interest in the products or services they discuss in their presentations or writings if that interest is not obvious in the authorship/ownership citations provided.

Standard III.4.7   School psychologists neither give nor receive any remuneration for referring children and other clients for professional services.

Standard III.4.8   School psychologists do not accept any remuneration in exchange for data from their client data base without the permission of their employer and a determination of whether the data release ethically requires informed client consent.

Standard III.4.9   School psychologists who provide school-based services and also engage in the provision of private practice services (dual setting practitioners) recognize the potential for conflict of interests between their two roles and take steps to avoid such conflicts. Dual setting practitioners:

- are obligated to inform parents or other potential clients of any psychological and educational services available at no cost from the schools prior to offering such services for remuneration;

---

[33] American Psychological Association. (2002). Ethical principles of psychologists and code of conduct. *American Psychologist, 57*, 1060–1073.

- may not offer or provide private practice services to a student of a school or special school program where the practitioner is currently assigned;
- may not offer or provide private practice services to the parents or family members of a student eligible to attend a school or special school program where the practitioner is currently assigned;
- may not offer or provide an independent evaluation as defined in special education law for a student who attends a local or cooperative school district where the practitioner is employed;
- do not use tests, materials, equipment, facilities, secretarial assistance, or other services belonging to the public sector employer unless approved in advance by the employer;
- conduct all private practice outside of the hours of contracted public employment; and
- hold appropriate credentials for practice in both the public and private sectors.

IV. Responsibility to Schools, Families, Communities, the Profession, and Society

School psychologists promote healthy school, family, and community environments. They assume a proactive role in identifying social injustices that affect children and schools and strive to reform systems-level patterns of injustice. They maintain the public trust in school psychologists by respecting law and encouraging ethical conduct. School psychologists advance professional excellence by mentoring less experienced practitioners and contributing to the school psychology knowledge base.

Principle IV.1 Promoting Healthy School, Family, and Community Environments

School psychologists use their expertise in psychology and education to promote school, family, and community environments that are safe and healthy for children.

Standard IV.1.1   To provide effective services and systems consultation, school psychologists are knowledgeable about the organization, philosophy, goals, objectives, culture, and methodologies of the settings in which they provide services. In addition, school psychologists develop partnerships and networks with community service providers and agencies to provide seamless services to children and families.

Standard IV.1.2   School psychologists use their professional expertise to promote changes in schools and community service systems that will benefit children and other clients. They advocate for school policies and practices that are in the best interests of children and that respect and protect the legal rights of students and parents.[34]

Principle IV.2 Respect for Law and the Relationship of Law and Ethics

School psychologists are knowledgeable of and respect laws pertinent to the practice of school psychology. In choosing an appropriate course of action, they consider the relationship between law and the *Principles for Professional Ethics*.

---

[34]Prilleltensky, I. (1991). The social ethics of school psychology: A priority for the 1990s. School Psychology Quarterly, 6, 200–222.

Standard IV.2.1   School psychologists recognize that an understanding of the goals, procedures, and legal requirements of their particular workplace is essential for effective functioning within that setting.

Standard IV.2.2   School psychologists respect the law and the civil and legal rights of students and other clients. The *Principles for Professional Ethics* may require a more stringent standard of conduct than law, and in those situations school psychologists are expected to adhere to the *Principles*.

Standard IV.2.3   When conflicts between ethics and law occur, school psychologists take steps to resolve the conflict through positive, respected, and legal channels. If not able to resolve the conflict in this manner, they may abide by the law, as long as the resulting actions do not violate basic human rights.[35]

Standard IV.2.4   School psychologists may act as individual citizens to bring about change in a lawful manner. They identify when they are speaking as private citizens rather than as employees. They also identify when they speak as individual professionals rather than as representatives of a professional association.

Principle IV.3 Maintaining Public Trust by Self-Monitoring and Peer Monitoring

School psychologists accept responsibility to monitor their own conduct and the conduct of other school psychologists to ensure it conforms to ethical standards.

Standard IV.3.1   School psychologists know the *Principles for Professional Ethics* and thoughtfully apply them to situations within their employment context. In difficult situations, school psychologists consult experienced school psychologists or state associations or NASP.

Standard IV.3.2   When a school psychologist suspects that another school psychologist or another professional has engaged in unethical practices, he or she attempts to resolve the suspected problem through a collegial problem-solving process, if feasible.

Standard IV.3.3   If a collegial problem-solving process is not possible or productive, school psychologists take further action appropriate to the situation, including discussing the situation with a supervisor in the employment setting, consulting state association ethics committees, and, if necessary, filing a formal ethical violation complaint with state associations, state credentialing bodies, or the NASP Ethical and Professional Practices Committee in accordance with their procedures.

Standard IV.3.4   When school psychologists are concerned about unethical practices by professionals who are not NASP members or do not hold the NCSP, informal contact is made to discuss the concern if feasible. If the situation cannot be resolved in this manner, discussing the situation with the professional's supervisor should be considered. If necessary, an appropriate professional organization or state credentialing agency could be contacted to determine the procedures established by that professional association or agency for examining the practices in question.

---

[35]American Psychological Association. (2002). Ethical principles of psychologists and code of conduct. American Psychologist, 57, 1060–1073.

Principle IV.4 Contributing to the Profession by Mentoring, Teaching, and Supervision

As part of their obligation to students, schools, society, and their profession, school psychologists mentor less experienced practitioners and graduate students to assure high quality services, and they serve as role models for sound ethical and professional practices and decision making.

Standard IV.4.1   School psychologists who serve as directors of graduate education programs provide current and prospective graduate students with accurate information regarding program accreditation, goals and objectives, graduate program policies and requirements, and likely outcomes and benefits.

Standard IV.4.2   School psychologists who supervise practicum students and interns are responsible for all professional practices of the supervisees. They ensure that practicum students and interns are adequately supervised as outlined in the NASP *Graduate Preparation Standards for School Psychologists*. Interns and graduate students are identified as such, and their work is co-signed by the supervising school psychologist.

Standard IV.4.3   School psychologists who employ, supervise, or train professionals provide appropriate working conditions, fair and timely evaluation, constructive supervision, and continuing professional development opportunities.

Standard IV.4.4   School psychologists who are faculty members at universities or who supervise graduate education field experiences apply these ethical principles in all work with school psychology graduate students. In addition, they promote the ethical practice of graduate students by providing specific and comprehensive instruction, feedback, and mentoring.

Principle IV.5 Contributing to the School Psychology Knowledge Base

To improve services to children, families, and schools, and to promote the welfare of children, school psychologists are encouraged to contribute to the school psychology knowledge base by participating in, assisting in, or conducting and disseminating research.

Standard IV.5.1   When designing and conducting research in schools, school psychologists choose topics and employ research methodology, research participant selection procedures, data-gathering methods, and analysis and reporting techniques that are grounded in sound research practice. School psychologists identify their level of training and graduate degree to potential research participants.

Standard IV.5.2   School psychologists respect the rights, and protect the well-being, of research participants. School psychologists obtain appropriate review and approval of proposed research prior to beginning their data collection.

- Prior to initiating research, school psychologists and graduate students affiliated with a university, hospital, or other agency subject to the U.S. Department of Health and Human Services (DHHS) regulation of research first obtain approval for their research from their Institutional Review Board for Research Involving Human Subjects (IRB) as well as the school or other agency in which the research will be conducted. Research proposals that have not been subject to IRB approval should be reviewed by individuals knowledgeable about research methodology and ethics and approved by the school administration or other appropriate authority.

- In planning research, school psychologists are ethically obligated to consider carefully whether the informed consent of research participants is needed for their study, recognizing that research involving more than minimum risk requires informed consent, and that research with students involving activities that are not part of ordinary, typical schooling requires informed consent. Consent and assent protocols provide the information necessary for potential research participants to make an informed and voluntary choice about participation. School psychologists evaluate the potential risks (including risks of physical or psychological harm, intrusions on privacy, breach of confidentiality) and benefits of their research and only conduct studies in which the risks to participants are minimized and acceptable.

Standard IV.5.3   School psychologists who use their assessment, intervention, or consultation cases in lectures, presentations, or publications obtain written prior client consent or they remove and disguise identifying client information.

Standard IV.5.4   School psychologists do not publish or present fabricated or falsified data or results in their publications and presentations.

Standard IV.5.5   School psychologists make available their data or other information that provided the basis for findings and conclusions reported in publications and presentations, if such data are needed to address a legitimate concern or need and under the condition that the confidentiality and other rights of research participants are protected.

Standard IV.5.6   If errors are discovered after the publication or presentation of research or other information, school psychologists make efforts to correct errors by publishing errata, retractions, or corrections.

Standard IV.5.7   School psychologists only publish data or other information that make original contributions to the professional literature. They do not report the same study in a second publication without acknowledging previous publication of the same data. They do not duplicate significant portions of their own or others' previous publications without permission of copyright holders.

Standard IV.5.8   When publishing or presenting research or other work, school psychologists do not plagiarize the works or ideas of others. They appropriately cite and reference all sources, print or digital, and assign credit to those whose ideas are reflected. In inservice or conference presentations, school psychologists give credit to others whose ideas have been used or adapted.

Standard IV.5.9   School psychologists accurately reflect the contributions of authors and other individuals who contributed to presentations and publications. Authorship credit is given only to individuals who have made a substantial professional contribution to the research, publication, or presentation. Authors discuss and resolve issues related to publication credit as early as feasible in the research and publication process.

Standard IV.5.10   School psychologists who participate in reviews of manuscripts, proposals, and other materials respect the confidentiality and proprietary rights of the authors. They limit their use of the materials to the activities relevant to the purposes of the professional review. School psychologists who review professional materials do not communicate the identity of the author, quote from the materials, or duplicate or circulate copies of the materials without the author's permission.

Appendix B

*AMERICAN PSYCHOLOGICAL ASSOCIATION ETHICAL PRINCIPLES OF PSYCHOLOGISTS AND CODE OF CONDUCT WITH THE 2010 AMENDMENTS**

INTRODUCTION AND APPLICABILITY

The American Psychological Association's (APA's) Ethical Principles of Psychologists and Code of Conduct (hereinafter referred to as the Ethics Code) consists of an Introduction, a Preamble, five General Principles (A–E), and specific Ethical Standards. The Introduction discusses the intent, organization, procedural considerations, and scope of application of the Ethics Code. The Preamble and General Principles are aspirational goals to guide psychologists toward the highest ideals of psychology. Although the Preamble and General Principles are not themselves enforceable rules, they should be considered by psychologists in arriving at an ethical course of action. The Ethical Standards set forth enforceable rules for conduct as psychologists. Most of the Ethical Standards are written broadly, in order to apply to psychologists in varied roles, although the application of an Ethical Standard may vary depending on the context. The Ethical Standards are not exhaustive. The fact that a given conduct is not specifically addressed by an Ethical Standard does not mean that it is necessarily either ethical or unethical.

This Ethics Code applies only to psychologists' activities that are part of their scientific, educational, or professional roles as psychologists. Areas covered include but are not limited to the clinical, counseling, and school practice of psychology; research; teaching; supervision of trainees; public service; policy development; social intervention; development of assessment instruments; conducting assessments; educational counseling; organizational consulting; forensic activities; program design and evaluation; and administration. This Ethics Code applies to these activities across a variety of contexts, such as in person, postal, telephone, internet, and other electronic transmissions. These activities shall be distinguished from the purely private conduct of psychologists, which is not within the purview of the Ethics Code.

Membership in the APA commits members and student affiliates to comply with the standards of the APA Ethics Code and to the rules and procedures used to enforce them. Lack of awareness or misunderstanding of an Ethical Standard is not itself a defense to a charge of unethical conduct.

The procedures for filing, investigating, and resolving complaints of unethical conduct are described in the current Rules and Procedures of the APA Ethics Committee. APA may impose sanctions on its members for violations of the standards of the Ethics Code, including termination of APA membership, and may notify other bodies and individuals of its actions. Actions that violate the standards of the Ethics Code may also lead to the imposition of sanctions on the psychologists or students whether or not they are APA members by bodies other than APA, including state psychological associations, other professional groups, psychology boards, other state or federal agencies, and payors for health services. In addition, APA may take action against a member after his or her conviction of a felony, expulsion or suspension from an affiliated state psychological association, or suspension or loss of licensure. When the sanction to be imposed by APA is less than expulsion, the 2001 Rules and Procedures do not guarantee an opportunity for an in-person hearing, but generally provide that complaints will be resolved only on the basis of a submitted record.

The Ethics Code is intended to provide guidance for psychologists and standards of professional conduct that can be applied by the APA and by other bodies that choose to adopt them. The Ethics Code is not intended to be a basis of civil liability. Whether a psychologist has violated the Ethics Code does not by itself determine whether the psychologist is legally liable in a court action, whether a contract is enforceable, or whether other legal consequences occur.

The modifiers used in some of the standards of this Ethics Code (e.g., reasonably, appropriate, potentially) are included in the standards when they would (1) allow professional judgment on the part of psychologists, (2) eliminate injustice or inequality that would occur without the modifier, (3) ensure applicability across the broad range of activities conducted by psychologists, or (4) guard against a set of rigid rules that might be quickly outdated. As used in this Ethics Code, the term reasonable means the prevailing professional judgment of psychologists engaged in similar activities in similar circumstances, given the knowledge the psychologist had or should have had at the time.

In the process of making decisions regarding their professional behavior, psychologists must consider this Ethics Code in addition to applicable laws and psychology board regulations. In applying the Ethics Code to their professional work, psychologists may consider other materials and guidelines that have been adopted or endorsed by scientific and professional psychological organizations and the dictates of their own conscience, as well as consult with others within the field. If this Ethics Code establishes a higher standard of conduct than is required by law, psychologists must meet the higher ethical standard. If psychologists' ethical responsibilities conflict with law, regulations, or other governing legal authority, psychologists make known their commitment to this Ethics Code and take steps to resolve the conflict in a responsible manner in keeping with basic principles of human rights.

PREAMBLE

Psychologists are committed to increasing scientific and professional knowledge of behavior and people's understanding of themselves and others and to the use of such knowledge to improve the condition of individuals, organizations, and society. Psychologists respect and protect civil and human rights and the central importance of freedom of inquiry and expression in research, teaching, and publication. They strive to help the public in developing informed judgments and choices concerning human behavior. In doing so, they perform many roles, such as researcher, educator, diagnostician, therapist, supervisor, consultant, administrator, social interventionist, and expert witness. This Ethics Code provides a common set of principles and standards upon which psychologists build their professional and scientific work.

This Ethics Code is intended to provide specific standards to cover most situations encountered by psychologists. It has as its goals the welfare and protection of the individuals and groups with whom psychologists work and the education of members, students, and the public regarding ethical standards of the discipline.

The development of a dynamic set of ethical standards for psychologists' work-related conduct requires a personal commitment and lifelong effort to act ethically; to encourage ethical behavior by students, supervisees, employees, and colleagues; and to consult with others concerning ethical problems.

GENERAL PRINCIPLES

This section consists of General Principles. General Principles, as opposed to Ethical Standards, are aspirational in nature. Their intent is to guide and inspire psychologists toward the very highest ethical ideals of the profession. General Principles, in contrast to Ethical Standards, do not represent obligations and should not form the basis for imposing sanctions. Relying upon General Principles for either of these reasons distorts both their meaning and purpose.

Principle A: Beneficence and Non-Maleficence

Psychologists strive to benefit those with whom they work and take care to do no harm. In their professional actions, psychologists seek to safeguard the welfare and rights of those with whom they interact professionally and other affected persons, and the welfare of animal subjects of research. When conflicts occur among psychologists' obligations or concerns, they attempt to resolve these conflicts in a responsible fashion that avoids or minimizes harm. Because psychologists' scientific and professional judgments and actions may affect the lives of others, they are alert to and guard against personal, financial, social, organizational, or political factors that might lead to misuse of their influence. Psychologists strive to be aware of the possible effect of their own physical and mental health on their ability to help those with whom they work.

Principle B: Fidelity and Responsibility

Psychologists establish relationships of trust with those with whom they work. They are aware of their professional and scientific responsibilities to society and to the specific communities in which they work. Psychologists uphold professional standards of conduct, clarify their professional roles and obligations, accept appropriate responsibility for their behavior, and seek to manage conflicts of interest that could lead to exploitation or harm. Psychologists consult with, refer to, or cooperate with other professionals and institutions to the extent needed to serve the best interests of those with whom they work. They are concerned about the ethical compliance of their colleagues' scientific and professional conduct. Psychologists strive to contribute a portion of their professional time for little or no compensation or personal advantage.

Principle C: Integrity

Psychologists seek to promote accuracy, honesty, and truthfulness in the science, teaching, and practice of psychology. In these activities psychologists do not steal, cheat, or engage in fraud, subterfuge, or intentional misrepresentation of fact. Psychologists strive to keep their promises and to avoid unwise or unclear commitments. In situations in which deception may be ethically justifiable to maximize benefits and minimize harm, psychologists have a serious obligation to consider the need for, the possible consequences of, and their responsibility to correct any resulting mistrust or other harmful effects that arise from the use of such techniques.

Principle D: Justice

Psychologists recognize that fairness and justice entitle all persons to access to and benefit from the contributions of psychology and equal quality in the processes, procedures, and services being conducted by psychologists. Psychologists exercise reasonable judgment and take precautions to ensure that their potential biases, the boundaries of their competence, and the limitations of their expertise do not lead to or condone unjust practices.

Principle E: Respect for People's Rights and Dignity

Psychologists respect the dignity and worth of all people, and the rights of individuals to privacy, confidentiality, and self-determination. Psychologists are aware that special safeguards may be necessary to protect the rights and welfare of persons or communities whose vulnerabilities impair autonomous decision making. Psychologists are aware of and respect cultural, individual, and role differences, including those based on age, gender, gender identity, race, ethnicity, culture, national origin, religion, sexual orientation, disability, language, and socioeconomic status and consider these factors when working with members of such groups. Psychologists try to eliminate the effect on their work of biases based on those factors, and they do not knowingly participate in or condone activities of others based upon such prejudices.

ETHICAL STANDARDS

Standard 1: Resolving Ethical Issues

1.01 Misuse of Psychologists' Work

If psychologists learn of misuse or misrepresentation of their work, they take reasonable steps to correct or minimize the misuse or misrepresentation.

1.02 Conflicts Between Ethics and Law, Regulations, or Other Governing Legal Authority

If psychologists' ethical responsibilities conflict with law, regulations, or other governing legal authority, psychologists clarify the nature of the conflict, make known their commitment to the Ethics Code, and take reasonable steps to resolve the conflict consistent with the General Principles and Ethical Standards of the Ethics Code. Under no circumstances may this standard be used to justify or defend violating human rights.

1.03 Conflicts Between Ethics and Organizational Demands

If the demands of an organization with which psychologists are affiliated or for whom they are working are in conflict with this Ethics Code, psychologists clarify the nature of the conflict, make known their commitment to the Ethics Code, and take reasonable steps to resolve the conflict consistent with the General Principles and Ethical Standards of the Ethics Code. Under no circumstances may this standard be used to justify or defend violating human rights.

1.04 Informal Resolution of Ethical Violations

When psychologists believe that there may have been an ethical violation by another psychologist, they attempt to resolve the issue by bringing it to the attention of that individual, if an informal resolution appears appropriate and the intervention does not violate any confidentiality rights that may be involved. (See also Standard 1.02, Conflicts Between Ethics and Law, Regulations, or Other Governing Legal Authority, and 1.03, Conflicts Between Ethics and Organizational Demands.)

1.05 Reporting Ethical Violations

If an apparent ethical violation has substantially harmed or is likely to substantially harm a person or organization and is not appropriate for informal resolution under Standard 1.04, Informal Resolution of Ethical Violations, or is not resolved properly in that fashion, psychologists take further action appropriate to the situation. Such action might include referral to state or national committees on professional ethics, to state licensing boards, or to the appropriate institutional authorities. This standard does not apply when an intervention would violate confidentiality rights or when psychologists have been retained to review the work of another psychologist whose professional conduct is in question. (See also Standard 1.02, Conflicts Between Ethics and Law, Regulations, or Other Governing Legal Authority.)

1.06 Cooperating with Ethics Committees

Psychologists cooperate in ethics investigations, proceedings, and resulting requirements of the APA or any affiliated state psychological association to which they belong. In doing so, they address any confidentiality issues. Failure to cooperate is itself an ethics violation. However, making a request for deferment of adjudication of an ethics complaint pending the outcome of litigation does not alone constitute noncooperation.

1.07 Improper Complaints

Psychologists do not file or encourage the filing of ethics complaints that are made with reckless disregard for or willful ignorance of facts that would disprove the allegation.

1.08 Unfair Discrimination Against Complainants and Respondents

Psychologists do not deny persons employment, advancement, admissions to academic or other programs, tenure, or promotion, based solely upon their having made or their being the subject of an ethics complaint. This does not preclude taking action based upon the outcome of such proceedings or considering other appropriate information.

Standard 2: Competence

2.01 Boundaries of Competence

(a) Psychologists provide services, teach, and conduct research with populations and in areas only within the boundaries of their competence, based on their education, training, supervised experience, consultation, study, or professional experience.

(b) Where scientific or professional knowledge in the discipline of psychology establishes that an understanding of factors associated with age, gender, gender identity, race, ethnicity, culture, national origin, religion, sexual orientation, disability, language, or socioeconomic status is essential for effective implementation of their services or research, psychologists have or obtain the training, experience, consultation, or supervision necessary to ensure the competence of their services, or they make appropriate referrals, except as provided in Standard 2.02, Providing Services in Emergencies.

(c) Psychologists planning to provide services, teach, or conduct research involving populations, areas, techniques, or technologies new to them undertake relevant education, training, supervised experience, consultation, or study.

(d) When psychologists are asked to provide services to individuals for whom appropriate mental health services are not available and for which psychologists have not obtained the competence necessary, psychologists with closely related prior training or experience may provide such services in order to ensure that services are not denied if they make a reasonable effort to obtain the competence required by using relevant research, training, consultation, or study.

(e) In those emerging areas in which generally recognized standards for preparatory training do not yet exist, psychologists nevertheless take reasonable steps to ensure the competence of their work and to protect clients/patients, students, supervisees, research participants, organizational clients, and others from harm.

(f) When assuming forensic roles, psychologists are or become reasonably familiar with the judicial or administrative rules governing their roles.

2.02 Providing Services in Emergencies

In emergencies, when psychologists provide services to individuals for whom other mental health services are not available and for which psychologists have not obtained the necessary training, psychologists may provide such services in order to ensure that services are not denied. The services are discontinued as soon as the emergency has ended or appropriate services are available.

2.03 Maintaining Competence

Psychologists undertake ongoing efforts to develop and maintain their competence.

2.04 Bases for Scientific and Professional Judgments

Psychologists' work is based upon established scientific and professional knowledge of the discipline. (See also Standards 2.01e, Boundaries of Competence, and 10.01b, Informed Consent to Therapy.)

2.05 Delegation of Work to Others

Psychologists who delegate work to employees, supervisees, or research or teaching assistants or who use the services of others, such as interpreters, take reasonable steps to (1) avoid delegating such work to persons who have a multiple relationship with those being served that would likely lead to exploitation or loss of objectivity; (2) authorize only those responsibilities that such persons can be expected to perform competently on the basis of their education, training, or experience, either independently or with the level of supervision being provided; and (3) see that such persons perform these services competently. (See also Standards 2.02, Providing Services in Emergencies; 3.05, Multiple

Relationships; 4.01, Maintaining Confidentiality; 9.01, Bases for Assessments; 9.02, Use of Assessments; 9.03, Informed Consent in Assessments; and 9.07, Assessment by Unqualified Persons.)

2.06 Personal Problems and Conflicts

(a) Psychologists refrain from initiating an activity when they know or should know that there is a substantial likelihood that their personal problems will prevent them from performing their work-related activities in a competent manner.

(b) When psychologists become aware of personal problems that may interfere with their performing work-related duties adequately, they take appropriate measures, such as obtaining professional consultation or assistance, and determine whether they should limit, suspend, or terminate their work-related duties. (See also Standard 10.10, Terminating Therapy.)

Standard 3: Human Relations

3.01 Unfair Discrimination

In their work-related activities, psychologists do not engage in unfair discrimination based on age, gender, gender identity, race, ethnicity, culture, national origin, religion, sexual orientation, disability, socioeconomic status, or any basis proscribed by law.

3.02 Sexual Harassment

Psychologists do not engage in sexual harassment. Sexual harassment is sexual solicitation, physical advances, or verbal or nonverbal conduct that is sexual in nature, that occurs in connection with the psychologist's activities or roles as a psychologist, and that either (1) is unwelcome, is offensive, or creates a hostile workplace or educational environment, and the psychologist knows or is told this or (2) is sufficiently severe or intense to be abusive to a reasonable person in the context. Sexual harassment can consist of a single intense or severe act or of multiple persistent or pervasive acts. (See also Standard 1.08, Unfair Discrimination Against Complainants and Respondents.)

3.03 Other Harassment

Psychologists do not knowingly engage in behavior that is harassing or demeaning to persons with whom they interact in their work based on factors such as those persons' age, gender, gender identity, race, ethnicity, culture, national origin, religion, sexual orientation, disability, language, or socioeconomic status.

3.04 Avoiding Harm

Psychologists take reasonable steps to avoid harming their clients/patients, students, supervisees, research participants, organizational clients, and others with whom they work, and to minimize harm where it is foreseeable and unavoidable.

3.05 Multiple Relationships

(a) A multiple relationship occurs when a psychologist is in a professional role with a person and (1) at the same time is in another role with the same person, (2) at the same time is in a relationship with a person closely associated with or related to the person with whom the psychologist has the professional relationship, or

(3) promises to enter into another relationship in the future with the person or a person closely associated with or related to the person.

A psychologist refrains from entering into a multiple relationship if the multiple relationship could reasonably be expected to impair the psychologist's objectivity, competence, or effectiveness in performing his or her functions as a psychologist, or otherwise risks exploitation or harm to the person with whom the professional relationship exists.

Multiple relationships that would not reasonably be expected to cause impairment or risk exploitation or harm are not unethical.

(b) If a psychologist finds that, due to unforeseen factors, a potentially harmful multiple relationship has arisen, the psychologist takes reasonable steps to resolve it with due regard for the best interests of the affected person and maximal compliance with the Ethics Code.

(c) When psychologists are required by law, institutional policy, or extraordinary circumstances to serve in more than one role in judicial or administrative proceedings, at the outset they clarify role expectations and the extent of confidentiality and thereafter as changes occur. (See also Standards 3.04, Avoiding Harm, and 3.07, Third-Party Requests for Services.)

3.06 Conflict of Interest

Psychologists refrain from taking on a professional role when personal, scientific, professional, legal, financial, or other interests or relationships could reasonably be expected to (1) impair their objectivity, competence, or effectiveness in performing their functions as psychologists or (2) expose the person or organization with whom the professional relationship exists to harm or exploitation.

3.07 Third-Party Requests for Services

When psychologists agree to provide services to a person or entity at the request of a third party, psychologists attempt to clarify at the outset of the service the nature of the relationship with all individuals or organizations involved. This clarification includes the role of the psychologist (e.g., therapist, consultant, diagnostician, or expert witness), an identification of who is the client, the probable uses of the services provided or the information obtained, and the fact that there may be limits to confidentiality. (See also Standards 3.05, Multiple Relationships, and 4.02, Discussing the Limits of Confidentiality.)

3.08 Exploitative Relationships

Psychologists do not exploit persons over whom they have supervisory, evaluative, or other authority such as clients/patients, students, supervisees, research participants, and employees. (See also Standards 3.05, Multiple Relationships; 6.04, Fees and Financial Arrangements; 6.05, Barter with Clients/Patients; 7.07, Sexual Relationships with Students and Supervisees; 10.05, Sexual Intimacies with Current Therapy Clients/Patients; 10.06, Sexual Intimacies with Relatives or Significant Others of Current Therapy Clients/Patients; 10.07, Therapy with Former Sexual Partners; and 10.08, Sexual Intimacies with Former Therapy Clients/Patients.)

3.09 Cooperation With Other Professionals

When indicated and professionally appropriate, psychologists cooperate with other professionals in order to serve their clients/patients effectively and appropriately. (See also Standard 4.05, Disclosures.)

3.10 Informed Consent

(a) When psychologists conduct research or provide assessment, therapy, counseling, or consulting services in person or via electronic transmission or other forms of communication, they obtain the informed consent of the individual or individuals using language that is reasonably understandable to that person or persons except when conducting such activities without consent is mandated by law or governmental regulation or as otherwise provided in this Ethics Code. (See also Standards 8.02, Informed Consent to Research; 9.03, Informed Consent in Assessments; and 10.01, Informed Consent to Therapy.)

(b) For persons who are legally incapable of giving informed consent, psychologists nevertheless (1) provide an appropriate explanation, (2) seek the individual's assent, (3) consider such persons' preferences and best interests, and (4) obtain appropriate permission from a legally authorized person, if such substitute consent is permitted or required by law. When consent by a legally authorized person is not permitted or required by law, psychologists take reasonable steps to protect the individual's rights and welfare.

(c) When psychological services are court ordered or otherwise mandated, psychologists inform the individual of the nature of the anticipated services, including whether the services are court ordered or mandated and any limits of confidentiality, before proceeding.

(d) Psychologists appropriately document written or oral consent, permission, and assent. (See also Standards 8.02, Informed Consent to Research; 9.03, Informed Consent in Assessments; and 10.01, Informed Consent to Therapy.)

3.11 Psychological Services Delivered To or Through Organizations

(a) Psychologists delivering services to or through organizations provide information beforehand to clients and when appropriate those directly affected by the services about (1) the nature and objectives of the services, (2) the intended recipients, (3) which of the individuals are clients, (4) the relationship the psychologist will have with each person and the organization, (5) the probable uses of services provided and information obtained, (6) who will have access to the information, and (7) limits of confidentiality. As soon as feasible, they provide information about the results and conclusions of such services to appropriate persons.

(b) If psychologists will be precluded by law or by organizational roles from providing such information to particular individuals or groups, they so inform those individuals or groups at the outset of the service.

3.12 Interruption of Psychological Services

Unless otherwise covered by contract, psychologists make reasonable efforts to plan for facilitating services in the event that psychological services are interrupted by factors such as the psychologist's illness, death, unavailability, relocation, or retirement or by the client's/patient's relocation or financial limitations. (See also Standard 6.02c, Maintenance, Dissemination, and Disposal of Confidential Records of Professional and Scientific Work.)

Standard 4: Privacy and Confidentiality

4.01 Maintaining Confidentiality

Psychologists have a primary obligation and take reasonable precautions to protect confidential information obtained through or stored in any medium, recognizing that the extent and limits of confidentiality may be regulated by law or established by institutional rules or professional or scientific relationship. (See also Standard 2.05, Delegation of Work to Others.)

4.02 Discussing the Limits of Confidentiality

(a) Psychologists discuss with persons (including, to the extent feasible, persons who are legally incapable of giving informed consent and their legal representatives) and organizations with whom they establish a scientific or professional relationship (1) the relevant limits of confidentiality and (2) the foreseeable uses of the information generated through their psychological activities. (See also Standard 3.10, Informed Consent.)

(b) Unless it is not feasible or is contraindicated, the discussion of confidentiality occurs at the outset of the relationship and thereafter as new circumstances may warrant.

(c) Psychologists who offer services, products, or information via electronic transmission inform clients/patients of the risks to privacy and limits of confidentiality.

4.03 Recording

Before recording the voices or images of individuals to whom they provide services, psychologists obtain permission from all such persons or their legal representatives. (See also Standards 8.03, Informed Consent for Recording Voices and Images in Research; 8.05, Dispensing With Informed Consent for Research; and 8.07, Deception in Research.)

4.04 Minimizing Intrusions on Privacy

(a) Psychologists include in written and oral reports and consultations, only information germane to the purpose for which the communication is made.

(b) Psychologists discuss confidential information obtained in their work only for appropriate scientific or professional purposes and only with persons clearly concerned with such matters.

4.05 Disclosures

(a) Psychologists may disclose confidential information with the appropriate consent of the organizational client, the individual client/patient, or another legally authorized person on behalf of the client/patient unless prohibited by law.

(b) Psychologists disclose confidential information without the consent of the individual only as mandated by law, or where permitted by law for a valid purpose such as to (1) provide needed professional services; (2) obtain appropriate professional consultations; (3) protect the client/patient, psychologist, or others from harm; or (4) obtain payment for services from a client/patient, in which instance disclosure is limited to the minimum that is necessary to achieve the purpose. (See also Standard 6.04e, Fees and Financial Arrangements.)

4.06 Consultations

When consulting with colleagues, (1) psychologists do not disclose confidential information that reasonably could lead to the identification of a client/patient, research participant, or other person or organization with whom they have a confidential relationship unless they have obtained the prior consent of the person or organization or the disclosure cannot be avoided, and (2) they disclose information only to the extent necessary to achieve the purposes of the consultation. (See also Standard 4.01, Maintaining Confidentiality.)

4.07 Use of Confidential Information for Didactic or Other Purposes

Psychologists do not disclose in their writings, lectures, or other public media, confidential, personally identifiable information concerning their clients/patients, students, research participants, organizational clients, or other recipients of their services that they obtained during the course of their work, unless (1) they take reasonable steps to disguise the person or organization, (2) the person or organization has consented in writing, or (3) there is legal authorization for doing so.

Standard 5: Advertising and Other Public Statements

5.01 Avoidance of False or Deceptive Statements

(a) Public statements include but are not limited to paid or unpaid advertising, product endorsements, grant applications, licensing applications, other credentialing applications, brochures, printed matter, directory listings, personal resumes or curricula vitae, or comments for use in media such as print or electronic transmission, statements in legal proceedings, lectures and public oral presentations, and published materials. Psychologists do not knowingly make public statements that are false, deceptive, or fraudulent concerning their research, practice, or other work activities or those of persons or organizations with which they are affiliated.

(b) Psychologists do not make false, deceptive, or fraudulent statements concerning (1) their training, experience, or competence; (2) their academic degrees; (3) their credentials; (4) their institutional or association affiliations; (5) their services; (6) the scientific or clinical basis for, or results or degree of success of, their services; (7) their fees; or (8) their publications or research findings.

(c) Psychologists claim degrees as credentials for their health services only if those degrees (1) were earned from a regionally accredited educational institution or (2) were the basis for psychology licensure by the state in which they practice.

5.02 Statements by Others

(a) Psychologists who engage others to create or place public statements that promote their professional practice, products, or activities retain professional responsibility for such statements.

(b) Psychologists do not compensate employees of press, radio, television, or other communication media in return for publicity in a news item. (See also Standard 1.01, Misuse of Psychologists' Work.)

(c) A paid advertisement relating to psychologists' activities must be identified or clearly recognizable as such.

5.03 Descriptions of Workshops and Non-Degree-Granting Educational Programs

To the degree to which they exercise control, psychologists responsible for announcements, catalogs, brochures, or advertisements describing workshops, seminars, or other non-degree-granting educational programs ensure that they accurately describe the audience for which the program is intended, the educational objectives, the presenters, and the fees involved.

5.04 Media Presentations

When psychologists provide public advice or comment via print, Internet, or other electronic transmission, they take precautions to ensure that statements (1) are based on their professional knowledge, training, or experience in accord with appropriate psychological literature and practice; (2) are otherwise consistent with this Ethics Code; and (3) do not indicate that a professional relationship has been established with the recipient. (See also Standard 2.04, Bases for Scientific and Professional Judgments.)

5.05 Testimonials

Psychologists do not solicit testimonials from current therapy clients/patients or other persons who because of their particular circumstances are vulnerable to undue influence.

5.06 In-Person Solicitation

Psychologists do not engage, directly or through agents, in uninvited in-person solicitation of business from actual or potential therapy clients/patients or other persons who because of their particular circumstances are vulnerable to undue influence. However, this prohibition does not preclude (1) attempting to implement appropriate collateral contacts for the purpose of benefiting an already engaged therapy client/patient or (2) providing disaster or community outreach services.

Standard 6: Record Keeping and Fees

6.01 Documentation of Professional and Scientific Work and Maintenance of Records

Psychologists create, and, to the extent the records are under their control, maintain, disseminate, store, retain, and dispose of records and data relating to their professional and scientific work in order to (1) facilitate provision of services later by them or by other professionals, (2) allow for replication of research design and analyses, (3) meet institutional requirements, (4) ensure accuracy of billing and payments, and (5) ensure compliance with law. (See also Standard 4.01, Maintaining Confidentiality.)

6.02 Maintenance, Dissemination, and Disposal of Confidential Records of Professional and Scientific Work

(a) Psychologists maintain confidentiality in creating, storing, accessing, transferring, and disposing of records under their control, whether these are written, automated, or in any other medium. (See also Standards 4.01, Maintaining Confidentiality, and 6.01, Documentation of Professional and Scientific Work and Maintenance of Records.)

(b) If confidential information concerning recipients of psychological services is entered into databases or systems of records available to persons whose access has not been consented to by the recipient, psychologists use coding or other techniques to avoid the inclusion of personal identifiers.

(c) Psychologists make plans in advance to facilitate the appropriate transfer and to protect the confidentiality of records and data in the event of psychologists' withdrawal from positions or practice. (See also Standards 3.12, Interruption of Psychological Services, and 10.09, Interruption of Therapy.)

6.03 Withholding Records for Nonpayment

Psychologists may not withhold records under their control that are requested and needed for a client's/patient's emergency treatment solely because payment has not been received.

6.04 Fees and Financial Arrangements

(a) As early as is feasible in a professional or scientific relationship, psychologists and recipients of psychological services reach an agreement specifying compensation and billing arrangements.

(b) Psychologists' fee practices are consistent with law.

(c) Psychologists do not misrepresent their fees.

(d) If limitations to services can be anticipated because of limitations in financing, this is discussed with the recipient of services as early as is feasible. (See also Standards 10.09, Interruption of Services, and 10.10, Terminating Therapy.)

(e) If the recipient of services does not pay for services as agreed, and if psychologists intend to use collection agencies or legal measures to collect the fees, psychologists first inform the person that such measures will be taken and provide that person an opportunity to make prompt payment. (See also Standards 4.05, Disclosures; 6.03, Withholding Records for Nonpayment; and 10.01, Informed Consent to Therapy.)

6.05 Barter with Clients/Patients

Barter is the acceptance of goods, services, or other nonmonetary remuneration from clients/patients in return for psychological services. Psychologists may barter only if (1) it is not clinically contraindicated, and (2) the resulting arrangement is not exploitative. (See also Standards 3.05, Multiple Relationships, and 6.04, Fees and Financial Arrangements.)

6.06 Accuracy in Reports to Payors and Funding Sources

In their reports to payors for services or sources of research funding, psychologists take reasonable steps to ensure the accurate reporting of the nature of the service provided or research conducted, the fees, charges, or payments, and where applicable, the identity of the provider, the findings, and the diagnosis. (See also Standards 4.01, Maintaining Confidentiality; 4.04, Minimizing Intrusions on Privacy; and 4.05, Disclosures.)

6.07 Referrals and Fees

When psychologists pay, receive payment from, or divide fees with another professional, other than in an employer-employee relationship, the payment to each is based on the services provided (clinical, consultative, administrative, or other) and is not based on the referral itself. (See also Standard 3.09, Cooperation with Other Professionals.)

Standard 7: Education and Training

7.01 Design of Education and Training Programs

Psychologists responsible for education and training programs take reasonable steps to ensure that the programs are designed to provide the appropriate knowledge and proper experiences, and to meet the requirements for licensure, certification, or other goals for which claims are made by the program. (See also Standard 5.03, Descriptions of Workshops and Non-Degree-Granting Educational Programs.)

7.02 Descriptions of Education and Training Programs

Psychologists responsible for education and training programs take reasonable steps to ensure that there is a current and accurate description of the program content (including participation in required course- or program-related counseling, psychotherapy, experiential groups, consulting projects, or community service), training goals and objectives, stipends and benefits, and requirements that must be met for satisfactory completion of the program. This information must be made readily available to all interested parties.

7.03 Accuracy in Teaching

(a) Psychologists take reasonable steps to ensure that course syllabi are accurate regarding the subject matter to be covered, bases for evaluating progress, and the nature of course experiences. This standard does not preclude an instructor from modifying course content or requirements when the instructor considers it pedagogically necessary or desirable, so long as students are made aware of these modifications in a manner that enables them to fulfill course requirements. (See also Standard 5.01, Avoidance of False or Deceptive Statements.)

(b) When engaged in teaching or training, psychologists present psychological information accurately. (See also Standard 2.03, Maintaining Competence.)

7.04 Student Disclosure of Personal Information

Psychologists do not require students or supervisees to disclose personal information in course- or program-related activities, either orally or in writing, regarding sexual history, history of abuse and neglect, psychological treatment, and relationships with parents, peers, and spouses or significant others except if (1) the program or training facility has clearly identified this requirement in its admissions and program materials or (2) the information is necessary to evaluate or obtain assistance for students whose personal problems could reasonably be judged to be preventing them from performing their training- or professionally related activities in a competent manner or posing a threat to the students or others.

7.05 Mandatory Individual or Group Therapy

(a) When individual or group therapy is a program or course requirement, psychologists responsible for that program allow students in undergraduate and graduate programs the option of selecting such therapy from practitioners unaffiliated with the program. (See also Standard 7.02, Descriptions of Education and Training Programs.)

(b) Faculty who are or are likely to be responsible for evaluating students' academic performance do not themselves provide that therapy. (See also Standard 3.05, Multiple Relationships.)

7.06 Assessing Student and Supervisee Performance

(a) In academic and supervisory relationships, psychologists establish a timely and specific process for providing feedback to students and supervisees. Information regarding the process is provided to the student at the beginning of supervision.

(b) Psychologists evaluate students and supervisees on the basis of their actual performance on relevant and established program requirements.

7.07 Sexual Relationships With Students and Supervisees

Psychologists do not engage in sexual relationships with students or supervisees who are in their department, agency, or training center or over whom psychologists have or are likely to have evaluative authority. (See also Standard 3.05, Multiple Relationships.)

Standard 8: Research and Publication

8.01 Institutional Approval

When institutional approval is required, psychologists provide accurate information about their research proposals and obtain approval prior to conducting the research. They conduct the research in accordance with the approved research protocol.

8.02 Informed Consent to Research

(a) When obtaining informed consent as required in Standard 3.10, Informed Consent, psychologists inform participants about (1) the purpose of the research, expected duration, and procedures; (2) their right to decline to participate and to withdraw from the research once participation has begun; (3) the foreseeable consequences of declining or withdrawing; (4) reasonably foreseeable factors that may be expected to influence their willingness to participate such as potential risks, discomfort, or adverse effects; (5) any prospective research benefits; (6) limits of confidentiality; (7) incentives for participation; and (8) whom to contact for questions about the research and research participants' rights. They provide opportunity for the prospective participants to ask questions and receive answers. (See also Standards 8.03, Informed Consent for Recording Voices and Images in Research; 8.05, Dispensing with Informed Consent for Research; and 8.07, Deception in Research.)

(b) Psychologists conducting intervention research involving the use of experimental treatments clarify to participants at the outset of the research (1) the experimental nature of the treatment; (2) the services that will or will not be available to the control group(s) if appropriate; (3) the means by which assignment to treatment and control groups will be made; (4) available treatment alternatives if an individual does not wish to participate in the research or wishes to withdraw once a study has begun; and (5) compensation for or monetary costs of participating including, if appropriate, whether reimbursement from the participant or a third-party payor will be sought. (See also Standard 8.02a, Informed Consent to Research.)

8.03 Informed Consent for Recording Voices and Images in Research

Psychologists obtain informed consent from research participants prior to recording their voices or images for data collection unless (1) the research consists solely of naturalistic observations in public places, and it is not anticipated that the recording will be used in a manner that could cause personal identification or harm, or (2) the research design includes deception, and consent for the use of the recording is obtained during debriefing. (See also Standard 8.07, Deception in Research.)

8.04 Client/Patient, Student, and Subordinate Research Participants

(a) When psychologists conduct research with clients/patients, students, or subordinates as participants, psychologists take steps to protect the prospective participants from adverse consequences of declining or withdrawing from participation.

(b) When research participation is a course requirement or opportunity for extra credit, the prospective participant is given the choice of equitable alternative activities.

8.05 Dispensing with Informed Consent for Research

Psychologists may dispense with informed consent only (1) where research would not reasonably be assumed to create distress or harm and involves (a) the study of normal educational practices, curricula, or classroom management methods conducted in educational settings; (b) only anonymous questionnaires, naturalistic observations, or archival research for which disclosure of responses would not place participants at risk of criminal or civil liability or damage their financial standing, employability, or reputation, and confidentiality is protected; or (c) the study of factors related to job or organization effectiveness conducted in organizational settings for which there is no risk to participants' employability and confidentiality is protected or (2) where otherwise permitted by law or federal or institutional regulations.

8.06 Offering Inducements for Research Participation

(a) Psychologists make reasonable efforts to avoid offering excessive or inappropriate financial or other inducements for research participation when such inducements are likely to coerce participation.

(b) When offering professional services as an inducement for research participation, psychologists clarify the nature of the services, as well as the risks, obligations, and limitations. (See also Standard 6.05, Barter with Clients/Patients.)

8.07 Deception in Research

(a) Psychologists do not conduct a study involving deception unless they have determined that the use of deceptive techniques is justified by the study's significant prospective scientific, educational, or applied value and that effective nondeceptive alternative procedures are not feasible.

(b) Psychologists do not deceive prospective participants about research that is reasonably expected to cause physical pain or severe emotional distress.

(c) Psychologists explain any deception that is an integral feature of the design and conduct of an experiment to participants as early as is feasible, preferably at the conclusion of their participation, but no later than at the conclusion of the data collection, and permit participants to withdraw their data. (See also Standard 8.08, Debriefing.)

8.08 Debriefing

(a) Psychologists provide a prompt opportunity for participants to obtain appropriate information about the nature, results, and conclusions of the research, and they take reasonable steps to correct any misconceptions that participants may have of which the psychologists are aware.

(b) If scientific or humane values justify delaying or withholding this information, psychologists take reasonable measures to reduce the risk of harm.

(c) When psychologists become aware that research procedures have harmed a participant, they take reasonable steps to minimize the harm.

8.09 Humane Care and Use of Animals in Research

(a) Psychologists acquire, care for, use, and dispose of animals in compliance with current federal, state, and local laws and regulations, and with professional standards.

(b) Psychologists trained in research methods and experienced in the care of laboratory animals supervise all procedures involving animals and are responsible for ensuring appropriate consideration of their comfort, health, and humane treatment.

(c) Psychologists ensure that all individuals under their supervision who are using animals have received instruction in research methods and in the care, maintenance, and handling of the species being used, to the extent appropriate to their role. (See also Standard 2.05, Delegation of Work to Others.)

(d) Psychologists make reasonable efforts to minimize the discomfort, infection, illness, and pain of animal subjects.

(e) Psychologists use a procedure subjecting animals to pain, stress, or privation only when an alternative procedure is unavailable and the goal is justified by its prospective scientific, educational, or applied value.

(f) Psychologists perform surgical procedures under appropriate anesthesia and follow techniques to avoid infection and minimize pain during and after surgery.

(g) When it is appropriate that an animal's life be terminated, psychologists proceed rapidly, with an effort to minimize pain and in accordance with accepted procedures.

8.10 Reporting Research Results

(a) Psychologists do not fabricate data. (See also Standard 5.01a, Avoidance of False or Deceptive Statements.)

(b) If psychologists discover significant errors in their published data, they take reasonable steps to correct such errors in a correction, retraction, erratum, or other appropriate publication means.

8.11 Plagiarism

Psychologists do not present portions of another's work or data as their own, even if the other work or data source is cited occasionally.

8.12 Publication Credit

(a) Psychologists take responsibility and credit, including authorship credit, only for work they have actually performed or to which they have substantially contributed. (See also Standard 8.12b, Publication Credit.)

(b) Principal authorship and other publication credits accurately reflect the relative scientific or professional contributions of the individuals involved, regardless of their relative status. Mere possession of an institutional position, such as department chair, does not justify authorship credit. Minor contributions to the research or to the writing for publications are acknowledged appropriately, such as in footnotes or in an introductory statement.

(c) Except under exceptional circumstances, a student is listed as principal author on any multiple-authored article that is substantially based on the student's doctoral dissertation. Faculty advisors discuss publication credit with students as early as feasible and throughout the research and publication process as appropriate. (See also Standard 8.12b, Publication Credit.)

8.13 Duplicate Publication of Data

Psychologists do not publish, as original data, data that have been previously published. This does not preclude republishing data when they are accompanied by proper acknowledgment.

8.14 Sharing Research Data for Verification

(a) After research results are published, psychologists do not withhold the data on which their conclusions are based from other competent professionals who seek to verify the substantive claims through reanalysis and who intend to use such data only for that purpose, provided that the confidentiality of the participants can be protected and unless legal rights concerning proprietary data preclude their release. This does not preclude psychologists from requiring that such individuals or groups be responsible for costs associated with the provision of such information.

(b) Psychologists who request data from other psychologists to verify the substantive claims through reanalysis may use shared data only for the declared purpose. Requesting psychologists obtain prior written agreement for all other uses of the data.

8.15 Reviewers

Psychologists who review material submitted for presentation, publication, grant, or research proposal review respect the confidentiality of and the proprietary rights in such information of those who submitted it.

Standard 9: Assessment

9.01 Bases for Assessments

(a) Psychologists base the opinions contained in their recommendations, reports, and diagnostic or evaluative statements, including forensic testimony, on information and techniques sufficient to substantiate their findings. (See also Standard 2.04, Bases for Scientific and Professional Judgments.)

(b) Except as noted in 9.01c, psychologists provide opinions of the psychological characteristics of individuals only after they have conducted an examination of the individuals adequate to support their statements or conclusions. When, despite reasonable efforts, such an examination is not practical, psychologists document the efforts they made and the result of those efforts, clarify the probable impact of their limited information on the reliability and validity of their opinions, and appropriately limit the nature and extent of their conclusions or recommendations. (See also Standards 2.01, Boundaries of Competence, and 9.06, Interpreting Assessment Results.)

(c) When psychologists conduct a record review or provide consultation or supervision and an individual examination is not warranted or necessary for the opinion, psychologists explain this and the sources of information on which they based their conclusions and recommendations.

9.02 Use of Assessments

(a) Psychologists administer, adapt, score, interpret, or use assessment techniques, interviews, tests, or instruments in a manner and for purposes that are appropriate in light of the research on or evidence of the usefulness and proper application of the techniques.

(b) Psychologists use assessment instruments whose validity and reliability have been established for use with members of the population tested. When such validity or reliability has not been established, psychologists describe the strengths and limitations of test results and interpretation.

(c) Psychologists use assessment methods that are appropriate to an individual's language preference and competence, unless the use of an alternative language is relevant to the assessment issues.

9.03 Informed Consent in Assessments

(a) Psychologists obtain informed consent for assessments, evaluations, or diagnostic services, as described in Standard 3.10, Informed Consent, except when (1) testing is mandated by law or governmental regulations; (2) informed consent is implied because testing is conducted as a routine educational, institutional, or organizational activity (e.g., when participants voluntarily agree to assessment when applying for a job); or (3) one purpose of the testing is to evaluate decisional capacity. Informed consent includes an explanation of the nature and purpose of the assessment, fees, involvement of third parties, and limits of confidentiality and sufficient opportunity for the client/patient to ask questions and receive answers.

(b) Psychologists inform persons with questionable capacity to consent or for whom testing is mandated by law or governmental regulations about the nature and purpose of the proposed assessment services, using language that is reasonably understandable to the person being assessed.

(c) Psychologists using the services of an interpreter obtain informed consent from the client/patient to use that interpreter, ensure that confidentiality of test results and test security are maintained, and include in their recommendations, reports, and diagnostic or evaluative statements, including forensic testimony, discussion of any limitations on the data obtained. (See also Standards 2.05, Delegation of Work to Others; 4.01, Maintaining Confidentiality; 9.01, Bases for Assessments; 9.06, Interpreting Assessment Results; and 9.07, Assessment by Unqualified Persons.)

9.04 Release of Test Data

(a) The term test data refers to raw and scaled scores, client/patient responses to test questions or stimuli, and psychologists' notes and recordings concerning client/patient statements and behavior during an examination. Those portions of test materials that include client/patient responses are included in the definition of test data. Pursuant to a client/patient release, psychologists provide test data to the client/patient or other persons identified in the release. Psychologists may refrain from releasing test data to protect a client/patient or others from substantial harm or misuse or misrepresentation of the data or the test, recognizing that in many instances release of confidential information under these circumstances is regulated by law. (See also Standard 9.11, Maintaining Test Security.)

(b) In the absence of a client/patient release, psychologists provide test data only as required by law or court order.

9.05 Test Construction

Psychologists who develop tests and other assessment techniques use appropriate psychometric procedures and current scientific or professional knowledge for test design, standardization, validation, reduction or elimination of bias, and recommendations for use.

9.06 Interpreting Assessment Results

When interpreting assessment results, including automated interpretations, psychologists take into account the purpose of the assessment as well as the various test factors, test-taking abilities, and other characteristics of the person being assessed, such as situational, personal, linguistic, and cultural differences, that might affect psychologists' judgments or reduce the accuracy of their interpretations. They indicate any significant limitations of their interpretations. (See also Standards 2.01b and c, Boundaries of Competence, and 3.01, Unfair Discrimination.)

9.07 Assessment by Unqualified Persons

Psychologists do not promote the use of psychological assessment techniques by unqualified persons, except when such use is conducted for training purposes with appropriate supervision. (See also Standard 2.05, Delegation of Work to Others.)

9.08 Obsolete Tests and Outdated Test Results

(a) Psychologists do not base their assessment or intervention decisions or recommendations on data or test results that are outdated for the current purpose.

(b) Psychologists do not base such decisions or recommendations on tests and measures that are obsolete and not useful for the current purpose.

9.09 Test Scoring and Interpretation Services

(a) Psychologists who offer assessment or scoring services to other professionals accurately describe the purpose, norms, validity, reliability, and applications of the procedures and any special qualifications applicable to their use.

(b) Psychologists select scoring and interpretation services (including automated services) on the basis of evidence of the validity of the program and procedures as well as on other appropriate considerations. (See also Standard 2.01b and c, Boundaries of Competence.)

(c) Psychologists retain responsibility for the appropriate application, interpretation, and use of assessment instruments, whether they score and interpret such tests themselves or use automated or other services.

9.10 Explaining Assessment Results

Regardless of whether the scoring and interpretation are done by psychologists, by employees or assistants, or by automated or other outside services, psychologists take reasonable steps to ensure that explanations of results are given to the individual or designated representative unless the nature of the relationship precludes provision of an explanation of results (such as in some organizational consulting, preemployment or security screenings, and forensic evaluations), and this fact has been clearly explained to the person being assessed in advance.

9.11 Maintaining Test Security

The term test materials refers to manuals, instruments, protocols, and test questions or stimuli and does not include test data as defined in Standard 9.04, Release of Test Data. Psychologists make reasonable efforts to maintain the integrity and security of test materials and other assessment techniques consistent with law and contractual obligations, and in a manner that permits adherence to this Ethics Code.

Standard 10: Therapy

10.01 Informed Consent to Therapy

(a) When obtaining informed consent to therapy as required in Standard 3.10, Informed Consent, psychologists inform clients/patients as early as is feasible in the therapeutic relationship about the nature and anticipated course of therapy, fees, involvement of third parties, and limits of confidentiality and provide sufficient opportunity for the client/patient to ask questions and receive answers. (See also Standards 4.02, Discussing the Limits of Confidentiality, and 6.04, Fees and Financial Arrangements.)

(b) When obtaining informed consent for treatment for which generally recognized techniques and procedures have not been established, psychologists inform their clients/patients of the developing nature of the treatment, the potential risks involved, alternative treatments that may be available, and the voluntary nature of their participation. (See also Standards 2.01e, Boundaries of Competence, and 3.10, Informed Consent.)

(c) When the therapist is a trainee and the legal responsibility for the treatment provided resides with the supervisor, the client/patient, as part of the informed consent procedure, is informed that the therapist is in training and is being supervised and is given the name of the supervisor.

10.02 Therapy Involving Couples or Families

(a) When psychologists agree to provide services to several persons who have a relationship (such as spouses, significant others, or parents and children), they take reasonable steps to clarify at the outset (1) which of the individuals are clients/patients and (2) the relationship the psychologist will have with each person. This clarification includes the psychologist's role and the probable uses of the services provided or the information obtained. (See also Standard 4.02, Discussing the Limits of Confidentiality.)

(b) If it becomes apparent that psychologists may be called on to perform potentially conflicting roles (such as family therapist and then witness for one party in divorce proceedings), psychologists take reasonable steps to clarify and modify, or withdraw from, roles appropriately. (See also Standard 3.05c, Multiple Relationships.)

10.03 Group Therapy

When psychologists provide services to several persons in a group setting, they describe at the outset the roles and responsibilities of all parties and the limits of confidentiality.

10.04 Providing Therapy to Those Served by Others

In deciding whether to offer or provide services to those already receiving mental health services elsewhere, psychologists carefully consider the treatment issues and the potential client's/patient's welfare. Psychologists discuss these issues with the client/patient or another legally authorized person on behalf of the client/patient in order to minimize the risk of confusion and conflict, consult with the other service providers when appropriate, and proceed with caution and sensitivity to the therapeutic issues.

10.05 Sexual Intimacies With Current Therapy Clients/Patients

Psychologists do not engage in sexual intimacies with current therapy clients/patients.

10.06 Sexual Intimacies With Relatives or Significant Others of Current Therapy Clients/Patients

Psychologists do not engage in sexual intimacies with individuals they know to be close relatives, guardians, or significant others of current clients/patients. Psychologists do not terminate therapy to circumvent this standard.

10.07 Therapy With Former Sexual Partners

Psychologists do not accept as therapy clients/patients persons with whom they have engaged in sexual intimacies.

10.08 Sexual Intimacies With Former Therapy Clients/Patients

(a) Psychologists do not engage in sexual intimacies with former clients/patients for at least two years after cessation or termination of therapy.

(b) Psychologists do not engage in sexual intimacies with former clients/patients even after a two-year interval except in the most unusual circumstances. Psychologists who engage in such activity after the two years following cessation or termination of therapy and of having no sexual contact with the former client/patient bear the burden of demonstrating that there has been no exploitation, in light of all relevant factors, including (1) the amount of time that has passed since therapy terminated; (2) the nature, duration, and intensity of the therapy; (3) the circumstances of termination; (4) the client's/patient's personal history; (5) the client's/patient's current mental status; (6) the likelihood of adverse impact on the client/patient; and (7) any statements or actions made by the therapist during the course of therapy suggesting or inviting the possibility of a post-termination sexual or romantic relationship with the client/patient. (See also Standard 3.05, Multiple Relationships.)

10.09 Interruption of Therapy

When entering into employment or contractual relationships, psychologists make reasonable efforts to provide for orderly and appropriate resolution of responsibility for client/patient care in the event that the employment or contractual relationship ends, with paramount consideration given to the welfare of the client/patient. (See also Standard 3.12, Interruption of Psychological Services.)

10.10 Terminating Therapy

(a) Psychologists terminate therapy when it becomes reasonably clear that the client/patient no longer needs the service, is not likely to benefit, or is being harmed by continued service.

(b) Psychologists may terminate therapy when threatened or otherwise endangered by the client/patient or another person with whom the client/patient has a relationship.

(c) Except where precluded by the actions of clients/patients or third-party payors, prior to termination psychologists provide pretermination counseling and suggest alternative service providers as appropriate.

HISTORY AND EFFECTIVE DATE

The American Psychological Association's Council of Representatives adopted this version of the APA Ethics Code during its meeting on August 21, 2002. The Code became effective on June 1, 2003. The Council of Representatives amended this version of the Ethics Code on February 20, 2010. The amendments became effective on June 1, 2010. Inquiries concerning the substance or interpretation of the APA Ethics Code should be addressed to the Director, Office of Ethics, American Psychological Association, 750 First Street, NE, Washington, DC 20002-4242. The standards in this Ethics Code will be used to adjudicate complaints brought concerning alleged conduct occurring on or after the effective date. Complaints will be adjudicated on the basis of the version of the Ethics Code that was in effect at the time the conduct occurred.

The APA has previously published its Ethics Code as follows:

American Psychological Association. (1953). Ethical standards of psychologists. Washington, DC: Author.

American Psychological Association. (1959). Ethical standards of psychologists. *American Psychologist, 14*, 279–282.

American Psychological Association. (1963). Ethical standards of psychologists. *American Psychologist, 18*, 56–60.

American Psychological Association. (1968). Ethical standards of psychologists. *American Psychologist, 23*, 357–361.

American Psychological Association. (1977, March). Ethical standards of psychologists. *APA Monitor*, 22–23.

American Psychological Association. (1979). Ethical standards of psychologists. Washington, DC: Author.

American Psychological Association. (1981). Ethical principles of psychologists. *American Psychologist, 36*, 633–638.

American Psychological Association. (1990). Ethical principles of psychologists (Amended June 2, 1989). *American Psychologist, 45*, 390–395.

American Psychological Association. (1992). Ethical principles of psychologists and code of conduct. *American Psychologist, 47*, 1597–1611.

Request copies of the APA's Ethical Principles of Psychologists and Code of Conduct from the APA Order Department, 750 First Street, NE, Washington, DC 20002-4242, or phone (202) 336-5510.

Appendix C

TABLE OF CASES

Agostini v. Felton, 522 U.S. 803, 118 S. Ct. 40, 139 L. Ed. 2d 8, 1997 U.S. LEXIS 4544, 66 U.S.L.W. 3253 (1997).

Alamo Heights Independent School District v. State Board of Education, 790 F.2d 1153 (5th Cir. 1986).

Altman v. Bedford Central School District, 45 F. Supp. 2d 368, 1999 U.S. Dist. LEXIS 7811 (S.D.N.Y. 1999).

A.P. v. Woodstock Board of Education, 572 F. Supp. 2d 221, 2008 U.S. Dist. LEXIS 63549 (D. Conn. 2008).

Armijo v. Wagon Mound Public Schools, 159 F.3d 1253 (10th Cir. 1998).

Arnold v. Board of Education of Escambia, 754 F. Supp. 853, U.S. Dist. LEXIS 14593 (S.D. Ala. 1990).

A.W. v. Northwest R-1 School District, 813 F.2d 158 (8th Cir. 1987), *cert. den.*, 108 S. Ct. 144 (1987).

Baird v. Rose, 192 F.3d 462, 1999 U.S. App. LEXIS 23001, 9 Am. Disabilities Cas. (BNA) 13322 (4th Cir. 1999).

Baker v. Owen, 395 F. Supp. 294 (M.D. N.C., 1975), *aff'd*, 423 U.S. 908 (1975).

Bellotti v. Baird, 443 U.S. 662 (1979).

Benskin v. Taft City School District, 14 Clearinghouse Review 529 (1980).

Bethel School Dis. No. 403 v. Fraser, 478 U.S. 675, 106 S. Ct. 3159, 92 L. Ed. 2d 549 (1986).

Biggs v. Board of Education of Cecil County, 229 F. Supp. 2d 437; 2002 U.S. Dist. LEXIS 3799 (D. Md. 2002).

Board of Education of the Hendrick Hudson Central School District v. Rowley, 458 U.S. 176, 102 S. Ct. 3034 (1982).

Brillon v. Klein Independent School District, 100 Fed. Appx. 309, 2004 U.S. App. LEXIS 11235 (5th Cir. 2004).

Brown v. Board of Education, 347 U.S. 483 (1954).

Burnside v. Byars, 363 F.2d 744 (5th Cir. 1966).

California Association of School Psychologists v. Superintendent of Public Instruction, 21 IDELR 130 (N.D. Cal. 1994).

Cedar Rapids Community School District v. Garret F. by Charlene F., 526 U.S. 66; 119 S. Ct. 992, 143 L. Ed. 2d 154, 1999 U.S. LEXIS 1709, 67 U.S.L.W. 4165, 161 A.L.R. Fed. 683, 99 Cal. Daily Op. Service 1582, 99 Daily Journal DAR 2029, 1999 Colo. J. C.A.R. 1126, 12 Fla. L. Weekly Fed. S 129 (1999).

Clevenger v. Oak Ridge School Board, 774 F.2d 514 (6th Cir. 1984).

Cordrey v. Euckert, 917 F.2d 1460 (6th Cir. 1990).

Crawford v. Honig, 37 F.3d 485 (9th Cir. 1994).

Daniel R.R. v. Texas Board of Education, El Paso Independent School District, 874 F.2d 1036 (5th Cir. 1989).

Darlene L. v. Illinois State Board of Education, 563 F. Supp. 1340 (N.D. Ill. 1983).

Davis v. Monroe County Board of Education, 526 U.S. 629, 119 S. Ct. 1661, 1999 U.S. LEXIS 3452, 143 L. Ed. 2d 839, 67 U.S.L.W. 4329, 99 Cal. Daily Op. Service 3861, 99 Daily Journal DAR 4931, 12 Fla. Law W. Fed. S 280, 1999 Colo. J. C.A.R. 2948 (1999).

Davison v. Santa Barbara High School, 48 F. Supp. 2d 1225, 1998 U.S. Dist. LEXIS 22407 (C.D. Cal. 1998).

Debra P. v. Turlington, 730 F.2d 1405 (11th Cir. 1984).

Denita Harris v. District of Columbia, 561 F. Supp. 2d 63, 2008 U.S. Dist. LEXIS 48022 (D.D.C. 2008).

Detsel v. Board of Education of the Auburn Enlarged City School District, 637 F. Supp. 1022 (N.D.N.Y. 1986), *aff'd*, 820 F.2d 587 (2nd Cir. 1987), *cert. den.*, 108 S. Ct. 495 (1987).

Devries v. Fairfax County School Board, 882 F.2d 876 (4th Cir. 1989).

Diana v. State Board of Education, Civ. Act. No. C-70-37 (N.D. Cal., 1970, *further order*, 1973).

Dickens by Dickens v. Johnson County Board of Education, 661 F. Supp. 155 (E.D. Tenn. 1987).

District 27 Community School Board v. Board of Education of the City of New York, 502 N.Y.S.2d 325 (N.Y. 1986).

Doe v. Belleville Public School District No. 118, 672 F. Supp. 342 (S.D. Ill. 1987).

Donohue v. Copiague Union Free School District, 391 N.E.2d 1352 (N.Y. 1979).

Eisel v. Board of Education of Montgomery County, 597 A.2d 447 (Md. 1991).

Elizabeth S. v. Thomas K. Gilhool, 558 Educ. of the Handicapped L. Rep. 461 (M.D. Pa. 1987).

Epperson v. State of Arkansas, 393 U.S. 97, 89 S. Ct. 266 (1968).

Fay v. South Colonie Central School District, 802 F.2d 21 (2nd Cir. 1986).

Flour Bluff Independent School District v. Katherine M., 24 IDELR 673 (5th Cir. 1996).

Forest Grove School District v. T.A., 129 S. Ct. 2484, 174 L. Ed. 2d 168, 2009 U.S. LEXIS 4645, 21 Fla. L. Weekly Fed. S 983, 13 Accom. Disabilities Dec. (CCH) P13-253 (2009).

Garcetti v. Ceballos, 126 S. Ct. 1951, 2006 U.S. LEXIS 4341 (2006).

Garcia by Garcia v. Miera, 817 F.2d 650 (10th Cir. 1987).

Georgia State Conference of Branches of NAACP v. State of Georgia, 775 F.2d 1403 (11th Cir. 1985).

Gonzaga University v. John Doe, 122 S. Ct. 2268, 2002 U.S. LEXIS 4649, 70 U.S.L.W. 4577 (2002).

Goss v. Lopez, 419 U.S. 565, 95 S. Ct. 729 (1975).

Greer v. Rome City School District, 950 F.2d 688 (11th Cir. 1991).

Guadalupe Organization, Inc. v. Tempe Elementary School District No. 3, Civ. No. 71-435 (D. Ariz. 1972).

Hall v. Tawney, 621 F.2d 607 (4th Cir. 1980).

Harlow v. Fitzgerald, 457 U.S. 800, 102 S. Ct. 2727 (1982).

Hayes v. Unified School District No. 377, 669 F. Supp. 1519 (D. Kan. 1987).

Hensley v. Eckerhart, 461 U.S. 424, 103 S. Ct. 1933, 76 L. Ed. 2d 40, 1983 U.S. LEXIS 160 (1983).

Hobson v. Hansen, 269 F. Supp. 401, 514 (D.D.C. 1967), *aff'd sub nom Smuck v. Hobson*, 408 F.2d 175 (D.C. Cir. 1969).

Honig v. Doe, 108 S. Ct. 592 (1988).

In re the "A" Family, 602 P.2d 157 (Mont. 1979).

Ingraham v. Wright, 430 U.S. 651, 97 S. Ct. 1404 (1977).

Irving Independent School District v. Tatro, 468 U.S. 883, 104 S. Ct. 3371 (1984).

Jaffee v. Redmond, 51 F.3d 1346, 1358, 116 S. Ct. 334 (1996).

J.N. v. Bellingham School District No. 501, 74 Wn. App. 49, 871 P.2d 1106, 1994 Wash. App. LEXIS 197 (Wash. App. 1994).

John K. and Mary K. v. Board of Education for School District #65, Cook County, 504 N.E.2d 797 (Ill. App. 1987).

Johnson v. Independent School District No. 4 of Bixby, Tulsa County, Oklahoma, 921 F.2d 1022 (10th Cir. 1990).

Johnson v. Upland, 26 Fed. Appx. 689, 2002 U.S. App. LEXIS 515 *(9th Cir. 2002).*

Kelson v. The City of Springfield, 767 F.2d 651 (9th Cir. 1985).

K.M. ex rel. D.G. v. Hyde Park Central School District, 381 F. Supp. 2d 343 (S.D.N.Y. 2005).

Landstrom v. Illinois Department of Children and Family Services, 892 F.2d 670 (7th Cir. 1990).

Larry P. v. Riles, 343 F. Supp. 1306 (D.C. N.D. Cal., 1972), *aff'd*, 502 F.2d 963 (9th Cir. 1974), *further proceedings*, 495 F. Supp. 926 (D.C. N.D. Cal., 1979), *aff'd*, 502 F.2d 693 (9th Cir. 1984).

Lau v. Nichols, 414 U.S. 563 (1974).

Lee v. Lee County Bd. of Education, 476 F. Supp. 2d 1356, 2007 U.S. Dist. LEXIS 16859 (M.D. Ala. 2007).

Lyons by Alexander v. Smith, 829 F. Supp. 414 (D.D.C. 1993).

Marshall v. American Psychological Association, No. 87-1316 (D.D.C. 1987).

Martinez v. The School Board of Hillsborough County, Florida, 675 F. Supp. 1574 (M.D. Fla. 1987).

Max M. v. Thompson, 566 F. Supp. 1330, 1388 (N.D. Ill. 1983) (Max I), 592 F. Supp. 1437, 1450 (N.D. Ill. 1984) (Max II).

McDuff v. Tamborlane, 1999 Conn. Super. LEXIS 1771 (Conn. Super. 1999).

McKenzie v. Jefferson, 566 F. Supp. 404 (D.D.C. 1983).

Merriken v. Cressman, 364 F. Supp. 913 (E.D. Pa. 1973).

Milligan et al. v. City of Slidell, No. 98-31335, 2000 WL 1285260 (5th Cir. 2000).

Mills v. Board of Education of District of Columbia, 348 F. Supp. 866 (1972); *contempt proceedings*, 551 Educ. of the Handicapped L. Rep. 643 (D.D.C. 1980).

Mirand v. Board of Education of the City of New York, 84 N.Y.2d 44, 637 N.E.2d 263, 1994 N.Y. LEXIS 1345, 614 N.Y.S.2d 372 (N.Y. 1994).

Morales v. Turman, 383 F. Supp. 53 (E.D. Tex. 1974).

Nabozny v. Podlesny, 92 F.3d 446, 1996 U.S. App. LEXIS 18866 (7th Cir. 1996).

New Jersey v. T.L.O., 469 U.S. 325 (1985).

Newport-Mesa Unified School District v. State of California Department of Education, 371 F. Supp. 2d 1170, 2005 U.S. Dist. LEXIS 10290 (C.D. Cal. 2005).

New York State Association for Retarded Children v. Carey, 393 F. Supp. 715 (E.D.N.Y. 1975).

Parents Against Abuse in Schools v. Williamsport Area School District, 594 A.2d 796 (Pa. Commw. 1991).

Parents in Action in Special Education (P.A.S.E.) v. Hannon, 506 F. Supp. 831 (N.D. Ill. 1980).

Parham v. J.R., 422 U.S. 584 (1979).

Pena v. New York State Division for Youth, 419 F. Supp. 203 (S.D.N.Y. 1976).

Pennsylvania Association for Retarded Children (P.A.R.C.) v. Commonwealth of Pennsylvania, 334 F. Supp. 1257 (D.C. E.D. Pa. 1971), 343 F. Supp. 279 (E.D. Pa. 1972).

People v. Vincent Moreno, 2005 N.Y. App. Div. LEXIS 2363 (N.Y. 2005).

Pesce v. J. Sterling Morton High School, 830 F.2d 789 (7th Cir. 1987).

Peter W. v. San Francisco Unified School District, 60 Cal. App. 3d 814 (1976).

Phillis P. v. Claremont Unified School District, 183 Cal. App. 3d 1193 (Cal. App. 1986).

Pickering v. Board of Education of Township High School District 205, Will County, 391 U.S. 563, 88 S. Ct. 1731, 20 L. Ed. 2d 811, 1968 U.S. LEXIS 1471, 1 I.E.R. Cas. (BNA) 8 (1968).

Planned Parenthood of Central Missouri v. Danforth, 428 U.S. 52 (1976).

Rettig v. Kent City School District, 788 F.2d 328 (6th Cir. 1986).

Reusch v. Fountain, 872 F. Supp. 1421 (D. Md. 1994).

Sacramento City Unified School District, Board of Education v. Holland, 786 F. Supp. 874 (E.D. Cal. 1992), *aff'd sub nom. Sacramento City Unified School District, Board of Education v.*

Rachel H., 14 F.3d 1398 (9th Cir. 1994), *cert. denied sub nom. Sacramento City Unified School District, Board of Education v. Holland*, 114 S. Ct. 2697 (1994).

Safford Unified School District No. 1 v. Redding, 129 S. Ct. 2633, 174 L. Ed. 2d 354, 2009 U.S. LEXIS 4735, 21 Fla. L. Weekly Fed. S 1011 (2009).

San Antonio Independent School District v. Rodriguez, 411 U.S. 1, 93 S. Ct. 1278 (1973).

Sandlin v. Johnson, 643 F.2d 1027 (4th Cir. 1981).

Schaffer v. Weast, 2005 U.S. LEXIS 8554; 74 U.S.L.W. 4009 (2005).

School Board of Nassau County, Florida v. Arline, 107 S. Ct. 1123 (1987).

Settlegoode v. Portland Public Schools, 371 F.3d 503, 2004 U.S. App. LEXIS 11329 (9th Cir. 2004).

Shore Regional High School v. P.S., 381 F.3d 194, 2004 U.S. App. LEXIS 17740, 1 Accom. Disabilities Dec. (CCH) 11-145 (3rd Cir. 2004).

Simmons v. Hooks, 843 F. Supp. 1296 (E.D. Ark. 1994).

State v. Grover, 437 N.W.2d 60 (Minn. 1989).

Sterling v. Borough of Minersville, 232 F.3d 190, 2000 U.S. App. LEXIS 27855 (3rd Cir. 2000).

Sutton v. United Air Lines, Inc., 527 U.S. 471 (1999).

Tarasoff v. Regents of California, 118 Cal. Rptr. 129, 529 P.2d 553 (Cal. 1974). (Tarasoff I). *Tarasoff v. Regents of California*, 131 Cal. Rptr. 14, 551 P.2d 334 (Cal. 1976). (Tarasoff II).

Thomas v. Atascadero Unified School District, 662 F. Supp. 376 (C.D. Cal. 1987).

Timothy W. v. Rochester, New Hampshire School District, 875 F.2d 954 (1st Cir. 1989).

Tinker v. Des Moines Independent Community School District, 393 U.S. 503, 89 S. Ct. 733 (1969).

Toyota Motor Manufacturing, Kentucky, Inc. v. Williams, 534 U.S. 181 (2002).

U.S. v. Farrar, 38 F.2d 515 (D. Mass. 1930).

Valerie J. v. Derry Coop. School District, 771 F. Supp. 492 (D.N.H. 1991).

Werth v. Board of Directors of the Public Schools of the City of Milwaukee, 472 F. Supp. 2d 113, 2007 U.S. Dist. LEXIS 4535 (E.D. Wis. 2007).

Winkelman v. Parma City School District, 550 U.S. 516, 127 S. Ct. 1994, 167 L. Ed. 2d 904, 2007 U.S. LEXIS 5902, 75 U.S.L.W. 4329, 20 Fla. L. Weekly Fed. S 287 (2007).

Wisconsin v. Constantineau, 400 U.S. 433 (1971).

Wolman v. Walter, 433 U.S. 229, 97 S. Ct. 2593 (1977).

Wyatt v. Stickney, 325 F. Supp. 781 (M.D. Ala. N.D. 1971), 334 F. Supp. 1341 (1971), 344 F. Supp. 373, 387 (M.D. Ala. N.D. 1972).

Wyke v. Polk County School Board, 129 F.3d 560, 1997 U.S. App. LEXIS 32945, 11 Fla. L. Weekly Fed. C 790 (11th Cir. 1997).

Zelman v. Simmons-Harris, 122 S. Ct. 2460, 153 L. Ed. 2d 604, 2002 U.S. LEXIS 4885, 70 U.S.L.W. 4683, 2002 Daily Journal DAR 7295, 15 Fla. L. Weekly Fed. S 490 (2002).

Appendix D

TABLE OF FEDERAL LEGISLATION [1]

Americans with Disabilities Act of 1990 or ADA (Pub. L. No. 101-336) is codified at 42 U.S.C. §§ 12101 *et seq*. Americans with Disabilities Amendments Act of 2008 (ADAA) language quoted in this book is based on the text of United State Code (Title 42, Chapter 126) as amended by ADAA and was retrieved from http://www.ada.gov/pubs/adastatute08mark.htm on April 17, 2009.

Bilingual Education Act of 1968 was added as an amendment to the Elementary and Secondary Education Act of 1965. The No Child Left Behind Act of 2001 (Pub. L. No. 107-110) continued funding for the education of children with limited English proficiency.

Child Abuse Prevention, Adoption, and Family Services Act of 1988 (Pub. L. No. 100-294), 42 U.S.C. § 1501.

Civil Rights Act of 1871 or "Section 1983," 42 U.S.C. § 1983.

Civil Rights Act of 1964 (Pub. L. No. 88-352), 42 U.S.C. § 2000d.

Education Amendments of 1972 (Pub. L. No. 92-318), 20 U.S.C. § 1681.

Education for All Handicapped Children Act of 1975 (Pub. L. No. 94-142), renamed the Individuals with Disabilities Education Act in 1990, 20 U.S.C. Chapter 33.

Education for the Handicapped Act Amendments of 1986 (Pub. L. No. 99-457); now Part C of the Individuals with Disabilities Education Act.

Elementary and Secondary Education Act of 1965 or ESEA (Pub. L. No. 89-750). The No Child Left Behind Act of 2001 (Pub. L. No. 107-110) includes the most recent amendments to ESEA. Available at http://www.ed.gov.

Family Educational Rights and Privacy Act of 1974 (a part of Pub. L. No. 93-380) is commonly called FERPA, 20 U.S.C. § 1232g. Regulations implementing FERPA appear at 34 C.F.R. § Part 99.

Handicapped Children's Protection Act of 1986 (Pub. L. No. 99-372), now part of the Individuals with Disabilities Education Act.

Health Insurance Portability and Accountability Act of 1996 (Pub. L. No. 104-191), 26 U.S.C. § 294, 42 U.S.C. §§ 201, 1395b-5. Regulations implementing the "Privacy Rule" can be found at 45 C.F.R. Part 160 and Part 164.

Individuals with Disabilities Education Act of 1990 (Pub. L. No. 101-476), 20 U.S.C. Chapter 33. Amended by Pub. L. No. 105-117 in June 1997. Amended by the Individuals with Disabilities Education Improvement Act of 2004 (Pub. L. No. 108-446) in December 2004, 20 U.S.C. §§ 1400 *et seq*. Regulations appear at 34 C.F.R. Part 300.

---

[1]Federal statutes are compiled and published in the *United States Code* (U.S.C.). Rules and regulations implementing a law first appear in a daily publication called the *Federal Register* (F.R.) and subsequently are published in the *Code of Federal Regulations* (C.F.R.). The *Code of Federal Regulations* has 50 titles, and each volume is updated once each calendar year. These government publications can be found at http://www.gpoaccess.gov and in state or university libraries. The U.S. Department of Education web site also has links to statutes and regulations pertinent to education (http://www.ed.gov).

Jacob K. Javits Gifted and Talented Students Education Act of 1988 (Pub. L. No. 100-297). Amended by No Child Left Behind Act of 2001 (Pub. L. No. 107-110).

National Research Act of 1974 (Pub. L. No. 93-348), 42 U.S.C. § 289. Regulations appear at 45 C.F.R. Part 46.

No Child Left Behind Act of 2001 (Pub. L. No. 107-110). Most recent set of amendments to the Elementary and Secondary Education Act of 1965. Available at http://www.ed.gov.

Protection of Pupil Rights Act (previously Hatch Amendment). A 1978 amendment to ESEA. Amended in 1994 by Pub. L. No. 103-227 and in 2001 by Pub. L. No. 107-110.

Rehabilitation Act of 1973 (Pub. L. No. 93-112), 29 U.S.C. § 794. Regulations implementing Section 504 appear at 34 C.F.R. Part 104.

References

Abramovitch, R., Freedman, J. L., Henry, K., & Van Brunschot, M. (1995). Children's capacity to agree to psychological research: Knowledge of risks and benefits and voluntariness. *Ethics and Behavior, 5*, 25–48.

Acalanes (CA) Union High School District Office for Civil Rights, Western Division, San Francisco (California). (2009). 109 LRP 32284. Retrieved October 29, 2009, from Special Education Connection, http://www.specialedconnection.com

ADD/ADHD students may be eligible under OHI. (1999, June). *California Special Education Alert, 5*(11). Retrieved November 14, 2001, from the LEXIS Legal News database.

Adler, T. (1993, September). APA, two other groups to revise test standards. *APA Monitor*, pp. 24–25.

Alan Guttmacher Institute. (2006, September). *U.S. teenage pregnancy statistics national and state trends and trends by race and ethnicity.* Retrieved December 28, 2009, from http://www.guttmacher.org/pubs/2006/09/12/USTPstats.pdf

Alan Guttmacher Institute. (2009a, December 1). *State policies in brief: Minors' access to contraceptive services.* Retrieved December 28, 2009, from http://www.guttmacher.org/statecenter/spibs/spib_MACS.pdf

Alan Guttmacher Institute. (2009b, December 1). *State policies in brief: Minors' access to STD services.* Retrieved December 28, 2009, from http://www.guttmacher.org/statecenter/spibs/spib_MASS.pdf

Alan Guttmacher Institute. (2009c, December 1). *State policies in brief: Parental involvement in minors' abortions.* Retrieved December 28, 2009, from http://www.guttmacher.org/statecenter/spibs/spib_OAL.pdf

Allen, J. (2007). A multicultural assessment supervision model to guide research and practice. *Professional Psychology: Research and Practice, 38*, 248–258.

American Association of University Professors. (2006). *Research on human subjects: Academic freedom and the institutional review board.* Report retrieved September 1, 2008, from http://www.aaup.org

American Educational Research Association, American Psychological Association, & National Council on Measurement in Education. (1999). *Standards for educational and psychological testing* (2nd ed.). Washington, DC: American Educational Research Association.

American Psychiatric Association. (2000). *Diagnostic and statistical manual of mental disorders* (4th ed., text rev.). Washington, DC: Author.

American Psychological Association. (1981). Ethical principles of psychologists. *American Psychologist, 36*, 633–638.

American Psychological Association. (1982). *Ethical principles in the conduct of research with human participants.* Washington, DC: Author.

American Psychological Association. (1986). *Guidelines for computer-based tests and interpretations.* Washington, DC: Author.

American Psychological Association. (1996). Statement on the disclosure of test data. *American Psychologist, 51*, 644–648.

American Psychological Association. (2001). *APA ethics committee rules and procedures*. Retrieved June 2, 2005, from http://www.apa.org/ethics/rules.html

American Psychological Association. (2002). Ethical principles of psychologists and code of conduct. *American Psychologist, 57*, 1060–1073.

American Psychological Association. (2007). Record keeping guidelines. *American Psychologist, 62*, 993–1004.

American Psychological Association. (2009). Report of the ethics committee, 2008. *American Psychologist, 64*, 464–473.

American Psychological Association Commission on Accreditation. (2009). *Guidelines and principles for accreditation of programs in professional psychology*. Retrieved November 25, 2009, from http://www.apa.org

American Psychological Association Committee on Legal Issues. (1996). Strategies for private practitioners coping with subpoenas or compelled testimony for client records or test data. *Professional Psychology: Research and Practice, 27*, 245–251.

American Psychological Association Committee on Professional Practice and Standards. (2003). Legal issues in the professional practice of psychology. *Professional Psychology: Research and Practice, 34*, 595–600.

Angold, A., Erkanli, A., Egger, H. L., & Costello, E. J. (2000). Stimulant treatment for children: A community perspective. *Journal of the American Academy of Child and Adolescent Psychiatry, 39*, 975–983.

Aponte, J. F., & Johnson, L. R. (2000). The impact of culture on the intervention and treatment of ethnic populations. In J. F. Aponte & J. Wohl (Eds.), *Psychological intervention and cultural diversity* (2nd ed., pp. 18–39). Boston: Allyn & Bacon.

Appelbaum, P. S., & Meisel, A. (1986). Therapists' obligations to report their patients' criminal acts. *Bulletin of the American Academy of Psychiatry and the Law, 14*, 221–230.

Armistead, L. D. (2008). Best practices in continuing professional development for school psychologists. In A. Thomas & J. Grimes (Eds.), *Best practices in school psychology V* (pp. 1975–1989). Bethesda, MD: National Association of School Psychologists.

Aronson, R. H. (2001). Symposium: The Uniform Rules of Evidence (1999): The mental health provider privilege in the wake of *Jaffee v. Redmond. Oklahoma Law Review, 54*, 591–612.

Atkinson, D. R. (1993). Who speaks for cross-cultural counseling research? *Counseling Psychologist, 21*, 218–224.

Austin, W., Rankel, M., Kagan, L., Bergum, V., & Lemermeyer, G. (2005). To stay or to go, to speak or stay silent, to act or not to act: Moral distress as experienced by psychologists. *Ethics & Behavior, 15*, 197–212.

Ayyash-Abdo, H. (2002). Adolescent suicide: An ecological approach. *Psychology in the Schools, 39*, 459–475.

Bailey, J. A. (1980, March). School counselors: Test your ethics. *School Counselor*, 285–293.

Baldick, T. L. (1980). Ethical discrimination ability of intern psychologists: A function of training in ethics. *Professional Psychology, 11*, 276–282.

Ballantine, H. T. (1979). The crisis in ethics, anno domini 1979. *New England Journal of Medicine, 301*, 634–638.

Barkley, R. A., & Edwards, G. (1998). Diagnostic interview, behavior rating scales, and the medical examination. In R. A. Barkley (Ed.), *Attention-deficit hyperactivity disorder: A handbook for diagnosis and treatment* (2nd ed., pp. 263–293). New York: Guilford Press.

Barnett, J. E., Baker, E. K., Elman, N. S., & Schoener, G. R. (2007). In pursuit of wellness: The self-care imperative. *Professional Psychology: Research and Practice, 38*, 603–612.

Barnett, J. E., Behnke, S. H., Rosenthal, S. L., & Koocher, G. P. (2007). In case of ethical dilemma, break glass: Commentary on ethical decision making in practice. *Professional Psychology: Research and Practice, 38*, 7–12.

Barnett, J. E., Doll, B., Younggren, J. N., & Rubin, N. J. (2007). Clinical competence for practicing psychologists: Clearly a work in progress. *Professional Psychology: Research and Practice, 38*, 510–517.

Barnett, J. E., Erickson Cornish, J. A., Goodyear, R. K., & Lichtenberg, J. W. (2007). Commentaries on the ethical and effective practice of clinical supervision. *Professional Psychology: Research and Practice, 38*, 268–275.

Barnett, J. E., Wise, E. H., Johnson-Greene, D., & Bucky, S. (2007). Informed consent: Too much of a good thing or not enough? *Professional Psychology: Research and Practice, 38*, 179–186.

Bashe, A., Anderson, S. K., Handelsman, M. M., & Klevansky, R. (2007). An acculturation model for ethics training: The ethics autobiography and beyond. *Professional Psychology: Research and Practice, 38*, 60–67.

Batsche, G. M., & Peterson, D. W. (1983). School psychology and projective assessment: A growing incompatibility. *School Psychology Review, 12*, 440–445.

Bauder, D. (1989, February 6). Misdiagnosed as mentally retarded, deaf man spent years in institutions. *Midland Daily News*, p. B-1.

Beauchamp, T., & Childress, J. (2001). *Principles of biomedical ethics* (5th ed.). New York: Oxford University Press.

Behavior Analyst Certification Board. (2004, August). Guidelines for responsible conduct for behavior analysts. Retrieved March 14, 2009, from http://www.bacb.com/Downloadfiles/BACBguidelines/40809_BACB_Guidelines.pdf

Behnke, S. (2003). Release of test data and APA's new ethics code. *Monitor on Psychology, 34*(7), 70–72.

Behring, S. T., Cabello, B., Kushida, D., & Murguia, A. (2000). Cultural modifications to current school-based consultation approaches reported by culturally diverse beginning consultants. *School Psychology Review, 29*, 354–367.

Benjamin, G. A. H., Kent, L., & Sirikantraporn, S. (2009). Duty to protect statutes. In J. L. Werth, E. R. Welfel, & G. A. H. Benjamin (Eds.), *The duty to protect: Ethical, legal, and professional responsibilities of mental health professionals* (pp. 9–28). Washington, DC: American Psychological Association.

Bennett, B. E., Bryant, B. K., VandenBos, G., & Greenwood, A. (1990). *Professional liability and risk management*. Washington, DC: American Psychological Association.

Bernard, J., & Jara, C. (1986). The failure of clinical psychology graduate students to apply understood ethical principles. *Professional Psychology: Research and Practice, 17*, 313–315.

Bernstein, B. E., & Hartsell, T. L. (1998). *The portable lawyer for mental health professionals*. New York: John Wiley & Sons.

Bersoff, D. N. (1979). Regarding psychologists testily: The legal regulation of psychological assessment in the public schools. *Maryland Law Review, 39*, 27–120.

Bersoff, D. N. (1982). Larry P. and PASE: Judicial report cards on the validity of individual intelligence tests. In T. Kratochwill (Ed.), *Advances in school psychology* (Vol. 2, pp. 61–95). Hillsdale, NJ: Lawrence Erlbaum.

Bersoff, D. N. (1983). Children as participants in psychoeducational assessment. In G. B. Melton, G. P. Koocher, & M. J. Saks (Eds.), *Children's competence to consent* (pp. 149–177). New York: Plenum Press.

Bersoff, D. N. (1994). Explicit ambiguity: The 1992 ethics code as an oxymoron. *Professional Psychology: Research and Practice, 25*, 382–387.

Bersoff, D. N., & Hofer, P. T. (1990). The legal regulation of school psychology. In C. R. Reynolds & T. B. Gutkin (Eds.), *The handbook of school psychology* (2nd ed., pp. 937–961). New York: John Wiley & Sons.

Bersoff, D. N., & Koeppl, P. M. (1993). The relation between ethical codes and moral principles. *Ethics and Behavior, 3*, 345–357.

Bersoff, D. N., & Prasse, D. (1978). Applied psychology and judicial decision making: Corporal punishment as a case in point. *Professional Psychology, 9*, 400–411.

Bersoff, D. N., & Ysseldyke, J. E. (1977). Non-discriminatory assessment: The law, litigation, and implications for the assessment of learning disabled children. In S. Jacob (Ed.), *The law: Assessment and placement of special education students* (pp. 65–92). Lansing: Michigan Department of Education.

Black, H. C. (1983). *Black's law dictionary* (5th ed., abridged). St. Paul, MN: West Group.

Black, M. M., & Ponirakis, A. (2000). Computer-administered interviews with children about maltreatment. *Journal of Interpersonal Violence, 15*, 682–695.

Blue-Banning, M., Summers, J. A., Frankland, H. C., Nelson, L. L., & Beegle, G. (2004). Dimensions of family and professional partnerships: Constructive guidelines for collaboration. *Exceptional Children, 70*, 167–184.

Boonstra, H., & Nash, E. (2000). *Minors and the right to consent to health care*. Retrieved June 15, 2009, from http://www.guttmacher.org/pubs/tgr/03/4/gr03404.pdf

Borum, R. (2000). Assessing violence risk among youth. *Journal of Clinical Psychology, 56*, 1263–1288.

Borum, R., Fein, R., Vossekuil, B., & Berglund, J. (1999). Threat assessment: Defining an approach for evaluating risk of targeted violence. *Behavioral Sciences and the Law, 17*, 323–337.

Bosk, C. L. (1979). *Forgive and remember: Managing medical failure*. Chicago: University of Chicago Press.

Bower, E. M. (1982). Defining emotional disturbance: Public policy and research. *Psychology in the Schools, 19*, 55–60.

Bowman, D. H. (2002, February 6). Survey's sexuality questions anger elementary parents. *Education Week*, p. 10.

Bowser, P. B. (2009, March). *Comment in NASP ethics public comment responses, compiled and provided to members of the Principles for Professional Ethics 2010 revision team*. Bethesda, MD: National Association of School Psychologists.

Braden, J. P., & Joyce, L. B. (2008). Best practices in making assessment accommodations. In A. Thomas & J. Grimes (Eds.), *Best practices in school psychology V* (pp. 589–603). Bethesda, MD: National Association of School Psychologists.

Braden, J. P., & Tayrose, M. P. (2008). Best practices in educational accountability: High-stakes testing and educational reform. In A. Thomas & J. Grimes (Eds.), *Best practices in school psychology V* (pp. 575–588). Bethesda, MD: National Association of School Psychologists.

Bradley, A. (2001, November 14). Police absolved in suit over gay student's suicide. *Education Week*, p. 4.

Bristol Township School District Pennsylvania State Educational Agency. (2009, August 11). 109 LRP 56531, SpecialEdConnection Case Report. Horsham, PA: LRP Publications. Retrieved September 29, 2009, from http://www.specialedconnection.com

Brock, S. E., Lazarus, P. J., & Jimerson, S. R. (2002). *Best practices in school crisis prevention and intervention*. Bethesda, MD: National Association of School Psychologists.

Brophy, J. E., & Good, T. L. (1974). *Teacher-student relationships*. New York: Holt, Rinehart & Winston.

Brown, D. T. (1979). Issues in accreditation certification, and licensure. In G. D. Phye & D. J. Reschly (Eds.), *School psychology: Perspectives and issues* (pp. 49–82). New York: Academic Press.

Brown, D., Pryzwansky, W. B., & Schulte, A. C. (1987). *Psychological consultation: Introduction to theory and practice*. Boston: Allyn & Bacon.

Brown, R. T., Reynolds, C. R., & Whitaker, J. S. (1999). Bias in mental testing since *Bias in Mental Testing. School Psychology Quarterly, 14*, 208–238.

Burgdorf, R. L. (1991). The Americans with Disabilities Act: Analysis and implications of a second-generation civil rights statute. *Harvard Civil Rights–Civil Liberties Law Review, 26*, 413–522.

Burns, M. K., Jacob, S., & Wagner, A. (2008). Ethical and legal issues associated with using responsiveness-to-intervention to assess learning disabilities. *Journal of School Psychology, 46*, 263–279.

Callahan, C. M. (2006). Giftedness. In G. G. Baer & K. M. Minke (Eds.), *Children's needs III: Development, prevention, and intervention* (pp. 443–458). Bethesda, MD: National Association of School Psychologists.

Callan, J. E., & Callan, M. E. (2005). An historical overview of basic approaches and issues in ethical and moral philosophy and principles: A foundation for understanding ethics in psychology. In S. F. Bucky, J. E. Callan, & G. Strickler (Eds.), *Ethical and legal issues for mental health professionals: A comprehensive handbook of principles and standards* (pp. 11–26). New York: Haworth Press.

Campbell, D. T., & Fiske, D. W. (1959). Convergent and discriminate validation by the multitrait-multimethod matrix. *Psychological Bulletin, 56*, 81–105.

Canadian Psychological Association. (2000). *Canadian code of ethics for psychologists* (3rd ed.). Available at http://www.cpa.ca

Canter, A. (1989, November). Is parent permission always necessary? *Communique*, p. 9.

Canter, A. (2001a, May). Test protocols: Pt. 1. Right to review and copy. *Communique*, pp. 30, 32.

Canter, A. (2001b, September). Test protocols: Pt. 2. Storage and disposal. *Communique*, pp. 16–19.

Carlson, J. (2008). Best practices in assessing the effects of psychotropic medications on student performance. In A. Thomas & J. Grimes (Eds.), *Best practices in school psychology V* (pp. 1377–1388). Bethesda, MD: National Association of School Psychologists.

Casey, A. (2006). School readiness. In G. G. Baer & K. M. Minke (Eds.), *Children's needs III: Development, prevention, and intervention* (pp. 541–551). Bethesda, MD: National Association of School Psychologists.

Centers for Disease Control and Prevention. (2009a, November 16). *Sexually transmitted diseases in the United States 2008*. Retrieved July 7, 2010, from: http://www.cdc.gov/std/stats08/trends.htm

Centers for Disease Control and Prevention. (2009b, February 18). *Estimated numbers of cases of HIV/AIDS, by year of diagnosis and selected characteristics, 2004–2007—34 states and 5 U.S. dependent areas with confidential name-based HIV infection reporting*. Retrieved December 24, 2009, from http://www.cdc.gov/hiv/topics/surveillance/resources/reports/2007/table1.htm

Chalfant, J., & Pysh, M. (1989). Teacher assistance teams: Five descriptive studies on 96 teams. *Remedial and Special Education, 10*(6), 49–58.

Chalk, R., Frankel, M. S., & Chafer, S. B. (1980). *AAAS professional ethics project*. Washington, DC: American Association for the Advancement of Science.

Chestnut, C. R. (2001, November 17). Jury awards $1 million to fired special ed teacher. *The Oregonian*. Retrieved November 18, 2001, from http://www.OregonLive.com

Chinn, P. C., & Hughes, S. (1987). Representation of minority students in special education classes. *Remedial and Special Education, 8*(4), 41–46.

Clarizio, H. F. (1987). Differentiating emotionally impaired from socially maladjusted students. *Psychology in the Schools, 24*, 237–242.

Clovis (CA) Unified School District, Office for Civil Rights, Western Division, San Francisco (CA). (April 23, 2009). 52 IDELR 167, 39 NDLR 162, 109 LRP 31672. SpecialEdConnection. Horsham, PA: LRP Publications. Retrieved September 29, 2009, from http://www.specialedconnection.com

Cobb County (GA) School District. (1992). OCR complaint investigation letter of findings. *Individuals with Disabilities Education Law Report, 19*, 29–32.

Cobia, D. C., & Boes, S. R. (2000). Professional disclosure statements and formal plans for supervision: Two strategies for minimizing the risk of ethical conflicts in post-master's supervision. *Journal of Counseling and Development, 78*, 293–296.

Cohn, S. D., Gelfman, M. H. B., & Schwab, N. C. (2005). Adolescent issues and rights of minors. In N. C. Schwab & M. H. B. Gelfman (Eds.), *Legal issues in school health services: A resource for school administrators, school attorneys, school nurses* (pp. 231–250). New York: Authors Choice Press.

Congress, E. P. (2001). Ethical issues in work with culturally diverse children and their families. In N. B. Webb (Ed.), *Culturally diverse parent-child and family relationships* (pp. 29–53). New York: Columbia University Press.

Conoley, J. C., & Conoley, C. W. (1982). *School consultation: A guide to practice and training.* New York: Pergamon Press.

Conoley, J. C., & Sullivan, J. R. (2002). Best practices in the supervision of interns. In A. Thomas & J. Grimes (Eds.), *Best practices in school psychology IV* (pp. 131–144). Bethesda, MD: National Association of School Psychologists.

Cooper, S. (1984). Minors' participation in therapy decisions: A written therapist-child agreement. *Journal of Child Adolescent Psychotherapy, 1,* 93–96.

Corrao, J., & Melton, G. B. (1988). Legal issues in school-based behavior therapy. In J. C. Witt, S. N. Elliot, & F. M. Gresham (Eds.), *Handbook of behavior therapy in education* (pp. 377–399). New York: Plenum Press.

Cottone, R. R., & Claus, R. E. (2000). Ethical decision-making models: A review of the literature. *Journal of Counseling and Development, 78,* 275–283.

Coughlin, E. K. (1988, November 30). Psychologist sentenced for giving false data to federal government. *Chronicle of Higher Education,* p. A5.

Council of Administrators of Special Education. (1999). *Section 504 and the ADA—Promoting student access.* Available from Council of Administrators of Special Education's online catalog, http://www.casecec.org

Curtis, M. J., Castillo, J. M., & Cohen, R. M. (2008). Best practices in system-level change. In A. Thomas & J. Grimes (Eds.), *Best practices in school psychology V* (pp. 887–901). Bethesda, MD: National Association of School Psychologists.

Dailor, A. N. (2007). *A national study of ethical transgressions and dilemmas reported by school psychology practitioners* (Unpublished master's thesis). Central Michigan University, Mt. Pleasant.

Dailor, A. N., & Jacob, S. (2010). Ethical and legal challenges: Negotiating change. In J. Kaufman, T. L. Hughes, & C. A. Riccio (Eds.), *Handbook of education, training, and supervision of school psychologists in school and community* (Vol. 2, pp. 153–168). New York: Routledge, Taylor & Francis Group.

Dana, R. H. (2000). Psychological assessment in the diagnosis and treatment of ethnic group members. In J. F. Aponte & J. Wohl (Eds.), *Psychological intervention and cultural diversity* (2nd ed., pp. 59–74). Boston: Allyn & Bacon.

Davis, J. L., & Mickelson, D. J. (1994). School counselors: Are you aware of ethical and legal aspects of counseling? *School Counselor, 42,* 5–13.

Davis, J. M., & Sandoval, J. (1982). Applied ethics for school-based consultants. *Professional Psychology, 13,* 543–551.

Dawson, M. M. (1987). Beyond ability grouping: A review of the effectiveness of ability grouping and its alternatives. *School Psychology Review, 16,* 348–369.

Debski, J., Spadafore, C. D., Jacob, S., Poole, D. A., & Hixson, M. D. (2007). Suicide intervention: Training, roles, and knowledge of school psychologists. *Psychology in the Schools, 44,* 157–170.

Decker, D. M., & Bolt, S. E. (2008). Challenges and opportunities for promoting student achievement through large-scale assessment results. *Assessment for Effective Intervention, 34,* 43–51.

Dee, J. (2005, June 26). Their unexpected adolescence. *New York Times.* Retrieved July 3, 2005, from http://www.nytimes.com/2005/06/26/magazine/26KIDS.html

Dekraai, M., Sales, B., & Hall, S. (1998). Informed consent, confidentiality, and duty to report laws in the conduct of child therapy. In T. R. Kratochwill & R. J. Morris (Eds.), *The practice of child therapy* (3rd ed., pp. 540–559). Boston: Allyn & Bacon.

de las Fuentes, C., & Willmuth, M. E. (2005). Competency training in ethics education and practice. *Professional Psychology: Research and Practice, 36*, 362–366.

Delaware College Preparatory Academy and the Red Clay Consolidated School District Delaware State Educational Agency. (2009). 109 LRP 59893. Retrieved October 29, 2009, from Special Education Connection, http://www.specialedconnection.com

Denig, S. J., & Quinn, T. (2001). Ethical dilemmas for school administrators. *The High School Journal, 84*(4), 43–49.

Diener, E., & Crandall, R. (1978). *Ethics in social and behavioral research.* Chicago: University of Chicago Press.

Discipline under Section 504. (1996, November 22). *Special Educator, 12*(1), 6–8.

Dreyfus, H. L. (1997). Intuitive, deliberative, and calculative models of expert performance. In C. E. Zsambok & G. Klein (Eds.), *Naturalistic decision making* (pp. 17–28). Mahwah, NJ: Lawrence Erlbaum Associates.

Duncan, B., & Fodness, R. (2008). Best practices in engaging in legislative activity to promote student academic achievement and mental health. In A. Thomas & J. Grimes (Eds.), *Best practices in school psychology V* (pp. 2013–2028). Bethesda, MD: National Association of School Psychologists.

Dunn, L. M. (1968). Special education for the mildly mentally retarded: Is much of it justifiable? *Exceptional Children, 35*, 5–22.

Dunst, C. J., & Trivette, C. M. (1987). Enabling and empowering families: Conceptual and intervention issues. *School Psychology Review, 16*, 443–456.

DuPaul, G. J., Barkley, R. A., & Connor, D. F. (1998). Stimulants. In R. A. Barkley (Ed.), *Attention-deficit hyperactivity disorder: A handbook for diagnosis and treatment* (2nd ed., pp. 510–551). New York: Guilford Press.

Eades, R. W. (1986). The school counselor or psychologist and problems of defamation. *Journal of School Law, 15*, 117–120.

East Lansing (MI) Public Schools. (1992). OCR complaint investigation letter of findings. *Individuals with Disabilities Education Law Report, 19*, 40–43.

Eberlein, L. (1987). Introducing ethics to beginning psychologists: A problem-solving approach. *Professional Psychology: Research and Practice, 18*, 353–359.

Epstein, M., Atkins, M., Cullinan, D., Kutash, K., & Weaver, R. (2008). *Reducing behavior problems in the elementary school classroom: A practice guide.* (NCEE #2008-012). Washington, DC: National Center for Education Evaluation and Regional Assistance, Institute of Education Sciences, U.S. Department of Education. Retrieved October 2, 2009, from http://ies.ed.gov/ncee/wwc/publications/practiceguides/

Erickson Cornish, J. A., Gorgens, K. A., Monson, S. P., Olkin, R., Palombi, B. J., & Abels, A. V. (2008). Perspectives on ethical practice with people who have disabilities. *Professional Psychology: Research and Practice, 39*, 488–497.

Ericsson, K. A., & Williams, A. M. (2007). Capturing naturally occurring superior performance in the laboratory: Translational research on expert performance. *Journal of Experimental Psychology: Applied, 13*, 115–123.

Esler, A. N., Godber, Y., & Christenson, S. L. (2008). Best practices in supporting school-family relationships. In A. Thomas & J. Grimes (Eds.), *Best practices in school psychology V* (pp. 917–936). Bethesda, MD: National Association of School Psychologists.

Esquivel, G. B., Lopez, E. C., & Nahari, S. (Eds.). (2007). *Multicultural handbook of school psychology: An interdisciplinary perspective.* Mahwah, NJ: Lawrence Erlbaum Associates.

Evans, W. J. (1997). Torts. In C. J. Russo (Ed.), *The yearbook of school law 1997* (pp. 183–212). Dayton, OH: Education Law Association.

Eversole, T. (1993, September). Lesbian, gay and bisexual youth in school. *Communique*, pp. 9–10.

Fagan, T. K., & Wise, P. S. (2007). *School psychology: Past, present, and future* (3rd ed.). Bethesda, MD: National Association of School Psychologists.

Failure to provide Section 504 to depressed teen was misjudgment. (2005, February 18). *The Special Educator, 20*(4). Horsham, PA: LRP Publications. Retrieved June 5, 2005, from LEXIS-NEXIS.

Falender, C. A., & Shafranske, E. P. (2007). Competence in competency-based supervision practice: Construct and application. *Professional Psychology: Research and Practice, 38*, 232–240.

Fanibanda, D. K. (1976). Ethical issues of mental health consultation. *Professional Psychology, 7*, 547–552.

FBI Academy. (2000). *The school shooter: A threat assessment perspective.* Retrieved November 3, 2002, from http://www.fbi.gov

Feinberg, T., & Jacob, S. (2002). Administrative considerations in preventing and responding to crisis: A risk management approach. In S. E. Brock, P. J. Lazarus, & S. R. Jimerson (Eds.), *Best practices in school crisis prevention and intervention* (pp. 95–108). Bethesda, MD: National Association of School Psychologists.

Felix, E., & Furlong, M. (2008). Best practices in bullying prevention. In A. Thomas & J. Grimes (Eds.), *Best practices in school psychology V* (pp. 1279–1289). Bethesda, MD: National Association of School Psychologists.

Ferguson, L. R. (1978). The competence and freedom of children to make choices regarding participation in research: A statement. *Journal of Social Issues, 34*, 114–121.

Fergusson, D. M., Beautrais, A. L., & Horwood, L. J. (2003). Vulnerability and resiliency to suicidal behaviours in young people. *Psychological Medicine, 33*, 61–73.

Figueroa, R. A. (1990). Best practices in the assessment of bilingual children. In A. Thomas & J. Grimes (Eds.), *Best practices in school psychology—II* (pp. 93–106). Washington, DC: National Association of School Psychologists.

Fine, M. A., & Ulrich, L. P. (1988). Integrating psychology and philosophy in teaching a graduate course in ethics. *Professional Psychology: Research and Practice, 19*, 542–546.

Finn, J. D. (1982). Patterns in special education placement as revealed by the OCR survey. In K. A. Heller, W. Holtzman, & S. Messick (Eds.), *Placing children in special education: A strategy for equity* (pp. 322–381). Washington, DC: National Academy Press.

Fischer, L., & Sorenson, G. P. (1996). *School law for counselors, psychologists, and social workers* (3rd ed.). White Plains, NY: Longman.

Fischetti, B. A., & Crespi, T. D. (1999). Clinical supervision for school psychologists: National practices, trends, and future implications. *School Psychology International, 20*, 278–288.

Fish, M. C. (2002). Best practices in collaborating with parents of children with disabilities. In A. Thomas & J. Grimes (Eds.), *Best practices in school psychology IV* (pp. 363–376). Bethesda, MD: National Association of School Psychologists.

Fisher, C. B. (2003). *Decoding the ethics code.* Thousand Oaks, CA: Sage.

Fisher, C. B., & Fryberg, D. (1994). Participant partners: College students weigh the costs and benefits of deceptive research. *American Psychologist, 49*, 417–427.

Fisher, M. A. (2008). Clarifying confidentiality with the ethical practice model. *American Psychologist, 63*, 624–625.

Fisher, M. A. (2009). Replacing "Who is the client?" with a different ethical question. *Professional Psychology: Research and Practice, 40*, 1–7.

Flanagan, R., Miller, J. A., & Jacob, S. (2005). The 2002 revision of APA's ethics code: Implications for school psychologists. *Psychology in the Schools, 42*, 433–445.

Flaugher, R. L. (1978). The many definitions of test bias. *American Psychologist, 33*, 671–679.

Fleming, E. R., & Fleming, D. C. (1987). Involvement of minors in special educational decision-making. *Journal of Law and Education, 16*, 389–402.

Forman, S. G., Bry, B. H., & Urga, P. (2006). Substance abuse. In G. G. Baer & K. M. Minke (Eds.), *Children's needs III: Development, prevention, and intervention* (pp. 1011–1023). Bethesda, MD: National Association of School Psychologists.

Frankel, M. S., & Siang, S. (1999). *Ethical and legal aspects of human subjects research.* Retrieved November 20, 2001, from http://www.aaas.org/spp/dspp/sfrl/projects/intres/main.htm

Friedman, S. L., Helm, D. T., & Marrone, J. (1999). Caring, control, and clinicians' influence: Ethical dilemmas in developmental disabilities. *Ethics and Behavior, 9,* 349–364.

Frisby, C. L. (1999a). Culture and test session behavior: Pt. 1. *School Psychology Quarterly, 14,* 263–280.

Frisby, C. L. (1999b). Culture and test session behavior: Pt. 2. *School Psychology Quarterly, 14,* 281–303.

Fuchs, D., Mock, D., Morgan, P. L., & Young, C. L. (2003). Responsiveness-to-intervention: Definitions, evidence, and implications for the learning disabilities construct. *Learning Disabilities Research and Practice, 18,* 157–171.

Gacono, C. B., & Hughes, T. L. (2004). Differentiating emotional disturbance from social maladjustment: Assessing psychopathy in aggressive youth. *Psychology in the Schools, 41,* 849–860.

Gallagher, J. J. (1989). A new policy initiative: Infants and toddlers with handicapping conditions. *American Psychologist, 44,* 387–391.

Gallessich, J. (1982). *The profession and practice of consultation.* San Francisco: Jossey- Bass.

Gelfman, M. H. B., & Schwab, N. C. (2005a). Discrimination in school: § 504, ADA, and Title IX. In N. C. Schwab & M. H. B. Gelfman (Eds.), *Legal issues in school health services* (pp. 335–371). New York: Authors Choice Press.

Gelfman, M. H. B., & Schwab, N. C. (2005b). School health records and documentation. In N. C. Schwab & M. H. B. Gelfman (Eds.), *Legal issues in school health services* (pp. 297–316). New York: Authors Choice Press.

Gersten, R., Compton, D., Connor, C. M., Dimino, J., Santoro, L., Linan-Thompson, S., et al. (2009). *Assisting students struggling with reading: Response to intervention (RTI) and multitier intervention for reading in the primary grades; IES practice guide.* (NCEE 2009-4045). Washington, DC: National Center for Education Evaluation and Regional Assistance, Institute of Education Sciences, U.S. Department of Education. Retrieved October 2, 2009, from http://ies.ed.gov/ncee/wwc/publications/practiceguides/

Gil, E. F., & Bob, S. (1999). Culturally competent research: An ethical perspective. *Clinical Psychology Review, 19,* 45–55.

Glosoff, H. L., Herlihy, B., & Spence, E. B. (2000). Privileged communication in the counselor-client relationship. *Journal of Counseling & Development, 78,* 454–462.

Gottlieb, M. C. (2006). A template for peer ethics consultation. *Ethics & Behavior, 16,* 151–162.

Gottlieb, M. C., Robinson, K., & Younggren, J. N. (2007). Multiple relations in supervision: Guidance for administrators, supervisors, and students. *Professional Psychology: Research and Practice, 38,* 241–247.

Gould, S. J. (1996). *The mismeasure of man.* New York: W.W. Norton.

Graden, J. L., Casey, A., & Bonstrom, O. (1985). Implementing a prereferral intervention system: Pt. 2. The data. *Exceptional Children, 51,* 487–496.

Gredler, G. R. (1992). *School readiness: Assessment and educational issues.* New York: John Wiley & Sons.

Gredler, G. R. (1997). Issues in school readiness. In G. G. Bear, K. M. Minke, & A. Thomas (Eds.), *Children's needs II: Development, problems, and alternatives* (pp. 489–499). Bethesda, MD: National Association of School Psychologists.

Gregory, R. J. (2007). *Psychological testing: History, principles, and applications* (5th ed.). Boston: Pearson.

Gresham, F. M. (2007). Response to intervention and emotional and behavioral disorders: Best practices in assessment for intervention. *Assessment for Effective Intervention, 32,* 214–222.

Gresham, F. M., Reschly, D. J., Tilly, W. D., Fletcher, J., Burns, M. K., Christ, T., et al. (2005). Comprehensive evaluation of learning disabilities: A response to intervention perspective. *School Psychologist, 59*(1), 26–30.

Grisso, T., & Vierling, L. (1978). Minor's consent to treatment: A developmental perspective. *Professional Psychology, 9*, 412–427.

Grunder, T. M. (1978). Two formulas for determining the readability of subject consent forms. *American Psychologist, 33*, 773–774.

Guard, P. J. (2007, August 7). *Letter to the Honorable Bill Shuster*. Retrieved September 9, 2009, from www.ed.gov/policy/speced/guid/idea/letters/revpolicy/tpconfedr.html

Gunsalus, C. K., Bruner, E. M., Burbules, N. C., Dash, L., Finkin, M., Goldberg, J. P., et al. (n.d.). *The Illinois white paper: Improving the system for protecting human subjects; Counteracting IRB "mission creep."* University of Illinois Law and Economics Research Paper No. LE06-016. Retrieved December 9, 2009, from http://ssrn.com/abstract=902995

Gutierrez, P. M., & Osman, A. (2009). Getting the best return on your screening investment: Maximizing sensitivity and specificity of the Suicide Ideation Questionnaire and the Reynolds Adolescent Depression Scale. *School Psychology Review, 38*, 200–217.

Gutkin, T. B., & Curtis, M. J. (1999). School-based consultation theory and practice: The art and science of indirect service delivery. In C. R. Reynolds & T. B. Gutkin (Eds.), *Handbook of school psychology* (3rd ed., pp. 598–637). New York: John Wiley & Sons.

Haas, L. J., & Malouf, J. L. (2005). *Keeping up the good work: A practitioner's guide to mental health ethics* (4th ed.). Sarasota, FL: Professional Resources Press.

Haas, L. J., Malouf, J. L., & Mayerson, N. H. (1986). Ethical dilemmas in psychological practice: Results of a national survey. *Professional Psychology: Research and Practice, 17*, 316–321.

HaileMariam, A., Bradley-Johnson, S., & Johnson, C. M. (2002). Pediatricians' preferences for ADHD information from schools. *School Psychology Review, 33*, 94–105.

Hammill, D. D., Brown, L., & Bryant, B. R. (1989). *A consumer's guide to tests in print*. Austin, TX: Pro-Ed.

Handelsman, M. M. (1986). Problems with ethics training by "osmosis." *Professional Psychology: Research and Practice, 17*, 371–372.

Handelsman, M. M., Gottlieb, M. C., & Knapp, S. (2005). Training ethical psychologists: An acculturation model. *Professional Psychology: Research and Practice, 36*, 59–65.

Hansen, J. C., Himes, B. S., & Meier, S. (1990). *Consultation: Concepts and practices*. Englewood Cliffs, NJ: Prentice-Hall.

Hansen, N. D., & Goldberg, S. G. (1999). Navigating the nuances: A matrix of considerations for ethical-legal dilemmas. *Professional Psychology: Research and Practice, 30*, 495–503.

Hansen, N. D., Pepitone-Arreola-Rockwell, F., & Greene, A. F. (2000). Multicultural competence: Criteria and case examples. *Professional Psychology: Research and Practice, 31*, 652–660.

Hanson, R. K. (2009). The psychological assessment of risk for crime and violence. *Canadian Psychology, 50*, 172–182.

Hare, R. (1981). The philosophical basis of psychiatric ethics. In S. Bloch & P. Chodoff (Eds.), *Psychiatric ethics* (pp. 31–45). Oxford, UK: Oxford University Press.

Harris, A., & Kapche, R. (1978). Behavior modification in schools: Ethical issues and suggested guidelines. *Journal of School Psychology, 16*, 25–33.

Harris, K. R. (1985). Definitional, parametric, and procedural considerations in timeout interventions and research. *Exceptional Children, 51*, 279–288.

Hartshorne, T. S. (2002). Mistaking courage for denial: Family resilience after the birth of a child with severe disabilities. *Journal of Individual Psychology, 58*, 263–278.

Harvey, V. S., & Carlson, J. F. (2003). Ethical and professional issues with computer-related technology. *School Psychology Review, 32*, 92–107.

Harvey, V. S., & Struzziero, J. A. (2008). *Professional development and supervision of school psychologists: From intern to expert* (2nd ed.). Thousand Oaks, CA: Joint Publication of National Association of School Psychologists and Corwin Press.

Havey, J. M. (1999). School psychologists' involvement in special education due process hearings. *Psychology in the Schools, 36*, 117–122.

Hays, P. A. (2001). *Addressing cultural complexities in practice*. Washington, DC: American Psychological Association.

Hehir, T. (1993, October 25). Response to letter of inquiry from McDonald. *Individuals with Disabilities Education Law Report, 20*, 1159–1160.

Helton, G. B., Ray, B. A., & Biderman, M. D. (2000). Responses of school psychologists and teachers to administrative pressures to practice unethically: A national survey. *Special Services in the Schools, 16*, 111–134.

Henderson, D. H. (1986). Constitutional implications involving the use of corporal punishment in the public schools. *Journal of Law and Education, 15*, 255–269.

Henker, B., & Whalen, C. K. (1989). Hyperactivity and attention deficits. *American Psychologist, 44*, 216–223.

Henning-Stout, M. (1996). ¿Que podemos hacer? Roles for school psychologists with Mexican and Latino migrant children and families. *School Psychology Review, 25*, 152–164.

Heumann, J. E. (1993). Response to letter of inquiry from G. Warrington. *Individuals with Disabilities Education Law Report, 20*, 539–540.

Hindman, S. E. (1986). The law, the courts, and the education of behaviorally disordered students. *Behavior Disorders, 11*, 280–289.

Holmes, D. S. (1976). Debriefing after psychological experiments: Pt. 2. Effectiveness of postexperimental desensitizing. *American Psychologist, 31*, 868–875.

Holmes, D. S., & Urie, R. C. (1975). Effects of preparing children for psychotherapy. *Journal of Consulting and Clinical Psychology, 43*, 311–318.

Hopkins, B. R., & Anderson, B. S. (1985). *The counselor and the law* (2nd ed.). Alexandria, VA: American Association for Counseling and Development.

Horton, C. B., & Cruise, T. K. (2001). *Child abuse and neglect: The school's response*. New York: Guilford Press.

Hosp, J. L., & Reschly, D. J. (2003). Referral rates for intervention and assessment: A meta-analysis of racial differences. *Journal of Special Education, 37*, 67–81.

Hostetler, A. J. (1988, June). Indictment: Congress sends message on fraud. *APA Monitor*, p. 5.

Hubsch, A. W. (1989). Education and self-government: The right to education under state constitutional law. *Journal of Law and Education, 18*, 93–133.

Hughes, J. N. (1986). Ethical issues in school consultation. *School Psychology Review, 15*, 489–499.

Hughes, T. L., & Bray, M. A. (2004). Differentiation of emotional disturbance and social maladjustment: Introduction to the special issue. *Psychology in the Schools, 41*, 819–821.

Hummel, D. L., Talbutt, L. C., & Alexander, M. D. (1985). *Law and ethics in counseling*. New York: Van Nostrand–Reinhold.

Huprich, S. K., Fuller, K. M., & Schneider, R. B. (2003). Divergent ethical perspectives on the duty-to-warn principle with HIV patients. *Ethics and Behavior, 13*, 263–278.

Hyman, I. A. (1990). *Reading, writing, and the hickory stick*. Lexington, MA: Lexington Books.

Hyman, I. A., Barrish, B. M., & Kaplan, J. (1997). Corporal punishment. In G. G. Baer, K. M. Minke, & A. Thomas (Eds.), *Children's needs II: Development, problems, and alternatives* (pp. 235–243). Bethesda, MD: National Association of School Psychologists.

Hyman, I. A., & Perone, D. C. (1998). The other side of school violence: Educator policies and practices that may contribute to student misbehavior. *Psychology in the Schools, 36*, 7–27.

Ingraham, C. L., & Meyers, J. (Guest Eds.). (2000). Mini-series: Multicultural and cross-cultural consultation in schools. *School Psychology Review, 29*, 315–428.

Is district to blame for student victimized by nondisabled peers? (2003, July 20). *Section 504 Compliance Advisor, 7*(6). Horsham, PA: LRP Publications. Retrieved July 3, 2005, from LEXIS-NEXIS.

Jacob, S. (2008). Best practices in developing ethical school psychological practice. In A. Thomas & J. Grimes (Eds.), *Best practices in school psychology V* (pp. 1921–1932). Bethesda, MD: National Association of School Psychologists.

Jacob, S. (2009). Putting it all together: Implications for school psychology. *School Psychology Review, 38*, 239–243.

Jacob, S., & Brantley, J. C. (1989). Ethics and computer-assisted assessment: Three case studies. *Psychology in the Schools, 26*, 163–167.

Jacob, S., Drevon, D. D., Abbuhl, C. M., & Taton, J. (2010). Preparing school psychologists to address the needs of gay, lesbian, biattractional, transgender, and questioning youth. In J. Kaufman, T. L. Hughes, & C. A. Riccio (Eds.), *Handbook of education, training and supervision of school psychologists in school and community* (Vol. 2, pp. 205–225). New York: Routledge, Taylor & Francis Group.

Jacob, S., & Feinberg, T. (2002). Legal and ethical issues in crisis prevention and response. In S. E. Brock, P. J. Lazarus, & S. R. Jimerson (Eds.), *Best practices in school crisis prevention and intervention* (pp. 709–732). Bethesda, MD: National Association of School Psychologists.

Jacob, S., & Powers, K. E. (2009). Privileged communication in the school psychologist-client relationship. *Psychology in the Schools, 46*, 307–318.

Jacob-Timm, S. (1996). Ethical and legal issues associated with the use of aversives in the public schools: The SIBIS controversy. *School Psychology Review, 2*, 184–198.

Jacob-Timm, S. (1999). Ethical dilemmas encountered by members of the National Association of School Psychologists. *Psychology in the Schools, 36*, 205–217.

Jimerson, S. R., & Furlong, M. J. (Eds.). (2006). *Handbook of school violence and school safety*. Mahwah, NJ: Lawrence Erlbaum Associates.

Jimerson, S. R., Graydon, K., Pletcher, S. M., Schnurr, B., Kundert, D., & Nickerson, A. (2006). Grade retention and promotion. In G. G. Baer & K. M. Minke (Eds.), *Children's needs III: Development, prevention, and intervention* (pp. 601–613). Bethesda, MD: National Association of School Psychologists.

Jobes, D. A., & Berman, A. L. (1993). Suicide and malpractice liability: Assessing and revising policies, procedures, and practice in outpatient settings. *Professional Psychology: Research and Practice, 24*, 91–99.

Johnson, W. B., Elman, N. S., Forrest, L., Robiner, W. N., Rodolfa, E., & Schaffer, J. B. (2008). Addressing professional competence problems in trainees: Some ethical considerations. *Professional Psychology: Research and Practice, 39*, 589–599.

Kalichman, S. C. (1999). *Mandated reporting of suspected child abuse: Ethics, law, and policy* (2nd ed.). Washington, DC: American Psychological Association.

Kaplan, M. S., Crisci, P. E., & Farling, W. (1974). Editorial comment [Special issue on ethical and legal issues]. *School Psychology Digest, 3*(1).

Kaser-Boyd, N., Adelman, H. S., & Taylor, L. (1985). Minors' ability to identify risks and benefits of therapy. *Professional Psychology: Research and Practice, 16*, 411–417.

Kaslow, N. J., Rubin, N. J., Bebeau, M. J., Leigh, I. W., Lichtenberg, J. W., Nelson, P. D., et al. (2007). Guiding principles and recommendations for the assessment of competence. *Professional Psychology: Research and Practice, 38*, 441–451.

Kaufman, A. S. (1994). *Intelligent testing with the WISC-III*. New York: John Wiley & Sons.

Keith-Spiegel, P. (1983). Children and consent to participate in research. In G. B. Melton, G. P. Koocher, & M. J. Saks (Eds.), *Children's competence to consent* (pp. 179–211). New York: Plenum Press.

Kenowa Hills (MI) Public Schools. (1992–1993). OCR complaint investigation letter of findings. *Individuals with Disabilities Education Law Report, 19*, 525–526.

Kirp, D. (1973). Schools as sorters. *University of Pennsylvania Law Review, 121*, 705–797.

Kitchener, K. S. (1986). Teaching applied ethics in counselor education: An integration of psychological processes and philosophical analysis. *Journal of Counseling and Development, 64*, 306–310.

Kitchener, K. S. (2000). *Foundations of ethical practice, research, and teaching*. Mahwah, NJ: Lawrence Erlbaum Associates.

Klotz, M. B., & Nealis, L. (2005). *The new IDEA: A summary of significant reforms*. Retrieved January 29, 2005, from http://www.nasponline.org

Knapp, S. (1980). A primer on malpractice for psychologists. *Professional Psychology, 11*, 606–612.

Knapp, S., Gottlieb, M., Berman, J., & Handelsman, M. M. (2007). When laws and ethics collide: What should psychologists do? *Professional Psychology: Research and Practice, 38*, 54–59.

Knapp, S., & VandeCreek, L. (1982). Tarasoff: Five years later. *Professional Psychology, 13*, 511–516.

Knapp, S., & VandeCreek, L. (1985). Psychotherapy and privileged communications in child custody cases. *Professional Psychology: Research and Practice, 16*, 398–407.

Knapp, S., & VandeCreek, L. (1997). Ethical and legal aspects of clinical supervision. In C. E. Watkins (Ed.), *Handbook of psychotherapy supervision* (pp. 589–599). New York: John Wiley & Sons.

Knapp, S., & VandeCreek, L. (2006). *Practical ethics for psychologists: A positive approach*. Washington, DC: American Psychological Association.

Knauss, L. K. (2001). Ethical issues in psychological assessment in school settings. *Journal of Personality Assessment, 77*, 231–241.

Koocher, G. P., & Keith-Spiegel, P. (2008). *Ethics in psychology and the mental health professions: Standards and cases*. New York: Oxford University Press.

Kozol, J. (1991). *Savage inequalities*. New York: Harper Perennial.

Kral, M. C., LaRosa, A., Brown, R. T., & Kubiszyn, T. (2006). Pediatric psychopharmacology. In G. G. Baer & K. M. Minke (Eds.), *Children's needs III: Development, prevention, and intervention* (pp. 1077–1088). Bethesda, MD: National Association of School Psychologists.

Kutz, G. D. (2009). *Seclusions and restraints: Selected cases of death and abuse at public and private schools and treatment centers*. GAO-09-719IT. Washington, DC: United States Government Accountability Office. Retrieved September 22, 2009, from http://www.gao.gov/new.items/d09719t.pdf

Lake Washington (WA) School District No. 414. (1985, June 28). OCR complaint investigation letter of findings. *Individuals with Disabilities Education Law Report, 257* (Suppl. 150), 611–615.

Lamb, D. H., Cochran, D. J., & Jackson, V. R. (1991). Training and organizational issues associated with identifying and responding to intern impairment. *Professional Psychology: Research and Practice, 22*, 291–296.

Landau, S., Meyers, A. B., & Pryor, J. B. (2006). HIV/AIDS. In G. G. Baer & K. M. Minke (Eds.), *Children's needs III: Development, prevention, and intervention* (pp. 871–884). Bethesda, MD: National Association of School Psychologists.

Larson, J. (2008). Best practices in school violence prevention. In A. Thomas & J. Grimes (Eds.), *Best practices in school psychology V* (pp. 1291–1307). Bethesda, MD: National Association of School Psychologists.

Lasser, J., & Klose, L. M. (2007). School psychologists' ethical decision making: Implications from selected social psychological phenomena. *School Psychology Review, 36*, 484–500.

Legal Information Institute. (2007, June). *Evidence*. Retrieved December 2, 2007, from http://www.law.cornell.edu/wex/index.php?title=Evidence&printable=yes

Legal Information Institute. (n.d.). *Law by source: Uniform laws*. Retrieved January 2, 2007, from http://www.law.cornell.edu/uniform/uniform.html

LeVay, S. (1996). *Queer science*. Cambridge, MA: MIT Press.

Levinson, W., Roter, D. L., Mullooly, J. O., Dull, V. T., & Frankel, R. M. (1997). Physician-patient communication: The relationship with malpractice claims among primary care physicians and surgeons. *Journal of the American Medical Association, 277*, 553–559.

Lieberman, R., Poland, S., & Cassel, R. (2008). Best practices in suicide intervention. In A. Thomas & J. Grimes (Eds.), *Best practices in school psychology V* (pp. 1457–1472). Bethesda, MD: National Association of School Psychologists.

Lim, J. (1993, May 19). OCR policy letter to regional offices. *Special Education Report*, p. 5.

Lindegren, M. L., Byers, R. H., Jr., Thomas, P., Davis, S. F., Caldwell, B., Rogers, M., et al. (1999). Trends in perinatal transmission of HIV/AIDS in the United States. *Journal of the American Medical Association, 282*, 531–538.

Lopez, E. C. (1997). The cognitive assessment of limited English proficient and bilingual children. In D. P. Flanagan, J. L. Genshaft, & P. L. Harrison (Eds.), *Contemporary intellectual assessment* (pp. 503–516). New York: Guilford Press.

Lopez, E. C. (2008). Best practices in working with school interpreters. In A. Thomas & J. Grimes (Eds.), *Best practices in school psychology V* (pp. 1751–1769). Bethesda, MD: National Association of School Psychologists.

Lopez, E. C., & Rogers, M. R. (2001). Conceptualizing cross-cultural school psychology competencies. *School Psychology Quarterly, 16*, 270–302.

Losen, D. J., & Orfield, G. E. (Eds.). (2002). *Racial inequity in special education*. Cambridge, MA: Harvard Educational Publishing Group.

Lynch, E. W., & Hanson, M. J. (1998). *Developing cross-cultural competence* (2nd ed.). Baltimore: Paul H. Brookes.

Marshall, E. (2000). Duke study faults overuse of stimulants for children. *Science, 289*, 721.

Marston, D. (2003, December). Comments on three papers addressing the question: "How many tiers are needed within RTI to achieve acceptable prevention outcomes and to achieve acceptable patterns of LD identification?" Paper presented at the National Research Center on Learning Disabilities Responsiveness-to-Intervention Symposium, Kansas City, MO.

Martens, B. K., Witt, J. C., Daly, E. J., & Vollmer, T. R. (1999). Behavior analysis: Theory and practice in educational settings. In C. R. Reynolds & T. B. Gutkin (Eds.), *Handbook of school psychology* (3rd ed., pp. 350–382). New York: John Wiley & Sons.

Martin, R. (1979). *Educating handicapped children: The legal mandate*. Champaign, IL: Research Press.

Martin, R. (1992). *Continuing challenges in special education law* (looseleaf notebook). Urbana, IL: Carle Media.

Masty, J., & Fisher, C. (2008). A goodness-of-fit approach to informed consent for pediatric intervention research. *Ethics & Behavior, 18*, 139–160.

Matarazzo, J. D. (1986). Computerized psychological test interpretations. *American Psychologist, 41*, 14–24.

McCarthy, M. M., Cambron-McCabe, N. H., & Thomas, S. B. (2004). *Legal rights of teachers and students*. Boston: Pearson Education.

McGivern, J. E., & McKevitt, B. C. (2002). Best practices in working with students using assistive technology. In A. Thomas & J. Grimes (Eds.), *Best practices in school psychology IV* (pp. 1537–1553). Bethesda, MD: National Association of School Psychologists.

McGue, M. (2000). Authorship and intellectual property. In B. D. Sales & S. Folkman (Eds.), *Ethics in research with human participants* (pp. 75–95). Washington, DC: American Psychological Association.

McIntosh, D. E., & Phelps, L. (2000). Supervision in school psychology: Where will the future take us? *Psychology in the Schools, 37*, 33–38.

McNamara, K. (2008). Best practices in the application of professional ethics. In A. Thomas & J. Grimes (Eds.), *Best practices in school psychology V* (pp. 1933–1941). Bethesda, MD: National Association of School Psychologists.

McNamara, K. (2009). Ethics and professional practices workgroup. In R. J. Armistead (Ed.), *Professional standards program area report to the delegate assembly*. Unpublished document. Bethesda, MD: National Association of School Psychologists.

McWilliams, M. (2003, February 16). School-wide information system (SWIS) discussion and issues of privacy. Retrieved April 6, 2003, from http://www.bridges4kids.org/articles/2-03/McWilliams1-16-03.html

Meddin, B. J., & Rosen, A. L. (1986). Child abuse and neglect: Prevention and reporting. *Young Children, 41*, 26–30.

Medway, F. J., & Rose, J. S. (1986). Grade retention. In T. R. Kratochwill (Ed.), *Advances in school psychology* (Vol. 5, pp. 141–175). Hillsdale, NJ: Lawrence Erlbaum.

Melton, G. B., Koocher, G. P., & Saks, M. J. (Eds.). (1983). *Children's competence to consent.* New York: Plenum Press.

Mercer, J. R. (1973). *Labeling the mentally retarded.* Berkeley: University of California Press.

Merrell, K. W., & Walker, H. M. (2004). Deconstructing a definition: Social maladjustment versus emotional disturbance and moving the EBD field forward. *Psychology in the Schools, 41*, 899–910.

Messick, S. (1965). Personality measurement and the ethics of assessment. *American Psychologist, 20*, 136–142.

Messick, S. (1980). Test validity and the ethics of assessment. *American Psychologist, 35*, 1012–1027.

Messick, S. (1984). Assessment in context: Appraising student performance in relation to instructional quality. *Educational Researcher, 13*, 3–8.

Messick, S. (1995). Validity of psychological assessment. *American Psychologist, 50*, 741–749.

Messina, D. J. (1988). Corporal punishment versus classroom discipline: A case of mistaken identity. *Loyola Law Review, 34*, 35–110.

Miller, D. D., & Kraft, N. P. (2008). Best practices in communicating with and involving parents. In A. Thomas & J. Grimes (Eds.), *Best practices in school psychology V* (pp. 937–951). Bethesda, MD: National Association of School Psychologists.

Miller, D. N., & Eckert, T. L. (2009). School-based suicide prevention: Research advances and practice implications [Special series]. *School Psychology Review, 38*, 153–248.

Miller, D. N., & Nickerson, A. (2007). Projective techniques and the school-based assessment of childhood internalizing disorders: A critical analysis. *Journal of Projective Psychology & Mental Health, 14*, 48–58.

Miller, F. L. (2009). Advocacy: The risks and rewards. *Communique, 38*, 17–18.

Miller, J. A., Williams, S. J., & McCoy, E. L. B. (2004). Using multimodal functional behavioral assessment to inform treatment selection for children with either emotional disturbance or social maladjustment. *Psychology in the Schools, 41*, 867–877.

Miller, V. A., Drotar, D., & Kodish, E. (2004). Children's competence for assent and consent: A review of empirical findings. *Ethics and Behavior, 14*, 255–295.

Minke, K. M., & Anderson, K. J. (2008). Best practices in facilitating family-school meetings. In A. Thomas & J. Grimes (Eds.), *Best practices in school psychology V* (pp. 969–981). Bethesda, MD: National Association of School Psychologists.

Monroe, S. J. (2007, December 26). *OCR Response to "Dear Colleague" letter.* Retrieved September 29, 2009, from http://www.specialedconnection.com

Mowder, B. (1983). Assessment and intervention in school psychological services. In G. W. Hynd (Ed.), *The school psychologist* (pp. 145–167). Syracuse, NY: Syracuse University Press.

Muehleman, T., Pickens, B. K., & Robinson, F. (1985). Informing clients about the limits to confidentiality, risks, and their rights: Is self-disclosure inhibited? *Professional Psychology: Research and Practice, 16*, 385–397.

Mulvey, E. P., & Cauffman, E. (2001). The inherent limits of predicting school violence. *American Psychologist, 56*, 797–802.

Naglieri, J. A., Drasgow, F., Schmit, M., Handler, I., Prifitera, A., Margolis, A., et al. (2004). Psychological testing on the Internet. *American Psychologist, 59*, 150–162.

Nastasi, B. K. (2008). Social justice and school psychology. *School Psychology Review, 37*, 487–492.

National Association of School Psychologists. (2008). *Ethical and Professional Practices Committee procedures.* Retrieved June 2, 2009, from http://www.nasponline.org

National Association of School Psychologists. (2009). *States that recognize the NCSP.* Retrieved June 11, 2009, from http://www.nasponline.org

National Association of School Psychologists. (2010a). *Standards for school psychology: Ethical and professional practices for school psychologists.* Bethesda, MD: Author. Electronic versions of the *Principles for Professional Ethics* and the *Model for Comprehensive and Integrated School Psychological Services* are available from http://www.nasponline.org

National Association of School Psychologists. (2010b). *Standards for school psychology: Graduate preparation and credentialing for school psychologists.* Bethesda, MD.

National Center for Education Statistics. (2008). *Indicators of school crime and safety: 2008.* Retrieved December 5, 2009, from http://www.nces.ed.gov/programs/crimeindicators/crimeindicators2008/key.asp

National Commission for the Protection of Human Subjects of Research. (1979). *The Belmont Report: Ethical principles and guidelines for the protection of human subjects of biomedical and behavioral research* (GPO 887-809). Washington, DC: U.S. Government Printing Office. Available from http://www.hhs.gov/ohrp/belmontArchive.html

National Institute of Mental Health. (2009, July 27). *Suicide in the U.S.: Statistics and prevention.* Retrieved December 27, 2009, from http://www.nimh.nih.gov/health/publications/suicide-in-the-us-statistics-and-prevention/index.shtml

National Institute on Drug Abuse. (2008, December). *NIDA infofacts: High school and youth trends.* Retrieved December 27, 2009, from http://www.nida.nih.gov/infofacts/HSYouthtrends.html

National Institutes of Health. (1991). National Institutes of Health consensus development conference statement. In *NIH consensus development conference on the treatment of destructive behaviors in persons with developmental disabilities.* NIH Publication No. 91-2410, pp. 1–29. Washington, DC: U.S. Government Printing Office.

National Research Council. (2003). *Protecting participants and facilitating social and behavioral sciences research.* C. F. Citro, D. R. Ilgen, & C. B. Marrett (Eds.). Washington, DC: National Academies Press.

National Task Force on Confidential Student Health Information. (2000). *Guidelines for protecting confidential student health information.* Kent, OH: American School Health Association.

Newman, J. L. (1993). Ethical issues in consultation. *Journal of Counseling and Development, 72,* 148–156.

Office for Civil Rights. (n.d.). *Frequently asked questions about sexual harassment.* Retrieved July 29, 2005, from http://www.ed.gov/about/offices.list.ocr/qasexharass.html

Olympia, D., Farley, M., Christiansen, E., Pettersson, H., Jenson, W., & Clark, E. (2004). Social maladjustment and students with behavioral and emotional disorders. *Psychology in the Schools, 41,* 835–847.

Ortiz, S. O. (2008). Best practices in nondiscriminatory assessment. In A. Thomas & J. Grimes (Eds.), *Best practices in school psychology V* (pp. 661–678). Bethesda, MD: National Association of School Psychologists.

Ortiz, S. O., Flanagan, D. P., & Dynda, A. M. (2008). Best practices in working with culturally diverse children and families. In A. Thomas & J. Grimes (Eds.), *Best practices in school psychology V* (pp. 1721–1738). Bethesda, MD: National Association of School Psychologists.

Osher, D., Sprague, J., Weissberg, R. P., Axelrod, J., Keenan, S., Kendziora, K., et al. (2008). A comprehensive approach to promoting social, emotional, and academic growth in contemporary schools. In A. Thomas & J. Grimes (Eds.), *Best practices in school psychology V* (pp. 1263–1278). Bethesda, MD: National Association of School Psychologists.

Page, E. B. (1980). Tests and decisions for the handicapped: A guide to evaluation under the new laws. *Journal of Special Education, 14,* 423–483.

Paredes Scribner, A. (2002). Best assessment and intervention practices with second language learners. In A. Thomas & J. Grimes (Eds.), *Best practices in school psychology IV* (pp. 337–351). Bethesda, MD: National Association of School Psychologists.

Physicians' desk reference. (2010). (64th ed.). Oradell, NJ: Medical Economics Co.

Picklo, D. M., & Christenson, S. L. (2005). Alternatives to retention and social promotion. *Remedial and Special Education, 26*, 258–268.

Pinard, M. (2003). From the classroom to the courtroom: Reassessing fourth amendment standards in public school searches involving law enforcement authorities. *Arizona Law Review, 45*, 1067–1125.

Pine-Richland (PA) School District. (2009, June 19). 53 IDELR 200, 13 FAB 2, 40 NDLR 151, 109 LRP 69515, Office for Civil Rights, Eastern Division, Philadelphia (Pennsylvania). Retrieved March 7, 2010, from http://www.specialedconnection.com

Pipes, R. B., Holstein, J. E., & Aguirre, M. G. (2005). Examining the personal-professional distinction. *American Psychologist, 60*, 325–334.

Pitcher, G., & Poland, S. (1992). *Crisis intervention in the schools*. New York: Guilford Press.

Poland, S. (1989). *Suicide intervention in the schools*. New York: Guilford Press.

Poole, D. A., & Dickinson, J. J. (2005). The future of the protocol movement: Commentary on Hershkowitz, Horowitz, & Lamb (2005). *Child Abuse & Neglect, 29*, 1197–1205.

Pope, K. S., Tabachnick, B. G., & Keith-Spiegel, P. (1987). The beliefs and behaviors of psychologists as therapists. *American Psychologist, 42*, 993–1006.

Power, T. J. (Ed.). (2007). The context of peer victimization [Special topic]. *School Psychology Review, 36*, 343–412.

Power, T. J. (Ed.). (2009). Research updates on teacher consultation for students with ADHD [Special topic]. *School Psychology Review, 38*, 3–44.

Prentice, E. D. (2005, July 28). *SACHRP chair letter to HHS secretary regarding recommendations*. Retrieved September 27, 2008, from http://www.hhs.gov/ohrp/sachrp/sachrpltrtohhssec.htm

Prilleltensky, I. (1991). The social ethics of school psychology: A priority for the 1990s. *School Psychology Quarterly, 6*, 200–222.

Prilleltensky, I. (1997). Values, assumptions, and practices: Assessing the moral implications of psychological discourse and action. *American Psychologist, 52*, 517–535.

Psychologist-patient privilege did not exist when student admitted homicide to school psychologist. (2002). *DOI Summaries, New York Law Journal, 222*, 17.

Pulliam, J. L. (1999). The attorney's role in responding to violence: A case study of Jonesboro, Arkansas. *School law in review 1999* (pp. 1–18). Alexandria, VA: National School Board Association.

Purcell, C. W. (1984). Limiting the use of corporal punishment in American schools: A call for more specific legal guidelines. *Journal of Law and Education, 13*, 183–195.

Redding, R. E. (1993). Children's competence to provide informed consent for mental health treatment. *Washington & Lee Law Review, 50*, 695–753.

Reddy, M., Borum, R., Berglund, J., Vossekuil, B., Fein, R., & Modzeleski, W. (2001). Evaluating risk for targeted violence in schools: Comparing risk assessment, threat assessment, and other approaches. *Psychology in the Schools, 38*, 157–172.

Repp, A. C., & Singh, N. N. (Eds.). (1990). *Perspectives on the use of nonaversive and aversive interventions with persons with developmental disabilities*. Pacific Grove, CA: Brooks/Cole.

Reschly, D. J. (1979). Nonbiased assessment. In G. D. Phye & D. J. Reschly (Eds.), *School psychology: Perspectives and issues* (pp. 215–253). New York: Academic Press.

Reschly, D. J. (1997). Diagnostic and treatment utility of intelligence tests. In D. P. Flanagan, J. L. Genshaft, & P. L. Harrison (Eds.), *Contemporary intellectual assessment* (pp. 437–456). New York: Guilford Press.

Reschly, D. J. (2000). Assessment and eligibility determination in the Individuals with Disabilities Education Act of 1997. In C. F. Telzrow & M. Tankersley (Eds.), *IDEA amendments of 1997* (pp. 65–104). Bethesda, MD: National Association of School Psychologists.

Reschly, D. J., & Bersoff, D. N. (1999). Law and school psychology. In C. R. Reynolds & T. B. Gutkin (Eds.), *Handbook of school psychology* (3rd ed., pp. 1077–1112). New York: John Wiley & Sons.

Reynolds, C. R., Lowe, P. A., & Saenz, A. L. (1999). The problem of bias in psychological assessment. In C. R. Reynolds & T. B. Gutkin (Eds.), *Handbook of school psychology* (2nd ed., pp. 549–595). New York: John Wiley & Sons.

Rhodes, R. L., Ochoa, S. H., & Ortiz, S. O. (2005). *Assessing culturally and linguistically diverse students: A practical guide.* New York: Guilford Press.

Rialto (CA) Unified School District. (1989). OCR complaint investigation letter of findings. *Education for the Handicapped Law Report, 353* (Suppl. 241), 201–204.

Roach, A. T., & Elliot, S. N. (2008). Best practices in facilitating and evaluating intervention integrity. In A. Thomas & J. Grimes (Eds.), *Best practices in school psychology V* (pp. 195–208). Bethesda, MD: National Association of School Psychologists.

Rogers, M. R., Ingraham, C. L., Bursztyn, A., Cajigas-Segredo, N., Esquivel, G., Hess, R., et al. (1999). Providing psychological services to racially, ethnically, culturally, and linguistically diverse individuals in the schools: Recommendations for practice. *School Psychology International, 20,* 243–264.

Rogers, M. R., & Lopez, E. C. (2002). Identifying critical cross-cultural school psychology competencies. *Journal of School Psychology, 40,* 115–141.

Rooker, L. S. (2005, September 13). *Letter to Mr. Gary S. Mathews.* Retrieved September 9, 2009, from the FERPA online library: http://www.ed.gov/policy/gen/guid/fpco/ferpa/library/carrollisd09305.html

Rooker, L. S. (2008, June 30). *Response to "Letter to Anonymous," Family Policy Compliance Office.* 12 FAB 27; 109 LRP 7789. SpecialEdConnection Case Report. Horsham, PA: LRP Publications. Retrieved December 12, 2009, from http://www.specialedconnection.com

Ross, R. P., & Harrison, P. L. (2006). Ability grouping. In G. G. Baer & K. M. Minke (Eds.), *Children's needs III: Development, prevention, and intervention* (pp. 579–588). Bethesda, MD: National Association of School Psychologists.

Ross, W. D. (1930). *The right and the good.* Oxford, UK: Clarendon Press.

Roy, L. (2001). Corporal punishment in American public schools and the rights of the child. *Journal of Law and Education, 30,* 554–563.

Russell Sage Foundation. (1970). *Guidelines for the collection, maintenance, and dissemination of pupil records.* Hartford: Connecticut Printers.

Russo, C. J. (2006). *Reutter's the law of public education* (5th ed.). New York: Foundation Press.

Ryan, D., & Martin, A. (2000). Lesbian, gay, bisexual, and transgender parents in the school systems. *School Psychology Review, 29,* 207–216.

Sales, B. D., Miller, M. O., & Hall, S. R. (2005). *Laws affecting clinical practice.* Washington, DC: American Psychological Association.

Sattler, J. M. (2008). *Assessment of children: Cognitive foundations* (5th ed.). San Diego, CA: Jerome M. Sattler.

Sattler, J. M., & Hoge, R. D. (2006). *Assessment of children: Behavioral, social, and clinical foundations* (5th ed.). San Diego, CA: Jerome M. Sattler.

Saunders, S. (2007, June 1). What you need to know about child abuse: A cautionary tale from Bedford Hills. *New York Teacher.* Retrieved November 11, 2009, from http://www.nysut.org/cps/rde/xchg/nysut/hs.xsl/newyorkteacher_7885.htm

Scarfone, K., Souppaya, M., & Sexton, M. (2007, November). *Guide to storage encryption technologies for end user devices.* National Institute of Standards and Technology, U.S. Department of Commerce. Retrieved December 3, 2009, from http://csrs.nist.gov/publications/nistpubs/800-111/SP800-111.pdf

Schill, K. (1993, Fall). Violence among students: Schools' liability under Section 1983. *School Law Bulletin,* 1–11.

Schimmel, D., & Fischer, L. (1977). *The rights of parents in the education of their children.* Columbia, MD: National Committee for Citizens in Education.

Schulenberg, S. E., & Yutrzenka, B. A. (2004). Ethical issues in the use of computerized assessment. *Computers in Human Behavior, 20,* 477–490.

Schwab, N. C., & Gelfman, M. H. B. (2005a). Confidentiality: Principles and practice issues. In N. C. Schwab & M. H. B. Gelfman (Eds.), *Legal issues in school health services: A resource for school administrators, school attorneys, school nurses* (pp. 261–295). New York: Authors Choice Press.

Schwab, N. C., & Gelfman, M. H. B. (Eds.). (2005b). *Legal issues in school health services: A resource for school administrators, school attorneys, school nurses.* New York: Authors Choice Press.

Schwab, N. C., Rubin, M., Maire, J. A., Gelfman, M. H. B., Bergren, M. D., Mazyck, D., et al. (2005). *Protecting and disclosing student health information: How to develop school district policies and procedures.* Kent, OH: American School Health Association.

Sheridan, S. M., Cowan, R. J., & Eagle, J. W. (2000). Partnering with parents in educational programming for students with special needs. In C. F. Telzrow & M. Tankersley (Eds.), *IDEA amendments of 1997* (pp. 307–349). Bethesda, MD: National Association of School Psychologists.

Sherry, P. (1991). Ethical issues in the conduct of supervision. *Counseling Psychologist, 19,* 566–584.

Shrag, J. A. (1991). Response to letter of inquiry from J. V. Osowaski. *Individuals with Disabilities Education Law Report, 18,* 532–543.

Shriberg, D., Bonner, M., Sarr, B. J., Walker, A. M., Hyland, M., & Chester, C. (2008). Social justice through a school psychology lens: Definition and applications. *School Psychology Review, 37,* 453–468.

Sieber, J. E. (2000). Planning research: Basic ethical decision-making. In B. D. Sales & S. Folkman (Eds.), *Ethics in research with human participants* (pp. 13–26). Washington, DC: American Psychological Association.

Siegel, M. (1979). Privacy, ethics, and confidentiality. *Professional Psychology, 10,* 249–258.

Simmonds, R. J., & Chanock, S. (1993). Medical issues related to caring for human immunodeficiency virus–infected children in and out of the home. *Pediatric Infectious Diseases Journal, 12,* 845–852.

Simon, R. I. (1999). The suicide prevention contract: Clinical, legal, and risk management issues. *Journal of the American Academy of Psychiatry and the Law, 27,* 445–450.

Sinclair, C. (1998). Nine unique features of the Canadian Code of Ethics for Psychologists. *Canadian Psychology, 39,* 167–176.

Skiba, R., & Rausch, M. K. (2006). School disciplinary systems: Alternatives to suspension and expulsion. In G. G. Baer & K. M. Minke (Eds.), *Children's needs III: Development, prevention, and intervention* (pp. 87–102). Bethesda, MD: National Association of School Psychologists.

Skiba, R. J., Simmons, A. B., Ritter, S., Gibb, A. C., Rausch, M. K., Cuadrado, J., et al. (2008). Achieving equity in special education: History, status, and current challenges. *Exceptional Children, 74,* 264–288.

Slenkovich, J. E. (1987a, June). Chemical dependency doesn't fit within "other health impaired." *Schools' Advocate,* p. 132.

Slenkovich, J. E. (1987b, December). Counseling not same as psychological services. *Schools' Advocate,* p. 143.

Slenkovich, J. E. (1988a, February). The seriously emotionally disturbed definition. *Schools' Advocate,* pp. 153–164.

Slenkovich, J. E. (1988b, March). When is a service a related service? *Schools' Advocate,* p. 168.

Small, M. A., Lyons, P. M., & Guy, L. S. (2002). Liability issues in child abuse and neglect reporting statutes. *Professional Psychology: Research and Practice, 33,* 13–18.

Smith, T. S., McGuire, J. M., Abbott, D. W., & Blau, B. I. (1991). Clinical ethical decision making: An investigation of the rationales used to justify doing less than one believes one should. *Professional Psychology: Research and Practice, 22,* 235–239.

Society for Research in Child Development. (2007). *SRCD ethical standards for research with children*. Retrieved December 3, 2009, from http://www.srcd.org

Solomon, R. S. (1984). *Ethics: A brief introduction*. New York: McGraw-Hill.

State of Michigan Governor's Task Force on Children's Justice, Department of Human Services. . (1998/2004). *State of Michigan Governor's Task Force on Children's Justice and Department of Human Services forensic interviewing protocol*. Retrieved September 23, 2007, from http://www.michigan.gov/documents/FIA-Pub779_13054_7.pdf

Steege, M. W., & Watson, T. S. (2008). Best practices in functional behavioral assessment. In A. Thomas & J. Grimes (Eds.), *Best practices in school psychology V* (pp. 337–347). Bethesda, MD: National Association of School Psychologists.

Stefkovich, J. A. (2006). *Best interests of the student: Applying ethical constructs to legal cases in education*. Mahwah, NJ: Lawrence Erlbaum Associates.

Steinberg, L., Cauffman, E., Woolard, J., Graham, S., & Banich, M. (2009). Are adolescents less mature than adults? *American Psychologist, 64*, 583–594.

Stephens, R. D. (1994). Planning for safer and better schools: School violence prevention and intervention strategies. *School Psychology Review, 23*, 204–215.

Stoiber, K. C., & McIntyre, H. (2006). Adolescent pregnancy and parenting. In G. G. Baer & K. M. Minke (Eds.), *Children's needs III: Development, prevention, and intervention* (pp. 705–719). Bethesda, MD: National Association of School Psychologists.

Swearer, S., & Espelage, D. L. (Eds.). (2008). Homophobia and bullying: Addressing research gaps [Special series]. *School Psychology Review, 37*, 155–227.

Taft, R. (1965). Comments of Senator Robert Taft. *U.S. Code Congressional and Administrative News*, p. 1450.

Talbot County (MD) Public Schools. (2008). *Individuals with Disabilities Education Law Report, 51*, 205 (OCR 2008). Retrieved September 29, 2009, from http://www.specialedconnection.com

Taylor, L., & Adelman, H. S. (1989). Reframing the confidentiality dilemma to work in children's best interests. *Professional Psychology: Research and Practice, 20*, 79–83.

Taylor, L., Adelman, H. S., & Kaser-Boyd, N. (1985). Minors' attitude and competence toward participation in psychoeducational decisions. *Professional Psychology: Research and Practice, 16*, 226–235.

Tharinger, D., & Stafford, M. (1995). Best practices in individual counseling of elementary age students. In A. Thomas & J. Grimes (Eds.), *Best practices in school psychology III* (pp. 893–907). Washington, DC: National Association of School Psychologists.

Thompson, R. A. (1990). Vulnerability in research: A developmental perspective on research risk. *Child Development, 61*, 1–16.

Tilly, W. D. (2008). The evolution of school psychology as a science-based practice: Problem-solving and the three-tiered model. In A. Thomas & J. Grimes (Eds.), *Best practices in school psychology V* (pp. 17–36). Bethesda, MD: National Association of School Psychologists.

Tilly, W. D., Knoster, T. P., & Ikeda, M. J. (2000). Functional behavioral assessment. In C. F. Telzrow & M. Tankersley (Eds.), *IDEA amendments of 1997* (pp. 151–197). Bethesda, MD: National Association of School Psychologists.

Tryon, G. S. (2000). Ethical transgressions of school psychology graduate students: A critical incidents survey. *Ethics and Behavior, 10*, 271–279.

Tryon, G. S. (2001). School psychology students' beliefs about their preparation and concern with ethical issues. *Ethics and Behavior, 11*, 375–394.

Turnbull, A. P., & Turnbull, H. R. (2001). *Families, professionals, and exceptionality: A special partnership collaborating for empowerment* (4th ed.). Upper Saddle River, NJ: Merrill.

Turnbull, H. R., & Turnbull, A. P. (2000). *Free appropriate public education* (6th ed.). Denver, CO: Love.

Turner, H. S., & Watson, T. S. (1999). Consultant's guide for the use of time-out in the preschool and elementary classroom. *Psychology in the Schools, 36*, 135–148.

Tymchuk, A. J. (1981). Ethical decision-making and psychological treatment. *Journal of Psychiatric Treatment and Evaluation, 3*, 507–513.

Tymchuk, A. J. (1985). Ethical decision-making and psychology students' attitudes toward training in ethics. *Professional Practice of Psychology, 6*, 219–232.

Tymchuk, A. J. (1986). Guidelines for ethical decision making. *Canadian Psychology, 27*, 36–43.

Uniform rules of evidence. (1999). Retrieved July 29, 2005, from http://www.law.upenn.edu/bll/ulc/ulc_frame.htm

U.S. Department of Education. (1991). Joint policy memorandum. *Individuals with Disabilities Education Law Report, 18*, 116–119.

U.S. Department of Education. (2010). *A blueprint for reform: The reauthorization of the Elementary and Secondary Education Act.* Retrieved March 16, 2010, from http://www2.ed.gov/policy/elsec/leg/blueprint/

U.S. Department of Education & Bias Crimes Task Force of the National Association of Attorneys General. (1999). *Protecting students from harassment and hate crime.* Available as an archived document from http://www2.ed.gov/offices/archives/Harassment/harass_intro.html

U.S. Department of Education, Office of Special Education Programs. (2002). *Specific learning disabilities: Finding common ground.* A report developed by 10 organizations participating in the Learning Disabilities Roundtable. Retrieved May 1, 2005, from http://www.nasponline.org/pdf/LD_OSEP.pdf

U.S. Department of Health and Human Services. (1991–1992). HHS policy clarification. *Individuals with Disabilities Education Law Report, 18*, 558–565.

U.S. Department of Health and Human Services. (2004, April 1). *HHS releases 2002 national statistics on child abuse and neglect.* Retrieved December 27, 2009, from http://www/hhs.gov/news/press/2004pres/20040401.html

U.S. Department of Health and Human Services. (2006, December 12). *HIPAA security guidance.* Retrieved November 24, 2009, from http://www/cms.hhs.gov/SecurityStandard/Downloads/SecurityGuidanceforRemoteUseFinal122806rev.pdf

U.S. Department of Health and Human Services & U.S. Department of Education. (2008, November). *Joint guidance on the application of the Family Educational Rights and Privacy Act (FERPA) and the Health Insurance Portability and Accountability Act of 1996 (HIPAA) to student health records.* Retrieved from http://www.ed.gov/policy/gen/guid/fpco/doc/ferpa-hippa-guidance.pdf

U.S. Equal Employment Opportunity Commission. (2005, March 2). *Sexual harassment.* Retrieved July 29, 2005, from http://www.eeoc.gov/types/sexual_harassment.html

Van Houten, R., Axelrod, S., Bailey, J. S., Favell, J. E., Foxx, R. N., Iwata, B. A., et al. (1988). The right to effective behavioral treatment. *Behavior Analyst, 11*, 111–114.

Vasquez, M. T. (1992). Psychologist as clinical supervisor: Promoting ethical practice. *Professional Psychology: Research and Practice, 23*, 196–202.

Vossekuil, B., Reddy, M., Fein, R., Borum, R., & Modzeleski, W. (2000). *U.S.S.S. safe school initiative: An interim report on the prevention of targeted violence in the schools.* Washington, DC: U.S. Secret Service, National Threat Assessment Center. Retrieved December 5, 2000, from http://www.treas.gov/usss

Ward, S. B. (2001). Intern supervision in school psychology. *School Psychology International, 22*, 269–284.

Webb, N. B. (2001). Strains and challenges of culturally diverse practice. In N. B. Webb (Ed.), *Culturally diverse parent-child and family relationships* (pp. 337–350). New York: Columbia University Press.

Weber, M. C. (2002). Disability harassment in the public schools. *William and Mary Law Review, 43*, 1079–1158.

Weber, M. C. (2007). Services for private school students under the Individuals with Disabilities Education Improvement Act: Issues of statutory entitlement, religious liberty, and procedural regularity. *Journal of Law & Education, 36*, 163–209.

Wechsler, D. (2002). Wechsler Preschool and Primary Scale of Intelligence III. San Antonio, TX: Psychological Corporation.

Wechsler, D. (2003). Wechsler Intelligence Scale for Children IV. San Antonio, TX: Harcourt Assessment.

Weirda, B. (1987, November). Related services—The medical exclusion. Schools' Advocate, pp. 137–139.

Weithorn, L. A. (1983). Involving children in decisions affecting their own welfare: Guidelines for professionals. In G. B. Melton, G. P. Koocher, & M. J. Saks (Eds.), Children's competence to consent (pp. 235–260). New York: Plenum Press.

Welfel, E. R. (1992). Psychologists as ethics educator: Successes, failures, and unanswered questions. Professional Psychology: Research and Practice, 23, 182–189.

Welfel, E. R., & Kitchener, K. S. (1992). Introduction to the special section: Ethics education— An agenda for the '90s. Professional Psychology: Research and Practice, 23, 179–181.

Welfel, E. R., & Lipsitz, N. E. (1984). Ethical behavior of professional psychologists: A critical analysis of the research. Counseling Psychologist, 12, 31–41.

White, R. M. (2000). Unraveling the Tuskegee study of untreated syphilis. Archives of Internal Medicine, 160, 585–598.

Willard, N. E. (2007). Cyberbullying and cyberthreats. Champaign, IL: Research Press.

Williams, B., Armistead, L., & Jacob, S. (2008). Professional ethics for school psychologists: A problem-solving model casebook. Bethesda, MD: National Association of School Psychologists.

Williams, B. B., Sinko, A., & Epifanio, F. J. (2010). Teaching ethical and legal issues. In J. Kaufman, T. L. Hughes, & C. A. Riccio (Eds.), Handbook of education, training, and supervision of school psychologists in school and community (Vol. 1, pp. 109–127). New York: Routledge, Taylor & Francis Group.

Winett, R. A., & Winkler, R. C. (1972). Current behavior modification in the classroom: Be still, be quiet, be docile. Journal of Applied Behavior Analysis, 5, 499–504.

Wonderly, D. (1989, April). Introductory comments. Ethical behavior: Is there adequate training and support? Symposia presented at the National Association of School Psychologists Convention, Boston.

Wood, R. C., & Chestnutt, M. D. (1995). Violence in U.S. schools: The problems and some responses. West's Education Law Quarterly, 4, 413–428.

Woody, R. H. (1988). Protecting your mental health practice. San Francisco: Jossey-Bass.

Yell, M. L., Drasgow, E., & Ford, L. (2000). The Individuals with Disabilities Education Act amendments of 1997: Implications for school-based teams. In C. E. Telzrow & M. Tankersley (Eds.), IDEA amendments of 1997 (pp. 1–27). Bethesda, MD: National Association of School Psychologists.

Ysseldyke, J., Burns, M., Dawson, P., Kelley, B., Morrison, D., Ortiz, S., et al. (2006). School psychology: A blueprint for training and practice III. Reprinted in A. Thomas & J. Grimes (Eds.), (2008), Best practices in school psychology V (pp. 37–69). Bethesda, MD: National Association of School Psychologists.

Ysseldyke, J. E., & Christenson, S. L. (1988). Linking assessment to intervention. In J. L. Graden, J. E. Zins, & M. J. Curtis (Eds.), Alternative educational delivery systems (pp. 91–109). Washington, DC: National Association of School Psychologists.

Yukon (OK) Public Schools. (2007). Individuals with Disabilities Education Law Report, 50. Office for Civil Rights, Midwestern Division, Kansas City, OK. Retrieved September 29, 2009, from http://www/specialedconnection.com

Zenere, F. J., & Lazarus, P. J. (2009). Research brief: The sustained reduction of youth suicidal behavior in an urban multicultural school district. School Psychology Review, 38, 189–199.

Zingaro, J. C. (1983). Confidentiality: To tell or not to tell. *Elementary School Guidance and Counseling, 17*, 261–267.

Zins, J. E., & Forman, S. G. (1988). Primary prevention in the schools: What are we waiting for? *School Psychology Review, 17*, 539–541.

Zirkel, P. A. (2008). Child advocacy and "freedom" of expression: Ethical obligation and the first amendment. *Communique, 36*, 1, 8–9.

Zirkel, P. (2009a). The ADAA and its effect on Section 504 students. *Journal of Special Education Leadership, 22*, 3–8.

Zirkel, P. (2009b). A step-by-step process for § 504/ADA eligibility determinations: An update. *West's Education Law Reporter, 239*, 333–343.

Zirkel, P. A. (2009c). Section 504: Student eligibility update. *The Clearing House, 82*, 209–211.

Zirkel, P. A., & Kincaid, J. M. (1993). *Section 504, the ADA, and the schools* (looseleaf). Horsham, PA: LRP Publications.

Zirkel, P. A., & Reichner, H. F. (1986). Is the *in loco parentis* doctrine dead? *Journal of Law and Education, 15*, 271–283.

Zirkel, P., & Rose, T. (2009). Special education law update X. *West's Education Law Reporter, 240*, 503–523.

Author Index

Subject Index

STUDY PACKAGE
CONTINUING EDUCATION
CREDIT INFORMATION

Ethics and Law for School Psychologists

Our goal is to provide you with current, accurate and practical information from the most experienced and knowledgeable speakers and authors.

Listed below are the continuing education credit(s) currently available for this self-study package. *Please note: Your state licensing board dictates whether self study is an acceptable form of continuing education. Please refer to your state rules and regulations.*

COUNSELORS: PESI, LLC is recognized by the National Board for Certified Counselors to offer continuing education for National Certified Counselors. Provider #: 5896. We adhere to NBCC Continuing Education Guidelines. This self-study package qualifies for **4.25** contact hours.

SOCIAL WORKERS: PESI, LLC, 1030, is approved as a provider for continuing education by the Association of Social Work Boards, 400 South Ridge Parkway, Suite B, Culpeper, VA 22701. www.aswb.org. Social workers should contact their regulatory board to determine course approval. Course Level: All Levels. Social Workers will receive **4.25** (Ethical) continuing education clock hours for completing this self-study package.

PSYCHOLOGISTS: PESI, LLC is approved by the American Psychological Association to sponsor continuing education for psychologists. PESI, LLC maintains responsibility for these materials and their content. PESI is offering these self- study materials for **4.0** hours of continuing education credit.

ADDICTION COUNSELORS: PESI, LLC is a Provider approved by NAADAC Approved Education Provider Program. Provider #: 366. This self-study package qualifies for **5.0** contact hours.

SCHOOL PSYCHOLOGISTS: This self study includes **4.0** hours of instructional content. Credit requirements vary per state jurisdiction. Please retain the certificate of completion you receive and contact your board for CE requirements.

Procedures:

1. Review the material and read the book.

2. If seeking credit, complete the posttest/evaluation form:

-Complete posttest/evaluation in entirety; including your email address to receive your certificate much faster versus by mail.

-Upon completion, mail to the address listed on the form along with the CE fee stated on the test. Tests will not be processed without the CE fee included.

-Completed posttests must be received 6 months from the date printed on the packing slip.

Your completed posttest/evaluation will be graded. If you receive a passing score (70% and above), you will be emailed/faxed/mailed a certificate of successful completion with earned continuing education credits. (Please write your email address on the posttest/evaluation form for fastest response) If you do not pass the posttest, you will be sent a letter indicating areas of deficiency, and another posttest to complete. The posttest must be resubmitted and receive a passing grade before credit can be awarded. We will allow you to re-take as many times as necessary to receive a certificate.

If you have any questions, please feel free to contact our customer service department at 1.800.844.8260.

PESI LLC
PO BOX 1000
Eau Claire, WI 54702-1000

Ethics and Law for School Psychologists

PESI

PO BOX 1000
Eau Claire, WI 54702
800-844-8260

Any persons interested in receiving credit may photocopy this form, complete and return with a payment of $20.00 per person CE fee. A certificate of successful completion will be sent to you. To receive your certificate sooner than two weeks, rush processing is available for a fee of $10. Please attach check or include credit card information below.

Mail to: PESI, PO Box 1000, Eau Claire, WI 54702 or fax to PESI (800) 554-9775 (both sides)

CE Fee: $20: (Rush processing fee: $10)   **Total to be charged** _____

Credit Card #: _____   **Exp Date:** _____ **V-Code*:** _____
(*MC/VISA/Discover: last 3-digit # on signature panel on back of card.) (*American Express: 4-digit # above account # on face of card.)

	LAST	FIRST	M.I.

Name (please print): _____   _____   _____

Address: _____ Daytime Phone: _____

City: _____ State: _____ Zip Code: _____

Signature: _____ Email: _____

Date Completed: _____ Actual time (# of hours) taken to complete this offering: _____hours

Program Objectives After completing this publication, I have been able to achieve these objectives:

1. Discuss the history of school psychology and describe its emergence as a major discipline.   1. Yes No

2. Describe the roles and functions of school psychologists and the scientist-practitioner model of service delivery.   2. Yes No

3. Understand the legal foundations of school-based practice.   3. Yes No

4. Discuss ethical principles, codes of ethics, and law pertinent to the delivery of school psychological services (e.g., NASP and APA codes of ethics, IDEA, FERPA, Section 504, and major court cases).   4. Yes No

5. Identify and discuss the ethical and legal aspects of situations that arise in professional practice, use ethical reasoning skills to anticipate and prevent problems from arising; and use a problem-solving model to make informed, well-reasoned choices in resolving problems when they do occur.   5. Yes No

6. Understand and value practice based on respect for the dignity of persons; responsible caring; integrity in professional relationships; and acceptance of responsibility to school, community, and society.   6. Yes No

7. Understand ways in which legislation and public policy can hinder or promote student learning and well being.   7. Yes No

PESI LLC
PO BOX 1000
Eau Claire, WI 54702-1000

ZNT042855   CE Release Date: 9/27/2010

Participant Profile:
1. Job Title: _____ Employment setting: _____

1. School psychologists can ensure that their professional conduct is ethical if they simply conform to the rules outlined in codes of ethics.
a. true
b. false

2. Codes of ethics, education law, and program accreditation are all types of _____ in the provision of school psychological services.
a. governmental regulation
b. professional regulation
c. self-regulation
d. quality control

3. With the passage of _____, Congress proposed that although "education is primarily a state function, the Federal Government has a secondary obligation to see that there is a basic floor under those essential services."
a. The Rehabilitation Act of 1973
b. The Elementary and Secondary Education Act
c. IDEA
d. FERPA

4. In emergency situations, parental consent to provide psychological services may be by-passed.
a. true
b. false

5. Even after an IEP Team determines that a child qualifies for special education, parents may refuse special education services for their child.
a. true
b. false

6. Under IDEA, states must offer special education and related services to pupils with severe disabilities, regardless of their ability to benefit. This is known as the:
a. zero reject principle
b. rebuttable presumption
c. LRE principle
d. a. & b

7. The definition of disability under ADAA EXCLUDES homosexuality, gender identity disorders, and transgender status.
a. true
b. false

8. Under 504, a student's accommodation plan should include:
a. A description of the nature of the concern
b. A description of how the physical or mental impairment affects a major life activity
c. The date when the plan will be reviewed or reassessed
d. all of the above

9. When child abuse is suspected, school personnel should investigate and be certain that it took place before contacting child protective services.
a. true
b. false

10. Education law and NASP's code of ethics obligate school psychologists to:
a. use a problem-solving process to develop interventions consistent with data collected
b. give preference to interventions reported in the research literature and found to be effective
c. ensure that interventions are implemented exactly as described in the literature
d. a & b

PESI LLC
PO BOX 1000
Eau Claire, WI 54702-1000